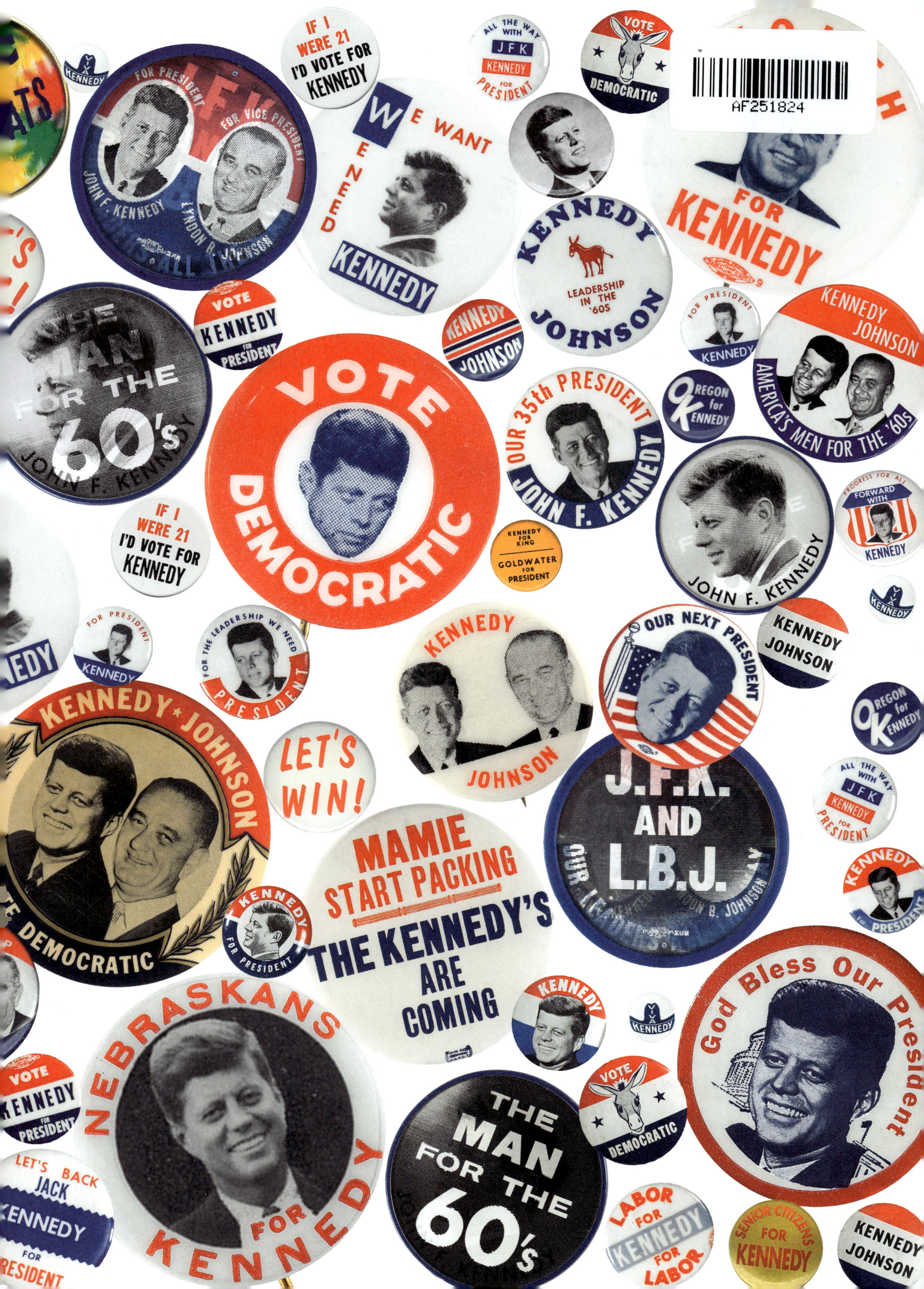

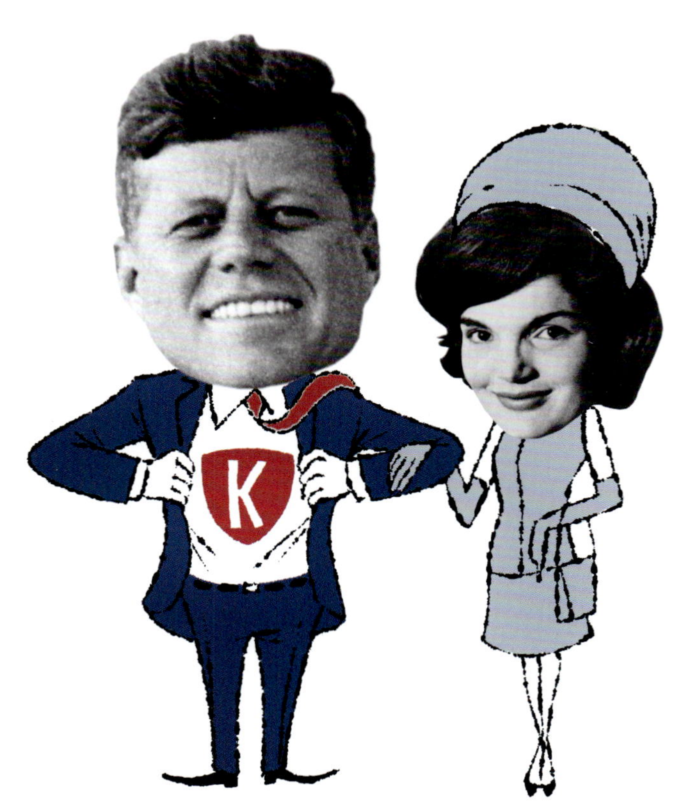

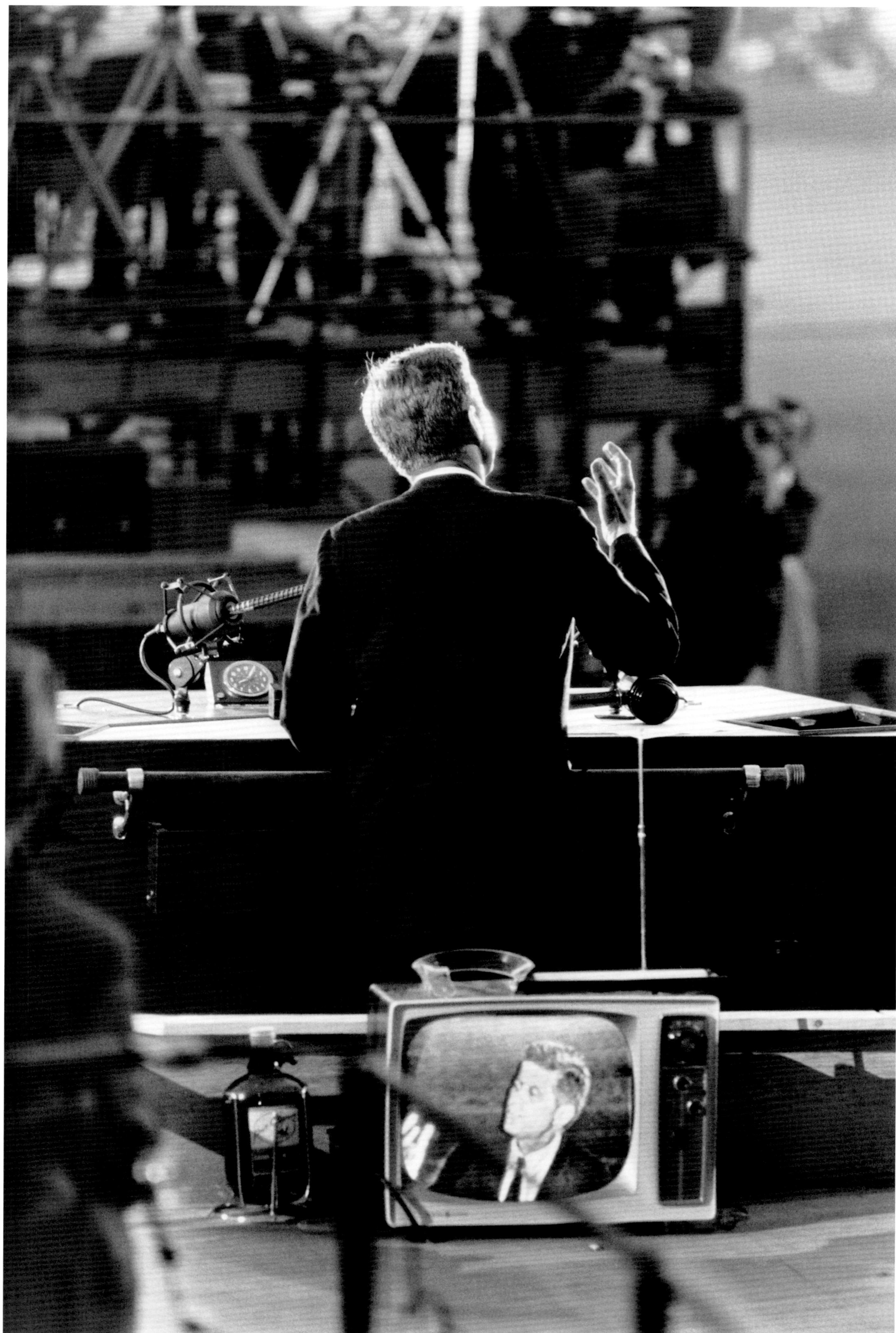

EDITED BY NINA WIENER   ART DIRECTION BY JOSH BAKER   INTRODUCTION BY J. MICHAEL LENNON   CONCEIVED BY LAWRENCE SCHILLER

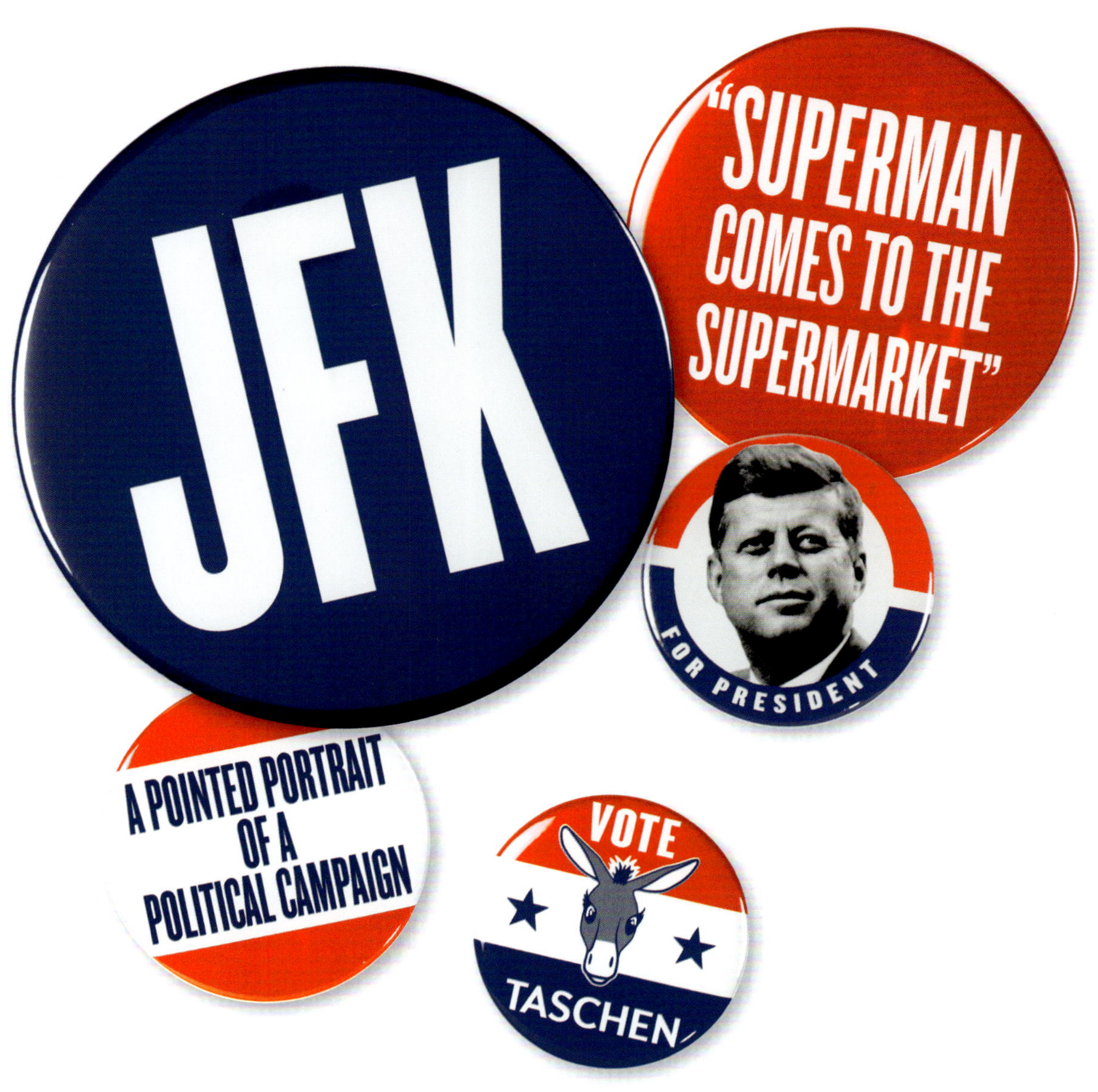

NORMAN MAILER

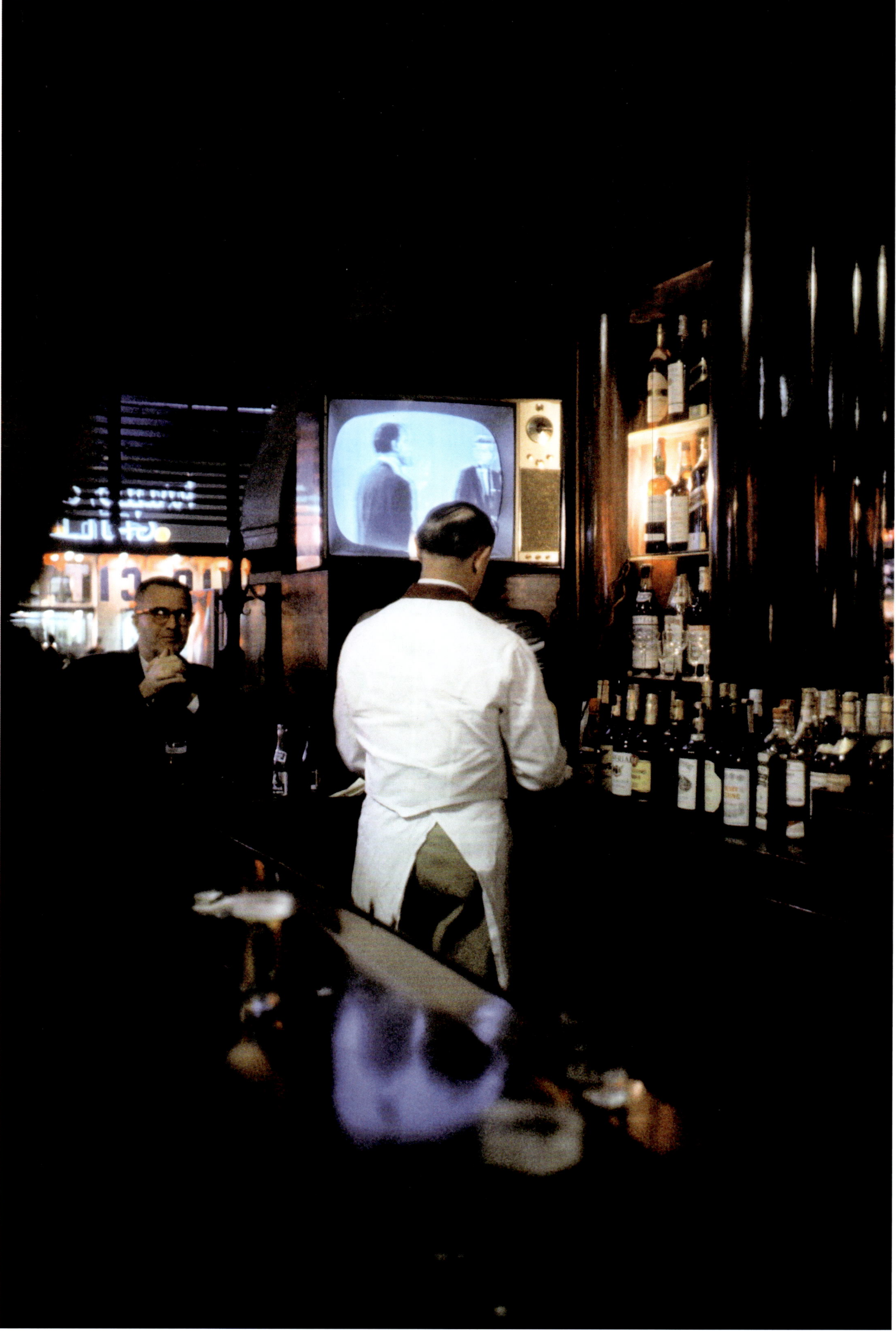

NORMAN MAILER JFK

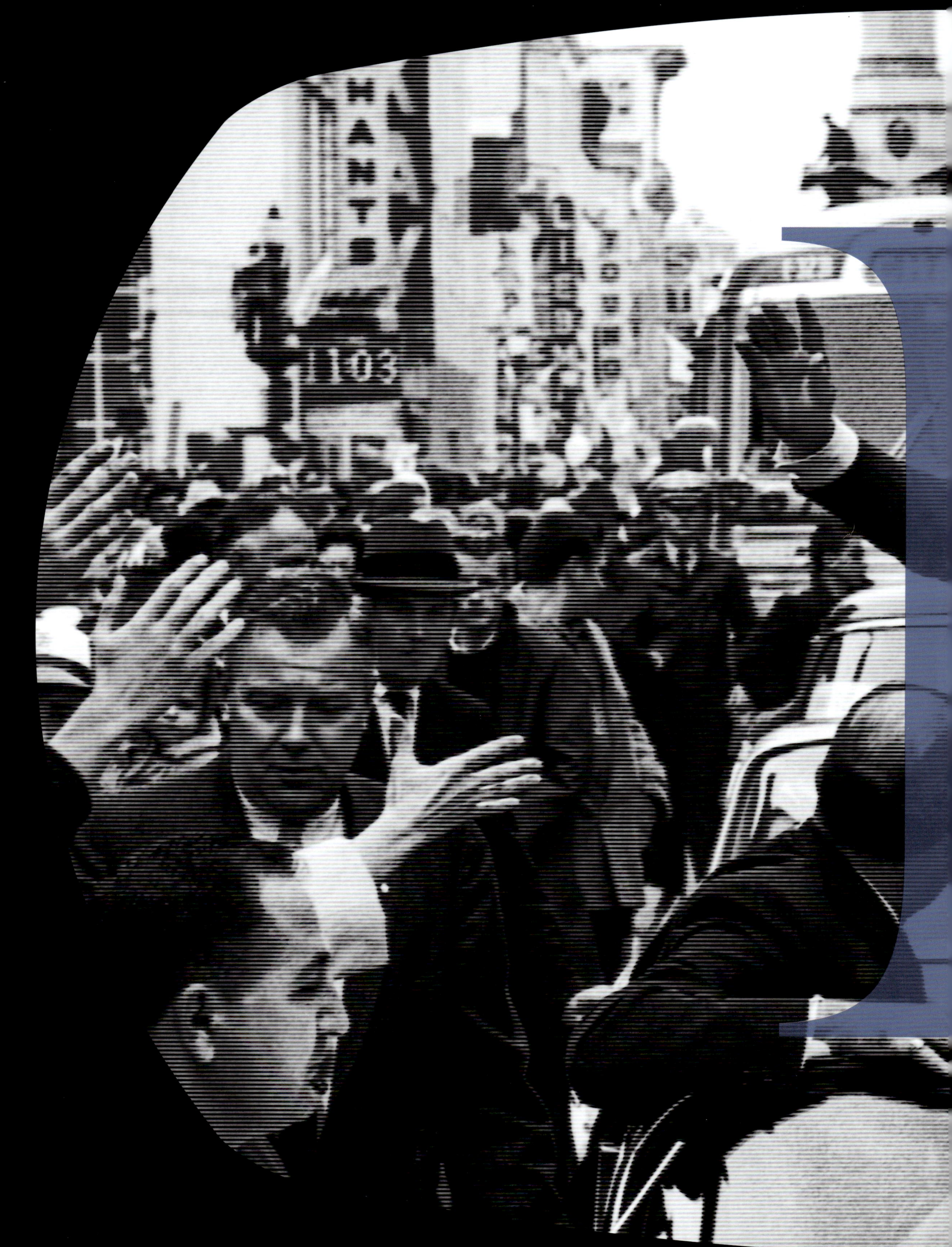

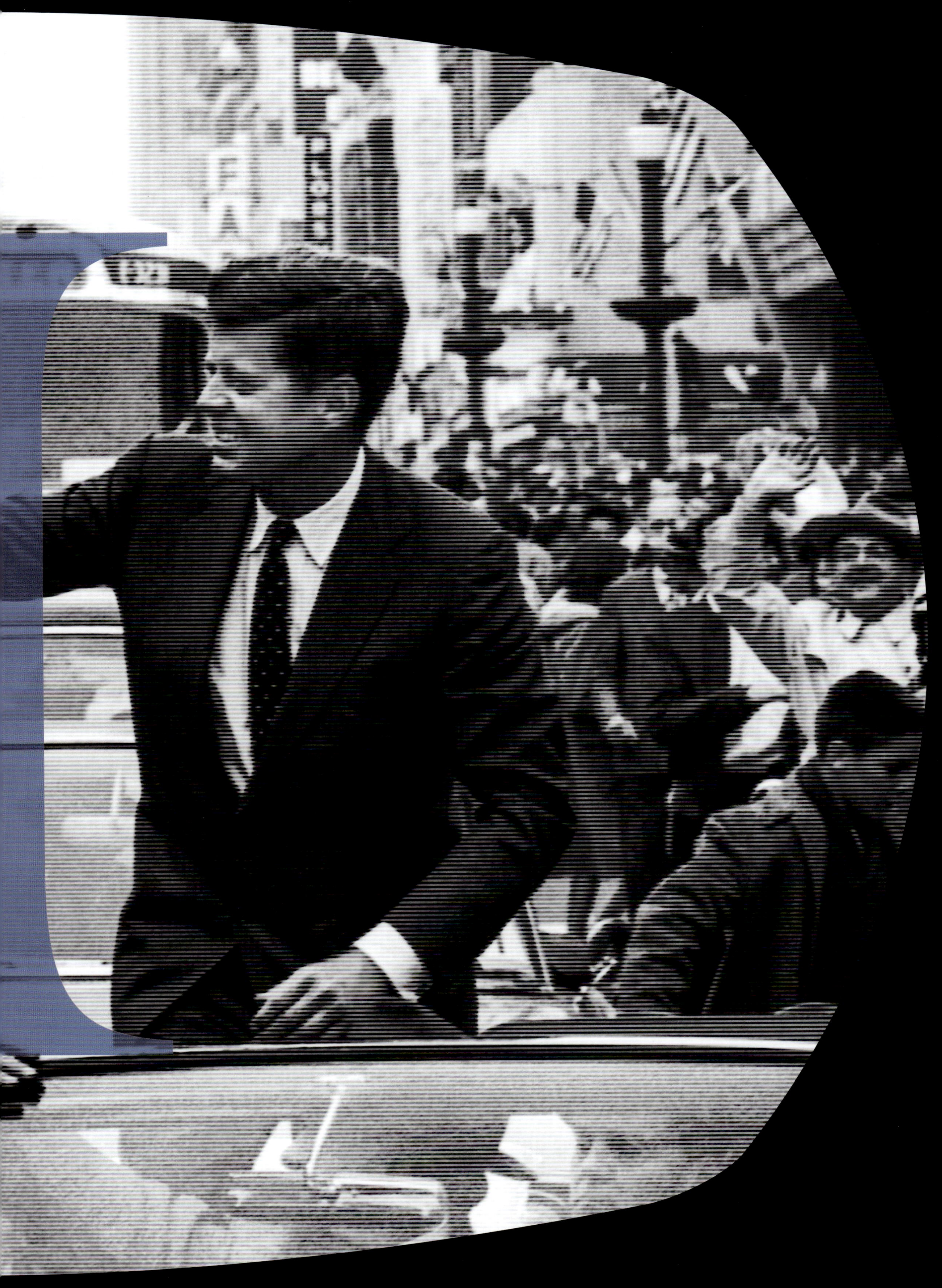

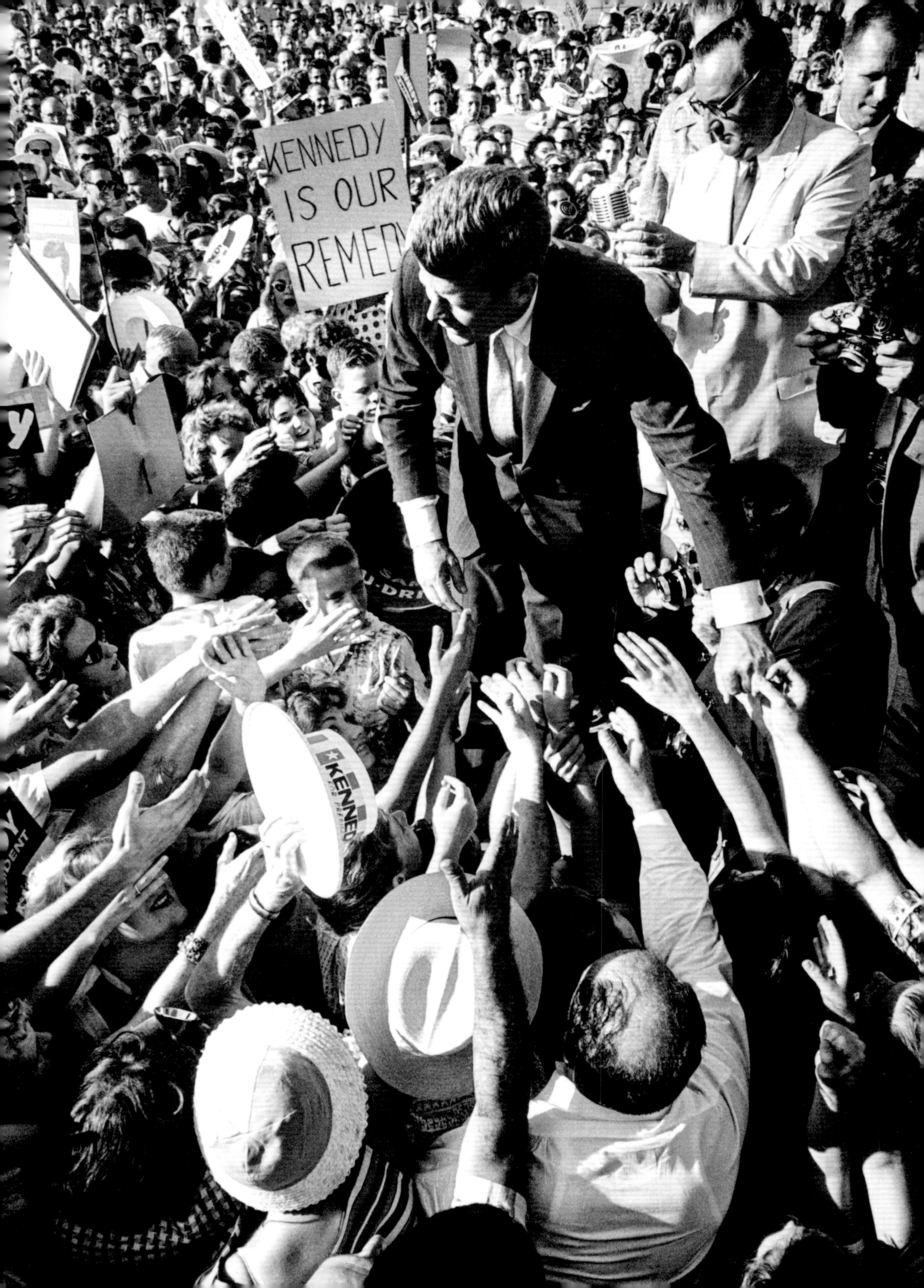

KENNEDY
IS OUR
REMEDY
KENNEDY
FOR PRESIDENT

TRIUMPH AT THE BILTMORE

Introduction by J. Michael Lennon

On November 3, 1960, five days before John F. Kennedy defeated Richard Nixon for the presidency by less than one percent of the popular vote, Norman Mailer wrote to Kennedy's wife, Jacqueline. He was replying to her letter thanking him for his extraordinarily favorable report on her husband's campaign, an essay published in *Esquire* magazine three weeks before the election titled "Superman Comes to the Supermarket." Mailer had depicted the campaign as the outcome of a dramatic morality play rather than as a realignment of voter preferences based on demographics and party promises. JFK was "a prince in the unstated aristocracy of the American dream," while Nixon was described as "sober, the apotheosis of opportunistic lead." Kennedy would win, Mailer predicted, because the nation was eager for change after eight dull, dispiriting years under President Dwight D. Eisenhower. There was a "subterranean river of untapped, ferocious, lonely and romantic desires" in the American psyche that Kennedy, a war hero with a Hollywood star's glamour, seemed ready to engage. Looking back

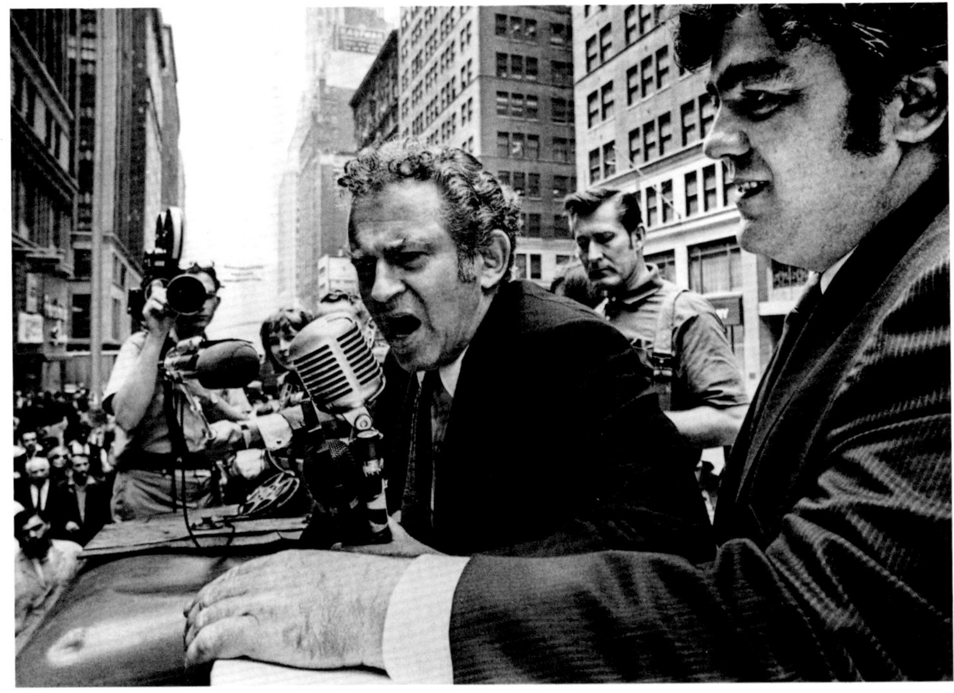

PREVIOUS SPREAD *October 28, 1960.* Center Square, Allentown, Pennsylvania. *Photo, Burton Berinsky*

OPPOSITE *September 9, 1960.* A sea of hands surge toward John F. Kennedy in Los Angeles. Buttressed by California Governor Pat Brown—one of many former rivals for the Democratic nomination—Kennedy enjoyed the full support of his party by the time of the general campaign. *Photo, Stanley Tretick*

LEFT *Spring 1969.* When Norman Mailer was assigned by *Esquire* to write about Kennedy's presidential race, he had not voted in an election since 1948. Inspired by what he saw, Mailer entered politics in 1969, running for mayor of New York City with fellow writer Jimmy Breslin. His "no more bullshit" platform won him 5 percent of the vote. *Photo, Neal Boenzi*

—Norman Mailer, "Superman Comes to the Supermarket," *Esquire*, November 1960

BELOW *June 1957.* Over the years, as JFK was testing the presidential waters—a process that began in 1957—thousands of people from across the country sent letters, postcards, and telegrams to his Senate office. Occasionally the letters were accompanied by photographs such as this snapshot, which included the prescient handwritten title and also a request: "After you are President, autograph and send back." *Photo, Anonymous*

many years later, Mailer said, "The country began to speed up, the sexual revolution began with Jack Kennedy…things began to open up."

Mailer told Mrs. Kennedy that he was troubled by her husband's disapproving, bellicose comments about Fidel Castro, who had just seized power in Cuba, but would nevertheless vote for him because "it is more important than ever that he win." It was the first vote Mailer had cast for a president since 1948 when he campaigned for third-party candidate Henry Wallace, who ran a distant third to Harry S. Truman and Thomas E. Dewey. The Kennedy mystique drew Mailer back into mainstream politics, and his essay became one of the earliest exemplars of the "New Journalism" (along with the work of Joan Didion, Gay Talese, and Tom Wolfe, among others), a new kind of writing that moved the observer onto the stage of the story. During the previous decade, Mailer had eschewed any part in conventional politics in favor of a frenetic,

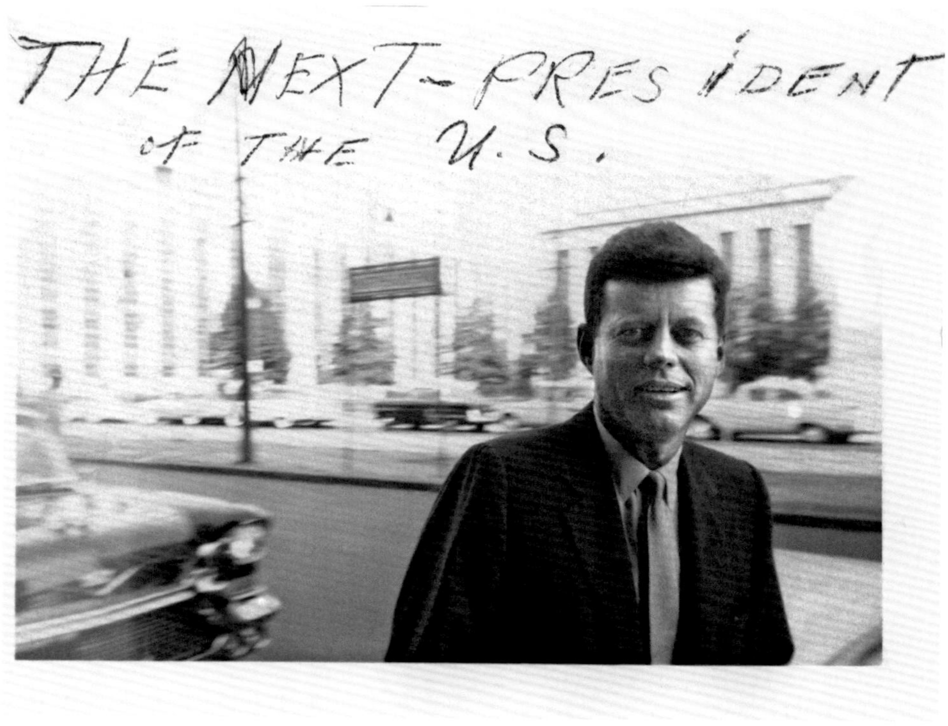

controversial role in the New York demimonde, where he extolled marijuana, jazz, and sexual freedom and celebrated the disenthralled lifestyles of African Americans in magazine essays and columns in *The Village Voice*, a weekly Greenwich Village newspaper that he cofounded and named. Bored and depressed by the kneejerk patriotism and family pieties of the tranquillized Eisenhower era, and oppressed by "the corporations, the FBI, the CIA, and the Mafia…working in an overt and covert association," Mailer saw Kennedy's election as "the hairline split in the American totalitarianism of the fifties." With the 43-year-old president and his elegant, cultured wife in the White House, politics had become exciting. In his speech accepting his party's nomination, Kennedy spoke of America as a "new frontier," a place of "unknown possibilities and perils."

Mailer was present in Los Angeles when Kennedy gave the speech, and was dazzled. He saw Kennedy as a hipster president, a bold, canny, ambitious politician who had "the remote and private air of a man who has traversed some lonely terrain of experience, of loss and gain, of nearness to death." For his services in helping get him elected, Mailer felt he was owed—at the very least—a meal, some drinks, and the president's ear, but his deeper desire was to become a key advisor, a cultural Cardinal Richelieu who would link the White House to the most exciting currents and actors on the American scene. He wanted a seat at the Camelot roundtable. Some in Kennedy's court called Mailer "an intellectual adventurer," and they had it right.

"Superman Comes to the Supermarket" was the brainchild of one of the top editors at *Esquire*, Clay Felker, who later founded *New York* magazine. He and another editor, the brilliantly irreverent Harold Hayes, as well as the magazine's cofounder and publisher, Arnold Gingrich (a fishing/drinking chum of Hemingway)—were properly impressed by the edgy, self-conscious style Mailer displayed in the prefatory "advertisements" to his 1959 omnium-gatherum, *Advertisements for Myself.* Nevertheless, they believed that their magazine, which was rapidly emerging as the best place for the brightest literary talents of the new decade to publish, was elevating Mailer's name as much as he was lofting the name of the magazine. A contest of egos ensued. Gingrich decided that the last word in the title of Mailer's JFK essay should be "Supermart," not "Supermarket," and made the change before publication. Mailer protested, and was assured by Felker that restoration would be made. But it wasn't, and in an angry letter Mailer resigned from the magazine. "You print nice stuff, but you gotta treat

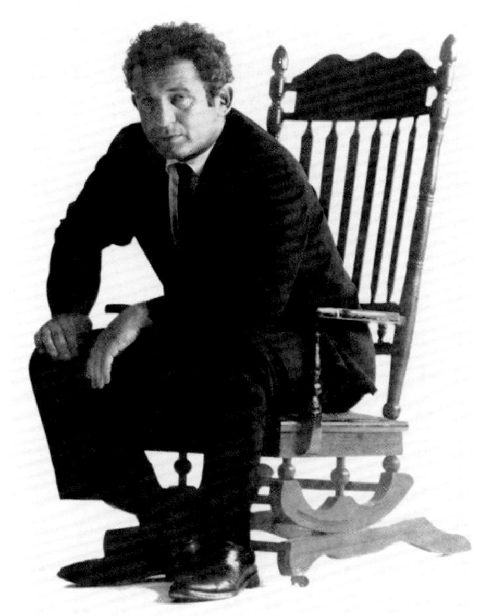

ABOVE *1963*. The original author photo for *The Presidential Papers* shows Mailer in a rocking chair, an irreverent reference to Kennedy's chair of choice. The book, which featured the essay "Superman Comes to the Supermarket," among others, had already gone to press when news of Kennedy's assassination arrived, and it was too late to change the jacket photo. The photograph was revised for the paperback edition. *Photo, Lester Krauss*

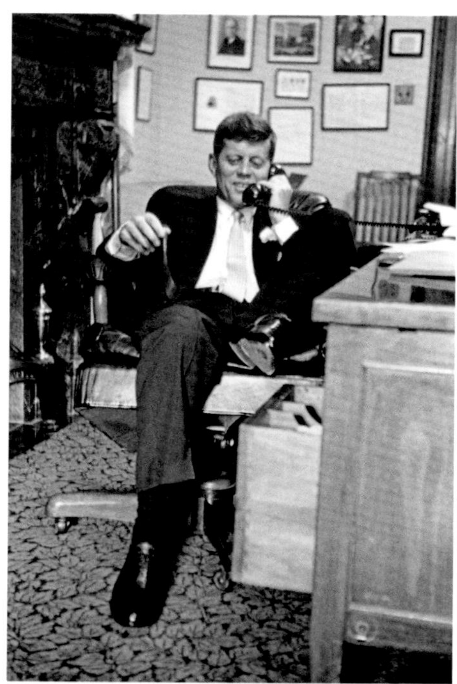

the hot writer right or you lose him like you just lost me. When I'm mayor, I'll pay you a visit and see if you've cleaned the stable." In later years, when admirers asked Mailer to sign a copy of the magazine containing his essay, he invariably crossed out "Supermart" and replaced it with the original word.

Mailer was not joshing about his ambition to become New York's next mayor. Bloated by the success of his essay, he decided to run in the September 1961 mayoral primary elections—but not on the Democratic Party ticket. Instead, he planned to run on the ticket of the Existentialist Party, which at that time (and ever after) did not exist. His temper of mind, he wrote later, was "Napoleonic." His friends listened to his plans, but with no enthusiasm. Mailer expected them, and his family, to rally around him the way the Kennedy clan had worked for JFK. Mailer's family thought the idea was crazy, and his wife, Adele, was terrified by the possibility of becoming the first lady of the nation's largest city. He intended to announce his candidacy at a large party at their Manhattan apartment on November 19, 1960, two weeks after Kennedy's victory. Drunk and stoned on marijuana (which he believed unseated unhealthy repressions), a frazzled and belligerent Mailer got into fistfights with several of his guests at the crowded party. The worst was to come. At around five A. M. on the 20th, he stabbed his wife with a penknife after she delivered a taunt about his manhood. She almost died of the thrust, which nicked the sac surrounding her heart, the pericardium. Mailer received a suspended sentence and was placed on probation after Adele refused to testify against him. They divorced two years later. His literary career was suspended, and his political career seemed over.

But the influence of the essay was not diminished; indeed, it was enhanced by the notoriety surrounding Mailer at the time. Felker said that the essay had "an enormous impact," and Pete Hamill, a journalist and novelist who was close to Mailer, said it "went through journalism like a wave." Young journalists now recognized that the venerable inverted pyramid form learned in school—a form that front-loaded the most newsworthy information—had become dull and stodgy, partly because it ignored the array of narrative techniques developed by novelists over the previous century. Mailer used them all, including scene-by-scene construction, later fingered by Tom Wolfe as one of the most important techniques of the New Journalism. "Superman" is one of the foundation stones of this movement, one that changed the face of writing about

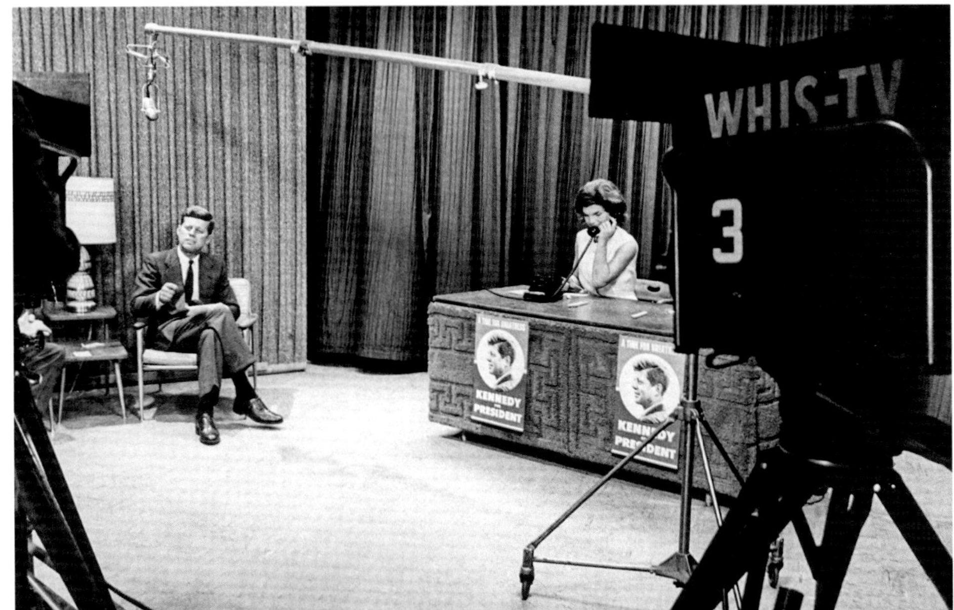

LEFT *April 26, 1960.* Jack and his wife, Jacqueline, appear on a local prime-time TV show in Bluefield, West Virginia, in the lead-up to the state's May 10th primary election, with Jackie fielding call-in questions from the audience for her husband. Earlier that day, JFK visited a string of towns and mingled with a crew of 200 coal miners during a shift change at the Pocahontas Fuel Company's Itmann coal mine near Mullens. *Photo, Hank Walker*

the news of the day. One difference between Wolfe's writing and Mailer's is that Mailer, extravagantly confident of the worth of his explorations, packed everything in: surmises about his subjects, larger speculations about the amazing changes in American life, and a filament of continuity extruded from Mailer's own personality. In his essays and nonfiction narratives of the 1960s and early 1970s, he consistently included his line of sight on events, coupled with the nuanced examination of his personal responses to them. His radar for the mood of events is unerring, and—to extend the metaphor— his sonar for the depths of his subjects' psyches has rarely been equaled. Identity and ambition were his touchstones.

In the middle of "Superman Comes to the Supermarket" Mailer describes his first meeting with then-Senator Kennedy at the family compound in Hyannis. The candidate tells the reporter that he is familiar with his novels, and after a slight but convincing hesitation says he has read Mailer's most recent and controversial, *The Deer Park*, passing over the one monotonously referred to by everyone else, *The Naked and the Dead* (his 1948 novel of Pacific combat that spent over a year on the bestseller list). Mailer is stunned, and ponders whether Kennedy is being truthful, or has been prepped to name *The Deer Park*, which deals with the lures and corruptions of contemporary Hollywood. He decides that it doesn't matter. If JFK's aides had advised him on what to say, Mailer concluded, it demonstrated the perspicacity of their boss and his predilection for hiring staff with subtle talents, and perhaps a sophisticated taste for literature. The encounter is the beginning of Mailer's lifelong admiration for Kennedy— this side of idolatry, as he sharply disagrees with many of his ideas and programs—a fealty that is burnished when Mrs. Kennedy writes to Mailer to say that her husband did indeed read *The Deer Park*, finishing it on a rainy day in Hyannis. Some years later, Mailer spoke of his attraction to Kennedy: "He was a little like [President Franklin D.] Roosevelt: both were enchanting, had personality, and made America more fun to live in. His spell, his wit, the rich and broad life he led conquered us to the point that we would have talked about him for years. I took to him right away. Rather, to be honest, before him I had taken to his wife."

In her letter, Mrs. Kennedy told Mailer that she also enjoyed his novel, and went on to say that before reading "Superman," she had "never dreamed that American politics could be written about that way." She lauded his talent, and encouraged him

"Politics is the art of the possible, and what is always possible is to reduce the amount of real suffering in a bad time, and to enrich the quality of life in a good time. This is precisely what is not being done in America."

—Norman Mailer, "Heroes and Leaders," *The Presidential Papers*, 1964

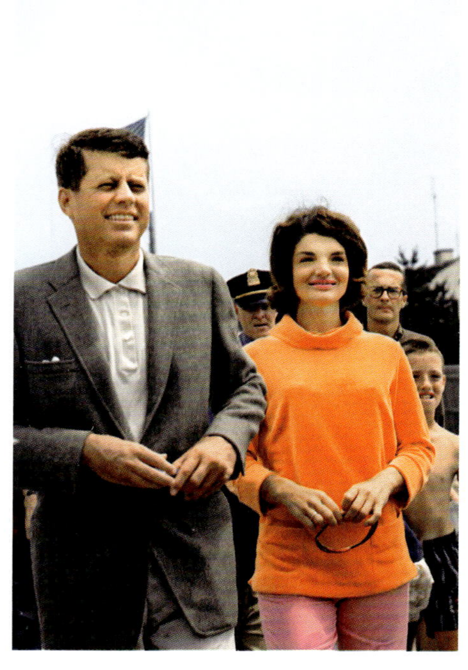

ABOVE *July 19, 1960.* Following his victory at the Democratic National Convention, Kennedy spent much of July and August shuttling between D.C., and the Kennedy compound in Hyannis Port, Massachusetts. A wealthy waterfront enclave, it afforded the Kennedys a relaxed atmosphere in which to interact with the media, and a modicum of privacy on sails around the cape. *Photo, Anonymous*

OPPOSITE *Spring 1960.* Early in the campaign, when Kennedy was staking out primary wins, Jackie often joined her husband on the campaign trail. *Photo, Stan Wayman*

to use it to write more nonfiction narratives. It was advice he took, writing accounts of subsequent presidential campaigns through 1972, and several novels set in earlier periods, most notably *Harlot's Ghost* (his 1991 novel about the CIA in the 1950s and 1960s) and his 1995 collaboration with Lawrence Schiller, *Oswald's Tale: An American Mystery*, a nonfiction book that explored the life of Kennedy's assassin. JFK's death is a crucial event in both books. Mailer never stopped worrying the bone of the Kennedy assassination (ultimately deciding that Oswald probably acted alone), and continued to ponder what might have been had Kennedy lived.

The slain president remained an inspiration, and in June 1969 Mailer ran in the New York City mayoral primary on the Democratic ticket. The popular newspaper columnist Jimmy Breslin ran for city council president on the same ticket. The key plank in their quixotic platform was making New York City the 51st state; their campaign slogan was "Vote the Rascals In." Mailer came in fourth in a field of five, and Breslin lost as well, and that was the end of Mailer's direct involvement in politics, although he and Senator Eugene McCarthy seriously discussed running in 1996—McCarthy for president and Mailer for vice president. (The idea died aborning.)

Mailer went on to report on the 1996 election for *George* at the behest of the magazine's chief editor and the martyred president's namesake, John F. Kennedy Jr. Mailer traveled around the country on the press planes of President Bill Clinton and his Republican opponent, Senator Robert J. Dole; and at 73, he was by far the oldest reporter covering the campaign, referred to by the others as "the Dean." The tutelary spirit of his *George* articles was President Kennedy himself, whom Mailer revered for the rest of his life as "a real man with a real set of desires to make a good and exciting and interesting change in history."

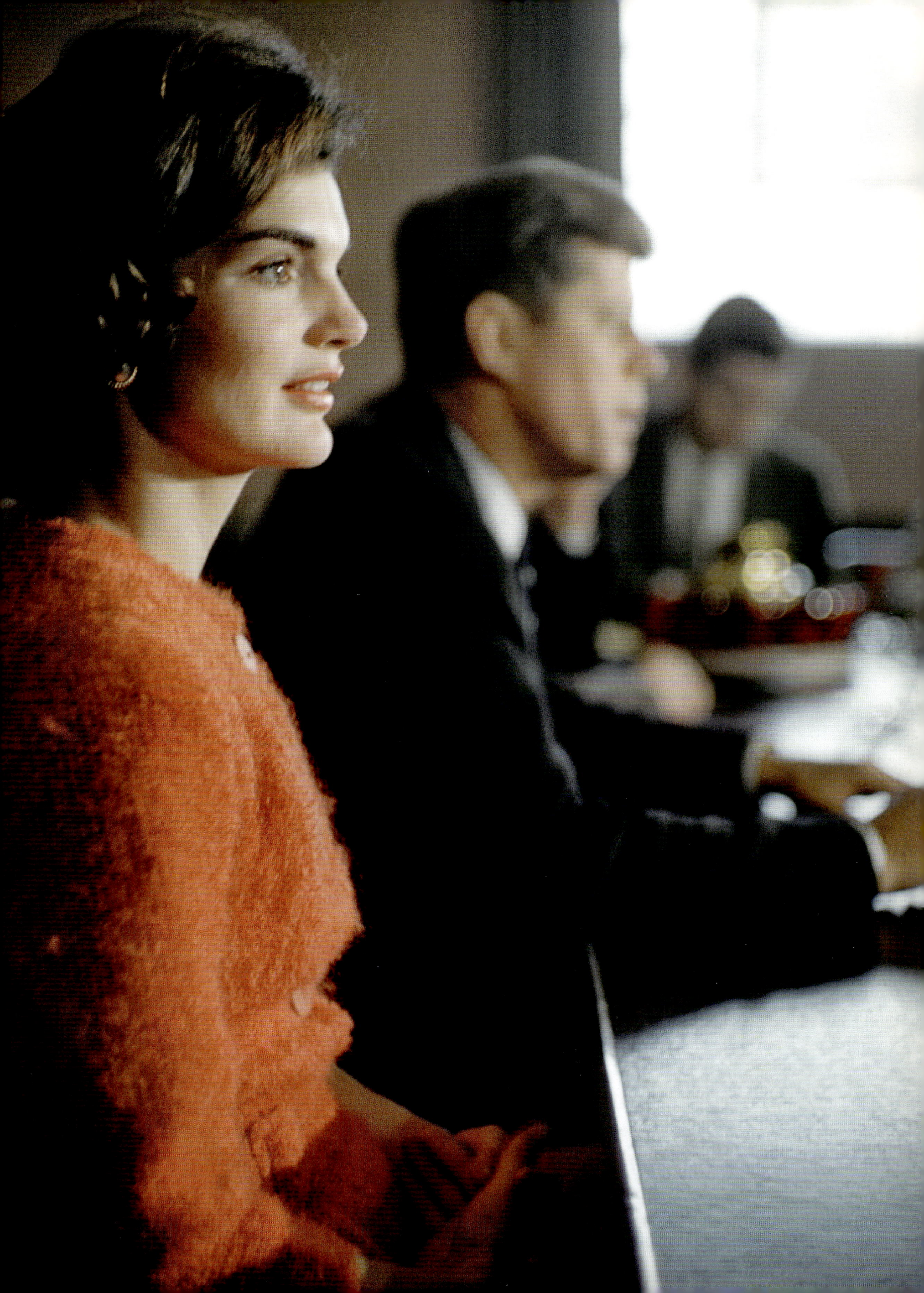

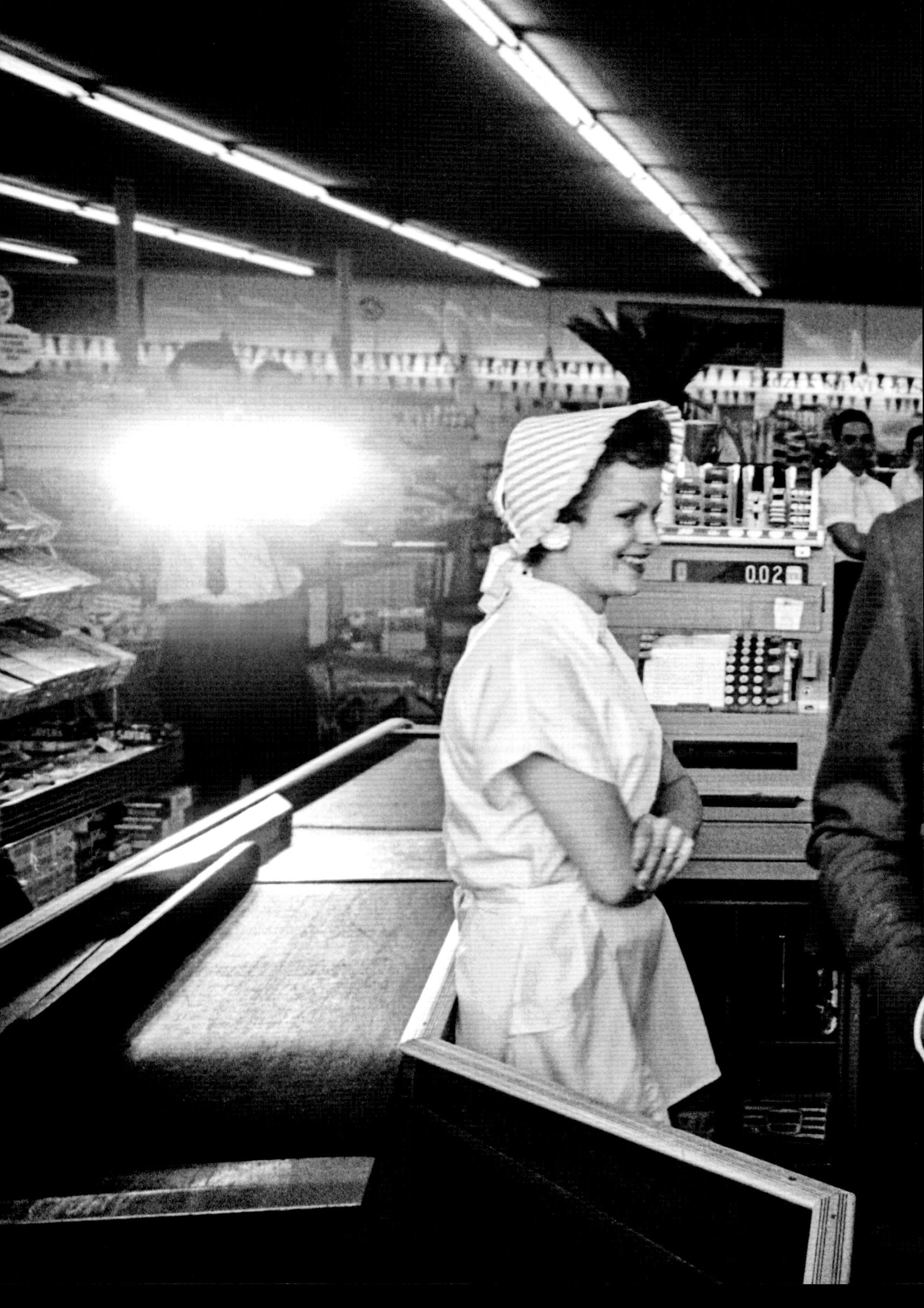

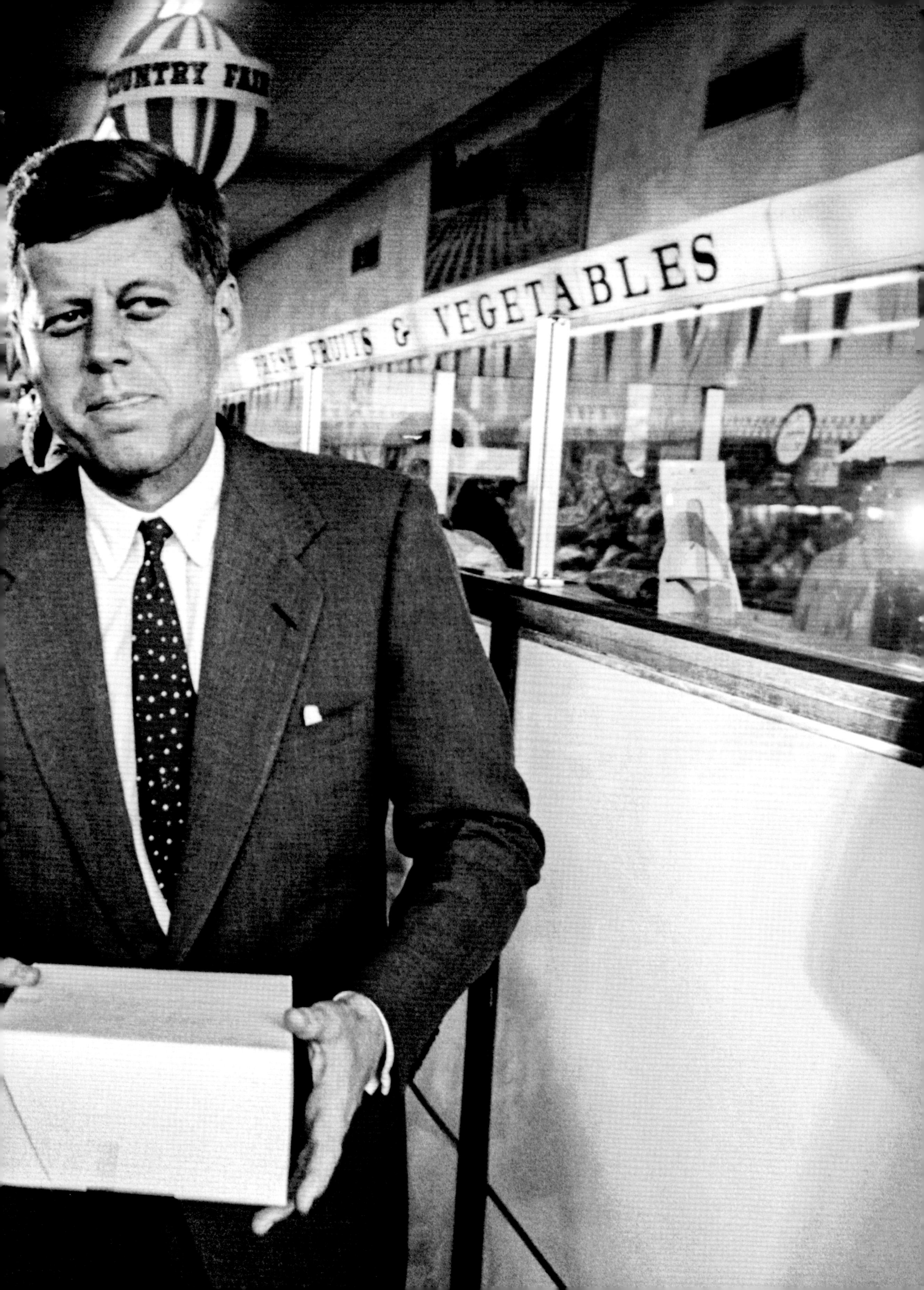

COUNTRY FAIR
THESE FRUITS & VEGETABLES

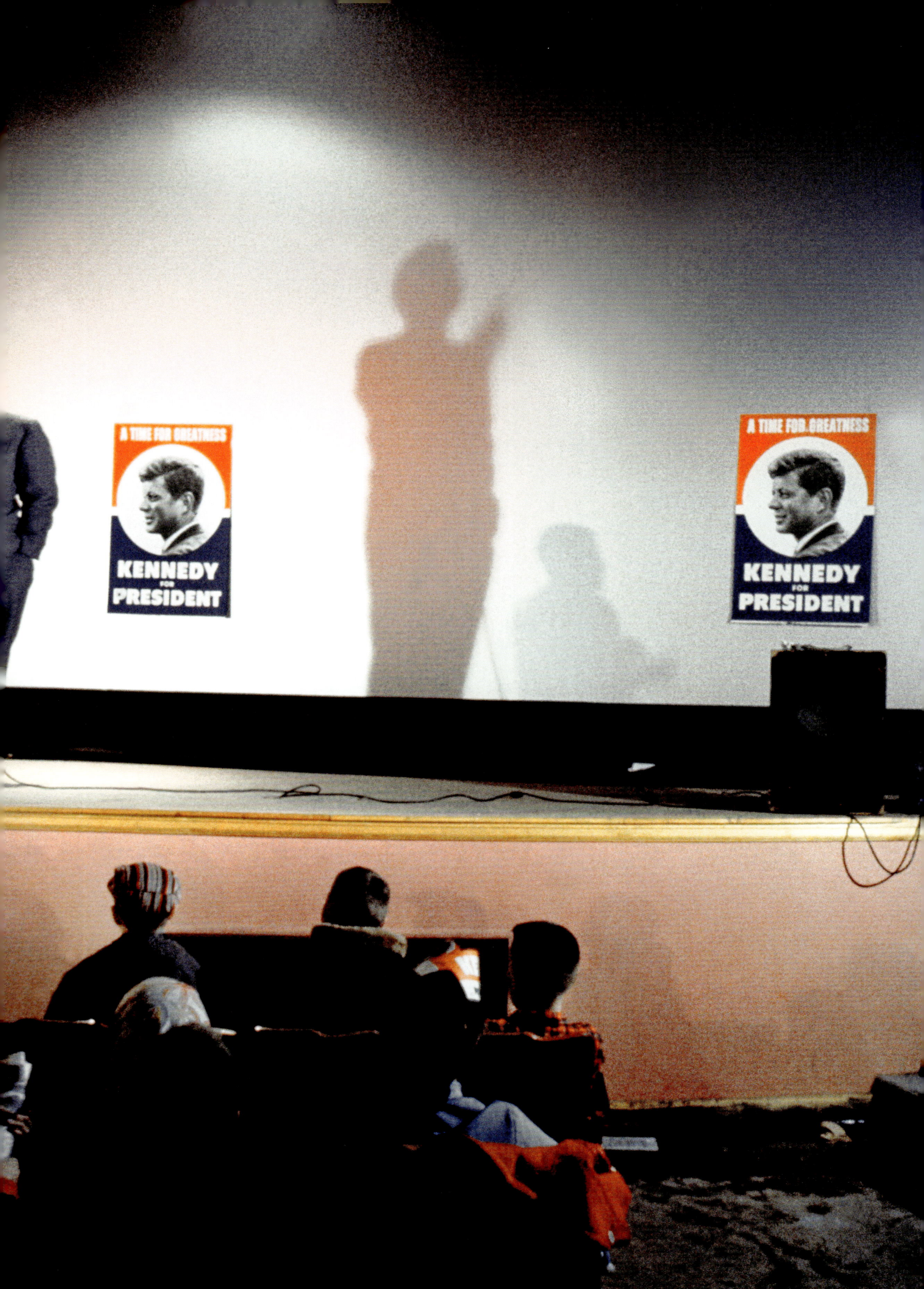
A TIME FOR GREATNESS
KENNEDY
FOR
PRESIDENT
A TIME FOR GREATNESS
KENNEDY
FOR
PRESIDENT

SUPERMAN COMES TO THE SUPERMARKET

By Norman Mailer

Not too much need be said for this piece; it is possible it can stand by itself. But perhaps its title should have been "Filling the Holes in No Man's Land." American politics is rarely interesting for its men, its ideas, or the style of its movements. It is usually more fascinating in its gaps, its absences, its uninvaded territories. We have used up our frontier, but the psychological frontier talked about in this piece is still alive with untouched possibilities and dire unhappy all-but-lost opportunities. In European politics the spaces are filled — the average politician, like the average European, knows what is possible and what is impossible for him. Their politics is like close trench warfare. But in America, one knows such close combat only for the more banal political activities. The play of political ideas is flaccid here in America because opposing armies never meet. The Right, the Center, and what there is of the Left have set up encampment on separate hills, they face one another across valleys, they send out small patrols to their front and vast communiqués to their rear. No Man's Land predominates. It is a situation which calls for guerrilla raiders. Any army which would dare to enter the valley in force might not only determine a few new political formations, but indeed could create more politics itself, even as the guerrilla raids of the Negro Left and Negro Right, the Freedom Riders and the Black Muslims, have discovered much of the secret nature of the American reality for us.

I wonder if I make myself clear. Conventional politics has had so little to do with the real subterranean life of America that none of us know much about the real — which is to say the potential — historic nature of America. That lies buried under apathy, platitudes, Rightist encomiums for the FBI, programmatic welfare from the liberal Center, and furious pips of protest from the Peace Movement's Left. The mass of Americans are not felt as a political reality. No one has any idea of how they would react to radically new sense. It is only when their heart-land, their no man's land, their valley is invaded, that one discovers the reality. In Birmingham during the days of this writing, the jails are filled with Negro children, two thousand of them. The militancy of the Negroes in Birmingham is startling, so too is the stubbornness of the Southern white, so too and unbelievable is the procrastination of the Kennedy administration. Three new realities have been discovered. The potential Left and potential Right of America are more vigorous than one would have expected and the Center is more irresolute. An existential political act, the drive by Southern Negroes, led by

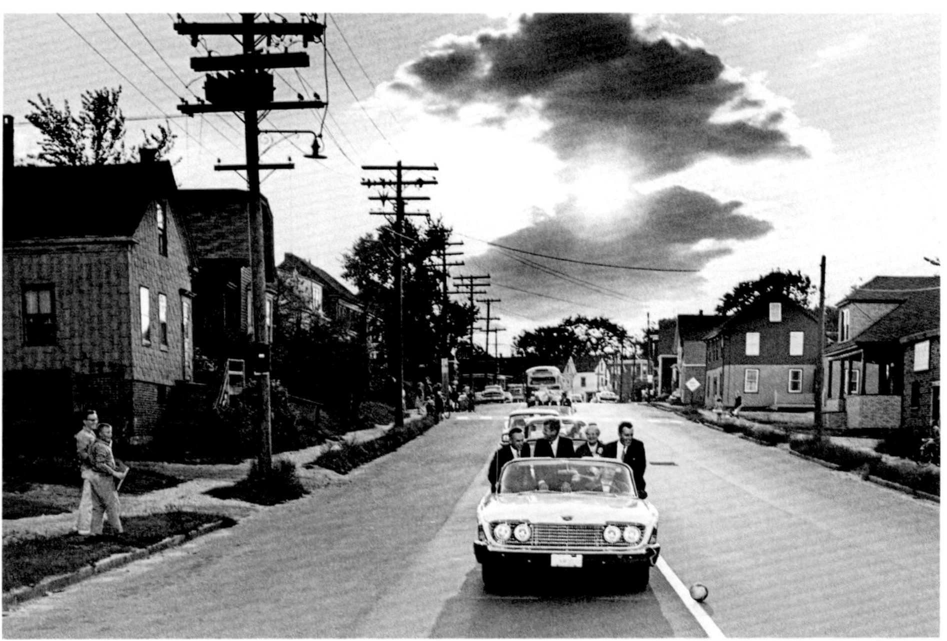

Martin Luther King, to end segregation in restaurants in Birmingham, an act which is existential precisely because its end is unknown, has succeeded en route in discovering more of the American reality to us.

If a public speaker in a small Midwestern town were to say, "J. Edgar Hoover has done more harm to the freedoms of America than Joseph Stalin," the act would be existential. Depending on the occasion and the town, he would be manhandled physically or secretly applauded. But he would create a new reality which would displace the old psychological reality that such a remark could not be made, even as for example the old Southern psychological reality that you couldn't get two Negroes to do anything together, let alone two thousand, has now been destroyed by a new and more accurate psychological reality: you can get two thousand Negroes to work in cooperation. The new psychological realities are closer to history and so closer to sanity and they exist because, and only because, the event has taken place.

It was Kennedy's potentiality to excite such activity which interested me most; that he was young, that he was physically handsome, and that his wife was attractive were not trifling accidental details but, rather, new major political facts. I knew if he became President, it would be an existential event: he would touch depths in American life which were uncharted. Regardless of his politics, and even then one could expect his politics would be as conventional as his personality was unconventional, indeed one could expect his politics to be pushed toward conventionality precisely to counteract his essential unconventionality, one knew nonetheless that regardless of his overt politics, America's tortured psychotic search for security would finally be torn loose from the feverish ghosts of its old generals, its MacArthurs and Eisenhowers — ghosts which Nixon could cling to — and we as a nation would finally be loose again in the historic seas of a national psyche which was willy-nilly and at last, again, adventurous. And that, I thought, that was the hope for America. So I swallowed my doubts, my disquiets, and my certain distastes for Kennedy's dullness of mind and prefabricated politics, and did my best to write a piece which would help him to get elected.

[Preface to "The Third Presidential Paper," *The Presidential Papers*, 1963]

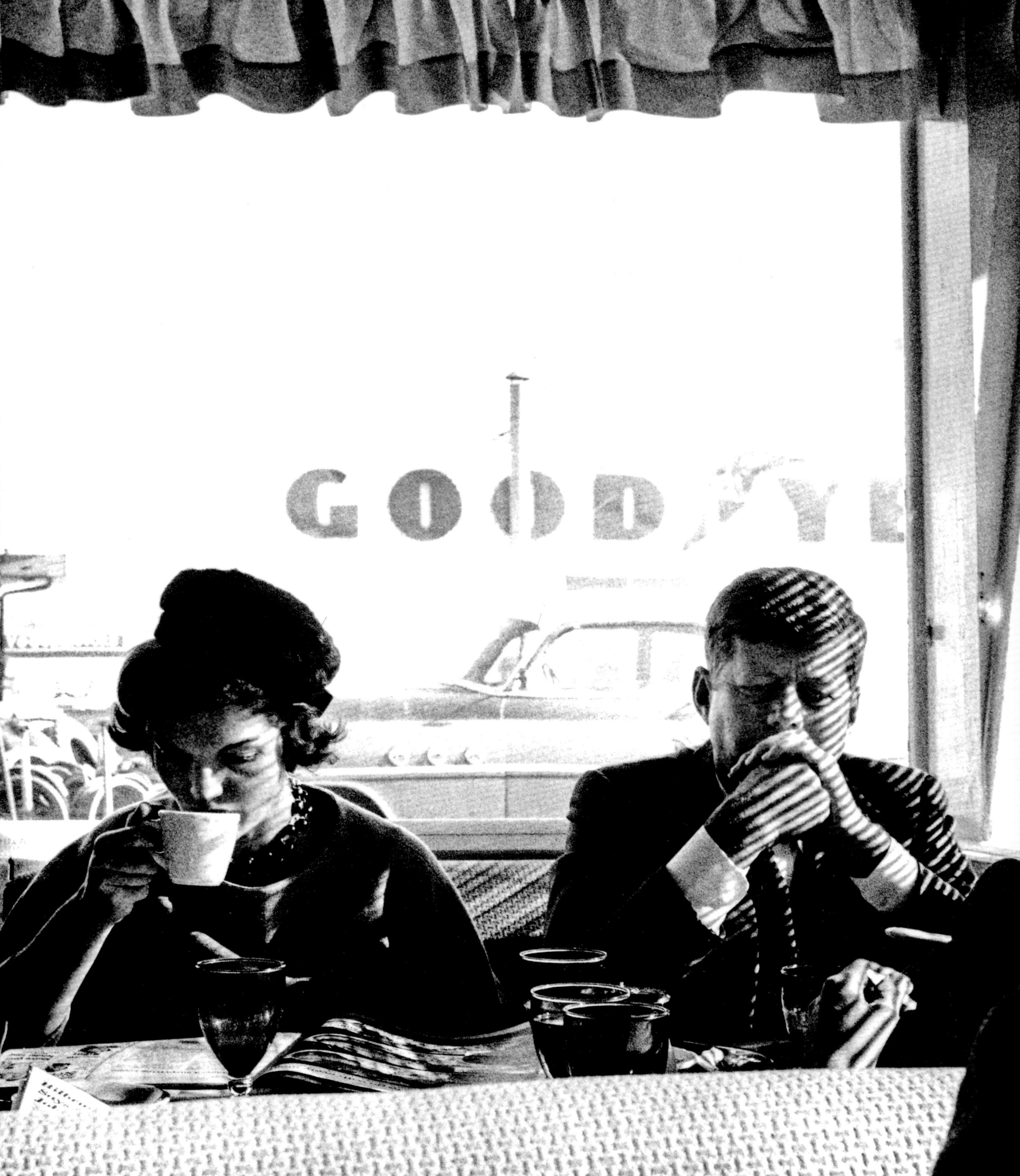
GOODYE

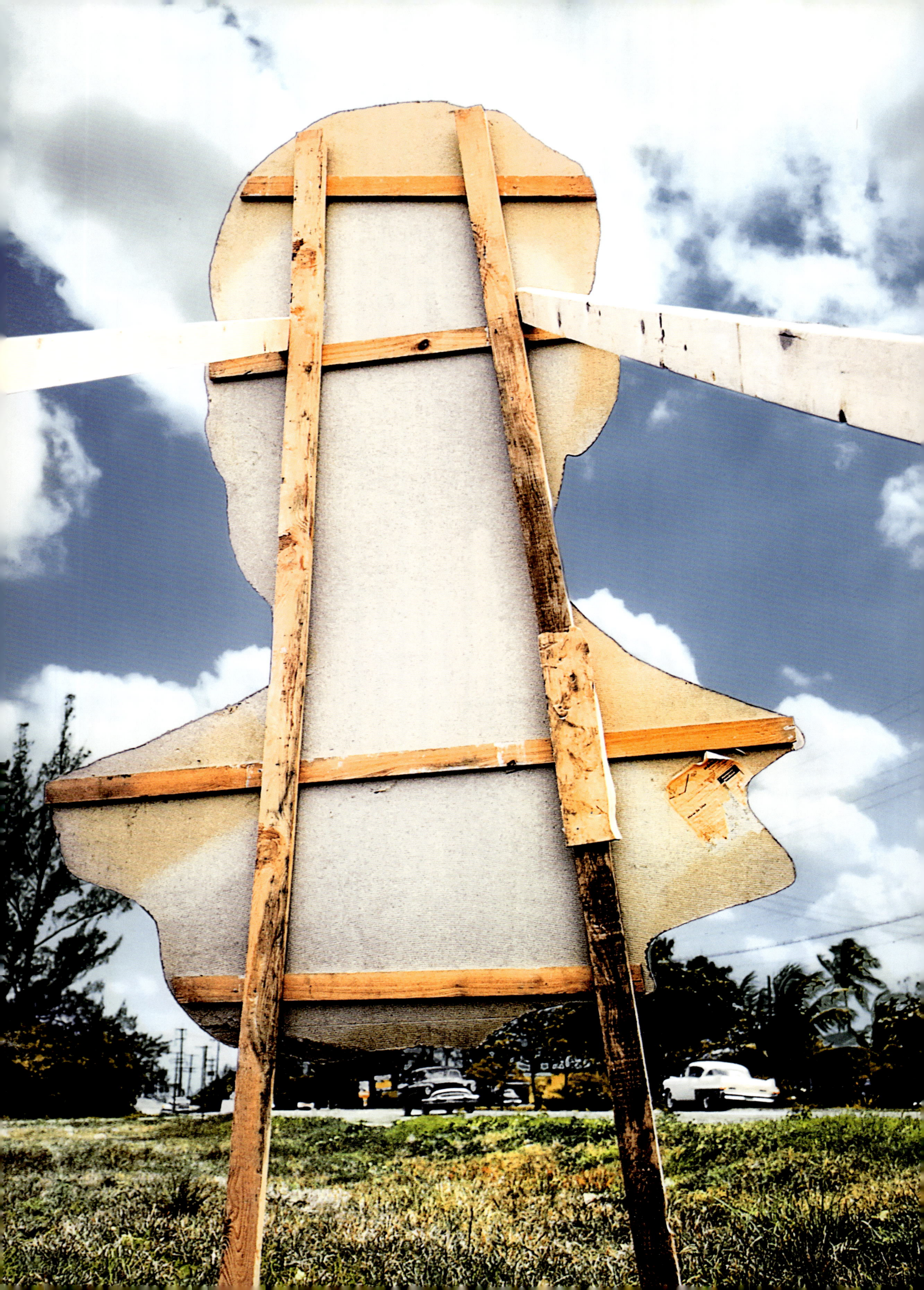

"Mysteries are irritated by facts, and the 1960 Democratic Convention began as one mystery and ended as another."

—Norman Mailer

For once let us try to think about a political convention without losing ourselves in housing projects of fact and issue. Politics has its virtues, all too many of them—it would not rank with baseball as a topic of conversation if it did not satisfy a great many things—but one can suspect that its secret appeal is close to nicotine. Smoking cigarettes insulates one from one's life, one does not feel as much, often happily so, and politics quarantines one from history; most of the people who nourish themselves in the political life are in the game not to make history but to be diverted from the history which is being made.

If that Democratic Convention which has now receded behind the brow of the Summer of 1960 is only half-remembered in the excitements of moving toward the election, it may be exactly the time to consider it again, because the mountain of facts which concealed its features last July has been blown away in the winds of High Television, and the man-in-the-street (that peculiar political term which refers to the quixotic voter who will pull the lever for some reason so salient as: "I had a brown-nose lieutenant once with Nixon's looks," or "that Kennedy must have false teeth"), the not so easily estimated man-in-the-street has forgotten most of what happened and could no more tell you who Kennedy was fighting against than you or I could place a bet on who was leading the American League in batting during the month of June.

So to try to talk about what happened is easier now than in the days of the convention, one does not have to put everything in—an act of writing which calls for a bulldozer rather than a pen—one can try to make one's little point and dress it with a ribbon or two of metaphor. All to the good. Because mysteries are irritated by facts, and the 1960 Democratic Convention began as one mystery and ended as another.

Since mystery is an emotion which is repugnant to a political animal (why else lead a life of bad banquet dinners, cigar smoke, camp chairs, foul breath, and excru-ciatingly dull jargon if not to avoid the echoes of what is not known), the psychic separation between what was happening on the floor, in the caucus rooms, in the headquarters, and what was happening in parallel to the history of the nation was mystery enough to drown the proceedings in gloom. It was on the one hand a dull convention, one of the less interesting by general agreement, relieved by local bits of color, given two half hours of excitement by two demonstrations for Stevenson, buoyed up by the class of the Kennedy machine, turned by the surprise of Johnson's

OPPOSITE *Spring 1960.* Cornell Capa had a keen interest in capturing the unseen moments and unnoticed mechanisms of political life. In a major story for the July 4, 1960, "U.S. Politics" special issue of *Life* magazine, he followed John F. Kennedy and other national and local candidates on the campaign trail from Pennsylvania to Wisconsin to New Mexico in the 1960 primary races. Shot entirely in color, none of his pictures of Kennedy made the editors' final cut. *Photo, Cornell Capa*

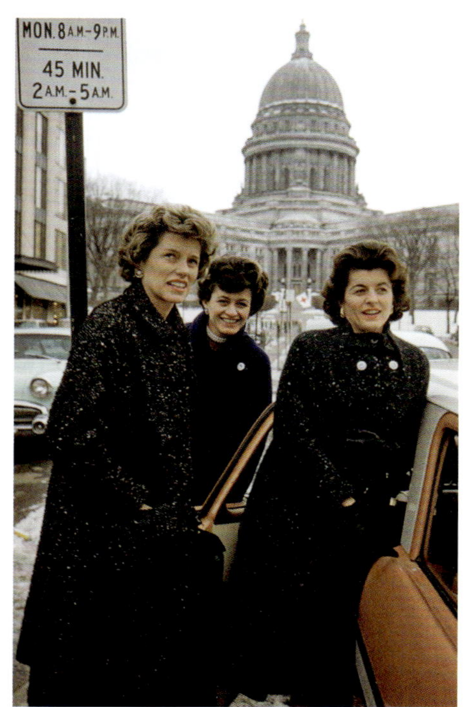

ABOVE *March 1960.* Jack's sisters—Eunice Shriver, Jean Smith, and Patricia Lawford—at work for their brother in Madison, Wisconsin (the State Capitol building appears in the background). The support of the entire Kennedy family during the campaign was crucial to JFK's victory, especially in hotly contested primaries. *Photo, Stan Wayman*

nomination as vice-president, but, all the same, dull, depressed in its overall tone, the big fiestas subdued, the gossip flat, no real air of excitement, just moments—or as they say in bullfighting—details. Yet it was also, one could argue—and one may argue this yet—it was also one of the most important conventions in America's history, it could prove conceivably to be the most important. The man it nominated was unlike any politician who had ever run for President in the history of the land, and if elected he would come to power in a year when America was in danger of drifting into a profound decline.

A Descriptive of the Delegates

Sons and Daughters of the Republic in a Legitimate Panic; Small-time Practitioners of Small-town Political Judo in the Big Town and the Big Time

Depression obviously has its several roots: it is the doubtful protection which comes from not recognizing failure, it is the psychic burden of exhaustion, and it is also, and very often, the discipline of the will or the ego which enables one to continue working when one's unadmitted emotion is panic. And panic it was I think which sat as the largest single sentiment in the breast of the collective delegates as they came to convene in Los Angeles. Delegates are not the noblest sons and daughters of the Republic; a man of taste, arrived from Mars, would take one look at a convention floor and leave forever, convinced he had seen one of the drearier squats of Hell. If one still smells the faint living echo of a carnival wine, the pepper of a bullfight, the rag, drag, and panoply of a jousting tourney, it is all swallowed and regurgitated by the senses into the fouler cud of a death gas one must rid oneself of—a cigar-smoking, stale-aired, slack-jawed, butt-littered, foul, bleak, hard-working, bureaucratic death gas of language and faces ("Yes, those *faces*," says the man from Mars: lawyers, judges, ward heelers, *mafiosos*, Southern goons and grandees, grand old ladies, trade unionists and finks), of pompous words and long pauses which lay like a leaden pain over fever, the fever that one is in, over, or is it that one is just behind history? A legitimate panic for a delegate. America is a nation of experts without roots; we are always creating tacticians who are blind to strategy and strategists who cannot take a step, and when the culture has finished its work the institutions handcuff the infirmity. A delegate is a man who picks a candidate for the largest office in the land, a President who must live with problems whose borders are in ethics, metaphysics, and now ontology; the delegate is prepared for this office of selection by emptying wastebaskets, toting garbage, and saying yes at the right time for twenty years in the small political machine of some small or large town; his reward, one of them anyway, is that he arrives at an invitation to the convention. An expert on local catch-as-catch-can, a small-time, often mediocre practitioner of small-town political judo, he comes to the big city with nine-tenths of his mind made up, he will follow the orders of the boss who brought him. Yet of course it is not altogether so mean as that: his opinion is listened to — the boss will consider what he has to say as one interesting factor among five hundred, and what is most important to the delegate, he has the illusion of partial freedom. He can, unless he is severely honest with himself — and if he is, why sweat

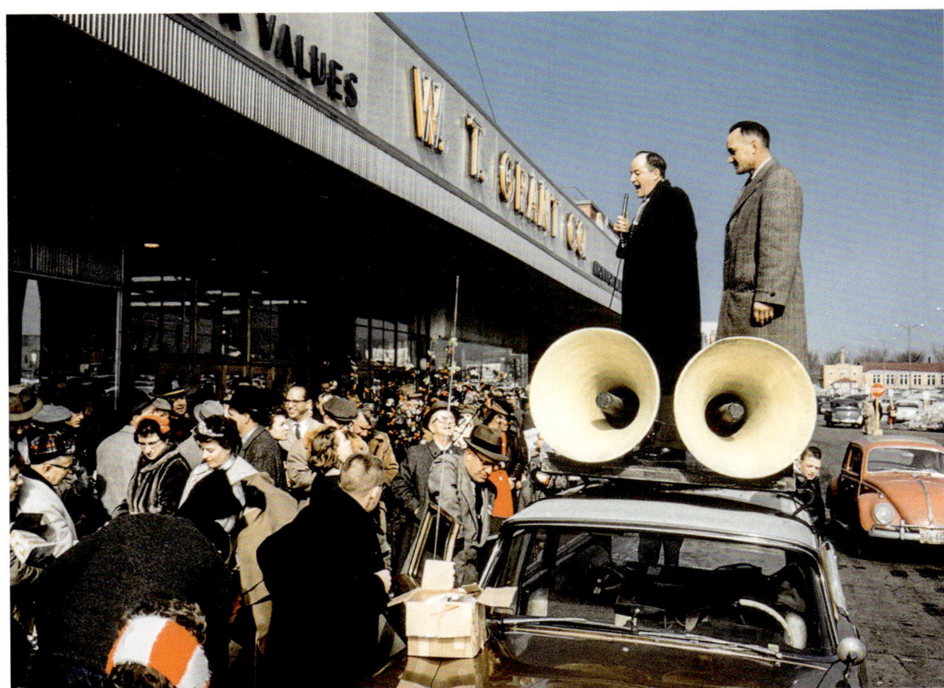

OPPOSITE *March 1960.* JFK signs autographs for high school students in the small town of Mayville, Wisconsin, prior to that state's primary. Kennedy was especially popular among young people all across the country. In the early 1960s, few photojournalists were shooting with color film—it was expensive and most magazines rarely published color except for covers—but Stan Wayman, on assignment for *Life*, used color to show the energy of this hotly contested primary race.
Photo, Stan Wayman

out the low levels of a political machine?—he can have the illusion that he has helped to choose the candidate, he can even worry most sincerely about his choice, flirt with defection from the boss, work out his own small political gains by the road of loyalty or the way of hard bargain. But even if he is there for more than the ride, his vote a certainty in the mind of the political boss, able to be thrown here or switched there as the boss decides, still in some peculiar sense he is reality to the boss, the delegate is the great American public, the bar he owns or the law practice, the piece of the union he represents, or the real-estate office, is a part of the political landscape which the boss uses as his own image of how the votes will go, and if the people will like the candidate. And if the boss is depressed by what he sees, if the candidate does not feel right to him, if he has a dull intimation that the candidate is not his sort (as, let us say, Harry Truman was his sort, or Symington might be his sort, or Lyndon Johnson), then vote for him the boss will if he must; he cannot be caught on the wrong side, but he does not feel the pleasure of a personal choice. Which is the center of the panic. Because if the boss is depressed, the delegate is doubly depressed, and the emotional fact is that Kennedy is not in focus, not in the old political focus, he is not comfortable; in fact it is a mystery to the boss how Kennedy got to where he is, not a mystery in its structures; Kennedy is rolling in money, Kennedy got the votes in primaries, and, most of all, Kennedy has a jewel of a political machine. It is as good as a crack Notre Dame team, all discipline and savvy and go-go-go, sound, drilled, never dull, quick as a knife, full of the salt of hipper-dipper, a beautiful machine; the boss could adore it if only a sensible candidate were driving it, a Truman, even a Stevenson, please God a Northern Lyndon Johnson, but it is run by a man who looks young enough to be coach of the Freshman team, and that is not comfortable at all. The boss knows political machines, he know issues, farm parity, Forand health bill, Landrum-Griffin, but this is not all so adequate after all to revolutionaries in Cuba who look like Beatniks, competitions in missiles, Negroes looting whites in the Congo, intricacies of nuclear fallout, and NAACP men one does well to call Sir. It is all out of hand, everything important is off the center, foreign affairs is now the lick of the heat, and senators are candidates instead of governors, a disaster to the old family style of political measure where a political boss knows his governor and knows who his governor knows. So the boss is depressed, profoundly depressed. He comes to this convention resigned to

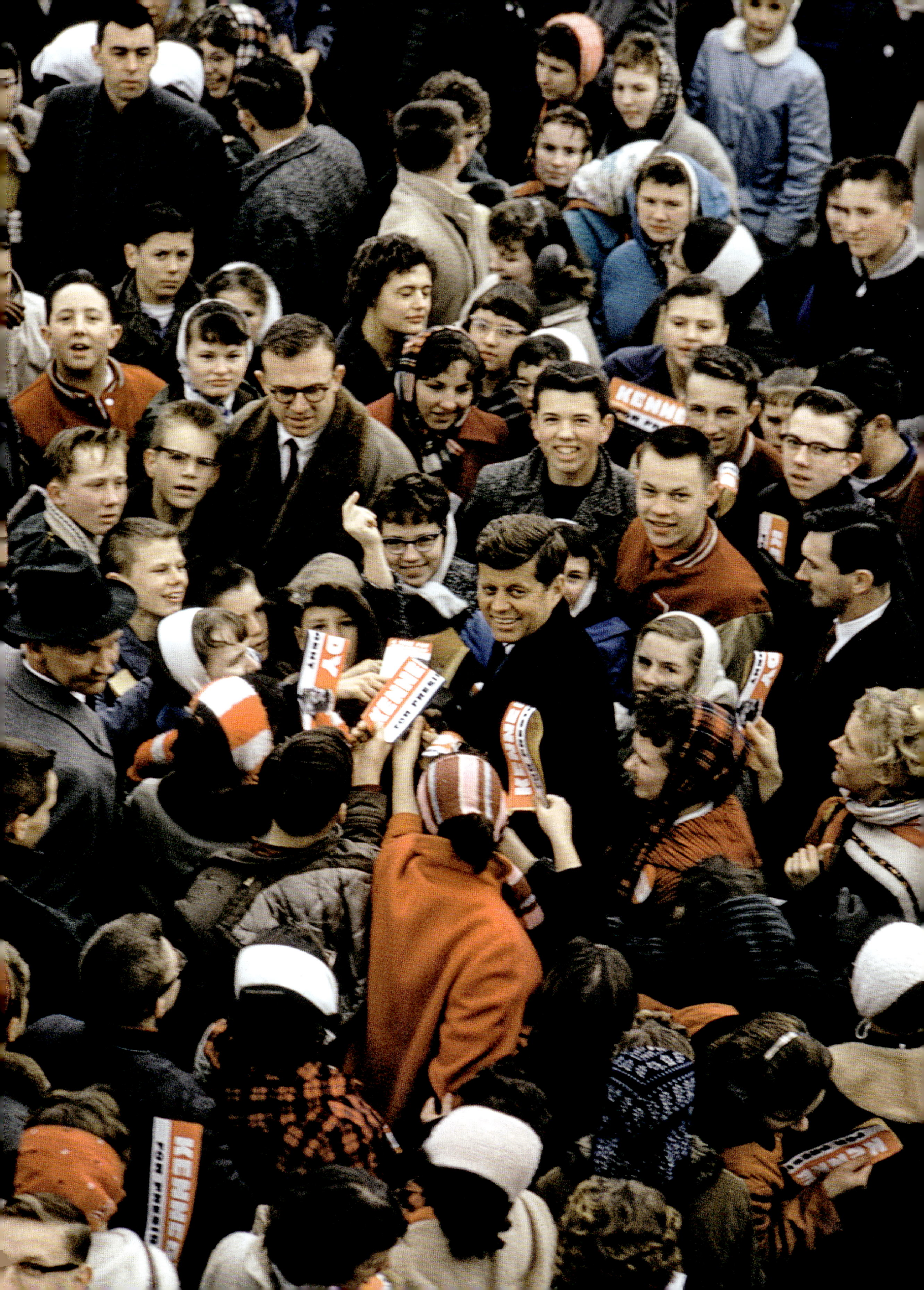

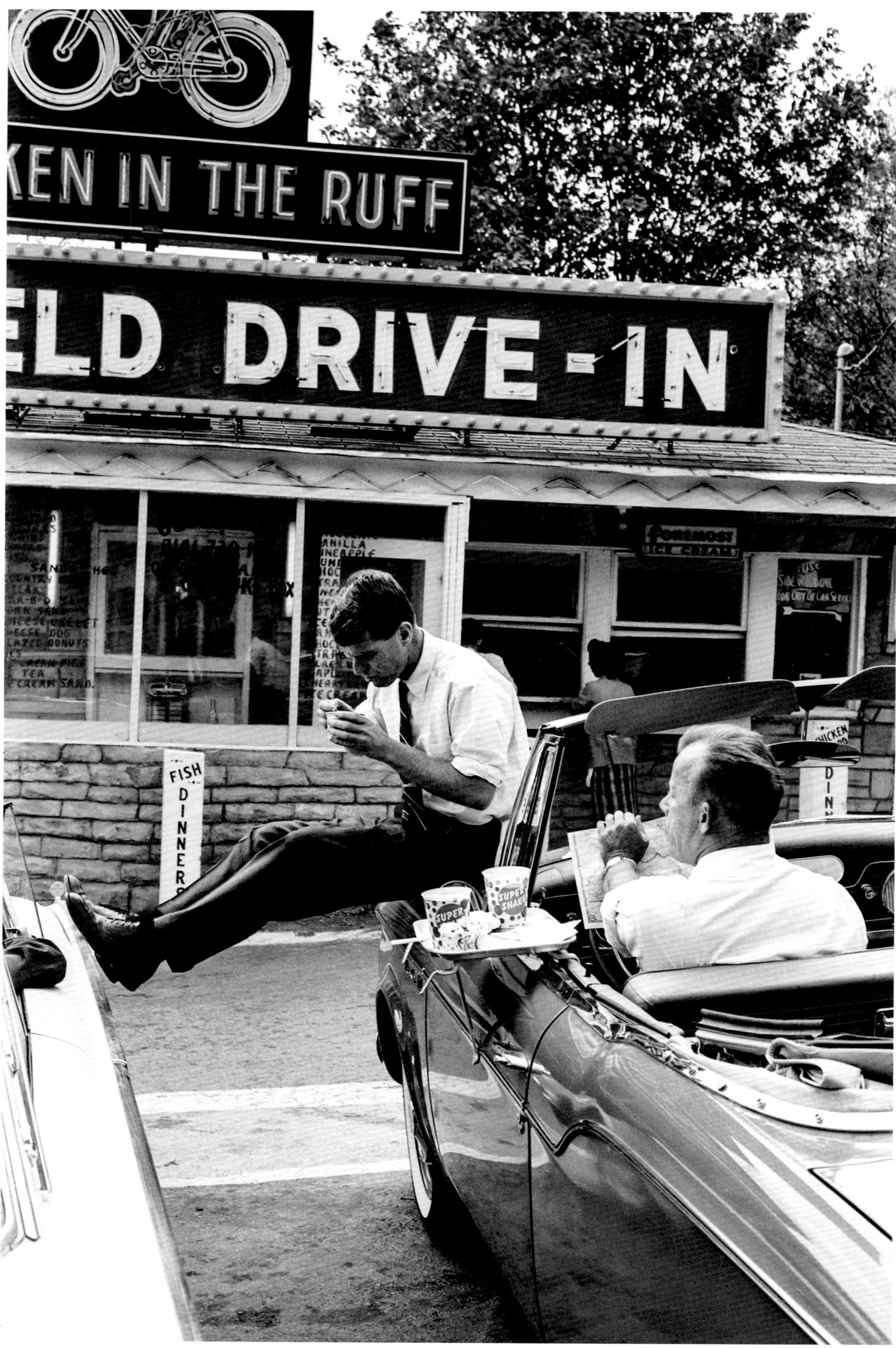
KEN IN THE RUFF
ELD DRIVE - IN
FISH DINNERS
SUPER SHAKE
SUPER SHAKE
FOREMOST
ICE CREAM

nominating a man he does not understand, or let us say that, so far as he understands the candidate who is to be nominated, he is not happy about the secrets of his appeal, not so far as he divines these secrets; they seem to have too little to do with politics and all too much to do with the private madnesses of the nation which had thousands—or was it hundreds of thousands—of people demonstrating in the long night before Chessman was killed, and a movie star, the greatest, Marlon the Brando out in the night with them. Yes, this candidate for all his record, his good, sound, conventional liberal record, has a patina of that other life, the second American life, the long electric night with the fires of neon leading down the highway to the murmur of jazz.

An Apparent Digression

A Vivid View of the "City of Lost Angels"; The Democrats Defined; A Pentagon of Traveling Salesmen; Some Pointed Portraits of the Politicians

"I was seeing Pershing Square, Los Angeles, now for the first time … the nervous fruithustlers darting in and out of the shadows, fugitives from Times Square, Market Street SF, the French Quarter—masculine hustlers looking for lonely fruits to score from, anything from the legendary $20 to a pad at night and breakfast in the morning and whatever you can clinch or clip; and the heat in their holy cop uniforms, holy because of the Almighty Stick and the Almightier Vagrancy Law; the scattered junkies, the small-time pushers, the queens, the sad panhandlers, the lonely, exiled nymphs haunting the entrance to the men's head, the fruits with the hungry eyes and jingling coins; the tough teen-age chicks—'dittybops'—making it with the lost hustlers … all amid the incongruous piped music and the flowers—twin fountains gushing rainbow colored: the world of Lonely America squeezed into Pershing Square, of the Cities of Terrible Night, downtown now trapped in the City of lost Angels … and the trees hang over it all like some type of apathetic fate." —John Rechy: *Big Table* 3

Seeing Los Angeles after ten years away, one realizes all over again that America is an unhappy contract between the East (that Faustian thrust of a most determined human will which reaches up and out above the eye into the skyscrapers of New York) and those flat lands of compromise and mediocre self-expression, those endless

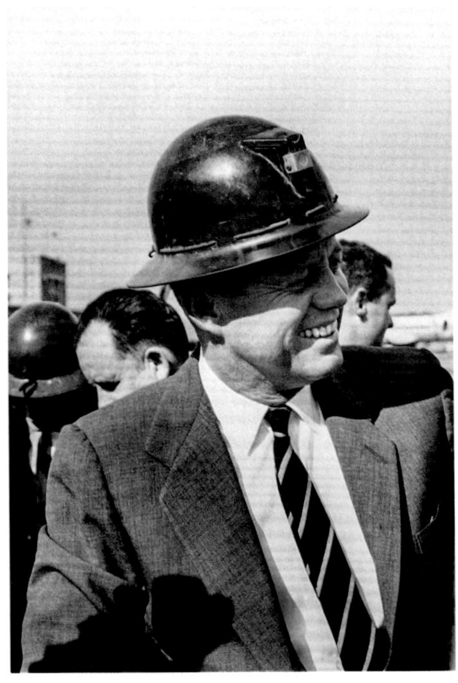

OPPOSITE *May 10, 1960.* Robert Francis Kennedy, JFK's younger brother and his campaign manager, takes a break in Bluefield, West Virginia. Renowned as a take-no-prisoners type—exhibited by his tough manner in taking on the Teamsters union as chief counsel to the Senate Select Committee investigating mob influence on labor unions—Bobby was a fierce competitor and major asset to his brother. *Photo, Bob Lerner*

ABOVE *1960.* JFK generally avoided having his picture taken while wearing hats for fear of looking foolish. However, there was one exception: hard hats. Whether coal miner or construction worker, Kennedy admired the workingman and was happy to appear as one. *Photo, Paul Schutzer*

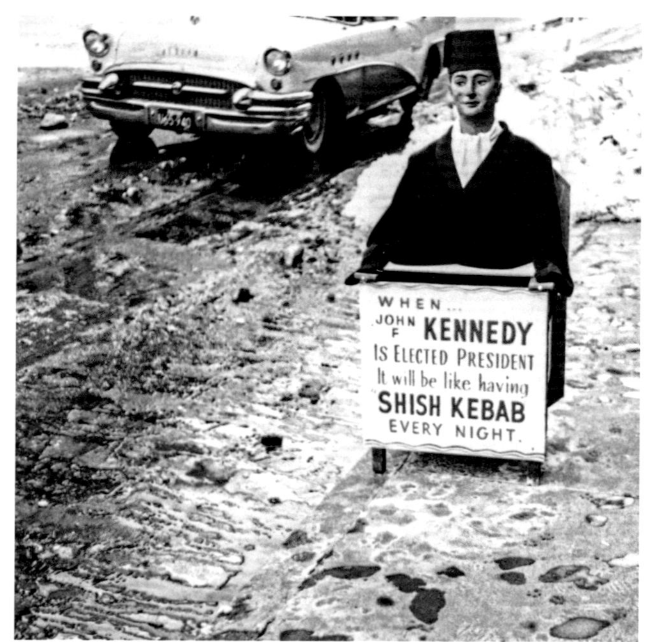

half-pretty repetitive small towns of the Middle and the West, whose spirit is forever horizontal and whose marrow comes to rendezvous in the pastel monotonies of Los Angeles architecture.

So far as America has a history, one can see it in the severe heights of New York City, in the glare from the Pittsburgh mills, by the color in the brick of Louisburg Square, along the knotted greedy facades of the small mansions on Chicago's North Side, in Natchez' antebellum homes, the wrought-iron balconies off Bourbon Street, a captain's house in Nantucket, by the curve of Commercial Street in Provincetown. One can make a list; it is probably finite. What culture we have made and what history has collected to it can be found in those few hard examples of an architecture which came to its artistic term, was born, lived and so collected some history about it. Not all the roots of American life are uprooted, but almost all, and the spirit of the supermarket, that homogeneous extension of stainless surfaces and psychoanalyzed people, packaged commodities and ranch homes, interchangeable, geographically unrecognizable, that essence of a new postwar SuperAmerica is found nowhere so perfectly as in Los Angeles' ubiquitous acres. One gets the impression that people come to Los Angeles in order to divorce themselves from the past, here to live or try to live in the rootless pleasure world of an adult child. One knows that if the cities of the world were destroyed by a new war, the architecture of the rebuilding would create a landscape which looked, subject to specifications of climate, exactly and entirely like the San Fernando Valley.

It is not that Los Angeles is altogether hideous, it is even by degrees pleasant, but for an Easterner there is never any salt in the wind; it is like Mexican cooking without chile, or Chinese egg rolls missing their mustard; as one travels through the endless repetitions of that city which is the capital of suburbia with its milky pinks, its washed-out oranges, its tainted lime-yellows of pastel on one pretty little architectural monstrosity after another, the colors not intense enough, the styles never pure, and never sufficiently impure to collide on the eye, one conceives the people who live here— they have come out to express themselves, Los Angeles is the home of self-expression, but the artists are middle-class and middling-minded; no passions will calcify here for years in the gloom to be revealed a decade later as the tessellations of hard and fertile work, no, it is all open, promiscuous, borrowed, half bought, a city without

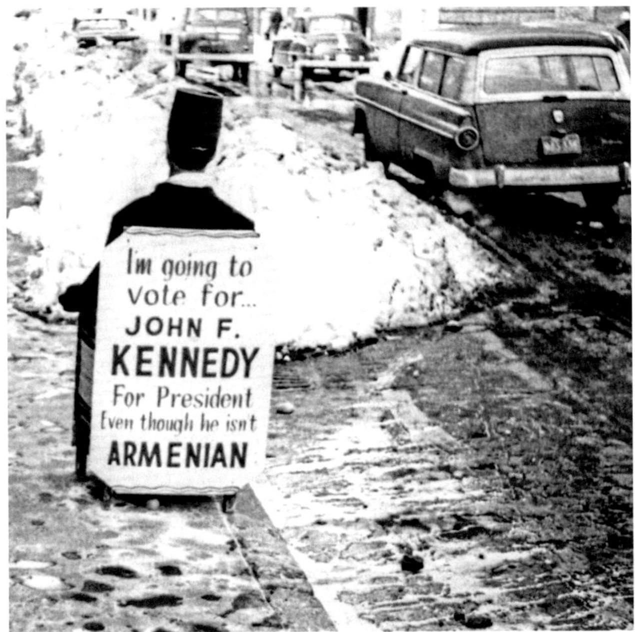

ABOVE AND OPPOSITE *Early 1960*. A pair of snapshots shows a humorous endorsement for Senator Kennedy in Boston's South End. The accompanying letter sent by Paul A. Wolf of Braintree, Massachusetts, on April 24, 1960, said, "When the going gets tough, 'Jack' remember it is they who deal in <u>innuendo</u> and prejudice who are hurting themselves." Kennedy wrote back in June, "All members of my staff, including myself, found them very amusing." *Photos, Paul A. Wolf*

iron, eschewing wood, a kingdom of stucco, the playground for mass men — one has the feeling it was built by television sets giving orders to men. And in this land of the pretty-pretty, the virility is in the barbarisms, the vulgarities, it is in the huge billboards, the screamers of the neon lighting, the shouting farm-utensil colors of the gas stations and monster drugstores, it is in the swing of the sports cars, hot rods, convertibles, Los Angeles is a city to drive in, the boulevards are wide, the traffic is nervous and fast, the radio stations play bouncing, blooping, rippling tunes, one digs the pop in a pop tune, no one of character would make love by it but the sound is good for swinging a car, electronic guitars and Hawaiian harps.

So this is the town the Democrats came to, and with their unerring instinct (after being with them a week, one thinks of this party as a crazy, half-rich family, loaded with poor cousins, traveling always in caravans with Cadillacs and Okie Fords, Lincolns and quarter-horse mules, putting up every night in tents to hear the chamber quartet of Great Cousin Eleanor invaded by the Texas-twanging steel-stringing geetarists of Bubber Lyndon, carrying its own mean high school principal, Doc Symington, chided for its manners by good Uncle Adlai, told the route of march by Navigator Jack, cut off every six months from the rich will of Uncle Jim Farley, never listening to the mechanic of the caravan, Bald Sam Rayburn, who assures them they'll all break down unless Cousin Bubber gets the concession on the garage; it's the Snopes family married to Henry James, with the labor unions thrown in like a Yankee dollar, and yet it's true, in tranquility one recollects them with affection, their instinct is good, crazy family good) and this instinct now led the caravan to pick the Biltmore Hotel in downtown Los Angeles for their family get-together and reunion.

The Biltmore is one of the ugliest hotels in the world. Patterned after the flat roofs of an Italian Renaissance palace, it is eighty-eight times as large, and one-millionth as valuable to the continuation of man, and it would be intolerable if it were not for the presence of Pershing Square, that square block of park with cactus and palm trees, the three-hundred-and-sixty-five-day-a-year convention of every junkie, pot-head, pusher, queen (but you have read that good writing already). For years Pershing Square has been one of the three or four places in America famous to homosexuals, famous not for its posh, the chic is round-heeled here, but because it is one of the avatars of the good old masturbatory sex, dirty with the crusted sugars of smut, dirty rooming houses

31

"This candidate for all his record, his good, sound, conventional liberal record has a patina of that other life, the second American life, the long electric night with the fires of neon leading down the highway to the murmur of jazz."

—Norman Mailer

around the corner where the score is made, dirty book and photograph stores down the street, old-fashioned out-of-the-Thirties burlesque houses, cruising bars, jukeboxes, movie houses; Pershing Square is the town plaza for all those lonely, respectable, small-town homosexuals who lead a family life, make children, and have the Philbrick psychology (How I Joined the Communist Party and Led Three Lives). Yes, it is the open-air convention hall for the small-town inverts who live like spies, and it sits in the center of Los Angeles, facing the Biltmore, that hotel which is a mausoleum, that Pentagon of traveling salesmen the Party chose to house the headquarters of the Convention.

So here came that family, cursed before it began by the thundering absence of Great-Uncle Truman, the delegates dispersed over a run of thirty miles and twenty-seven hotels: the Olympian Motor Hotel, the Ambassador, the Beverly Wilshire, the Santa Ynez Inn (where rumor has it the delegates from Louisiana had some midnight swim), the Mayan, the Commodore, the Mayfair, the Sheraton-West, the

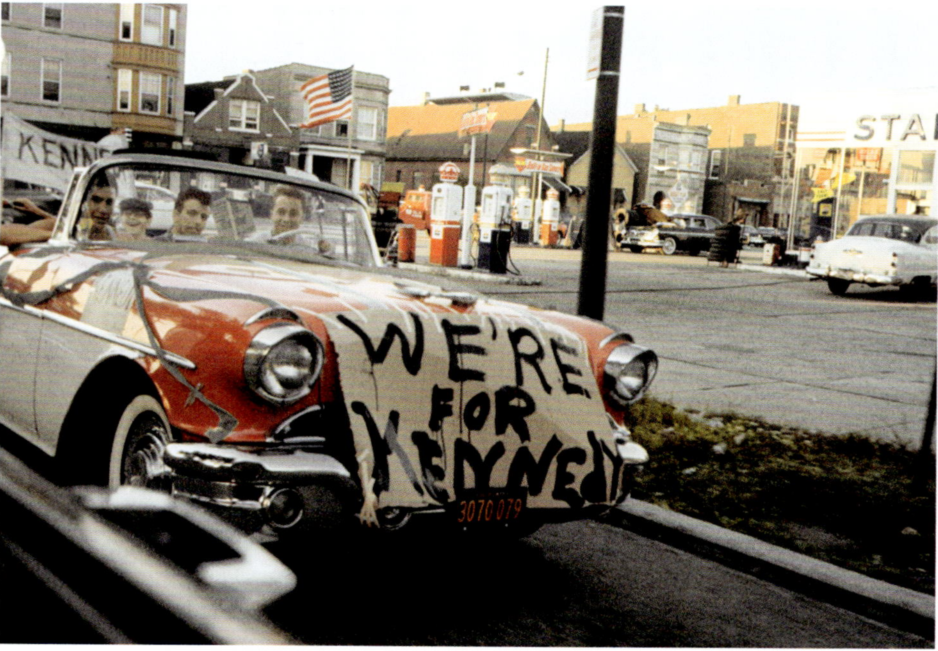

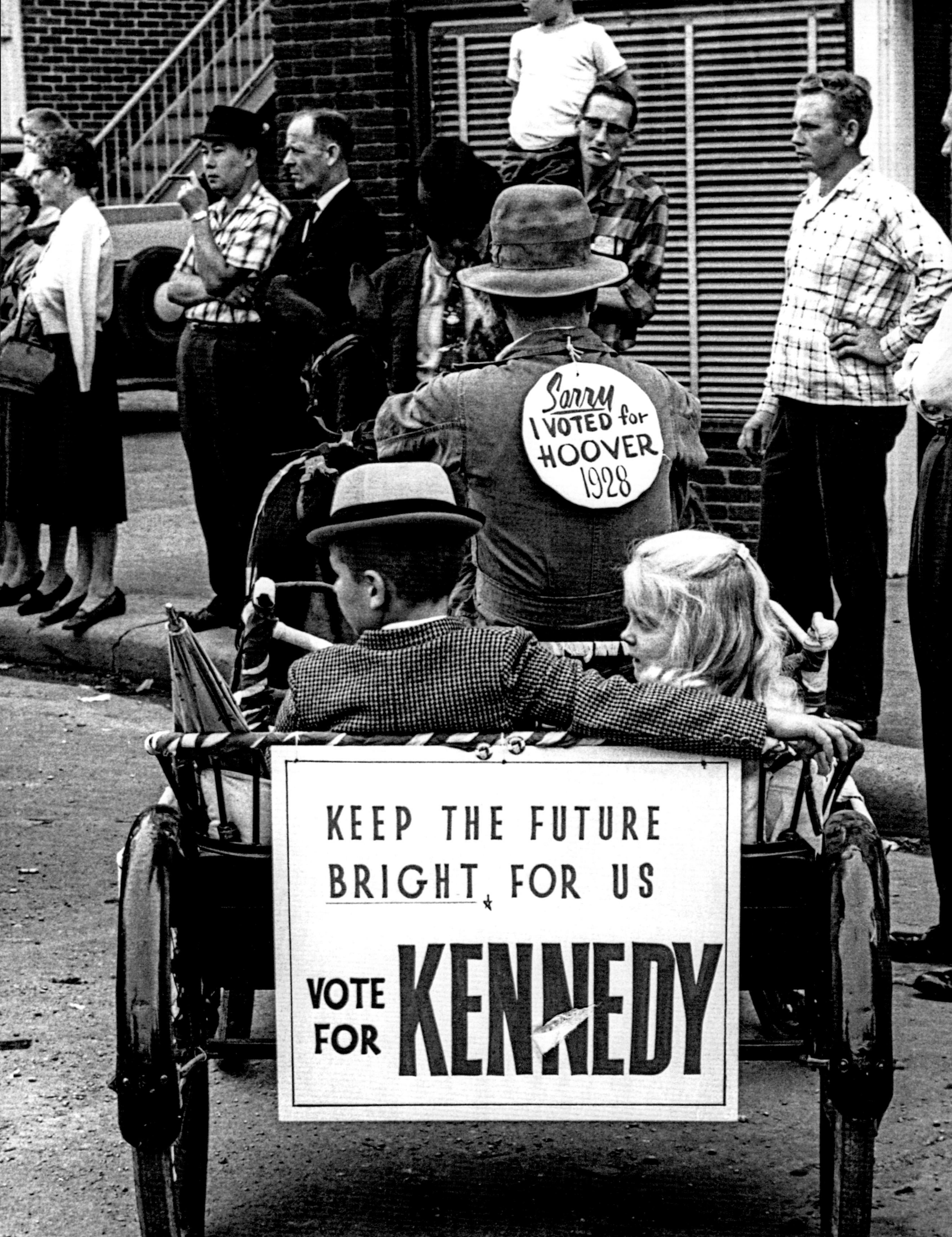
Sorry
I VOTED for
HOOVER
1928
KEEP THE FUTURE
BRIGHT FOR US
VOTE FOR KENNEDY

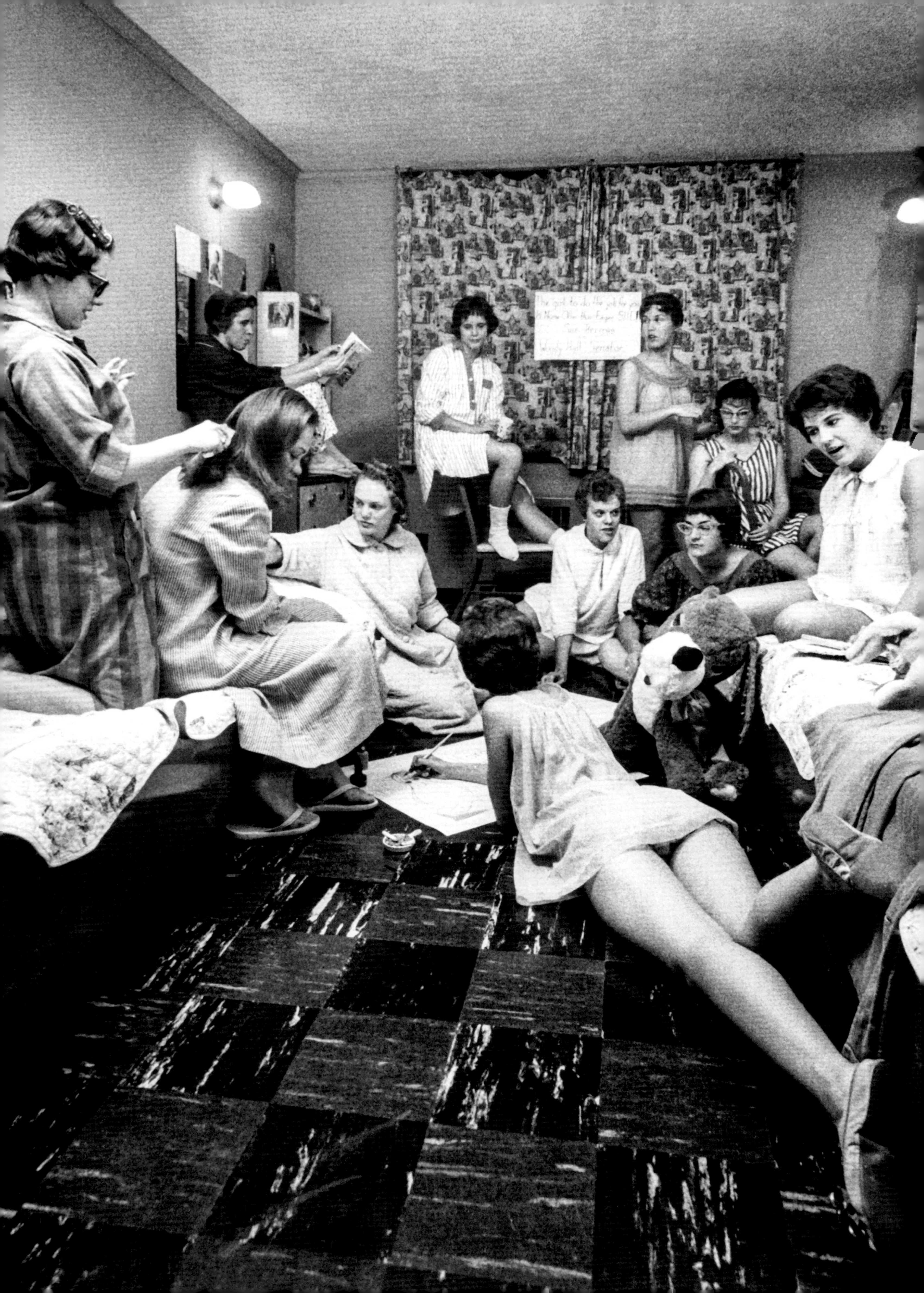

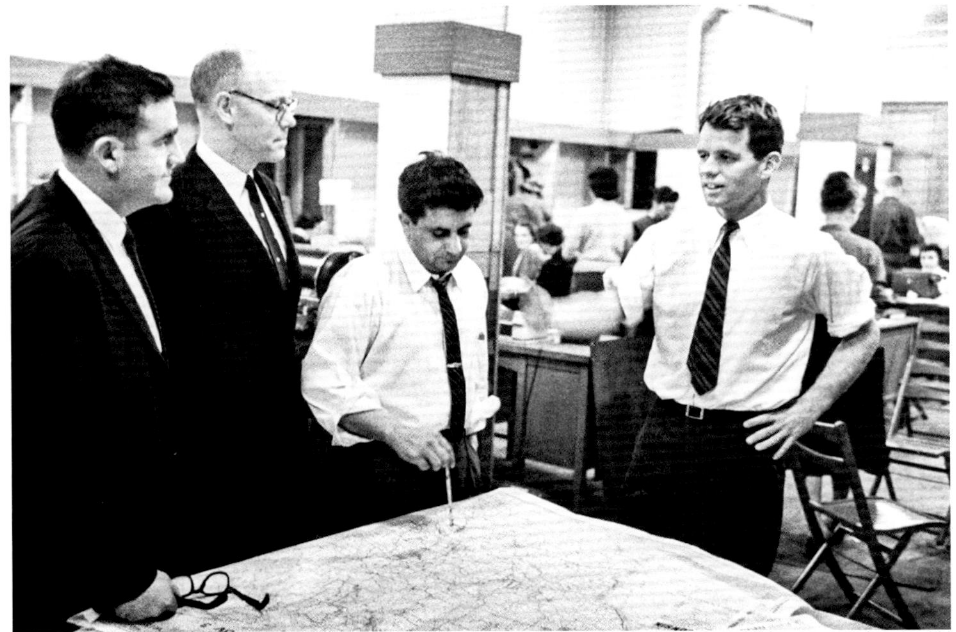

Huntington-Sheraton, the Green, the Hayward, the Gates, the Figueroa, the Statler
Hilton, the Hollywood Knickerbocker — does one have to be a collector to list such
names? — beauties all, with that up-from-the-farm Los Angeles décor, plate-glass
windows, patio and terrace, foam-rubber mattress, pastel paints, all of them pretty as
an ad in full-page color, all but the Biltmore where everybody gathered every day —
the newsmen, the TV, radio, magazine, and foreign newspaperman, the delegates,
the politicos, the tourists, the campaign managers, the runners, the flunkies, the cousins
and aunts, the wives, the grandfathers, the eight-year-old girls, and the twenty-eight-
year-old girls in the Kennedy costumes, red and white and blue, the Symingteeners,
the Johnson Ladies, the Stevenson Ladies, everybody — and for three days before
the convention and four days into it, everybody collected at the Biltmore, in the lobby,
in the grill, in the Biltmore Bowl, in the elevators, along the corridors, three hundred
deep always outside the Kennedy suite, milling everywhere, every dark-carpeted
grey-brown hall of the hotel, but it was in the Gallery of the Biltmore where one
first felt the mood which pervaded all proceedings until the convention was almost
over, that heavy, thick, witless depression which was to dominate every move as the
delegates wandered and gawked and paraded and set for a spell, there in the Gallery
of the Biltmore, that huge depressing alley with its inimitable hotel color, that faded
depth of chiaroscuro which unhappily has no depth, that brown which is not a
brown, that grey which has no pearl in it, that color which can be described only as
hotel-color because the beiges, the tans, the walnuts, the mahoganies, the dull blood
rugs, the moaning yellows, the sick greens, the greys and all those dumb browns
merge into that lack of color which is an over-large hotel at convention time, with all
the small-towners wearing their set, starched faces, that look they get at carnival, all
fever and suspicion, and proud to be there, eddying slowly back and forth in that high
block-long tunnel of a room with its arched ceiling and square recesses filling every
rib of the arch with art work, escutcheons and blazons and other art, pictures I think,
I cannot even remember, there was such a hill of cigar smoke the eye had to travel
on its way to the ceiling, and at one end there was galvanized-pipe scaffolding and
workmen repairing some part of the ceiling, one of them touching up one of the endless
squares of painted plaster in the arch, and another worker, passing by, yelled up to
the one who was working on the ceiling: "Hey, Michelangelo!"

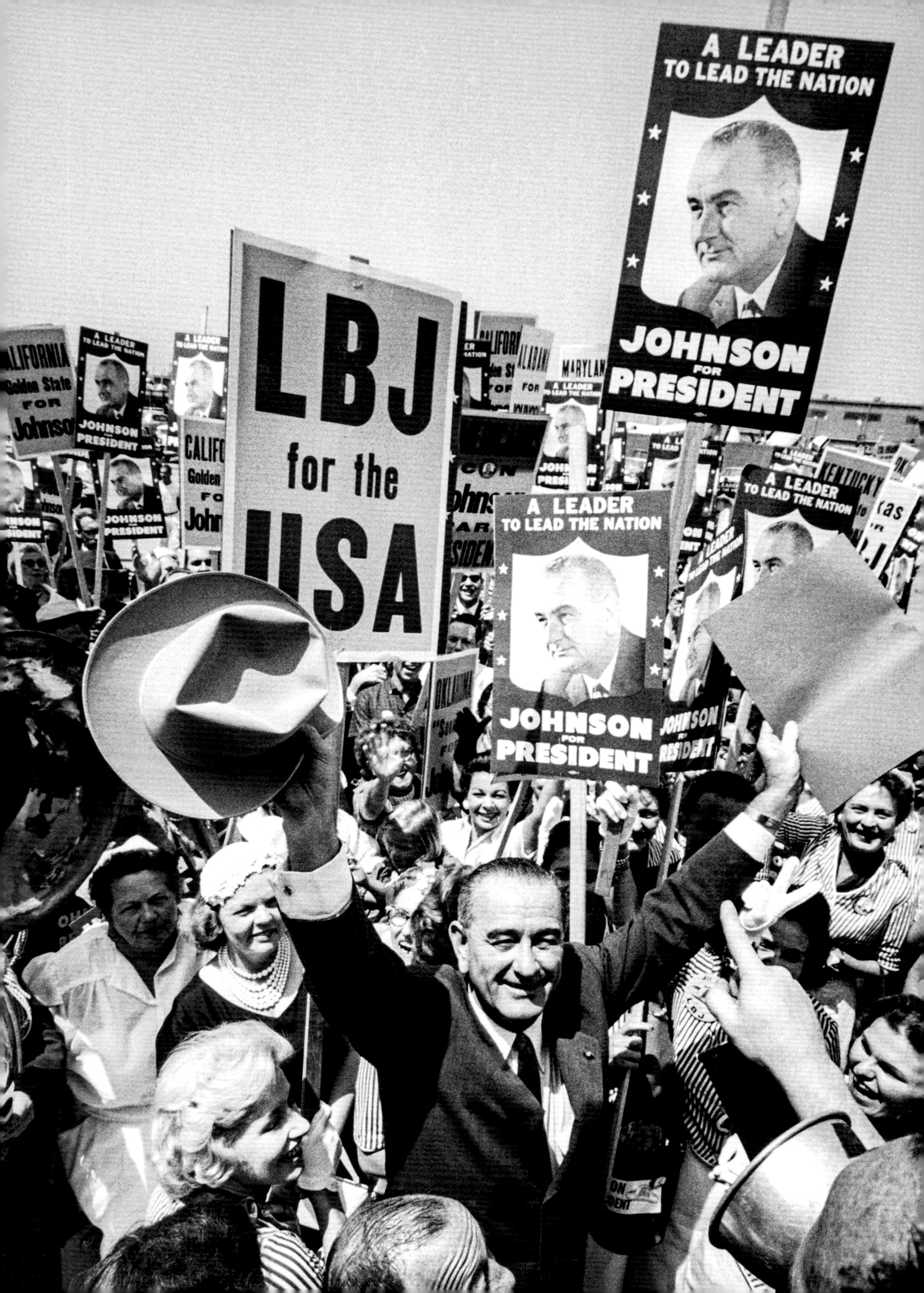

A LEADER
TO LEAD THE NATION
JOHNSON
FOR
PRESIDENT
LBJ
for the
USA
A LEADER
TO LEAD THE NATION
JOHNSON
FOR
PRESIDENT
JOHNSON
FOR
PRESIDENT
CALIFORNIA
Golden State
FOR
Johnson
CALIFORNIA
Golden State
FOR
Johnson
JOHNSON
FOR
PRESIDENT
ALABAMA
MARYLAND
KENTUCKY
A LEADER
TO LEAD THE NATION

Later, of course, it began to emerge and there were portraits one could keep, Symington, dogged at a press conference, declaring with no conviction that he knew he had a good chance to win, the disappointment eating at his good looks so that he came off hard-faced, mean, and yet slack—a desperate dullness came off the best of his intentions. There was Johnson who had compromised too many contradictions and now the contradictions were in his face: when he smiled the corners of his mouth squeezed gloom; when he was pious, his eyes twinkled irony; when he spoke in a righteous tone, he looked corrupt; when he jested, the ham in his jowls looked to quiver. He was not convincing. He was a Southern politician, a Texas Democrat, a liberal Eisenhower; he would do no harm, he would do no good, he would react to the machine, good fellow, nice friend—the Russians would understand him better than his own.

Stevenson had the patina. He came into the room and the room was different, not stronger perhaps (which is why ultimately he did not win), but warmer. One knew why

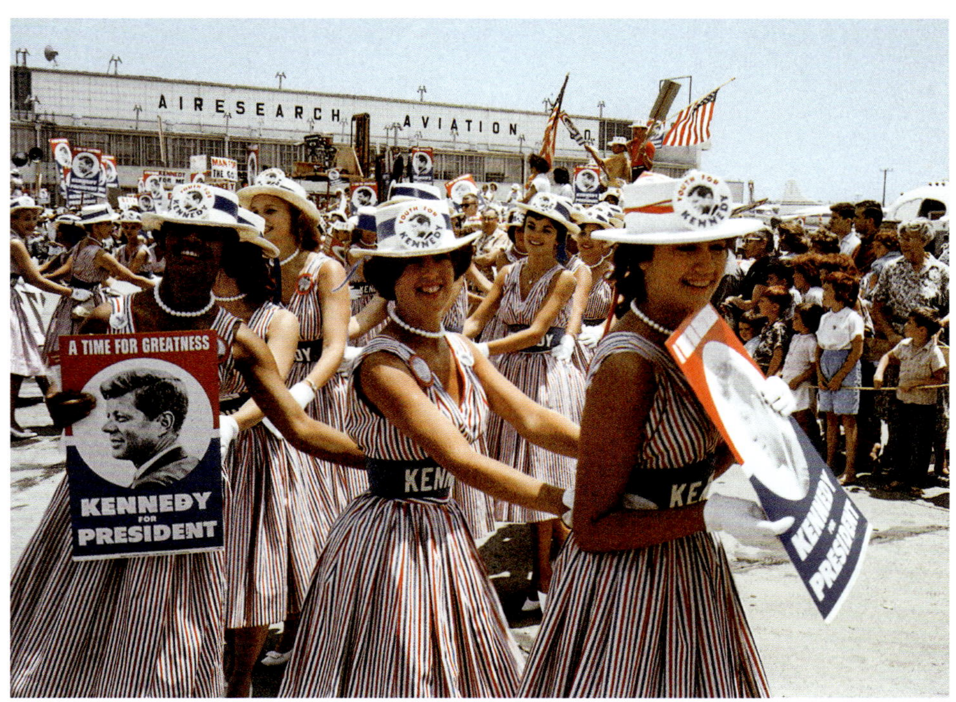

OPPOSITE *ca. July 8–11, 1960.* JFK's top competitor for the presidential nomination was U.S. Senate Majority Leader Lyndon Baines Johnson of Texas. When he arrived at the Democratic National Convention in Los Angeles, LBJ claimed he had at least 500 delegates, even though he had not run in a single primary. Instead, he had orchestrated a "cloakroom campaign" in Washington, gathering commitments from congressmen, senators, and other party insiders. *Photo, Thomas D. McAvoy*

LEFT *July 9, 1960.* A conga line of "Kennedy girls" give "Prince Jack" a "great big, brassy, honky-tonk, hysterical, razzmatazz welcome" at a private landing strip near Los Angeles International Airport. Reporting from the tarmac that day, BBC reporter Robin Day went on to declare, "Senator Kennedy is young, rich, and handsome; he's the son of a multi-millionaire; he's the idol of the bobbysoxers; and… the envy of all politicians." *Photo, Hank Walker*

"He had the deep orange-brown suntan of a ski instructor, and when he smiled at the crowd his teeth were amazingly white...one expected at any moment to see him lifted to its shoulders like a matador being carried back to the city after a triumph in the plaza."

—Norman Mailer

OPPOSITE *July 9, 1960.* JFK makes his way through a crowd of supporters and journalists upon his arrival at the Democratic National Convention, and his chances of winning the nomination are very good. His hard work traveling the country for over three years, 10 victories in presidential primary elections, plus the detailed organization he and his team have built with Bobby Kennedy at the helm, place him in good standing to win the nomination on the first ballot. Still, nothing is certain at political conventions, and Kennedy will have to fight for the last round of Democratic holdouts. *Photo, Anonymous*

some adored him; he did not look like other people, not with press lights on his flesh; he looked like a lover, the simple truth, he had the sweet happiness of an adolescent who has just been given his first major kiss. And so he glowed, and one was reminded of Chaplin, not because they were the least alike in features, but because Charlie Chaplin was luminous when one met him and Stevenson had something of that light.

There was Eleanor Roosevelt, fine, precise, hand-worked like ivory. Her voice was almost attractive as she explained in the firm, sad tones of the first lady in this small town why she could not admit Mr. Kennedy, who was no doubt a gentleman, into her political house. One had the impression of a lady who was finally becoming a woman, which is to say that she was just a little bitchy about it all; nice bitchy, charming, it had a touch of art to it, but it made one wonder if she were not now satisfying the last passion of them all, which was to become physically attractive, for she was better-looking than she had ever been as she spurned the possibilities of a young suitor.

Jim Farley. Huge. Cold as a bishop. The hell he would consign you to was cold as ice.

Bobby Kennedy, that archetype Bobby Kennedy, looked like a West Point cadet, or, better, one of those reconstructed Irishmen from Kirkland House one always used to have to face in the line in Harvard house football games. "Hello," you would say to the ones who looked like him as you lined up for the scrimmage after the kickoff, and his type would nod and look away, one rock glint of recognition your due for living across the hall from one another all through Freshman year, and then bang, as the ball was passed back, you'd get a bony king-hell knee in the crotch. He was the kind of man never to put on the gloves with if you wanted to do some social boxing, because after two minutes it would be a war, and ego-bastards last long in a war.

Carmine DeSapio and Kenneth Galbraith on the same part of the convention floor. DeSapio is bigger than one expects, keen and florid, great big smoked glasses, a suntan like Man-tan—he is the kind of heavyweight Italian who could get by with a name like Romeo—and Galbraith is tall-tall, as actors say, six foot six it could be, terribly thin, enormously attentive, exquisitely polite, birdlike, he is sensitive to the stirring of reeds in a wind over the next hill. "Our grey eminence," whispered the intelligent observer next to me.

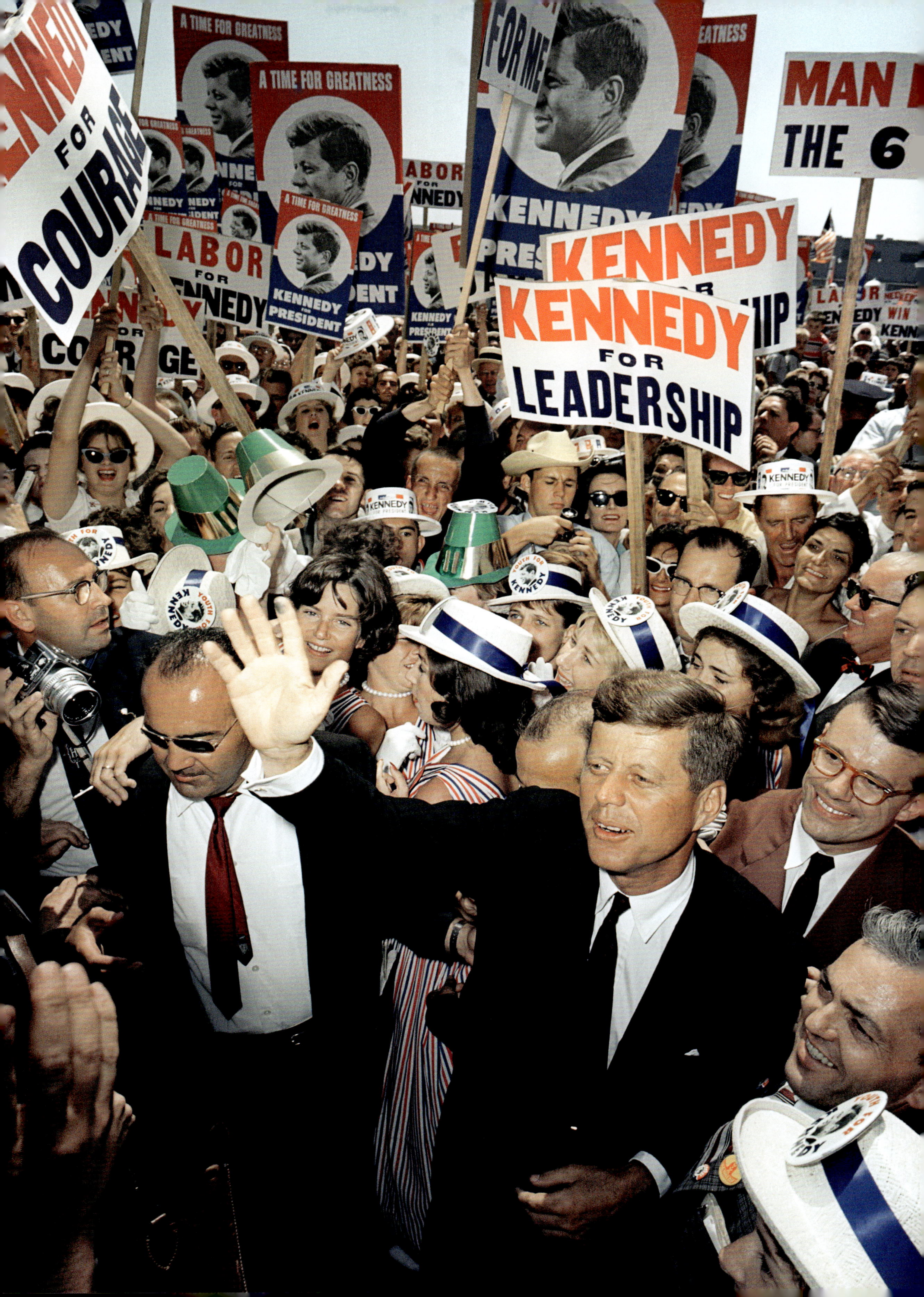

KENNEDY FOR COURAGE
A TIME FOR GREATNESS
LABOR FOR KENNEDY
KENNEDY FOR PRESIDENT
A TIME FOR GREATNESS
KENNEDY FOR PRESIDENT
MAN THE 6
KENNEDY KENNEDY FOR LEADERSHIP
LABOR FOR KENNEDY WIN
YOUTH FOR KENNEDY

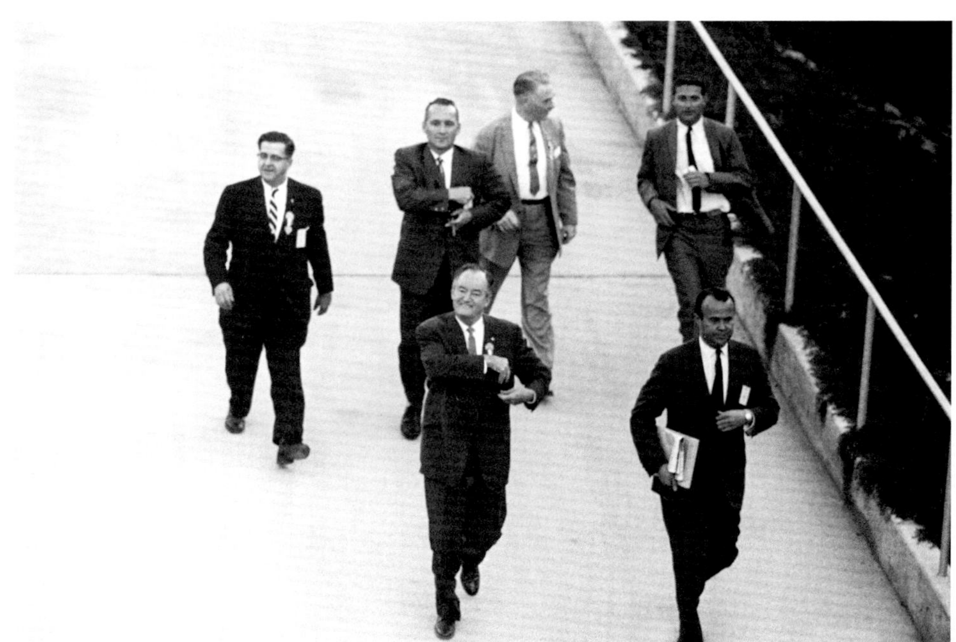

Bob Wagner, the mayor of New York, a little man, plump, groomed, blank. He had the blank, pomaded, slightly worried look of the first barber in a good barbershop, the kind who would go to the track on his day off and wear a green transparent stone in a gold ring.

And then there was Kennedy, the edge of the mystery. But a sketch will no longer suffice.

Perspective from the Biltmore Balcony

The Colorful Arrival of the Hero with Orange-brown Suntan and Amazingly White Teeth; Revelation of the Two Rivers Political Theory

> *"…it can be said with a fair amount of certainty that the essence of his political attractiveness is his extraordinary political intelligence. He has a mind quite unlike that of any other Democrat of this century. It is not literary, metaphysical and moral, as Adlai Stevenson's is. Kennedy is articulate and often witty, but he does not seek verbal polish. No one can doubt the seriousness of his concern with the most serious political matters, but one feels that whereas Mr. Stevenson's political views derive from a view of life that holds politics to be a mere fraction of existence, Senator Kennedy's primary interest is in politics. The easy way in which he disposes of the question of Church and State — as if he felt that any reasonable man could quite easily resolve any possible conflict of loyalties — suggests that the organization of society is the one thing that really engages his interest."* —Richard Rovere: *The New Yorker,* July 23, 1960

The afternoon he arrived at the convention from the airport, there was of course a large crowd on the street outside the Biltmore, and the best way to get a view was to get up on an outdoor balcony of the Biltmore, two flights above the street, and look down on the event. One waited thirty minutes, and then a honking of horns as wild as the getaway after an Italian wedding sounded around the corner, and the Kennedy cortege came into sight, circled Pershing Square, the men in the open and leading convertibles sitting backwards to look at their leader, and finally came to a halt in a space cleared for them by the police in the crowd. The television cameras were out,

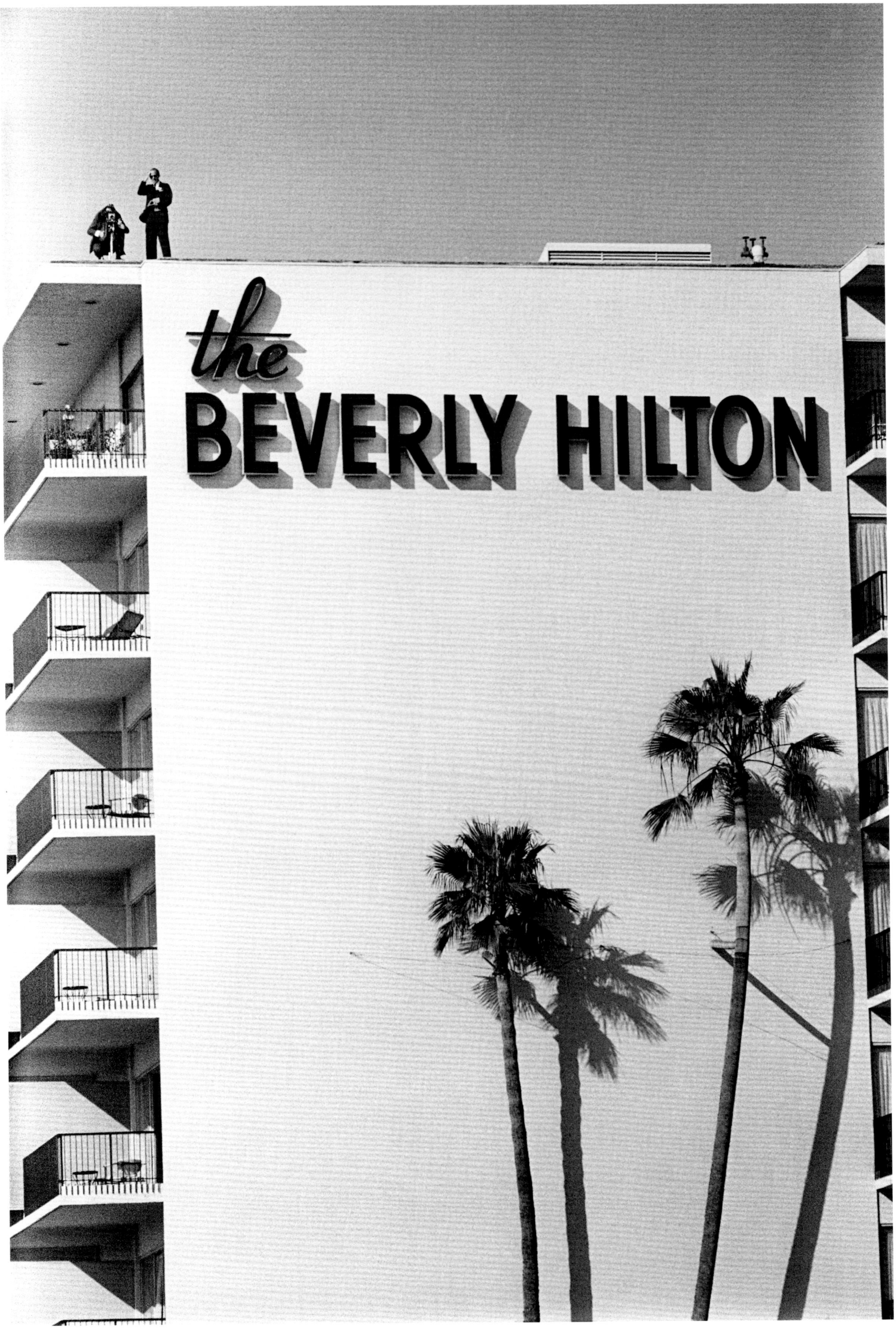

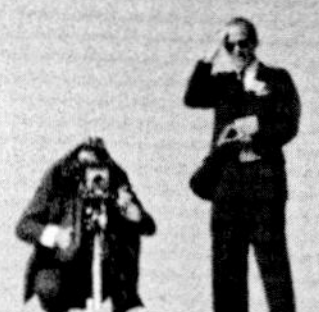

the
BEVERLY HILTON

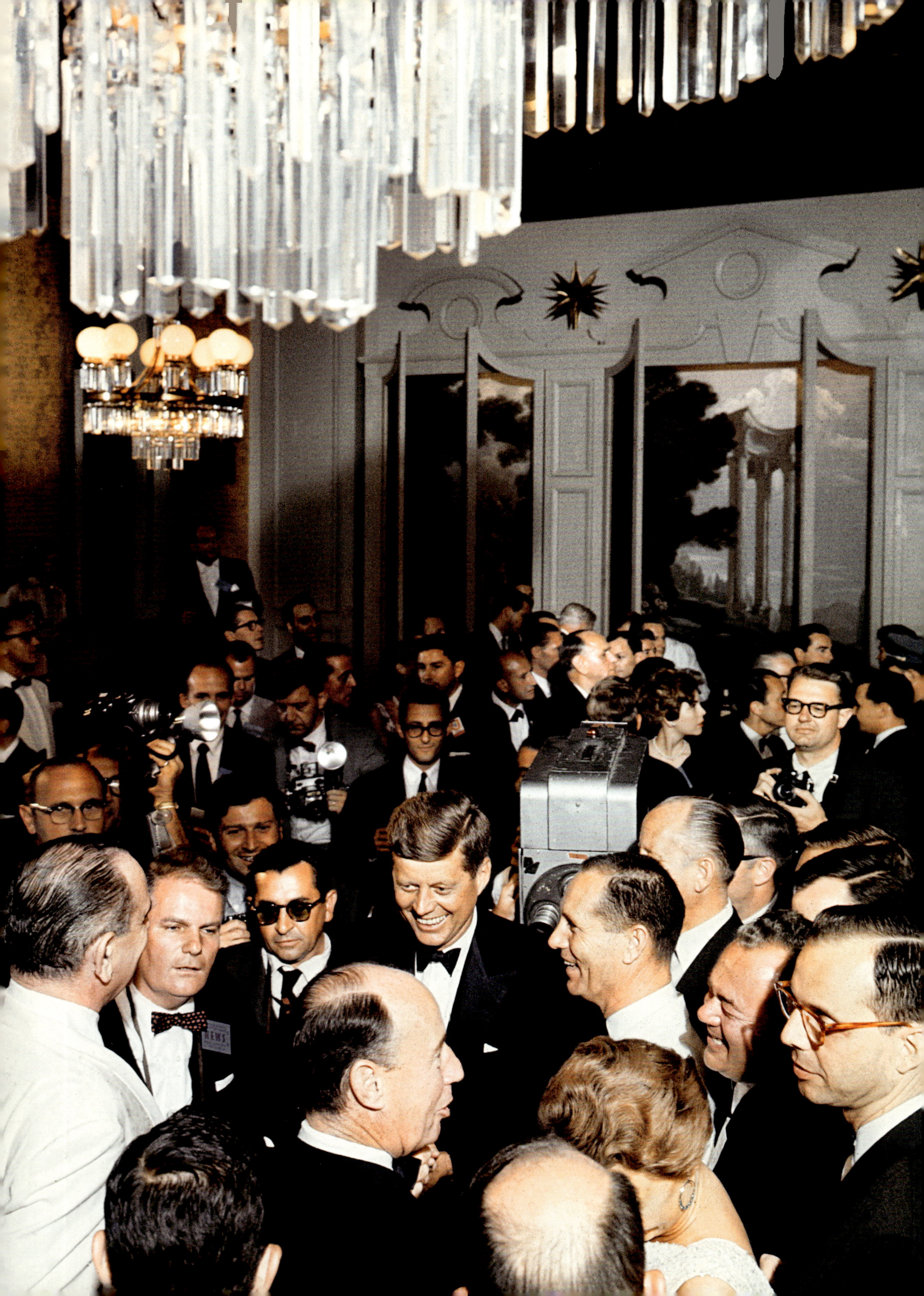

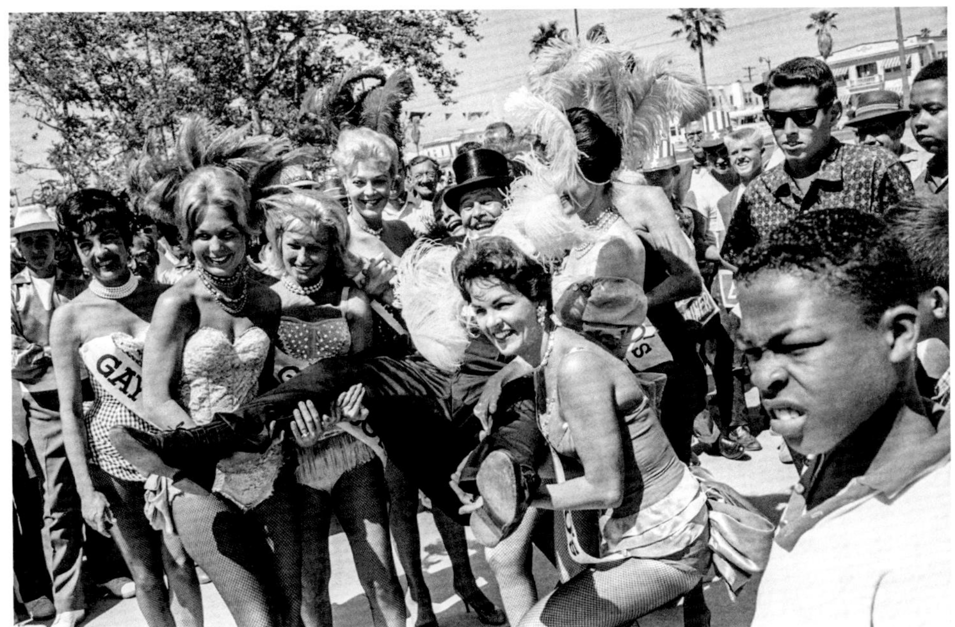

and a Kennedy band was playing some circus music. One saw him immediately. He had the deep orange-brown suntan of a ski instructor, and when he smiled at the crowd his teeth were amazingly white and clearly visible at a distance of fifty yards. For one moment he saluted Pershing Square, and Pershing Square saluted him back, the prince and the beggars of glamour staring at one another across a city street, one of those very special moments in the underground history of the world, and then with a quick move he was out of his car and by choice headed into the crowd instead of the lane cleared for him into the hotel by the police, so that he made his way inside surrounded by a mob, and one expected at any moment to see him lifted to its shoulders like a matador being carried back to the city after a triumph in the plaza. All the while the band kept playing the campaign tunes, sashaying circus music, and one had a moment of clarity, intense as a *déjà vu,* for the scene which had taken place had been glimpsed before in a dozen musical comedies; it was the scene where the hero, the matinee idol, the movie star comes to the palace to claim the princess, or what is the same, and more to our soil, the football hero, the campus king, arrives at the dean's home surrounded by a court of open-singing students to plead with the dean for his daughter's kiss and permission to put on the big musical that night. And suddenly I saw the convention, it came into focus for me, and I understood the mood of depression which had lain over the convention, because finally it was simple: the Democrats were going to nominate a man who, no matter how serious his political dedication might be, was indisputably and willy-nilly going to be seen as a great box-office actor, and the consequences of that were staggering and not at all easy to calculate.

Since the First World War Americans have been leading a double life, and our history has moved on two rivers, one visible, the other underground; there has been the history of politics which is concrete, factual, practical and unbelievably dull if not for the consequences of the actions of some of these men; and there is a subterranean river of untapped, ferocious, lonely and romantic desires, that concentration of ecstasy and violence which is the dream life of the nation.

The twentieth century may yet be seen as that era when civilized man and underprivileged man were melted together into mass man, the iron and steel of the nineteenth century giving way to electronic circuits which communicated their messages into men, the unmistakable tendency of the new century seeming to be the

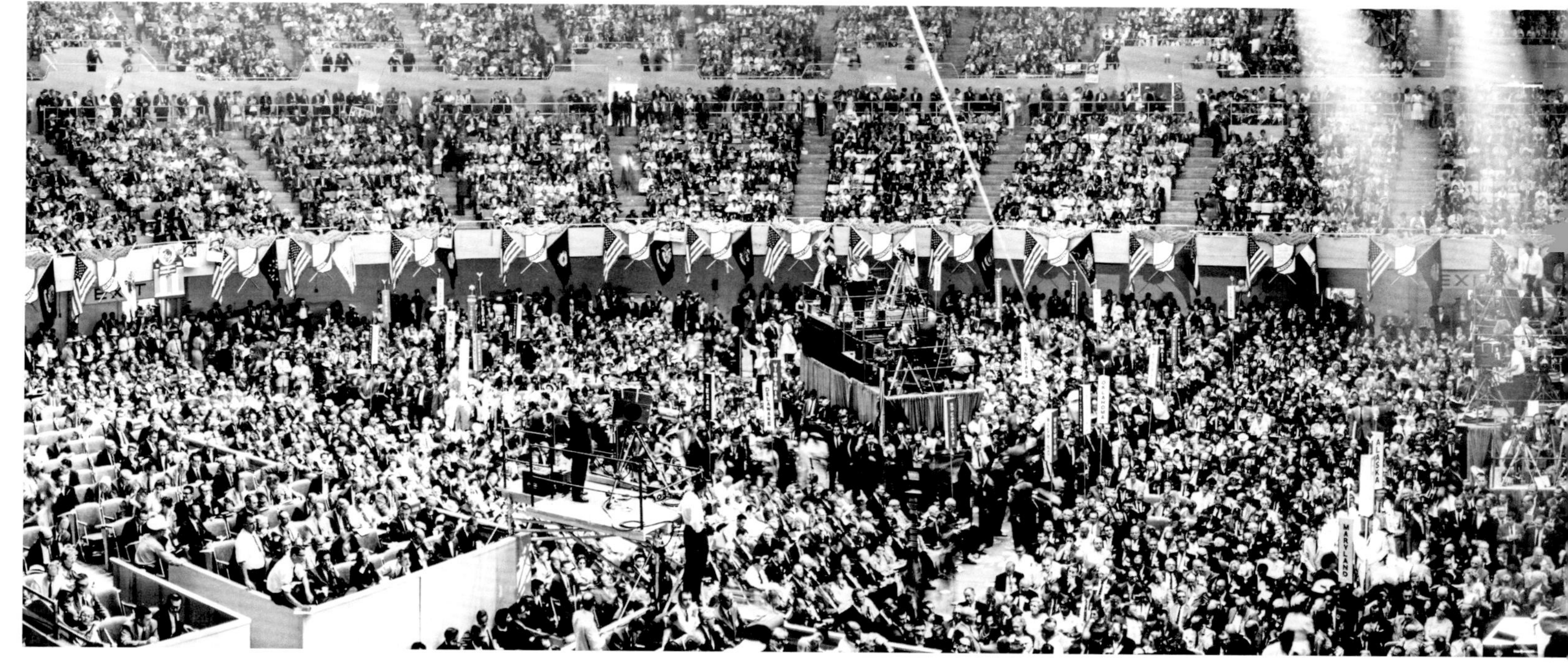

ABOVE *ca. July 11–13, 1960.* Some 45,000 people—delegates, press, politicians, and assorted fans—assemble for the weeklong nomination process inside the Los Angeles Memorial Sports Arena. There were the politicos: minor players urging delegates to consider their candidate during the day and at nighttime impassioned speeches from major players. And there was the media: photographers with walkie-talkies to arrange film pickups and deliveries, journalists doing on-the-spot interviews and TV news people reporting from the floor, copy boys rushing errands. *Photo, Irving Brent*

creation of men as interchangeable as commodities, their extremes of personality singed out of existence by the psychic fields of force the communicators would impose. This loss of personality was a catastrophe to the future of the imagination, but billions of people might first benefit from it by having enough to eat—one did not know—and there remained citadels of resistance in Europe where the culture was deep and roots were visible in the architecture of the past.

Nowhere, as in America, however, was this fall from individual man to mass man felt so acutely, for America was at once the first and most prolific creator of mass communications, and the most rootless of countries, since almost no American could lay claim to the line of a family which had not once at least severed its roots by migrating here. But, if rootless, it was then the most vulnerable of countries to its own homogenization. Yet America was also the country in which the dynamic myth of the Renaissance—that every man was potentially extraordinary—knew its most passionate persistence. Simply, America was the land where people still believed in heroes: George Washington; Billy the Kid; Lincoln, Jefferson; Mark Twain, Jack London, Hemingway; Joe Louis, Dempsey, Gentleman Jim; America believed in athletes, rum-runners, aviators; even lovers, by the time Valentino died. It was a country which had grown by the leap of one hero past another—is there a county in all of our ground which does not have its legendary figure? And when the West was filled, the expansion turned inward, became part of an agitated, overexcited, superheated dream life. The film studios threw up their searchlights as the frontier was finally sealed, and the romantic possibilities of the old conquest of land turned into a vertical myth, trapped within the skull, of a new kind of heroic life, each choosing his own archetype of a neo-renaissance man, be it Barrymore, Cagney, Flynn, Bogart, Brando or Sinatra, but it was almost as if there were no peace unless one could fight well, kill well (if always with honor), love well and love many, be cool, be daring, be dashing, be wild, be wily, be resourceful, be a brave gun. And this myth, that each of us was born to be free, to wander, to have adventure and to grow on the waves of the violent, the perfumed, and the unexpected, had a force which could not be tamed no matter how the nation's regulators—politicians, medicos, policemen, professors, priests, rabbis, ministers, *idéologues*, psychoanalysts, builders, executives and endless communicators—would brick-in the modern life with hygiene upon sanity, and

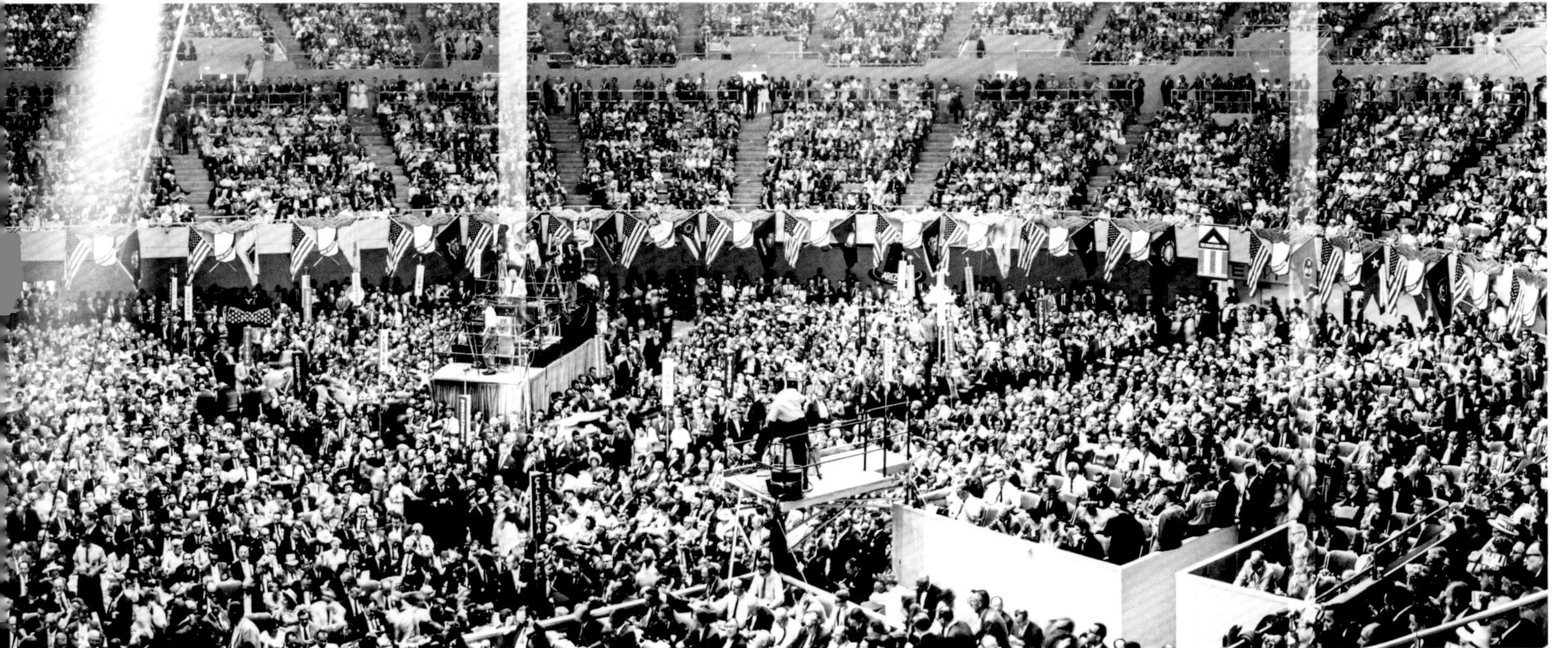

middle-brow homily over platitude; the myth would not die. Indeed a quarter of the nation's business must have depended upon its existence. But it stayed alive for more than that—it was as if the message in the labyrinth of the genes would insist that violence was locked with creativity, and adventure was the secret of love.

Once, in the Second World War and in the year or two which followed, the underground river returned to earth, and the life of the nation was intense, of the present, electric; as a lady said, "That was the time when we gave parties which changed people's lives." The Forties was a decade when the speed with which one's own events occurred seemed as rapid as the history of the battlefields, and for the mass of people in America a forced march into a new jungle of emotion was the result. The surprises, the failures, and the dangers of that life must have terrified some nerve of awareness in the power and the mass, for, as if stricken by the orgiastic vistas the myth had carried up from underground, the retreat to a more conservative existence was disorderly, the fear of communism spread like an irrational hail of boils. To anyone who could see, the excessive hysteria of the Red wave was no preparation to face an enemy, but rather a terror of the national self: free-loving, lust-looting, atheistic, implacable—absurdity beyond absurdity to label communism so, for the moral products of Stalinism had been Victorian sex and a ponderous machine of material theology.

Forced underground again, deep beneath all *Reader's Digest* hospital dressings of Mental Health in Your Community, the myth continued to flow, fed by television and the film. The fissure in the national psyche widened to the danger point. The last large appearance of the myth was the vote which tricked the polls and gave Harry Truman his victory in '48. That was the last. Came the Korean War, the shadow of the H-bomb, and we were ready for the General. Uncle Harry gave way to Father, and security, regularity, order, and the life of no imagination were the command of the day. If one had any doubt of this, there was Joe McCarthy with his built-in treason detector, furnished by God, and the damage was done. In the totalitarian wind of those days, anyone who worked in Government formed the habit of being not too original, and many a mind atrophied from disuse and private shame. At the summit there was benevolence without leadership, regularity without vision, security without safety, rhetoric without life. The ship drifted on, that enormous warship of the United States, led by a Secretary of State whose cells were seceding to cancer,

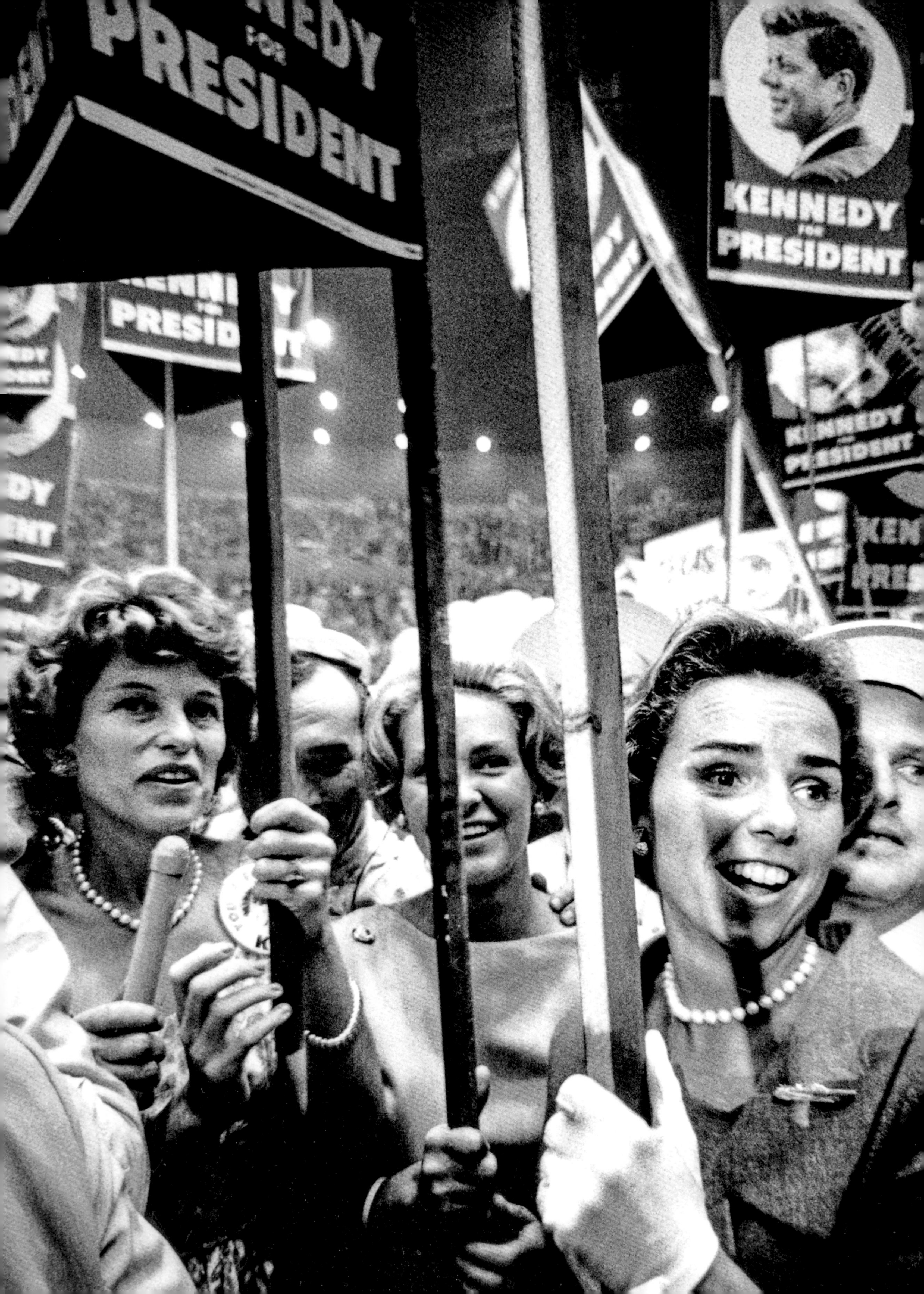

KENNEDY
FOR
PRESIDENT
KENNEDY
FOR
PRESIDENT
KENNEDY
FOR
PRESIDENT
KENNEDY
FOR
PRESIDENT

and as the world became more fantastic—Africa turning itself upside down, while some new kind of machine man was being made in China—two events occurred which stunned in the confidence of America into a new night: the Russians put up their Sputnik, and Civil Rights—that reluctant gift to the American Negro, granted for its effect on foreign affairs—spewed into real life at Little Rock. The national Ego was in shock: the Russians were now in some ways our technological superiors, and we had an internal problem of subject populations equal conceivably in its difficulty to the Soviet and its satellites. The fatherly calm of the General began to seem like the uxorious mellifluences of the undertaker.

Underneath it all was a larger problem. The life of politics and the life of myth had diverged too far, and the energies of the people one knew everywhere had slowed down. Twenty years ago a post-Depression generation had gone to war and formed a lively, grousing, by times inefficient, carousing, pleasure-seeking, not altogether inadequate

OPPOSITE *July 11, 1960*. JFK's assets were varied and many, but of utmost importance were the Kennedy women, beginning with Jackie and extending through matriarch, Rose, the sisters—Eunice (left), Jean, and Pat—and the sisters-in-law—Joan and Ethel (center and right). All worked hard for the cause, whether in genteel afternoon teas or out-on-the-hustings campaigning. *Photo, Jacques Lowe*

BELOW *July 13, 1960*. Working the DNC floor, Bobby is charged with keeping an eye on delegate votes. "Bobby Kennedy," observed Norman Mailer, "was the kind of man never to put on the gloves with if you wanted to do some social boxing, because after two minutes it would be a war, and ego-bastards last long in a war." *Photo, Ralph Crane*

FOLLOWING SPREAD *ca. July 11–13, 1960*. During the DNC, the floor was arranged by state, a vast region of delegates to be wooed by floor managers seeking to bring wavering or undecided delegates to their man. *Photo, John Bryson*

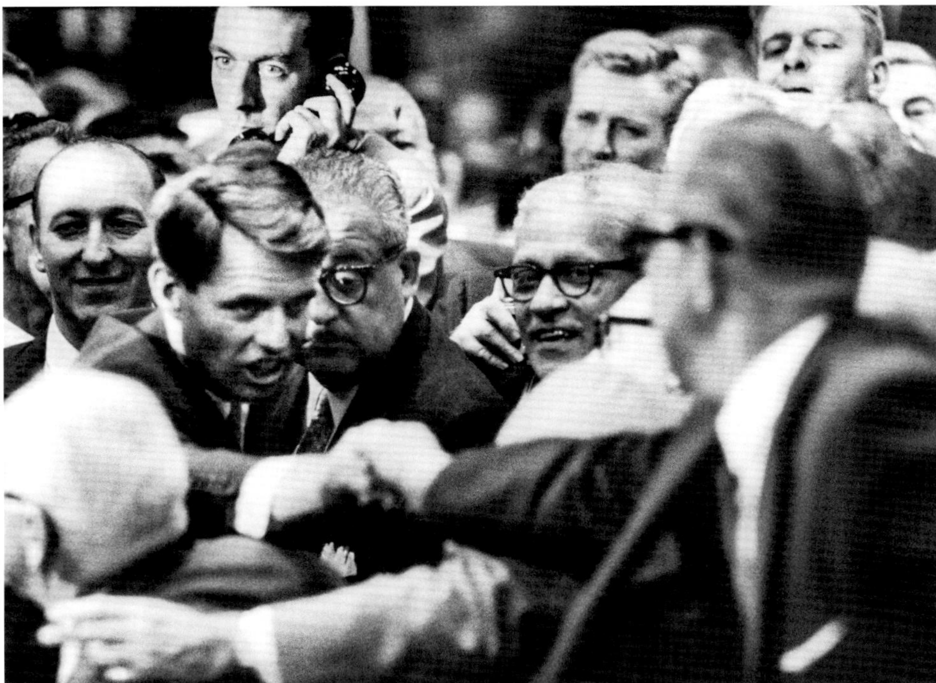

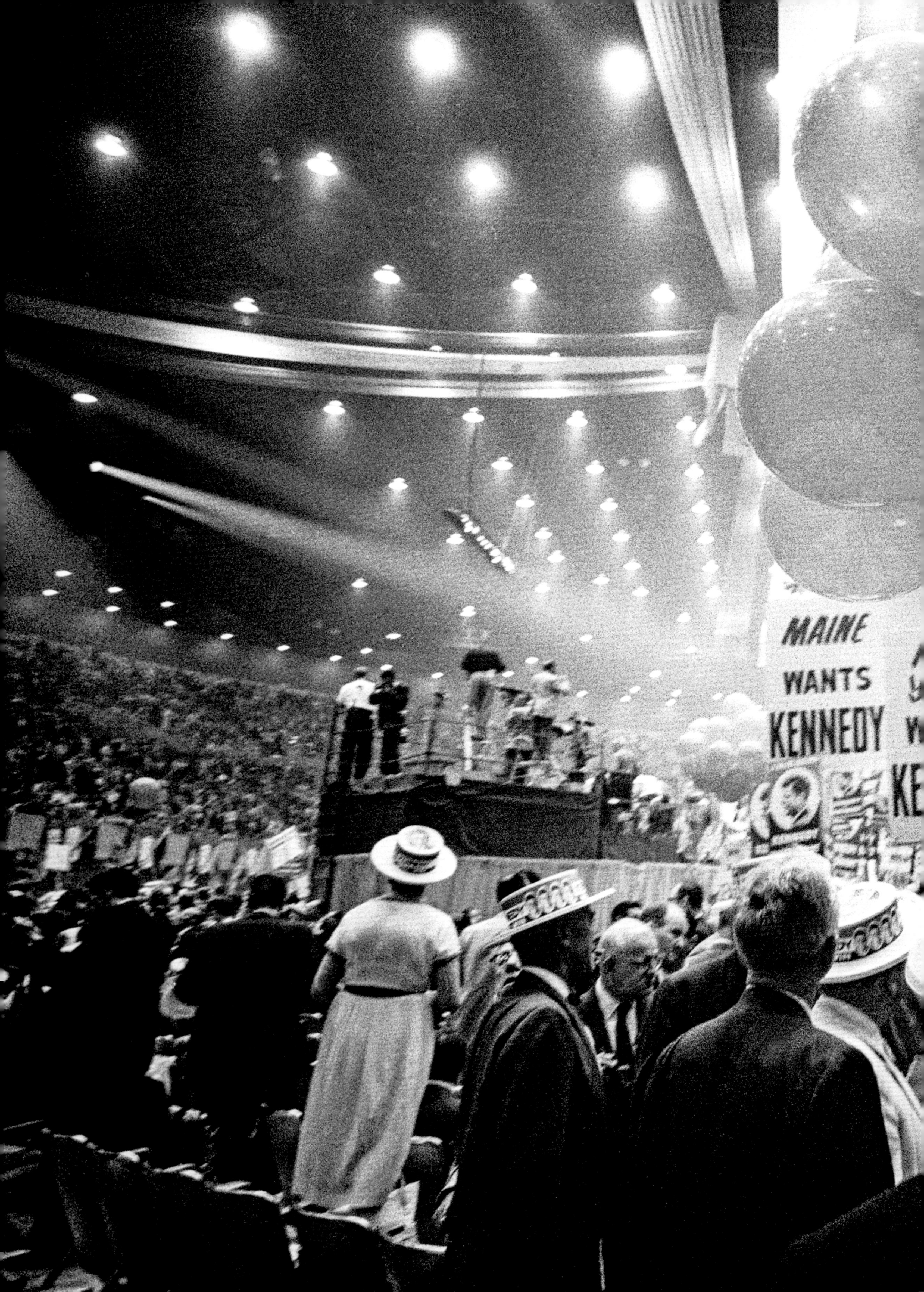
MAINE
WANTS
KENNEDY

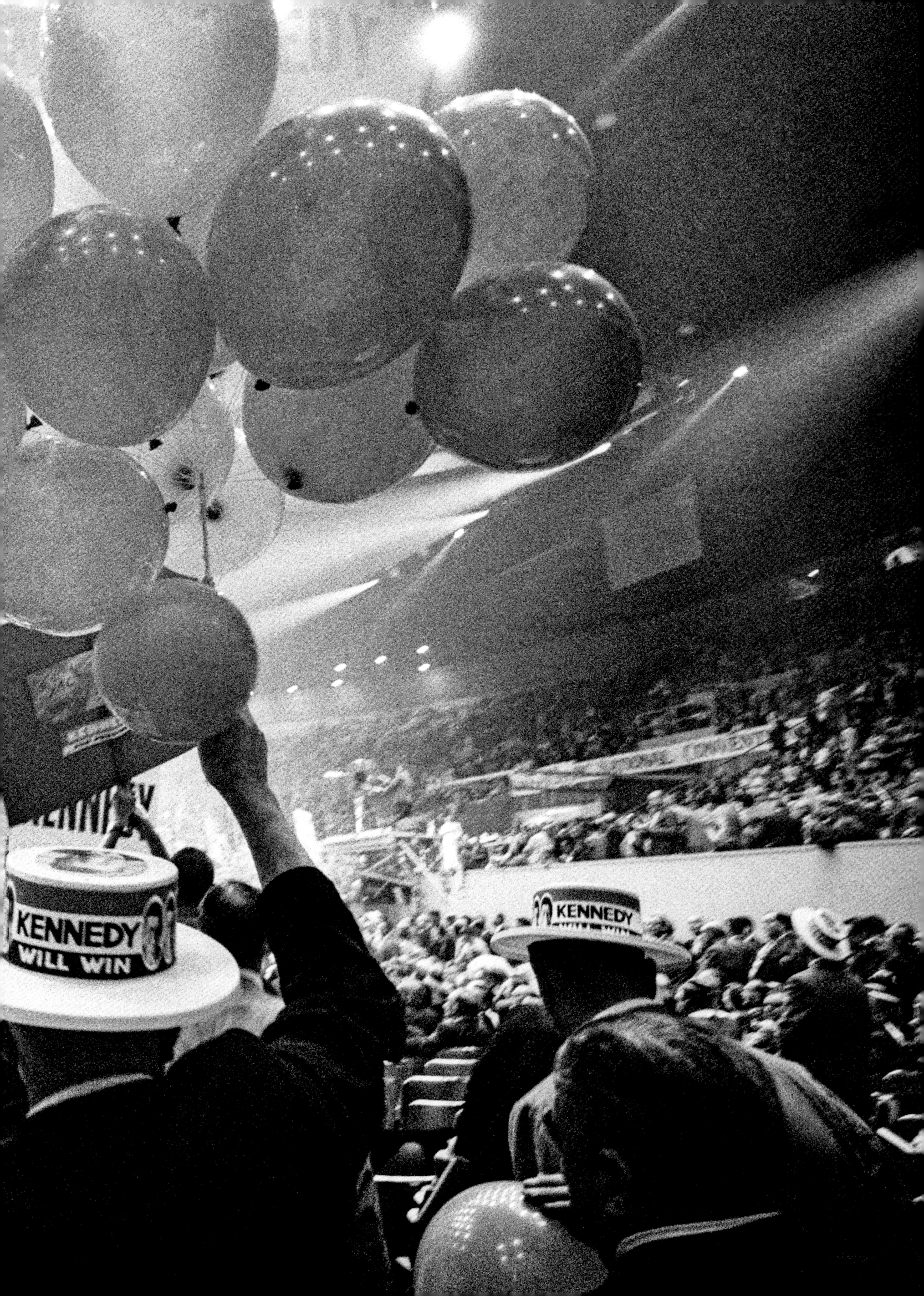

KENNEDY
WILL WIN
KENNEDY

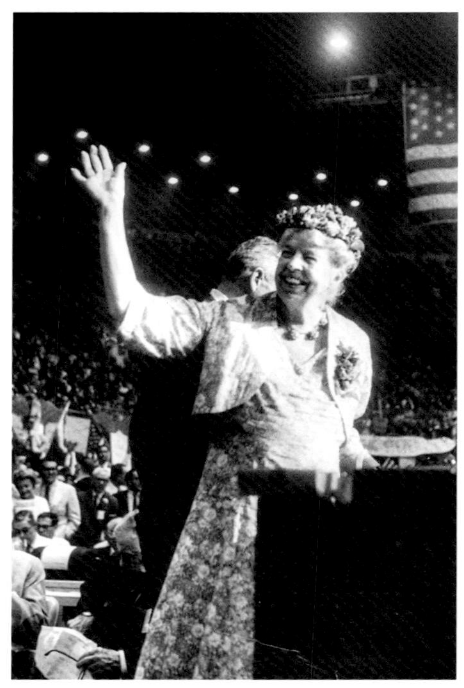

ABOVE *July 13, 1960.* Eleanor Roosevelt, the
grand dame of the Democratic Party, supported
former Illinois Governor Adlai Stevenson for the
nomination, as did many party liberals. Knowing
her importance, Kennedy tried to win her over—
and eventually would after he was nominated.
Photo, Ed Clark

OPPOSITE *July 12, 1960.* When Stevenson was
nominated by Minnesota Senator Eugene McCarthy
at the DNC, his delegation erupted in a demonstration so intense that the convention organizers
turned off the lights to try to end it. For the two
previous election cycles, Stevenson's liberalism
had been burnished deeply by a faithful faction of
the party who could not let go of their candidate.
Photo, Frank Q. Brown

army. It did part of what it was supposed to do, and many, out of combat, picked up
a kind of private life on the fly, and had their good time despite the yaws of the
military system. But today in America the generation which respected the code of the
myth was Beat, a horde of half-begotten Christs with scraggly beards, heroes none,
saints all, weak before the strong, empty conformisms of the authority. The sanction
for finding one's growth was no longer one's flag, one's career, one's sex, one's
adventure, not even one's booze. Among the best in this newest of the generations,
the myth had found its voice in marijuana, and the joke of the underground was that
when the Russians came over they could never dare to occupy us for long because
America was too Hip. Gallows humor. The poorer truth might be that America was
too Beat, the instinct of the nation so separated from its public mind that apathy,
schizophrenia, and private beatitudes might be the pride of the welcoming committee
any underground could offer.

Yes, the life of politics and the life of the myth had diverged too far. There was
nothing to return them to one another, no common danger, no cause, no desire, and,
most essentially, no hero. It was a hero America needed, a hero central to his time,
a man whose personality might suggest contradiction and mysteries which could reach
into the alienated circuits of the underground, because only a hero can capture the
secret imagination of a people, and so be good for the vitality of his nation; a hero
embodies the fantasy and so allows each private mind the liberty to consider its fantasy
and find a way to grow. Each mind can become more conscious of its desire and
waste less strength in hiding from itself. Roosevelt was such a hero, and Churchill,
Lenin and DeGaulle; even Hitler, to take the most odious example of this thesis, was
a hero, the hero-as-monster, embodying what had become the monstrous fantasy of
a people, but the horror upon which the radical mind and liberal temperament foun-
dered was that he gave outlet to the energies of the Germans and so presented the
twentieth century with an index of how horrible had become the secret heart of its
desire. Roosevelt is of course a happier example of the hero; from his paralytic leg to
the royal elegance of his geniality he seemed to contain the country within himself;
everyone from the meanest starving cripple to an ambitious young man could expand
into the optimism of an improving future because the man offered an unspoken
promise of a future which would be rich. The sexual and the sex-starved, the poor,

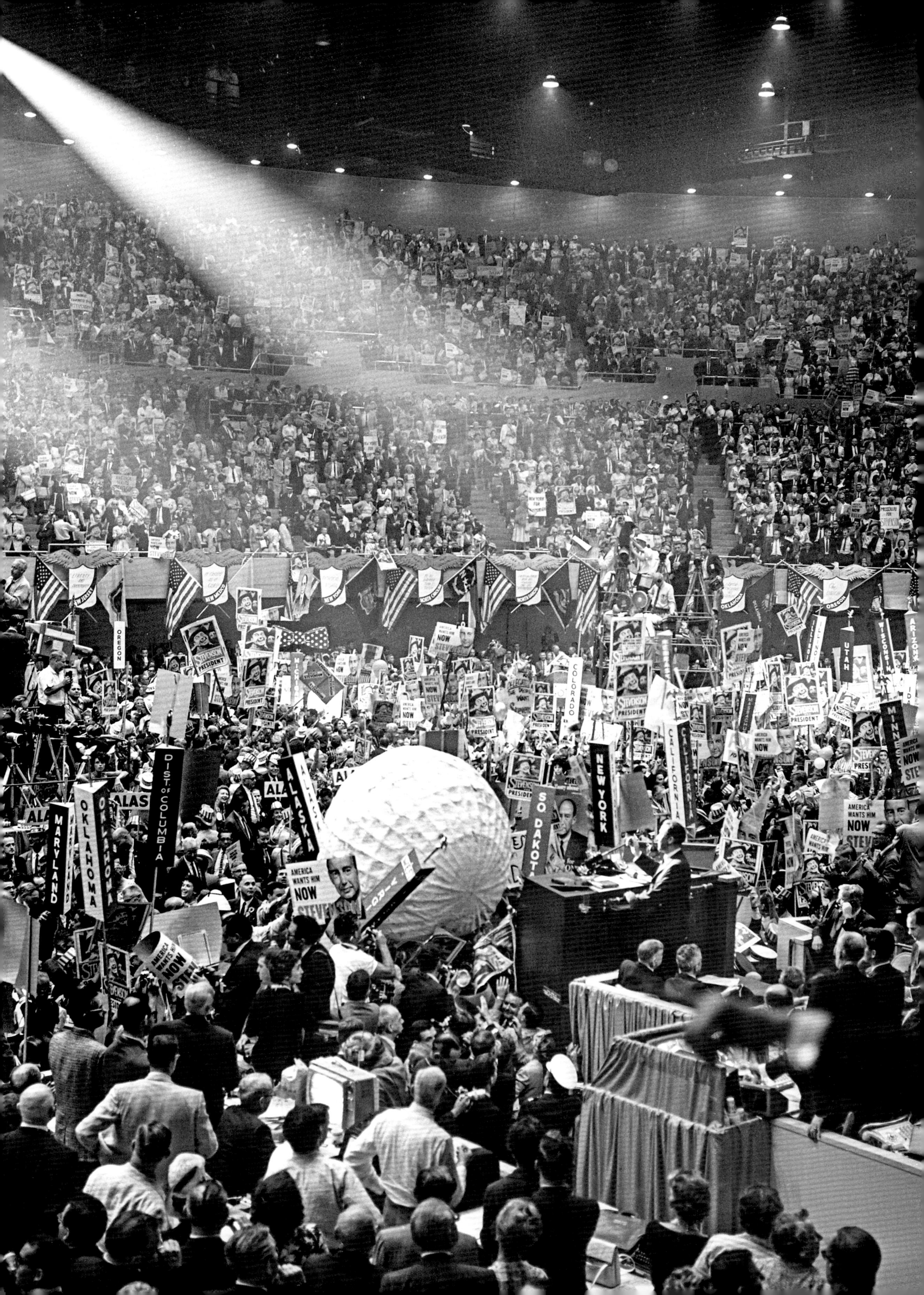

OREGON
DIST. OF COLUMBIA
MARYLAND
OKLAHOMA
ALA
ALASKA
NEW YORK
SO DAKOTA
COLORADO
CALIFORNIA
UTAH
MINNESOTA
ILLINOIS
STEVENSON FOR PRESIDENT
AMERICA WANTS HIM NOW STEVENSON

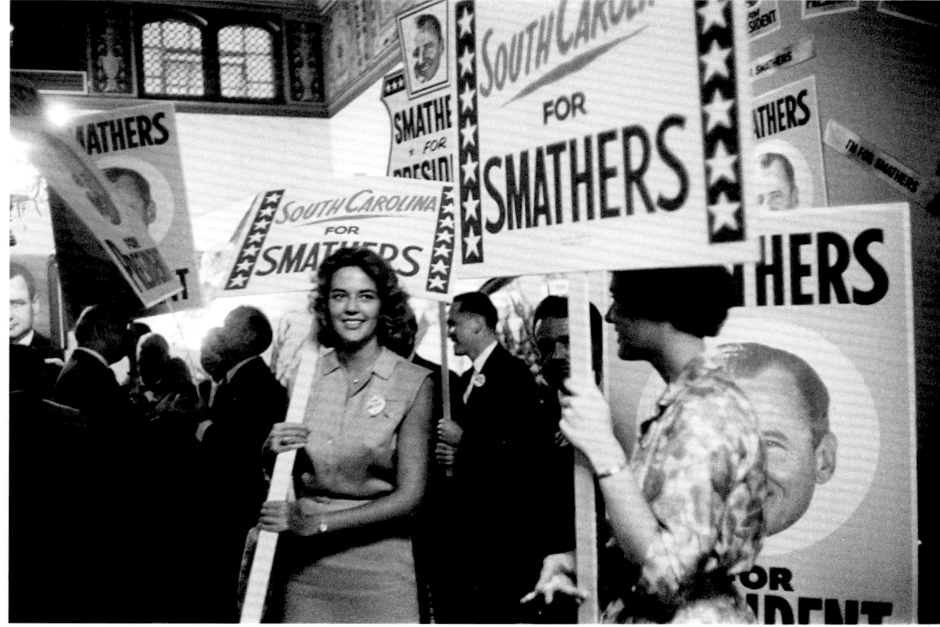

RIGHT *ca. July 11–13, 1960.* Florida Senator George Smathers, a close friend of JFK's (he served as a groomsman in Kennedy's wedding), ran in the Florida primary even though he had no intention of entering the national race. He ran as a favorite son to keep LBJ and JFK from running in his state's primary, as he feared they would split the Democratic Party there. *Photo, Garry Winogrand*

BELOW *July 13, 1960.* Stevenson supporters, loyal and committed, made their presence known at the DNC. Though he had been the Democratic presidential nominee in 1952 and 1956 (twice defeated by Eisenhower), he was coy about his candidacy for the 1960 election, announcing it just before the convention began. Unpopular among party insiders, he had no real chance at the nomination, but his candidacy did prove to be something of a spoiler for others. *Photo, Garry Winogrand*

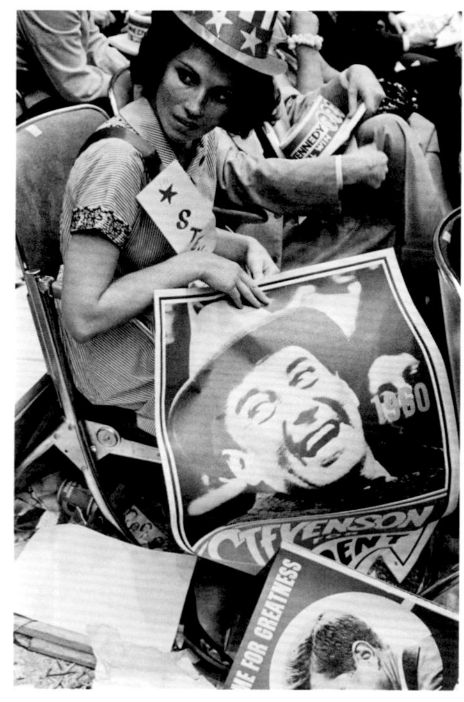

the hard-working and the imaginative well-to-do could see themselves in the President, could believe him to be like themselves. So a large part of the country was able to discover its energies because not as much was wasted in feeling that the country was a poisonous nutrient which stifled the day.

Too simple? No doubt. One tries to construct a simple model. The thesis is after all not so mysterious; it would merely nudge the notion that a hero embodies his time and is not so very much better than his time, but he is larger than life and so is capable of giving direction to the time, able to encourage a nation to discover the deepest colors of its character. At bottom the concept of hero is antagonistic to impersonal social progress, to the belief that social ills can be solved by social legislating, for it sees a country as all-but-trapped in its character until it has a hero who reveals the character of the country to itself. The implication is that without such a hero the nation turns sluggish. Truman for example was not such a hero, he was not sufficiently larger than life, he inspired familiarity without excitement, he was a character but his proportions came from soap opera: Uncle Harry, full of salty common-sense and small-minded certainty, a storekeeping uncle.

Whereas Eisenhower has been the anti-Hero, the regulator. Nations do not necessarily and inevitably seek for heroes. In periods of dull anxiety, one is more likely to look for security than a dramatic confrontation, and Eisenhower could stand as a hero only for that large number of Americans who were most proud of their lack of imagination. In American life, the unspoken war of the century has taken place between the city and the small town; the city which is dynamic, orgiastic, unsettling, explosive and accelerating to the psyche; the small town which is rooted, narrow, cautious and planted in the life-logic of the family. The need of the city is to accelerate growth; the pride of the small town is to retard it. But since America has been passing through a period of enormous expansion since the war, the double-four years of Dwight Eisenhower could not retard the expansion, it could only denude it of color, character, and the development of novelty. The small-town mind is rooted — it is rooted in the small town — and when it attempts to direct history the results are disastrously colorless because the instrument of world power which is used by the small-town mind is the committee. Committees do not create, they merely proliferate, and the incredible dullness wreaked upon the American landscape in Eisenhower's eight years has been the triumph of the corporation. A tasteless, sexless, odorless sanctity in architecture, manners, modes, styles has been the result. Eisenhower embodied half the needs of the nation, the needs of the timid, the petrified, the sanctimonious, and the sluggish. What was even worse, he did not divide the nation as a hero might (with a dramatic dialogue as the result); he merely excluded one part of the nation from the other. The result was an alienation of the best minds and bravest impulses from the faltering history which was made. America's need in those years was to take an existential turn, to walk into the nightmare, to face into that terrible logic of history which demanded that the country and its people must become more extraordinary and more adventurous, or else perish, since the only alternative was to offer a false security in the power and the panacea of organized religion, family, and the FBI, a totalitarianization of the psyche by the stultifying techniques of the mass media which would seep into everyone's most private associations and so leave the country powerless against the Russians even if the denouement were to take fifty years, for in a competition between totalitarianisms the first maxim of the prizefight manager would doubtless apply: "Hungry fighters win fights."

The Hipster as Presidential Candidate

Thoughts on a Public Man's Eighteenth-Century Wife; Face-to-Face with the Hero; Significance of a Personal Note, or the Meaning of His Having Read an Author's Novel

Some part of these thoughts must have been in one's mind at the moment there was that first glimpse of Kennedy entering the Biltmore Hotel; and in the days which followed, the first mystery — the profound air of depression which hung over the convention — gave way to a second mystery which can be answered only by history. The depression of the delegates was understandable: no one had too much doubt that Kennedy would be nominated, but if elected he would be not only the youngest President ever to be chosen by voters, he would be the most conventionally attractive young man ever to sit in the White House, and his wife — some would claim it — might be the most beautiful first lady in our history. Of necessity the myth would emerge once more, because America's politics would now be also America's favorite movie,

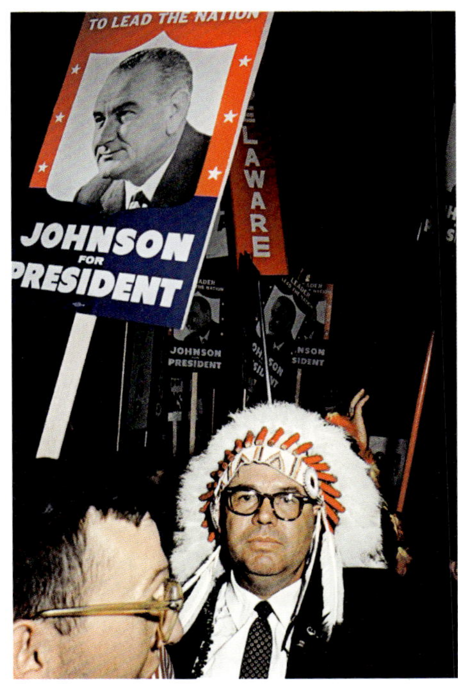

ABOVE *ca. July 11–13, 1960.* In the spirit of political spectacle, a delegate dons a Native American war bonnet. It was not uncommon for delegates to wear costumes of all sorts. According to former L.A. city council member and DNC organizer Rosalind Wyman, "people would try to outdo each other. They dressed up as mariachis, Groucho Marx, cowboys…" she said. "And you would allow so much time for their parades. Today there's nothing like it because the outcome is known in advance." *Photo, Anonymous*

"If Stevenson had campaigned for a year before the convention, it is possible that he could have stopped Kennedy. At the least, the convention would have been enormously more exciting…"

—Norman Mailer

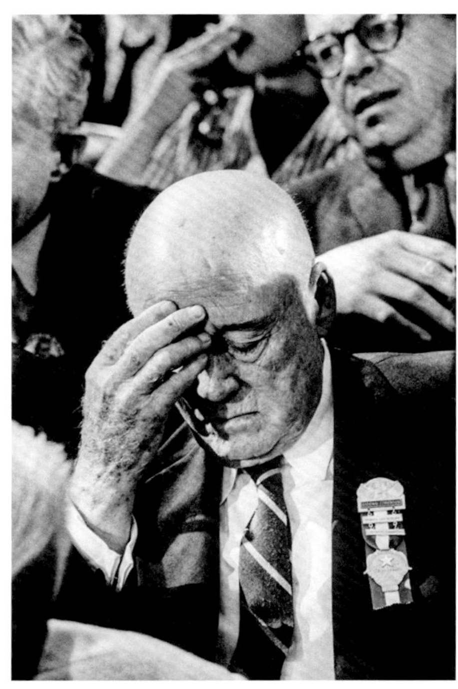

ABOVE *July 13, 1960.* Sam Rayburn, congressman from Texas and speaker of the U.S. House of Representatives from 1955 to 1961, reacts to Kennedy's nomination at the DNC. As LBJ's chief backer, Rayburn had many doubts about Kennedy, especially that a Catholic could win the national election. *Photo, Howard Sochurek*

OPPOSITE *July 11, 1960.* A sober Adlai Stevenson retreats to his hotel room while the headlines of the day announce JFK's growing momentum. Beaten twice by Eisenhower, and now by Kennedy, this would be Stevenson's last attempt to seek the presidency. However, he would become a key Kennedy ally and statesman, appointed by JFK to serve as the U.S. ambassador to the U.N. *Photo, Cornell Capa*

America's first soap opera, America's best-seller. One thinks of the talents of writers like Taylor Caldwell or Frank Yerby, or is it rather *The Fountainhead* which would contain such a fleshing of the romantic prescription? Or is it indeed one's own work which is called into question? "Well, there's your first hipster," says a writer one knows at the convention, "Sergius O'Shaugnessy born rich," and the temptation is to nod, for it could be true, a war hero, and the heroism is bona fide, even exceptional, a man who has lived with death, who, crippled in the back, took on an operation which would kill him or restore him to power, who chose to marry a lady whose face might be too imaginative for the taste of a democracy which likes its first ladies to be executives of home-management, a man who courts political suicide by choosing to go all out for a nomination four, eight, or twelve years before his political elders think he is ready, a man who announces a week prior to the convention that the young are better fitted to direct history than the old. Yes, it captures the attention. This is no routine candidate calling every shot by safety's routine book ("Yes," Nixon said, naturally but terribly tired an hour after his nomination, the TV cameras and lights and microphones bringing out a sweat of fatigue on his face, the words coming very slowly from the tired brain, somber, modest, sober, slow, slow enough so that one could touch emphatically the cautions behind each word, "Yes, I want to say," said Nixon, "that whatever abilities I have, I got from my mother." A tired pause…dull moment of warning, "…and my father." The connection now made, the rest comes easy, "…and my school and my church." Such men are capable of anything.)

One had the opportunity to study Kennedy a bit in the days that followed. His style in the press conferences was interesting. Not terribly popular with the reporters (too much a contemporary, and yet too difficult to understand, he received nothing like the rounds of applause given to Eleanor Roosevelt, Stevenson, Humphrey, or even Johnson), he carried himself nonetheless with a cool grace which seemed indifferent to applause, his manner somehow similar to the poise of a fine boxer, quick with his hands, neat in his timing, and two feet away from his corner when the bell ended the round. There was a good lithe wit to his responses, a dry Harvard wit, a keen sense of proportion in disposing of difficult questions — invariably he gave enough of an answer to be formally satisfactory without ever opening himself to a new question which might go further than the first. Asked by a reporter, "Are you for Adlai

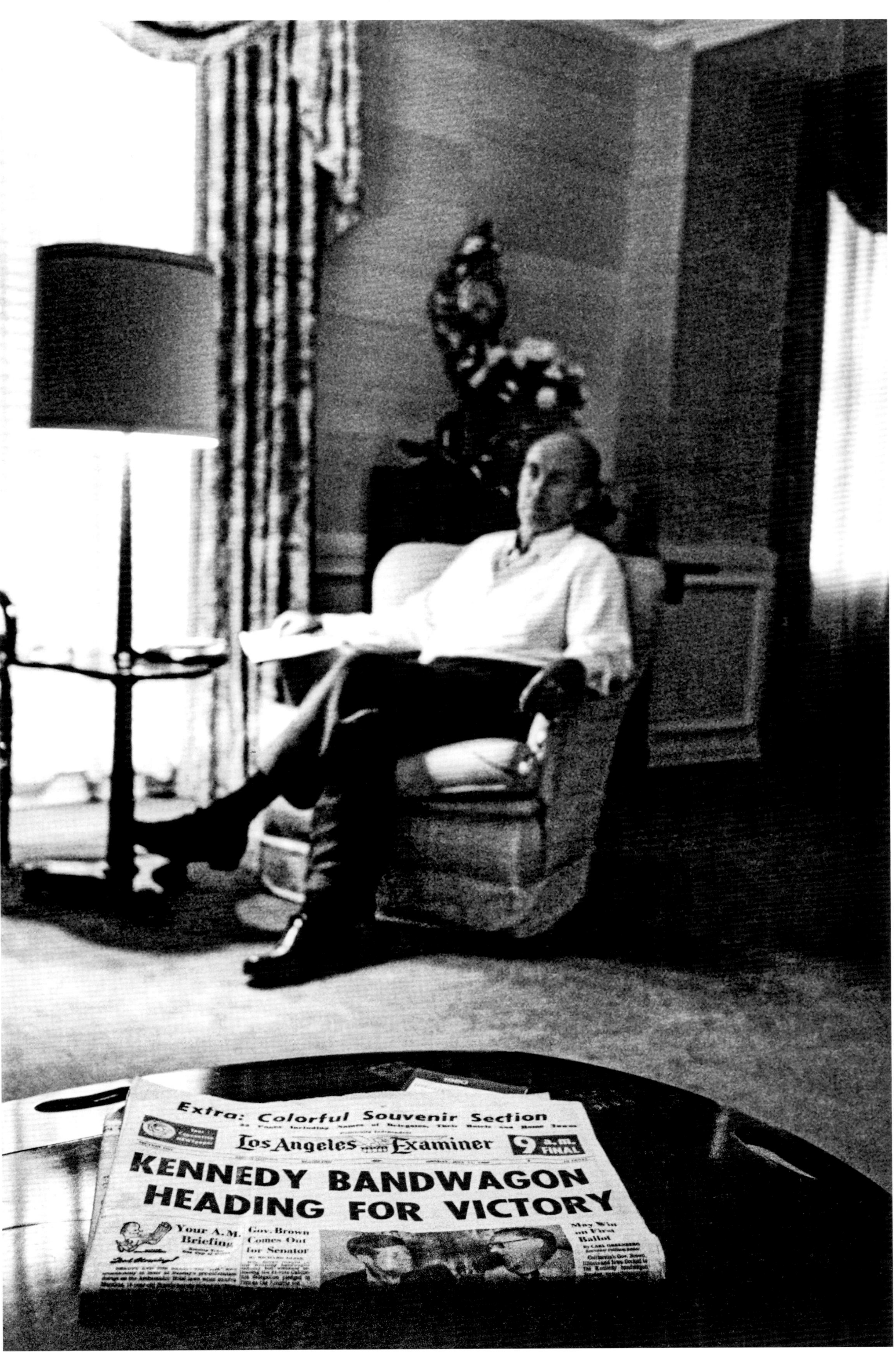

Extra: Colorful Souvenir Section
Los Angeles Examiner
9 A.M. FINAL
KENNEDY BANDWAGON
HEADING FOR VICTORY
Your A.M. Briefing
Gov. Brown Comes Out for Senator
May Win on First Ballot

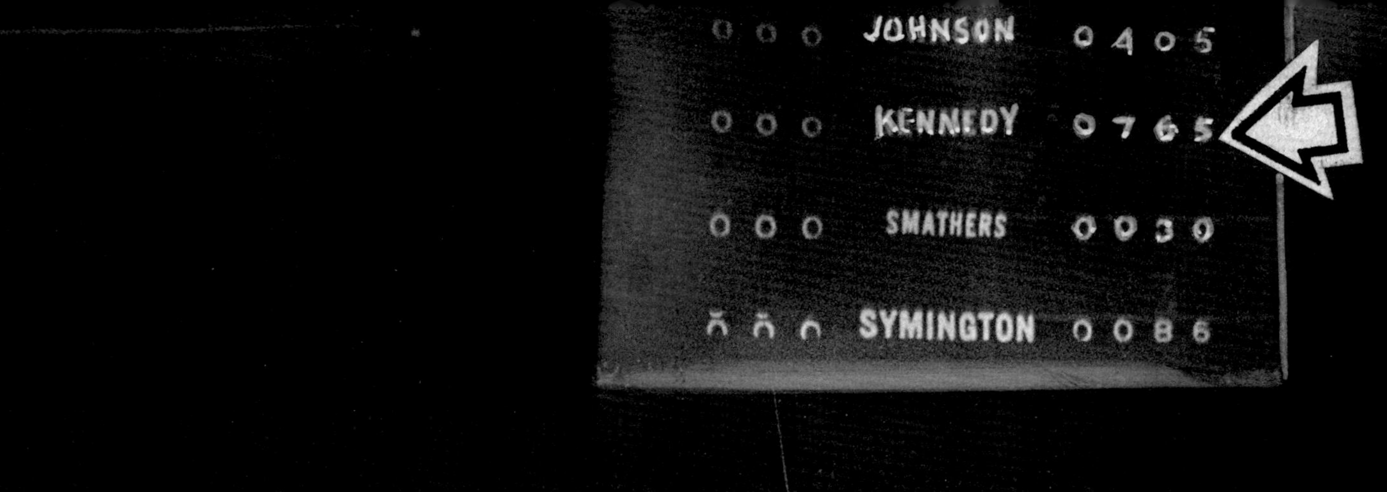

JOHNSON 0405
KENNEDY 0765
SMATHERS 0030
SYMINGTON 0086

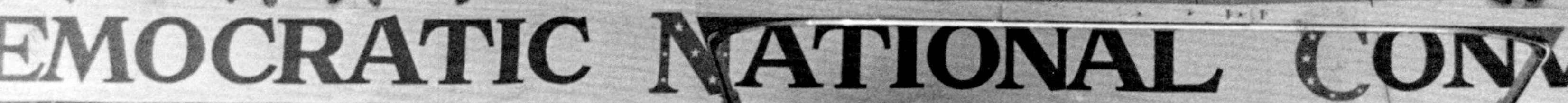

DEMOCRATIC NATIONAL CONV

DEMOCRATIC NATIONAL CONVENTION
1960

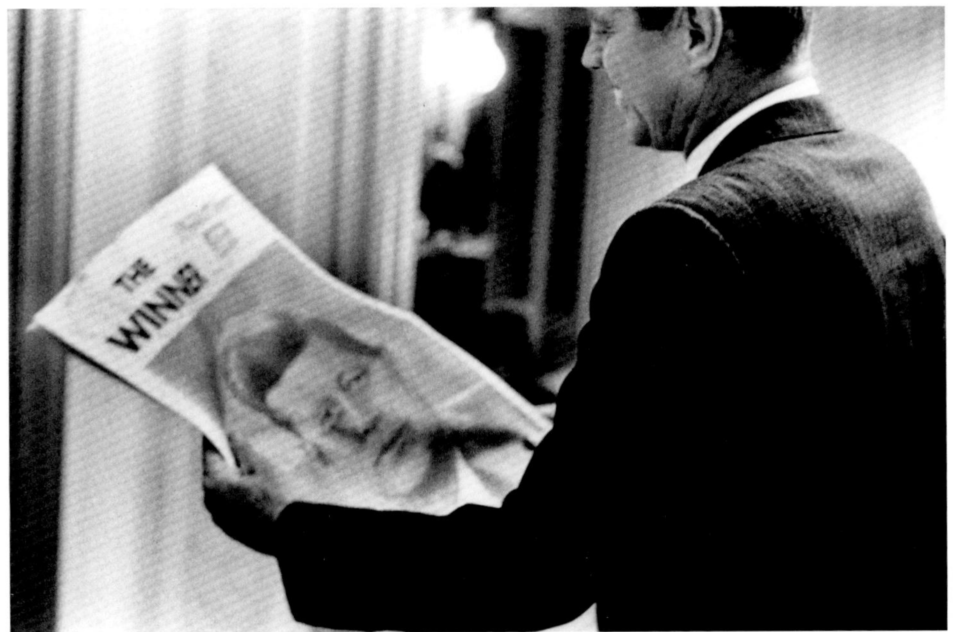

as vice-president?" the grin came forth and the voice turned very dry, "No, I cannot say we have considered *Adlai* as a vice-president." Yet there was an elusive detachment to everything he did. One did not have the feeling of a man present in the room with all his weight and all his mind. Johnson gave you all of himself, he was a political animal, he breathed like an animal, sweated like one, you knew his mind was entirely absorbed with the compendium of political fact and maneuver; Kennedy seemed at times like a young professor whose manner was adequate for the classroom, but whose mind was off in some intricacy of the Ph.D. thesis he was writing. Perhaps one can give a sense of the discrepancy by saying that he was like an actor who had been cast as the candidate, a good actor, but not a great one—you were aware all the time that the role was one thing and the man another—they did not coincide, the actor seemed a touch too aloof (as, let us say, Gregory Peck is usually too aloof) to become the part. Yet one had little sense of whether to value this elusiveness, or to beware of it. One could be witnessing the fortitude of a superior sensitivity or the detachment of a man who was not quite real to himself. And his voice gave no clue. When Johnson spoke, one could separate what was fraudulent from what was felt, he would have been satisfying as an actor the way Broderick Crawford or Paul Douglas are satisfying; one saw into his emotions, or at least had the illusion that one did. Kennedy's voice, however, was only a fair voice, too reedy, near to strident, it had the metallic snap of a cricket in it somewhere, it was more impersonal than the man, and so became the least-impressive quality in a face, a body, a selection of language, and a style of movement which made up a better-than-decent presentation, better than one had expected.

With all of that, it would not do to pass over the quality in Kennedy which is most difficult to describe. And in fact some touches should be added to this hint of a portrait, for later (after the convention), one had a short session alone with him, and the next day, another. As one had suspected in advance the interviews were not altogether satisfactory, they hardly could have been. A man running for President is altogether different from a man elected President: the hazards of the campaign make it impossible for a candidate to be as interesting as he might like to be (assuming he has such a desire). One kept advancing the argument that this campaign would be a contest of personalities, and Kennedy kept returning the discussion to politics. After a while one recognized this was an inevitable caution for him. So there would be not

"The Republican Party was still a party of church ushers, undertakers, choirboys, prison wardens, bank presidents, small-town police chiefs, state troopers,…tax-board assessors, community leaders, surgeons, Pullman porters, head nurses and the fat sons of rich fathers."

—Norman Mailer

too much point to reconstructing the dialogue since Kennedy is hardly inarticulate about his political attitudes and there will be a library vault of text devoted to it in the newspapers. What struck me most about the interview was a passing remark whose importance was invisible on the scale of politics, but was altogether meaningful to my particular competence. As we sat down for the first time, Kennedy smiled nicely and said that he had read my books. One muttered one's pleasure. "Yes," he said, "I've read…" and then there was a short pause which did not last long enough to be embarrassing in which it was yet obvious no title came instantly to his mind, an omission one was not ready to mind altogether since a man in such a position must be obliged to carry a hundred thousand facts and names in his head, but the hesitation lasted no longer than three seconds or four, and then he said, "I've read *The Deer Park* and…the others," which startled me for it was the first time in a hundred similar situations, talking to someone whose knowledge of my work was casual, that the sentence did not come out, "I've read *The Naked and the Dead*…and the others." If one

RIGHT *ca. July 11–13, 1960.* A protester's sign describes a not uncommon fear about a Kennedy candidacy. Some thought his religion would ensure a Nixon win, while others believed he was too young and inexperienced. *Photo, Garry Winogrand*

OPPOSITE *July 28, 1960.* At the Republican National Convention, held in Chicago's International Amphitheatre, delegates cheer as Richard Nixon and Henry Cabot Lodge win the party's nomination for president and vice president. Nixon, a two-term incumbent vice president, had arrived at the RNC unopposed, so there was little drama. On July 29, 1960, a day after the RNC concluded, NBC-TV chairman Robert W. Sarnoff sent telegrams to Nixon and JFK suggesting, for the first time in history, a series of televised debates. *Photo, Anonymous*

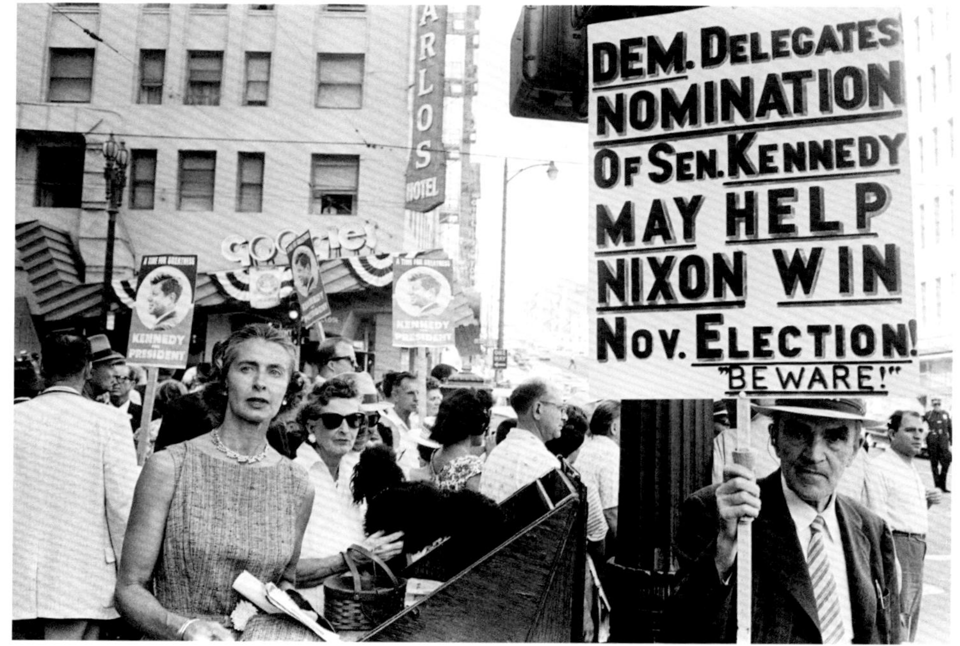

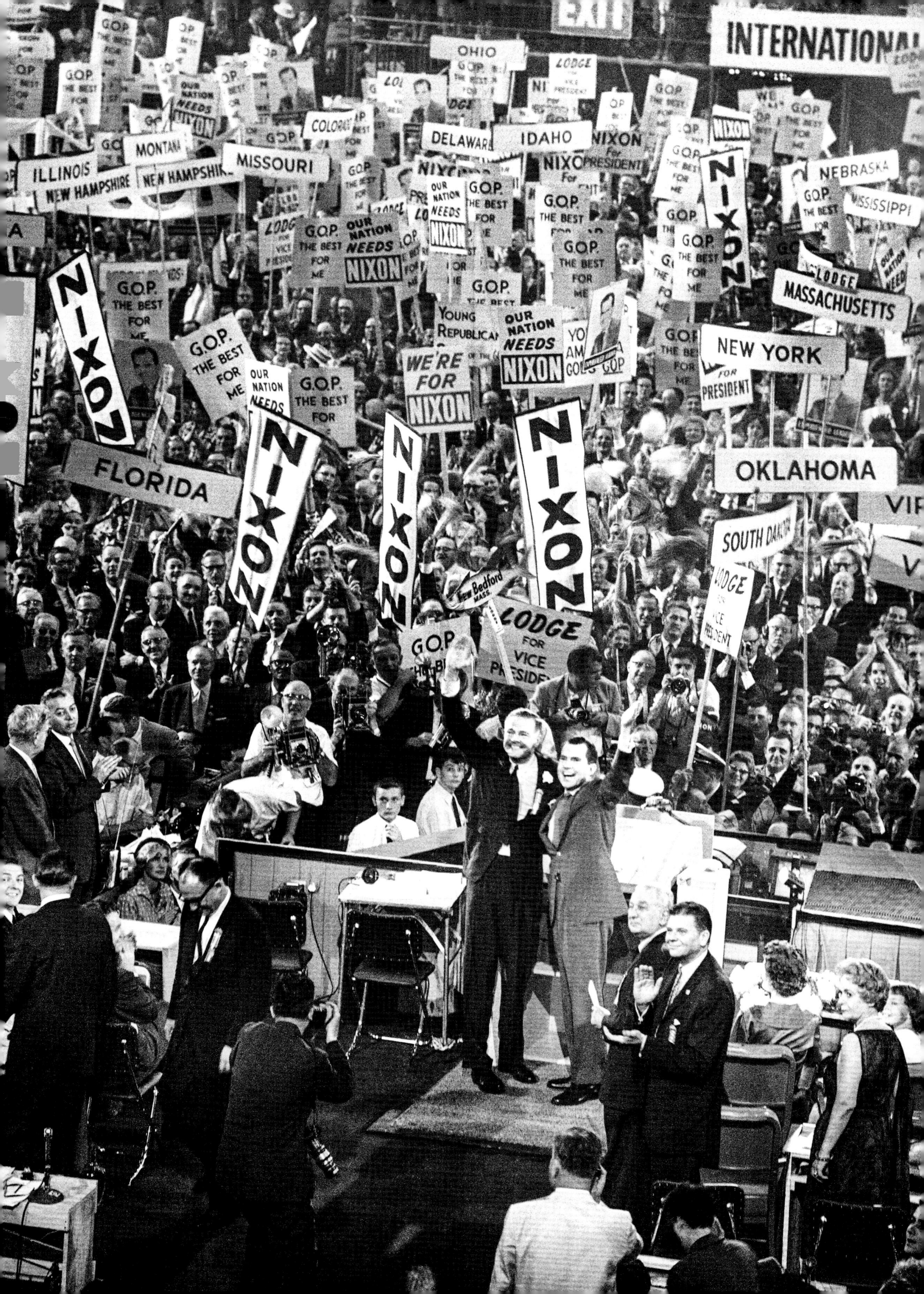

EXIT
INTERNATIONAL
ILLINOIS
NEW HAMPSHIRE
MONTANA
NEW HAMPSHIRE
MISSOURI
OHIO
DELAWARE
IDAHO
NEBRASKA
MISSISSIPPI
MASSACHUSETTS
NEW YORK
OKLAHOMA
FLORIDA
SOUTH DAKOTA
COLORADO
NIXON
NIXON FOR PRESIDENT
NIXON for PRESIDENT
NIXON
LODGE
G.O.P. THE BEST FOR ME
OUR NATION NEEDS NIXON
WE'RE FOR NIXON
LODGE FOR VICE PRESIDENT
LODGE FOR VICE PRESIDENT
G.O.P.
New Bedford MASS.
Young Republican

is to take the worst and assume that Kennedy was briefed for this interview (which is most doubtful), it still speaks well for the striking instincts of his advisers.

What was retained later is an impression of Kennedy's manners which were excellent, even artful, better than the formal good manners of Choate and Harvard, almost as if what was creative in the man had been given to the manners. In a room with one or two people, his voice improved, became low-pitched, even pleasant—it seemed obvious that in all these years he had never become a natural public speaker and so his voice was constricted in public, the symptom of all orators who are ambitious, throttled, and determined.

His personal quality had a subtle, not quite describable intensity, a suggestion of dry pent heat perhaps, his eyes large, the pupils grey, the whites prominent, almost shocking, his most forceful feature: he had the eyes of a mountaineer. His appearance changed with his mood, strikingly so, and this made him always more interesting than what he was saying. He would seem at one moment older than his age, forty-eight or fifty, a tall, slim, sunburned professor with a pleasant weathered face, not even particularly handsome; five minutes later, talking to a press conference on his lawn, three microphones before him, a television camera turning, his appearance would have gone through a metamorphosis, he would look again like a movie star, his coloring vivid, his manner rich, his gestures strong and quick, alive with that concentration of vitality a successful actor always seems to radiate. Kennedy had a dozen faces. Although they were not at all similar as people, the quality was reminiscent of someone like Brando whose expression rarely changes, but whose appearances seems to shift from one person into another as the minutes go by, and one bothers with this comparison because, like Brando, Kennedy's most characteristic quality is the remote and private air of a man who has traversed some lonely terrain of experience, of loss and gain, of nearness to death, which leaves him isolated from the mass of others.

The next day while they waited in vain for rescuers, the wrecked half of the boat turned over in the water and they saw that it would soon sink. The group decided to swim to a small island three miles away. There were other islands bigger and nearer, but the Navy officers knew that they were occupied by the Japanese. On one island, only one mile to the south, they could see a Japanese camp. McMahon, the engineer whose legs were disabled by

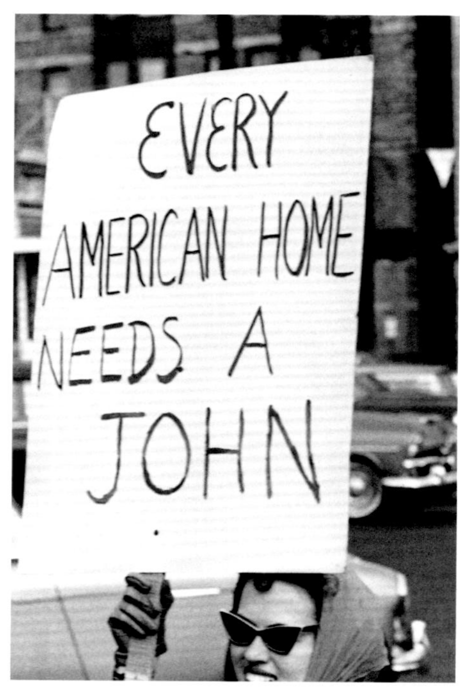

ABOVE *November 6, 1960.* A woman with a clever homemade sign in Newark, New Jersey, draws the attention of photographer Burton Berinsky, who often turned his camera on Kennedy's crowds. Berinsky, who had worked as an organizer with the International Ladies' Garment Workers' Union, met Kennedy through the ILGW in 1960 and joined his entourage on many of the campaign's East Coast stops. *Photo, Burton Berinsky*

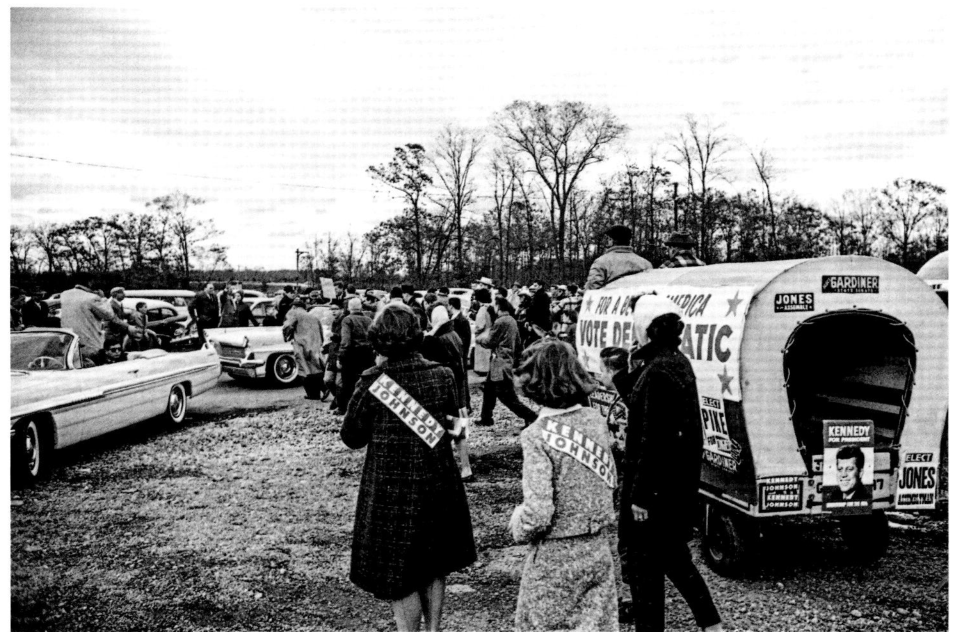

LEFT *November 6, 1960.* Journalists and supporters surround the candidate's white Lincoln convertible outside the Long Island Arena in New York's staunchly Republican Suffolk County. A crowd of 9,000 overflowed the stadium's 4,000-seat capacity as Kennedy proposed federal education funding to make college accessible to an individual based on merit rather than "his race or means." *Photo, Burton Berinsky*

BELOW *October 26, 1960.* Attendees at a rally in Mount Clemens, Michigan, demonstrate their eagerness to leave the conservative 1950s behind. *Photo, Paul Schutzer*

burns, was unable to swim. Despite his own painfully crippled back, Kennedy swam the three miles with a breast stroke, towing behind him by a life-belt strap that he held between his teeth the helpless McMahon…it took Kennedy and the suffering engineer five hours to reach the island.

The quotation is from a book which has for its dedicated unilateral title, *The Remarkable Kennedys*, but the prose is by one of the best of the war reporters, the former *Yank* editor, Joe McCarthy, and so presumably may be trusted in such details as this. Physical bravery does not of course guarantee a man's abilities in the White House — all too often men with physical courage are disappointing in their moral imagination — but the heroism here is remarkable for its tenacity. The above is merely one episode in a continuing saga which went on for five days in and out of the water, and left Kennedy at one point "miraculously saved from drowning (in a storm) by a group of Solomon Island natives who suddenly came up beside him in a large dugout canoe." Afterward, his back still injured (that precise back injury which was to put him on crutches eleven years later, and have him search for "spinal-fusion surgery" despite a warning that his chances of living through the operation were "extremely limited") afterward, he asked to go back on duty and became so bold in the attacks he made with his PT boat "that the crew didn't like to go out with him because he took so many chances."

It is the wisdom of a man who senses death within him and gambles that he can cure it by risking his life. It is the therapy of the instinct, and who is so wise as to call it irrational? Before he went into the Navy, Kennedy had been ailing. Washed out of Freshman year at Princeton by a prolonged trough of yellow jaundice, sick for a year at Harvard, weak already in the back from an injury at football, his trials suggest the self-hatred of a man whose resentment and ambition are too large for his body. Not everyone can discharge their furies on an analyst's couch, for some angers can be relaxed only by winning power, some rages are sufficiently monumental to demand that one try to become a hero or else fall back into that death which is already within the cells. But if one succeeds, the energy aroused can be exceptional. Talking to a man who had been with Kennedy in Hyannis Port the week before the convention, I heard that he was in a state of deep fatigue.

"Well, he didn't look tired at the convention," one commented.

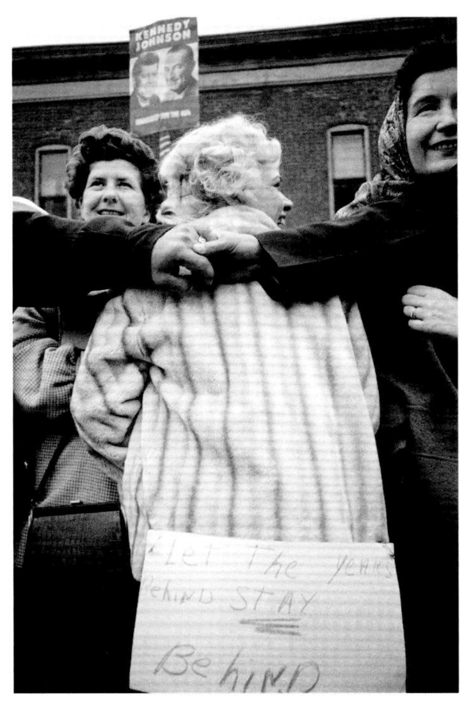

61

"Oh, he had three days of rest. Three days of rest for him is like six months for us."

One thinks of that three-mile swim with the belt in his mouth and McMahon holding it behind him. There are pestilences which sit in the mouth and rot the teeth— in those five hours how much of the psyche must have been remade, for to give vent to the bite in one's jaws and yet use that rage to save a life: it is not so very many men who have the apocalyptic sense that heroism is the First Doctor.

If one had a profound criticism of Kennedy it was that his public mind was too conventional, but that seemed to matter less than the fact of such a man in office because the law of political life had become so dreary that only a conventional mind could win an election. Indeed there could be no politics which gave warmth to one's body until the country had recovered its imagination, its pioneer lust for the unexpected and incalculable. It was the changes that might come afterward on which one could put one's hope. With such a man in office the myth of the nation would again be

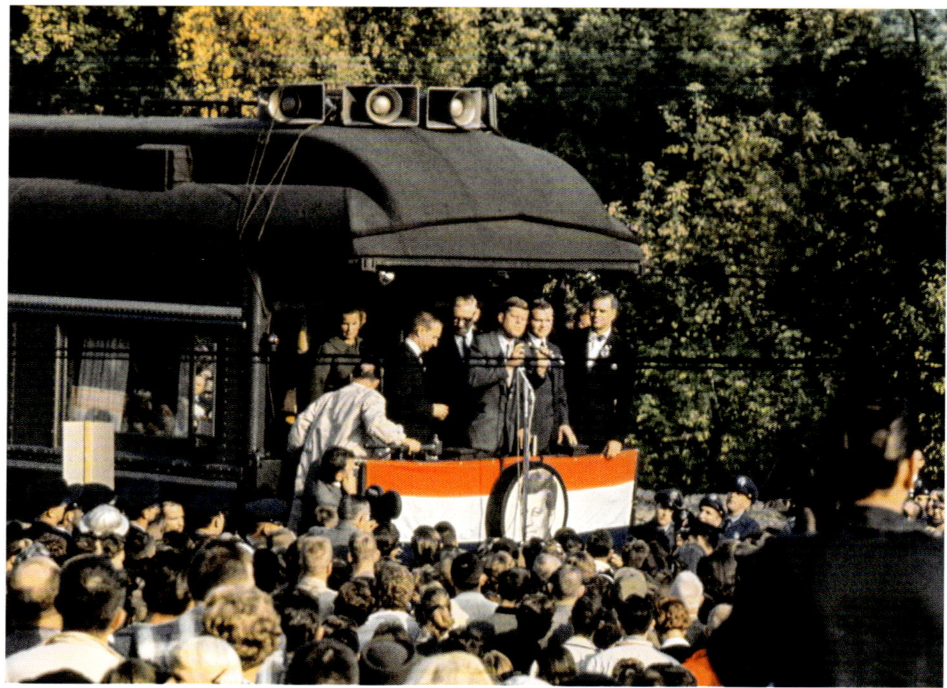

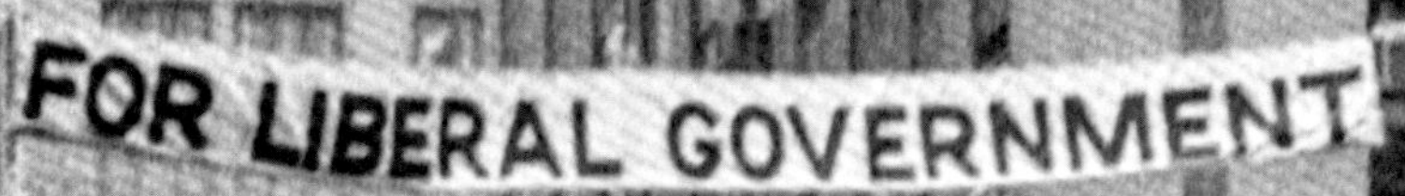
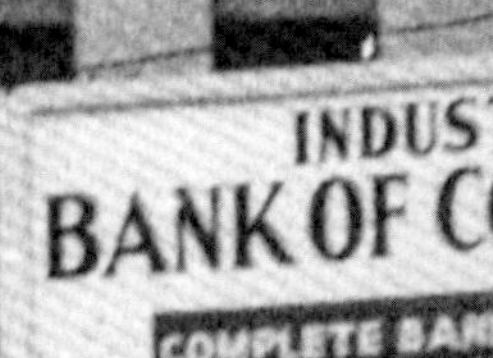
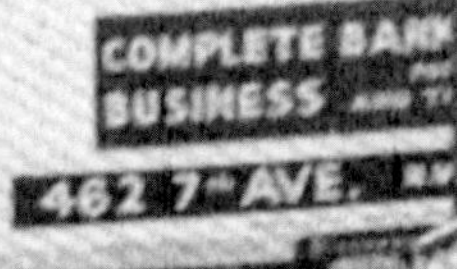
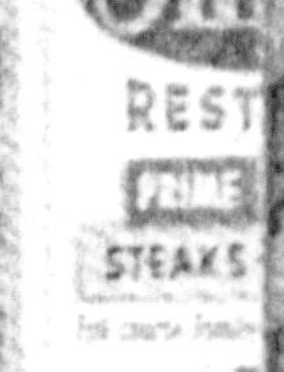
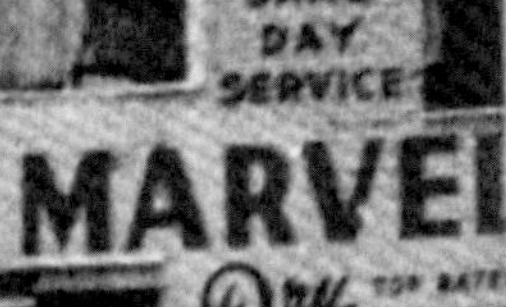
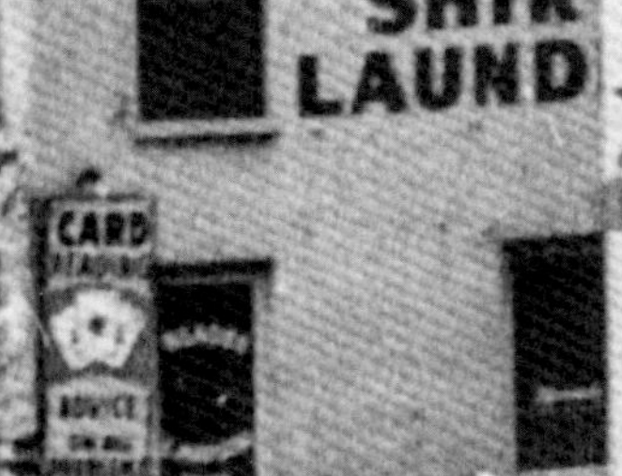
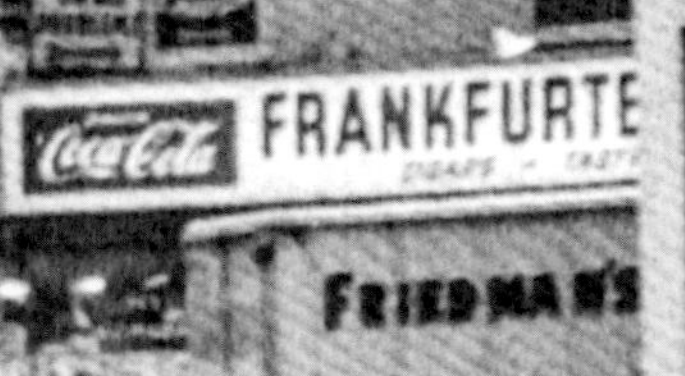
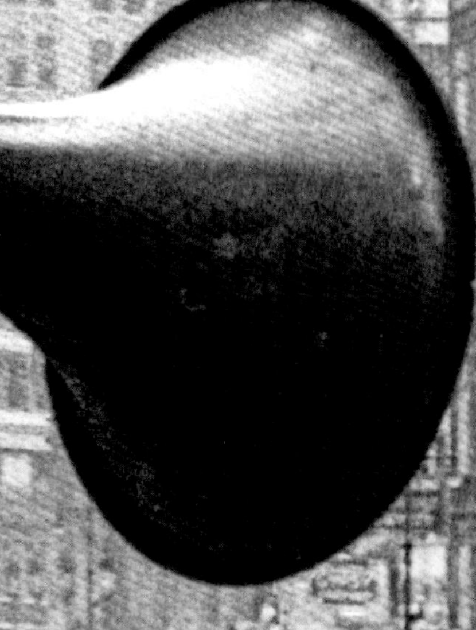

VOTE FOR
JOHN F. KENNEDY FOR PRESIDENT
LYNDON B. JOHNSON FOR VICE-PRESIDENT
VOTE LIBERAL PARTY ROW C
FOR LIBERAL GOVERNMENT
INDUST
BANK OF C
COMPLETE BANK
BUSINESS
462 7th AVE
SAME DAY SERVICE
MARVEL
Dry CLEAN
GARMENT
INDUST
212 W. 35
Same DAY
SHIRT
LAUNDRY
SH
REST
PRIME
STEAKS
LOANS
BEAUTY SALON
CARD
READ
COCA-COLA
FRANKFURTE
FRIEDMAN'S

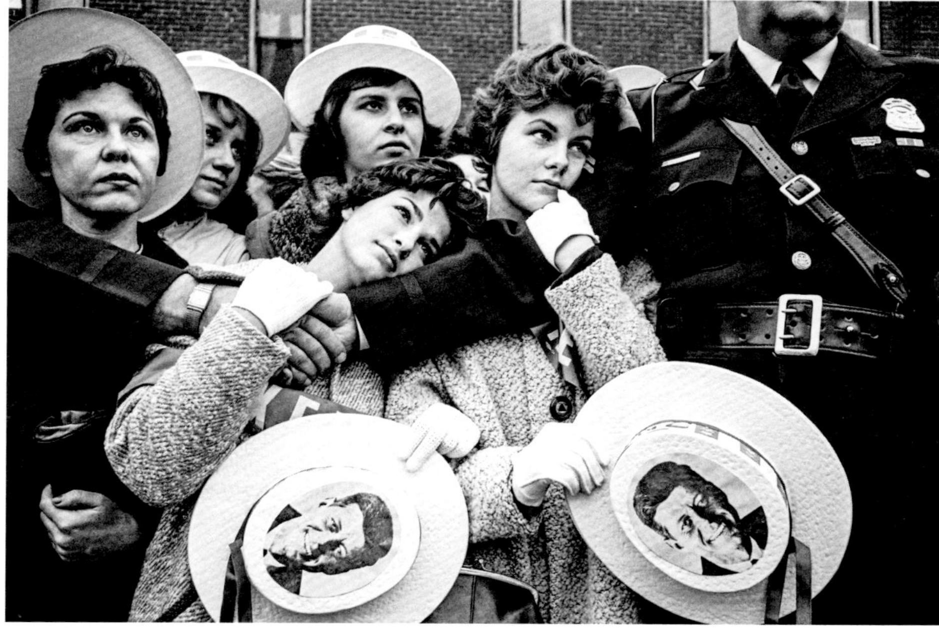

RIGHT *October 26, 1960.* Two teenage girls hang on the arms of state police officers at a rally in Mount Clemens. According to a *Life* magazine story published the day before the general election, "The blissful fog of feminine adoration surrounding Jack Kennedy. . . grew even thicker in the last days of his tour," a critical consideration with women of voting age outnumbering men "56.1 million to 52.7 million." *Photo, Paul Schutzer*

BELOW *October 30, 1960.* At a rally in Levittown, Pennsylvania, a message is sent to the sitting First Lady. Mamie and "Ike" Eisenhower would be leaving the White House no matter the outcome of the election, but the symbolic resonance of the old guard being replaced by the dynamic Kennedys proved to hold sway with the young. *Photo, Burton Berinsky*

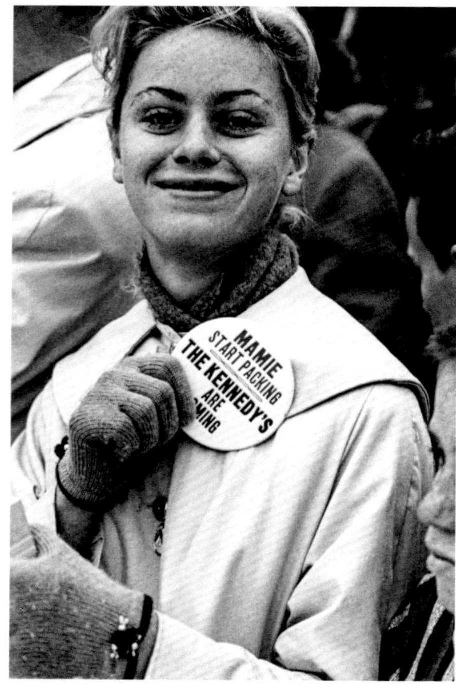

engaged, and the fact that he was Catholic would shiver a first existential vibration of consciousness into the mind of the White Protestant. For the first time in our history, the Protestant would have the pain and creative luxury of feeling himself in some tiny degree part of a minority, and that was an experience which might be incommensurable in its value to the best of them.

A Vignette of Adlai Stevenson; The Speeches

What Happened When the Teleprompter Jammed: How U.S. Senator Eugene McCarthy Played the Matador. An Observation on the Name Fitzgerald

As yet we have said hardly a word about Stevenson. And his actions must remain a puzzle unless one dares a speculation about his motive, or was it his need?

So far as the people at the convention had affection for anyone, it was Stevenson, so far as they were able to generate any spontaneous enthusiasm, their cheers were again for Stevenson. Yet it was obvious he never had much chance because so soon as a chance would present itself he seemed quick to dissipate the opportunity. The day before the nominations, he entered the Sports Arena to take his seat as a delegate—the demonstration was spontaneous, noisy and prolonged; it was quieted only by Governor Collins' invitation for Stevenson to speak to the delegates. In obedience perhaps to the scruple that a candidate must not appear before the convention until nominations are done, Stevenson said no more than: "I am grateful for this tumultuous and moving welcome. After getting in and out of the Biltmore Hotel and this hall, I have decided I know whom you are going to nominate. It will be the last survivor." This dry reminder of the ruthlessness of politics broke the roar of excitement for his presence. The applause as he left the platform was like the dying fall-and-moan of a baseball crowd when a home run curves foul. The next day, a New York columnist talking about it said bitterly, "If he'd only gone through the motions, if he had just said that now he wanted to run, that he would work hard, and he hoped the delegates would vote for him. Instead he made that lame joke." One wonders. It seems almost as if he did not wish to win unless victory came despite himself, and then was overwhelming. There are men who are not heroes because they are too good for their

time, and it is natural that defeats leave them bitter, tired, and doubtful of their right
to make new history. If Stevenson had campaigned for a year before the convention,
it is possible that he could have stopped Kennedy. At the least, the convention would
have been enormously more exciting, and the nominations might have gone through
half-a-dozen ballots before a winner was hammered into shape. But then Stevenson
might also have shortened his life. One had the impression of a tired man who (for a
politician) was sickened unduly by compromise. A year of maneuvering, broken promises,
and detestable partners might have gutted him for the election campaign. If elected,
it might have ruined him as a President. There is the possibility that he sensed his
situation exactly this way, and knew that if he were to run for President, win and make
a good one, he would first have to be restored, as one can indeed be restored, by an
exceptional demonstration of love—love, in this case, meaning that the Party had a
profound desire to keep him as their leader. The emotional truth of a last-minute
victory for Stevenson over the Kennedy machine might have given him new energy;
it would certainly have given him new faith in a country and a party whose good motives
he was possibly beginning to doubt. Perhaps the fault he saw with his candidacy was
that he attracted only the nicest people to himself and there were not enough of them.
(One of the private amusements of the convention was to divine some of the qualities
of the candidates by the style of the young women who put on hats and clothing and
politicked in the colors of one presidential gent or another. Of course, half of them
must have been hired models, but someone did the hiring and so it was fair to look for
a common denominator. The Johnson girls tended to be plump, pie-faced, dumb sexy
Southern; the Symingteeners seemed a touch mulish, stubborn, good-looking pluggers;
the Kennedy ladies were the handsomest; healthy, attractive, tough, a little spoiled—
they looked like the kind of girls who had gotten all the dances in high school and/or
worked for a year as an airline hostess before marrying well. But the Stevenson
girls looked to be doing it for no money; they were good sorts, slightly horsy-faced,
one had the impression they had played field hockey in college.) It was indeed the
pure, the saintly, the clean-living, the pacifistic, the vegetarian who seemed most for
Stevenson, and the less humorous in the Kennedy camp were heard to remark bitterly
that Stevenson had nothing going for him but a bunch of Goddamn Beatnicks. This
might even have had its sour truth. The demonstrations outside the Sports Arena

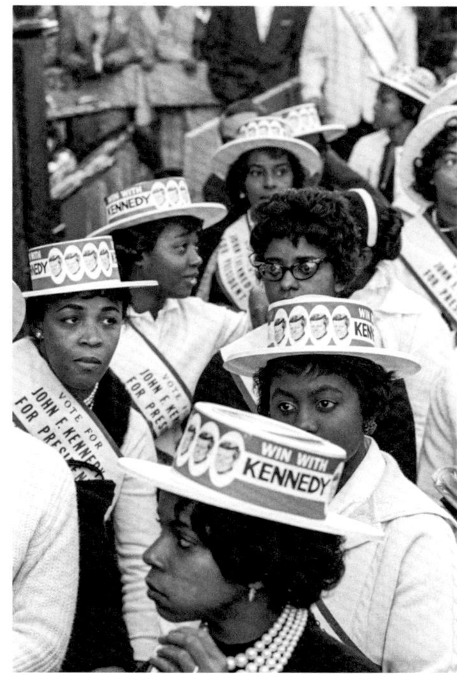

ABOVE *October 12, 1960.* Rally in Harlem, New York.
While the campaign worked hard to project modernity
and progressive ideals in its marketing efforts, it
was impossible to entirely transcend its charismatic
leader's well-heeled roots. Observed Mailer: "[T]he
personnel had something of the Kennedy élan, those
paper hats designed to look like straw boaters…the
elegance always giving its subtle echo of the Twenties."
Photo, Burton Berinsky

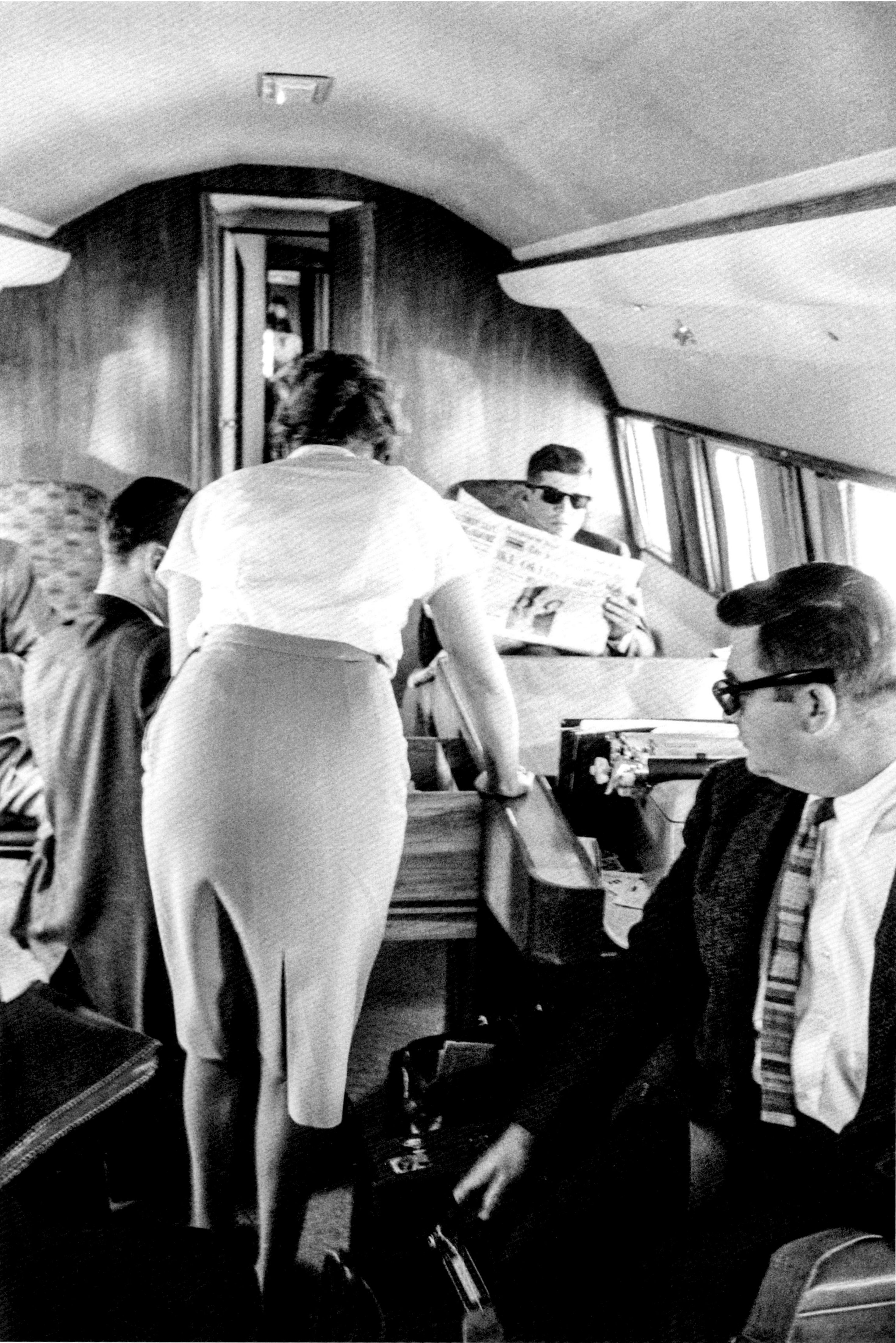

for Stevenson seemed to have more than a fair proportion of tall, emaciated young men with thin, wry beards and three-string guitars accompanied (again in undue proportion) by a contingent of ascetic, face-washed young Beat ladies in sweaters and dungarees. Not to mention all the Holden Caulfields one could see from here to the horizon. But of course it is unfair to limit it so, for the Democratic gentry were also committed half en masse for Stevenson, as well as a considerable number of movie stars, Shelley Winters for one: after the convention she remarked sweetly, "Tell me something nice about Kennedy so I can get excited about him."

What was properly astonishing was the way this horde of political half-breeds and amateurs came within distance of turning the convention from its preconceived purpose, and managed at least to bring the only hour of thoroughgoing excitement the convention could offer.

But then nominating day was the best day of the week and enough happened to suggest that a convention out of control would be a spectacle as extraordinary in the American scale of spectator values as a close seventh game in the World Series or a tied fourth quarter in a professional-football championship. A political convention is after all not a meeting of a corporation's board of directors; it is a fiesta, a carnival, a pig-rooting, horse-snorting, band-playing, voice-screaming medieval get-together of greed, practical lust, compromised idealism, career-advancement, meeting, feud, vendetta, conciliation, of rabble-rousers, fist fights (as it used to be), embraces, drunks (again as it used to be) and collective rivers of animal sweat. It is a reminder that no matter how the country might pretend it has grown up and become tidy in its manners, bodiless in its legislative language, hygienic in its separation of high politics from private life, that the roots still come grubby from the soil, and that politics in America is still different from politics anywhere else because the politics has arisen out of the immediate needs, ambitions, and cupidities of the people, that our politics still smell of the bedroom and the kitchen, rather than having descended to us from the chill punctilio of aristocratic negotiation.

So. The Sports Arena was new, too pretty of course, tasteless in its design — it was somehow pleasing that the acoustics were so bad for one did not wish the architects well; there had been so little imagination in their design, and this arena would have none of the harsh grandeur of Madison Square Garden when it was aged by spectators'

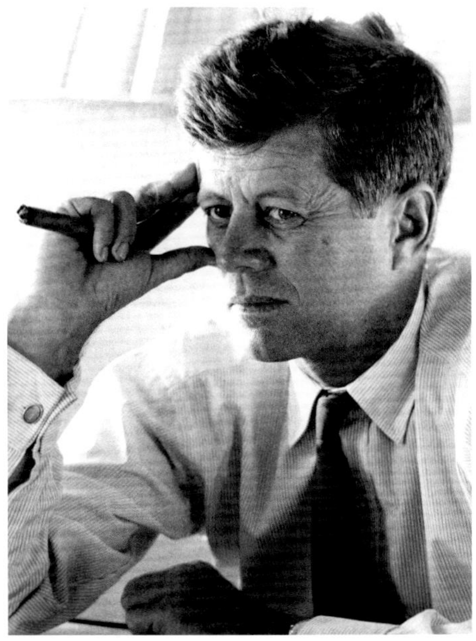

OPPOSITE *1960.* **A significant advantage to the Kennedy campaign was its private plane, named the** *Caroline* **(after JFK's daughter). It included its own pilot, cook, and flight attendant (Janet Des Rosiers, center). Starting in September 1959, the** *Caroline* **would log many miles crisscrossing the country with JFK, sometimes Jackie, and an assortment of media, friends, and staff (including press secretary Pierre Salinger, right) on board.** *Photo, Jacques Lowe*

ABOVE *Early 1960.* **Kennedy was traveling from West Virginia to Nebraska aboard the** *Caroline* **when Jacques Lowe snapped this photograph of Kennedy engaged in conversation with his advisors. According to Lowe, cigars were one of Kennedy's "calming props," used only in private, both lit and unlit, as he worked on speeches and strategy.** *Photo, Jacques Lowe*

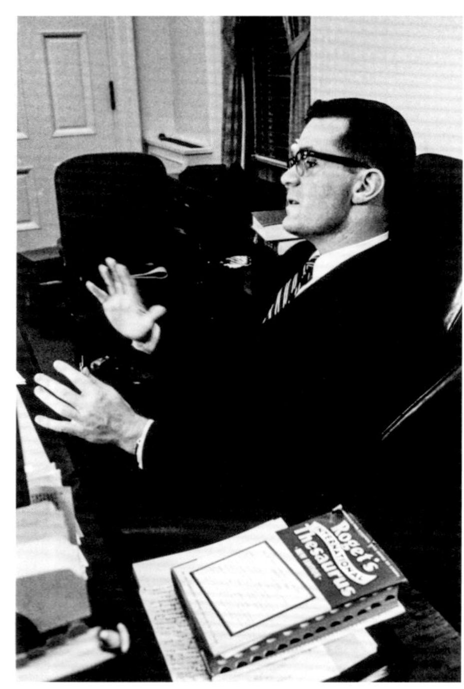

phlegm and feet over the next twenty years. Still it had some atmosphere; seen from the streets, with the spectators moving to the ticket gates, the bands playing, the green hot-shot special editions of the Los Angeles newspapers being hawked by the newsboys, there was a touch of the air of promise that precedes a bullfight, not something so good as the approach to the Plaza Mexico, but good, let us say, like the entrance into El Toreo of Mexico City, another architectural monstrosity, also with seats painted, as I remember, in rose-pink, and dark, milky sky-blue.

Inside, it was also different this nominating day. On Monday and Tuesday the air had been desultory, no one listened to the speakers, and everybody milled from one easy chatting conversation to another—it had been like a tepid Kaffeeklatsch for fifteen thousand people. But today there was a whip of anticipation in the air, the seats on the floor were filled, the press section was working, and in the gallery people were sitting in the aisles.

Sam Rayburn had just finished nominating Johnson as one came in, and the rebel yells went up, delegates started filing out of their seats and climbing over seats, and a pullulating dance of bodies and bands began to snake through the aisles, the posters jogging and whirling in time to the music. The dun color of the floor (faces, suits, seats, and floor boards), so monotonous the first two days, now lit up with life as if an iridescent caterpillar had emerged from a fold of wet leaves. It was more vivid than one had expected, it was right, it felt finally like a convention, and from up close when one got down to the floor (where your presence was illegal and so consummated by sneaking in one time as demonstrators were going out, and again by slipping a five-dollar bill to a guard) the nearness to the demonstrators took on high color, that electric vividness one feels on the side lines of a football game when it is necessary to duck back as the ballcarrier goes by, his face tortured in the concentration of the moment, the thwomp of his tackle as acute as if one had been hit oneself.

That was the way the demonstrators looked on the floor. Nearly all had the rapt, private look of a passion or a tension which would finally be worked off by one's limbs, three hundred football players, everything from seedy delegates with jowl-sweating shivers to livid models, paid for their work that day, but stomping out their beat on the floor with the hypnotic adulatory grimaces of ladies who had lived for Lyndon these last ten years.

Then from the funereal rostrum, whose color was not so rich as mahogany nor so dead as a cigar, came the last of the requests for the delegates to take their seats.

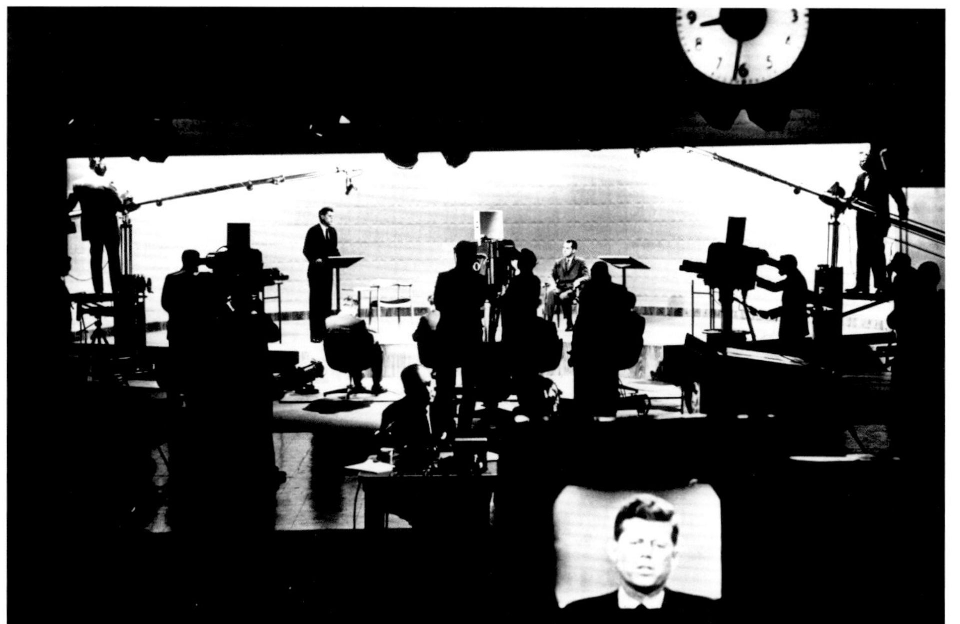

The seconding speeches began, one minute each; they ran for three and four, the minor-league speakers running on the longest as if the electric antennae of television was the lure of the Sirens, leading them out. Bored cheers applauded their concluding Götterdämmerungen and the nominations were open again. A favorite son, a modest demonstration, five seconding speeches, tedium.

Next was Kennedy's occasion. Governor Freeman of Minnesota made the speech. On the second or third sentence his television prompter jammed, an accident. Few could be aware of it at the moment; the speech seemed merely flat and surprisingly void of bravura. He was obviously no giant of extempore. Then the demonstration. Well-run, bigger than Johnson's, jazzier, the caliber of the costumes and decorations better chosen: the placards were broad enough, "Let's Back Jack," the floats were garish, particularly a papier-mâché or plastic balloon of Kennedy's head, six feet in diameter, which had nonetheless the slightly shrunken, over-red, rubbery look of a toy for practical jokers in one of those sleazy off-Times Square magic-and-gimmick stores; the band was suitably corny; and yet one had the impression this demonstration had been designed by some hands-to-hip interior decorator who said, "Oh, joy, let's have fun, let's make this *true* beer hall."

Besides, the personnel had something of the Kennedy *élan*, those paper hats designed to look like straw boaters with Kennedy's face on the crown, and small photographs of him on the ribbon, those hats which had come to symbolize the crack speed of the Kennedy team, that Madison Avenue cachet which one finds in the bars like P. J. Clarke's, the elegance always giving its subtle echo of the Twenties so that the raccoon coats seem more numerous than their real count, and the colored waistcoats are measured by the charm they would have drawn from Scott Fitzgerald's eye. But there, it occurred to one for the first time that Kennedy's middle name was just that, Fitzgerald, and the tone of his crack lieutenants, the unstated style, was true to Scott. The legend of Fitzgerald had an army at last, formed around the self-image in the mind of every superior Madison Avenue opportunist that he was hard, he was young, he was In, his conversation was lean as wit, and if the work was not always scrupulous, well the style could aspire. If there came a good day…he could meet the occasion.

The Kennedy snake dance ran its thirty lively minutes, cheered its seconding speeches, and sat back. They were so sure of winning, there had been so many victories

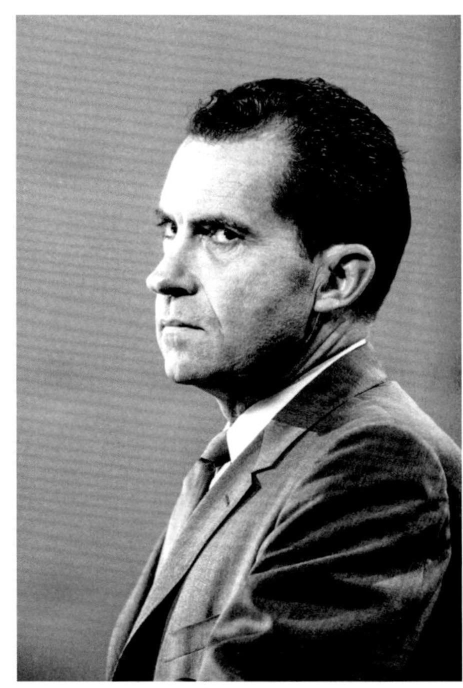

69

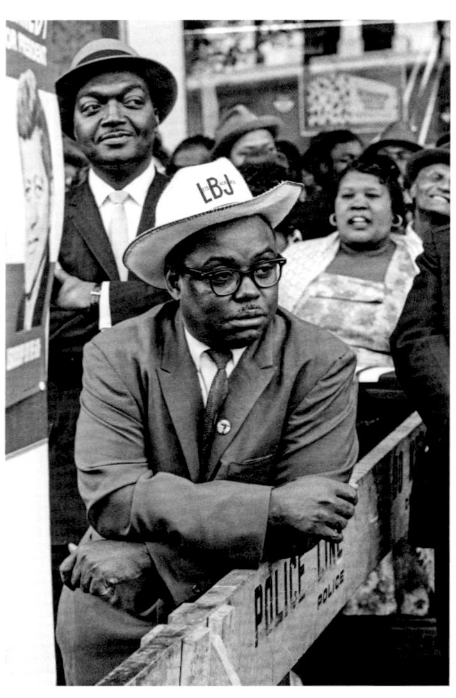

before this one, and this one had been scouted and managed so well, that hysteria could hardly be the mood. Besides, everyone was waiting for the Stevenson barrage which should be at least diverting. But now came a long tedium. Favorite sons were nominated, fat mayors shook their hips, seconders told the word to constituents back in Ponderwaygot County, treacly demonstrations tried to hold the floor, and the afternoon went by; Symington's hour came and went, a good demonstration, good as Johnson's (for good cause — they had pooled their demonstrators). More favorite sons, Governor Docking of Kansas declared "a genius" by one of his lady speakers in a tense go-back-to-religion voice. The hours went by, two, three, four hours, it seemed forever before they would get to Stevenson. It was evening when Senator Eugene McCarthy of Minnesota got up to nominate him.

The gallery was ready, the floor was responsive, the demonstrators were milling like bulls in their pen waiting for the *toril* to fly open — it would have been hard not to wake the crowd up, not to make a good speech. McCarthy made a great one. Great it was by the measure of convention oratory, and he held the crowd like a matador, timing their *olés!*, building them up, easing them back, correcting any sag in attention, gathering their emotion, discharging it, creating new emotion on the wave of the last, driving his passes tighter and tighter as he readied for the kill. "Do not reject this man who made us all proud to be called Democrats, do not leave the prophet without honor in his own party." One had not heard a speech like this since 1948 when Vito Marcantonio's voice, his harsh, shrill, bitter, street urchin's voice screeched through the loud-speakers at Yankee Stadium and lashed seventy thousand people into an uproar.

"There was only one man who said let's talk sense to the American people," McCarthy went on, his muleta furled for the *naturales*. "There was only one man who said let's talk sense to the American people," he repeated. "He said the promise of America is the promise of greatness. This was his call to greatness....Do not forget this man....Ladies and Gentlemen, I present to you not the favorite son of one state, but the favorite son of the fifty states, the favorite son of every country he has visited, the favorite son of every country which has not seen him but is secretly thrilled by his name." Bedlam. The kill. "Ladies and Gentlemen, I present to you Adlai Stevenson of Illinois." Ears and tail. Hooves and bull. A roar went up like the roar one heard the day Bobby Thomson hit his home run at the Polo Grounds and the Giants won the

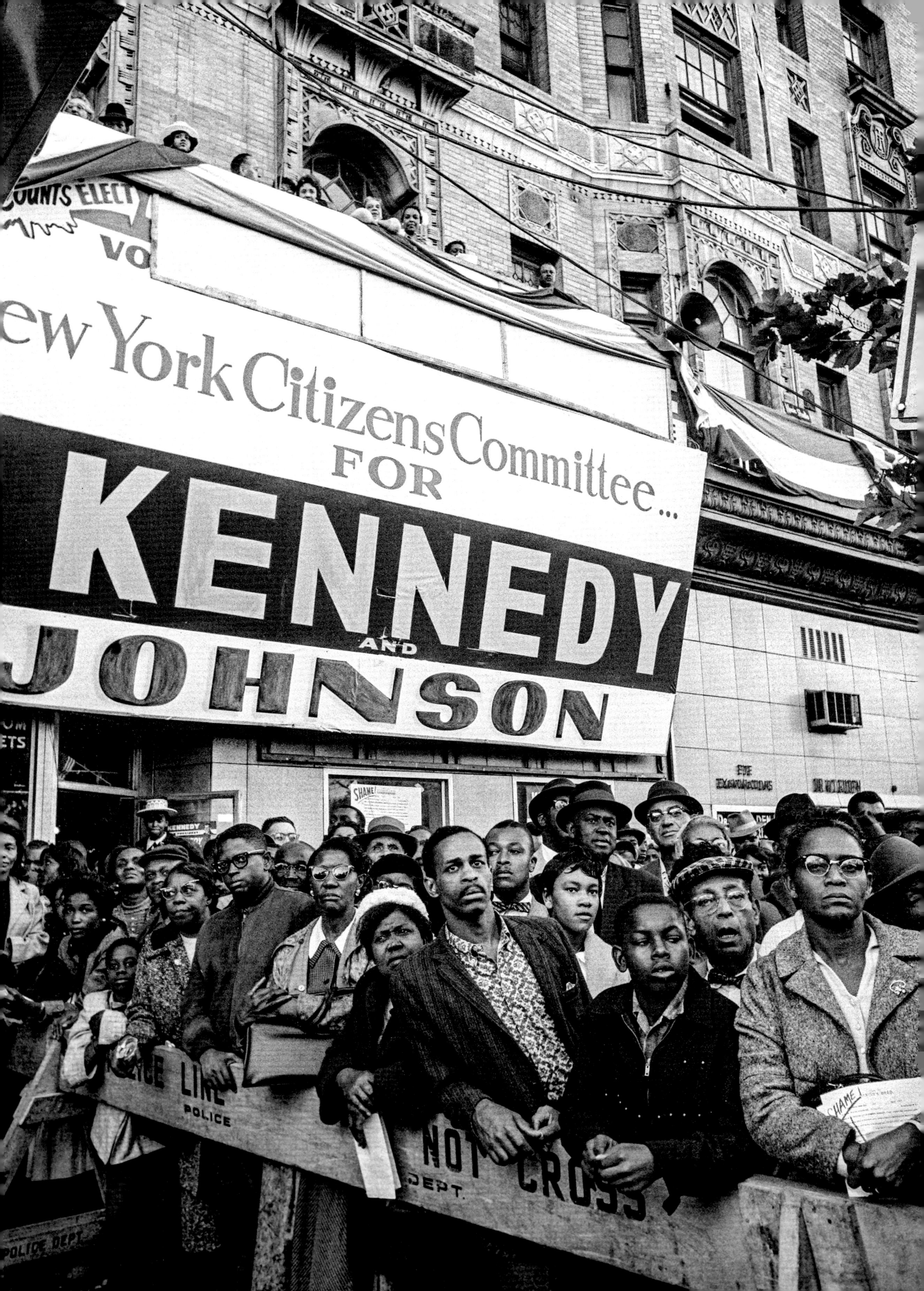
COUNTS ELECT
VO
ew York Citizens Committee...
FOR
KENNEDY
AND
JOHNSON
KENNEDY
FOR PRESIDENT
SHAME
EYE EXAMINATIONS
POLICE LINE
POLICE
DO NOT CROSS
DEPT.
POLICE DEPT.

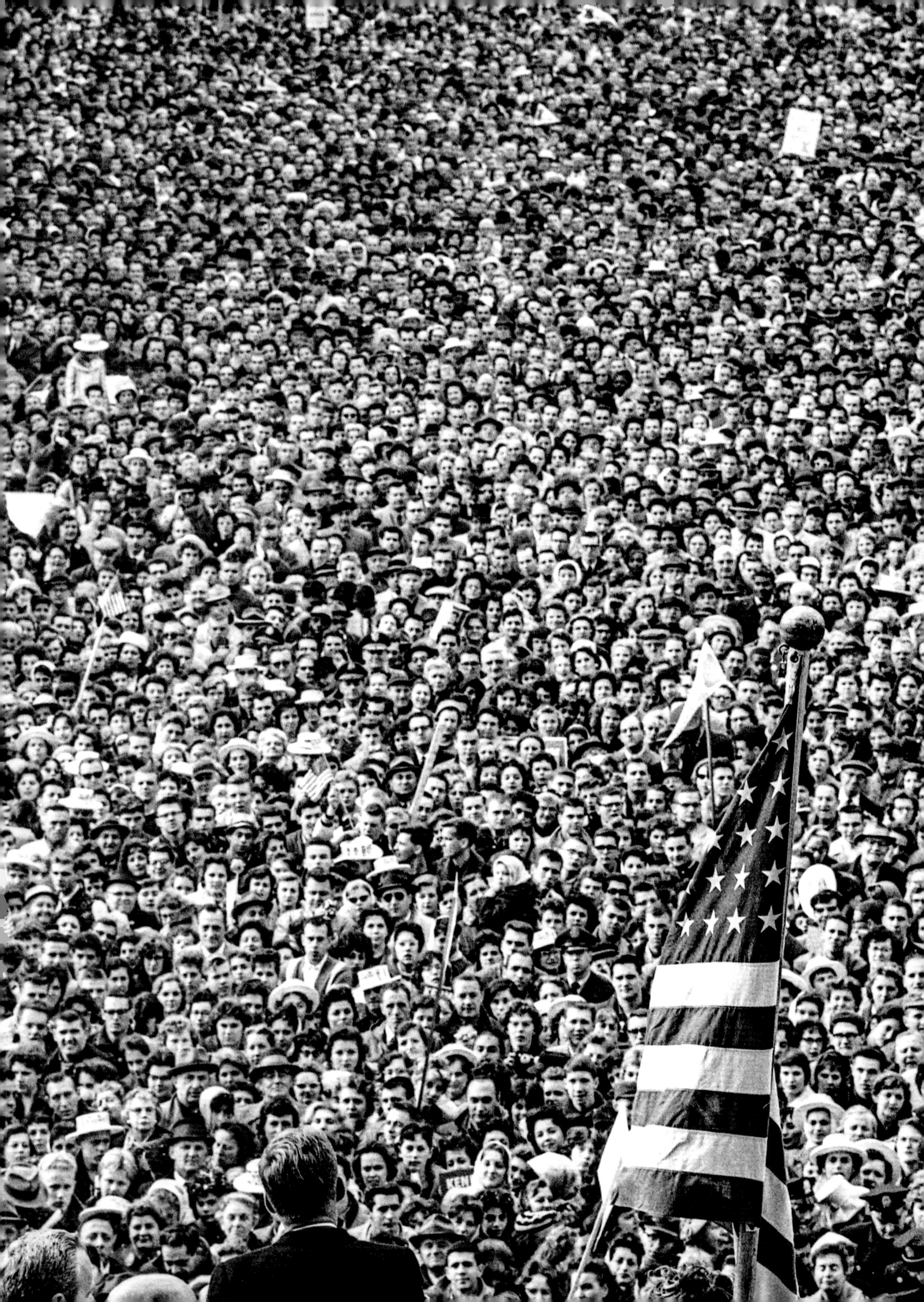

pennant from the Dodgers in the third playoff game of the 1951 season. The demonstration cascaded onto the floor, the gallery came to its feet, the Sports Arena sounded like the inside of a marching drum. A tidal pulse of hysteria, exaltation, defiance, exhilaration, anger and roaring desire flooded over the floor. The cry which had gone up on McCarthy's last sentence had not paused for breath in five minutes, and troop after troop of demonstrators jammed the floor (the Stevenson people to be scolded the next day for having collected floor passes and sent them out to bring in new demonstrators) and still the sound mounted. One felt the convention coming apart. There was a Kennedy girl in the seat in front of me, the Kennedy hat on her head, a dimpled healthy brunette; she had sat silently through McCarthy's speech, but now, like a woman paying her respects to the power of natural thrust, she took off her hat and began to clap herself. I saw a writer I knew in the next aisle; he had spent a year studying the Kennedy machine in order to write a book on how nomination is won.

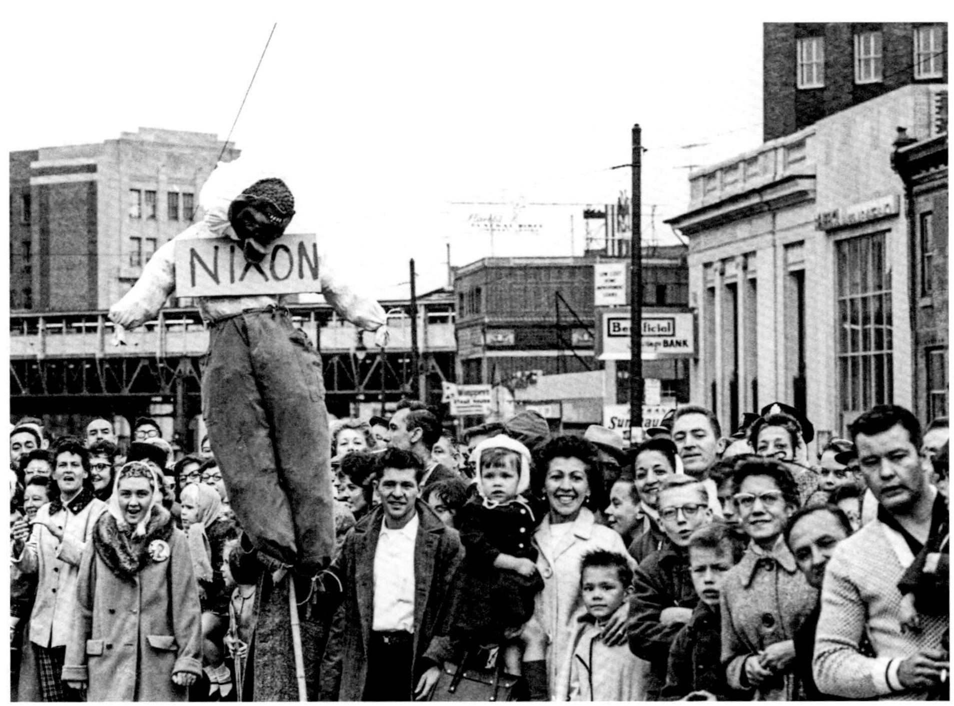

OPPOSITE *November 7, 1960.* JFK, at bottom center, addresses thousands in Hartford, Connecticut, just prior to Election Day. In the closing weeks of the campaign, throngs of enthusiasts went wherever he went—and at all hours. Just the night before, hordes of people had lined his route with torches and lights for 27 miles. When he finally arrived at the Roger Smith Hotel in Waterbury at 3 A.M., an estimated 40,000 people were waiting to catch a glimpse of him. *Photo, Burton Berinsky*

LEFT *October 30, 1960.* A crowd in Philadelphia expresses its displeasure with Nixon through an effigy. A rarity in American politics today, such crude caricatures, often made of straw or newspaper so they could be easily burnt, have a long history in global politics as stand-ins for individuals that have inspired public fury. *Photo, Burton Berinsky*

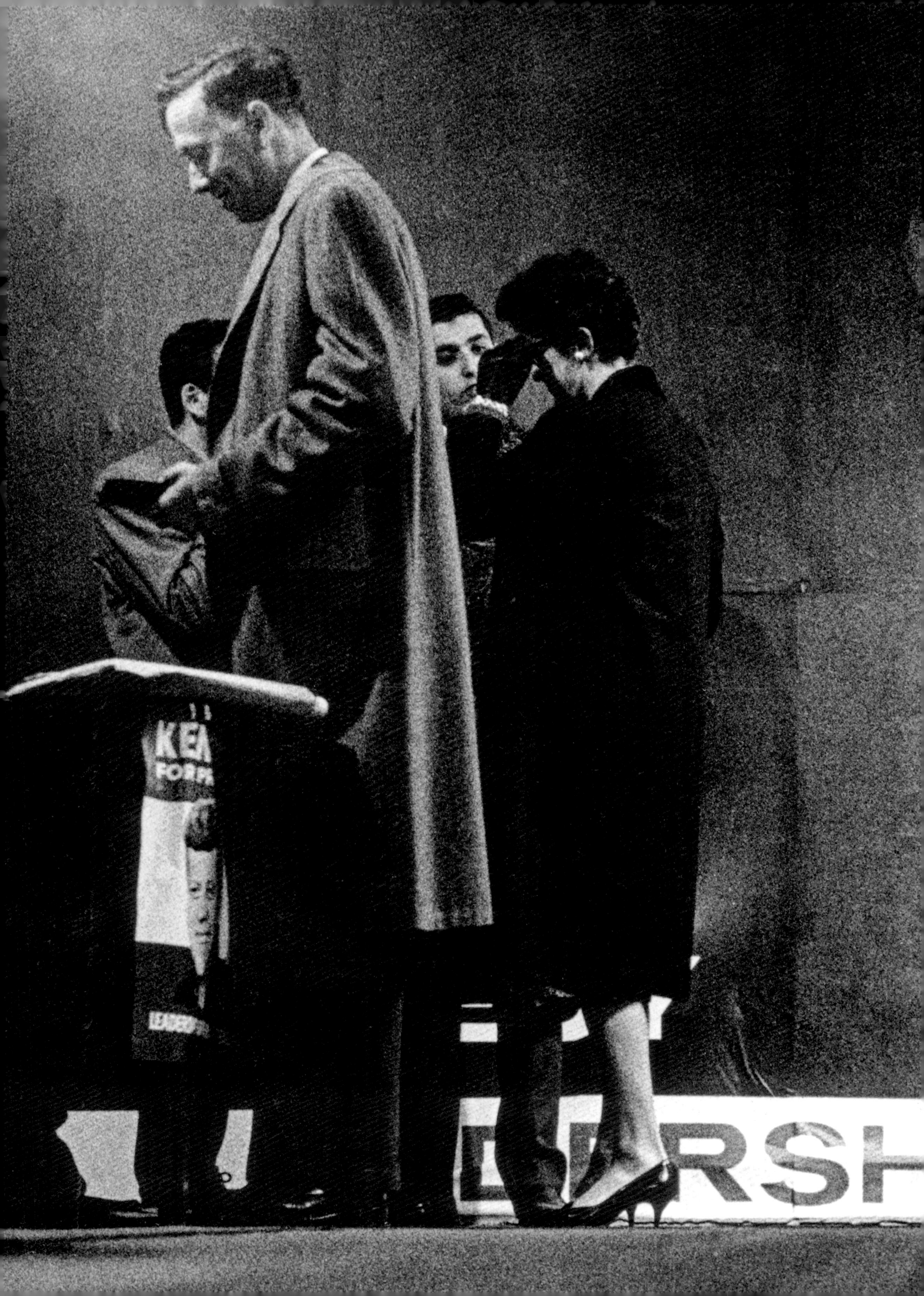
KE
FOR
LEADER
RSH

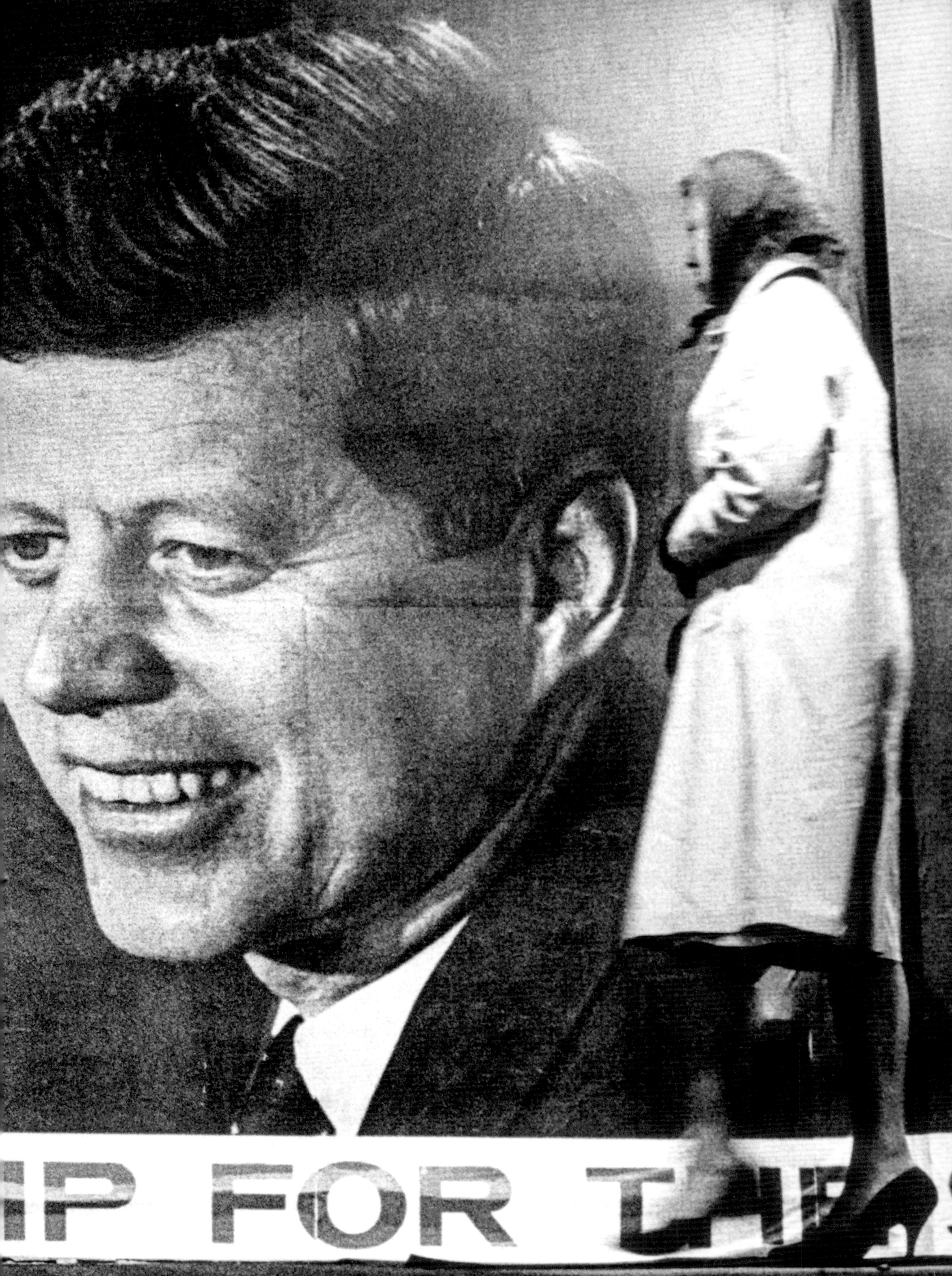
IP FOR THE

If Stevenson stampeded the convention, his work was lost. Like a reporter at a mine cave-in I inquired the present view of the widow. "Who can think," was the answer, half frantic, half elated, "just watch it, that's all." I found a cool one, a New York reporter, who smiled in rueful respect. "It's the biggest demonstration I've seen since Wendell Willkie's in 1940," he said, and added, "God, if Stevenson takes it, I can wire my wife and move the family on to Hawaii."

"I don't get it."

"Well, every story I wrote said it was locked up for Kennedy."

Still it went on, twenty minutes, thirty minutes, the chairman could hardly be heard, the demonstrators refused to leave. The lights were turned out, giving a sudden theatrical shift to the sense of a crowded church at midnight, and a new roar went up, louder, more passionate than anything heard before. It was the voice, it was the passion, if one insisted to call it that, of everything in America which was defeated, idealistic, innocent, alienated, outside and Beat, it was the potential voice of a new

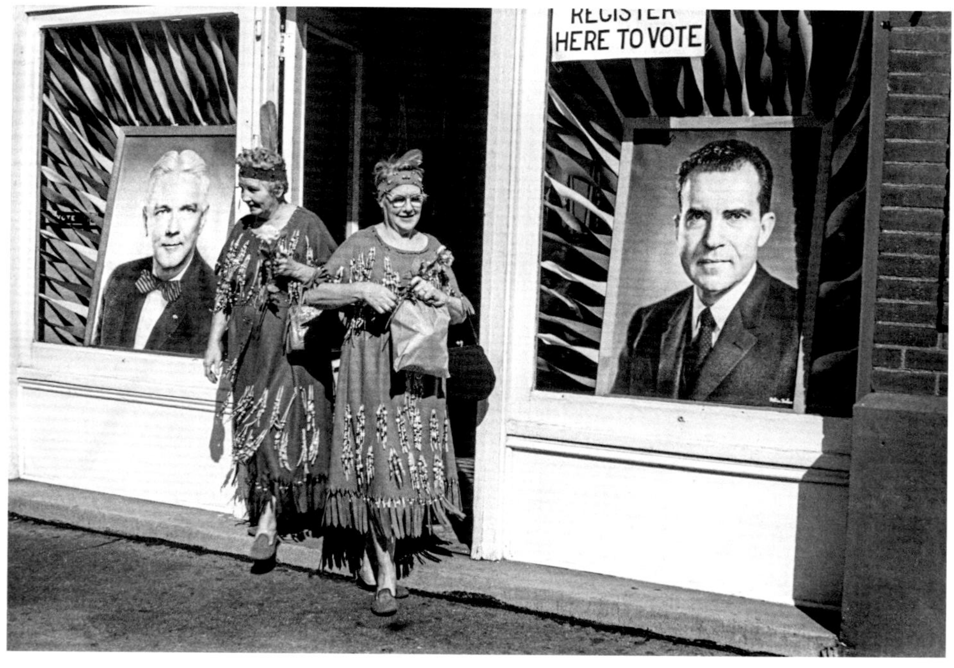

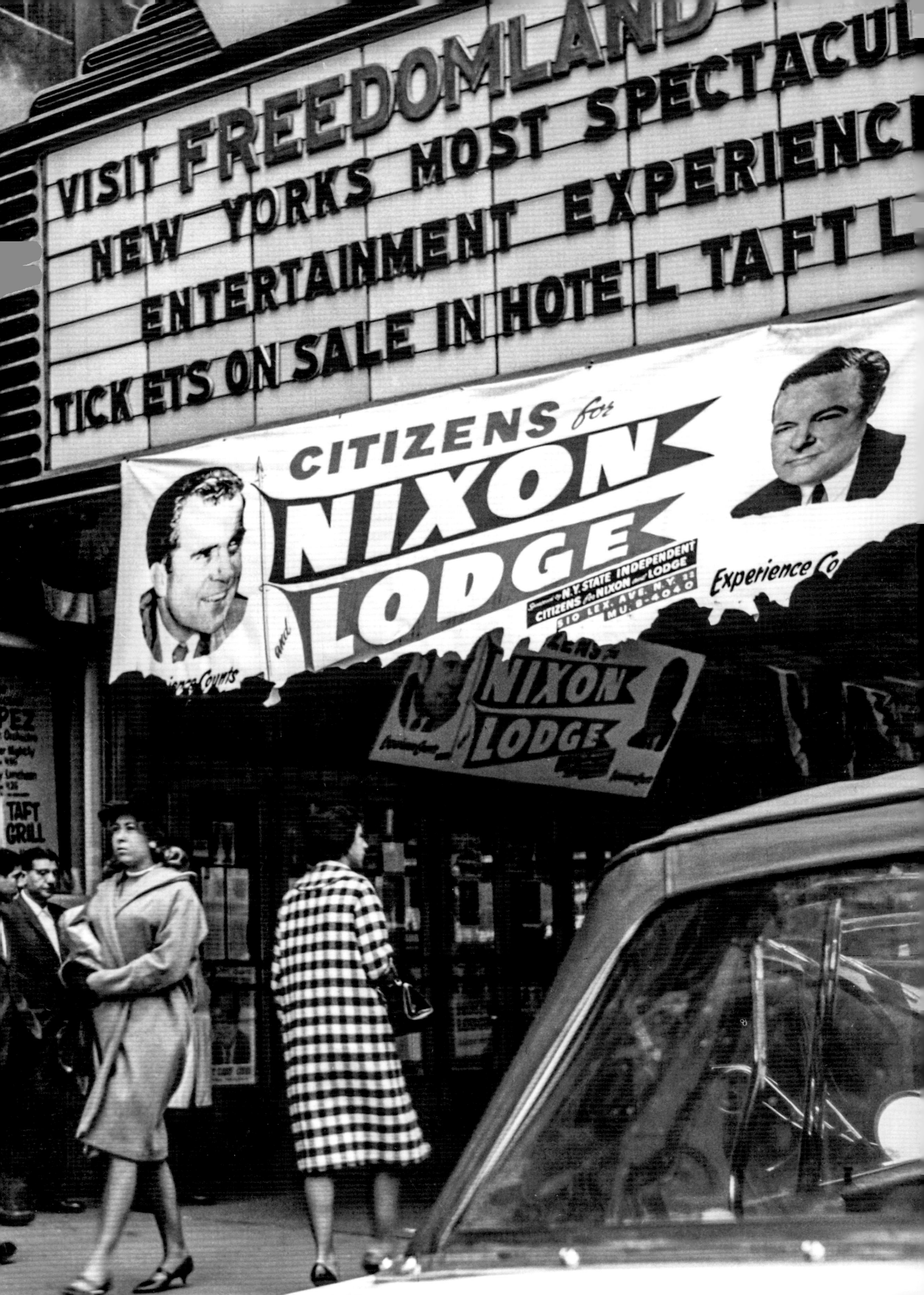

VISIT FREEDOMLAND
NEW YORKS MOST SPECTACUL
ENTERTAINMENT EXPERIENC
TICKETS ON SALE IN HOTEL TAFT L
CITIZENS for
NIXON
LODGE
N.Y. STATE INDEPENDENT
CITIZENS for NIXON and LODGE
510 LEX. AVE. N.Y.
MU. 8-4040
Experience Co
NIXON
LODGE
TAFT
GRILL
PEZ

third of the nation whose psyche was ill from cultural malnutrition, it was powerful, it was extraordinary, it was larger than the decent, humorous, finicky, half-noble man who had called it forth, it was a cry from the Thirties when Time was simple, it was a resentment of the slick technique, the oiled gears, and the superior generals of Fitzgerald's Army; but it was also—and for this reason one could not admire it altogether, except with one's excitement—it was also the plea of the bewildered who hunger for simplicity again, it was the adolescent counterpart of the boss's depression before the unpredictable dynamic of Kennedy as President, it was the return to the sentimental dream of Roosevelt rather than the approaching nightmare of history's oncoming night, and it was inspired by a terror of the future as much as a revulsion of the present.

Fitz's Army held; after the demonstration was finally down, the convention languished for ninety minutes while Meyner and others were nominated, a fatal lapse of time because Stevenson had perhaps a chance to stop Kennedy if the voting had begun on the echo of the last cry for him, but in an hour and a half depression crept in again and emotions spent, the delegates who had wavered were rounded into line. When the vote was taken, Stevenson had made no gains. The brunette who had taken off her hat was wearing it again, and she clapped and squealed when Wyoming delivered the duke and Kennedy was in. The air was sheepish, like the mood of a suburban couple who forgive each other for cutting in and out of somebody else's automobile while the country club dance is on. Again, tonight, no miracle would occur. In the morning the papers would be moderate in their description of Stevenson's last charge.

A Sketch of the Republicans Gathered in Convention

The Choice Between the Venturesome and the Safe; What May Happen at Three O'clock in the Morning on a Long Dark Night

One did not go to the other convention. It was seen on television, and so too much cannot be said of that. It did however confirm one's earlier bias that the Republican Party was still a party of church ushers, undertakers, choirboys, prison wardens, bank presidents, small-town police chiefs, state troopers, psychiatrists, beauty-parlor operators, corporation executives, Boy-Scout leaders, fraternity presidents, tax-board assessors,

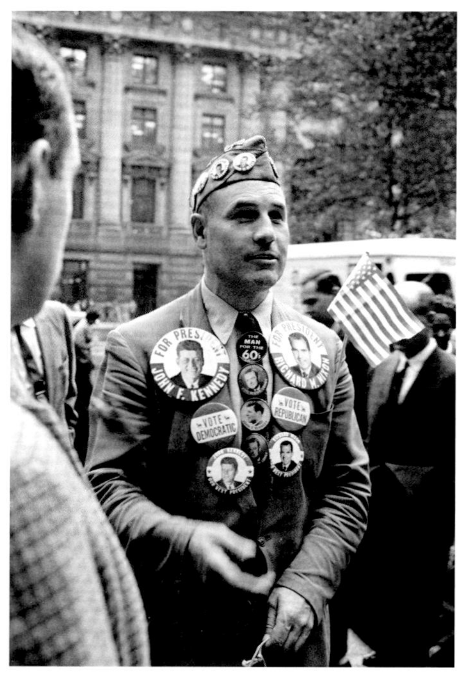

ABOVE *October 19, 1960.* Posters, banners, brochures, hats, tie tacks, money clips, cuff links: if a candidate's name and slogan could be printed on it, it was, and Kennedy and Nixon clubs across the country spent thousands stocking up on campaign products, including the ubiquitous buttons. During the race, "more than 100 million of them" would be produced in one season. As reported by *The New York Times Magazine* in August 1960, that amounted to "over $1 million" to "be distributed by Election Day." *Photo, Henri Dauman*

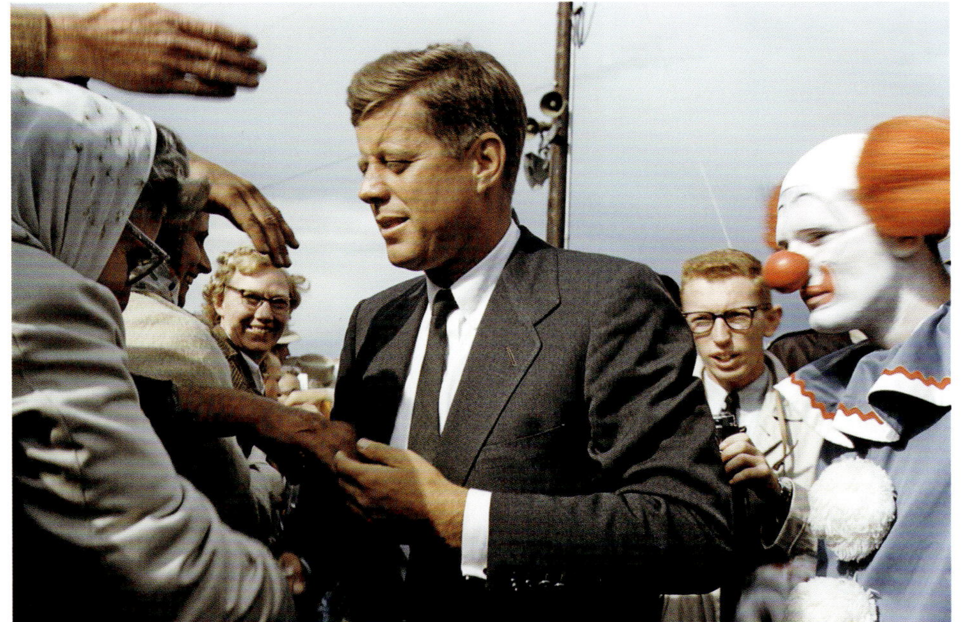

community leaders, surgeons, Pullman porters, head nurses and the fat sons of rich fathers. Its candidate would be given the manufactured image of an ordinary man, and his campaign, so far as it was a psychological campaign (and this would be far indeed), would present him as a simple, honest, dependable, hard-working, ready-to-learn, modest, humble, decent, sober young man whose greatest qualification for president was his profound abasement before the glories of the Republic, the stability of the mediocre, and his own unworthiness. The apocalyptic hour of Uriah Heep.

It would then be a campaign unlike the ones which had preceded it. Counting by the full spectrum of complete Right to absolute Left, the political differences would be minor, but what would be not at all minor was the power of each man to radiate his appeal into some fundamental depths of the American character. One would have an inkling at last if the desire of America was for drama or stability, for adventure or monotony. And this, this appeal to the psychic direction America would now choose for itself was the element most promising about this election, for it gave the possibility that the country might be able finally to rise above the deadening verbiage of its issues, its politics, its jargon, and live again by an image of itself. For in some part of themselves the people might know (since these candidates were not old enough to be revered) that they had chosen one young man for his mystery, for his promise that the country would grow or disintegrate by the unwilling charge he gave to the intensity of the myth, or had chosen another young man for his unstated oath that he would do all in his power to keep the myth buried and so convert the remains of Renaissance man as rapidly as possible into mass man. One might expect them to choose the enigma in preference to the deadening certainty. Yet one must doubt America's bravery. This lurching, unhappy, pompous and most corrupt nation— could it have the courage finally to take on a new image for itself, was it brave enough to put into office not only one of its ablest men, its most efficient, its most conquistadorial (for Kennedy's capture of the Democratic Party deserves the word), but also one of its more mysterious men (the national psyche must shiver in its sleep at the image of Mickey Mantle-cum-Lindbergh in office, and a First Lady with an eighteenth-century face). Yes, America was at last engaging the fate of its myth, its consciousness about to be accelerated or cruelly depressed in its choice between two young men in their forties who, no matter how close, dull, or indifferent their

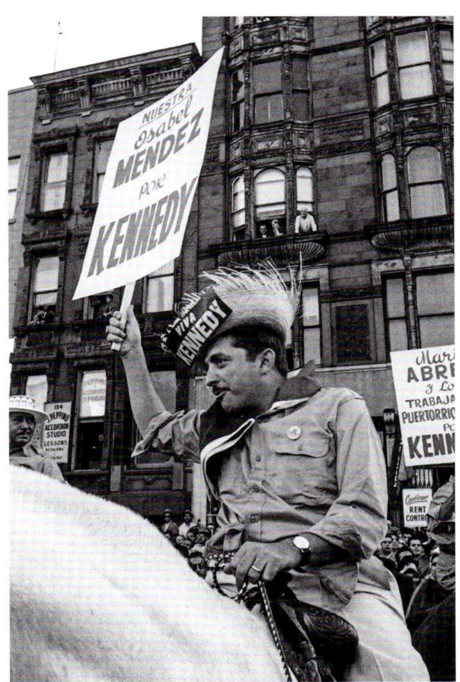

PART I · SUPERMAN COMES TO THE SUPERMARKET

—Norman Mailer

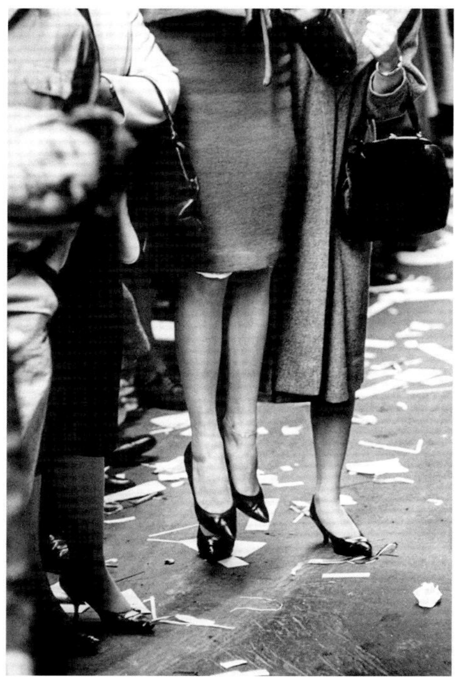

ABOVE *October 19, 1960.* A woman tries to catch a
glimpse of Kennedy at Rockefeller Center in New
York City. *Photo, Paul Schutzer*

OPPOSITE *October 19, 1960.* Thirty-one-year-old
Jackie Kennedy was magnetic on the campaign trail.
While her travel had been limited due to pregnancy,
she reemerged on an important swing through
New York City in October. Kenny O'Donnell would
later write: "She was always cheerful and obliging,
never complaining, and...did not bother to put on a
phony show about everything that she saw and every
local politician whom she met. The crowds sensed
that and it impressed them." *Photo, Henri Dauman*

stated politics might be, were radical poles apart, for one was sober, the apotheosis of opportunistic lead, all radium spent, the other handsome as a prince in the unstated aristocracy of the American dream. So, finally, would come a choice which history had never presented to a nation before—one could vote for glamour or for ugliness, a staggering and most stunning choice—would the nation be brave enough to enlist the romantic dream of itself, would it vote for the image in the mirror of its unconscious, were the people indeed brave enough to hope for an acceleration of Time, for that new life of drama which would come from choosing a son to lead them who was heir apparent to the psychic loins? One could pause: it might be more difficult to be a President than it ever had before. Nothing less than greatness would do.

Yet if the nation voted to improve its face, what an impetus might come to the arts, to the practices, to the lives and to the imagination of the American. If the nation so voted. But one knew the unadmitted specter in the minds of the Democratic delegates: that America would go to sleep on election eve with the polls promising Kennedy a victory on the day to come, yet in its sleep some millions of Democrats and Independents would suffer a nightmare before the mystery of uncharted possibilities their man would suggest, and in a terror of all the creativities (and some violences) that mass man might now have to dare again, the undetermined would go out in the morning to vote for the psychic security of Nixon the way a middle-aged man past adventure holds to the stale bread of his marriage. Yes, this election might be fearful enough to betray the polls and no one in America could plan the new direction until the last vote was counted by the last heeler in the last ambivalent ward, no one indeed could know until then what had happened the night before, what had happened at three o'clock in the morning on that long dark night of America's search for a security cheaper than her soul.

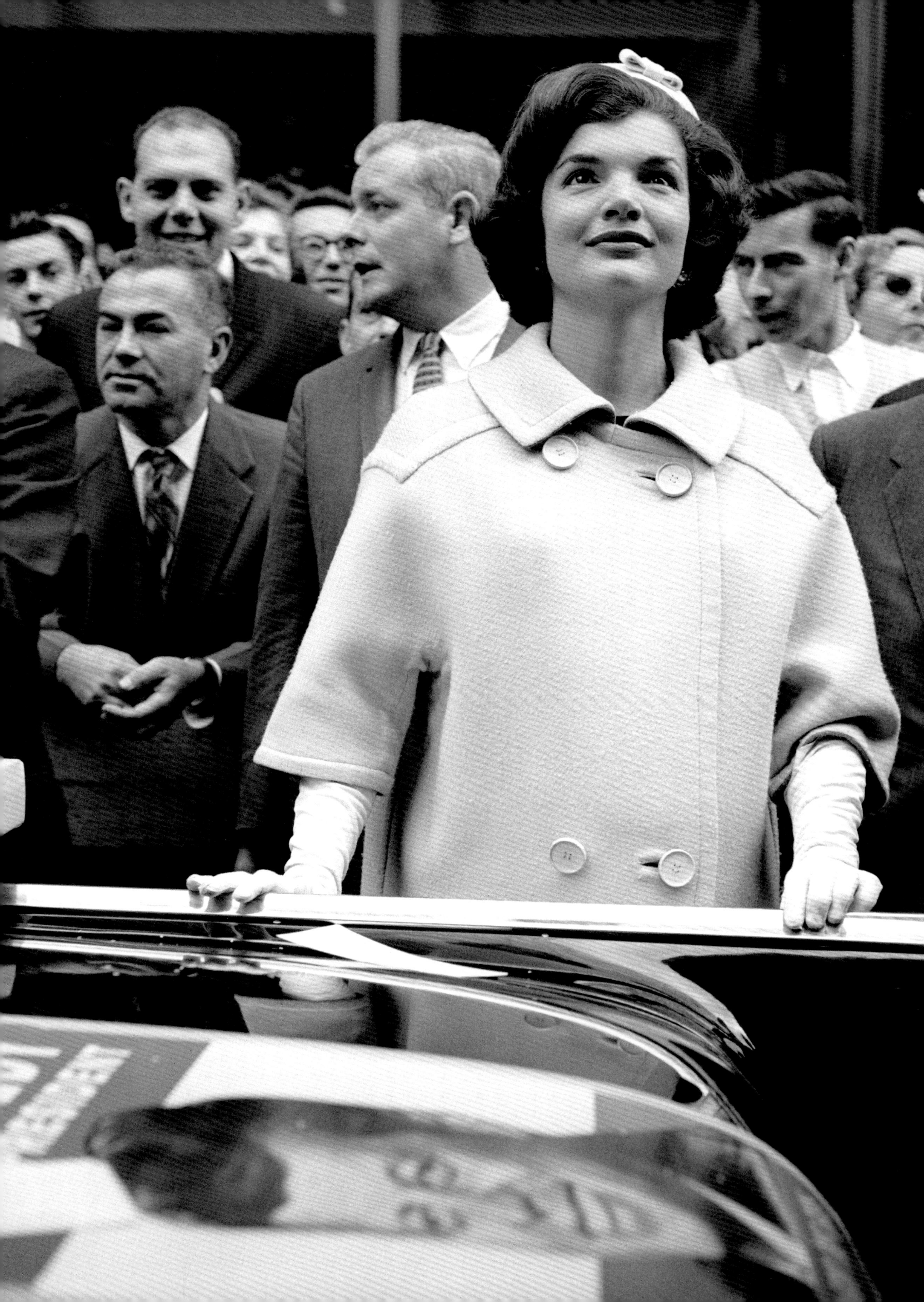

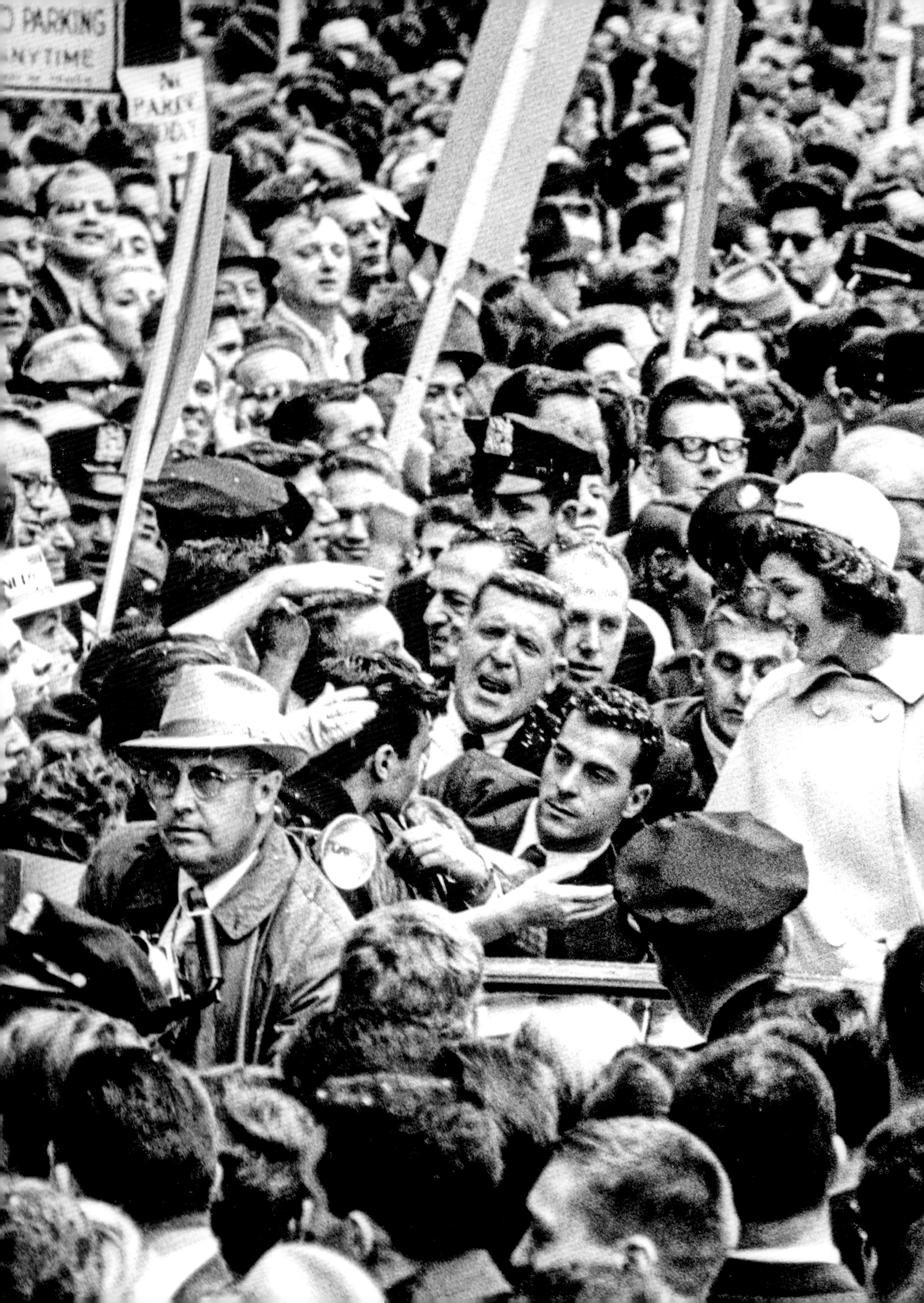
PARKING
NYTIME
NO
PARKING
TODAY

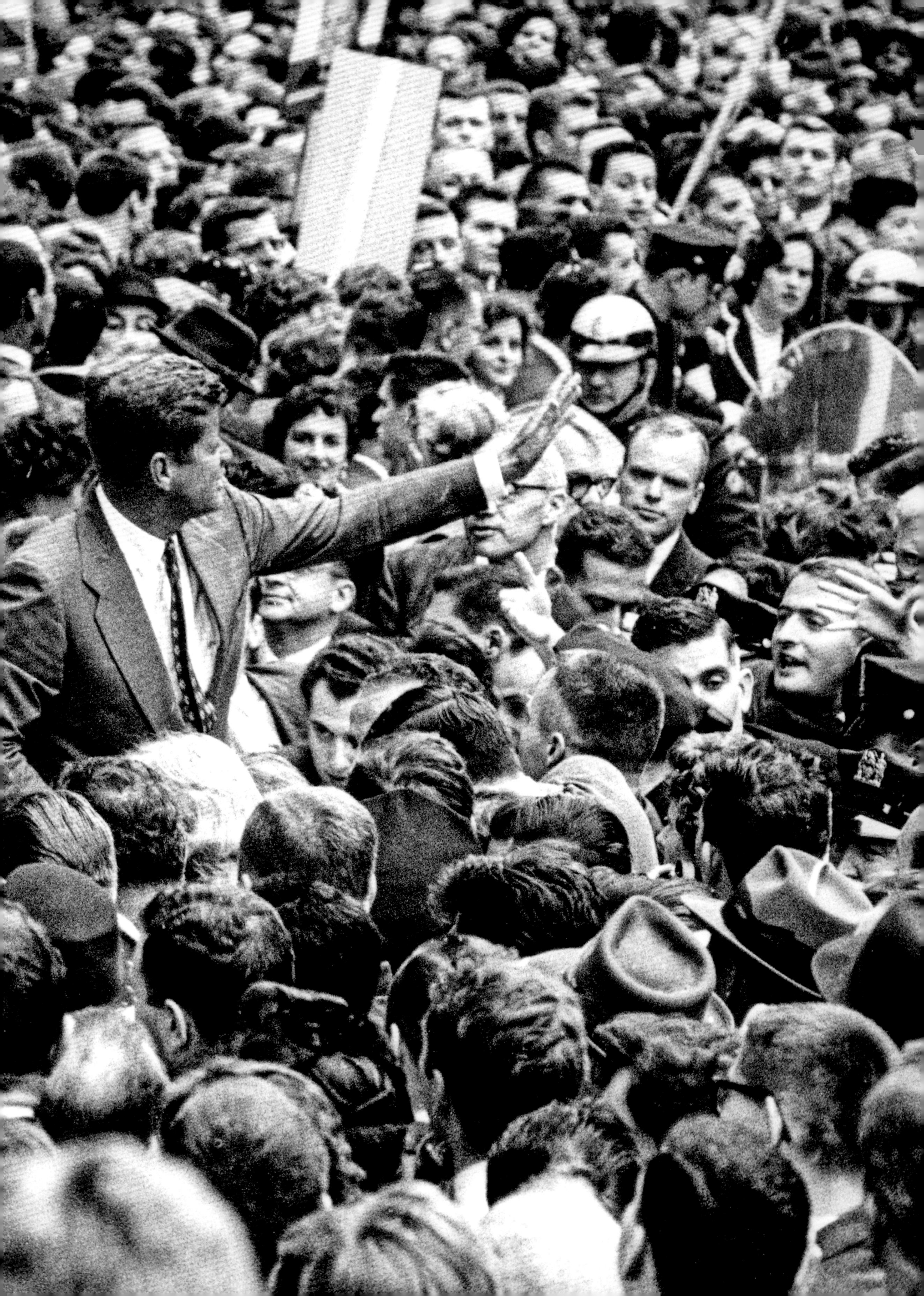

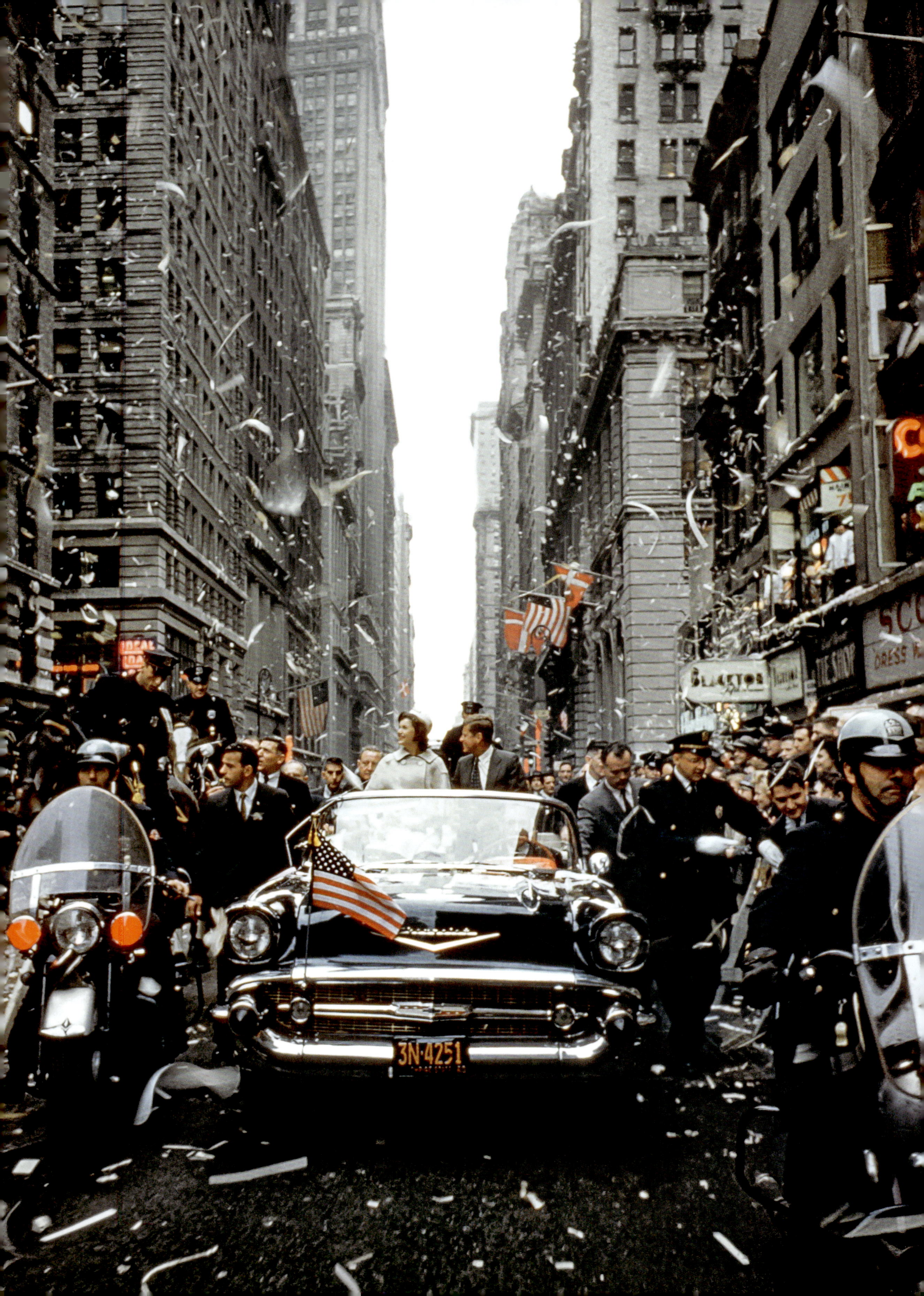

This piece had more effect than any other single work of mine, and I think this is due as much to its meretriciousness as to its merits. I was forcing a reality, I was bending reality like a field of space to curve the time I wished to create. I was not writing with the hope that perchance I could find reality by being sufficiently honest to perceive it, but on the contrary was distorting reality in the hope that thereby I could affect it. I was engaging in an act of propaganda.

During the period after Kennedy was nominated, there was great indifference to him among the Democrats I knew; disaffection was general; outright aversion was felt by most of the liberal Left—the white collar SANE sort of professional who had been for Stevenson. The Kennedy machine worked well to overcome apathy and inertia; so did the debates with Nixon. Through the early Fall, before the election, people who had been going along with the Democratic Party for years began somewhat resignedly to accept their fate: they would go out after all and vote for John F. Kennedy. But there was no real enthusiasm, no drive. My piece came at the right time for him—three weeks before the election. It added the one ingredient Kennedy had not been able to find for the stew—it made him seem exciting, it made the election appear important. Around New York there was a turn in sentiment; one could feel it; Kennedy now had glamour.

…I took to myself some of the critical credit for his victory. Whether I was right or wrong in fact may not be so important as its psychological reality in my own mind. I had invaded No Man's Land, I had created an archetype of Jack Kennedy in the public mind which might or might not be true, but which would induce people to vote for him, and so would tend to move him into the direction I had created. Naturally there would be forces thrusting him back out to No Man's Land, back to conventional politics, but so far as I had an effect, it was a Faustian one, much as if I had made a pact with Mephisto to give me an amulet, an art-work, which might arouse a djinn in history…

[Postscript to "The Third Presidential Paper," *The Presidential Papers*, 1963]

PREVIOUS SPREAD *October 19, 1960.* Well-wishers strain to reach Jack and Jackie Kennedy as their convertible inches down Broadway. More than 1.2 million New Yorkers crowded the parade route and rally sites on October 19, hoping to cheer their candidate on to victory. *Photo, Stanley Tretick*

OPPOSITE *October 19, 1960.* The Kennedys take a triumphant ride down New York City's "Canyon of Heroes" in a ticker-tape parade in their honor. *Photo, Cornell Capa*

FOLLOWING SPREAD *January 2, 1960.* Senator John F. Kennedy at a press conference on the day he officially entered the race for president of the United States. *Photo, Jacques Lowe*

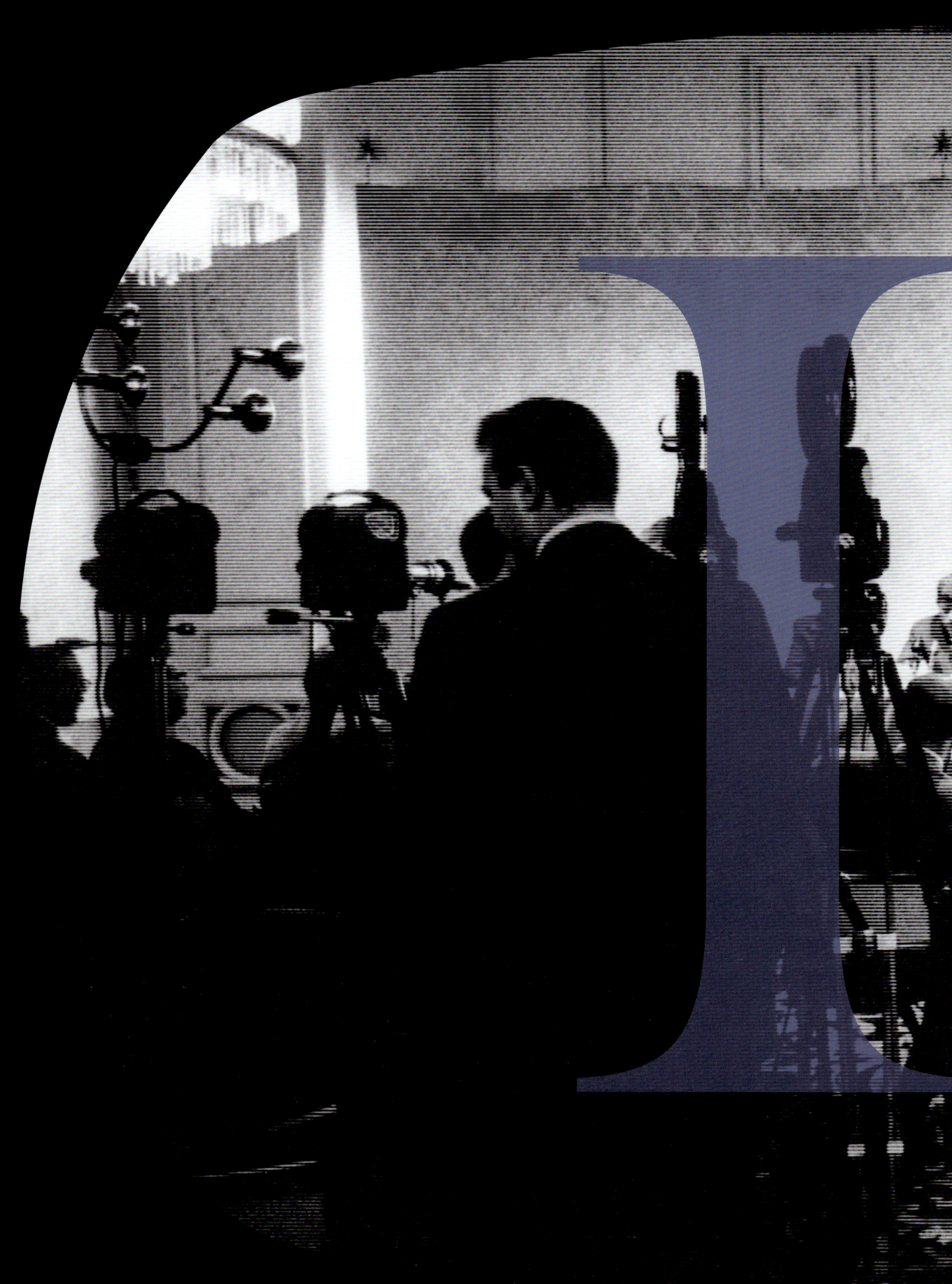

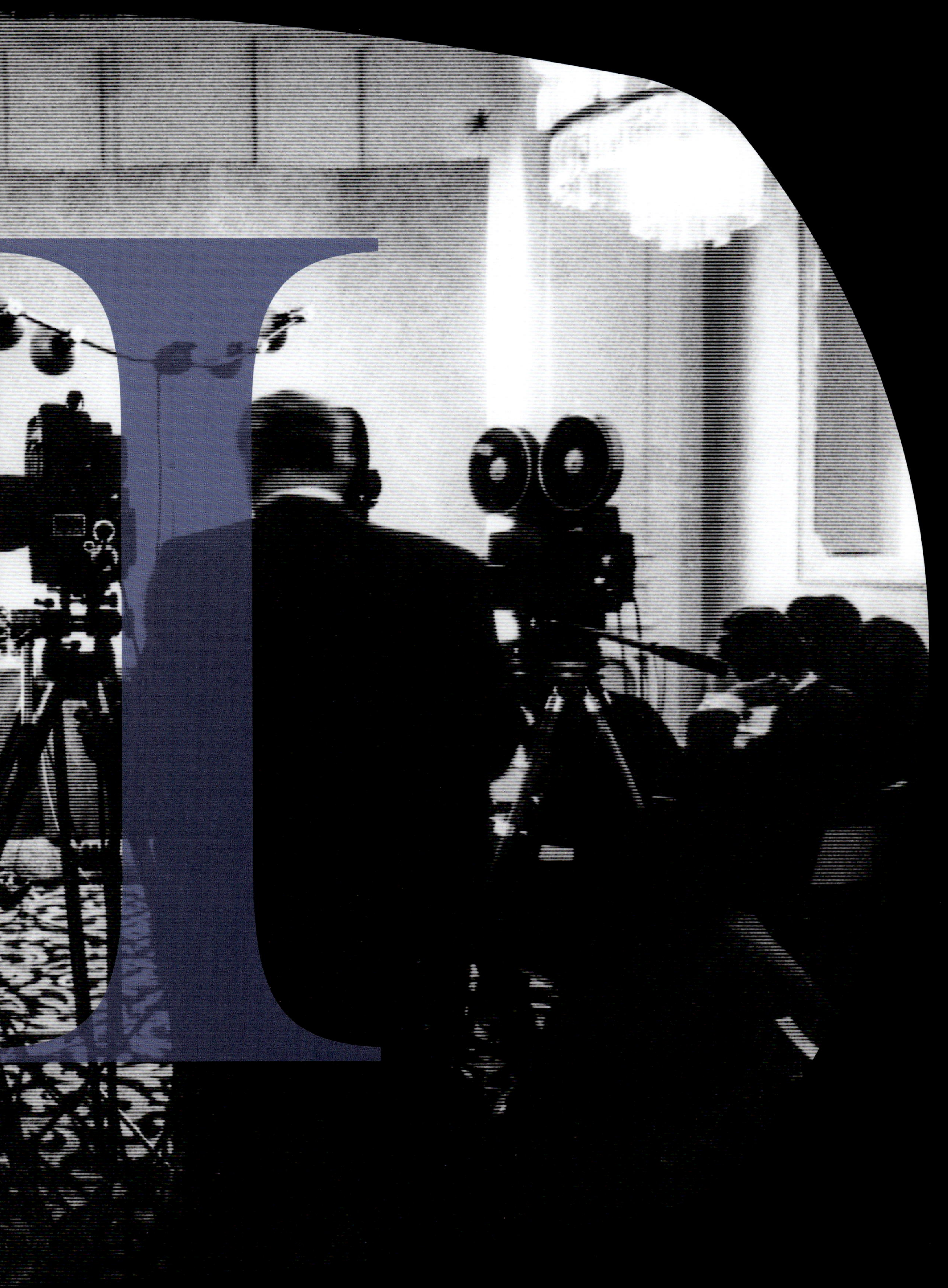

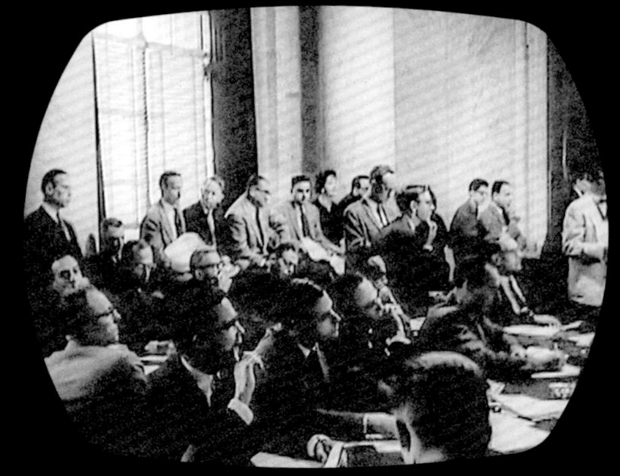

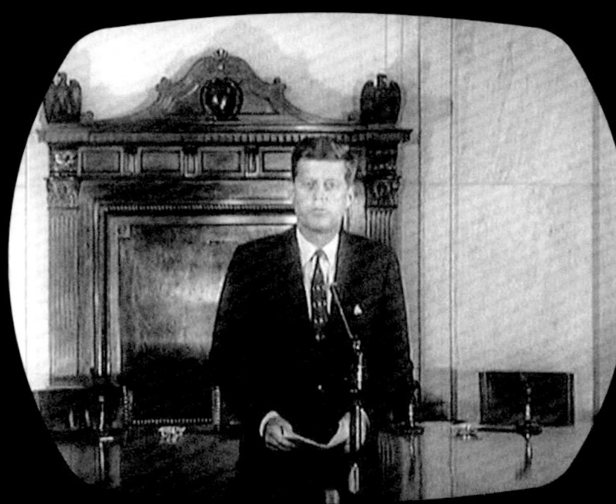

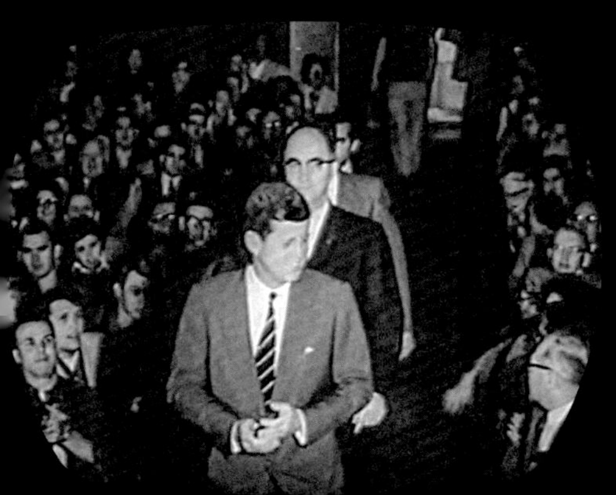
UNIVERSAL-INTERNATIONAL NEWS
KENNEDY
TOSSES HAT
IN THE RING
VOICE: ED HERLIHY

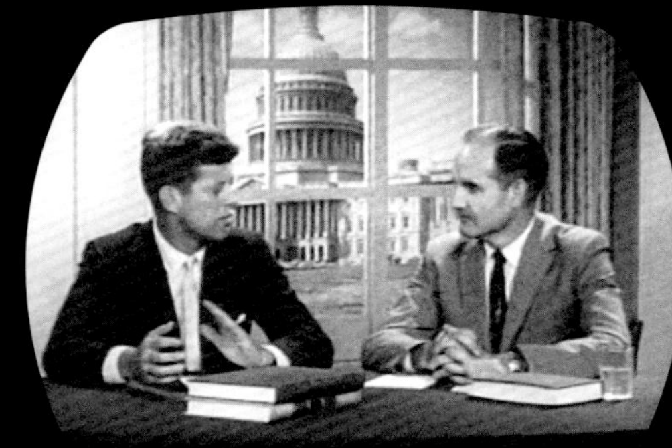

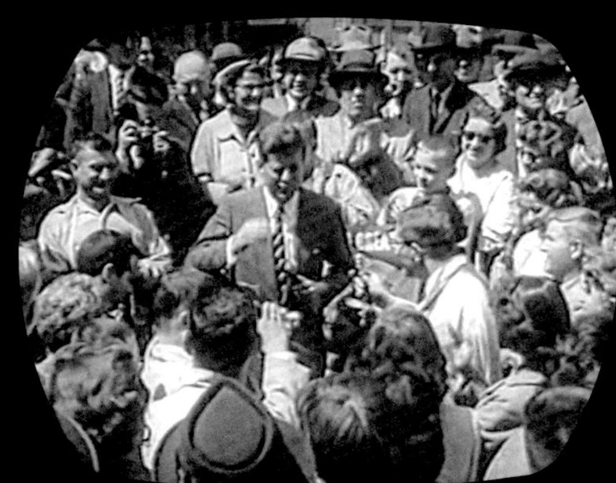

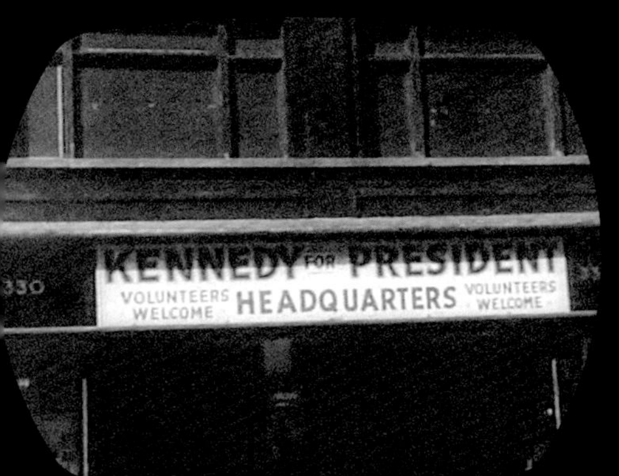
KENNEDY FOR PRESIDENT
VOLUNTEERS
WELCOME
HEADQUARTERS
VOLUNTEERS
WELCOME

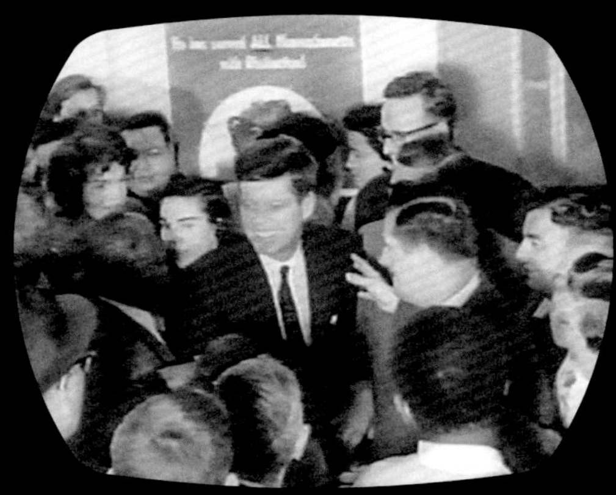

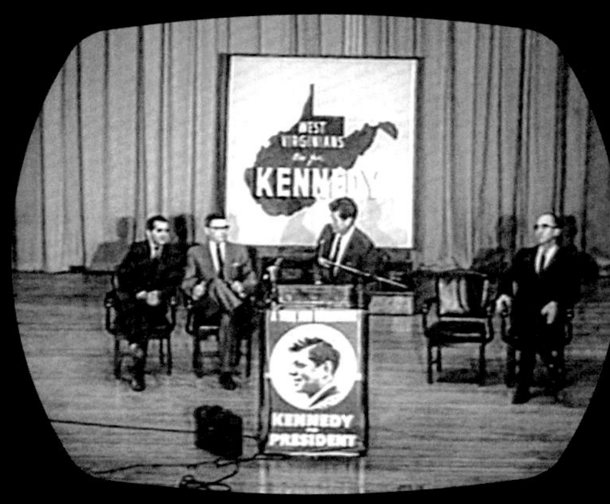
WEST VIRGINIANS
for
KENNEDY
KENNEDY
for
PRESIDENT

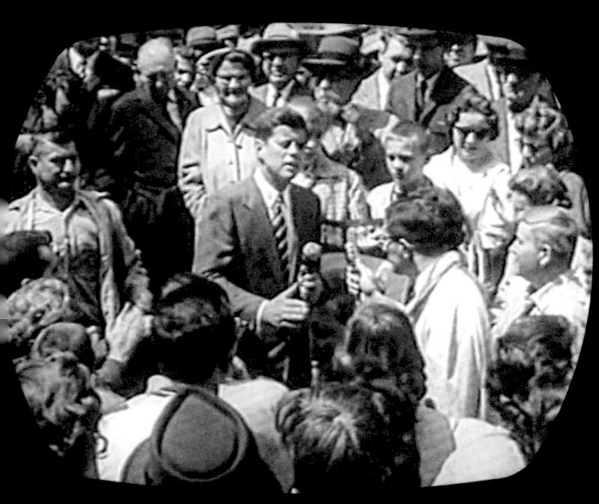

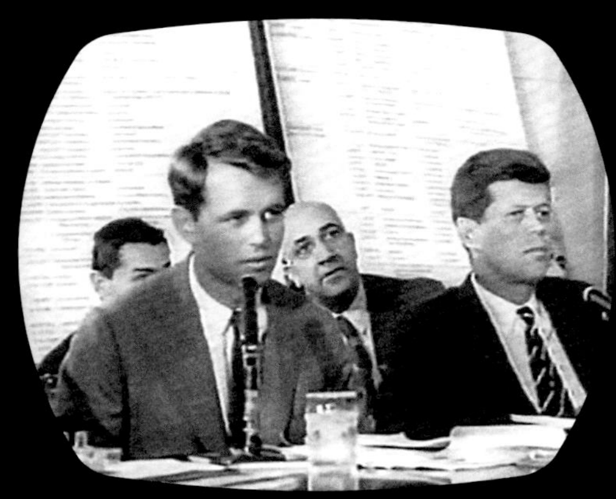

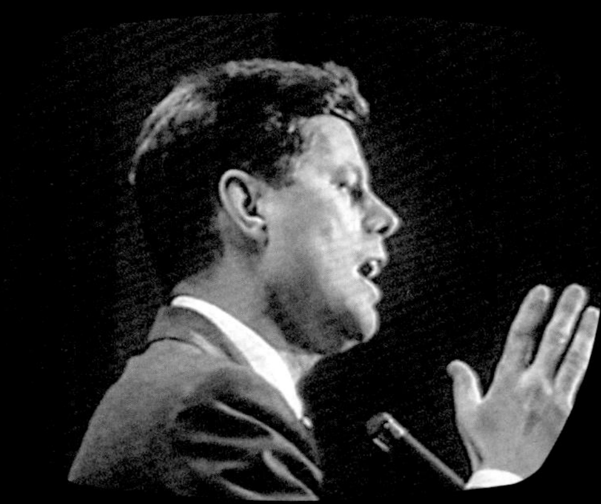

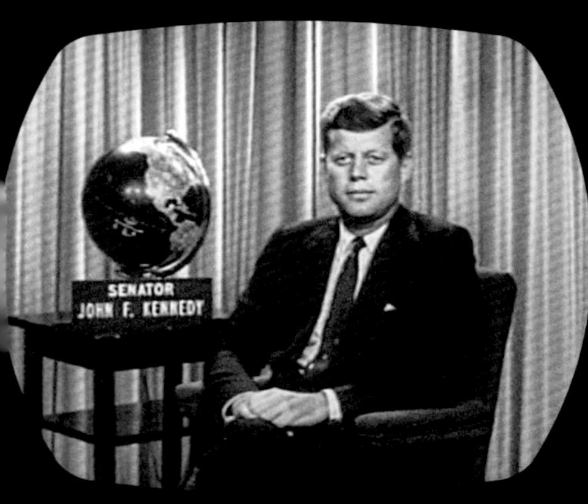
SENATOR
JOHN F. KENNEDY

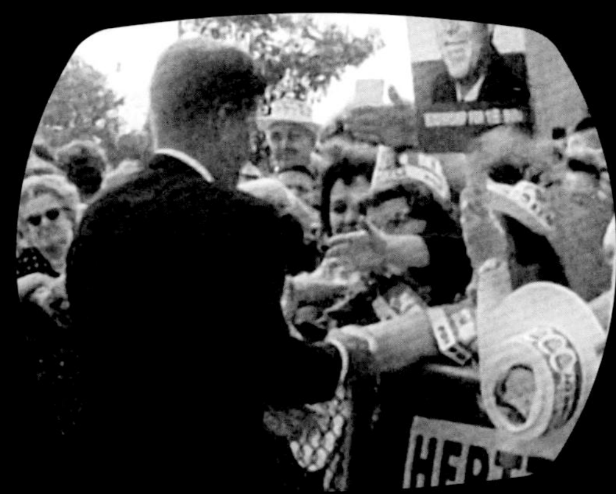

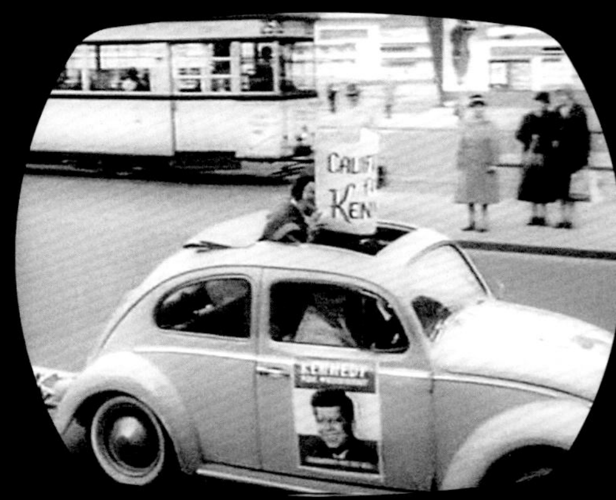

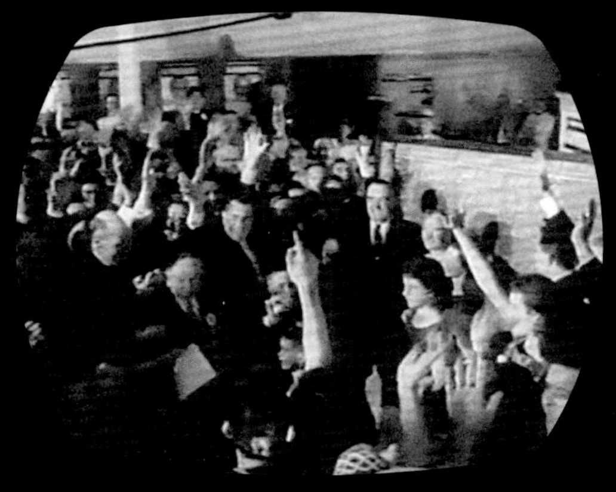
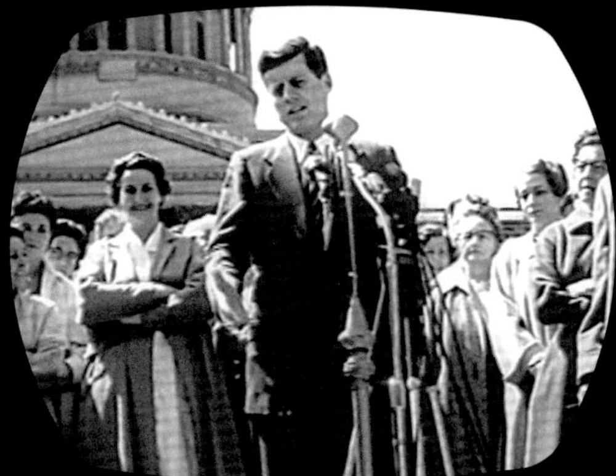
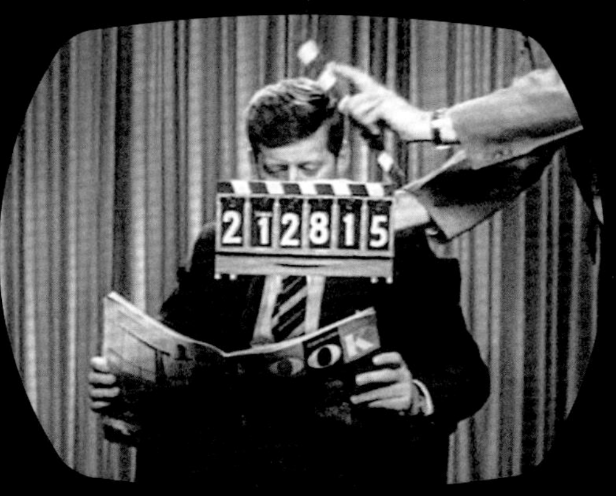
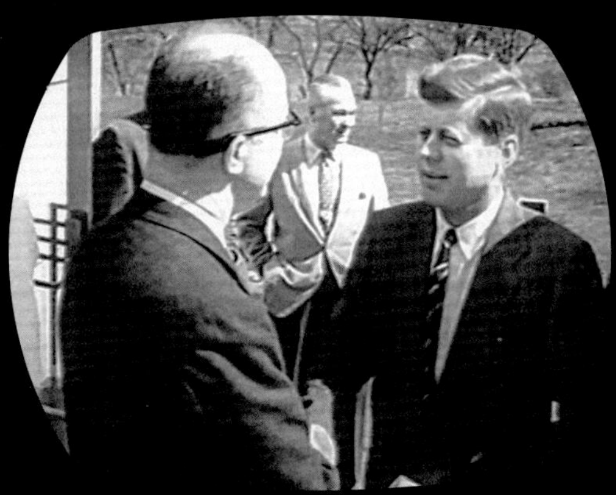
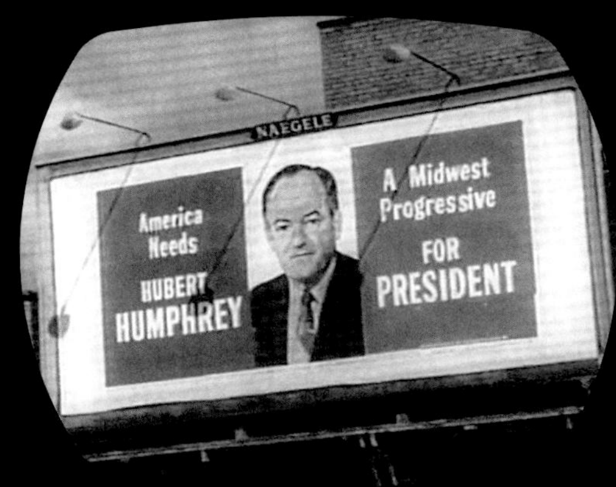
NAEGELE
America Needs
HUBERT HUMPHREY
A Midwest Progressive
FOR PRESIDENT
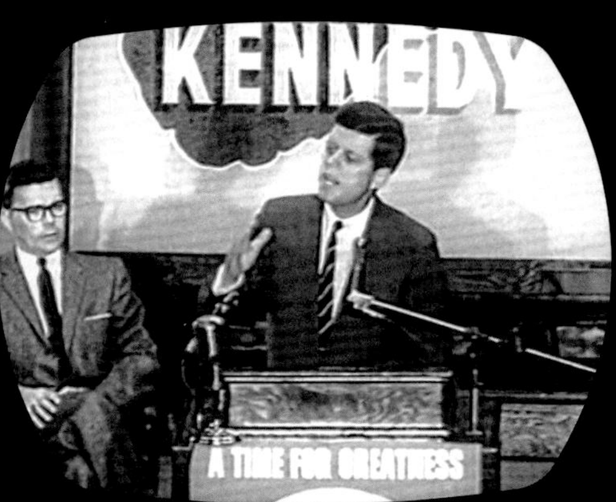
KENNEDY
A TIME FOR GREATNESS
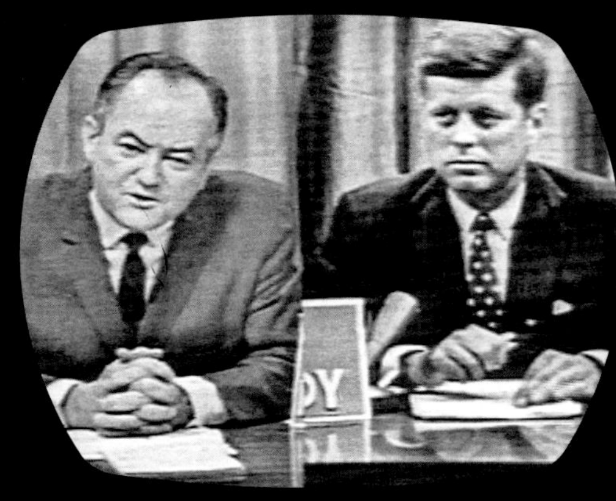
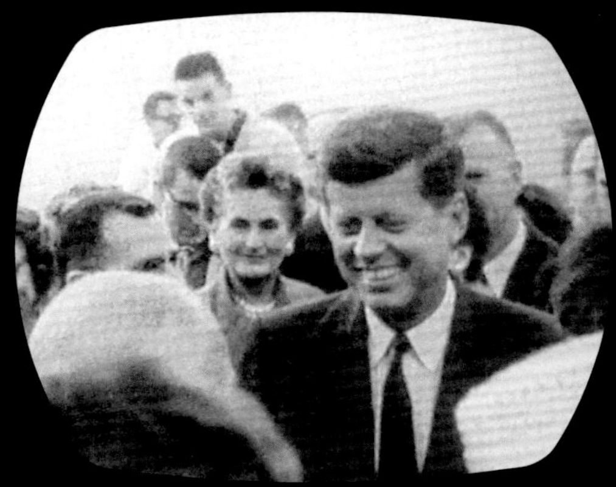
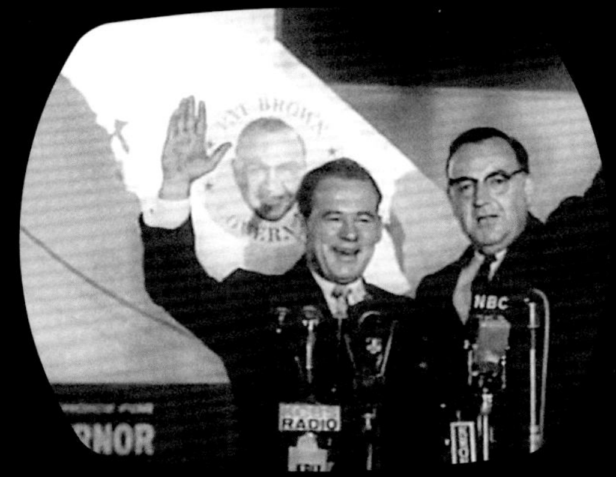
NBC
RADIO
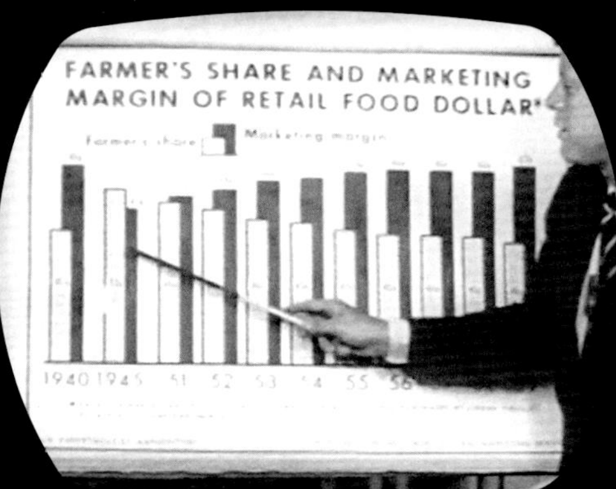
FARMER'S SHARE AND MARKETING
MARGIN OF RETAIL FOOD DOLLAR
Farmer's share   Marketing margin
1940 1945   51   52   53   54   55   56
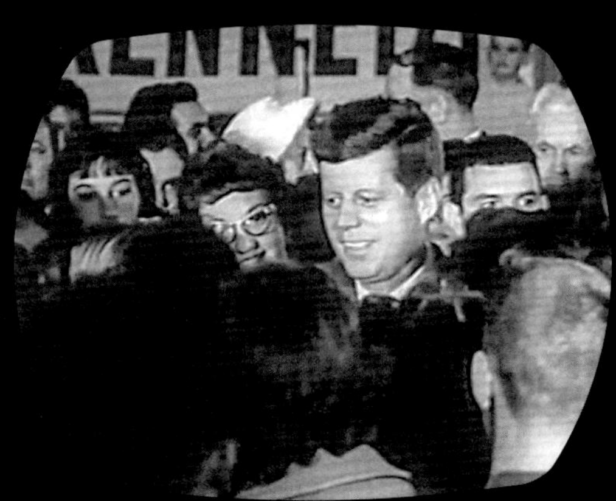
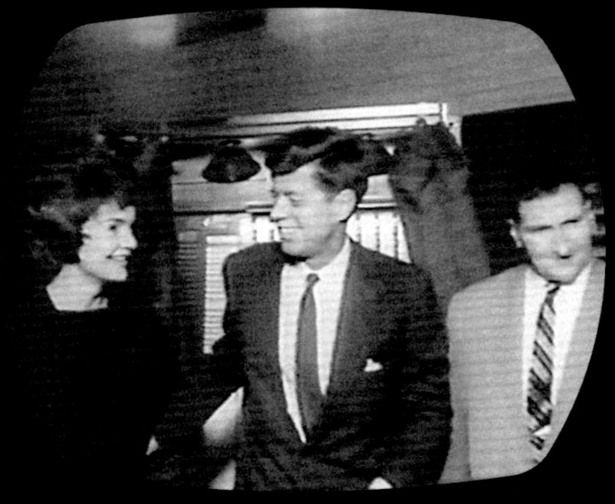
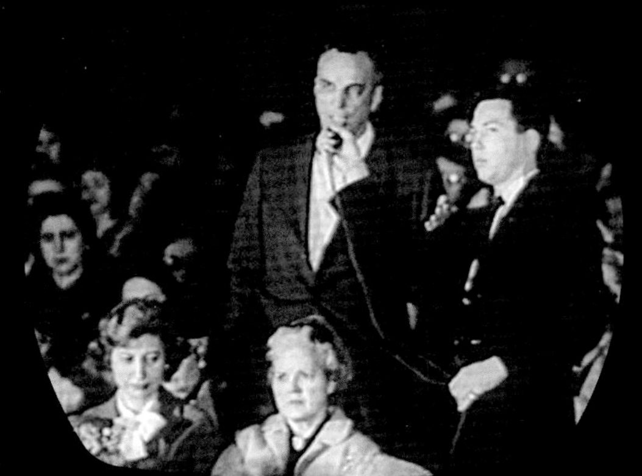
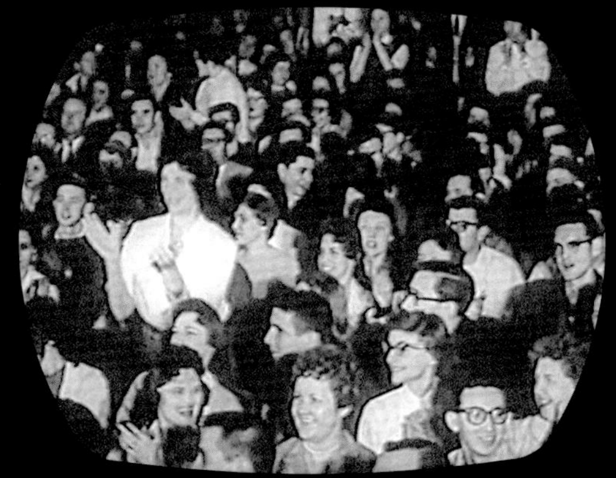
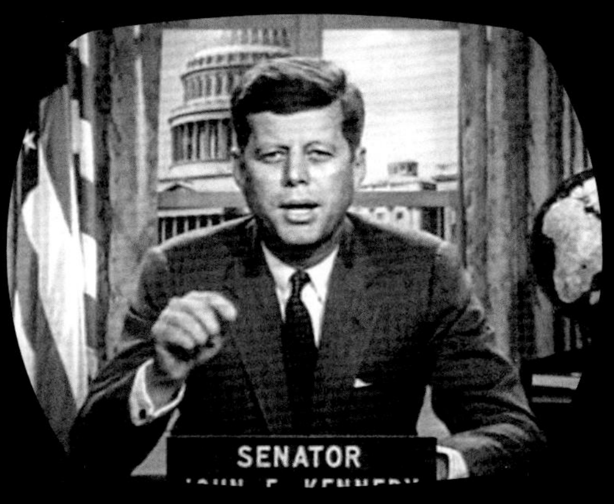
SENATOR
JOHN F. KENNEDY

TO SEEK THE PRESIDENCY

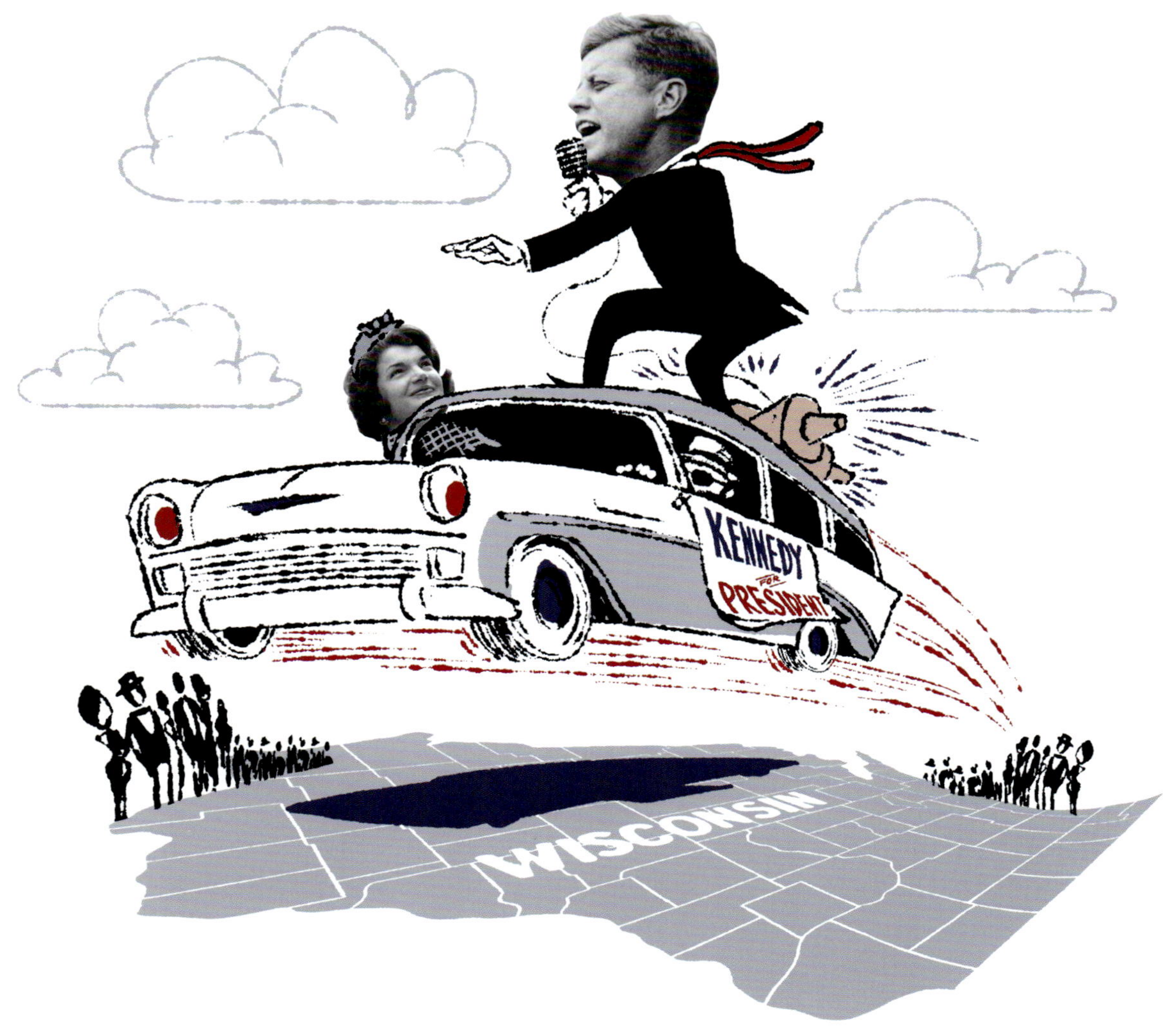

**THE PRIMARY CAMPAIGN
JANUARY – JUNE 1960**

I DID NOT UNDERTAKE LIGHTLY TO SEEK THE PRESIDENCY.

It is not a prize or a normal object of ambition. It is the greatest office
in the world…

It is true, of course, that almost all of the major world leaders today
on both sides of the Iron Curtain are men past the age of sixty-five. It is true
that the world today is largely in the hands of men whose education was
completed before the whole course of international events was altered by
two world wars.

But…the world is changing, the old ways will not do.

The balance of power is shifting. There are new and more terrible
weapons, new and uncertain nations, new pressures of population and
automation that were never considered before. And in many of these new
countries I have noticed, in both Africa and Asia, they are electing young
men to leadership — men who are not bound by the traditions of the past,
men who are not blinded by the old fears and rivalries, men who can
cast off the old slogans and illusions, and suspicions.

It is time for a new generation of leadership to cope with new problems
and new opportunities. For there is a new world to be won, a world of peace
and goodwill, a world of hope and abundance, and I want America to lead
the way to that new world.

Mr. Truman asked me if I think I am ready. I am reminded that one
hundred years ago Abraham Lincoln, not yet President and under fire from
veteran politicians, wrote these words: "I see the storm coming and I know
His hand is in it. If He has a place and work for me, I believe I am ready."

Today I say to you, with full knowledge of the responsibilities of that high
office, if the people of the nation select me to be their President, I believe
that I am ready.

—John F. Kennedy, Televised News Conference, New York City, July 4, 1960

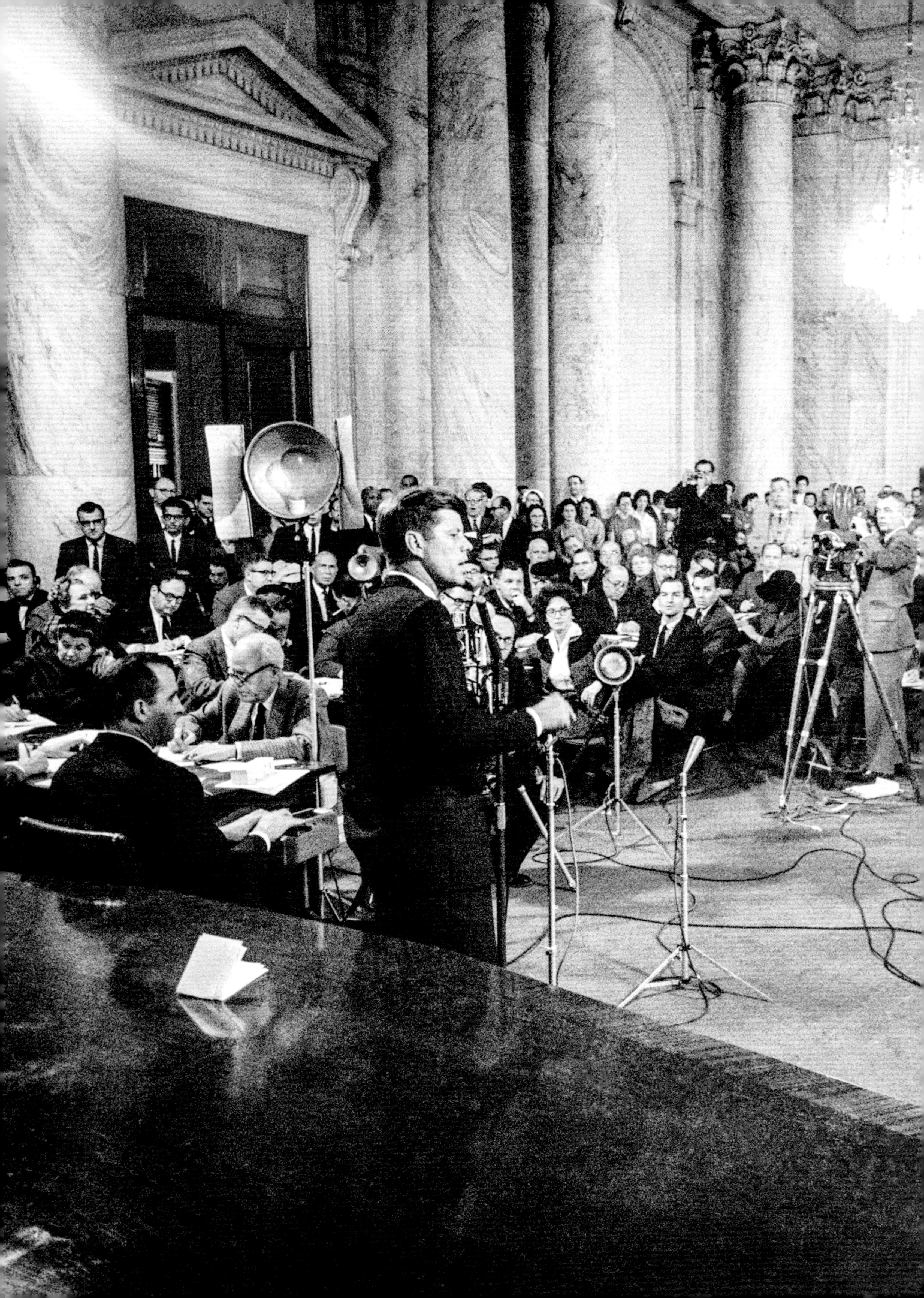

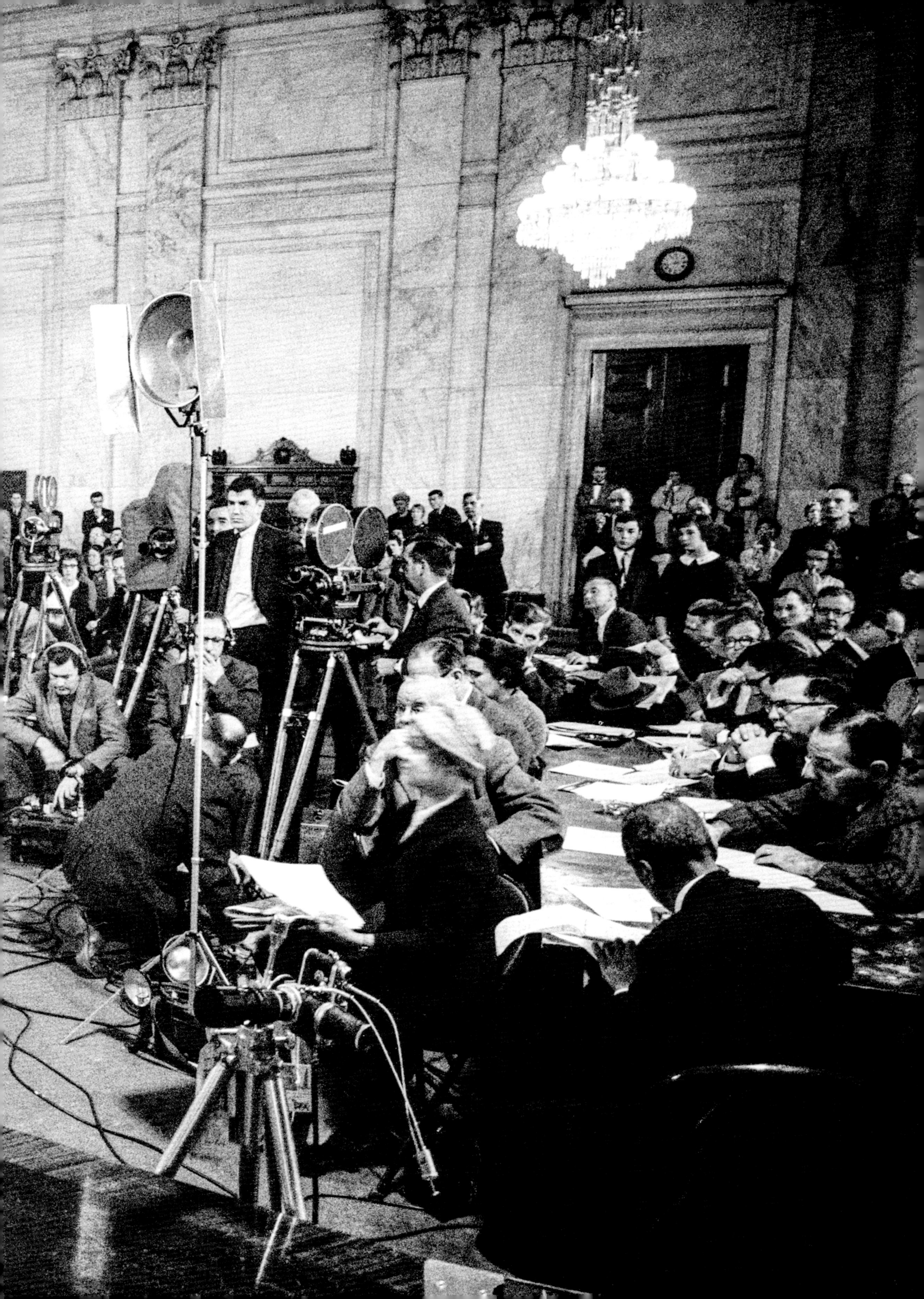

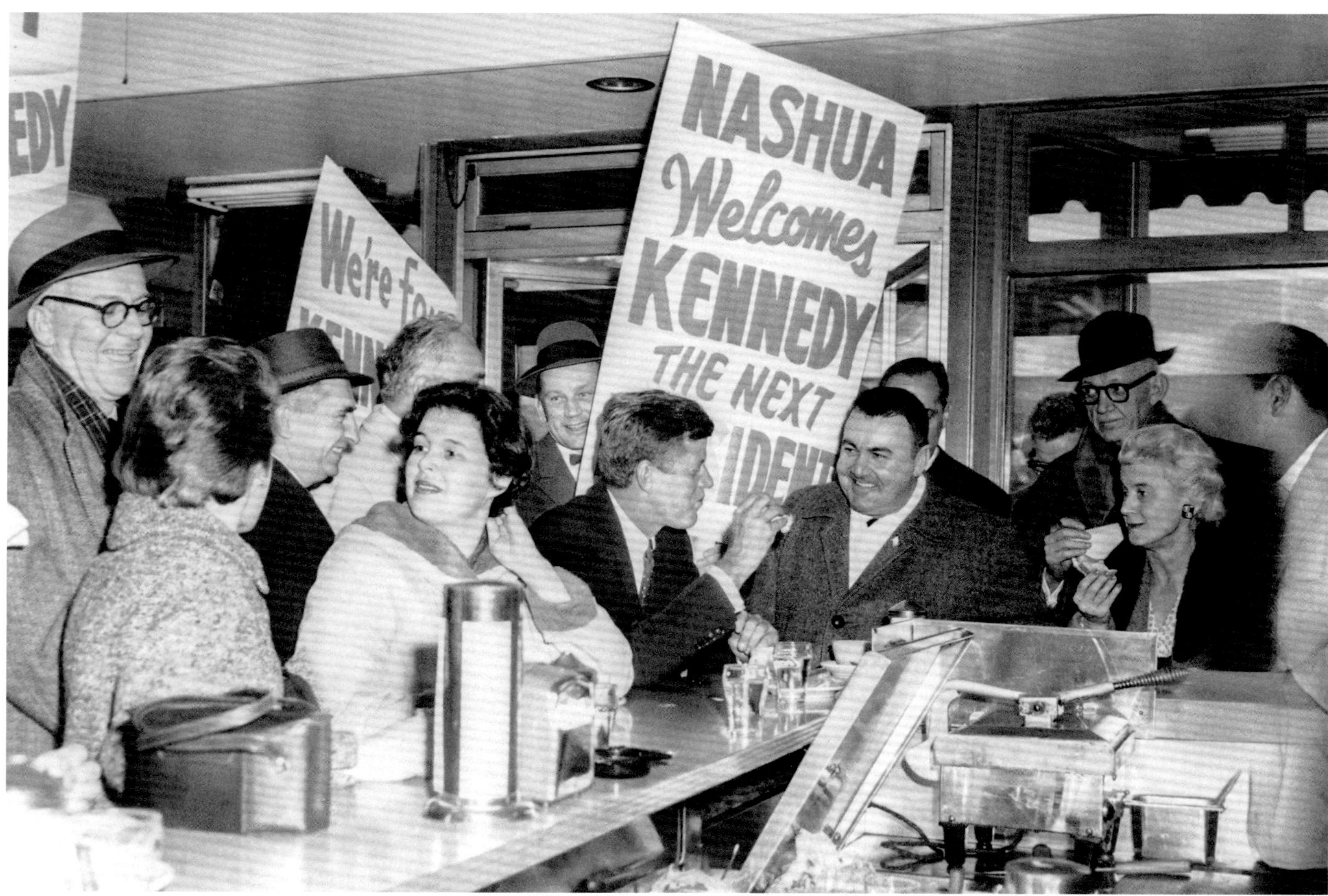

PREVIOUS SPREAD *January 2, 1960.* After nearly three years of unofficial campaigning, Kennedy formally announces his entry into the race for the presidency from the U.S. Senate Caucus Room in Washington, D.C. "In the past 40 months, I have toured every state in the Union and I have talked to Democrats in all walks of life," he stated. "My candidacy is therefore based on the conviction that I can win both the nomination and the election." His rivals were now on notice: Those that did not run in the primaries did not deserve to be taken seriously at the Democratic National Convention in July. *Photo, Anonymous*

ABOVE *January 25, 1960.* Kennedy chews the fat with locals at a diner in Nashua, New Hampshire, where the first primary election would be held in March. The next day the visit was front-page news: "Crowds Out To See Kennedy," said *The Nashua Telegraph* newspaper headline. From that point on, it was nonstop campaigning through November. *Photo, Anonymous*

OPPOSITE *ca. February 12, 1960.* Jack and Jackie on the *Caroline* en route to California. Before her pregnancy stopped her from traveling, Jackie often campaigned with her husband, and when the crowds were thin and the questions hostile, she was there to offer reassurance. An avid reader and lover of the arts, she also supplied JFK with many of the literary references and historical quotations he used in his speeches. *Photo, Jacques Lowe*

"In the decade that lies ahead — in the challenging revolutionary sixties — the American Presidency will demand more than ringing manifestoes issued from the rear of the battle. It will demand that the President place himself in the very thick of the fight…"

—John F. Kennedy, Address to the National Press Club, Washington, D.C., January 14, 1960

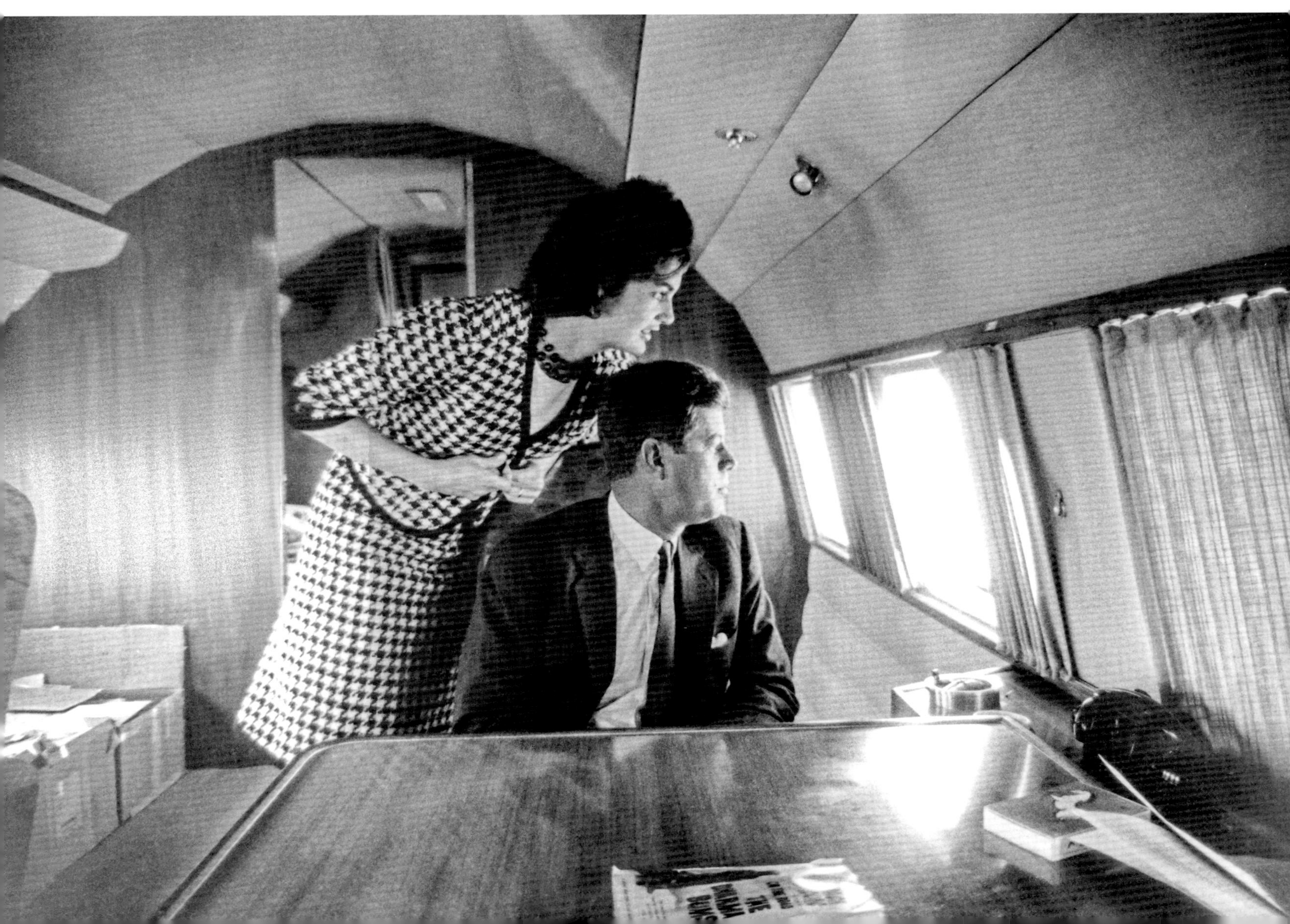

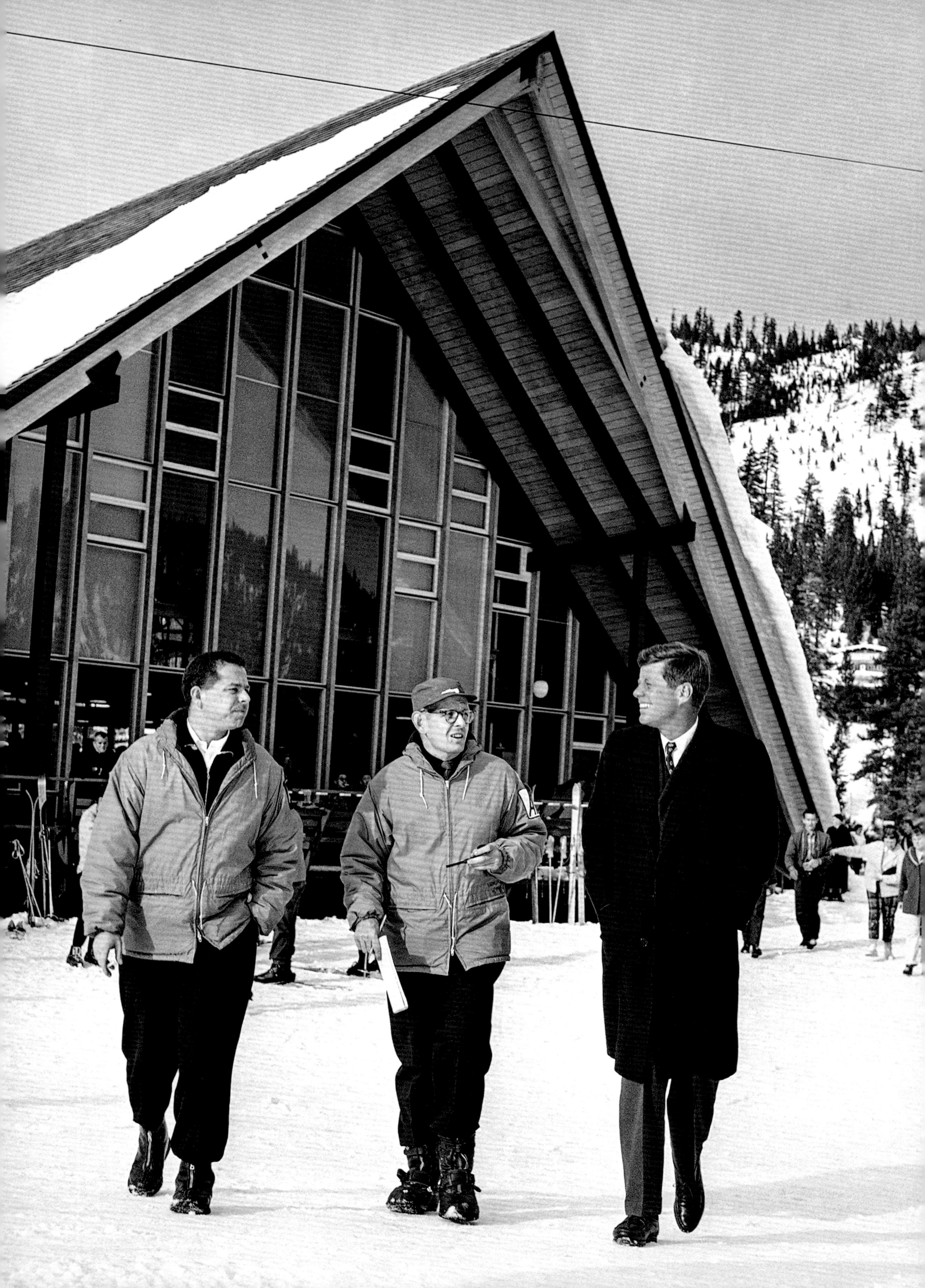

OPPOSITE *January 31, 1960.* JFK tours Squaw Valley, California, after flying to nearby Reno en route to address the Nevada State Legislature the following day. When he arrived at the airport he asked for a car, promised to show up for the speech, and took off at the wheel alone for Squaw Valley to see the final preparations for the Winter Olympics. While Kennedy explored the site, two reporters from Associated Press, Al Cline (left) and Jack Stevenson (center), got an impromptu interview. *Photo, Robert Houston*

BELOW *March 1960.* Senator Hubert H. Humphrey announced his candidacy for the Democratic nomination on December 30, 1959, a few days before Kennedy did. Here, in Wisconsin, Humphrey—a popular liberal from nearby Minnesota—posed a considerable threat. In fact, within JFK's inner circle there had been heated discussion over whether Kennedy should even run in Wisconsin, as the possibility of losing this primary could knock him out of the race altogether. *Photo, Stan Wayman*

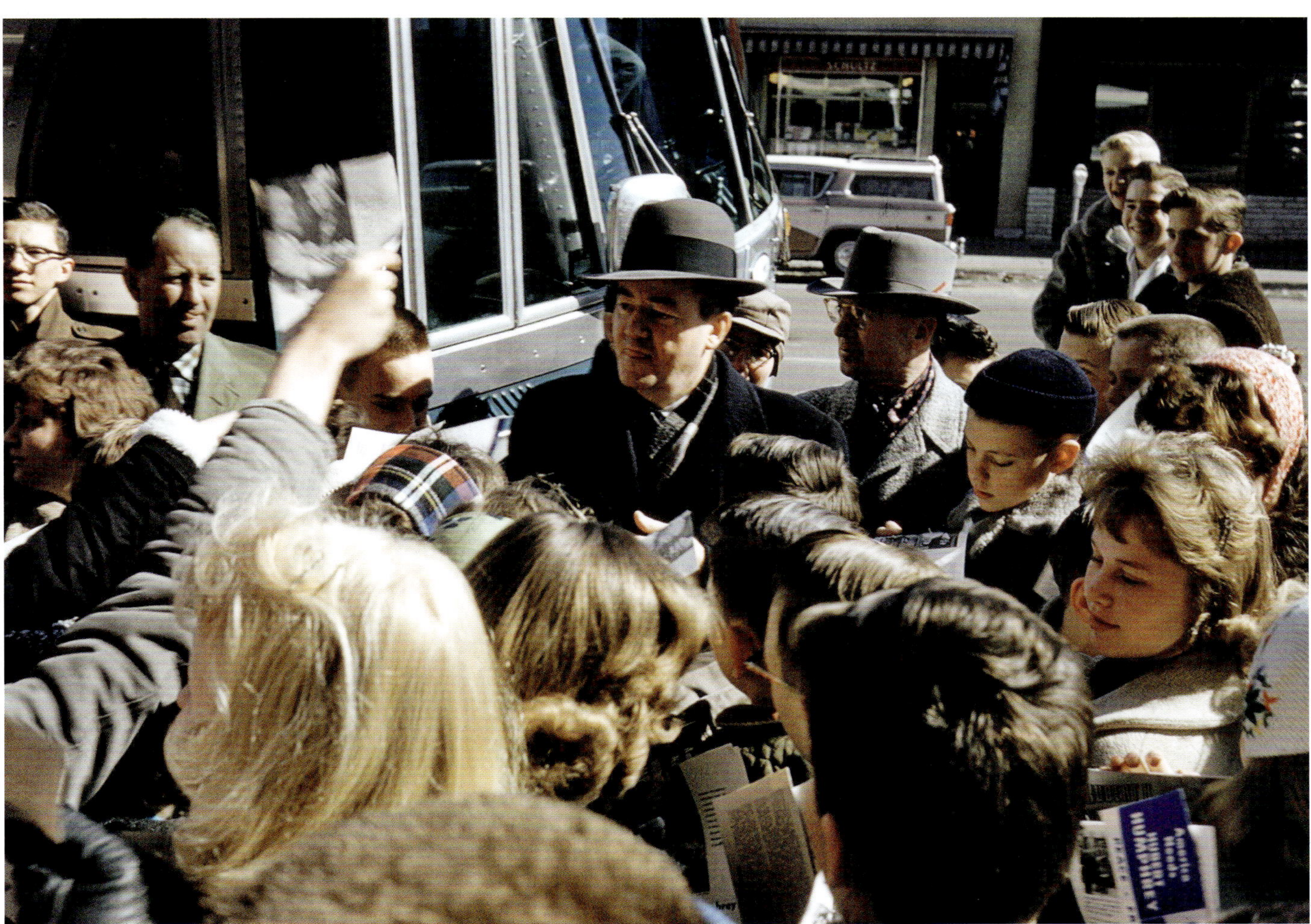

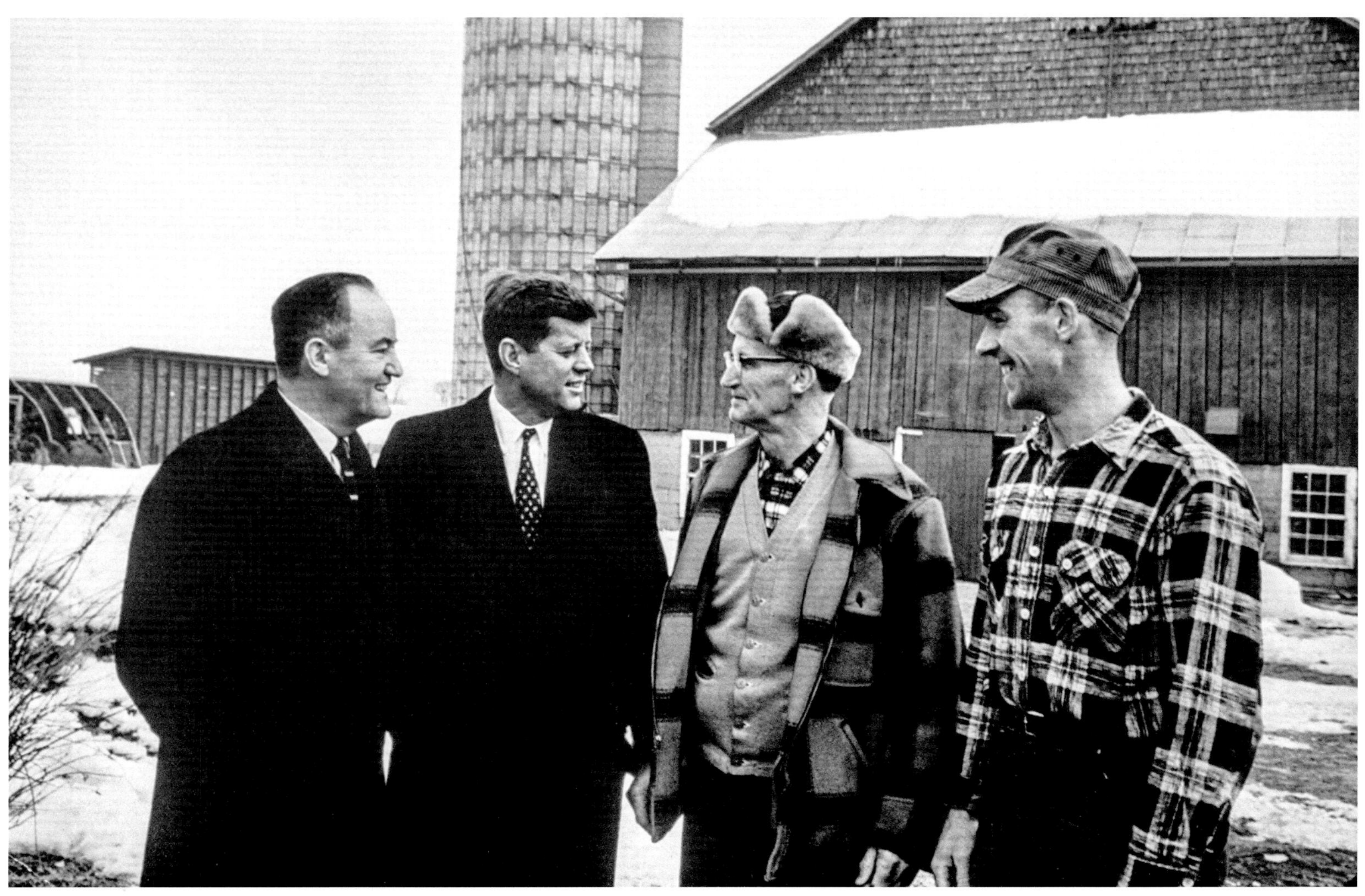

OPPOSITE *April 5, 1960.* On the evening of the Wisconsin primary, Senator Kennedy is interviewed by a Wisconsin TV news reporter. Of the 16 Democratic primaries that spring, Kennedy entered 10—avoiding states like Ohio, California, and Florida with "favorite sons" (governors or senators) in the race. Without the support of party insiders, Kennedy's team had devised a strategy to go to the people directly. Key wins in just enough primary races would demonstrate his potential to overcome his youth and his religion before the convention in July. Wins in Wisconsin and West Virginia emerged as key "momentum-builders," leading to a sweep of every race he entered. *Photo, Stan Wayman*

MJ-TV • THE MILWAUKEE JOURNAL WT

WISCONSIN PRIMAR

9:00		9:30		10:00		10:30		11:00	
5		5		5		5		5	AT LARGE
2½			2½	2½		2½		2½	FIRST DIST
2½		2½		2½			2½	2½	2ND
2½		2½		2½			2½		3RD
—	—	—	—	—		2½		2½	4TH
—	—	—	—	—		2½		2½	5TH
	2½	2½		2½		2½			
		2½		2½		2½			
	2½	2½		2½		2½			
		2½		2½		2½			
		2½		2½					
		2½		2½		2½			
	½	½	½			½			
	15½	10½	10½		10½	20½			

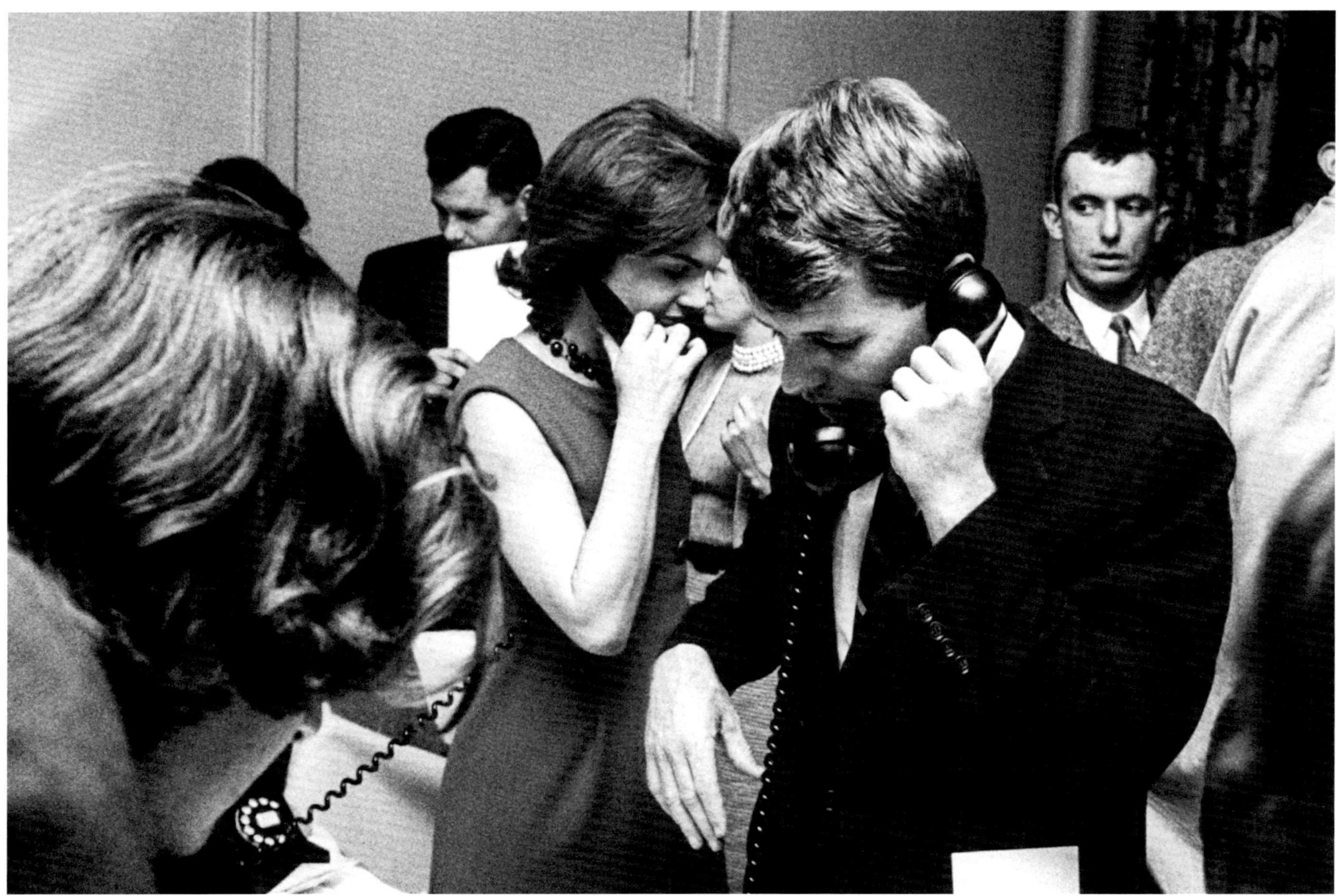

ABOVE AND OPPOSITE (TOP) *April 5, 1960.* The Kennedy family came out in full force the night of the Wisconsin primary vote. Bobby, who had run JFK's earliest campaigns for Congress and the U.S. Senate, was his most trusted aide and political confidante; but while Jack was canvassing Wisconsin for votes, Bobby already had his eyes on the next battle: "This campaign is being won in West Virginia right now. Not here," he told filmmaker Robert Drew on the night before the Wisconsin primary. "I am running the staff in West Virginia that's going to win this election." *Photos, Stan Wayman*

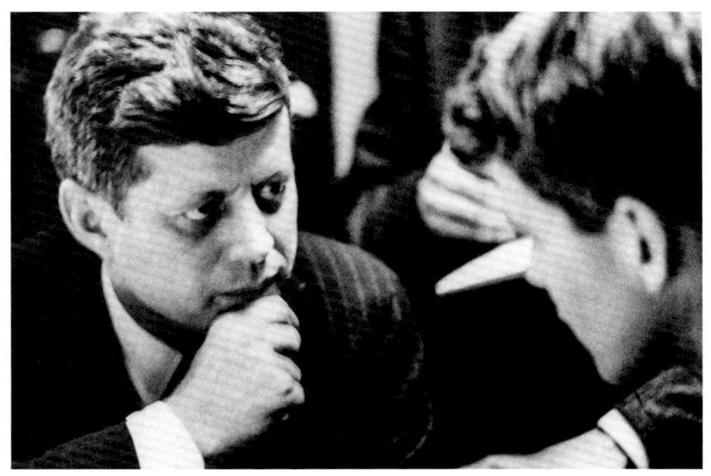

BELOW *April 5, 1960.* Returns come in the night of the Wisconsin primary at the television studios of CBS-affiliate WTTI in Milwaukee. Though Kennedy won the Wisconsin primary by an impressive 100,000-plus votes—beating Humphrey 478,118 to 372,034—his margin of victory came from heavily Catholic areas. He failed to carry a number of Protestant districts, and his victory did not impress party bosses, who remained doubtful of his broader appeal. That meant the next primary battle—in the heavily Protestant state of West Virginia—would be a key test for Kennedy. *Photo, Bob Sandberg*

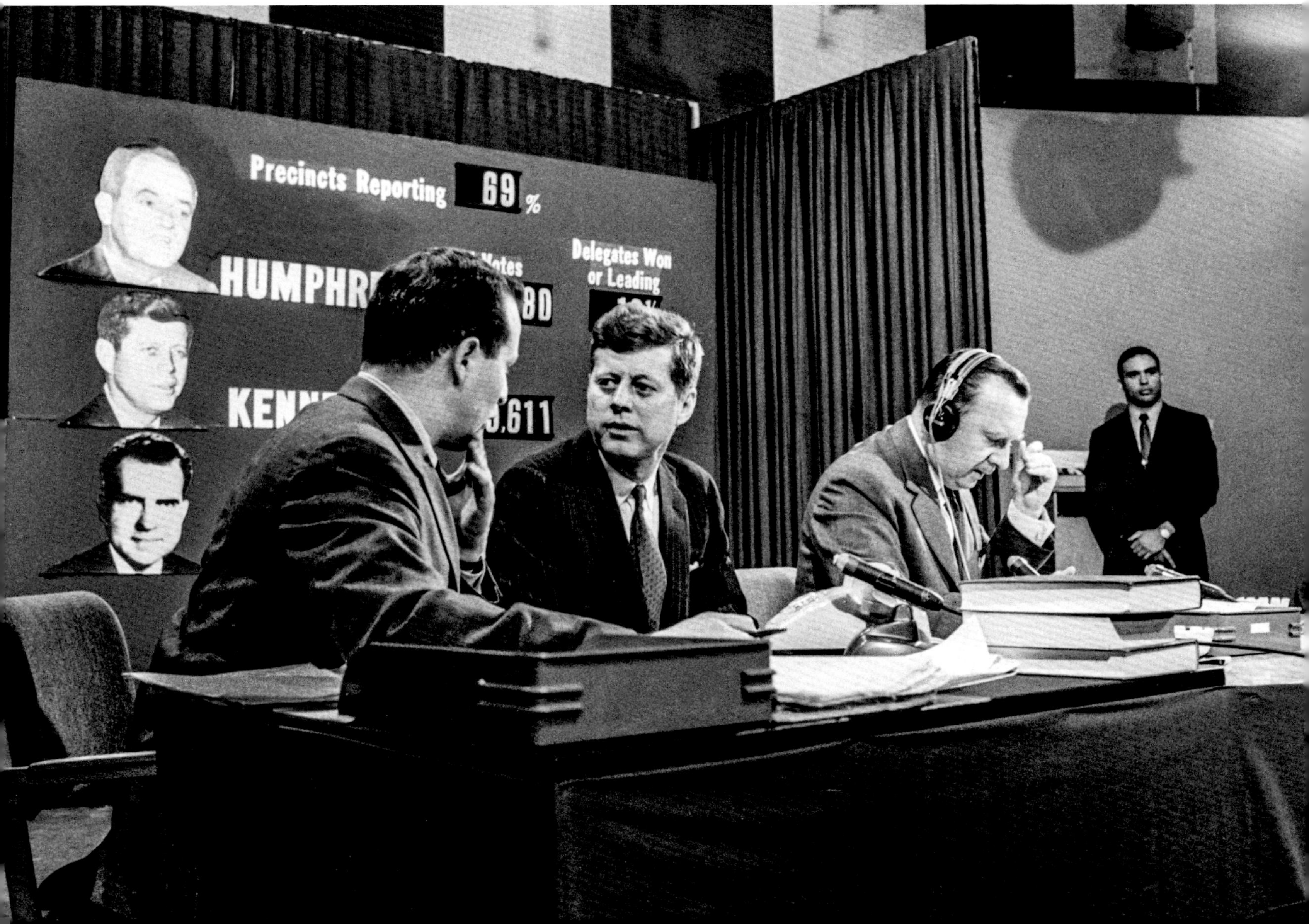

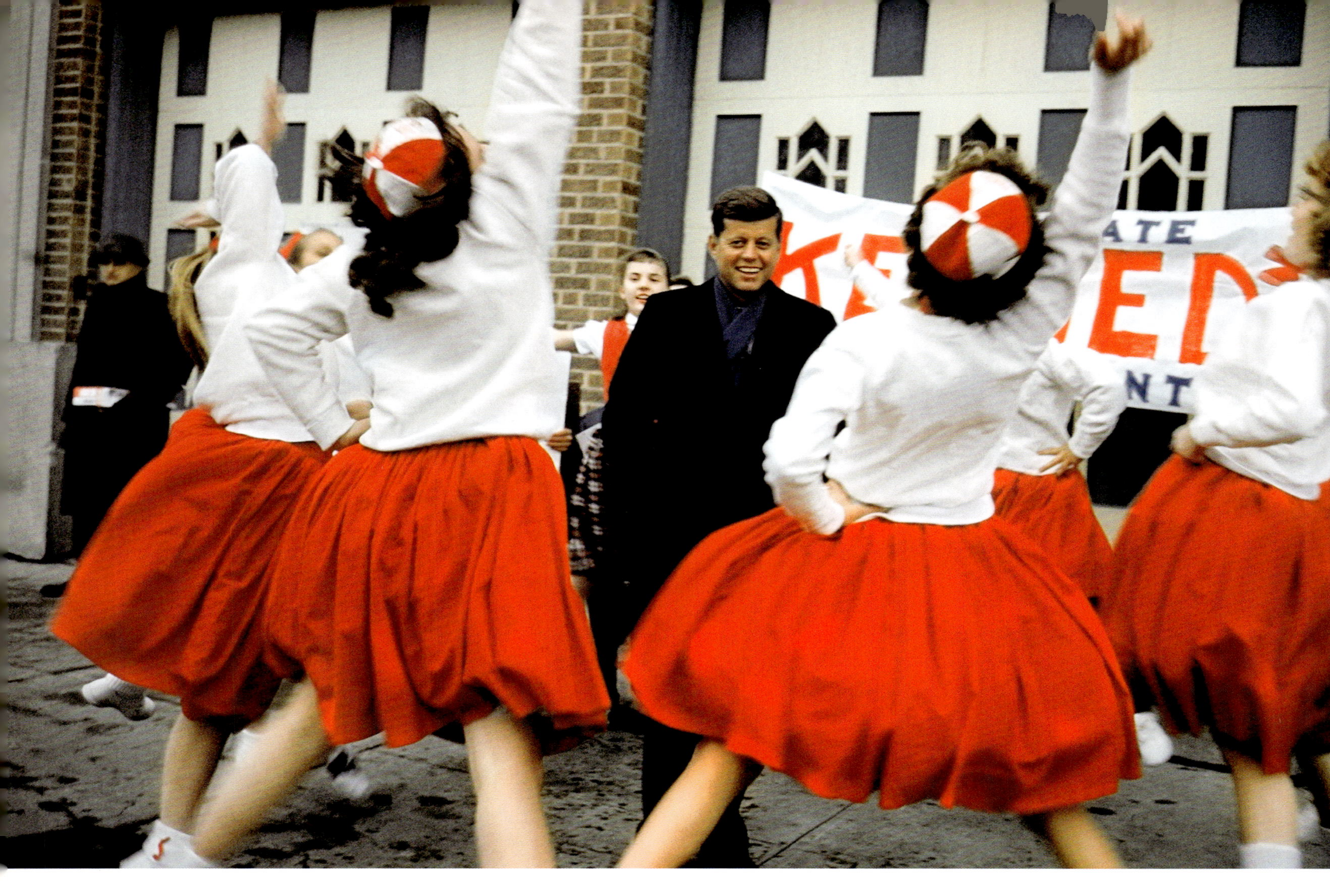

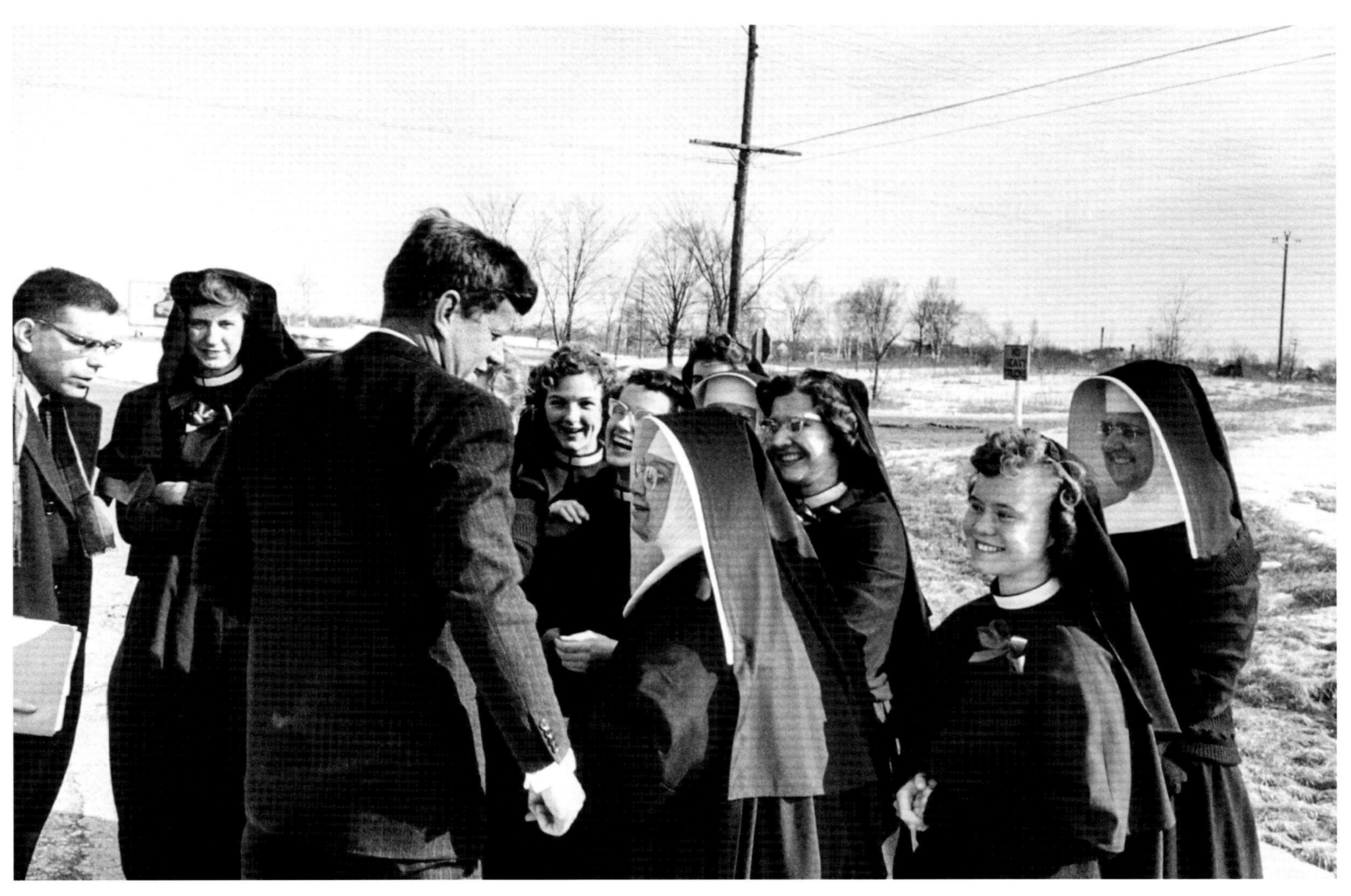

 March 1960. A squad of high school cheerleaders offers JFK an enthusiastic welcome in Wisconsin. Humphrey was popular with his folksy charm, but Kennedy was greeted like a rock star. *Photo, Stan Wayman*

 March 1960. While in Ladysmith, Wisconsin, JFK visited Catholic nuns and acolytes near the Lady of Sorrows convent. One of the nuns gave the candidate a shamrock, which he pinned to his lapel. However, mindful of the religion issue and his need to appeal to Protestant voters, Kennedy would never linger long with Catholic clergy members. He would later quip that while the priests and bishops would, as was typical, vote Republican, the nuns would go Democratic for him. *Photo, Stan Wayman*

BELOW *Spring 1960.* Jackie Kennedy rests mid-campaign. Though she had traveled extensively with Jack in his early campaigning, Jackie was forced to limit her travels after becoming pregnant in early 1960. When filmmaker Richard Leacock, who was on the campaign trail with the Kennedys in Wisconsin, asked her, "'Doesn't your hand hurt after all these handshakes?" her response was, "Well, did you ever try smiling 1,000 times a day? My face hurts." *Photo, Jacques Lowe*

OPPOSITE *Spring 1960.* En route to Wisconsin, Kennedy stages a strategy session on the fly at Chicago's O'Hare Airport. *Photo, Jacques Lowe*

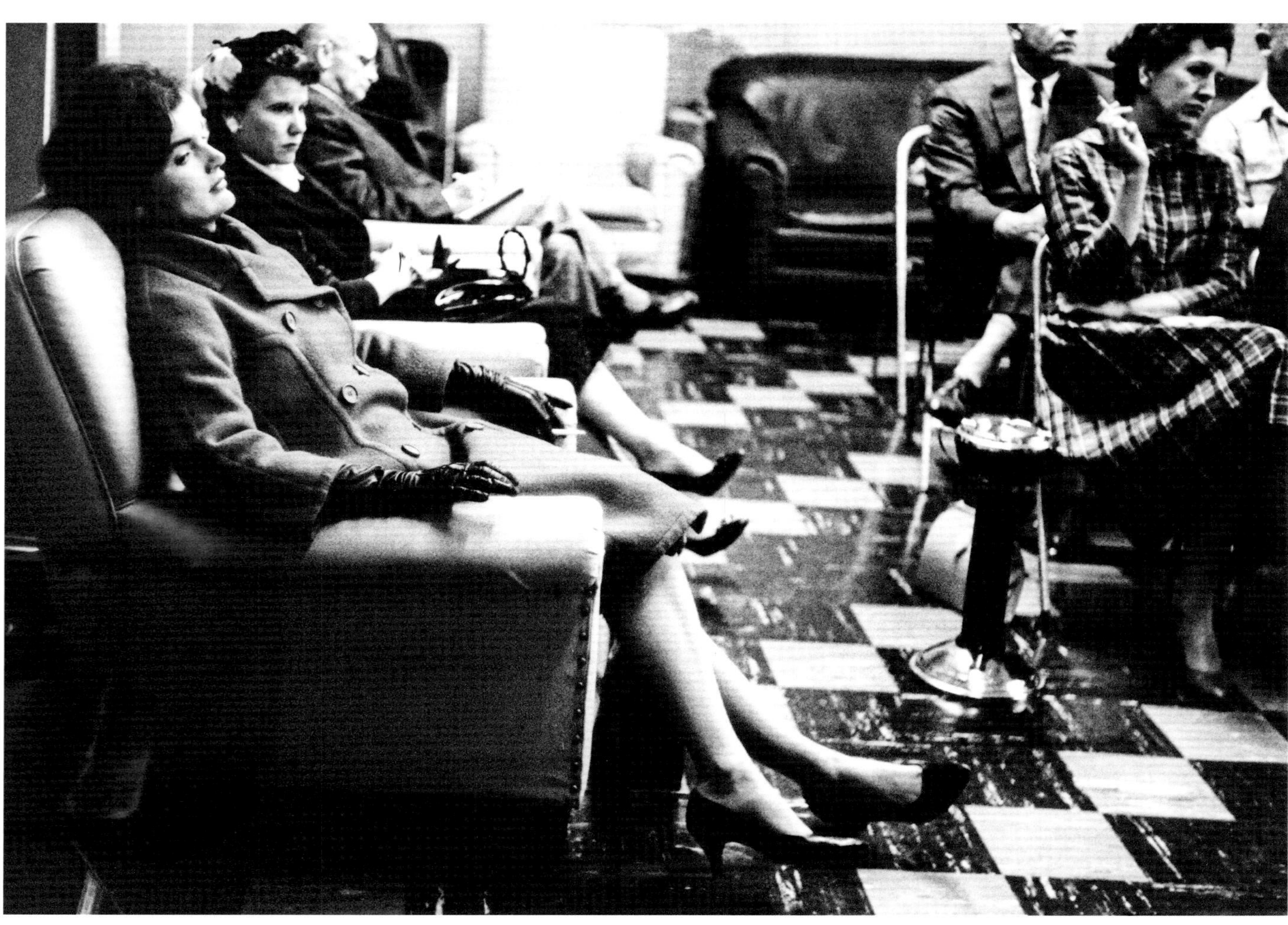

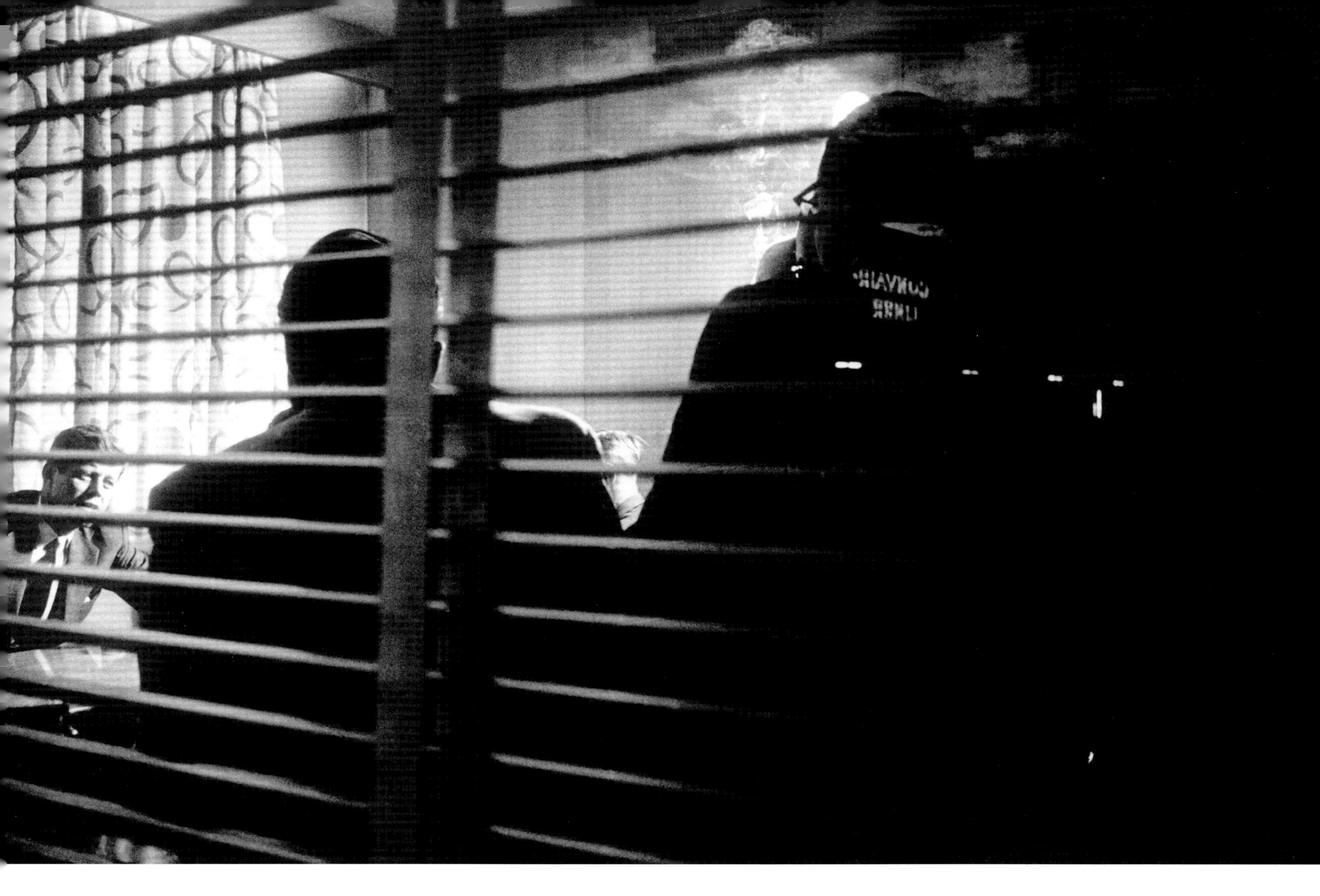

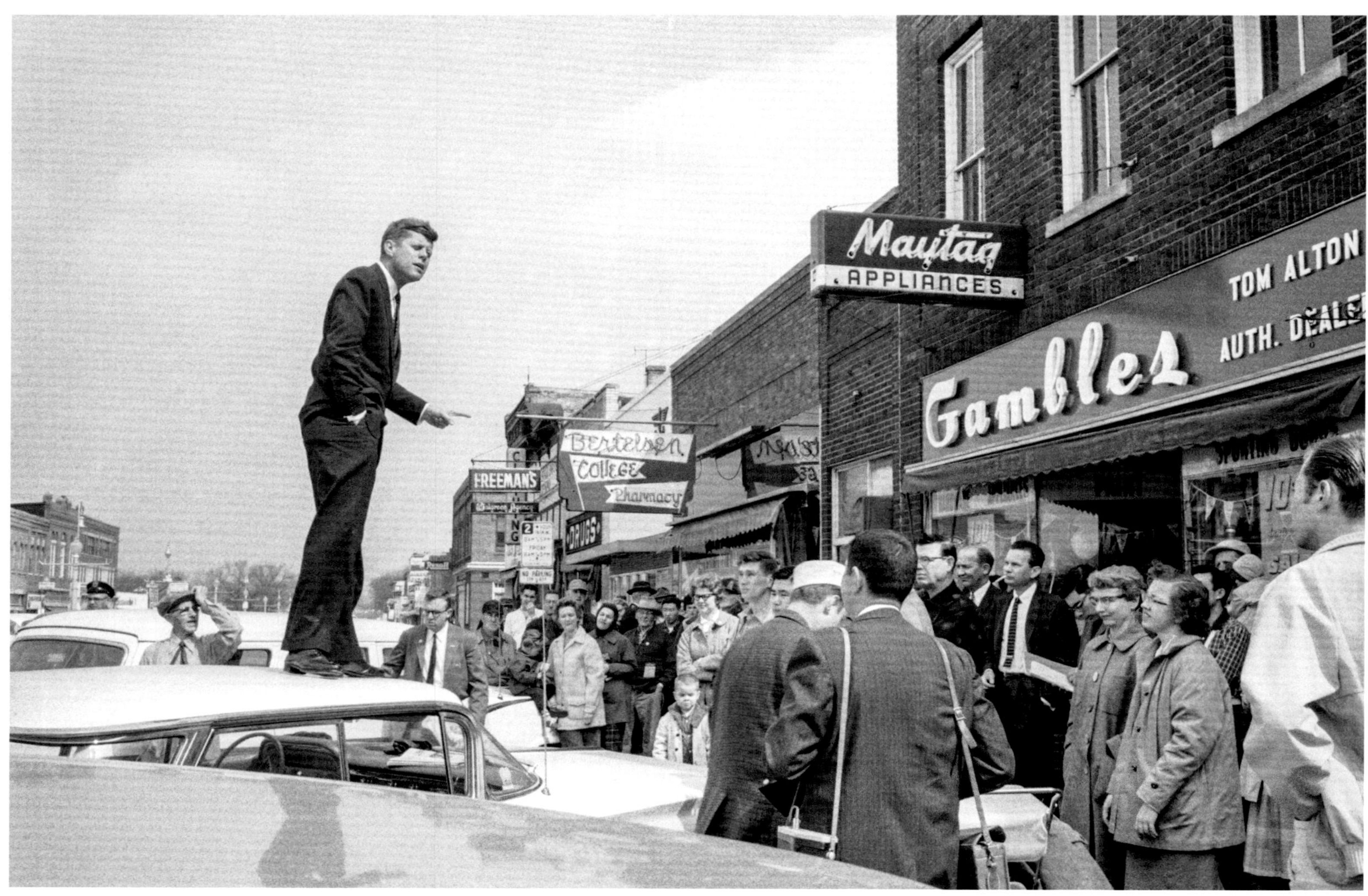

ABOVE *April 1960.* Kennedy wasn't fussy about his stage, and not all of his stump speeches were prearranged. He became known for his roadside stops any time he spied a group of voters to be converted, like this group in River Falls, Wisconsin. *Photo, Bob Sandberg*

OPPOSITE *April 11, 1960.* En route to Charleston, West Virginia, Kennedy hops atop a bulldozer to give an impromptu speech to schoolchildren. Having spoken at high schools across the country when few knew his name, Kennedy would always say that even though kids could not vote, they would bring word of his visit home to their parents. *Photo, Jacques Lowe*

FOLLOWING SPREAD *April 25, 1960.* A speech in Amherstdale, West Virginia, one of the mining towns Kennedy visited in Logan County. In early April 1960, Kennedy's campaign team discovered that JFK had suffered a dramatic reversal in the polls here. A prior poll had Kennedy winning the state, but as the "Catholic issue" became more prominent in press coverage, Humphrey gained advantage. Hence, West Virginia became a battleground between the two candidates, who enlisted everyone they could in the fight—celebrities, friends, family, and various local politicians, all of whom blanketed the state. *Photo, Hank Walker*

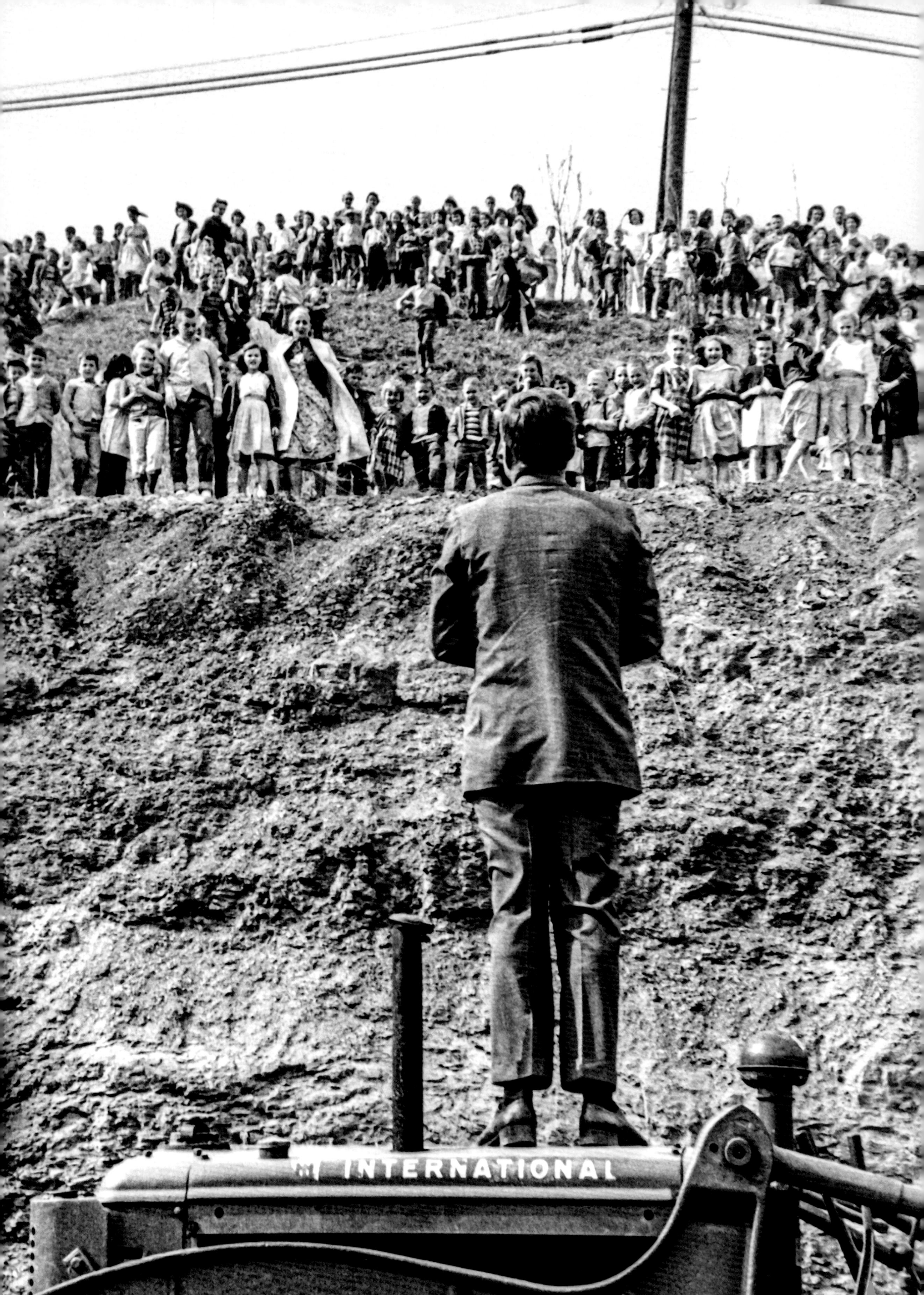

INTERNATIONAL

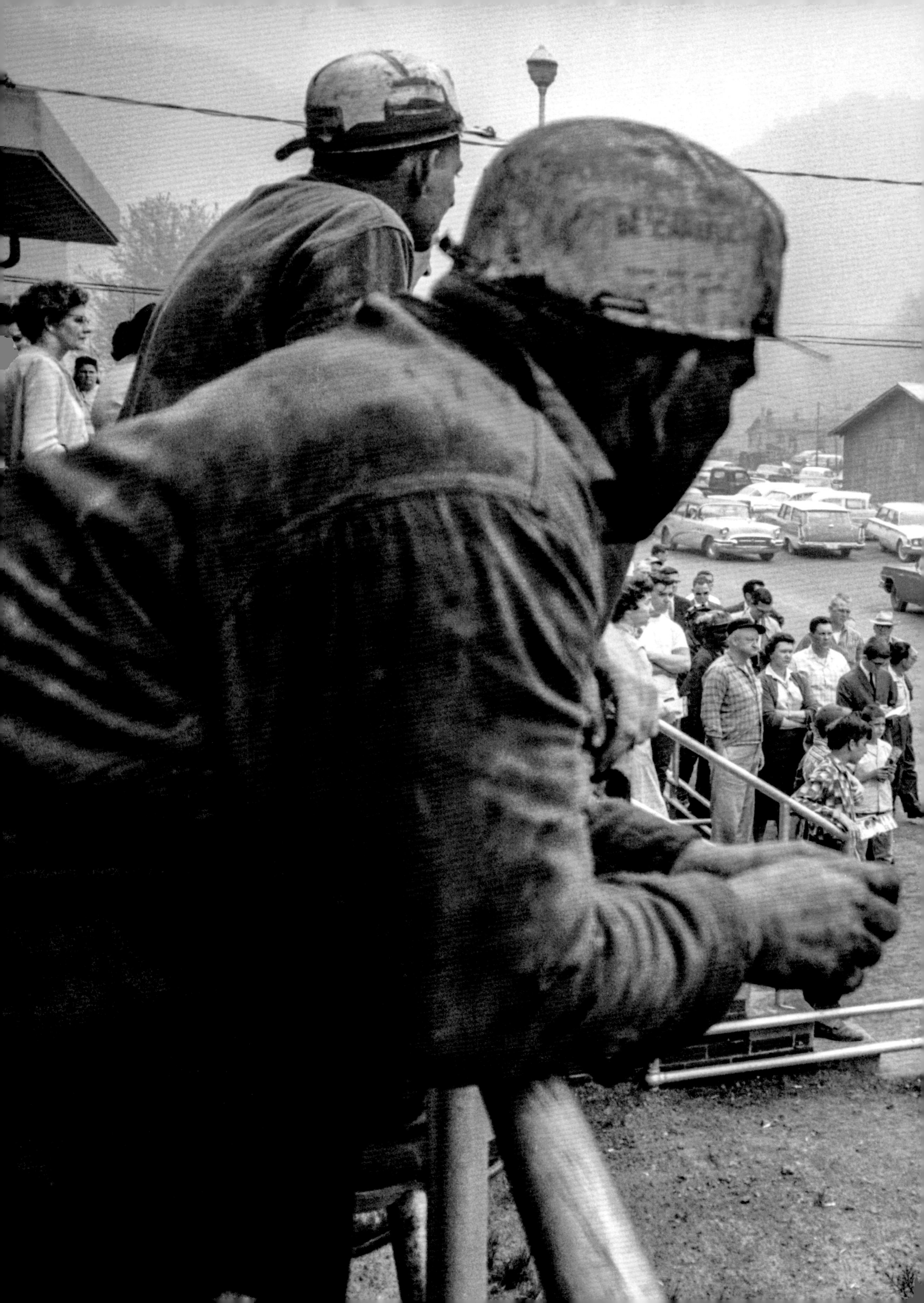

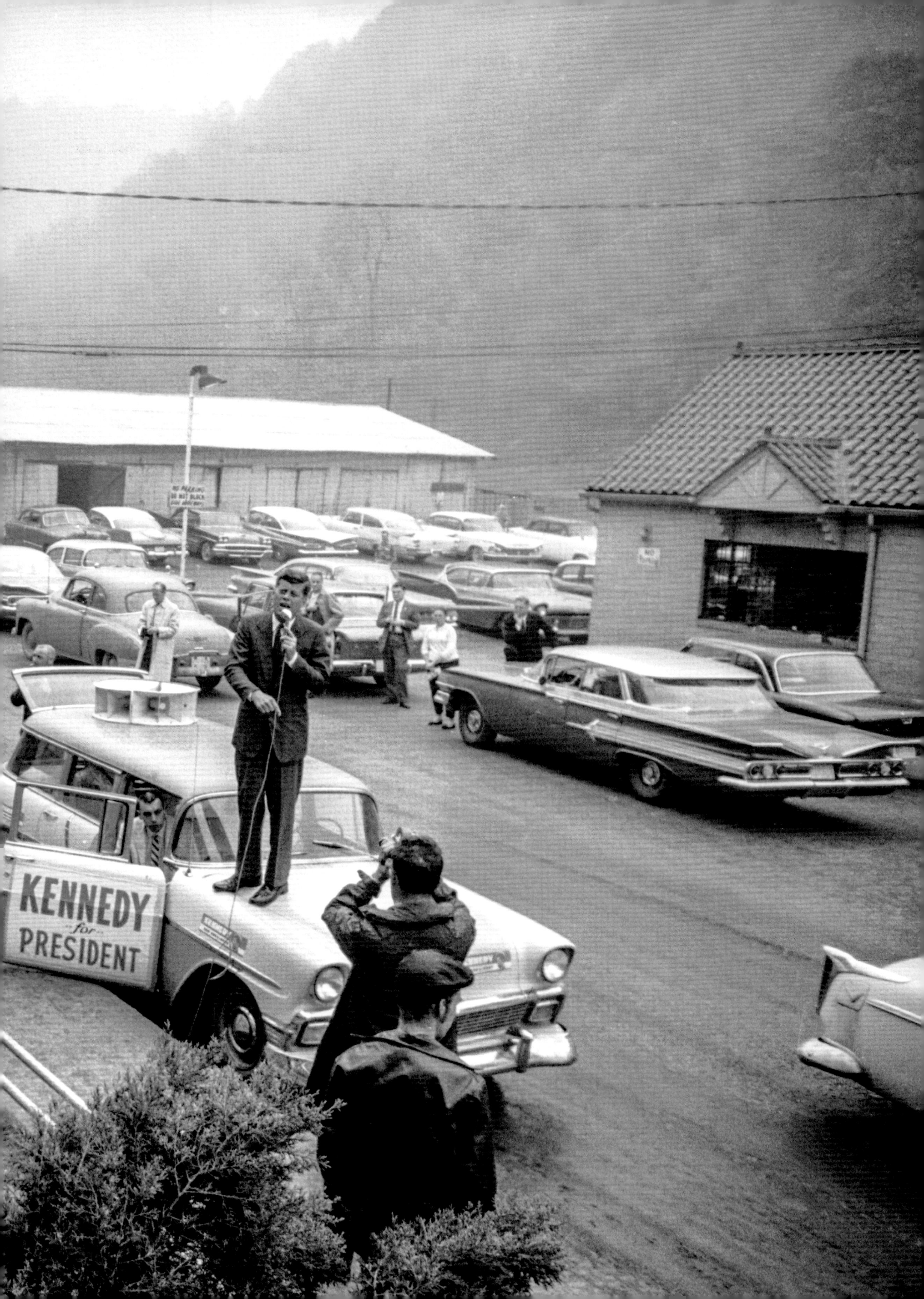

KENNEDY
-for-
PRESIDENT

"We have the most gadgets and the most gimmicks in our history, the biggest TV and tail-fins — but we also have the worst slums, the most crowded schools, and the greatest erosion of our natural resources and our national will. It may be, for some, an age of material prosperity — but it is also an age of spiritual poverty."

—John F. Kennedy, "Victory in '60" Luncheon, Salt Lake City, Utah, January 30, 1960

OPPOSITE *April 25, 1960.* JFK's precarious stance as he gave this speech in rural Logan County, might well be a metaphor for his campaign's position in the state. Aside from any personal reasons voters there might view him suspiciously, he also faced hard opposition and even subterfuge from other presidential contenders. Among West Virginia politicians, U.S. Senator Robert Byrd told voters: "If you are for Adlai Stevenson, Senator Stuart Symington, Senator Johnson, or John Doe, this primary may be your last chance to stop Kennedy." *Photo, Hank Walker*

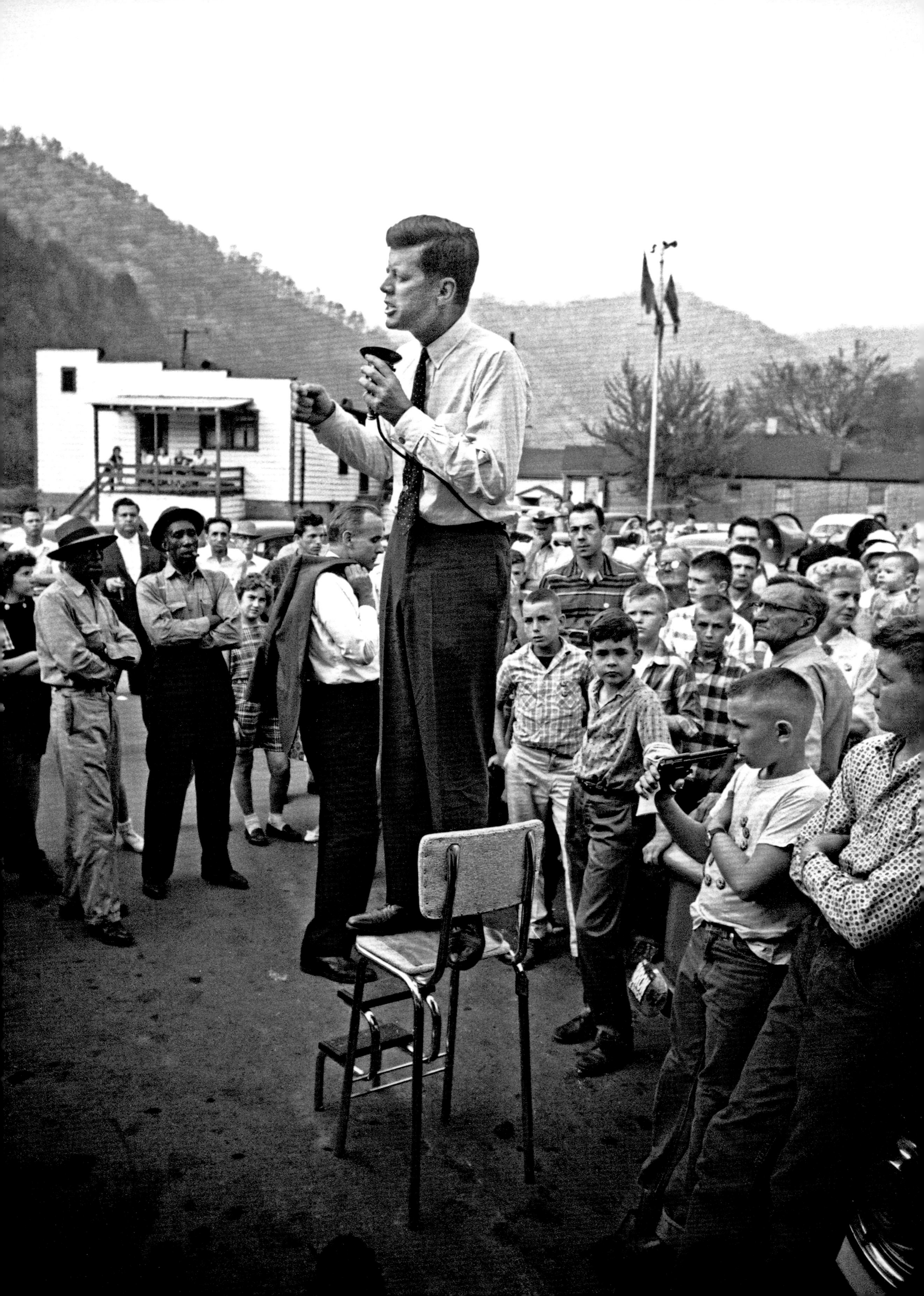

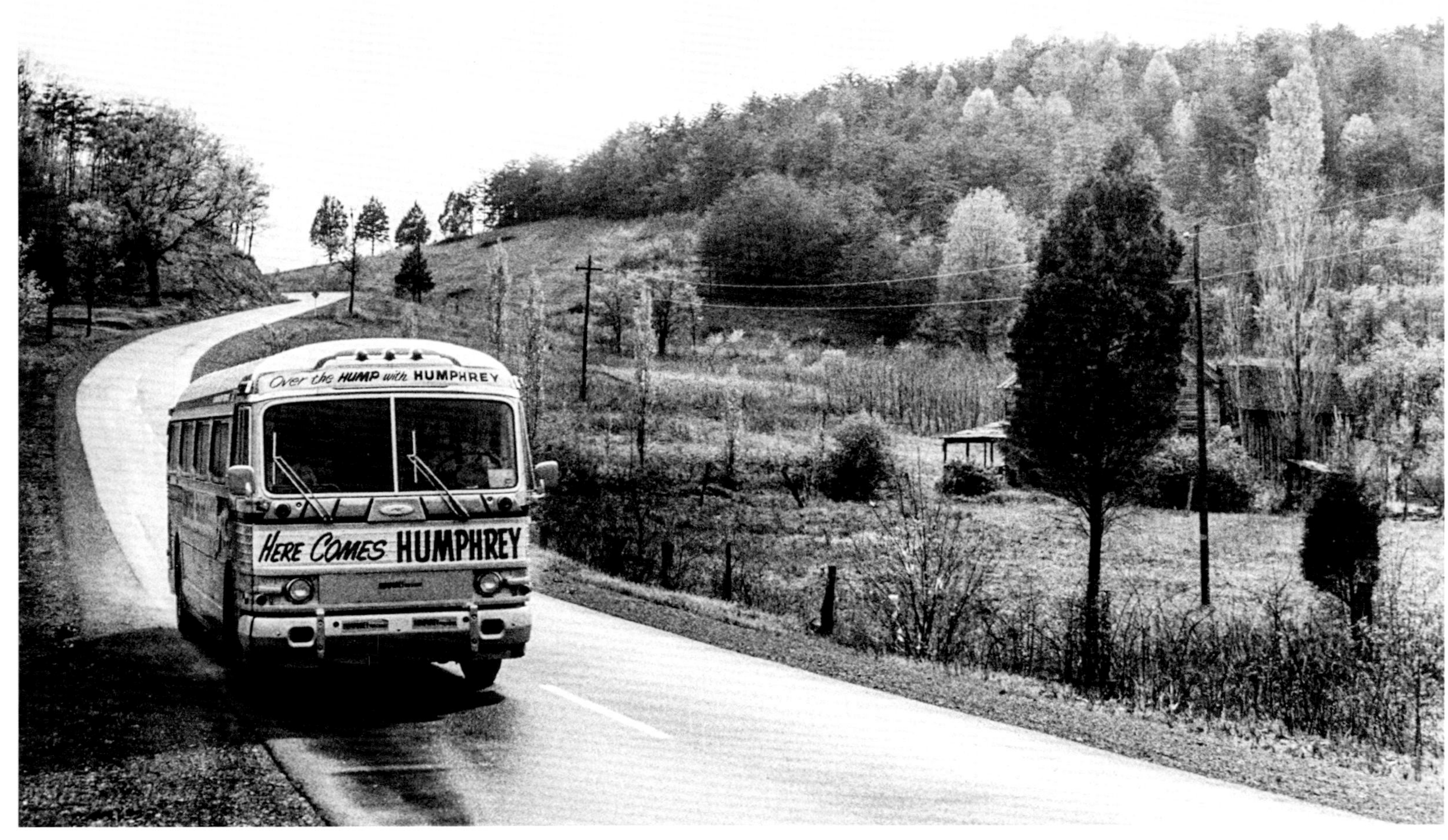

ABOVE *April 1960.* A campaign bus carries Humphrey through West Virginia's Morgan County—one of the few Republican areas in the largely Democratic state. Humphrey realized the state was an uphill battle after the loss to Kennedy in Wisconsin, but he had an advantage with voters in this struggling economy: He was once poor. As he often hit home on the campaign trail, "Anybody who hasn't known poverty is worse off for it." *Photo, Paul Schutzer*

OPPOSITE *April 25, 1960.* In West Virginia, old coal mining camps often became the basis for small towns. In Omar, one such town, Kennedy seeks the "front porch vote" of local residents. *Photo, Hank Walker*

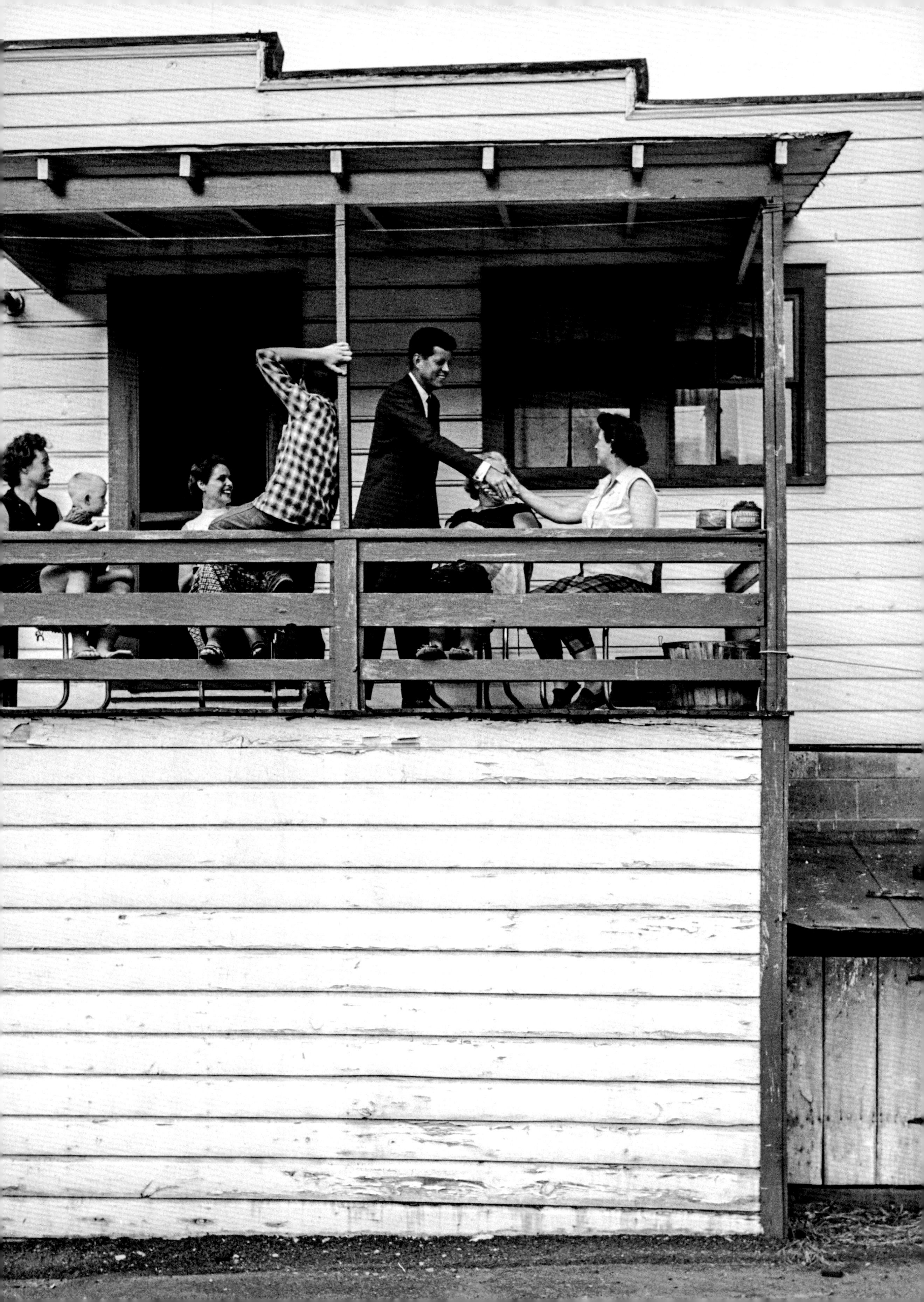

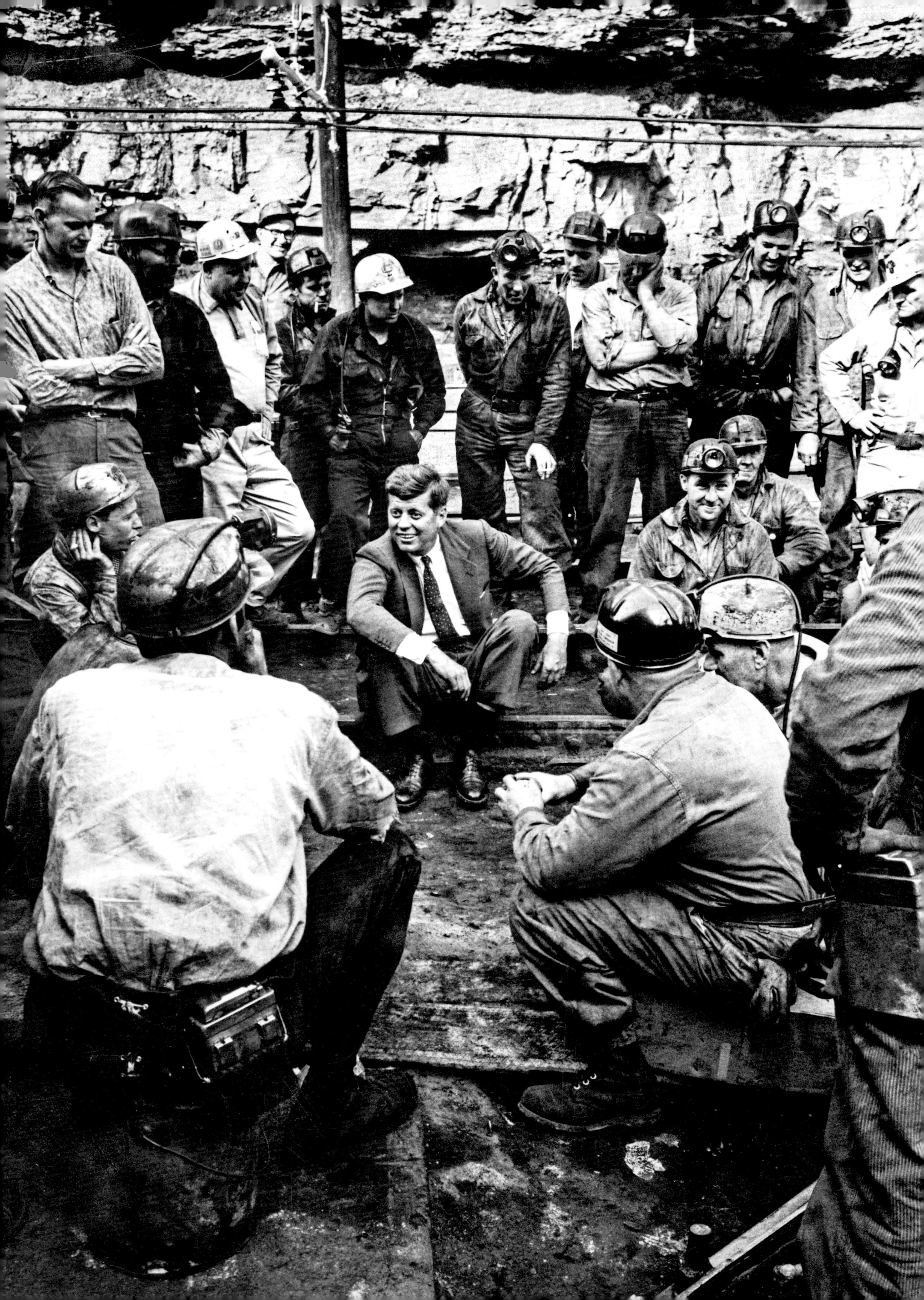

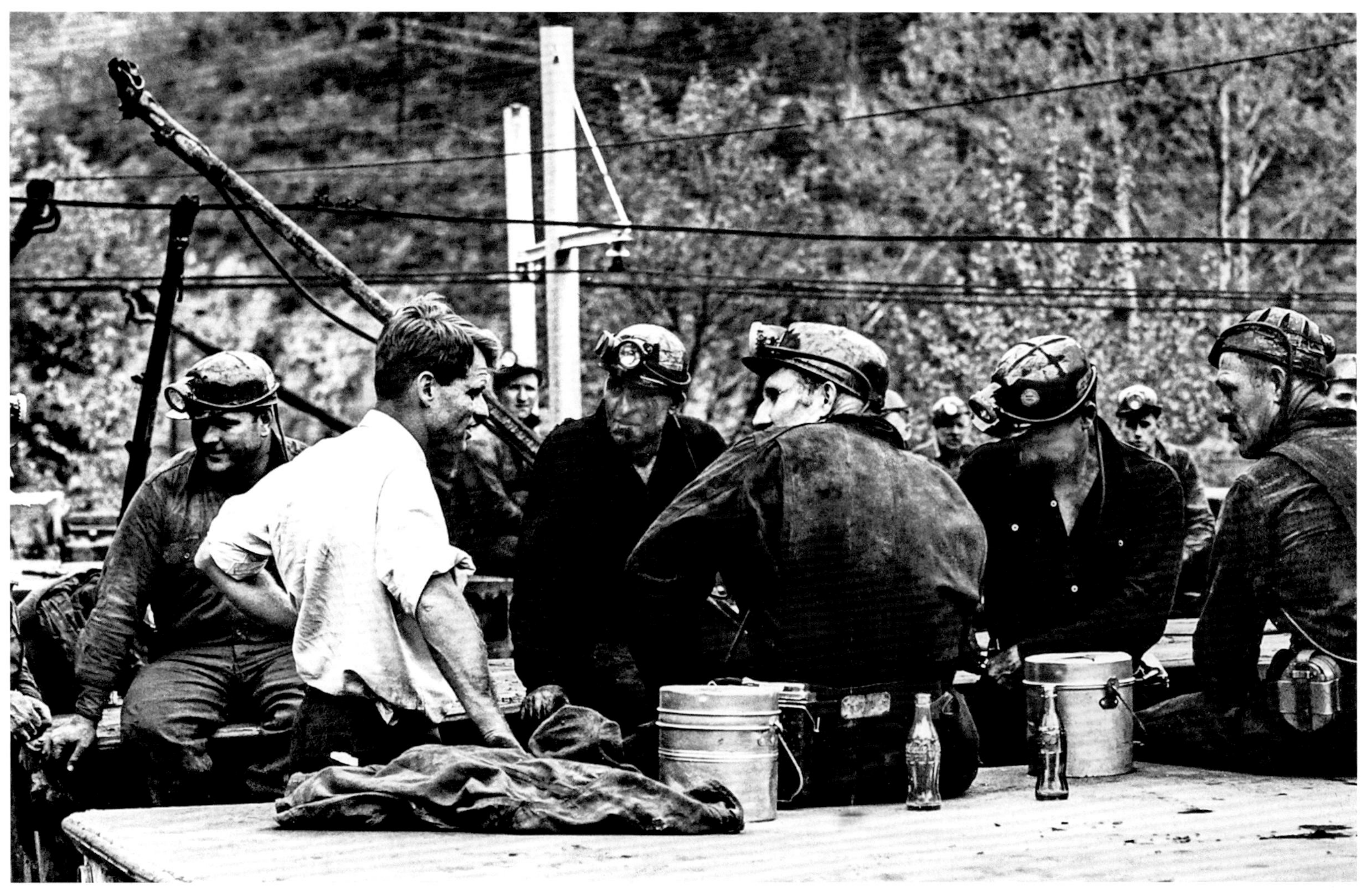

OPPOSITE *April 26, 1960.* Kennedy visited several working coal mines in West Virginia, including one near the town of Mullens, West Virginia, where he greeted miners during a midnight shift change. Some of them refused to shake his hand upon meeting, but once he began talking about their economic problems and what he might do as president to help, they often warmed to him. He would also draw parallels to the loss of manufacturing and milling jobs in his home state of Massachusetts. *Photo, Hank Walker*

ABOVE *April 26, 1960.* According to an article in *Look* magazine, Bobby was an indefatigable campaigner. "The most important thing in primary campaigns," the article quotes Jack as saying in the July 19, 1960, issue, "is personal contact. And my family multiplies the amount that I could do alone." Scenes like this one near Mullens would be repeated eight years later, when RFK would make his own bid for the Democratic presidential nomination. *Photo, Robert Lerner*

"I am not the Catholic candidate for President. I do not speak for the Catholic Church on issues of public policy — and no one in that Church speaks for me."

—John F. Kennedy, American Society of Newspaper Editors,
  Washington, D.C., April 21, 1960

OPPOSITE *Spring 1960.* In speeches and interviews, JFK spoke boldly and directly about issues, including the "Catholic problem." He told the American Society of Newspaper Editors, "the great bulk of West Virginians paid very little attention to my religion—until they read repeatedly in the nation's press that this was the decisive issue in West Virginia." And in Wheeling a heckler in a crowd asked him how he could reconcile being president with being Catholic. Kennedy responded, "I don't take orders from above." In the end the voters of West Virginia, a heavily Protestant state, demonstrated that a Catholic candidate could win a significant victory, which he did: 61 percent to 39 percent. *Photo, Cornell Capa*

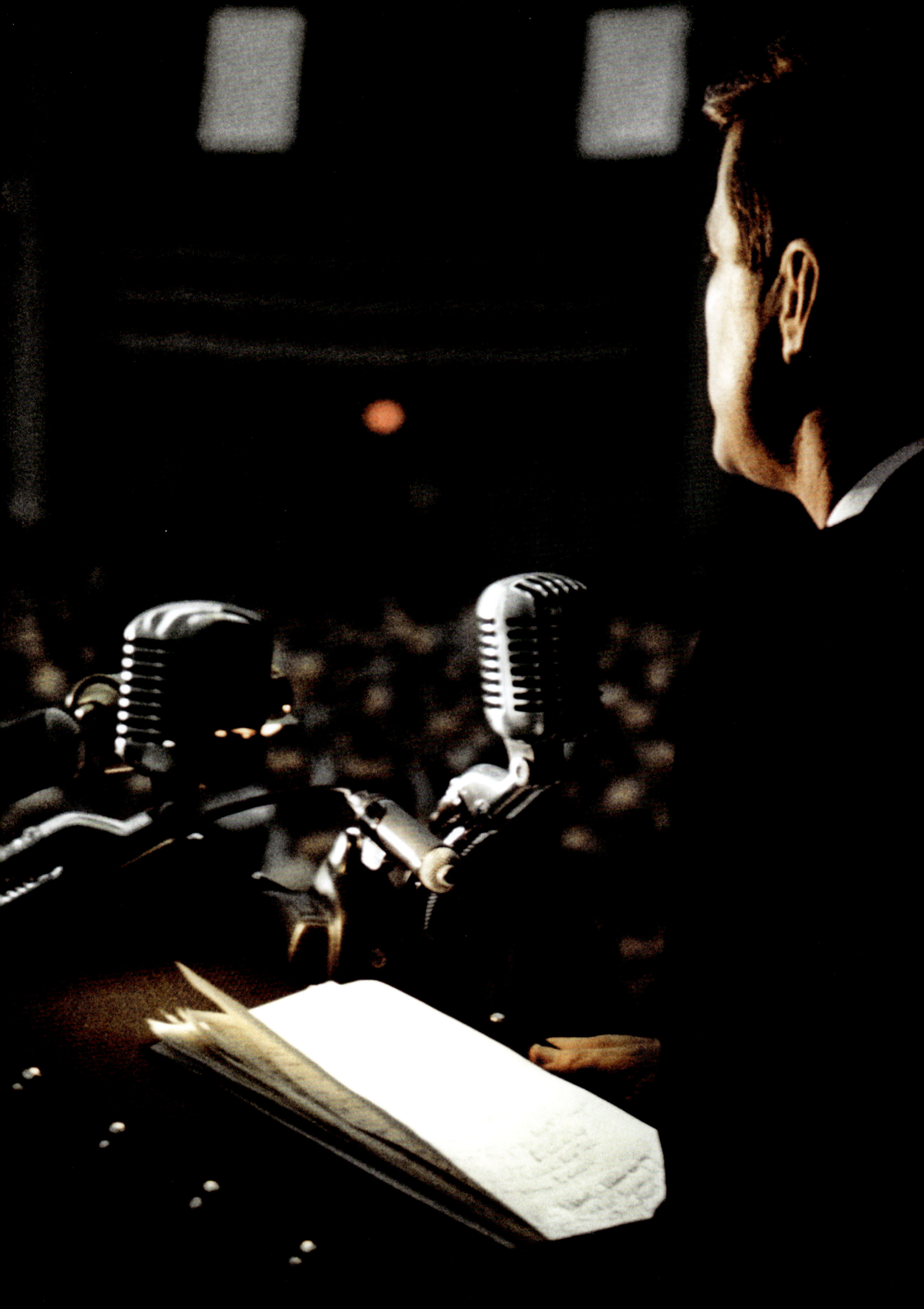

"If a candidate wishes to understand the needs and aspirations
of the people he seeks to serve — he must go among them....
He must listen as well as talk, see as well as be seen, learn as well
as teach....For after the nomination it is often too late — for the
candidate and for the country."

—John F. Kennedy, Weyerhaeuser Lumber Company, Eugene, Oregon, May 17, 1960

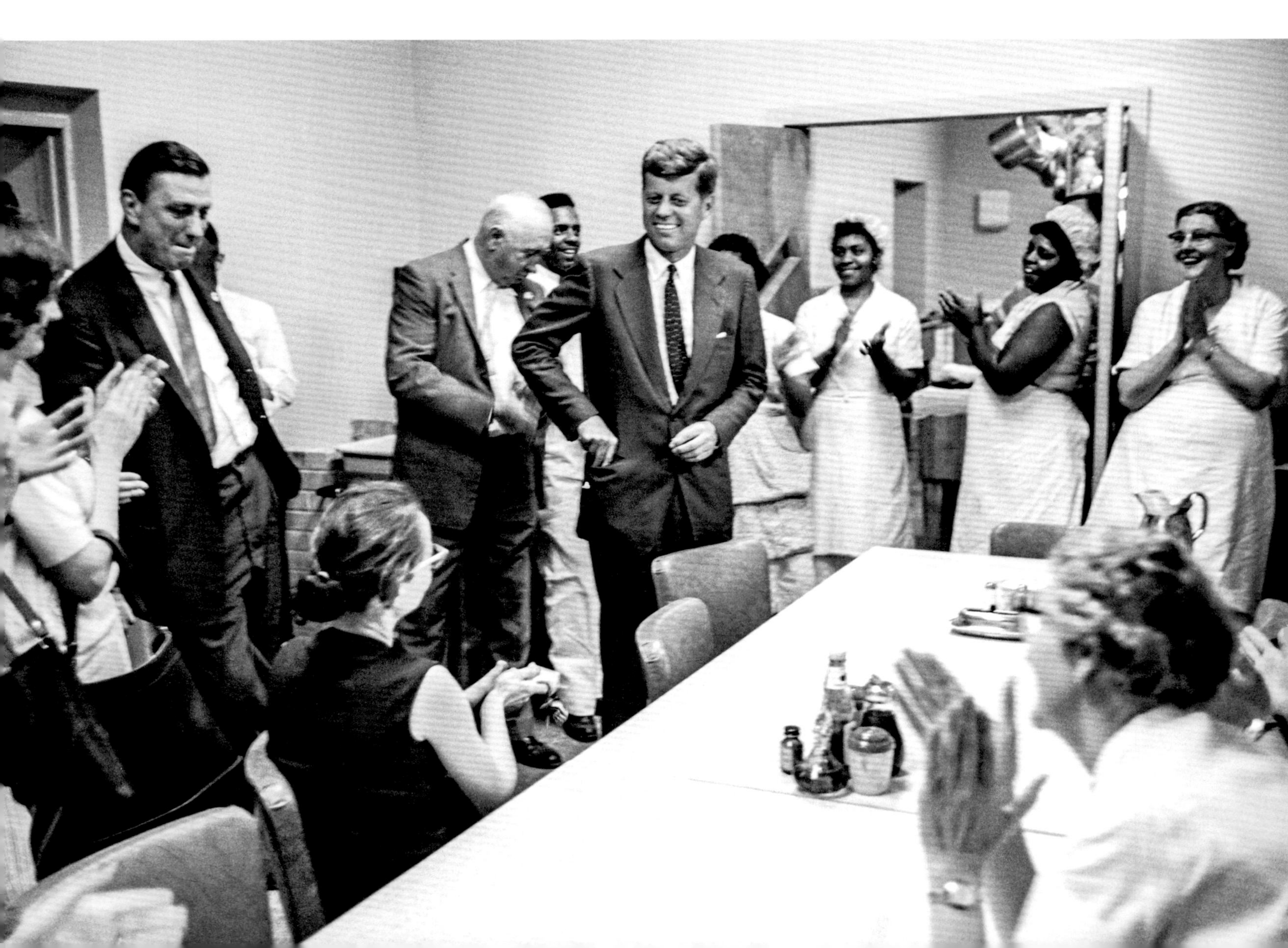

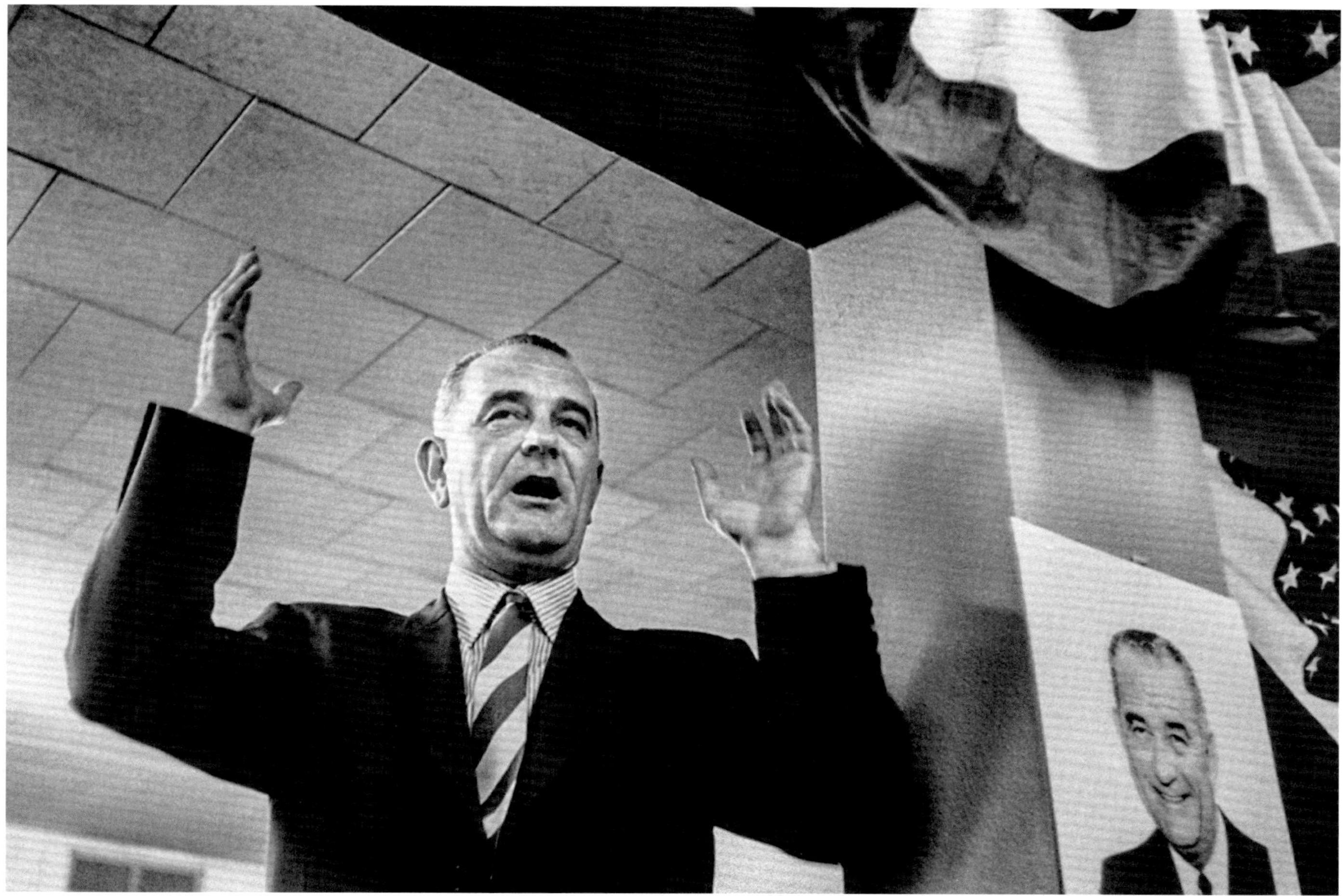

OPPOSITE *April 25, 1960.* Workers at the Wyoming General Hospital in Mullens applaud the candidate and Franklin D. Roosevelt Jr. (left), who was considered by insiders to be Kennedy's "most valuable campaigner in West Virginia." Knowing the Roosevelt name was revered throughout the state (President Roosevelt had greatly improved working conditions for coal miners), JFK's father had recruited FDR Jr. to help out. *Photo, Hank Walker*

ABOVE *April 5, 1960.* Senator Lyndon Johnson, an ambitious old-school politician with a domineering personality, worked the party bosses and did what he could to block or drain votes away from Kennedy in the primary elections. In West Virginia, a "stop Kennedy" drive was orchestrated by West Virginia Senator Robert Byrd, then a Lyndon Johnson supporter, in an attempt to derail JFK's bid. *Photo, Thomas D. McAvoy*

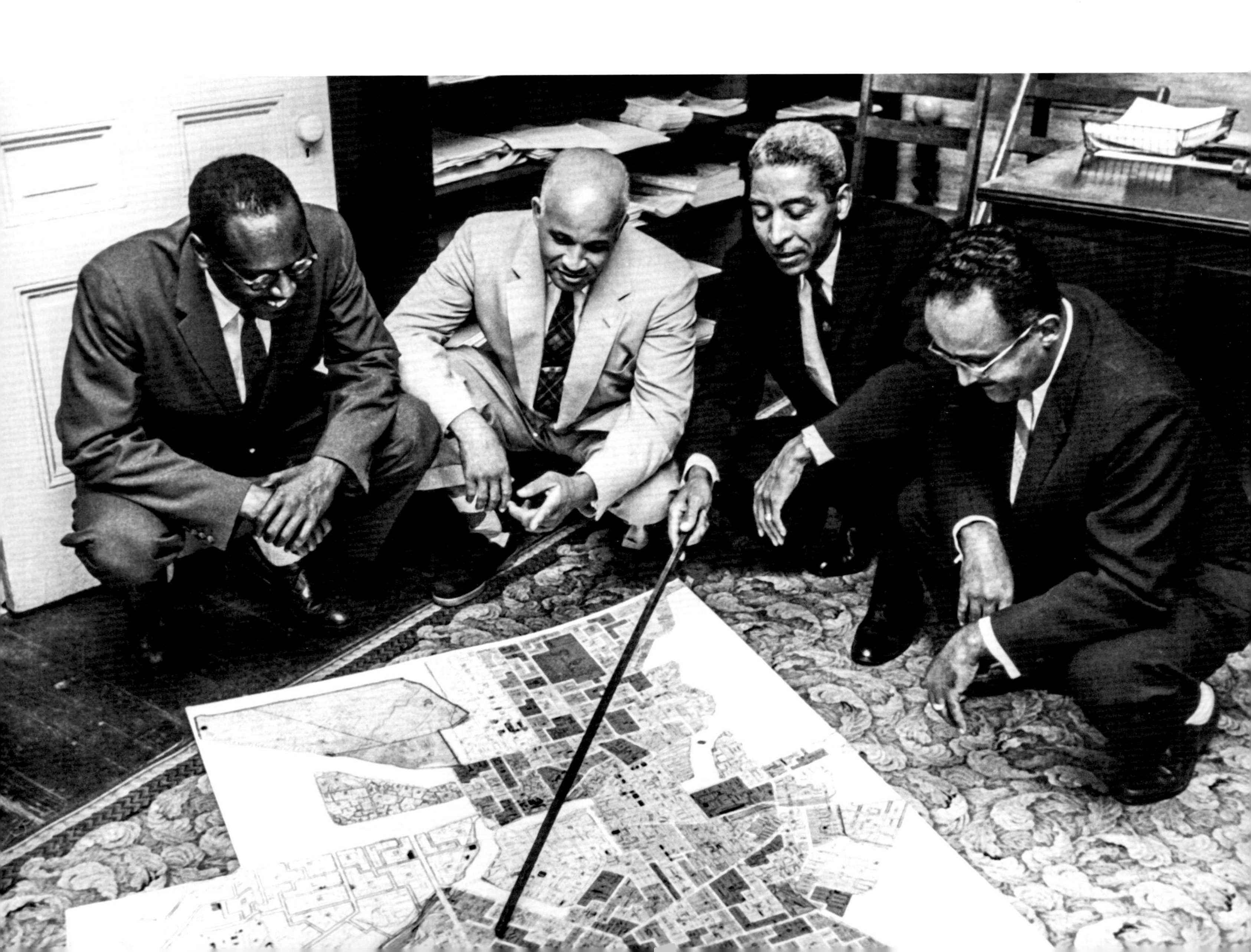

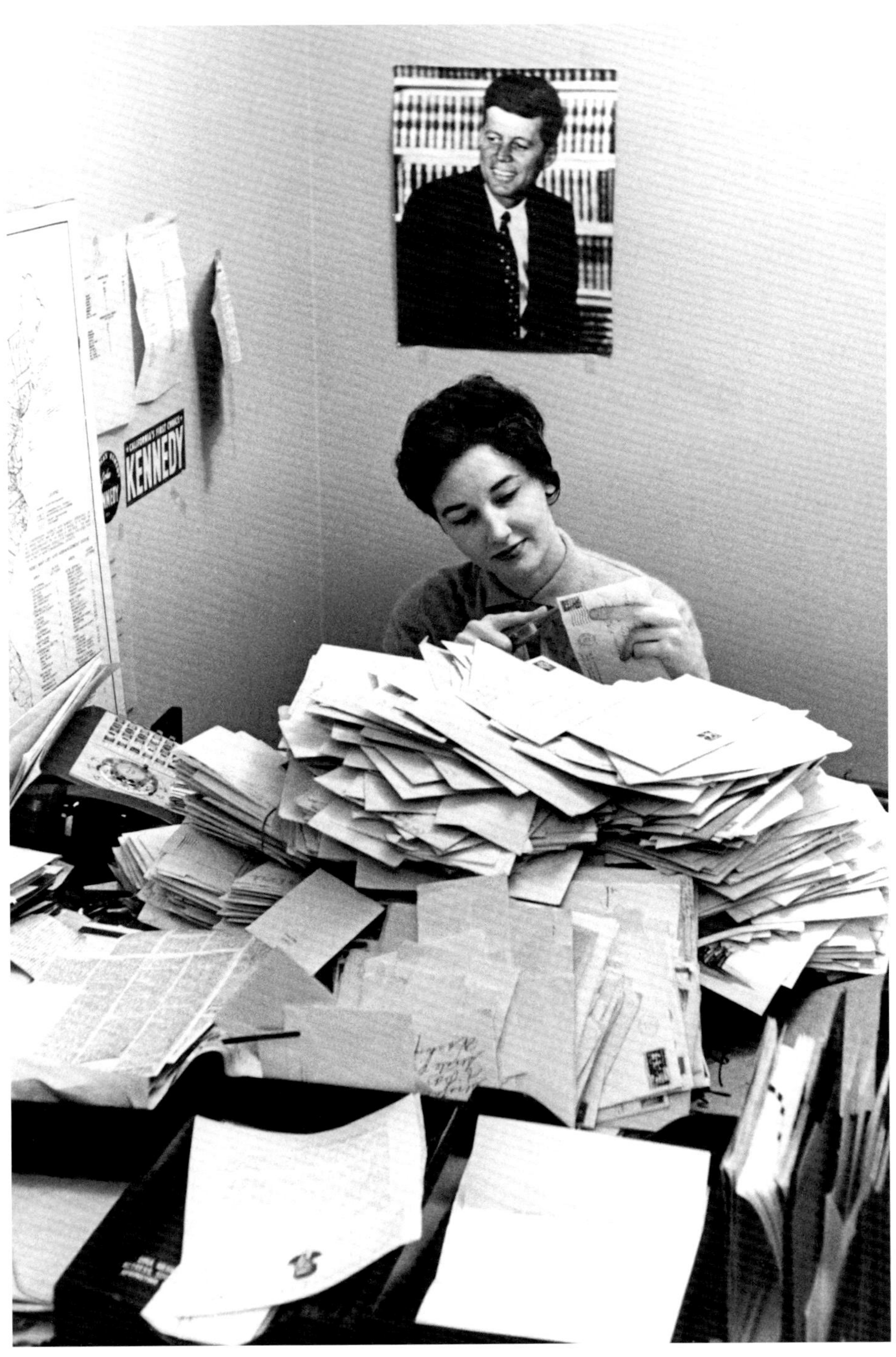

OPPOSITE *May 1960.* Leaders at the National Association for the Advancement of Colored People (NAACP) map out their plans for political action during the 1960 election season, including strategies for the July Democratic National Convention in Los Angeles. Civil rights activity and non-violent protests in the American South had begun to receive mainstream media attention and would play an important role in the presidential election. *Photo, Anonymous*

ABOVE *Spring 1960.* By late spring, once Kennedy had won several primaries, his campaign headquarters in Washington, D.C., began to be inundated with mail. Meanwhile, in Hyannis Port and Palm Beach, Florida, JFK's inner circle—anticipating a win at the July convention—had already prepared political strategy and mapped target states for the general campaign in the fall. *Photo, Anonymous*

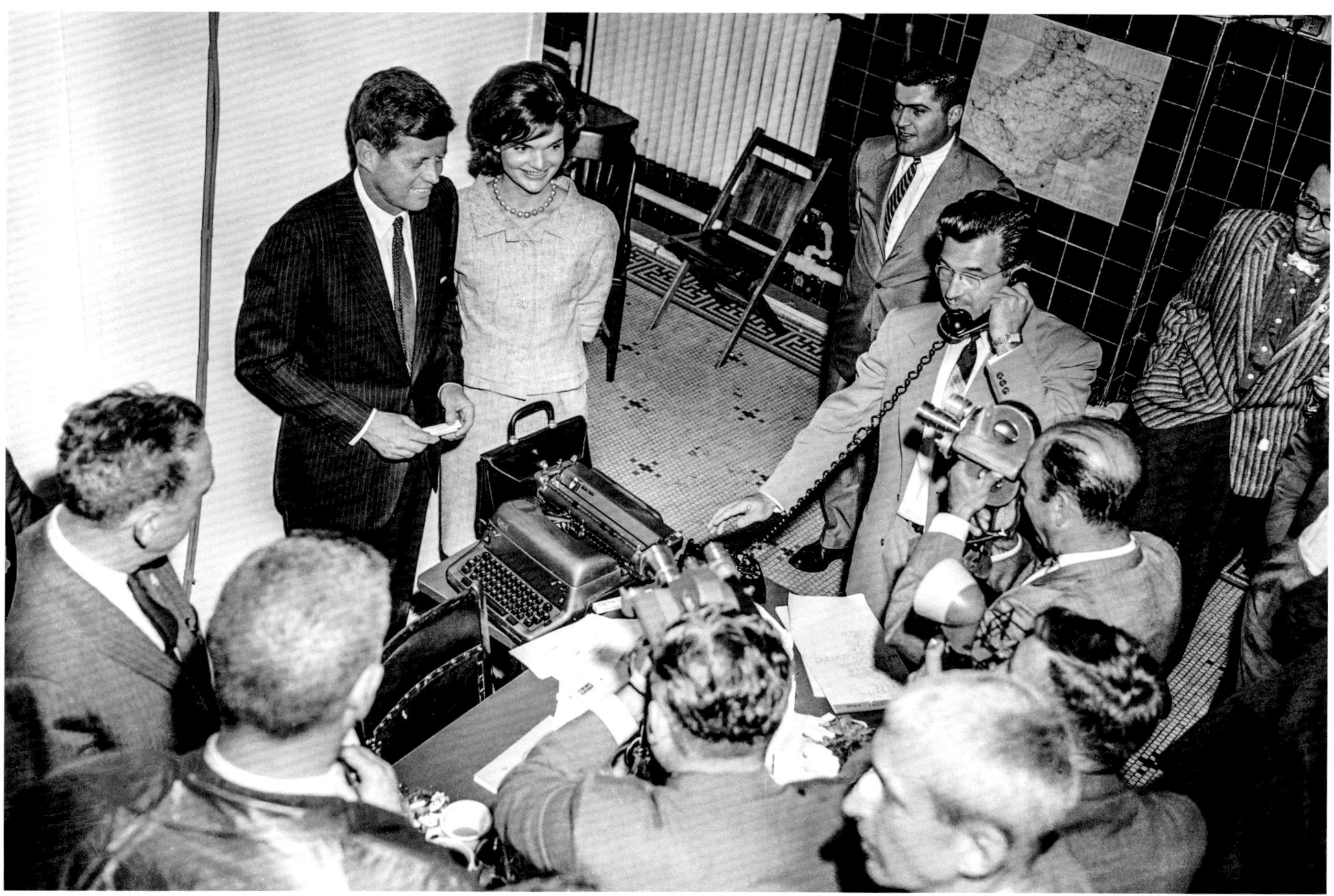

ABOVE *May 11, 1960.* The media meets Kennedy in Charleston after his decisive West Virginia win. Not optimistic about the race's outcome, JFK returned home to Washington on election night, and went to a movie with Jackie and two friends. When he learned of the results—61 percent of the vote and 48 of the 55 counties—at 11:30 P.M. that night, the Kennedys got ready to fly to Charleston early the next morning. "That spectacular performance in West Virginia wrapped up the nomination for Kennedy," writes Kenny O'Donnell. "It settled finally the one big question about his candidacy in the minds of the party leaders who controlled the delegates in the larger states—whether a Catholic could be elected." *Photo, Anonymous*

OPPOSITE *May 1960.* JFK, an obsessive reader of newspapers, uses the dim light from the Butler Aviation facility at LaGuardia Airport to catch up on the news during his primary campaign. *Photo, Ed Clark*

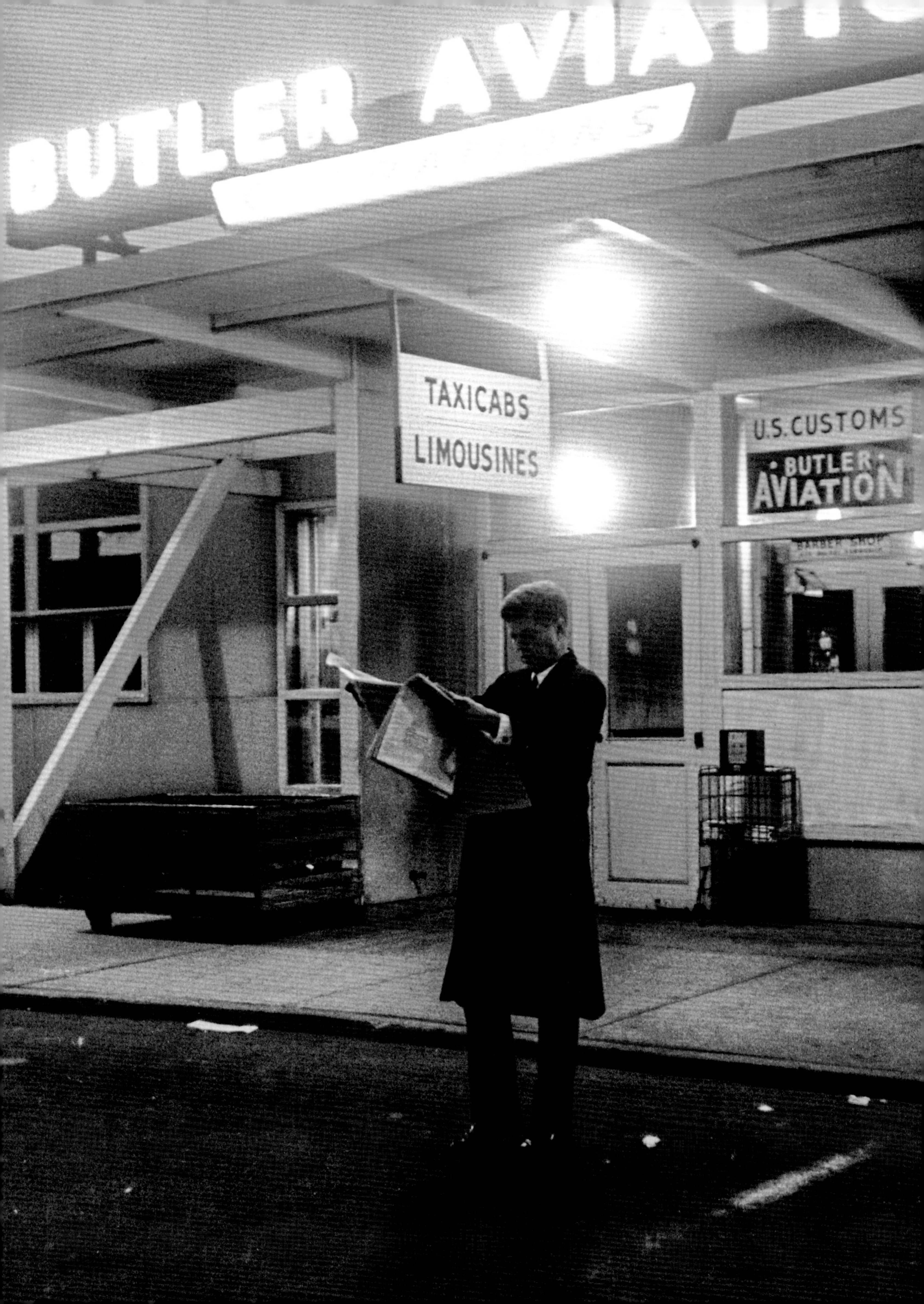

BUTLER AVIATION
TAXICABS
LIMOUSINES
U.S. CUSTOMS
BUTLER AVIATION
BARBER SHOP

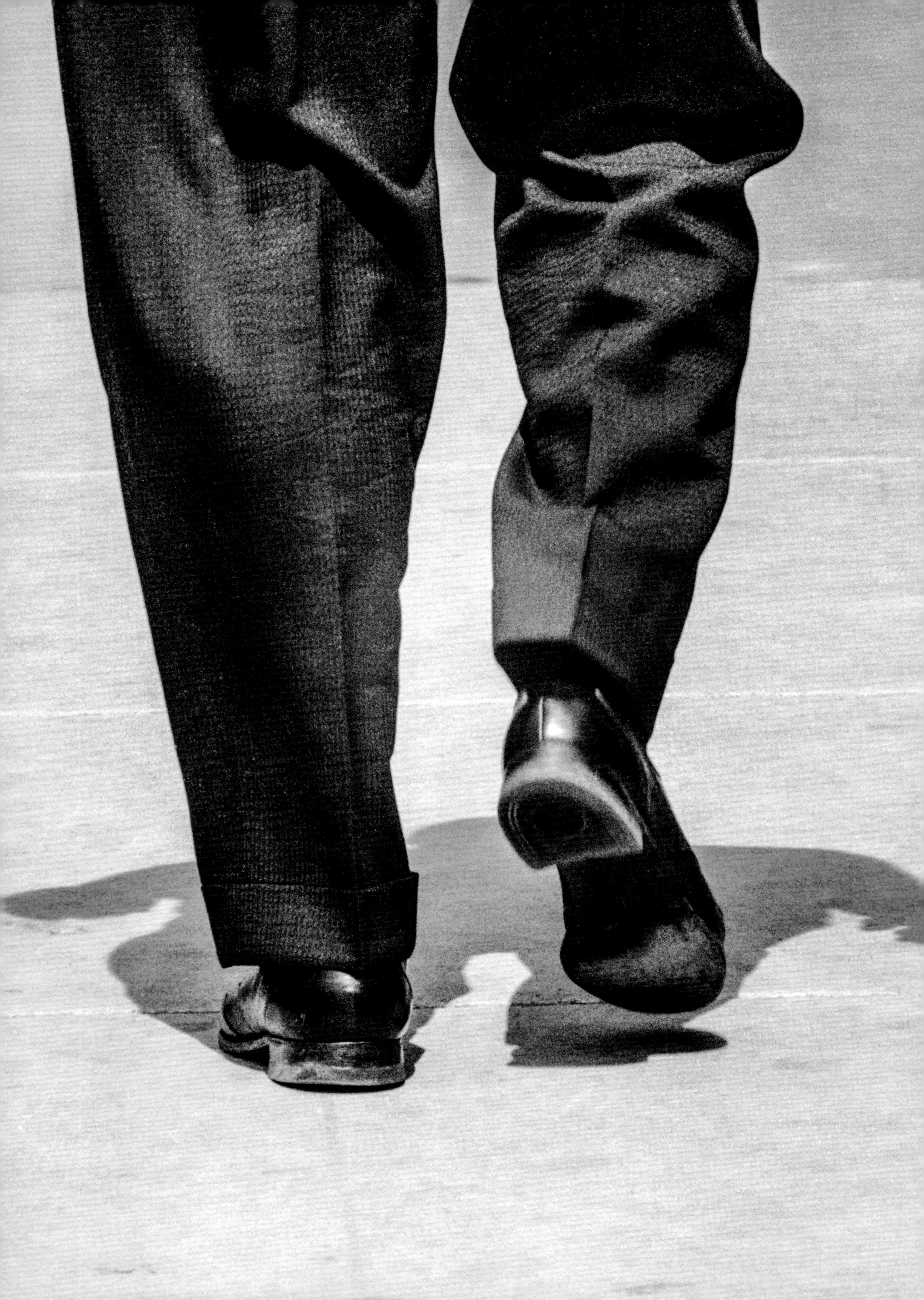

**"Of the many issues, which make up this many-sided debate —
none is more significant than the fight to secure the right to
vote to all Americans.... If men are not allowed to choose their
elected officials — then no person's place in society is secure."**

—John F. Kennedy, Milwaukee, Wisconsin, March 20, 1960

OPPOSITE *April 12, 1960.* Local foot soldiers such as
Democratic precinct captain Joe Formusa of Chicago,
Illinois, hit the pavement in cities and towns across the
U.S. and were essential to getting people to the polls.
Photo, Michael Rougier

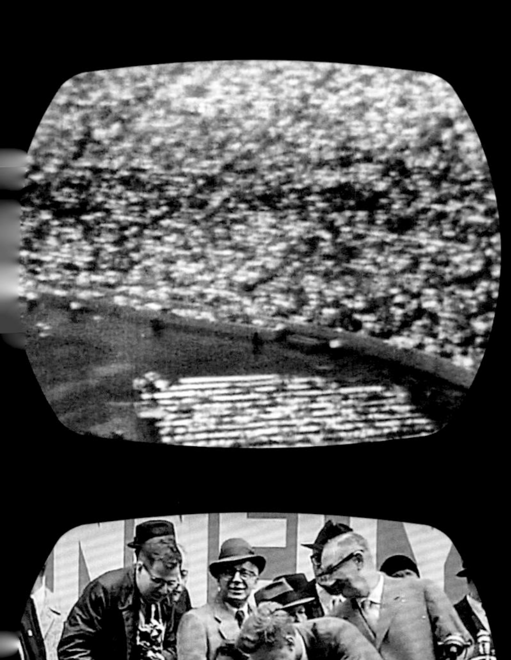
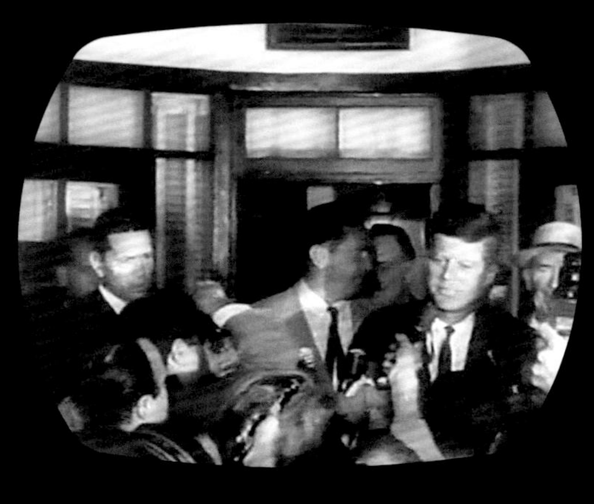
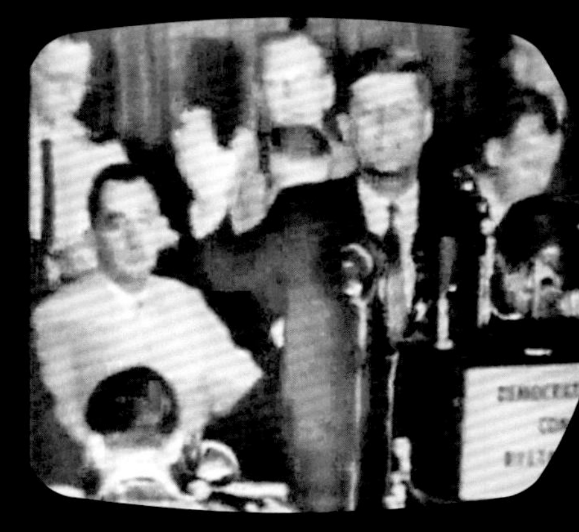
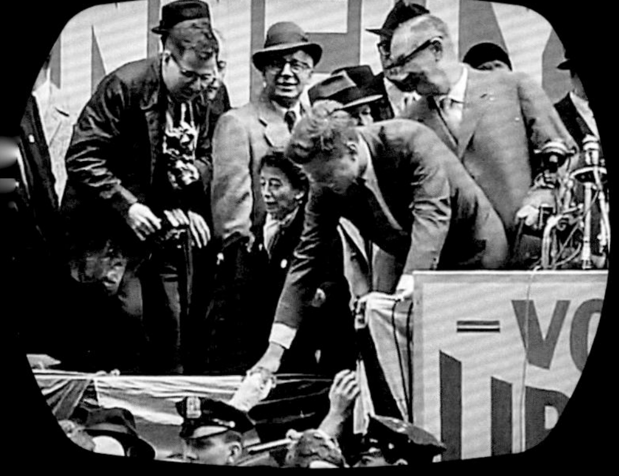
VO
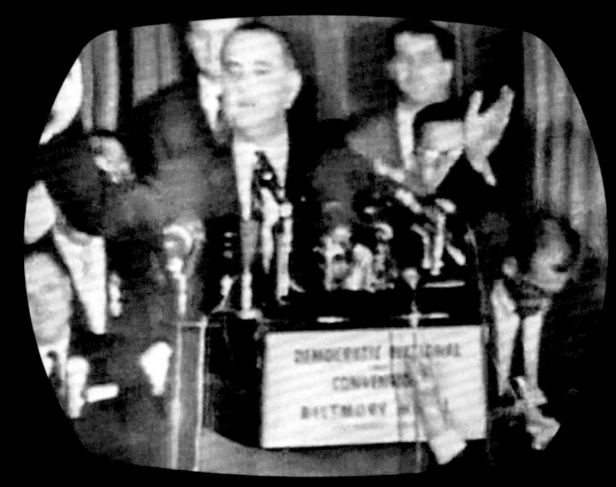
DEMOCRATIC NATIONAL
CONVENTION
BILTMORE
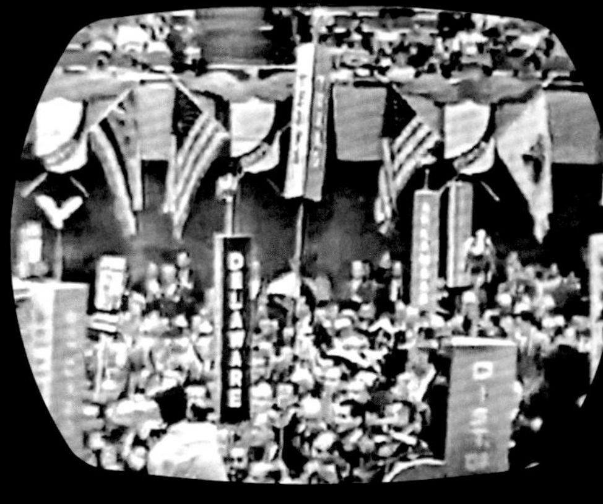
DELAWARE
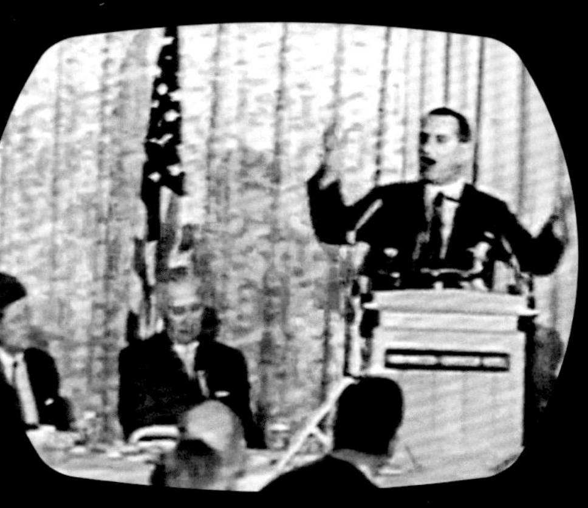
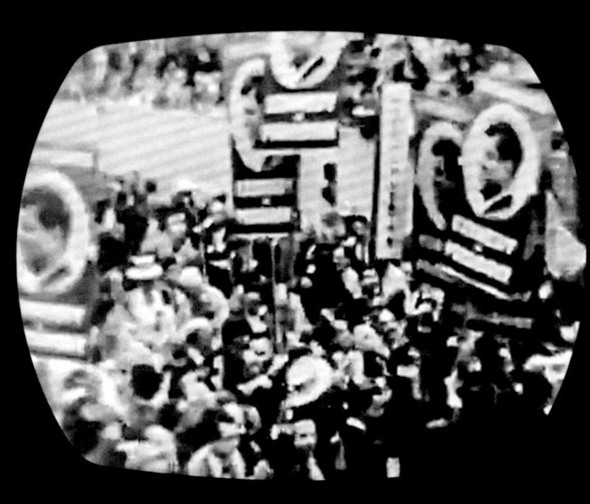
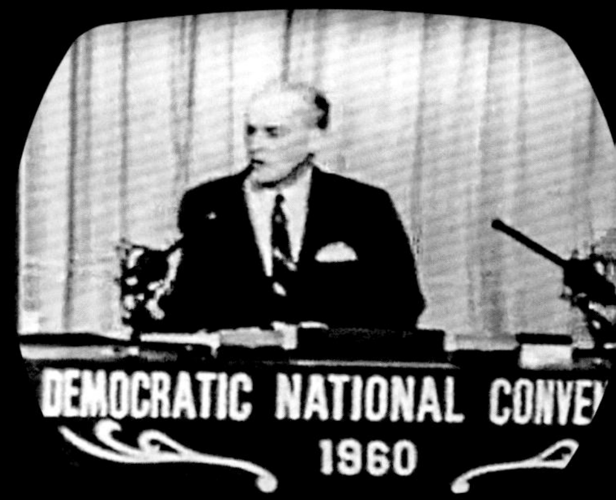
DEMOCRATIC NATIONAL CONVE
1960
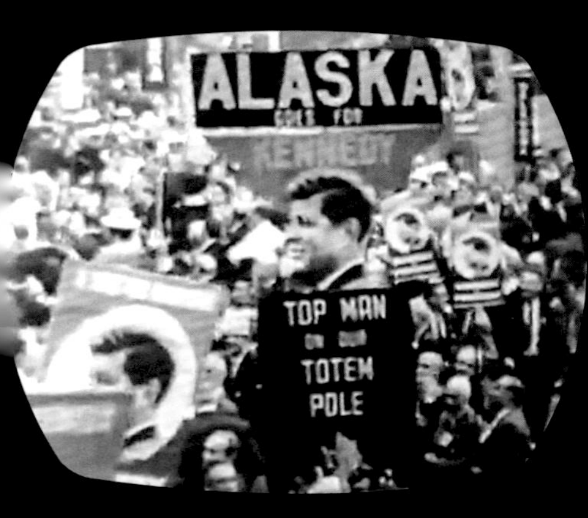
ALASKA
TOP MAN
ON OUR
TOTEM
POLE
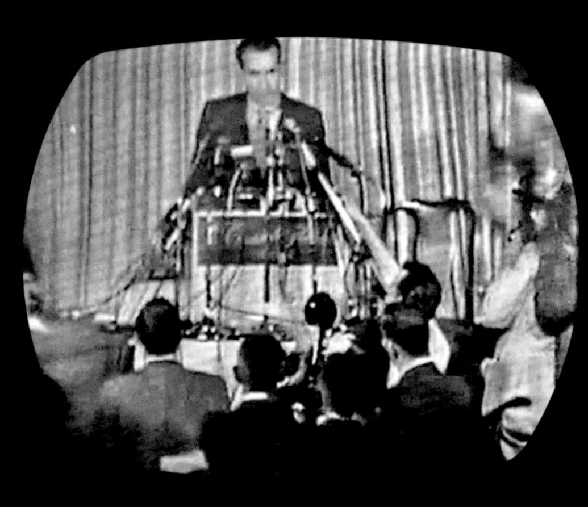
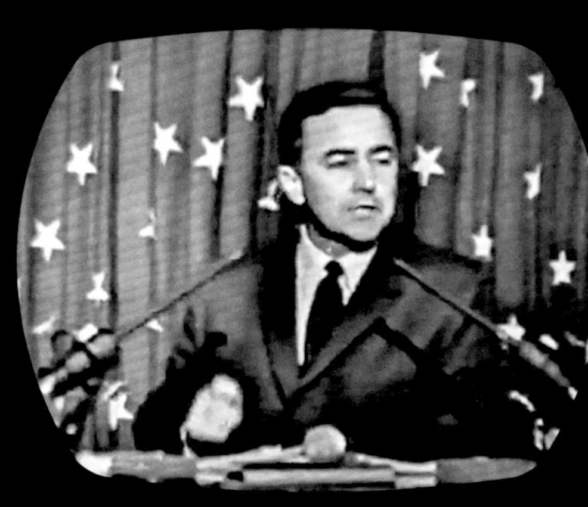
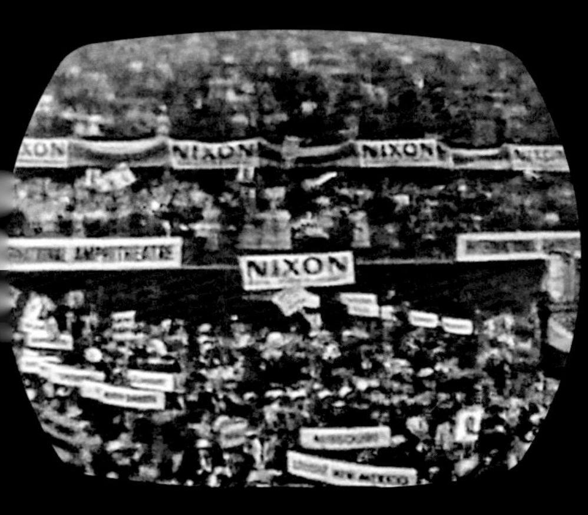
NIXON   NIXON   NIXON
NIXON
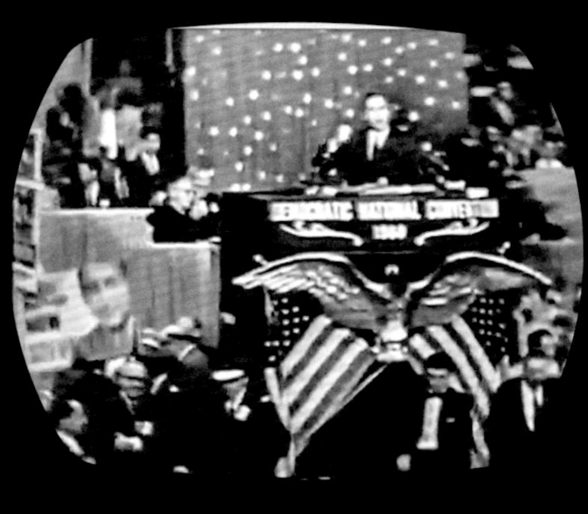
DEMOCRATIC NATIONAL CONVENTION
1960
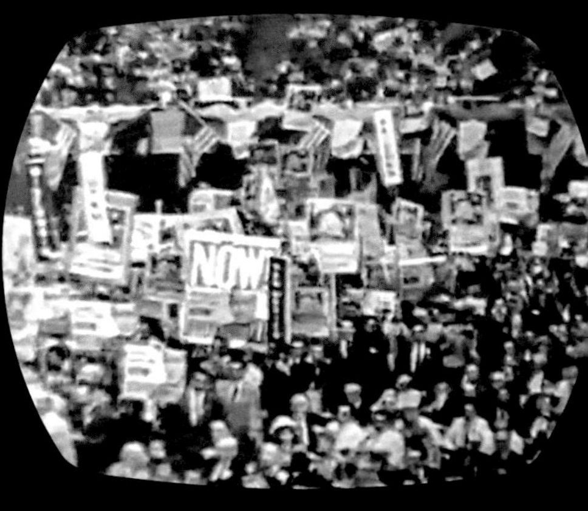
NOW

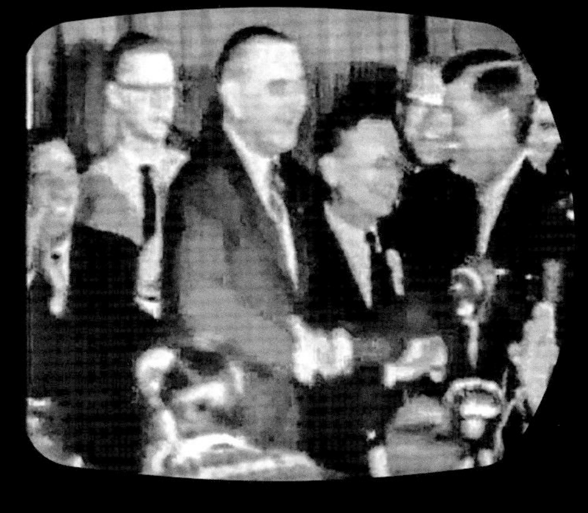
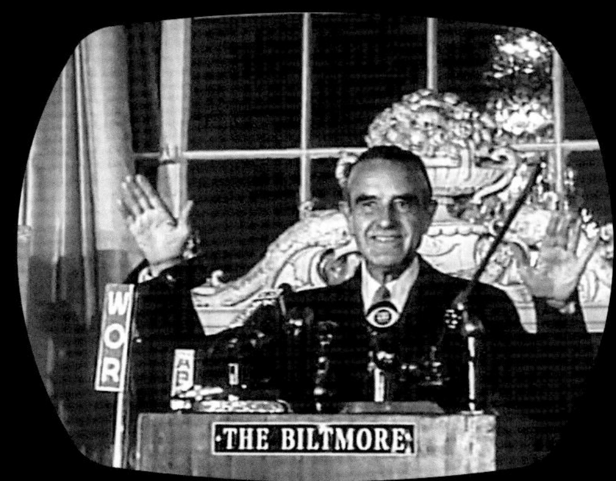

WOR
THE BILTMORE

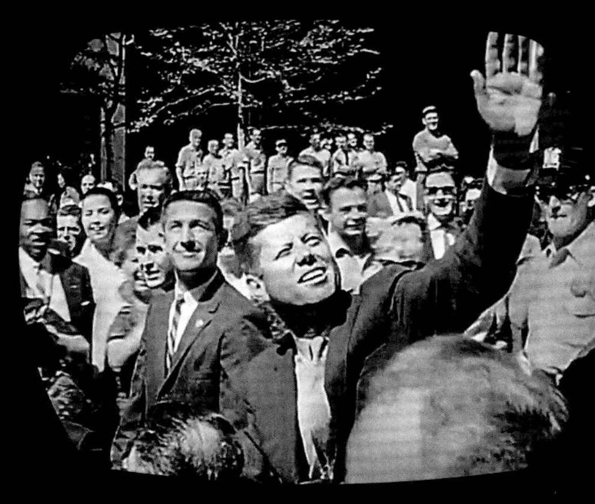
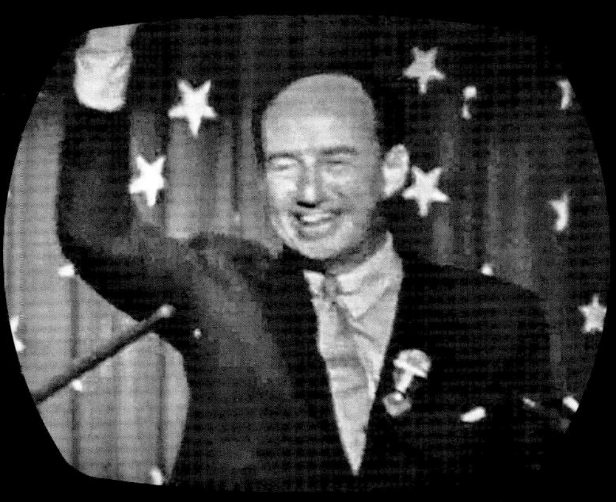
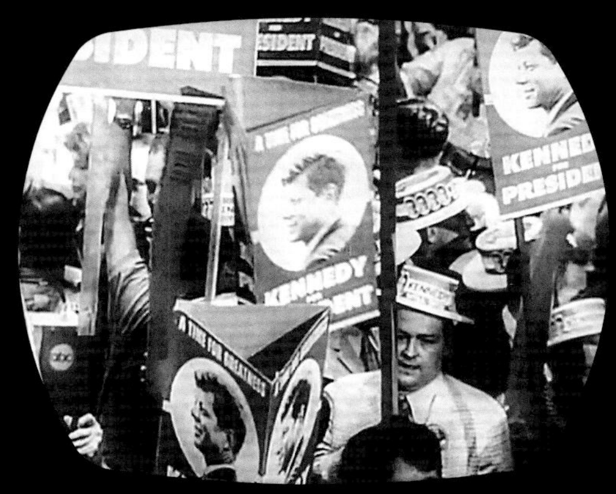

SIDENT
A TIME FOR GREATNESS
KENNEDY FOR PRESIDENT

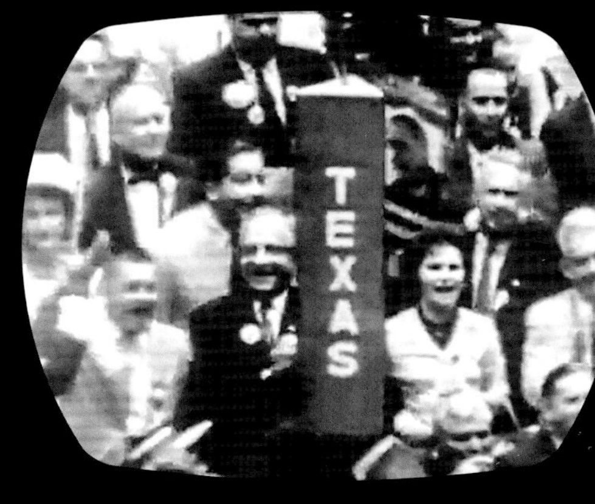

TEXAS

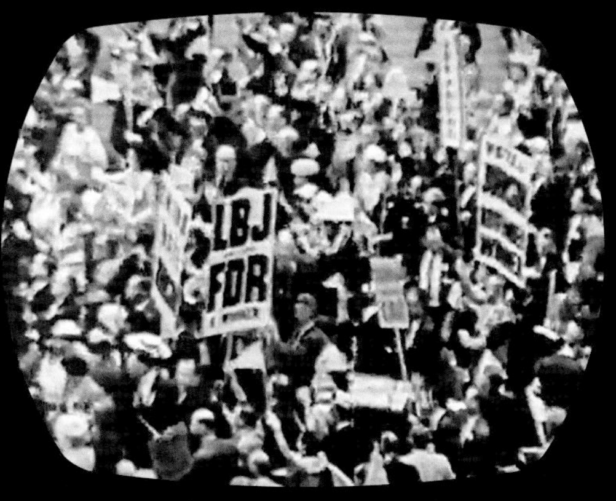

LBJ
FOR
FDR

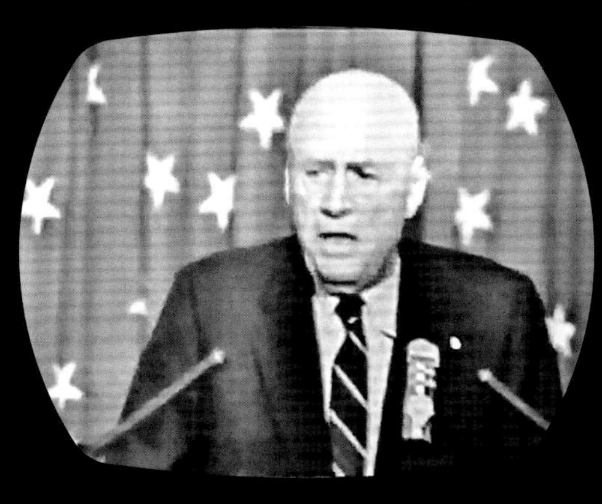
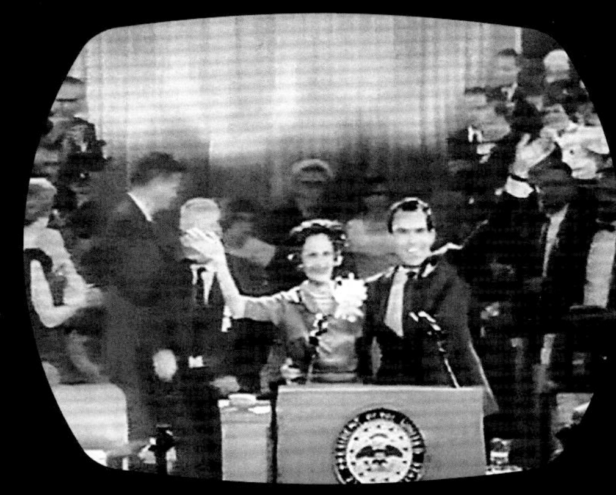
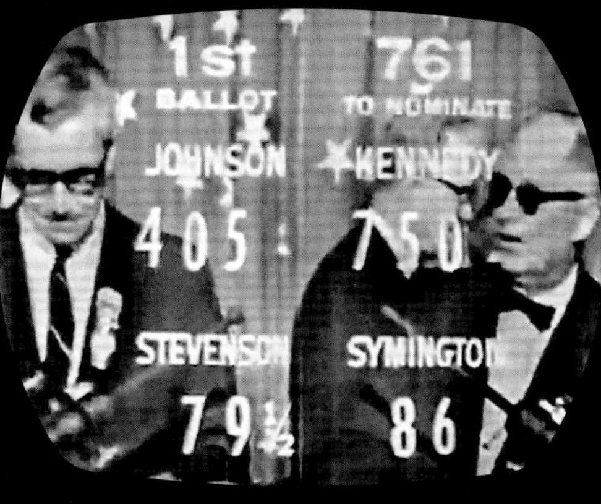

1st 761
BALLOT TO NOMINATE
JOHNSON KENNEDY
405 750
STEVENSON SYMINGTON
79½ 86

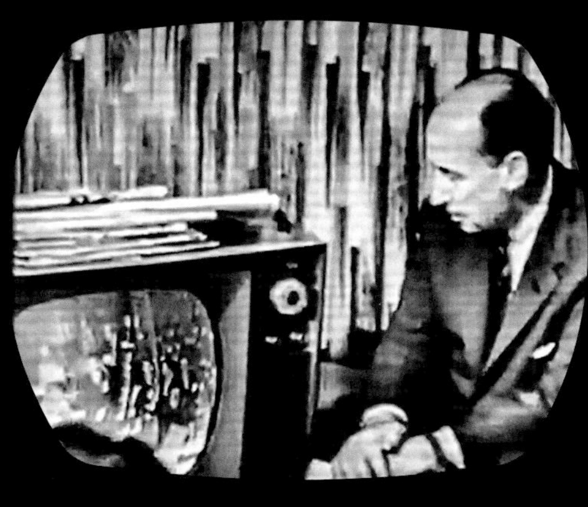
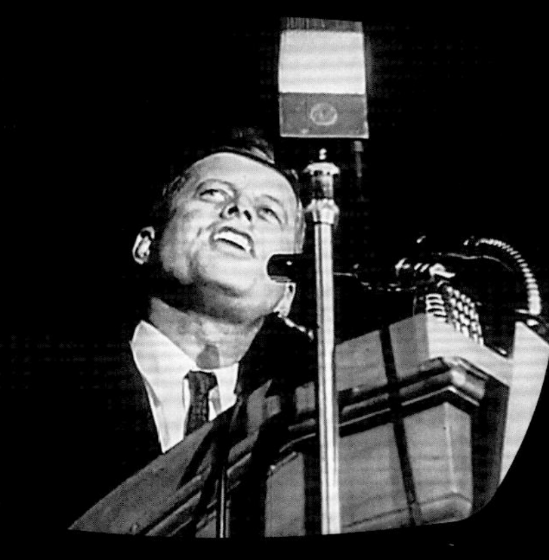
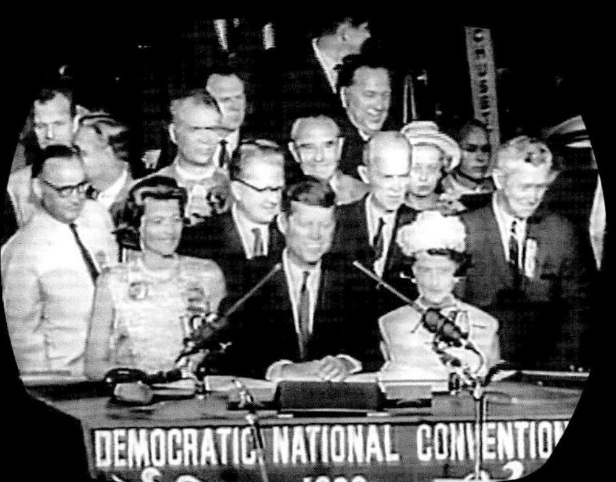

DEMOCRATIC NATIONAL CONVENTION
1960

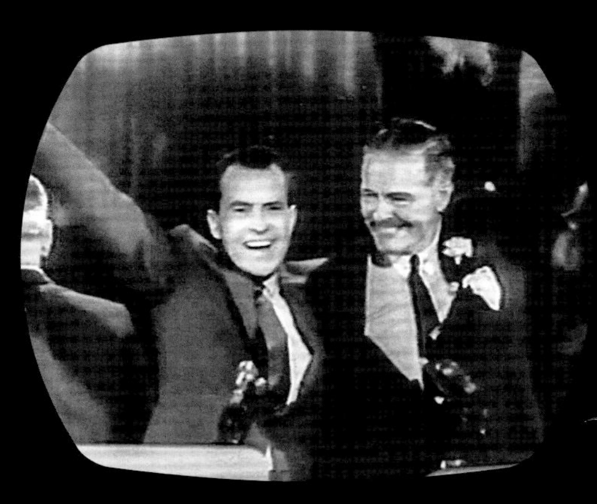
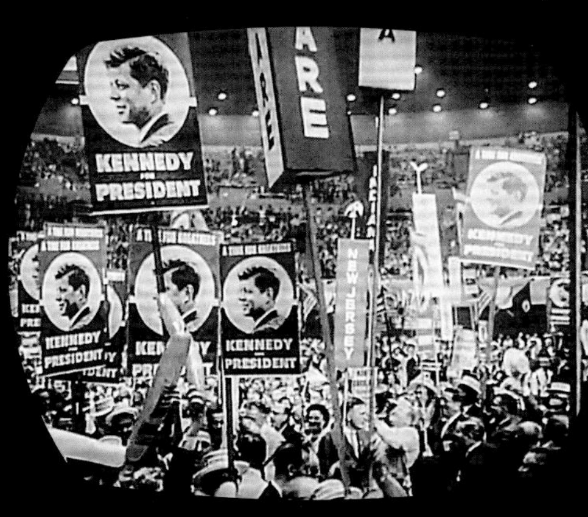

KENNEDY FOR PRESIDENT
KENNEDY PRESIDENT

THE NEW FRONTIER

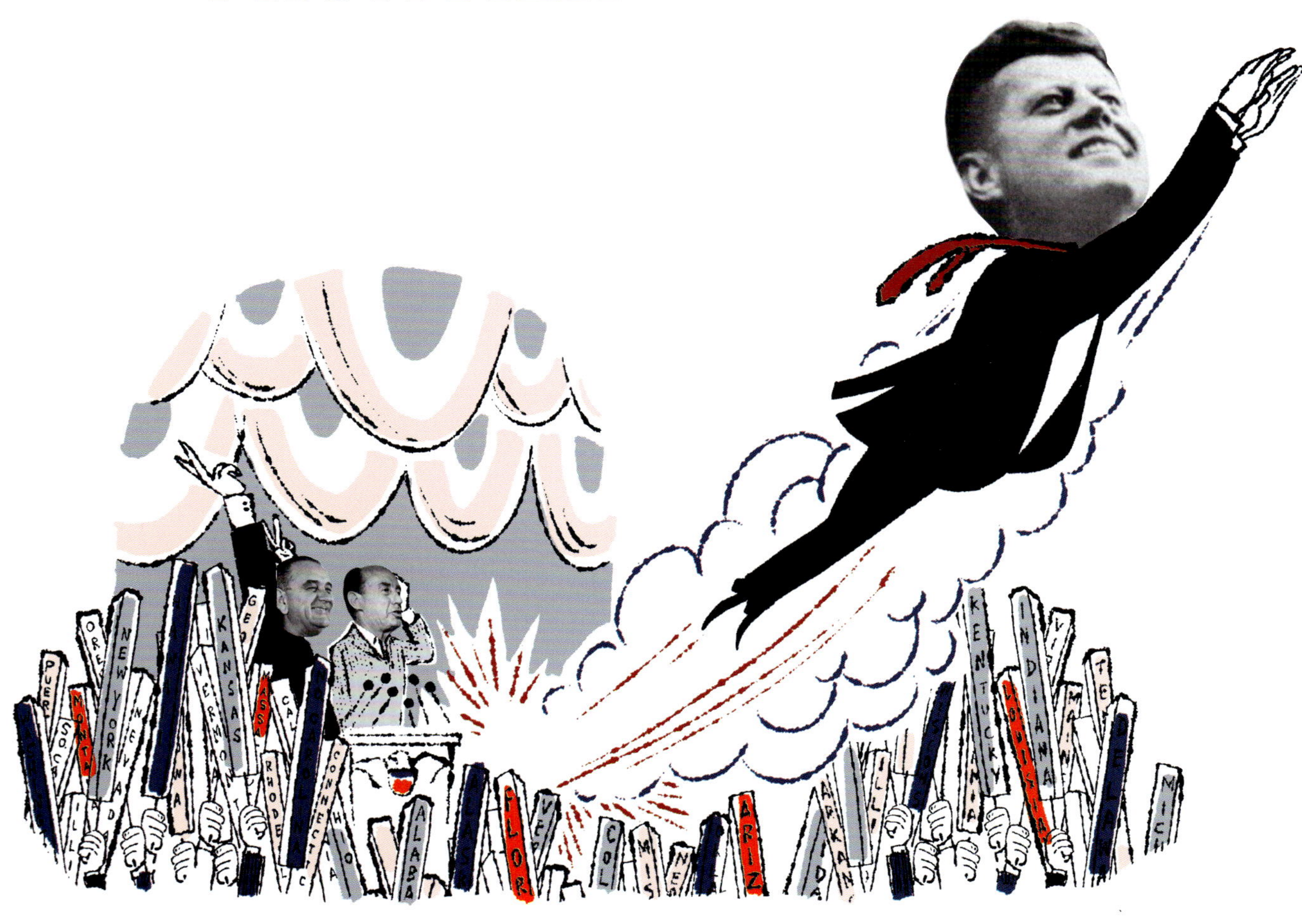

THE DEMOCRATIC NATIONAL
CONVENTION, JULY 1960

WE STAND TODAY ON THE EDGE OF A NEW FRONTIER —

the frontier of the 1960s — a frontier of unknown opportunities and perils — a frontier of unfulfilled hopes and threats. [...]

There may be those who wish to hear more — more promises to this group or that — more harsh rhetoric about the men in the Kremlin — more assurances of a golden future, where taxes are always low and subsidies ever high. But my promises are in the platform you have adopted — our ends will not be won by rhetoric and we can have faith in the future only if we have faith in ourselves.

For the harsh facts of the matter are that we stand on this frontier at a turning point in history. We must prove all over again whether this nation — or any nation so conceived — can long endure — whether our society — with its freedom of choice, its breadth of opportunity, its range of alternatives — can compete with the single-minded advance of the Communist system.

Can a nation organized and governed such as ours endure? That is the real question. Have we the nerve and the will? Can we carry through in an age where we will witness not only new breakthroughs in weapons of destruction — but also a race for mastery of the sky and the rain, the ocean and the tides, the far side of space and the inside of men's minds?

Are we up to the task — are we equal to the challenge? Are we willing to match the Russian sacrifice of the present for the future — or must we sacrifice our future in order to enjoy the present?

That is the question of the New Frontier. That is the choice our nation must make — a choice that lies not merely between two men or two parties, but between the public interest and private comfort — between national greatness and national decline — between the fresh air of progress and the stale, dank atmosphere of "normalcy" — between determined dedication and creeping mediocrity.

—John F. Kennedy, Acceptance Speech, Democratic National Convention,
   Los Angeles, California, July 15, 1960

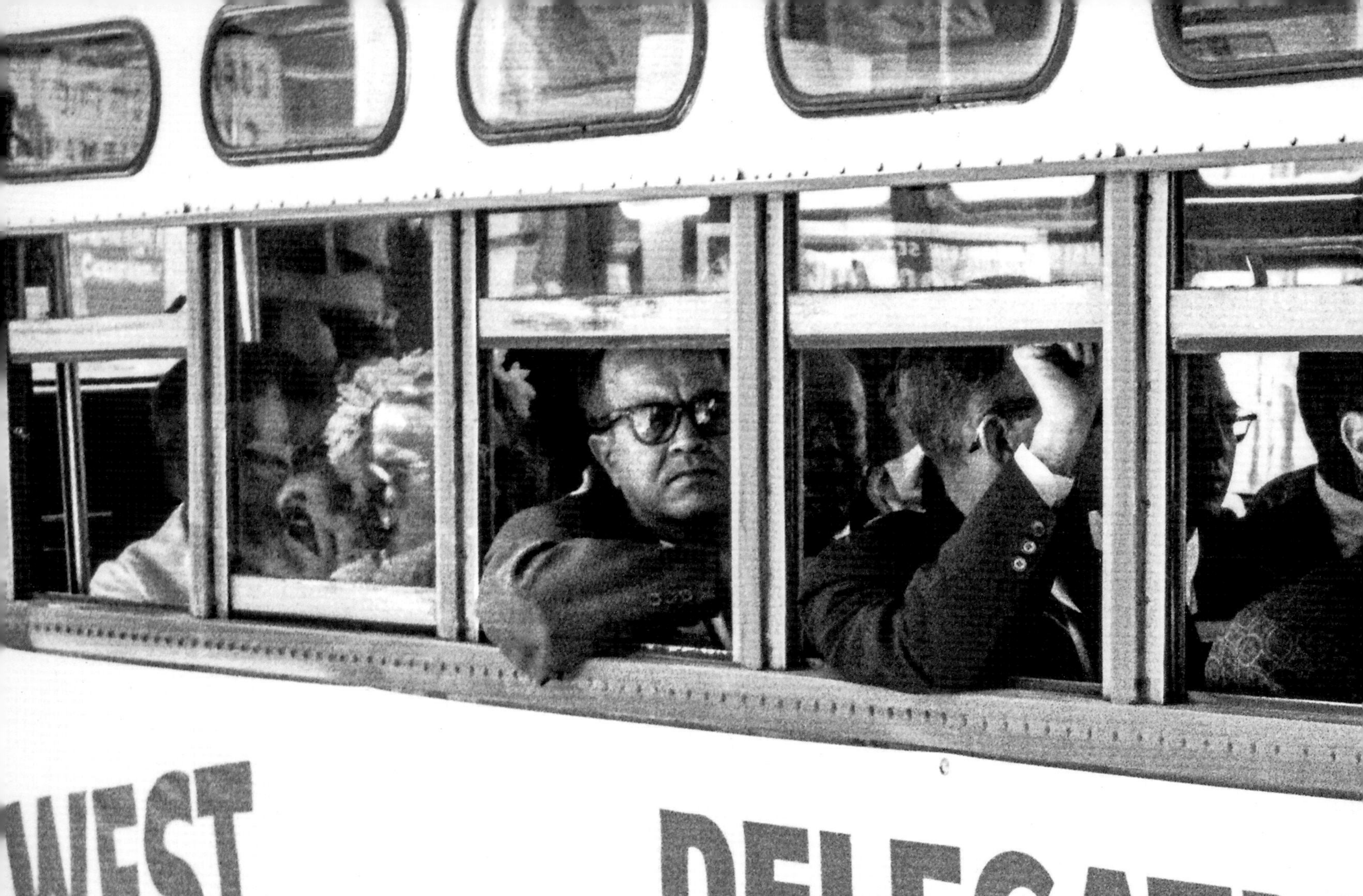

WEST
VIRGINIA
DELEGATIO
DEMOCRA
National Conver

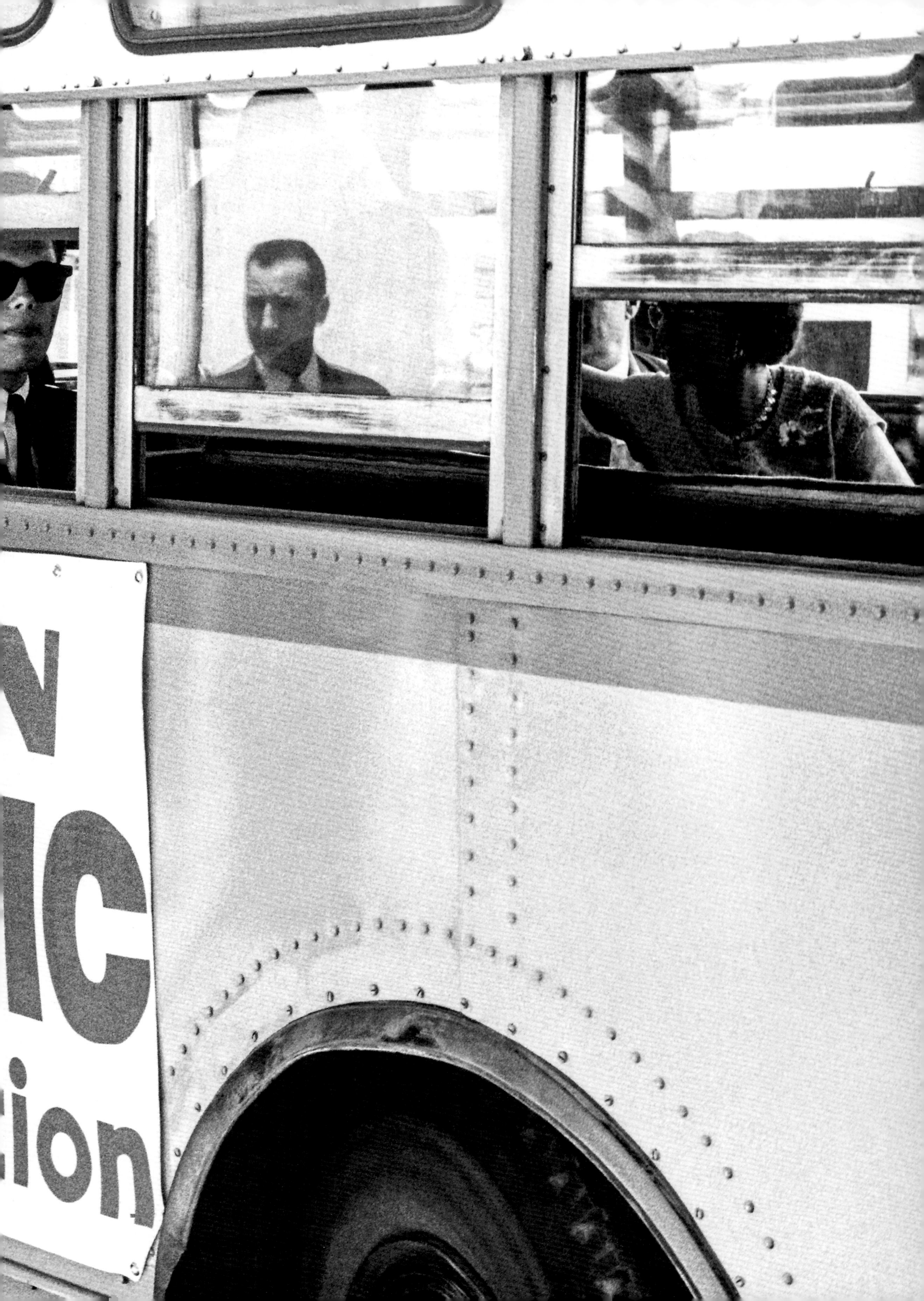

NIC
tion

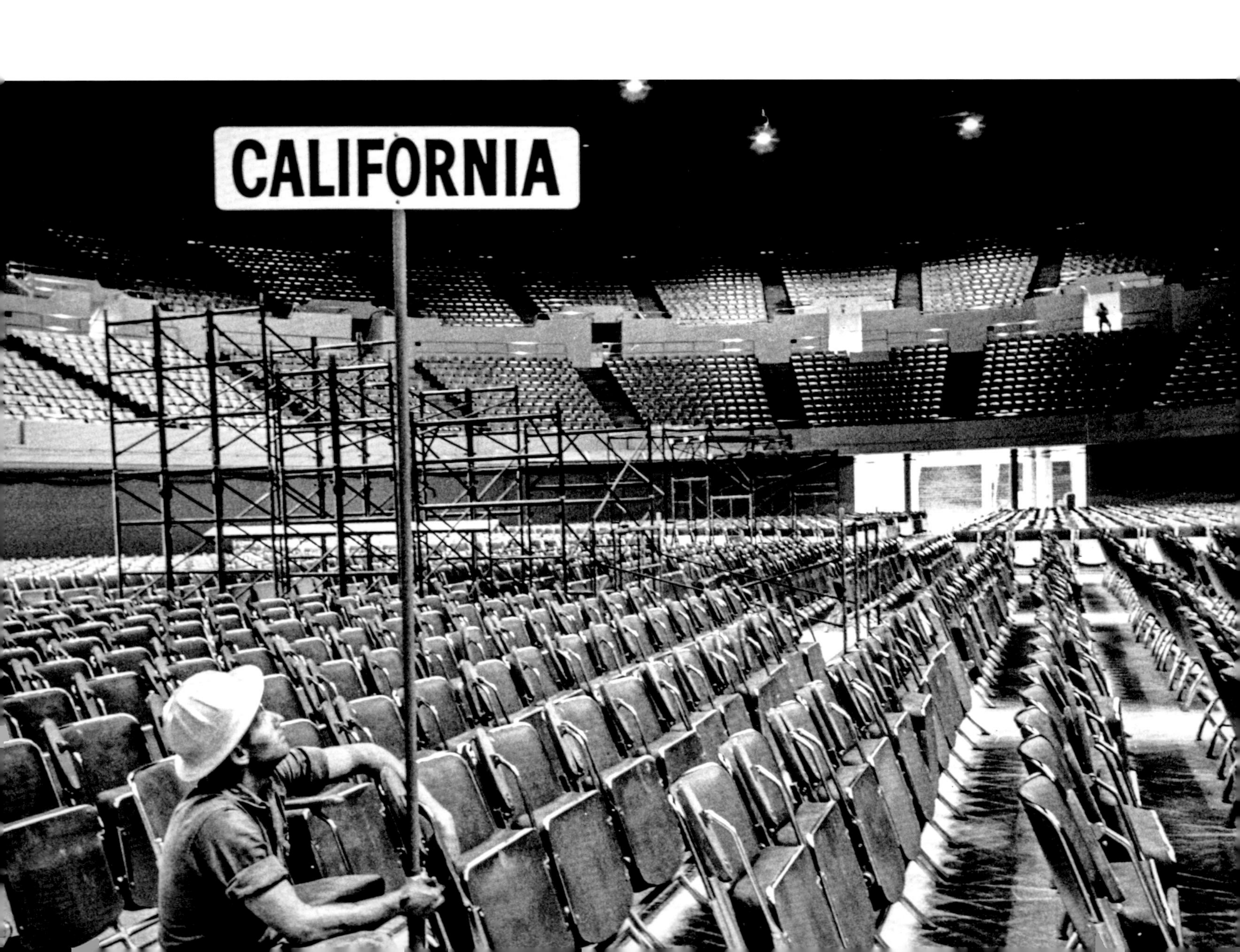

CALIFORNIA

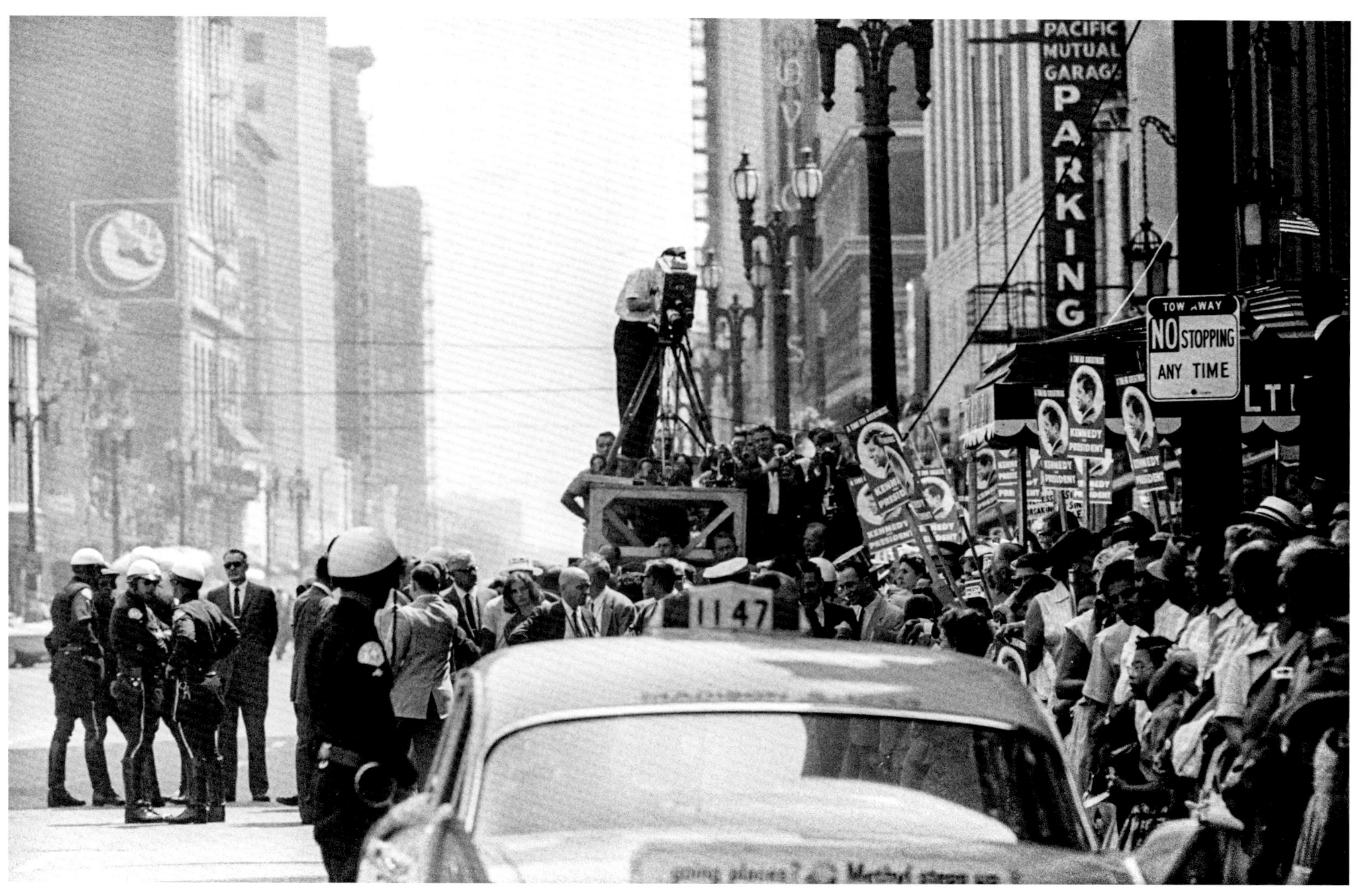

PREVIOUS SPREAD *July 1960.* The West Virginia delegation heads out for the convention, opening on Monday, July 11. *Photo, Anonymous*

OPPOSITE *June 29, 1960.* A workman tapes the first delegation placard in place at the cavernous Los Angeles Memorial Sports Arena, located adjacent to the Los Angeles Memorial Coliseum in Exposition Park. The Sports Arena opened on July 4, 1959, but it was the Democratic National Convention that really put the arena on the national stage. "That convention was really hot," said California delegate and former city council member Rosalind Wyman. "It was the next best thing to getting the Olympics." *Photo, Anonymous*

ABOVE *July 9, 1960.* Members of the media, arriving delegates, street campaigners, and city police stake out their positions near Pershing Square in downtown Los Angeles ahead of the Democratic National Convention. *Photo, Garry Winogrand*

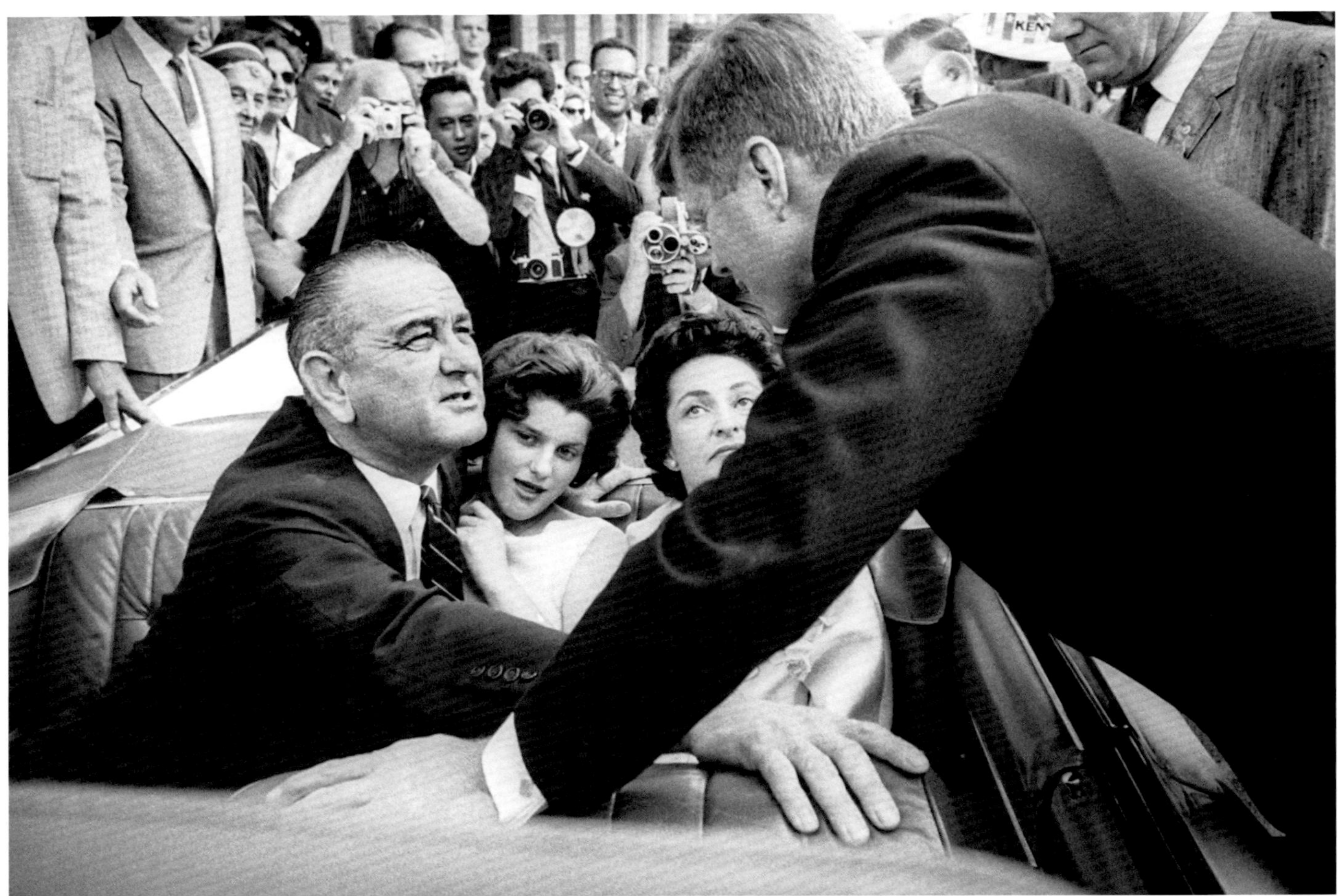

ABOVE *ca. July 9–15, 1960.* Kennedy greets Senator Lyndon Johnson, with his daughter Lynda and wife, Lady Bird. Harsh criticism and cutthroat tactics were part of LBJ's campaign: Just prior to the opening of the DNC, Johnson aides at a press conference charged that Kennedy had Addison's disease and couldn't survive without cortisone treatments. Kennedy's people, including Bobby, had falsely denied JFK's condition, and his doctors had earlier issued a carefully worded statement that also skirted the truth. *Photo, Paul Schutzer*

OPPOSITE *ca. July 9–13, 1960.* Kennedy supporters parade outside the Knickerbocker Hotel in Hollywood. With an estimated 45,000 to 50,000 delegates flooding the city, hotels were filled far beyond the downtown area. The largest demonstrations would be reserved for the main floor of the convention proceedings during the heart of the nomination process, but they also pervaded the galleries, hotel lobbies, and venues all across the city with the purpose of pushing their candidate to the fore. *Photo, Hank Walker*

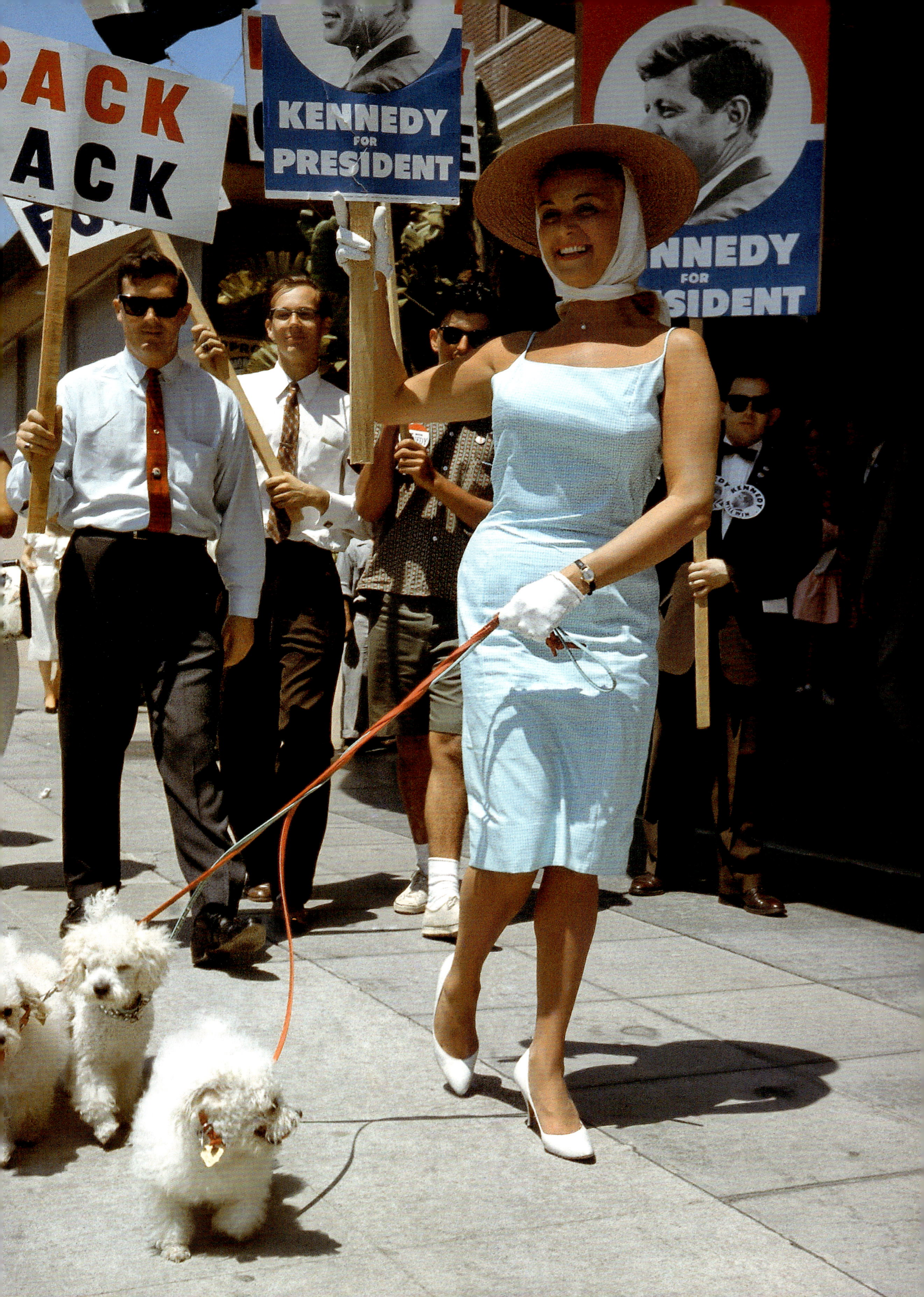
ACK
ACK
KENNEDY
FOR
PRESIDENT
KENNEDY
FOR
PRESIDENT

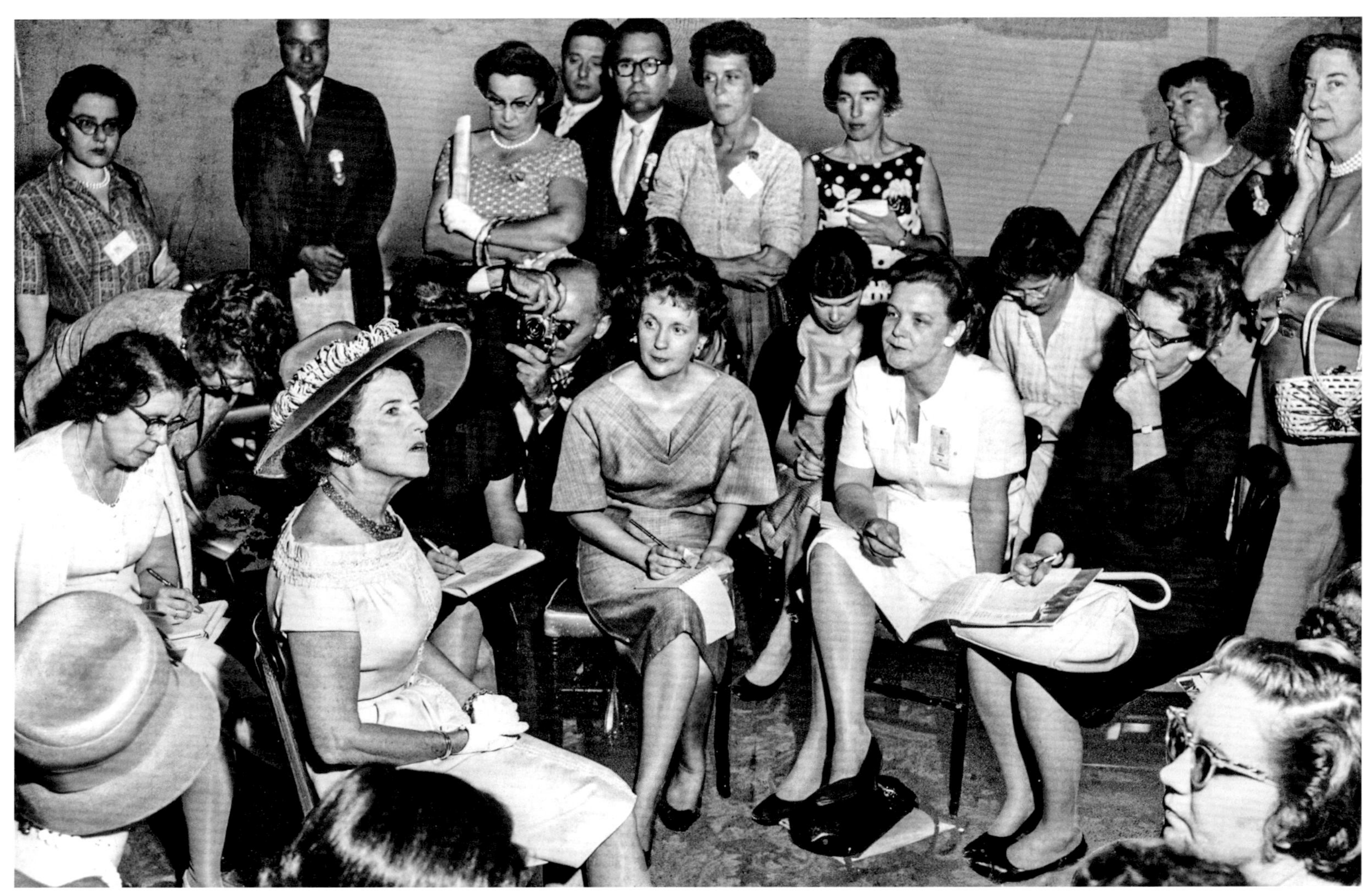

 July 12, 1960. JFK's mother, Rose Kennedy, talks to newspaper writers at the Biltmore Hotel in downtown Los Angeles. Earlier in the week, Rose and other Kennedy women had hosted a welcome reception for delegates. Many members of the family had come to L. A. for the DNC, including patriarch Joseph P. Kennedy, who rented a Beverly Hills villa from film star Marion Davies. Jackie Kennedy, then several months pregnant, stayed in Massachusetts. *Photo, Nelson Tiffany*

OPPOSITE *July 11, 1960.* Reverend Maurice A. Dawkins, a Los Angeles–based pastor who would become a national civil rights leader, engages in a 24-hour period of prayer and fasting outside the Sports Arena. As Dawkins and others protested outside, inside Kennedy's team helped push through and adopt a strong civil rights platform for the party that pledged to utilize Federal powers to end all forms of discrimination. The day before, JFK had addressed the NAACP, and though he was coolly received at first (some of the audience booed) Kennedy gained support when he vowed to end segregation. *Photo, Dick Oliver*

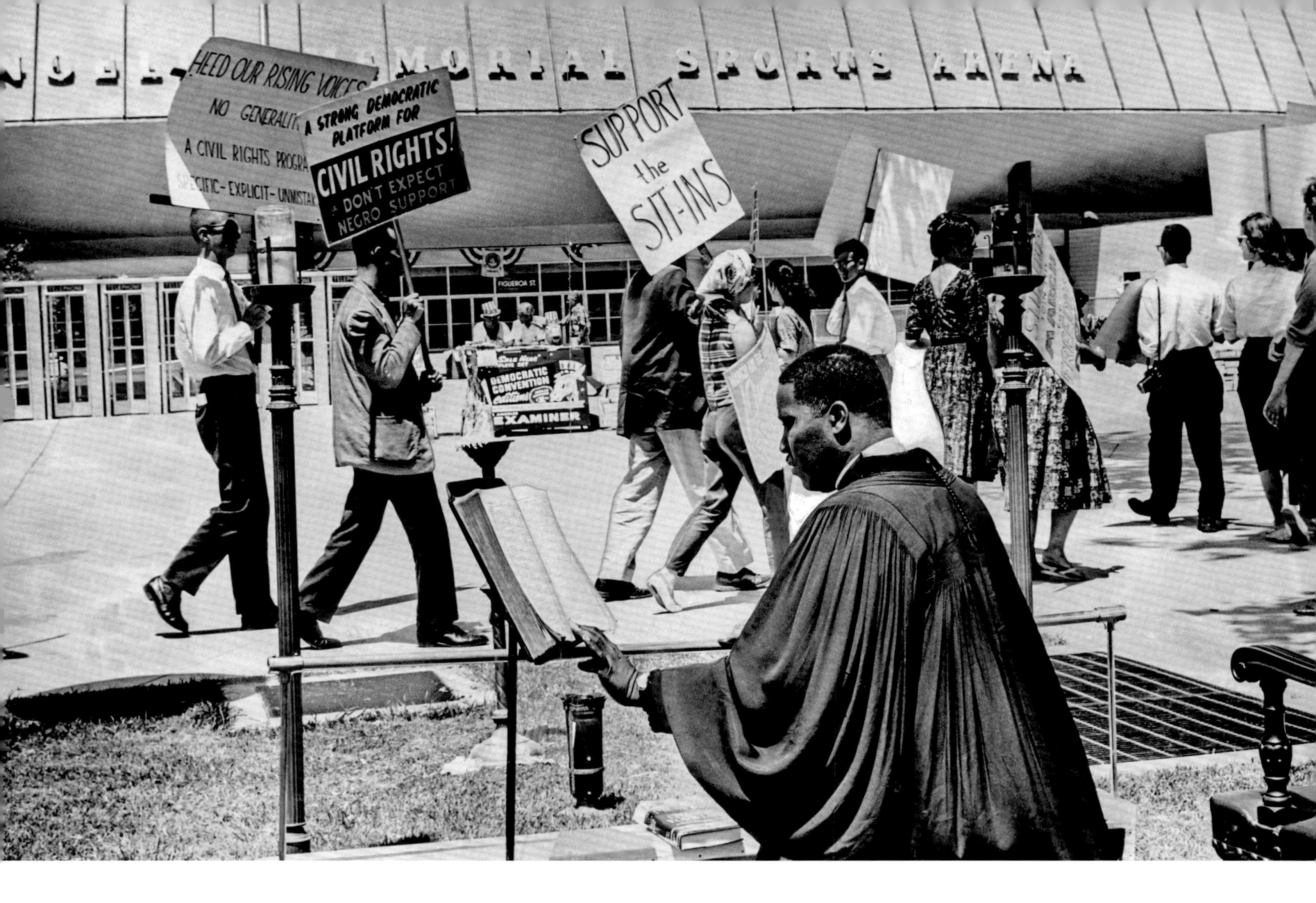
HEED OUR RISING VOICES
NO GENERALIT...
A CIVIL RIGHTS PROGRA
SPECIFIC - EXPLICIT - UNMISTAK
A STRONG DEMOCRATIC
PLATFORM FOR
CIVIL RIGHTS!
DON'T EXPECT
NEGRO SUPPORT
SUPPORT
the
SIT-INS
DEMOCRATIC
CONVENTION
Edition
EXAMINER
FIGUEROA ST
MORIAL SPORTS ARENA

**"My friends — if you are sober-minded enough to believe —
then — to the extent that these tasks require the support, the
guidance and the leadership of the American Presidency —
I am bold enough to try."**

—John F. Kennedy, Democratic National Committee Dinner,
   Los Angeles, California, July 10, 1960

OPPOSITE *July 10, 1960.* On the evening before the
convention's formal opening, Kennedy attended a
fund-raiser for the Democratic National Committee at
the Beverly Hilton. Though Frank Sinatra and Sammy
Davis Jr., were on hand to entertain guests, Kennedy
looks as though his mind is elsewhere—as if he's counting
votes and reviewing his convention week strategy
rather than enjoying the show. *Photo, Elliott Erwitt*

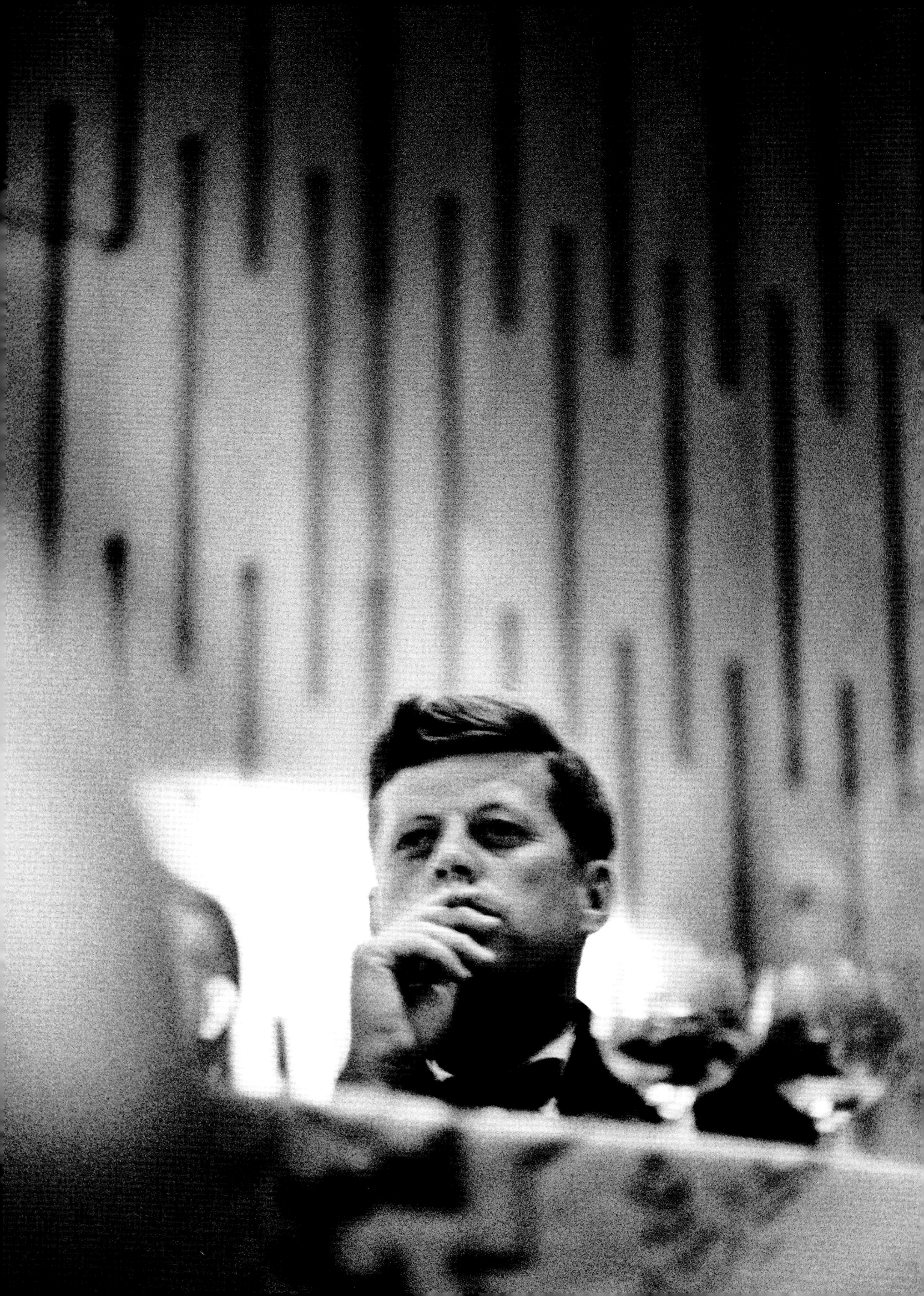

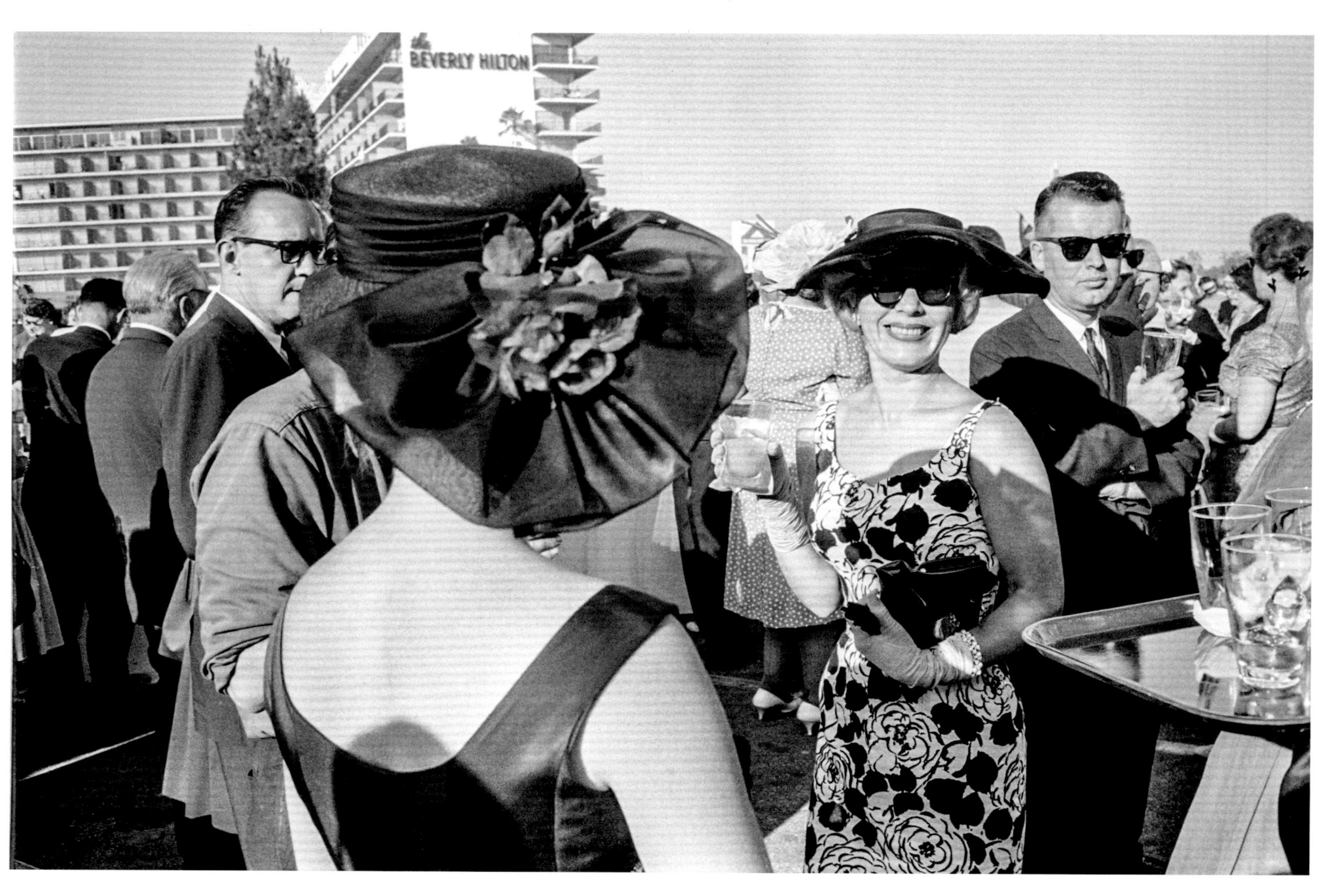
BEVERLY HILTON

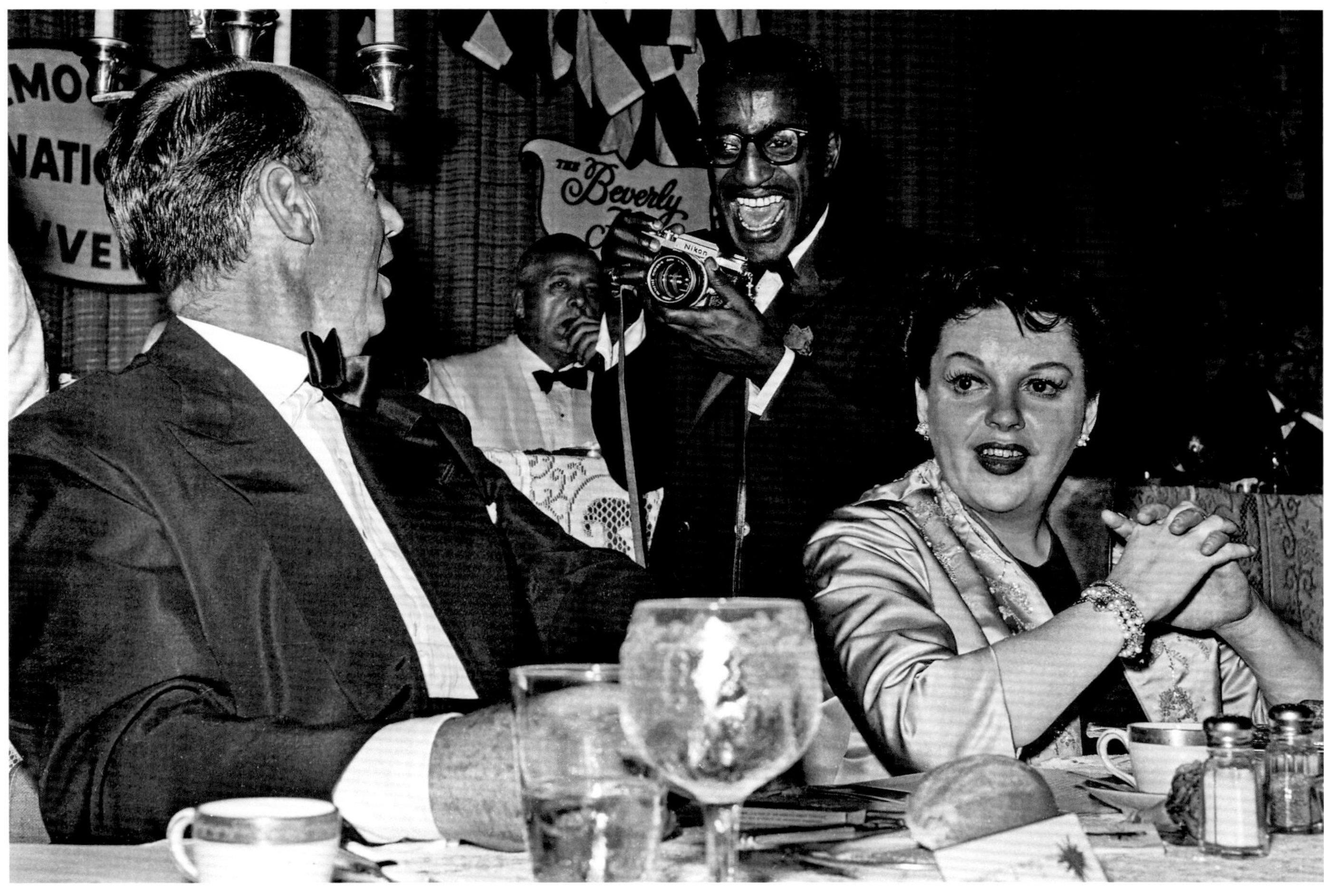

OPPOSITE *July 10, 1960.* The parking lot of the Beverly Hilton provided a sunny L. A. welcome to guests attending the Democratic Party's $100-a-plate gala. The battle for the top of the ticket was about to start downtown, but for one night the faithful would come together with a common agenda: raising money. *Photo, Garry Winogrand*

ABOVE *July 10, 1960.* Entertainer Sammy Davis Jr., also a photographer, takes a snapshot of Adlai Stevenson at the Beverly Hilton fund-raiser. Seated next to Stevenson is actress Judy Garland. The next day at the opening ceremony for the convention, delegates from Mississippi and Alabama booed Davis as he came onstage to sing the national anthem with Sinatra. His widely publicized engagement to a white woman, actress May Britt, had turned out to be a divisive issue for racist Southerners. Davis was devastated. Choked up, he managed to sing through the national anthem with Sinatra and others, but left the convention hall shortly thereafter. *Photo, Anonymous*

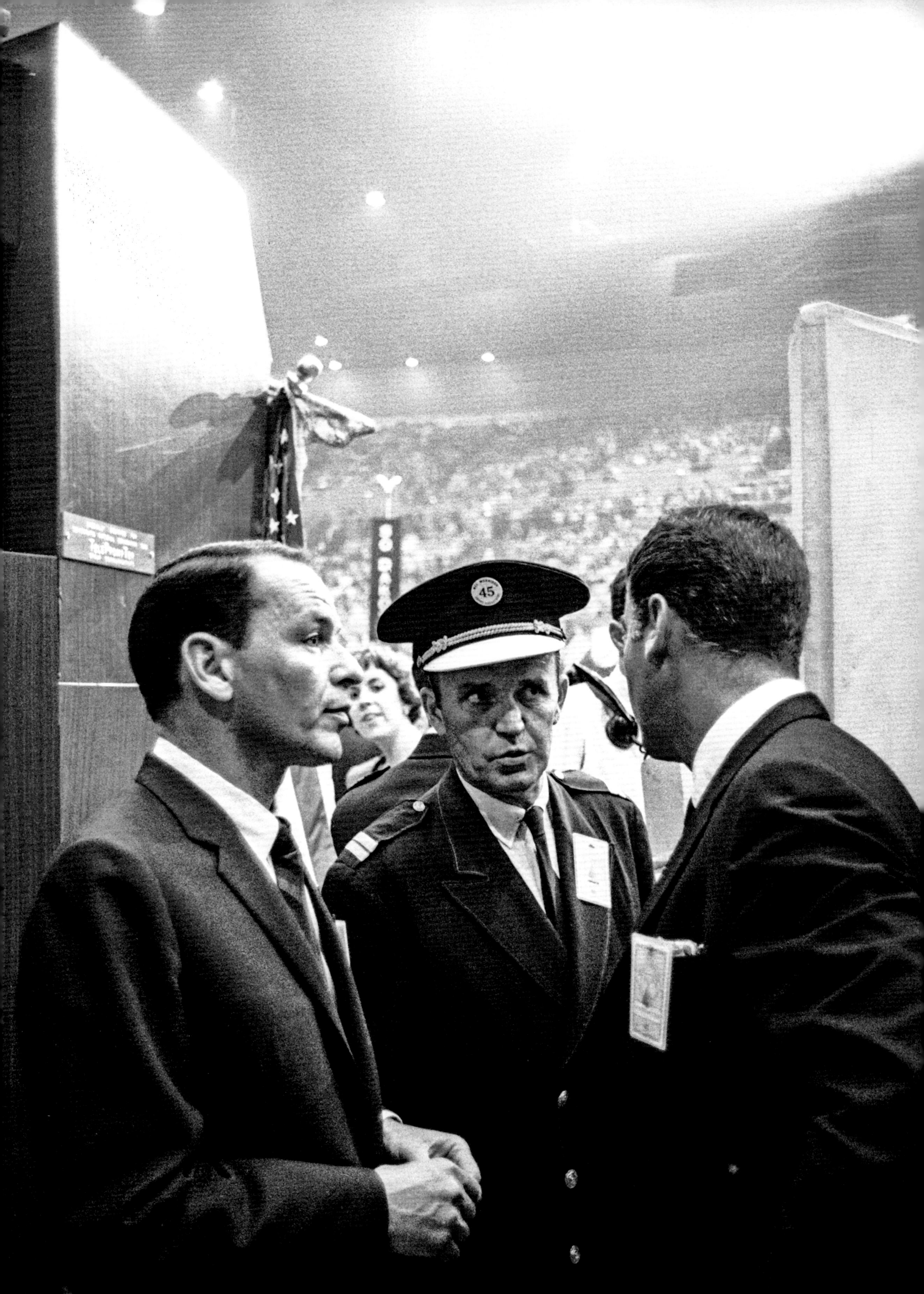

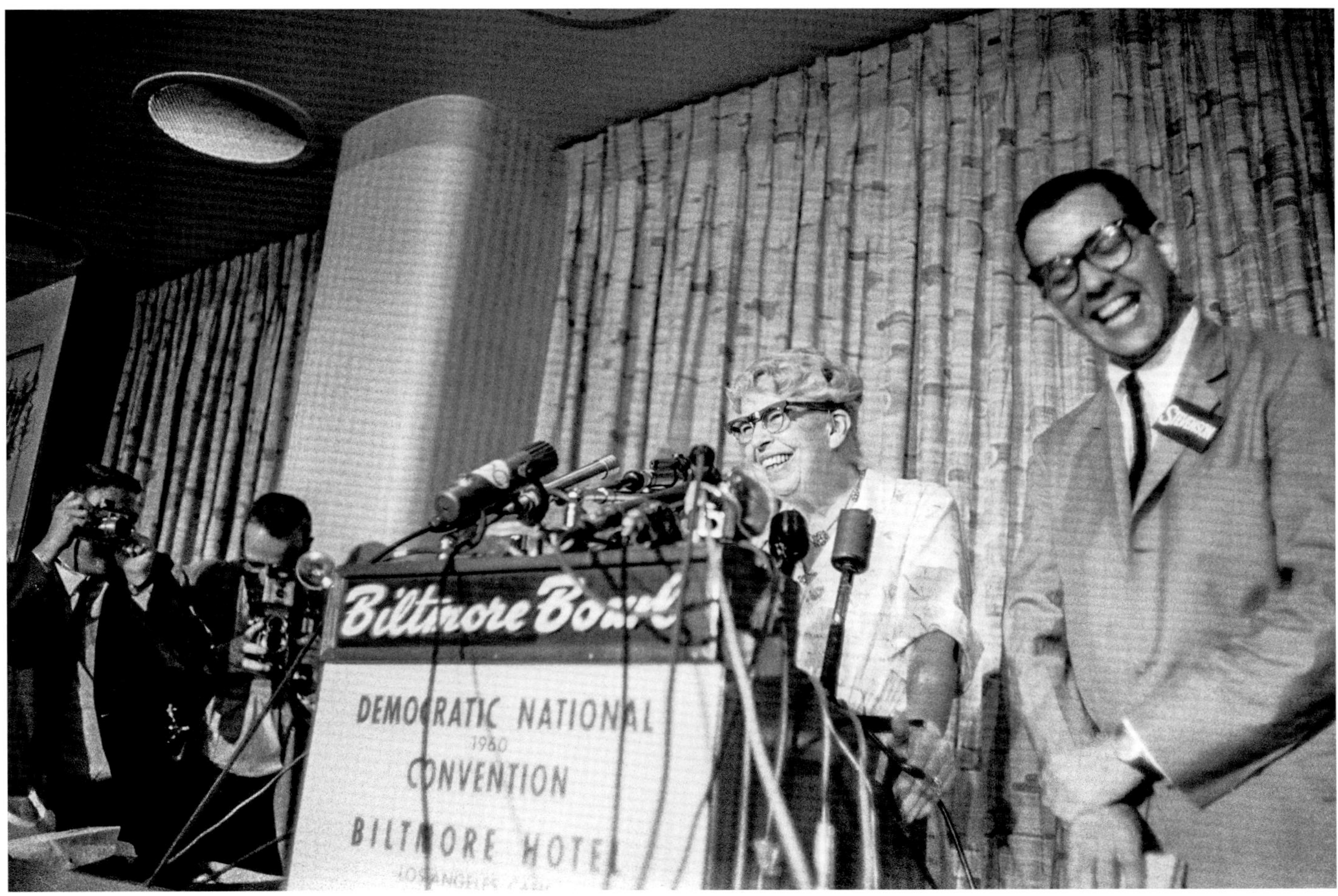

OPPOSITE *July 11, 1960.* Hollywood had a strong presence at the convention, due to its locale and especially the fact that Frank Sinatra (left) summoned his famous "Rat Pack" to support the cause. Appearing on stage as a part of the convention's opening ceremony were Sinatra, Sammy Davis Jr., Tony Curtis, Janet Leigh, Peter Lawford (right), and other Hollywood stars. *Photo, Ed Clark*

ABOVE *ca.* July 11, 1960. Eleanor Roosevelt, a die-hard Adlai Stevenson backer, arrived at the DNC on Sunday night, July 10, and soon began lobbying delegates to back a Stevenson candidacy. At a press conference on July 11 she suggested Kennedy should take the VP slot on the ticket—where he might "grow and learn"—and added that she believed JFK could not win the election. *Photo, Garry Winogrand*

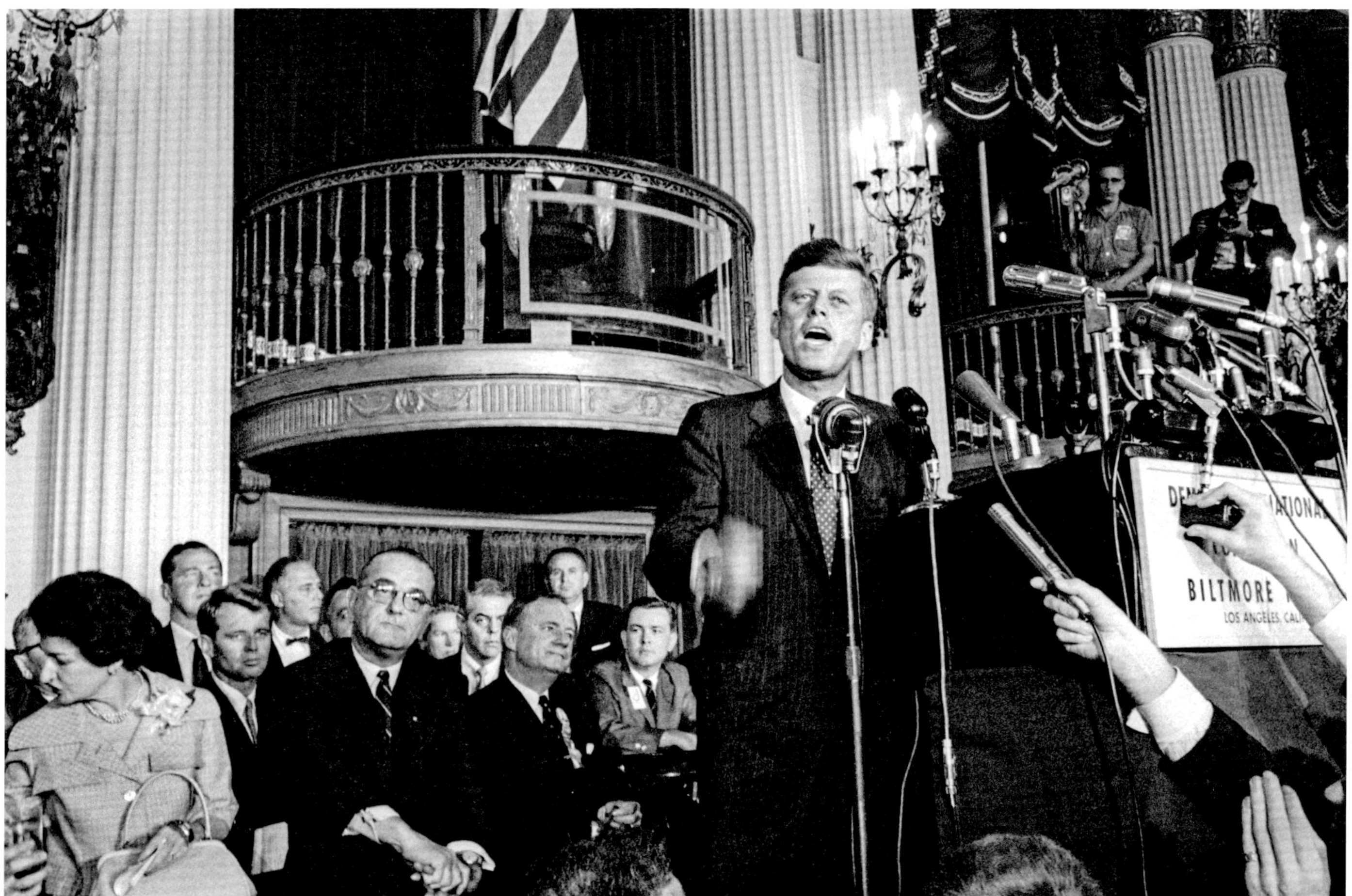

ABOVE *July 12, 1960.* In the Biltmore Hotel showdown between Johnson and Kennedy, LBJ made a last stand in his bid for the Democratic nomination but JFK's charm and wit won the day. "I come to you today full of admiration for Senator Johnson, full of affection for him, strongly in support of him as Majority Leader [of the U.S. Senate]," he said, "and I'm confident that in that position we're all going to be able to work together." *Photo, Cornell Capa*

OPPOSITE *July 12, 1960.* In a debate with Kennedy at the Biltmore Hotel before their respective state's delegations, Lyndon Johnson slams JFK's voting record in the Senate, arguing that the senator from Massachusetts was so busy campaigning that he had missed a number of important votes. *Photo, Jacques Lowe*

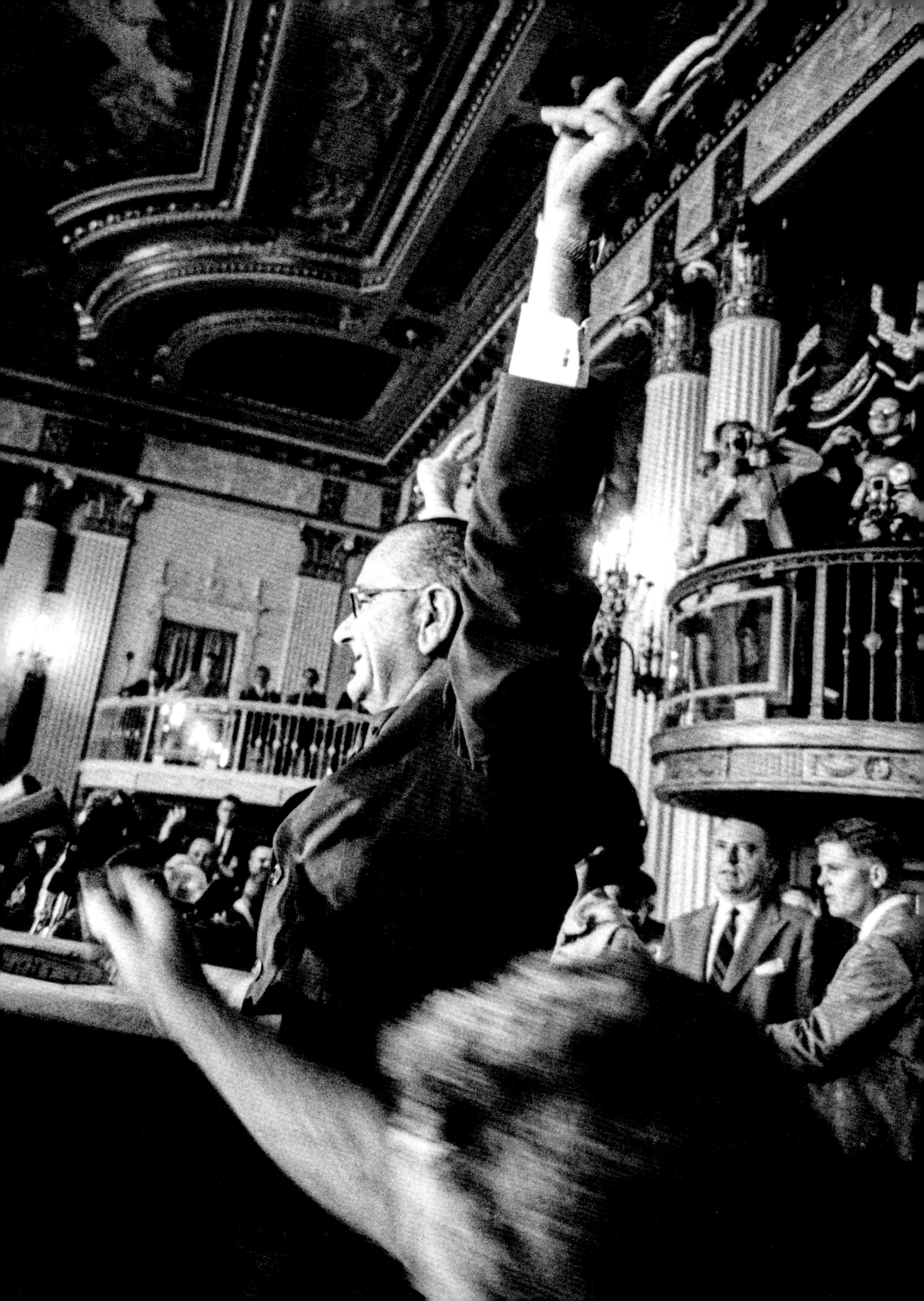

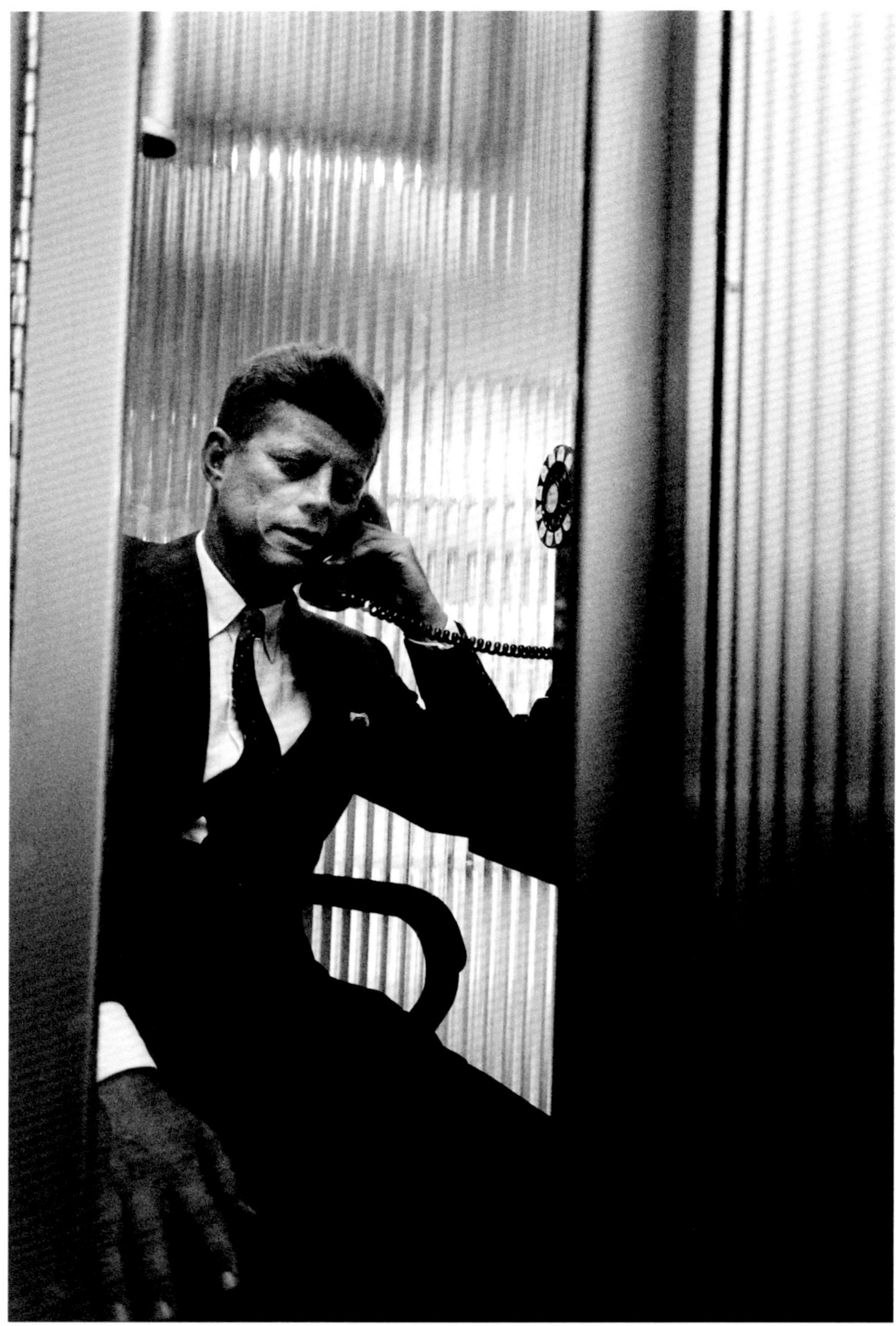

ABOVE *ca. July 11–13, 1960.* JFK in a phone booth at the Statler Hotel in Los Angeles during the convention. No, he isn't making some high-stakes political call or putting the arm on some party big-wig. Rather, according to *Life* magazine deputy editor Ben Cosgrove, he was nabbed by a businessman in the lobby of the hotel. "Come say hello to my wife," the man reportedly said, and handed the phone to Kennedy. Kennedy hopped on the line and told the New Jersey housewife that he "hoped she was taking care of her husband," and then went about his business. The man later told Schutzer his wife thought he was drunk. *Photo, Paul Schutzer*

OPPOSITE *ca. July 9–10, 1960.* Carmine G. DeSapio (far left), an influential politician from New York City, and other New York delegates huddle before the convention. DeSapio, who oversaw a resurgence of Tammany Hall, the late eighteenth-century New York City political machine, held particular sway in Manhattan. But by 1960 the Kennedy organization had made inroads throughout the rest of New York state, making him less of a power broker at the convention. Kennedy's national "going to the people" strategy via his primary wins and local list-making along the way signaled an end to the "nomination by political bosses" process. *Photo, Walter Sanders*

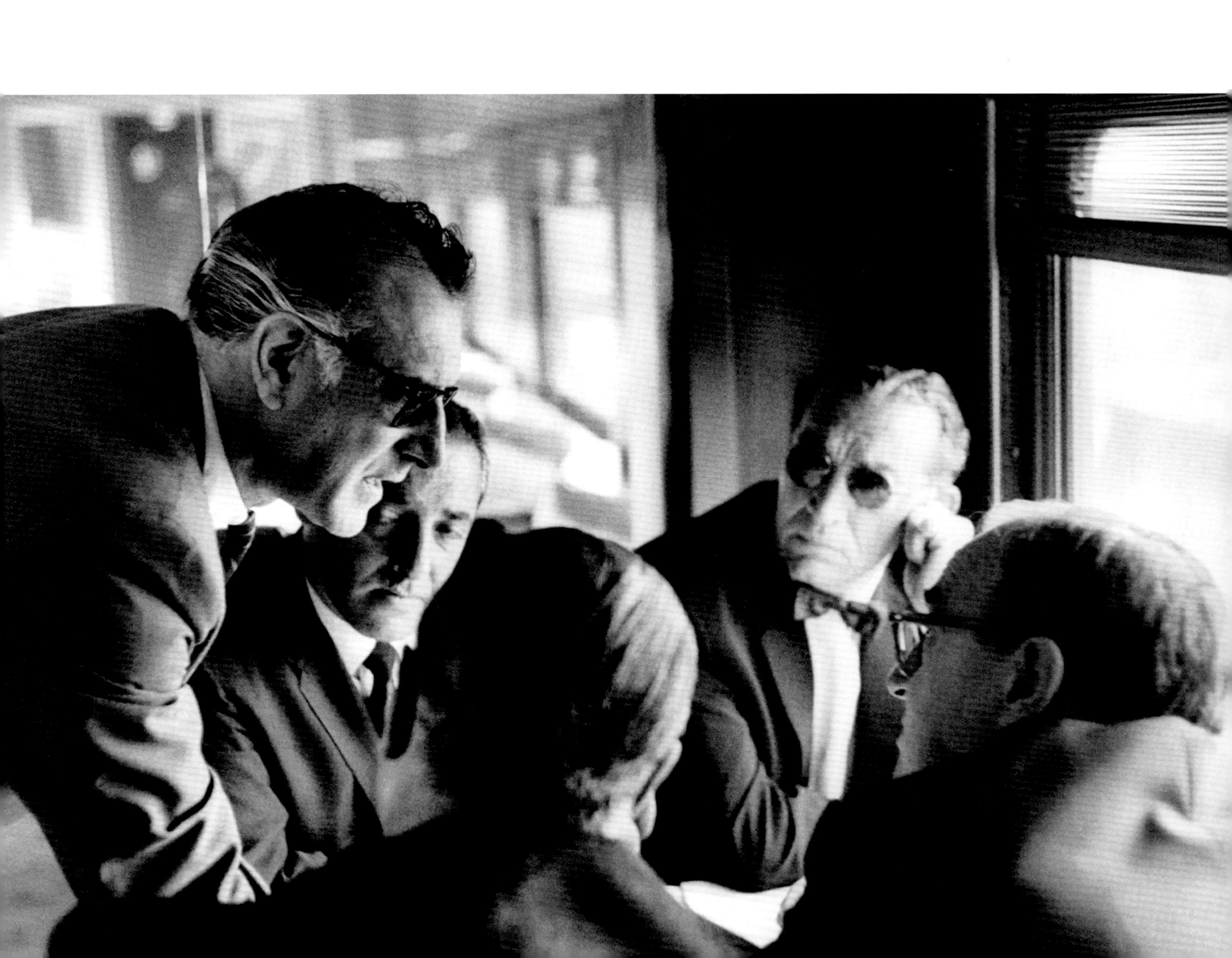

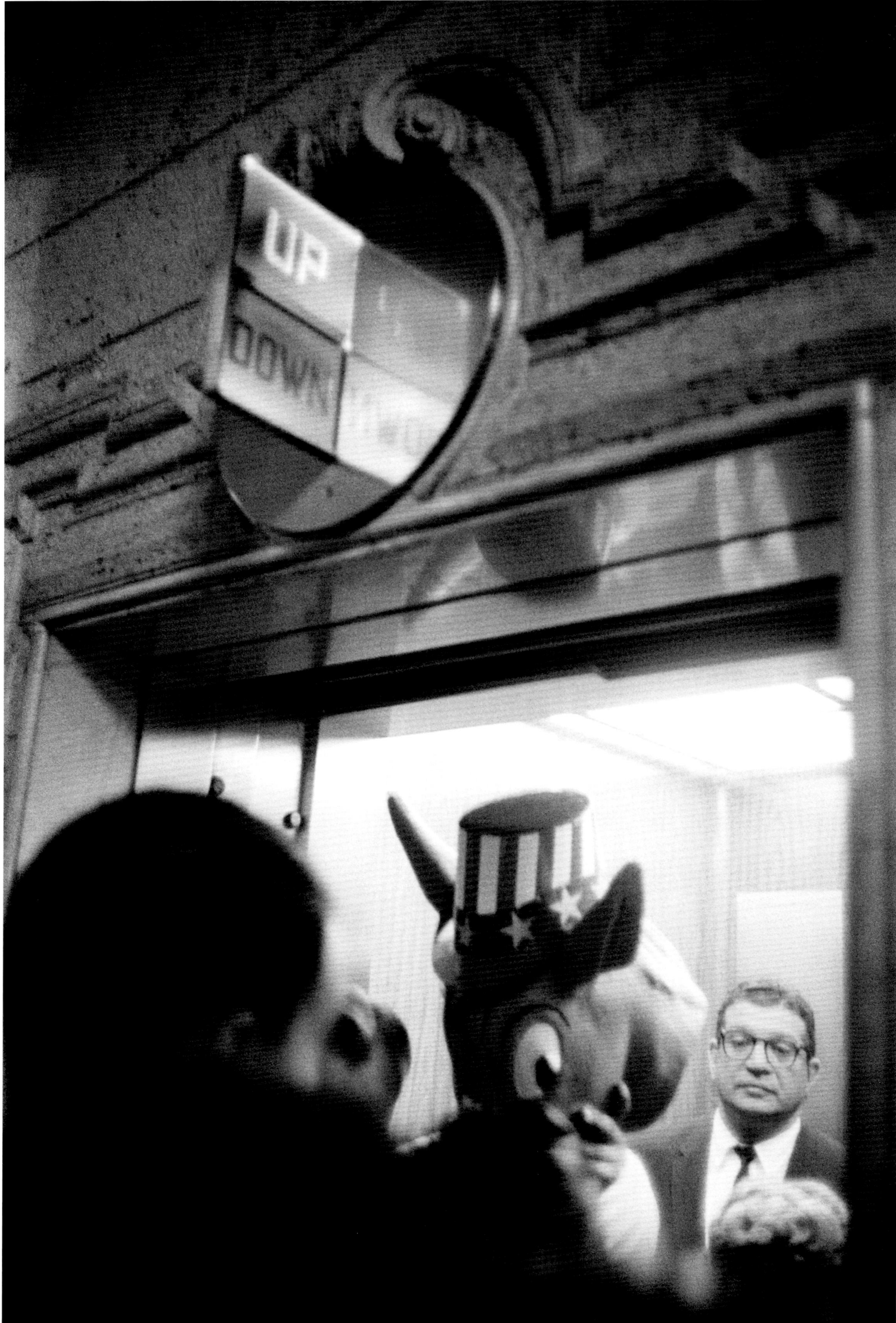
UP
DOWN

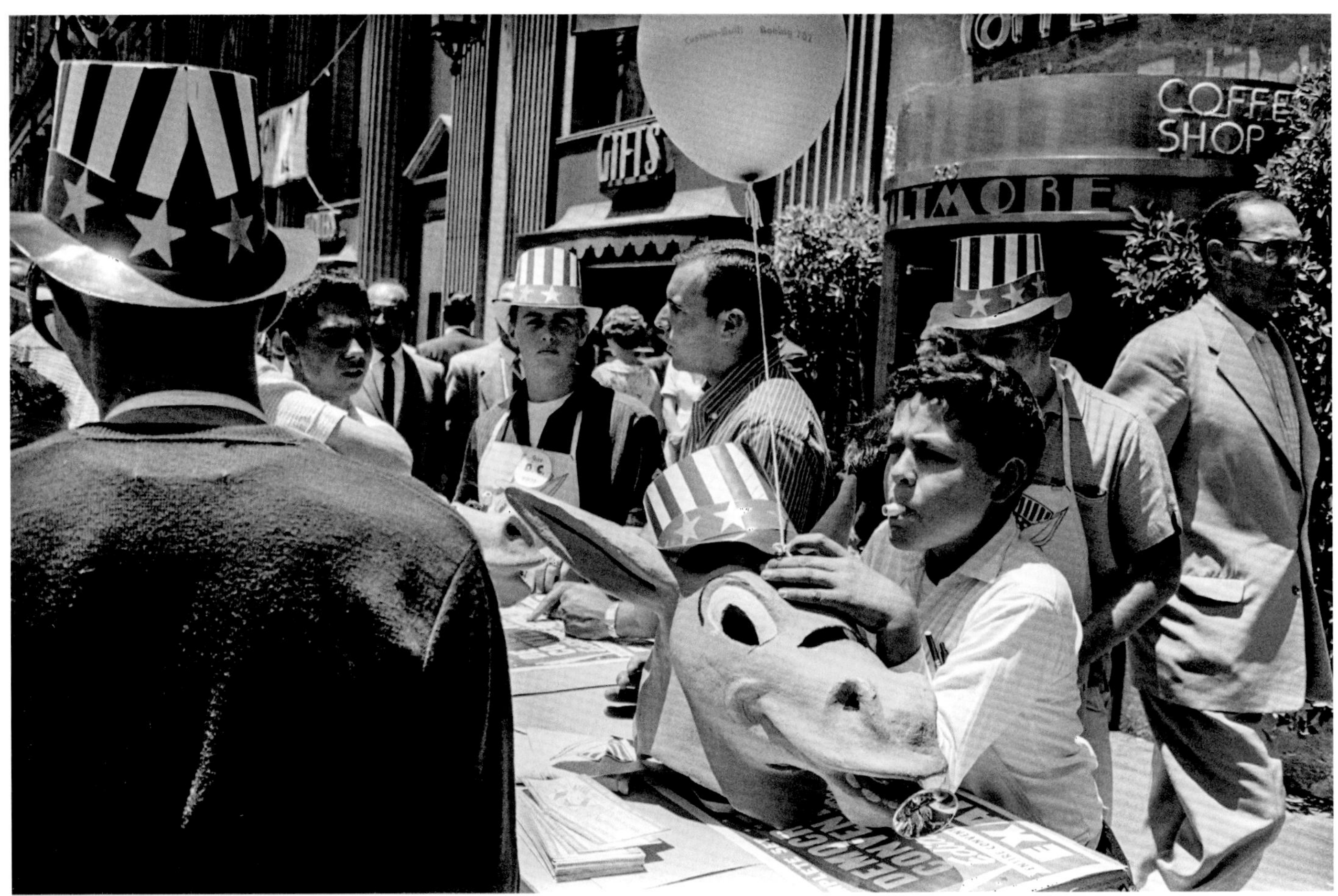

OPPOSITE AND ABOVE *ca. July 9–13, 1960.* According to Mailer, the Biltmore
Hotel was "where everybody gathered every day—the newsmen, the TV,
radio, magazine, and foreign newspaperman, the delegates, the politicos,
the tourists, the campaign managers, the runners, the flunkies, the
cousins and aunts, the wives, the grandfathers, the eight-year-old girls,
and the twenty-eight-year-old girls in the Kennedy costumes, red and white
and blue, the Symingteeners, the Johnson Ladies, the Stevenson Ladies,
everybody." It was a circus, and the animal at its center was the donkey—
a symbol of the party since the days of Andrew Jackson and the 1870
drawings of cartoonist Thomas Nast. *Photos, Garry Winogrand*

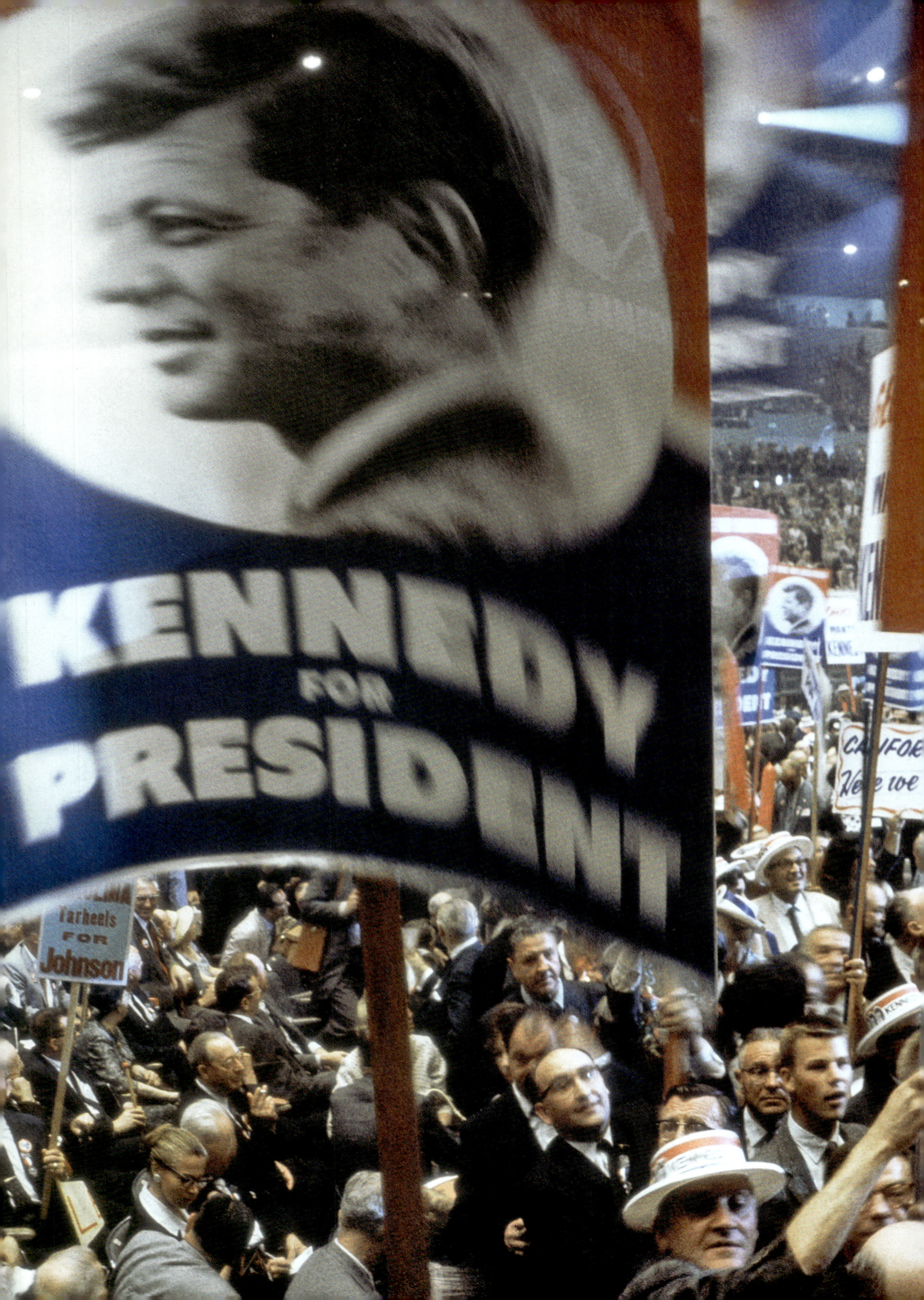

KENNEDY FOR PRESIDENT
Tarheels FOR Johnson
CALIFO
Here we
KENNE

"Delegates are not the noblest sons and daughters of the Republic; man of taste, arrived from Mars, would take one look at a convention floor and leave forever, convinced he had seen one of the drearier squats of Hell."

—Norman Mailer, "Superman Comes to the Supermarket," *Esquire*, November 1960

FOLDOUT *July 13, 1960.* "Floor demonstrations" are a big part of the theatrics common to American political conventions. Each candidate whose name is expected to be considered for nomination—whether insider or outsider, long shot or sure thing—typically has one or more moments during the convention where his or her supporters come forward en masse, cheering, whistling, stomping their feet, waving their banners and placards. Today they resemble a pep rally, but at the DNC in 1960 suspense filled the air for the first two days as to who would be the nominee for president, and floor demonstrations were lively and passionate. *Photo, Ralph Crane*

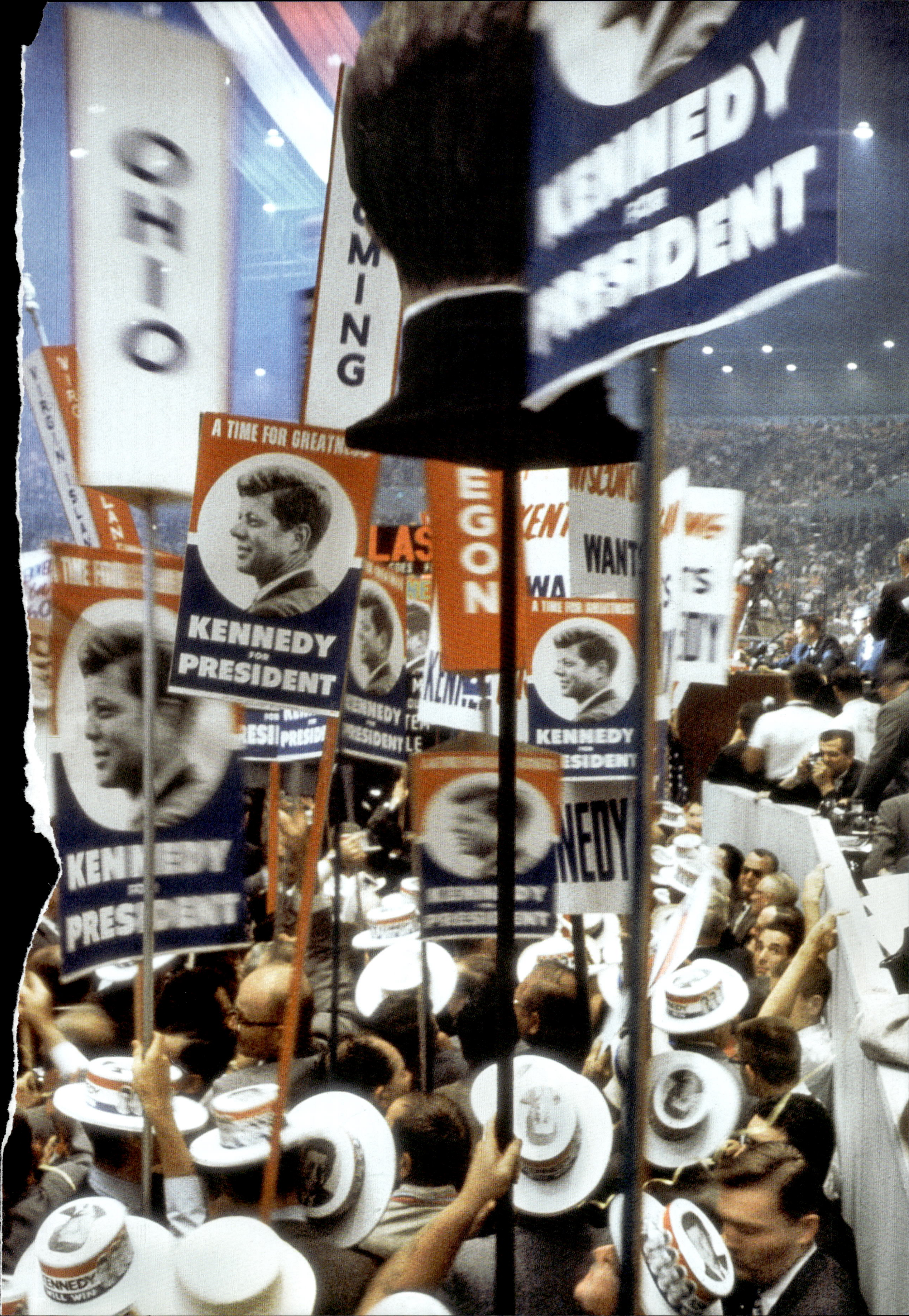

OHIO
OMING
KENNEDY FOR PRESIDENT
A TIME FOR GREATNESS
KENNEDY FOR PRESIDENT
EGON
WISCONSIN
WANTS
A TIME FOR GREATNESS
KENNEDY FOR PRESIDENT
KENNEDY FOR PRESIDENT
KENNEDY FOR PRESIDENT
KENNEDY
VIRGINIA
KENNEDY WILL WIN

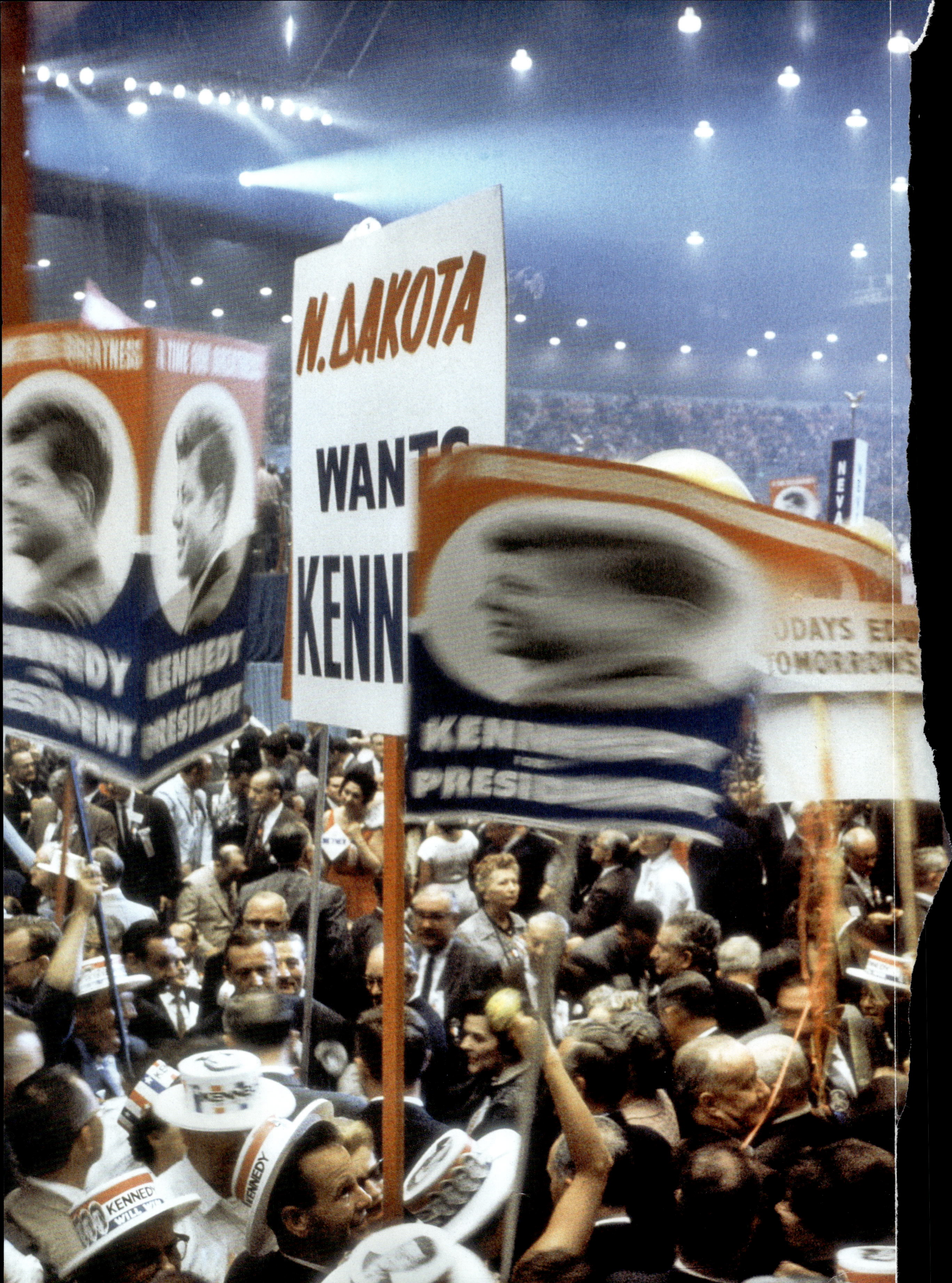

GREATNESS
A TIME FOR GREATNESS
N. DAKOTA
WANTS
KENN
KENNEDY
PRESIDENT
KENNEDY
for
PRESIDENT
KEN
PRESI
ODAYS E
TOMORROW
NEX
KENNEDY
KENNEDY
WILL WIN

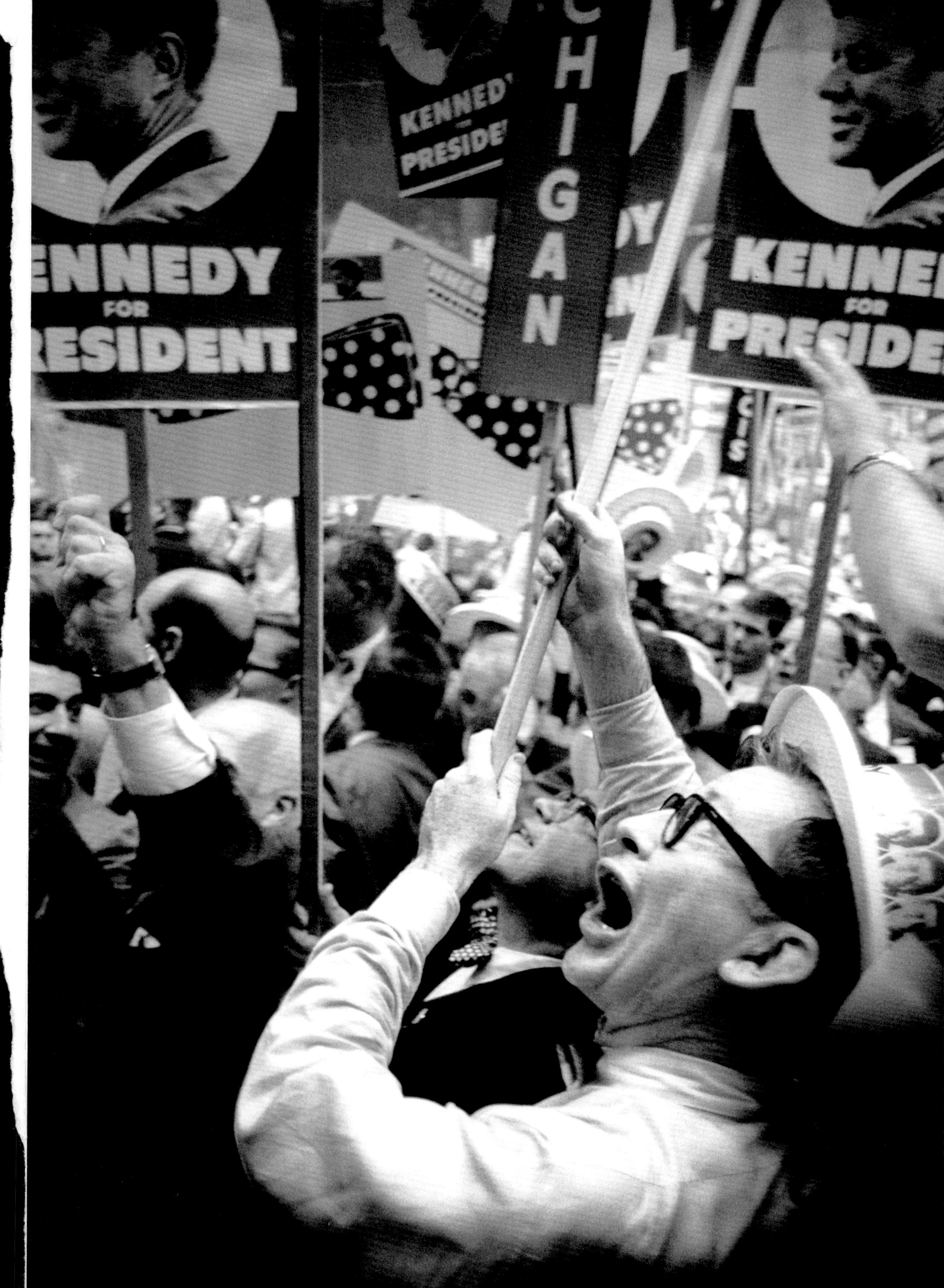

KENNEDY FOR PRESIDENT
KENNEDY FOR PRESIDENT
KENNEDY FOR PRESIDENT
CHIGAN

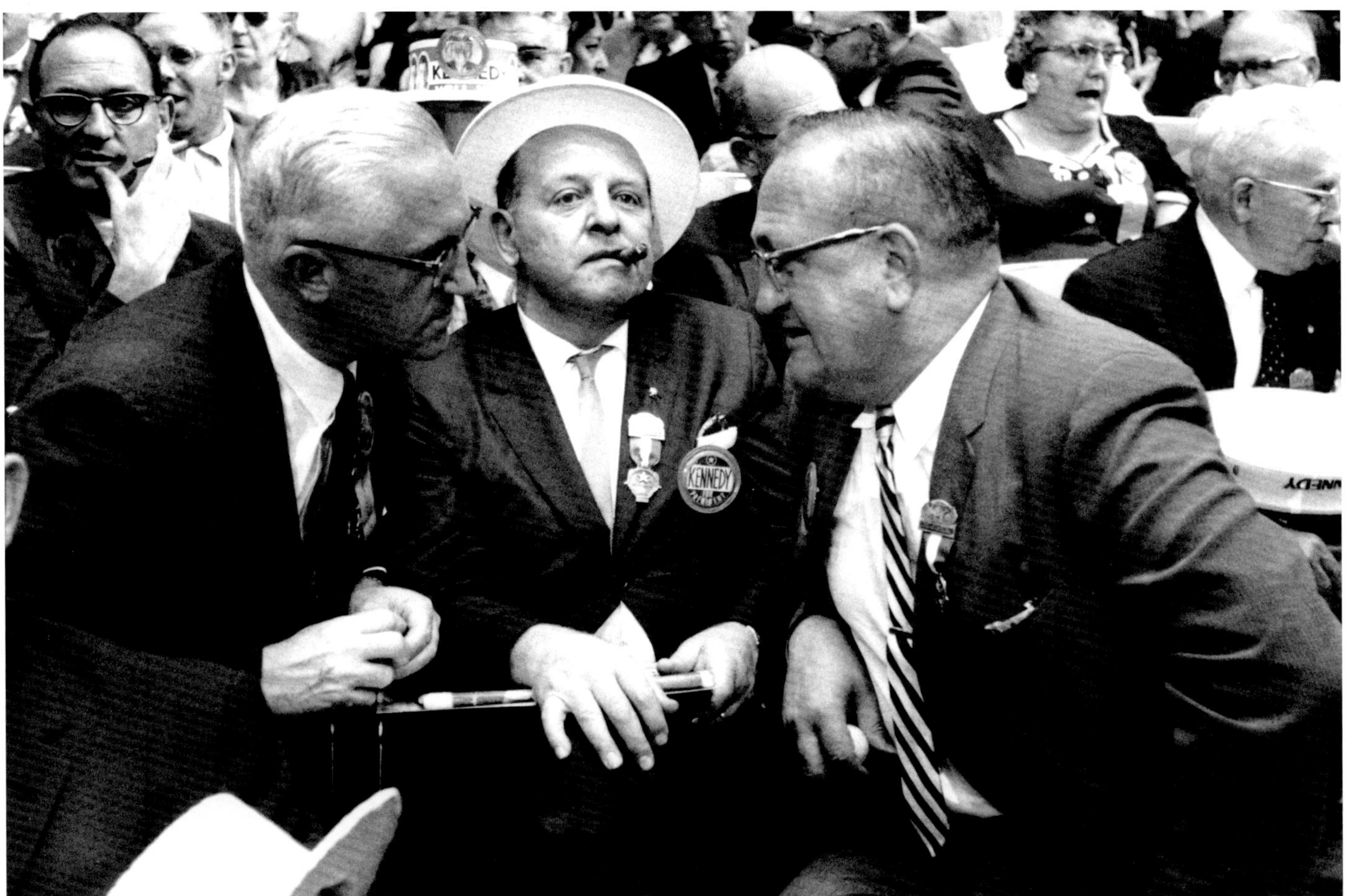

OPPOSITE *July 13, 1960.* Kennedy delegates engage in a floor demonstration for their candidate. By the time a delegate got to the convention, anticipation was running high, and the arena was already busy with activity. At the DNC in 1960, most of the prominent candidates had at least one floor demonstration, with that for Adlai Stevenson reportedly being the loudest and longest lasting, running at least 17 minutes by one count. *Photo, Grey Villet*

ABOVE *ca. July 11–13, 1960.* The more experienced party delegates, who'd been to one or more national political conventions, showed newcomers the ropes. *Photo, Jacques Lowe*

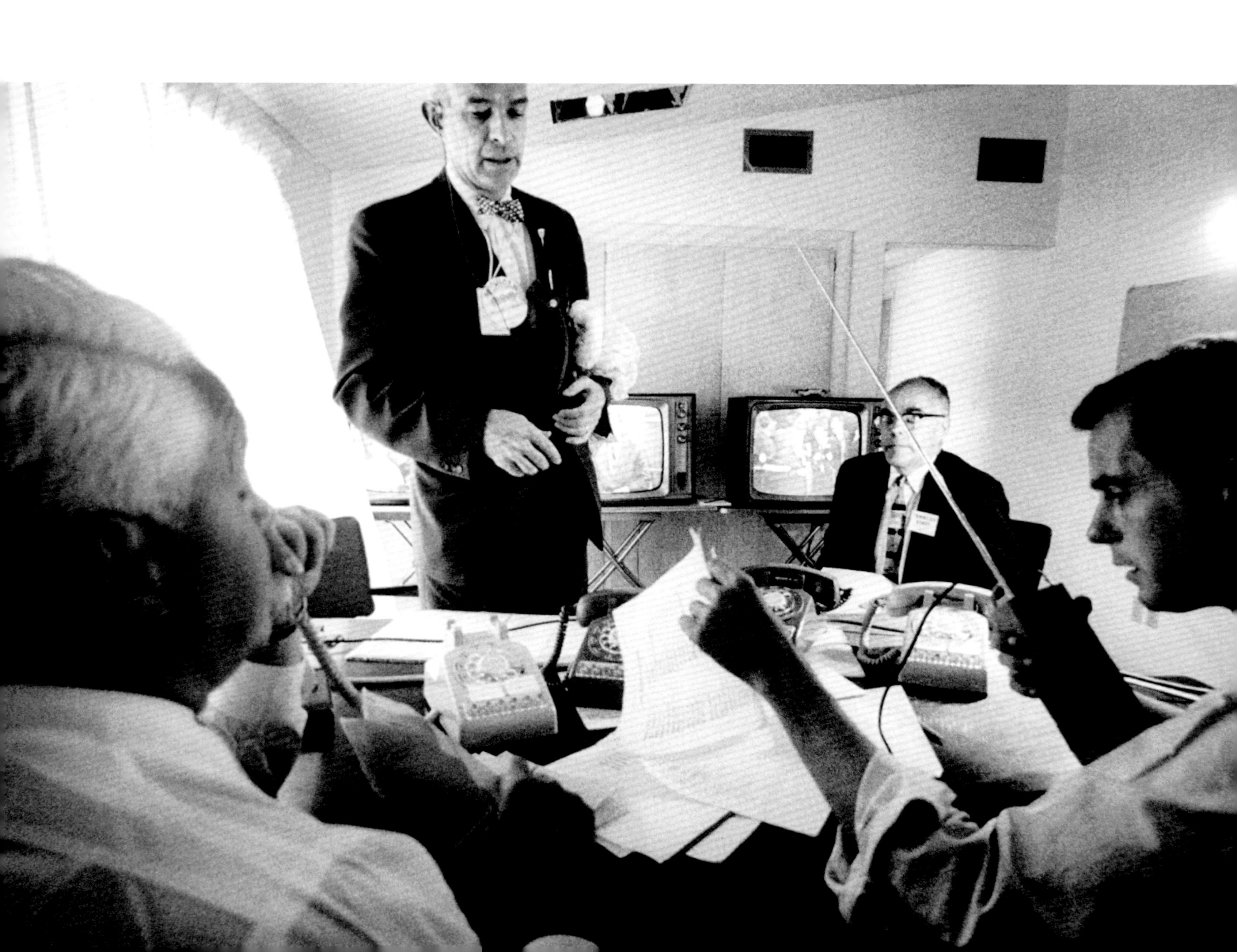

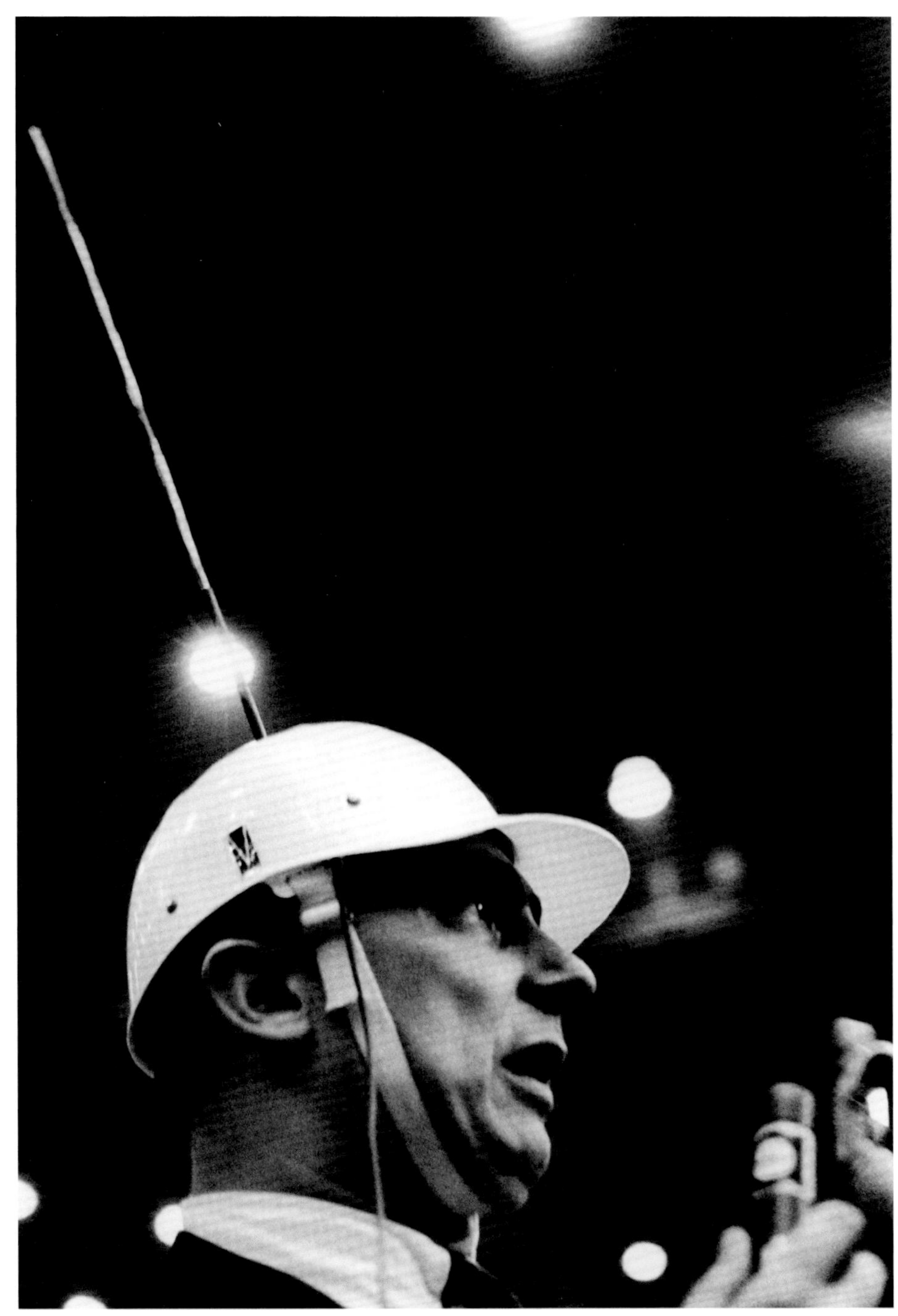

OPPOSITE *ca. July 11–13.* JFK staffers Hy Raskin (left) and Walter Spolar (right) at the Democratic Convention Arena Communications HQ. During the DNC, Kennedy's team had a detailed plan for coverage of floor activity and delegate whereabouts, with top-level aides assigned to specific state delegations, as their head count for the nomination was never taken for granted. *Photo, Howard Sochurek*

ABOVE *ca. July 11–13, 1960.* An ABC-TV staffer on the convention floor uses a mobile communications device to report back to the main broadcast office at the convention. Television and print coverage of the 1960 Democratic National Convention was intense, with hundreds of journalists and newsmen and -women on the scene. TV coverage grew in importance, continuing a trend that had begun with the 1952 conventions. In 1950 only 11 percent of households owned a television set; by 1960 that number was 88 percent. *Photo, Howard Sochurek*

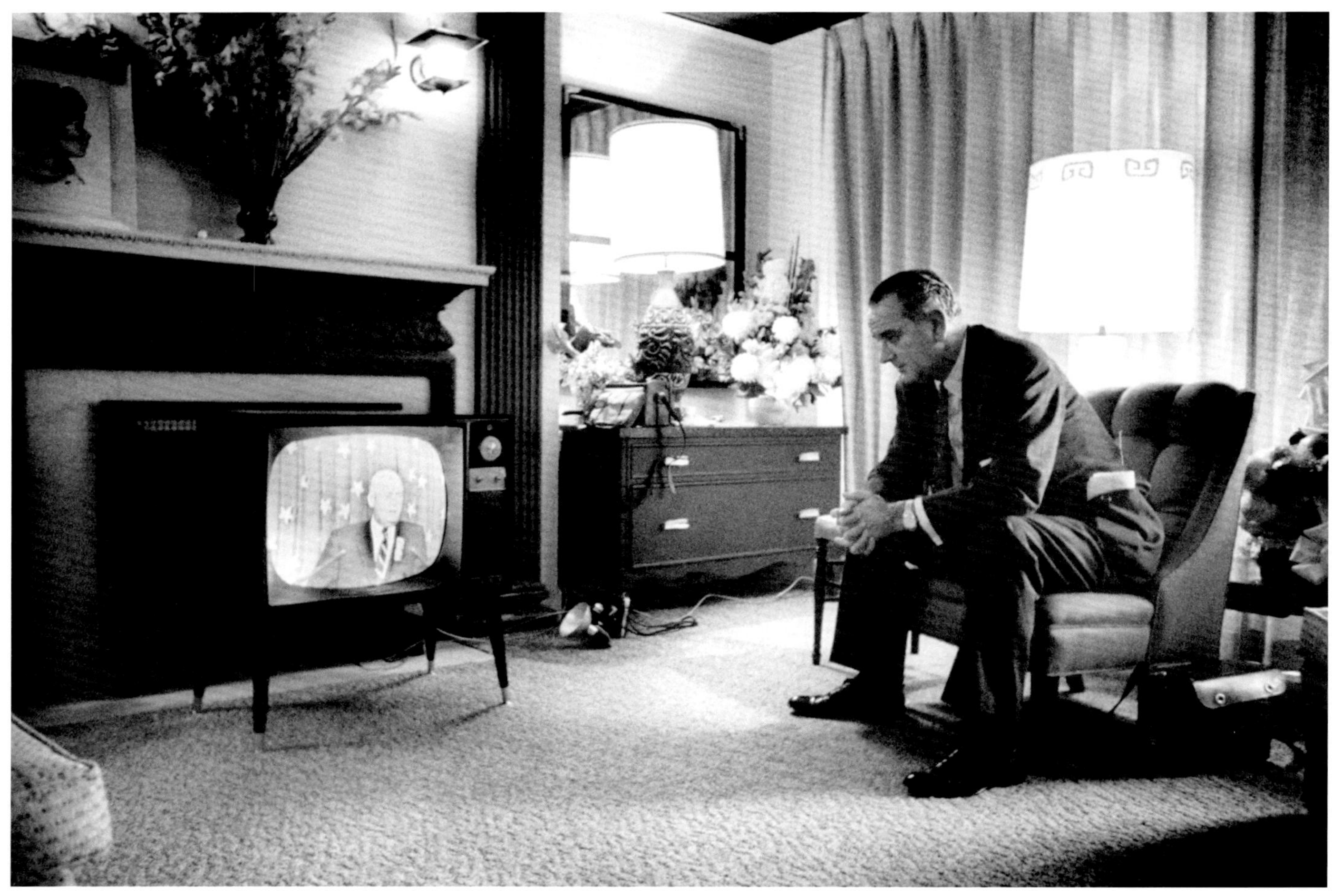

ABOVE *July 13, 1960.* Candidate Lyndon Johnson watches convention returns from his hotel room. Kennedy would win the nomination with more than enough votes at 806 to Johnson's 409. *Photo, Thomas D. McAvoy*

OPPOSITE *July 14, 1960.* TV reporters and camera crews descend on the Kennedy home in Hyannis Port, where Jackie is interviewed on an outside porch the morning after her husband's nomination. When one reporter asked her if she'd be meeting Jack at the airport on Sunday night, she quipped, "I'd like to. It depends how many of you will be there." *Photo, Ted Polumbaum*

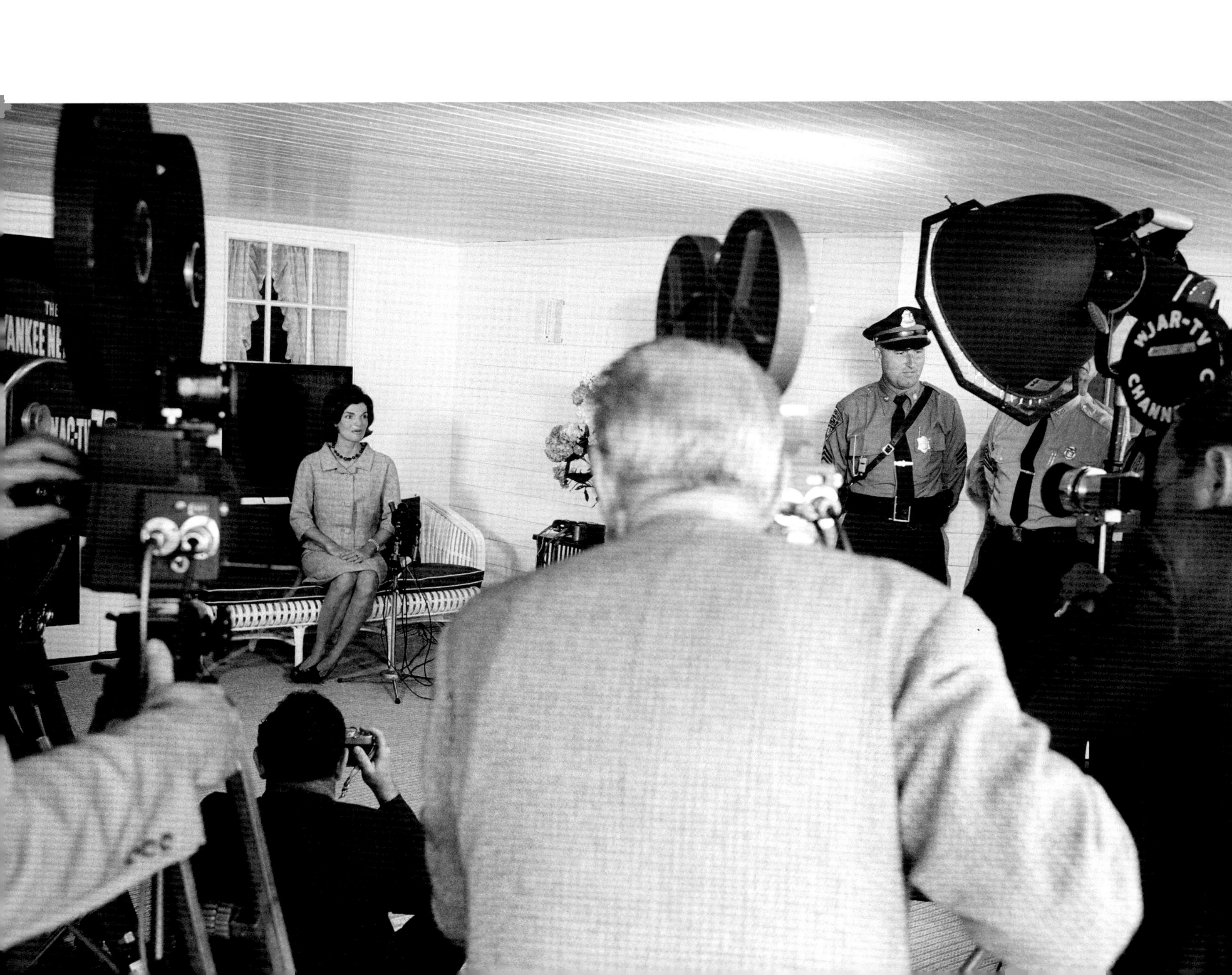

"[It was] one of the most important conventions in America's history... The man it nominated was unlike any politician who had ever run for President in the history of the land, and if elected he would come to power in a year when America was in danger of drifting into a profound decline."

—Norman Mailer, "Superman Comes to the Supermarket," *Esquire*, November 1960

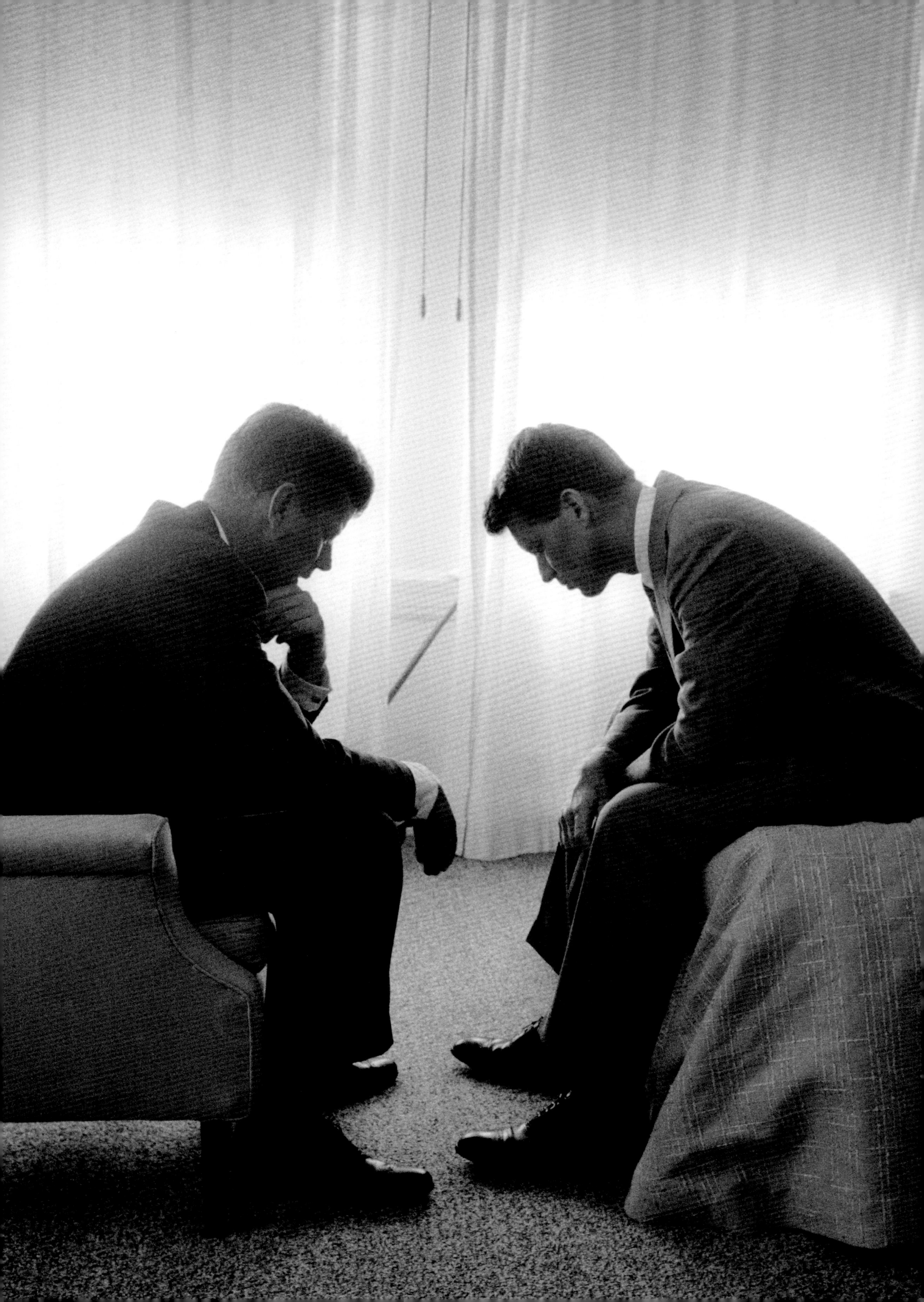

"In these days of great challenge Americans must have a Vice-President capable of dealing with the grave problems confronting this nation and the free world.... We need men of strength if we are to be strong...."

—John F. Kennedy, Press Conference, Biltmore Bowl,
Los Angeles, July 14, 1960

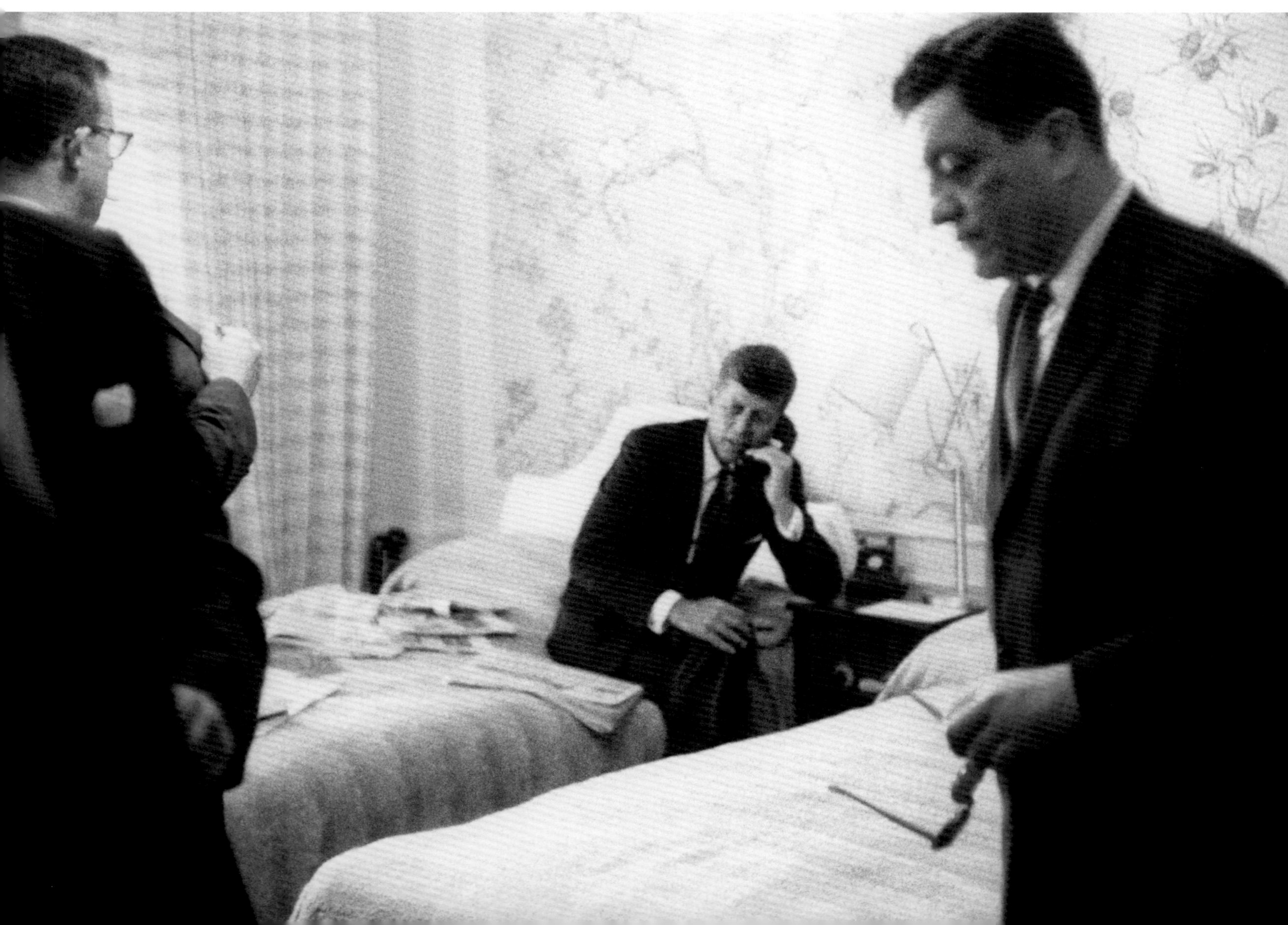

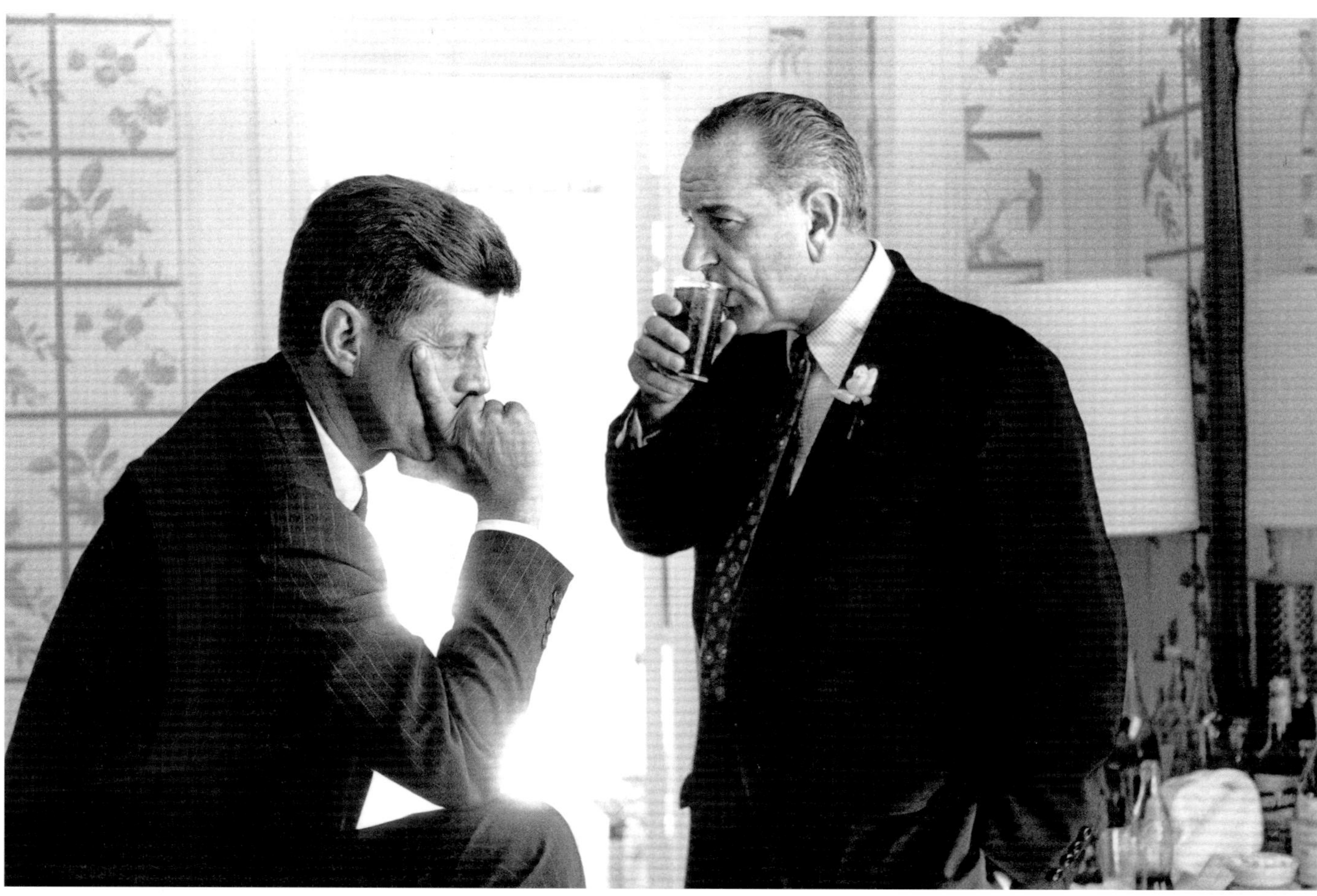

BELOW *July 14, 1960.* A delegate nods off during the succession of speakers
that preceded the nomination of Lyndon B. Johnson as the party's vice
presidential candidate, a fact announced by headlines from that morning's
Los Angeles Examiner, "worn" by the sleepy listener. *The Examiner*, part of
the Hearst newspaper syndicate, was a rival to the bigger *Los Angeles Times*.
There were also two other papers, the *Los Angeles Herald-Express* and the
Los Angeles Mirror (a sister *L.A. Times* afternoon tabloid). During the DNC
all four papers put out "convention specials," sometimes with morning and
evening editions to capture the latest news, rumors, and developments.
Photo, Anonymous

OPPOSITE *July 14, 1960.* With the convention winding down, the campaign
detritus of placards, banners, hats, and ribbons litters the arena floor, some
still reading of candidate hopes and promises. *Photo, Dirck Halstead*

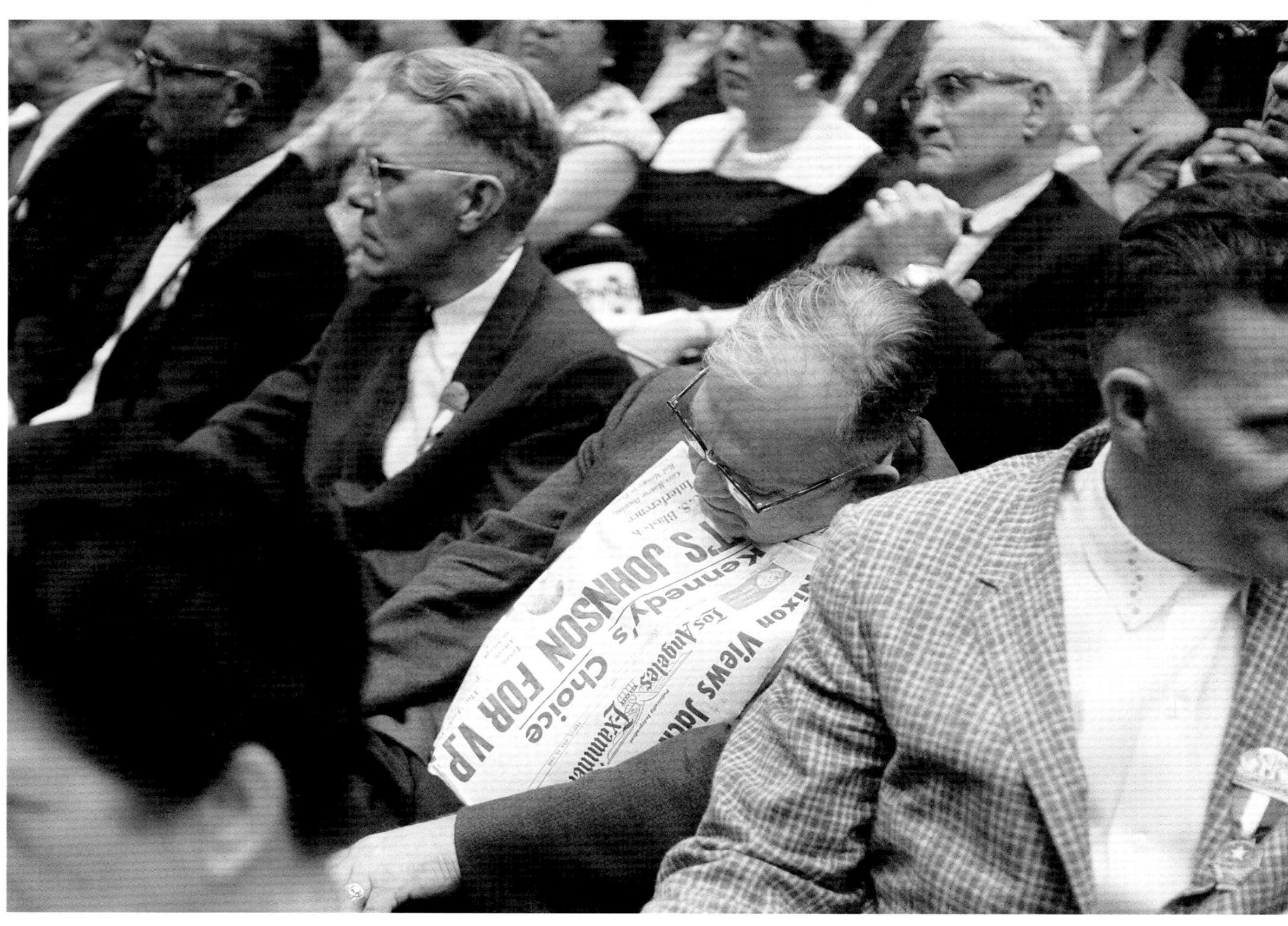

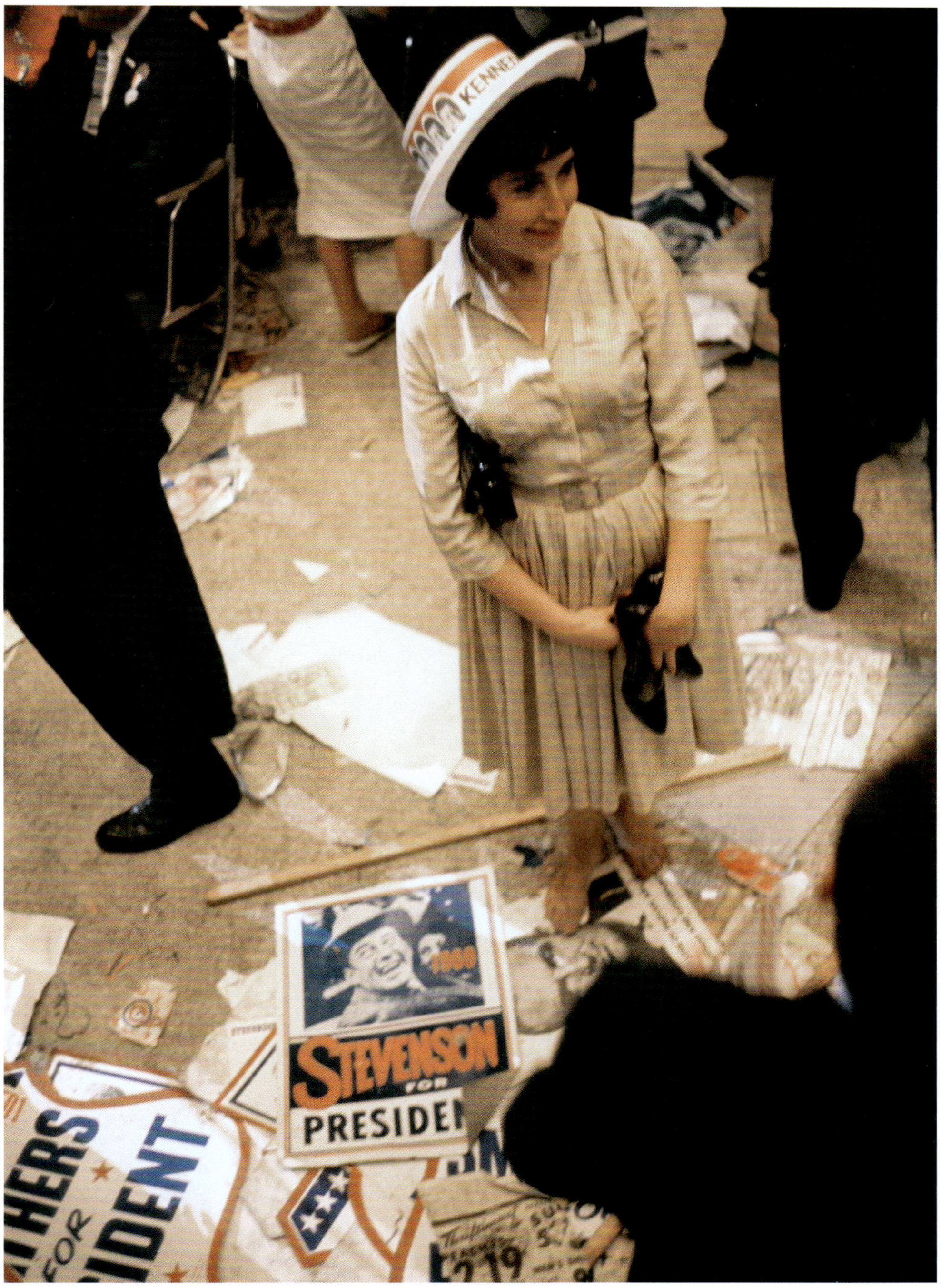
STEVENSON
FOR
PRESIDEN

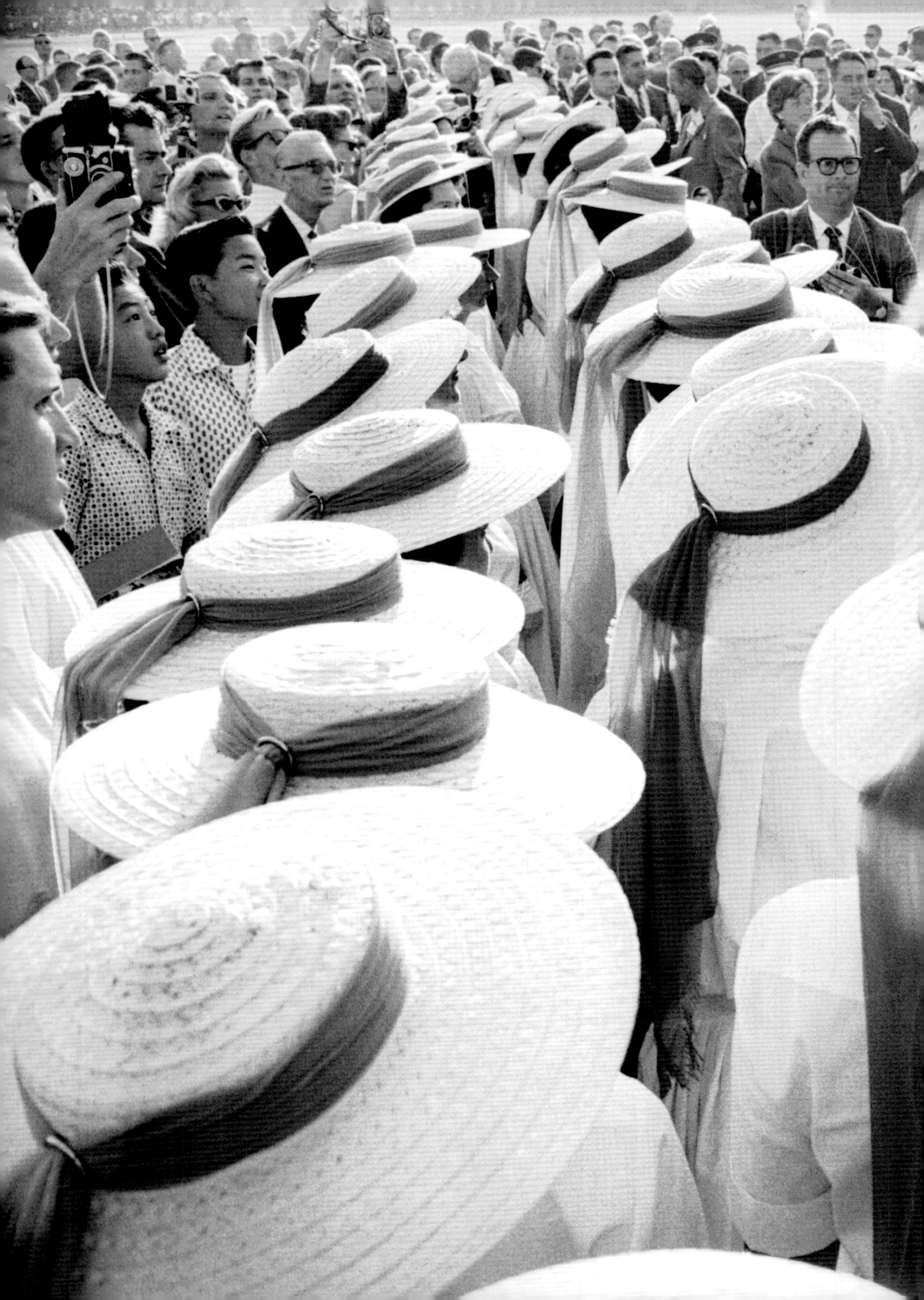

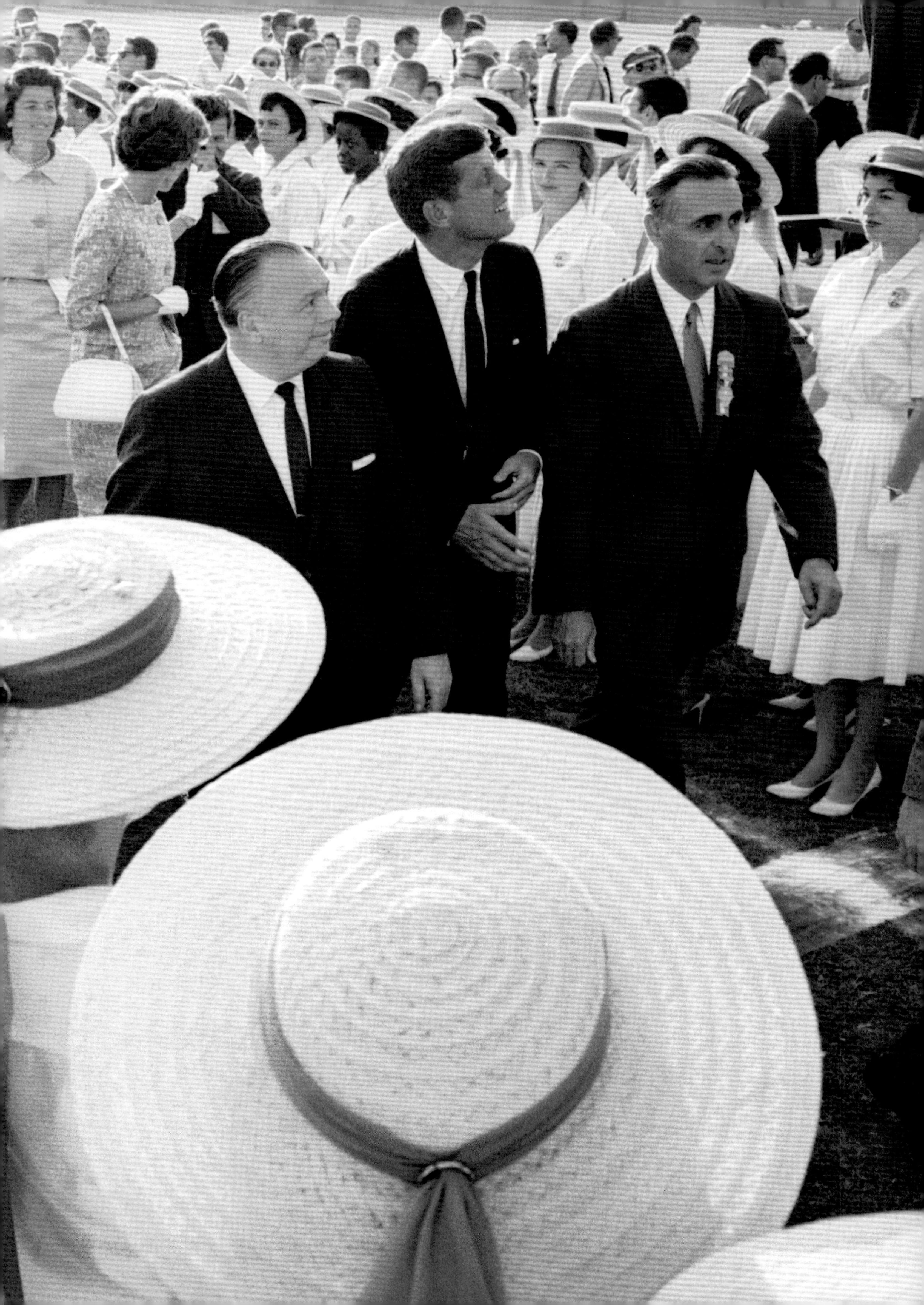

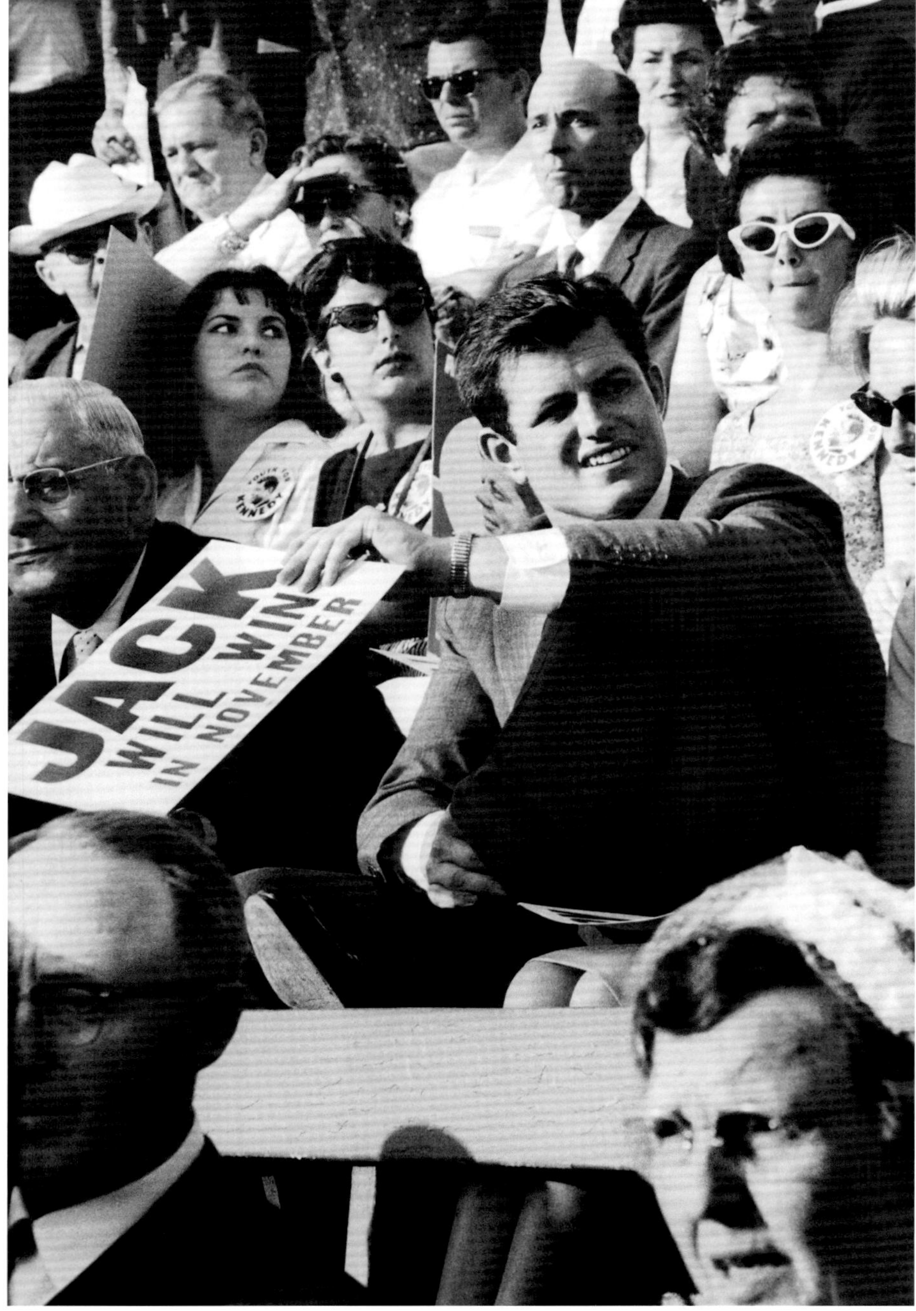

PREVIOUS SPREAD *July 15, 1960.* Flanked by Ohio Governor Michael V. DiSalle (left) and Connecticut Governor Abraham A. Ribicoff (right), and followed by sisters Eunice and Pat and brother-in-law Sargent Shriver, JFK arrives at the Memorial Coliseum to formally accept the nomination of his party. With media attention surrounding the nomination at a high level of intensity, party organizers smartly decided to make the keynote speech of the convention open to the public—a move that required relocating the event from the Los Angeles Sports Arena to the much larger coliseum nearby, which could accommodate an audience of up to 100,000 attendees. *Photo, Grey Villet*

ABOVE *July 15, 1960.* Ted Kennedy celebrates his brother's nomination from the stands of the coliseum. He was JFK's Western states organizer, and by the time of the DNC, had spent many hours on the road—in the West and the East—working on behalf of his brother. *Photo, Ralph Crane*

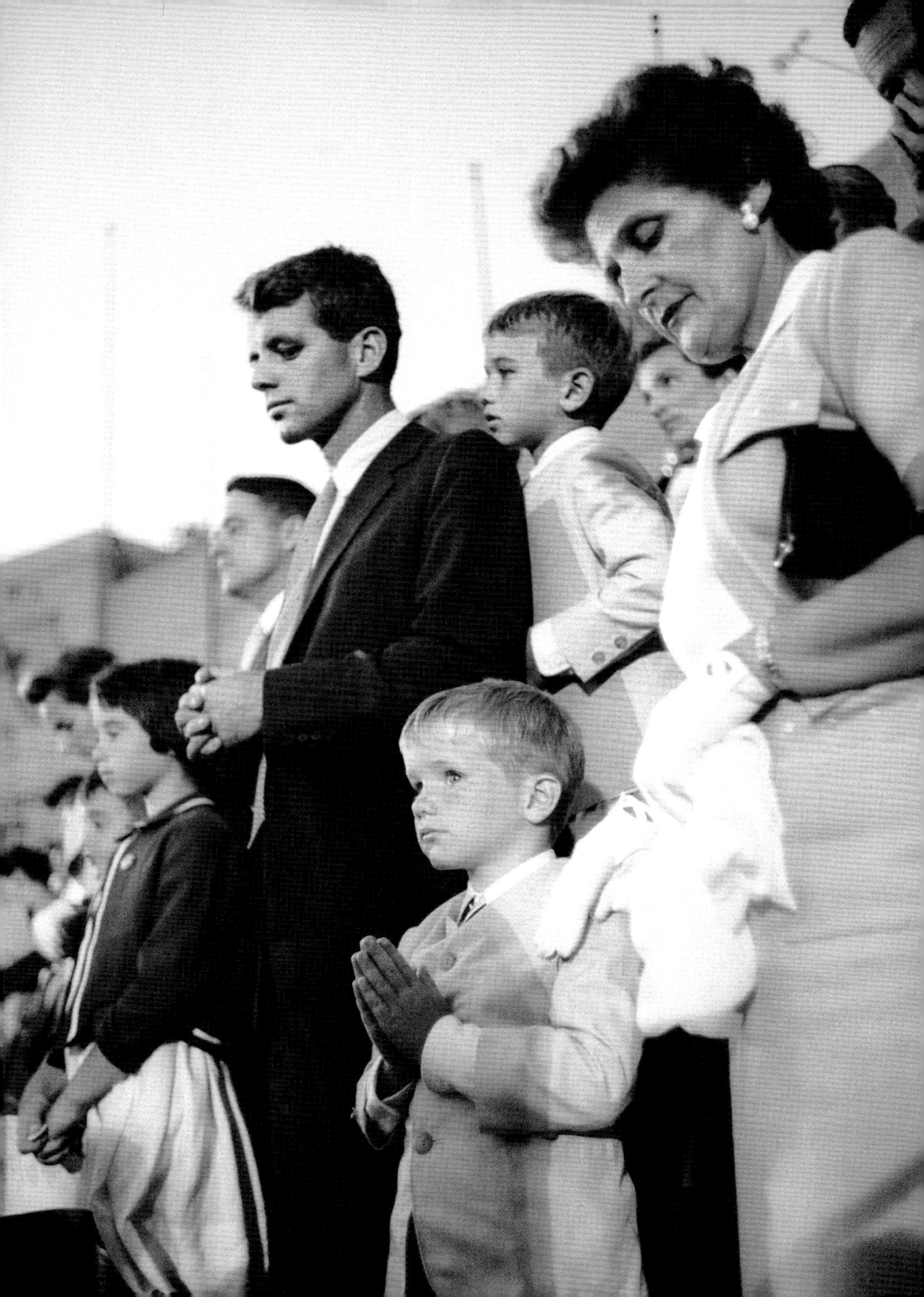

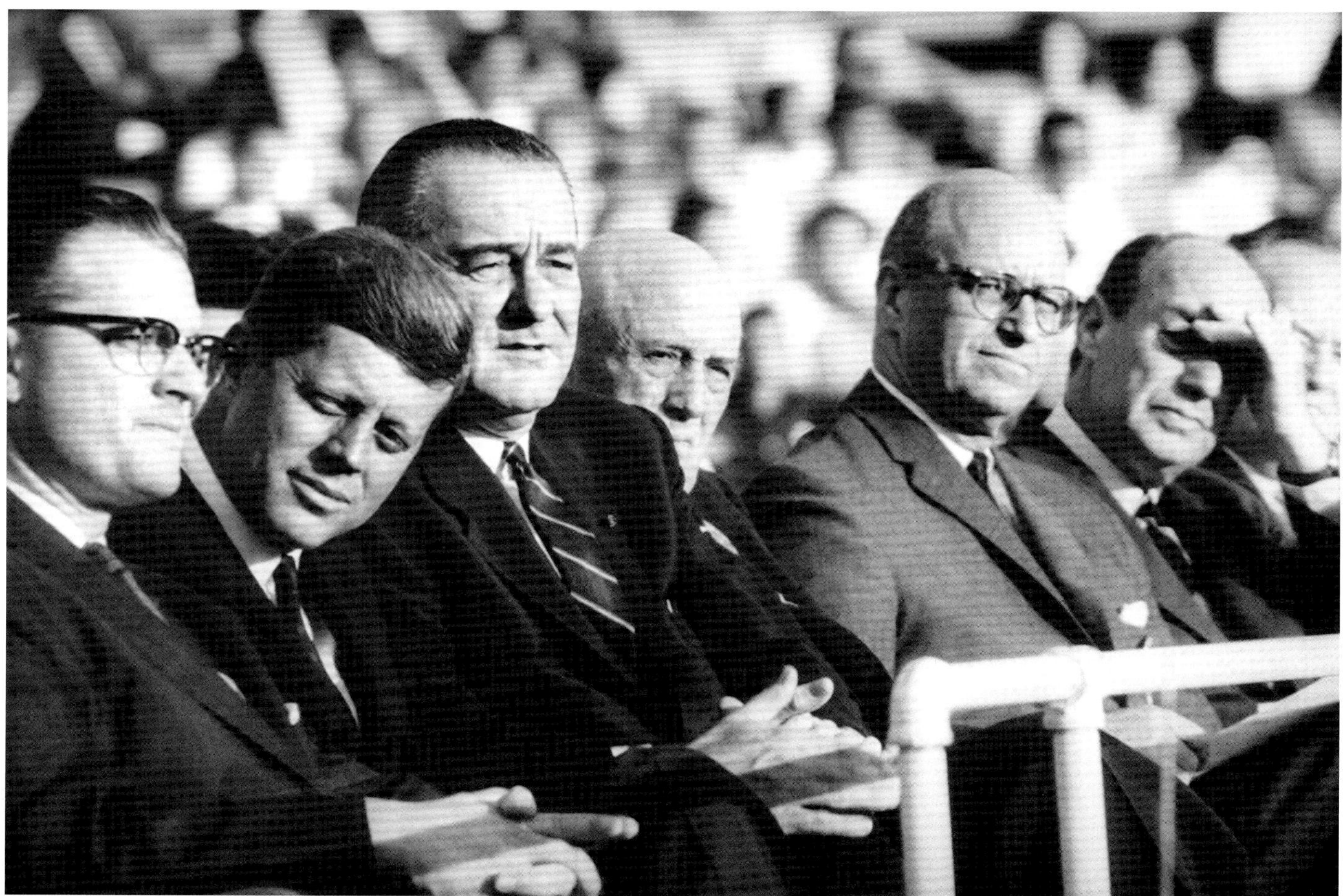

ABOVE *July 15, 1960.* Kennedy waits to speak in the early evening light of the coliseum. California Governor Edmund Brown sits to his left; Lyndon Johnson, Sam Rayburn, Franklin Roosevelt Jr., Adlai Stevenson, and Hubert Humphrey to his right. *Photo, Ed Clark*

OPPOSITE *July 15, 1960.* Kennedy's speech would end a long day of remarks from many of these and other politicians, as well as Eleanor Roosevelt—all aimed at unifying the party as it headed into the fall campaign. Kennedy introduced what would become a key theme of his fall campaign, and later, his administration—the New Frontier: "I tell you the New Frontier is here, whether we seek it or not." *Photo, Anonymous*

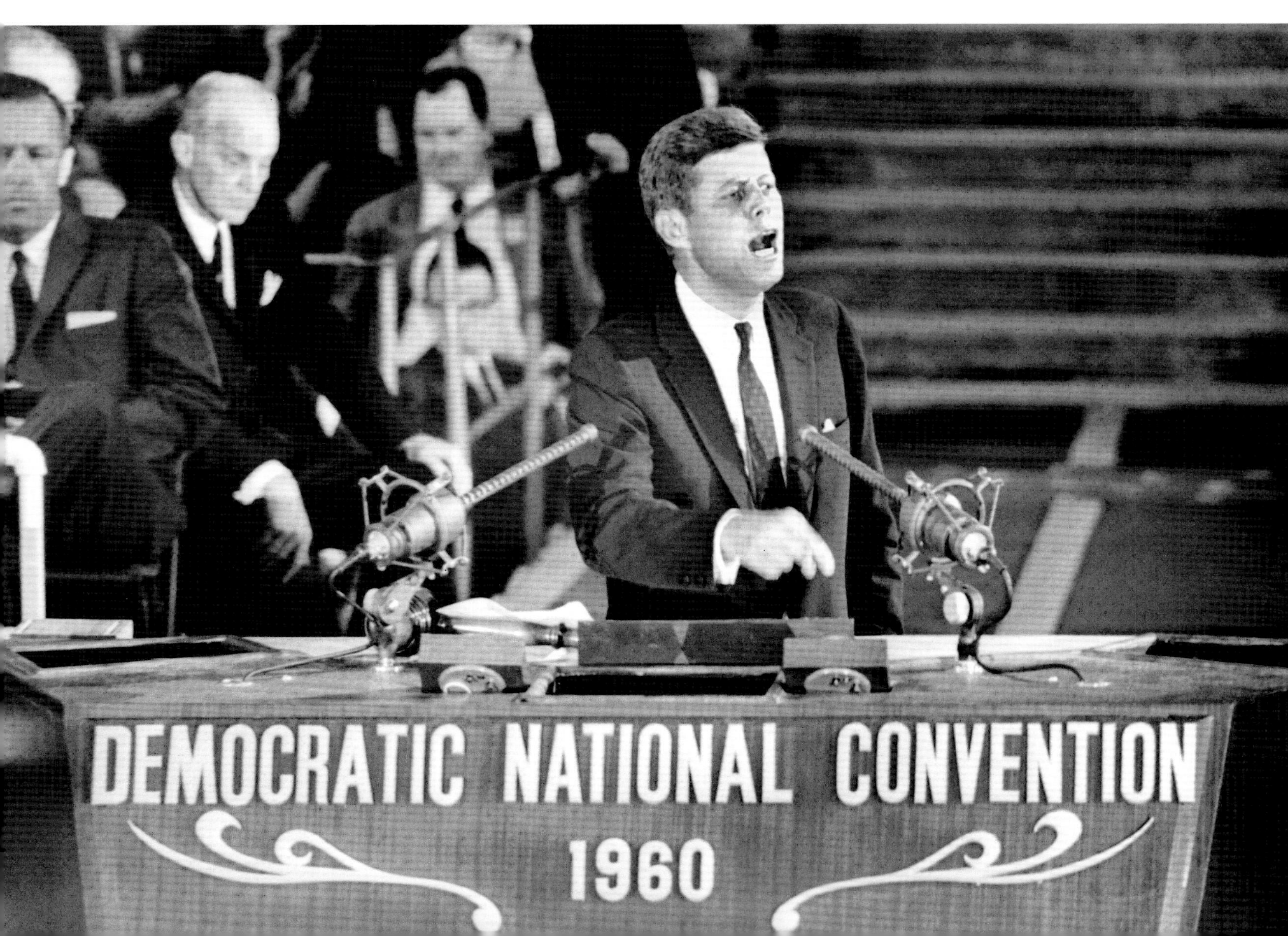

DEMOCRATIC NATIONAL CONVENTION
1960

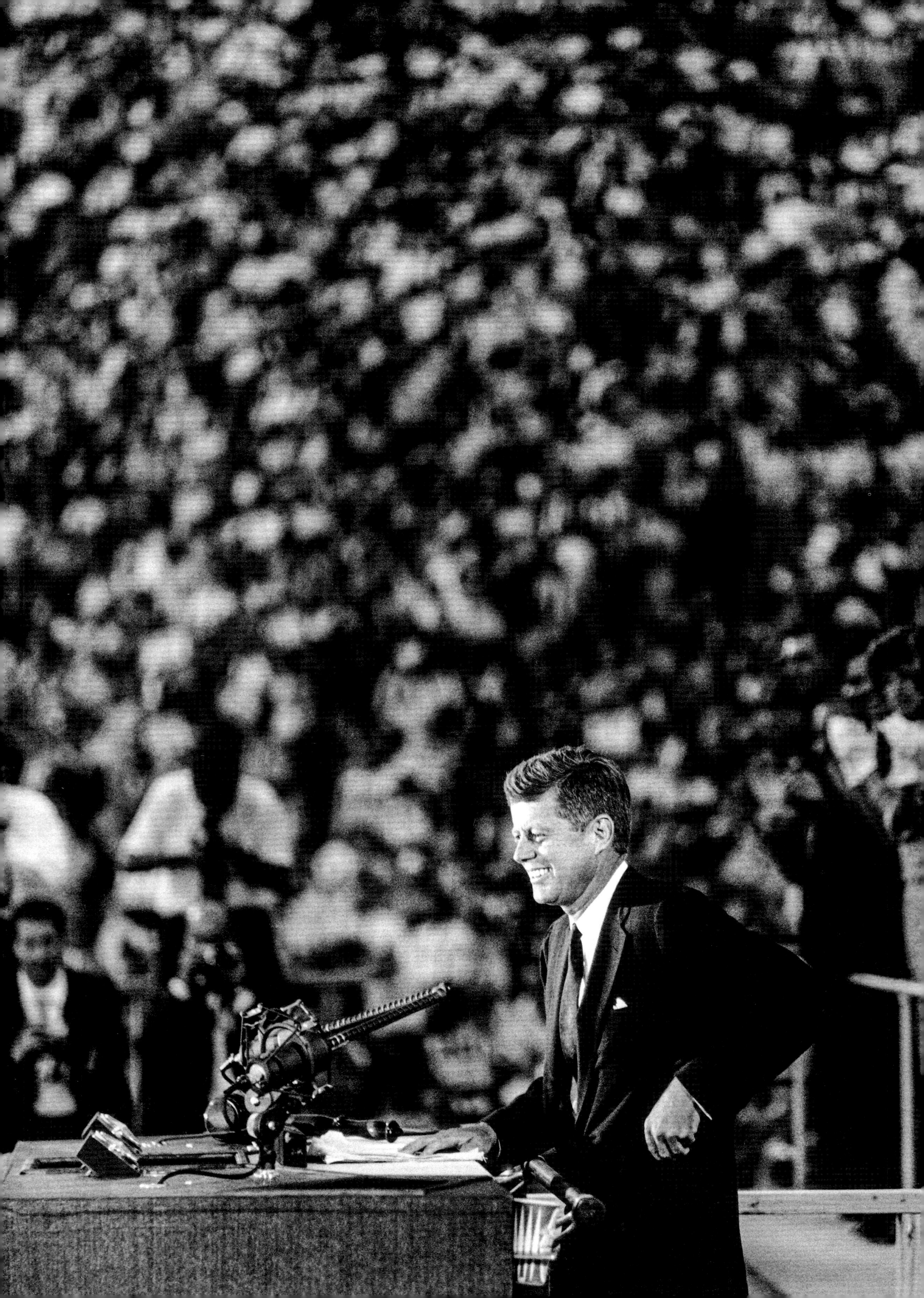

"I think the American people expect more from us than cries of indignation and attack. The times are too grave, the challenge too urgent, and the stakes too high to permit the customary passions of political debate. We are not here to curse the darkness, but to light the candle that can guide us through that darkness to a safe and sane future."

—John F. Kennedy, Acceptance Speech, Democratic National Convention,
 Los Angeles, California, July 15, 1960

OPPOSITE *July 15, 1960.* Thirty-five million people
watched Kennedy's nomination acceptance speech on
television. One of those tuning in to see JFK was his
father, Joseph P. Kennedy, who watched his son's speech
at the New York home of Republican Henry Luce, publisher
of *Time*, *Life*, and *Fortune* magazines (total circulation of
about 12 million in 1960). Still, Luce remained a Nixon
man: *Life* endorsed Nixon for president in October 1960,
and Luce personally voted for Nixon on Election Day.
Photo, Jacques Lowe

FOLLOWING SPREAD *July 17, 1960.* Kennedy returned home
to Hyannis Port to his family and an airport filled with
fans. *Photo, Jacques Lowe*

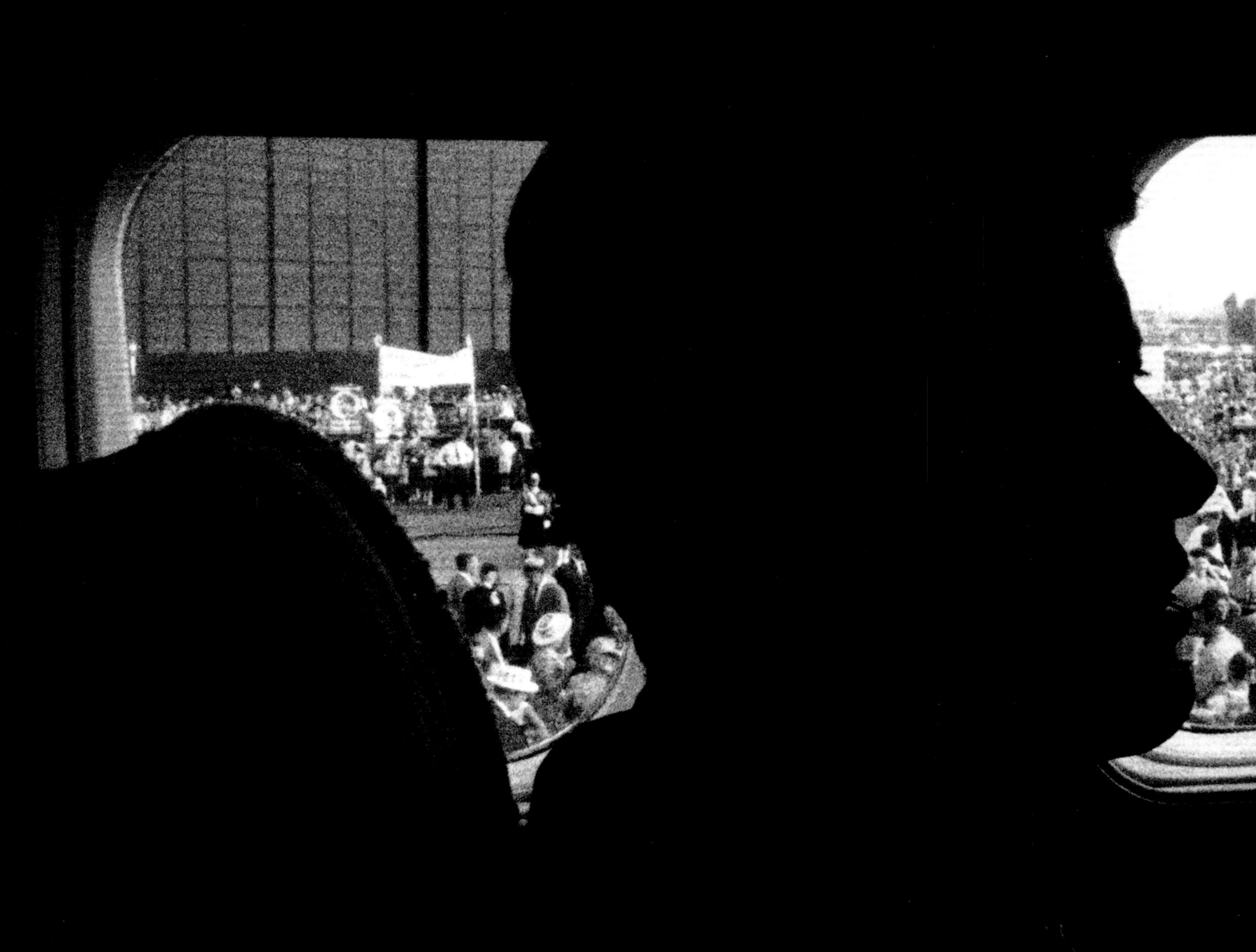

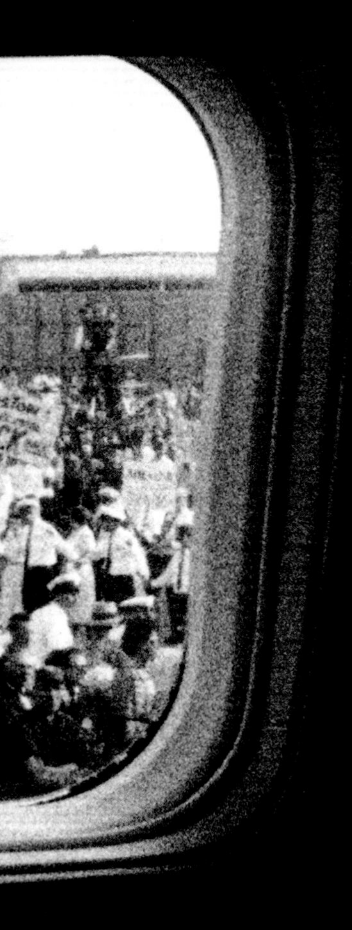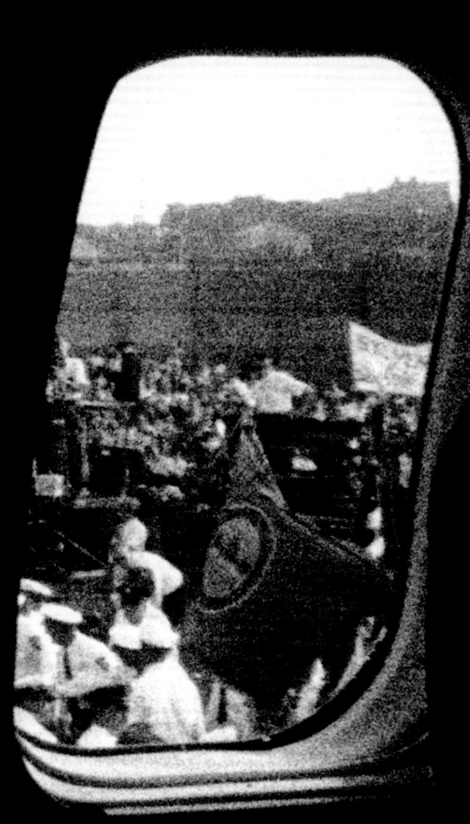

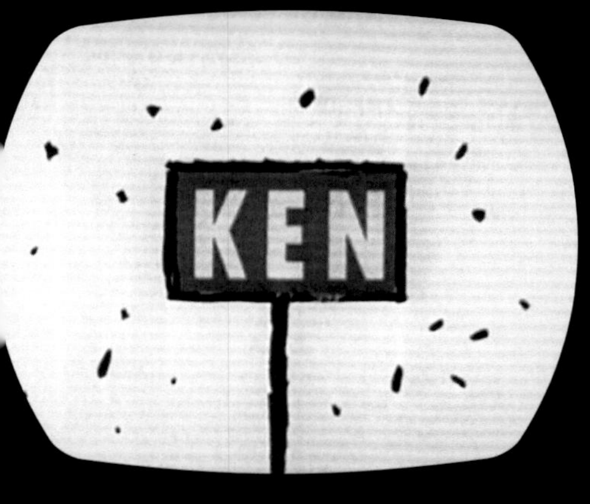
KEN
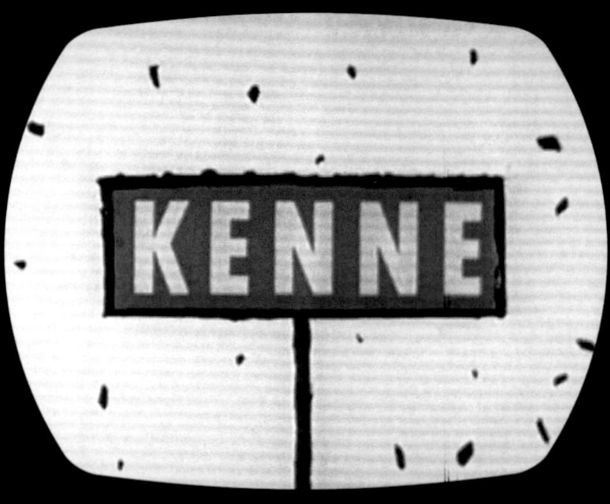
KENNE
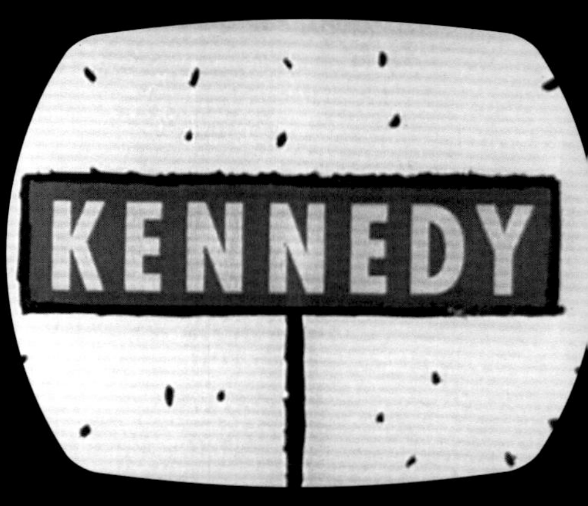
KENNEDY
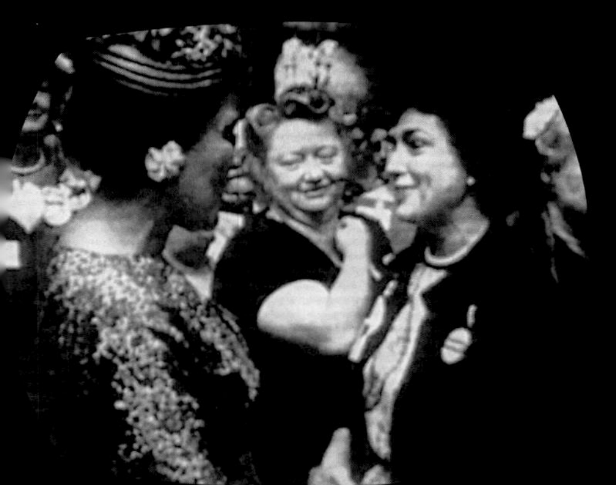
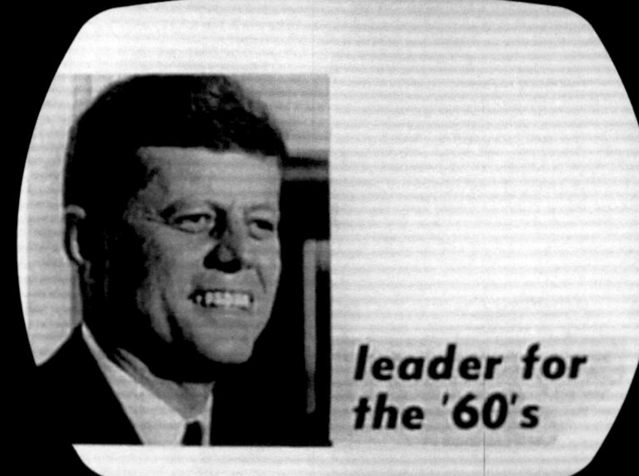
leader for
the '60's
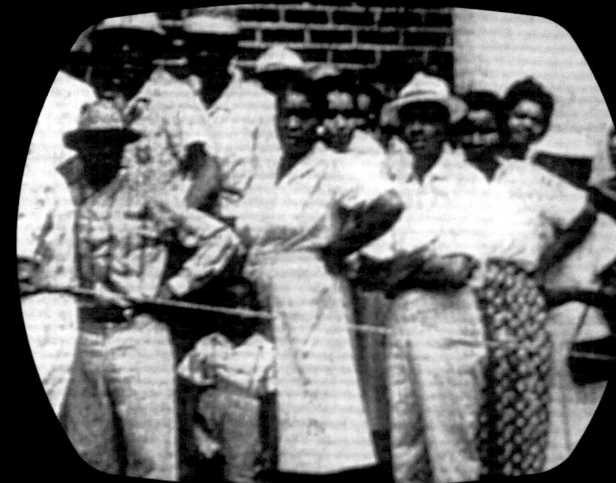
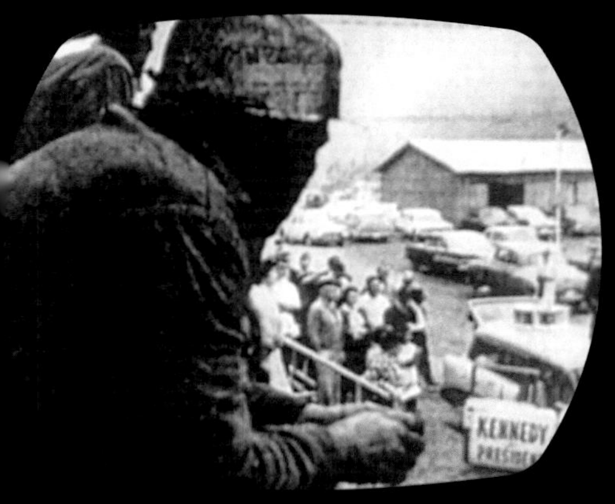
KENNEDY
PRESID
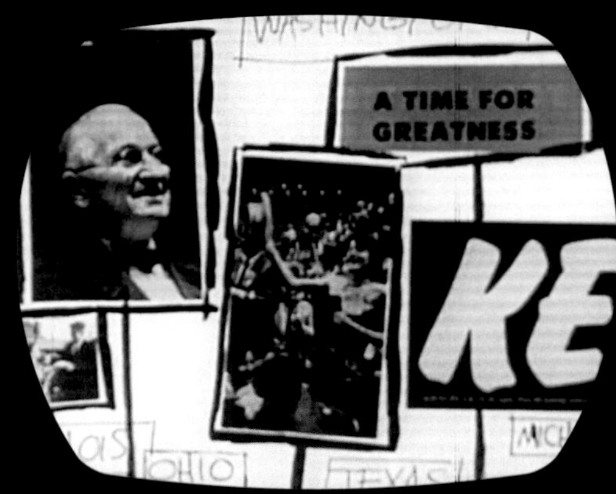
WASHINGTO
A TIME FOR
GREATNESS
KE
OHIO
TEXAS
MICH
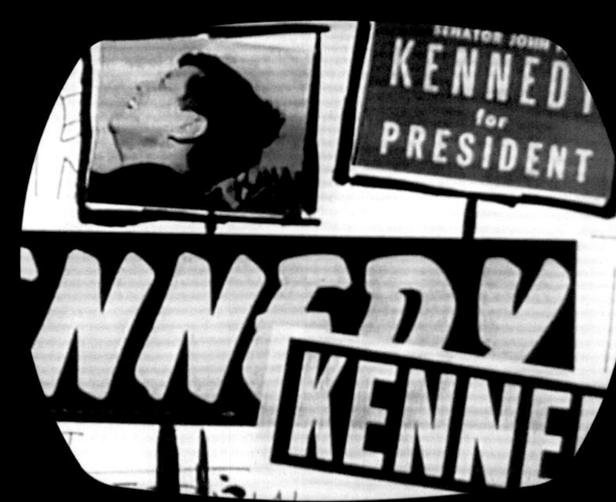
SENATOR JOHN
KENNEDY
for
PRESIDENT
NNEDY
KENNE
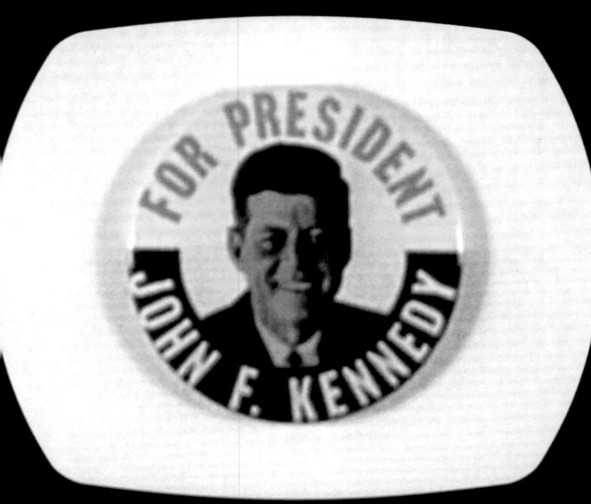
FOR PRESIDENT
JOHN F. KENNEDY
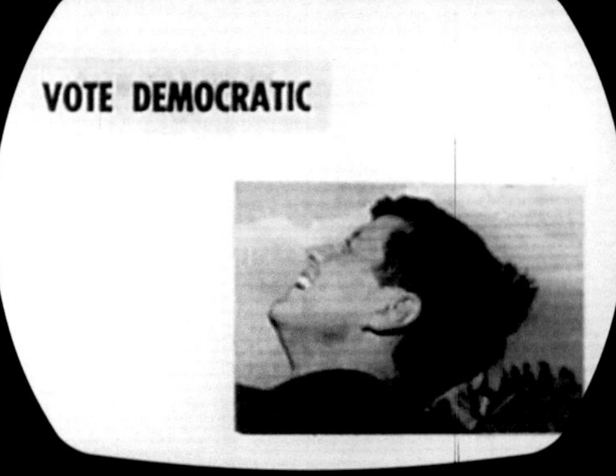
VOTE DEMOCRATIC
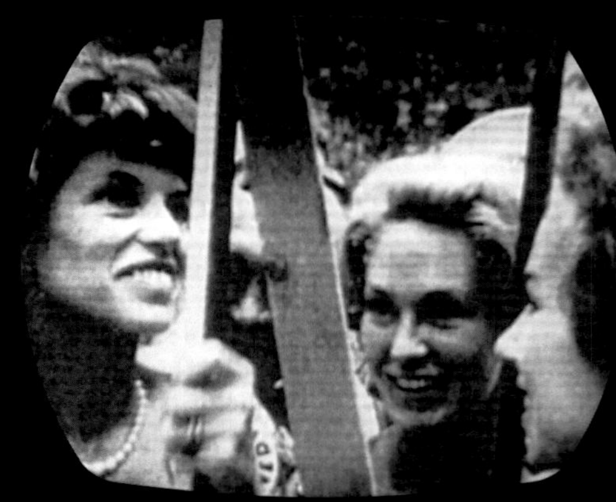
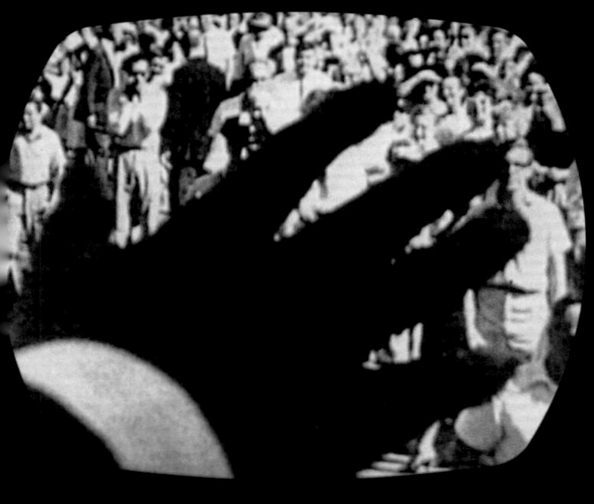
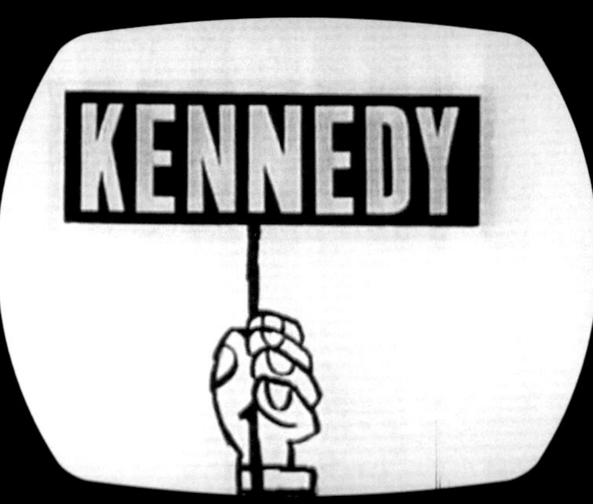
KENNEDY
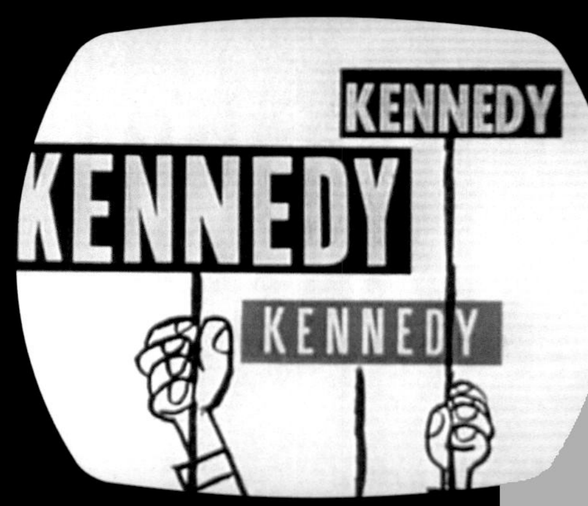
KENNEDY
KENNEDY
KENNEDY

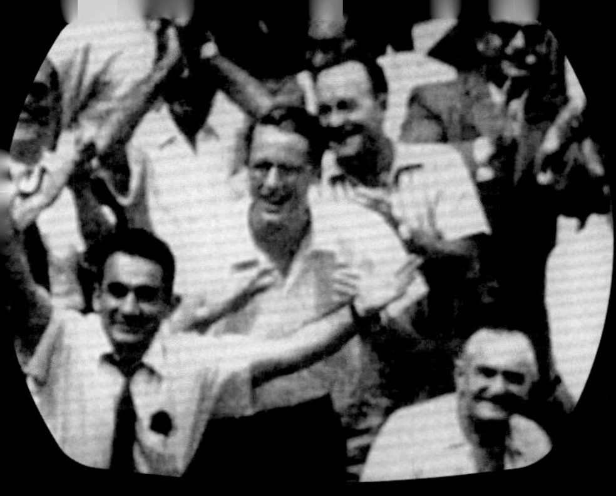
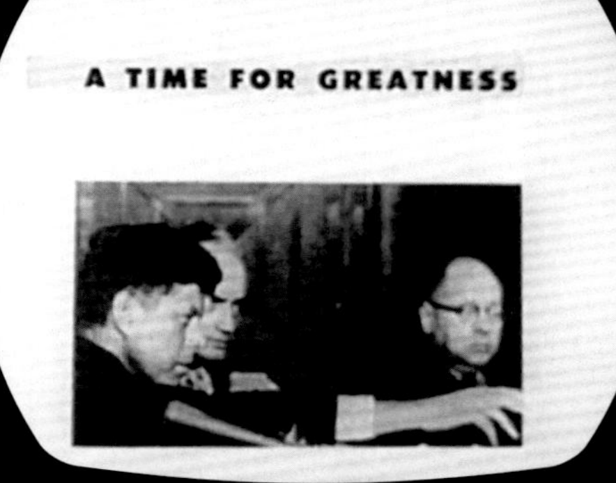
A TIME FOR GREATNESS
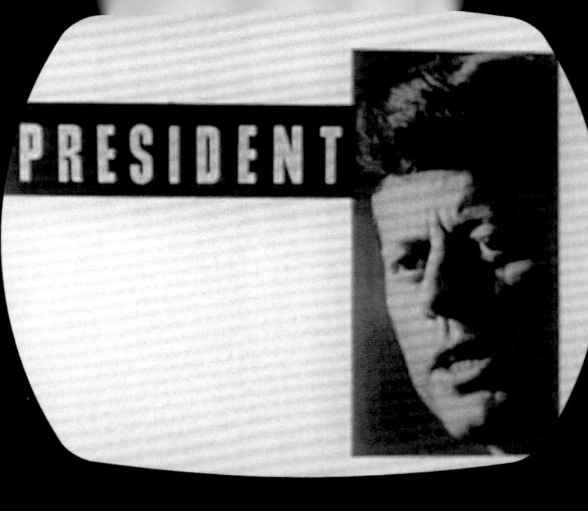
PRESIDENT
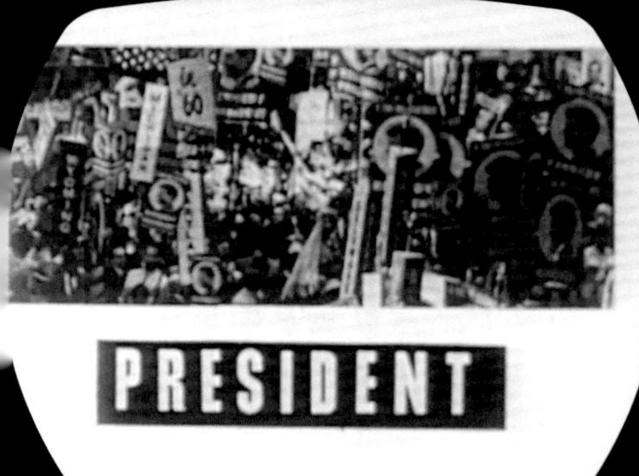
PRESIDENT
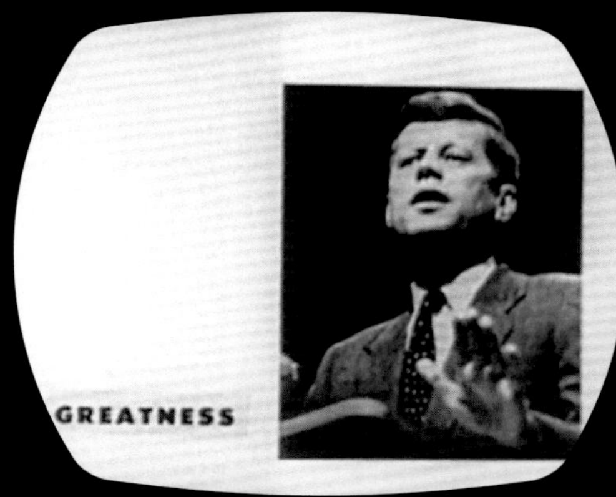
GREATNESS
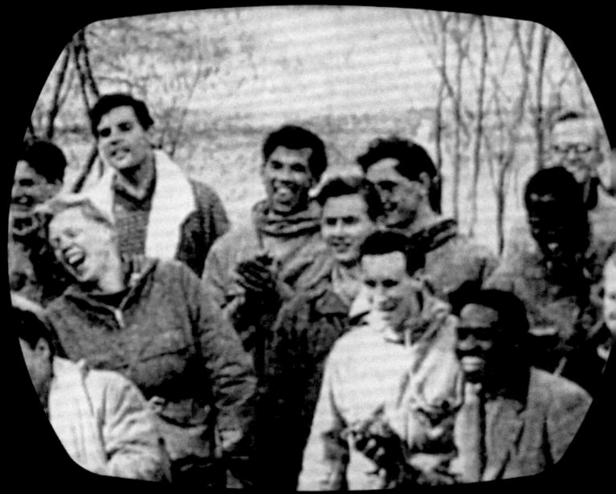
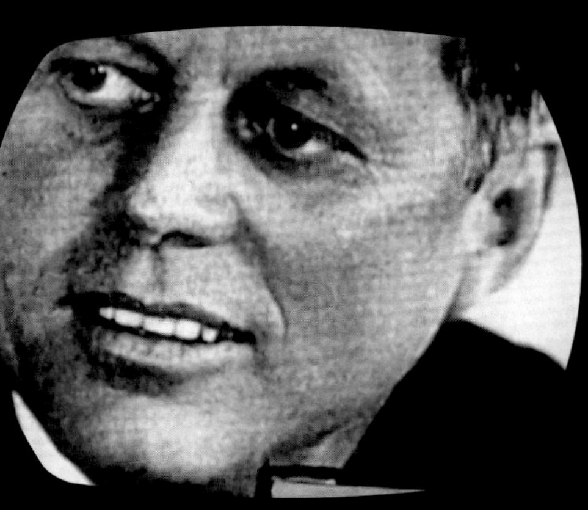
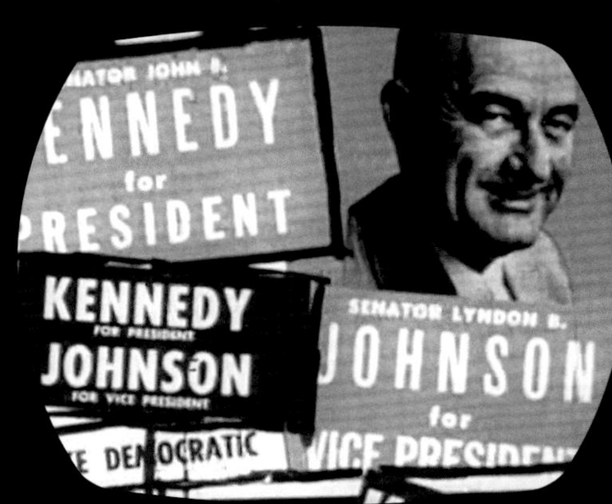
SENATOR JOHN B.
KENNEDY
for
PRESIDENT
KENNEDY
JOHNSON
FOR VICE PRESIDENT
SENATOR LYNDON B.
JOHNSON
for
VICE PRESIDENT
THE DEMOCRATIC
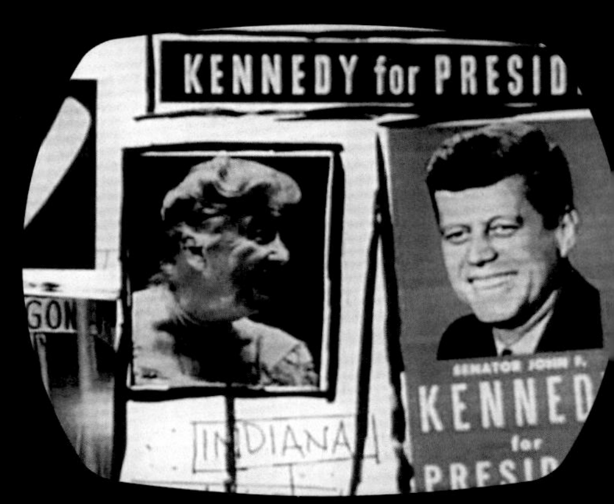
KENNEDY for PRESIDENT
INDIANA
SENATOR JOHN F.
KENNEDY
for
PRESID
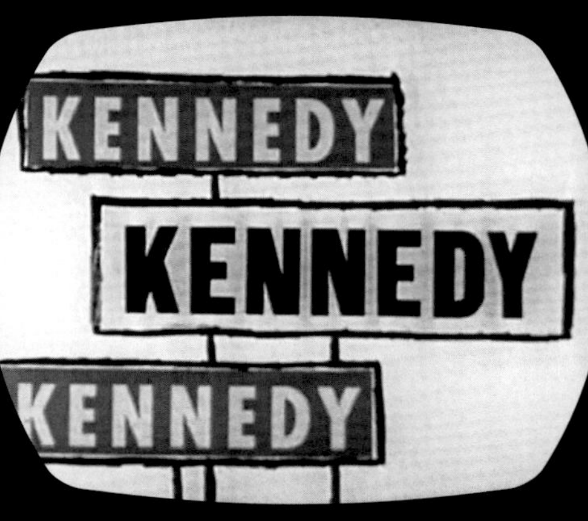
KENNEDY
KENNEDY
KENNEDY
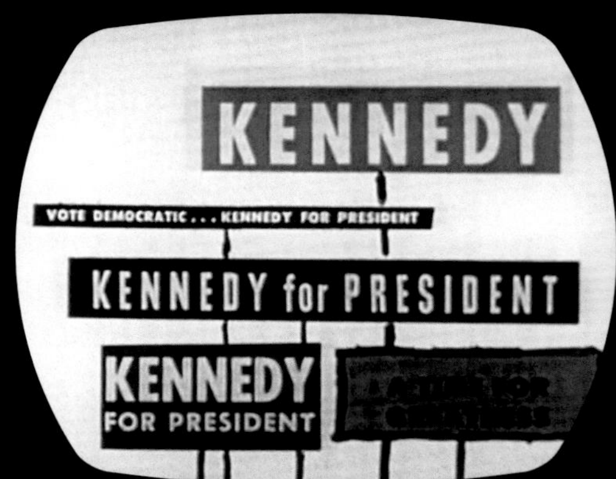
KENNEDY
VOTE DEMOCRATIC . . . KENNEDY FOR PRESIDENT
KENNEDY for PRESIDENT
KENNEDY
FOR PRESIDENT
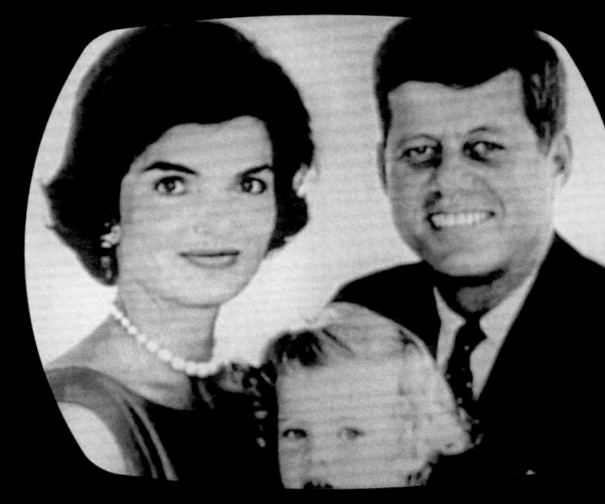
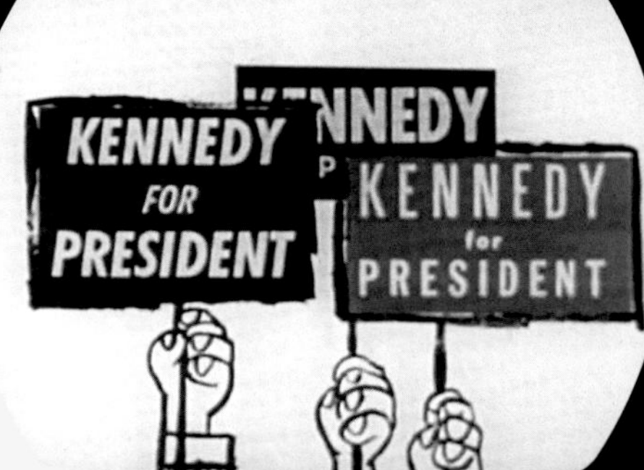
KENNEDY
FOR
PRESIDENT
KENNEDY
for
PRESIDENT
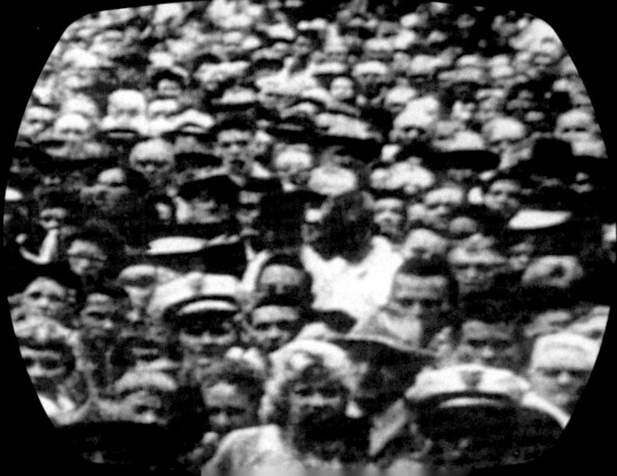
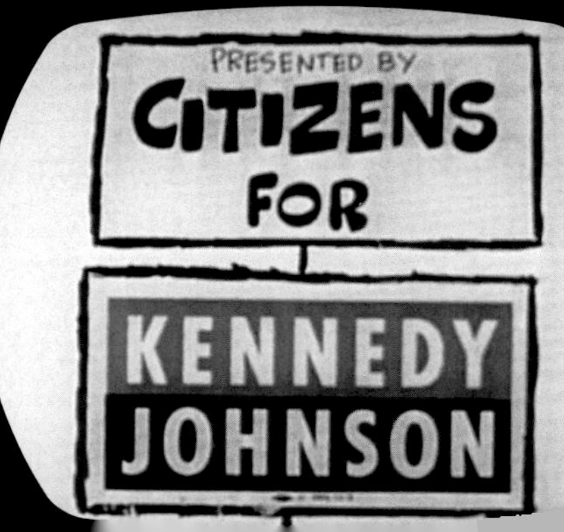
PRESENTED BY
CITIZENS
FOR
KENNEDY
JOHNSON

PREPARED TO LEAD

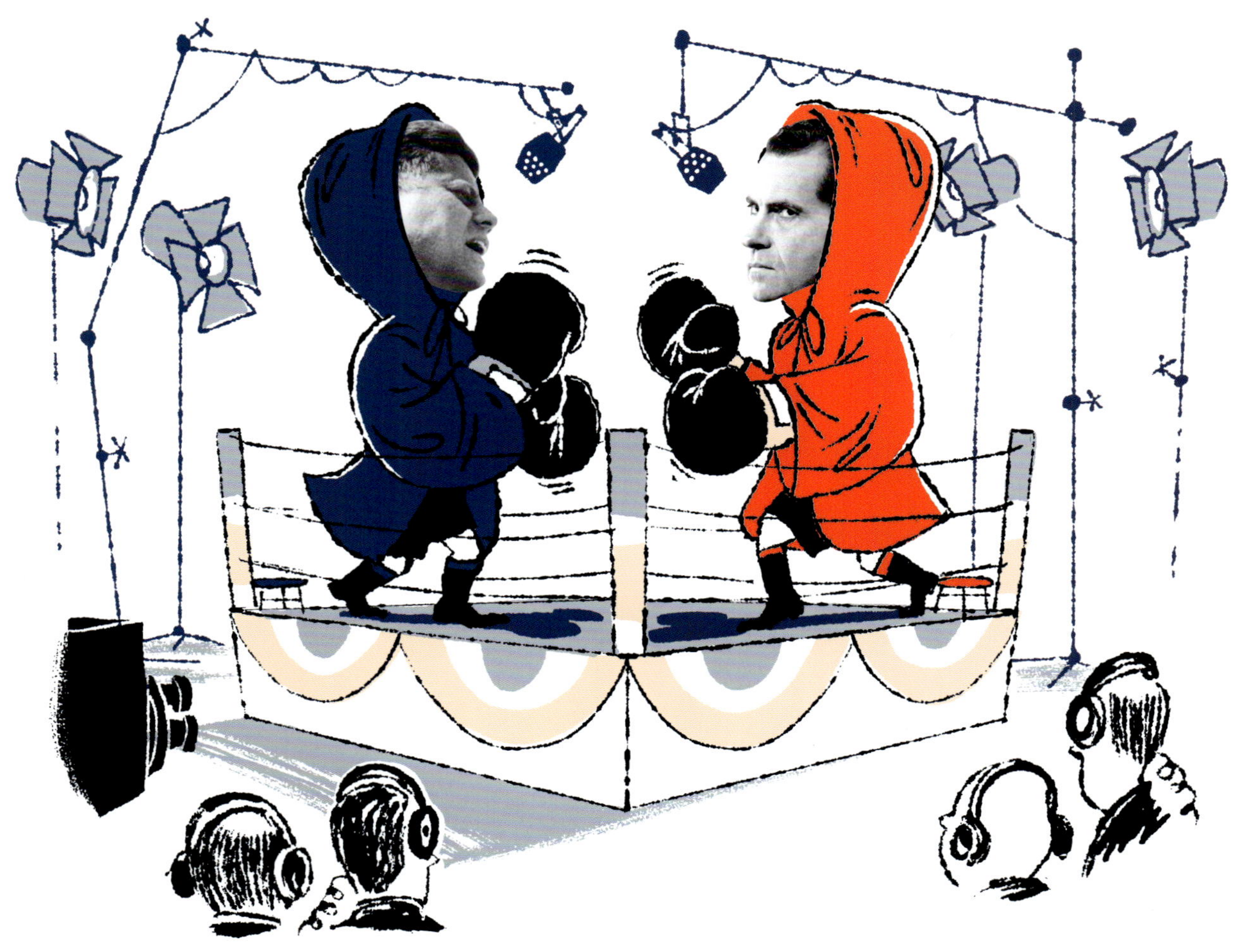

KENNEDY VS. NIXON
SEPTEMBER 5 – NOVEMBER 7, 1960

IF THERE IS ONE CONTRIBUTION OR ONE QUALITY FOR

which the Democratic Party has been noted since its earliest beginnings, since the time of Thomas Jefferson and Andrew Jackson, stretching through the Administrations of Wilson and Roosevelt and Truman, it has been its willingness to break new ground, to look ahead, not to stand still. No Democrat has ever run for the Presidency with a motto, "You never had it so good." Every Democratic President who has served this country in times of crisis has looked to the future. The slogans of our party in this century tell the story of our party; Woodrow Wilson's New Freedom, Franklin Roosevelt's New Deal, Harry Truman's Fair Deal, Adlai Stevenson's New America, and now I talk today in 1960 about the New Frontiers of the 1960s.

No Democrat has ever run for the Presidency standing pat with McKinley or returning to normalcy with Harding, or keeping cool with Coolidge. Those who are satisfied with things as they are, those who wish to stand still, those who look back to the good old days, I don't think they should come with us in the 1960's. But those who want to move this country, those who think we can do better, those who think that there are better days still ahead, those who think that it is time that the government and the people devoted themselves to the great unfinished business of our society—as Franklin Roosevelt did in his administration, and Woodrow Wilson in his, and Harry Truman in his—I hope they will come with us.

We don't promise an easy future at home and abroad because there is no easy life for a citizen of the United States who bears his responsibilities in 1960. But we can say to you that the Democratic Party as it has so often in the past is prepared to lead, and if we are successful this country will move again.

—John F. Kennedy, United Chemical Workers Convention, Ambassador Hotel,
Atlantic City, New Jersey, September 19, 1960

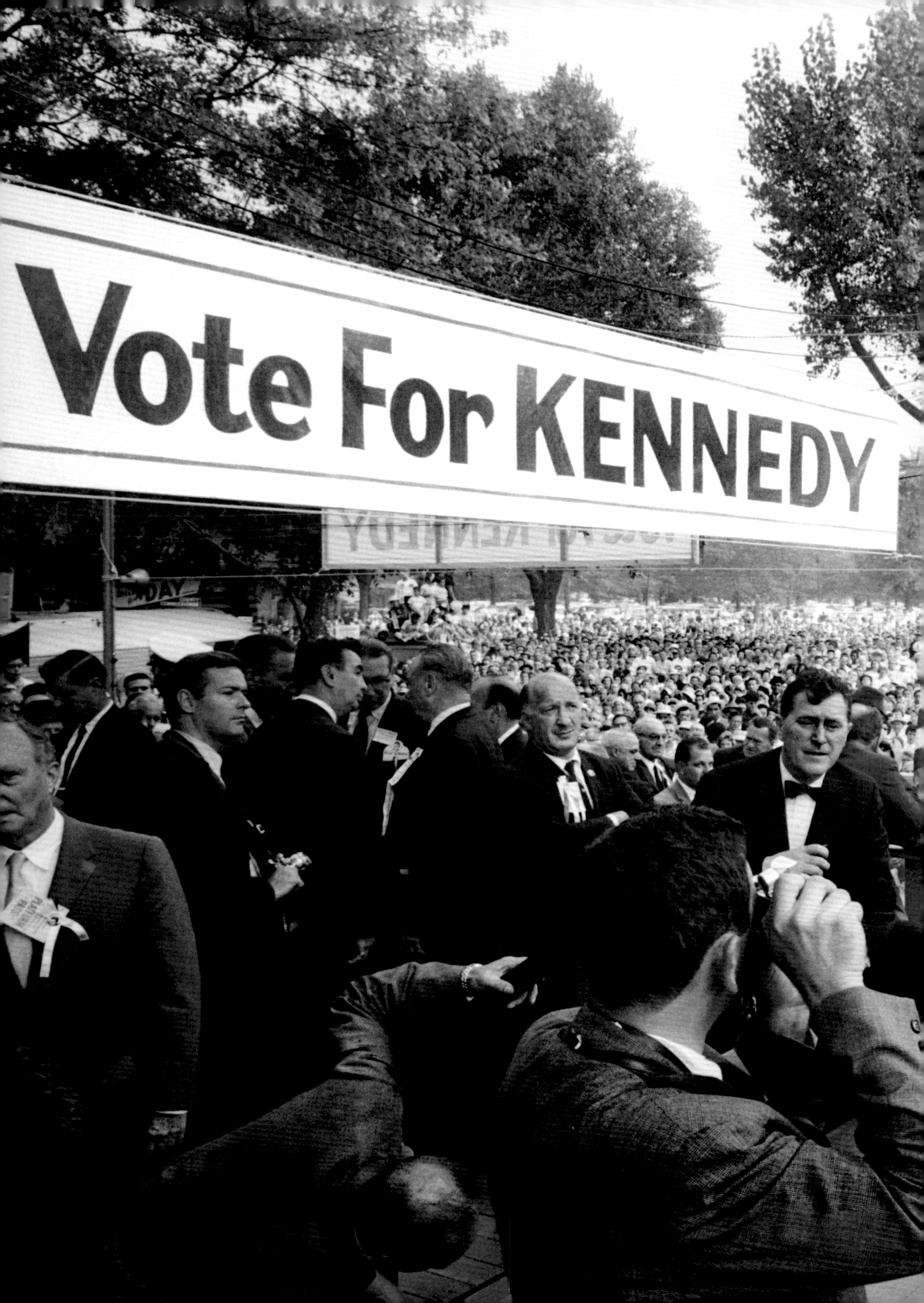

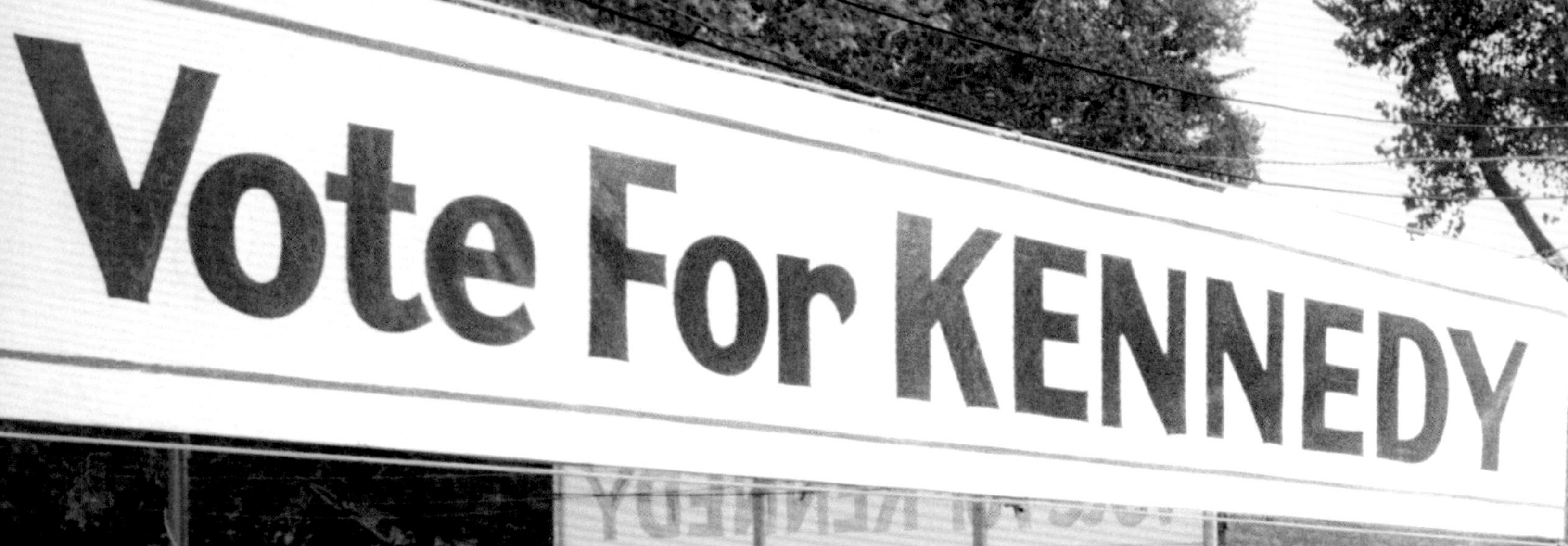

Vote For KENNEDY

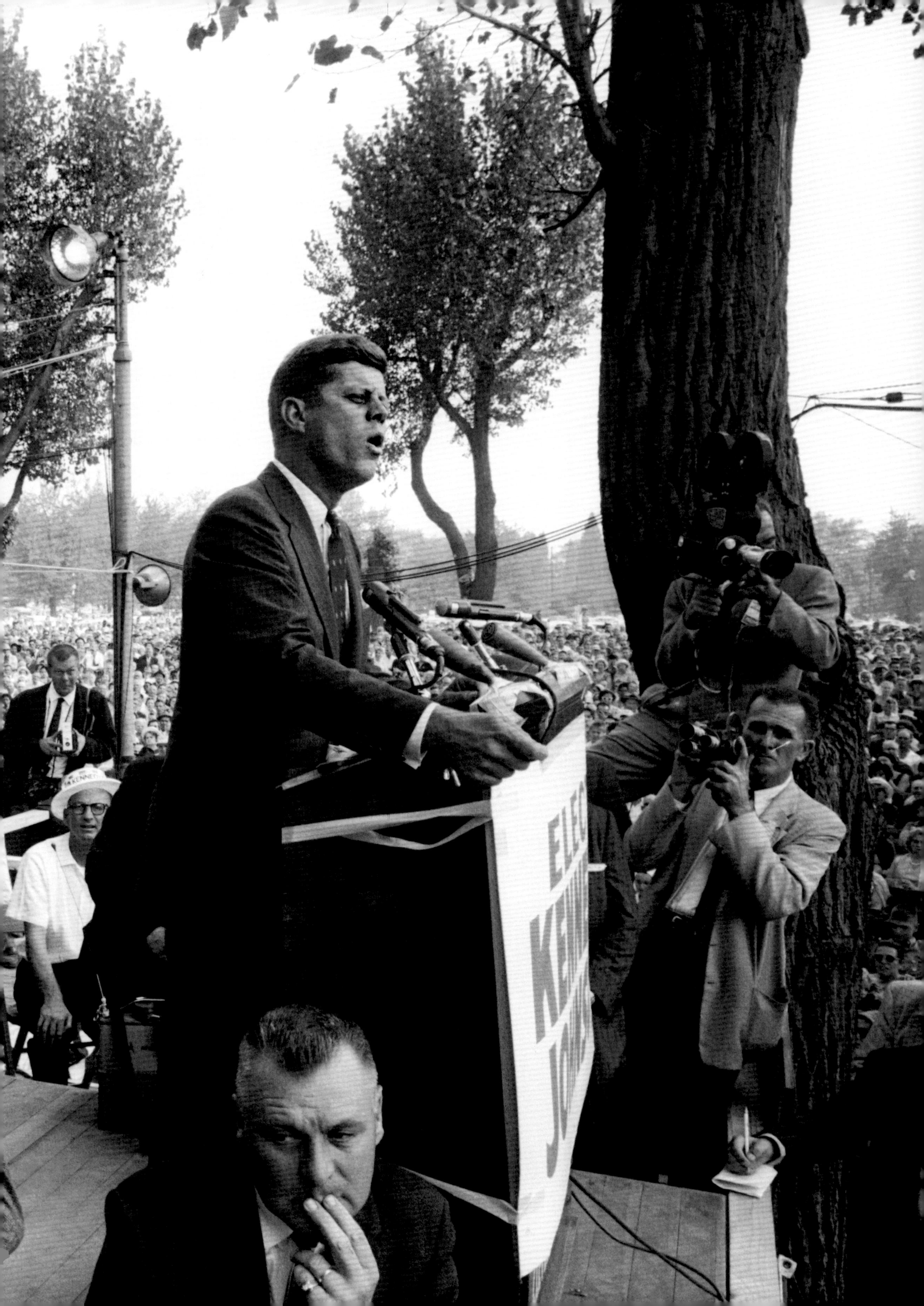
ELEC
KENN
JOH

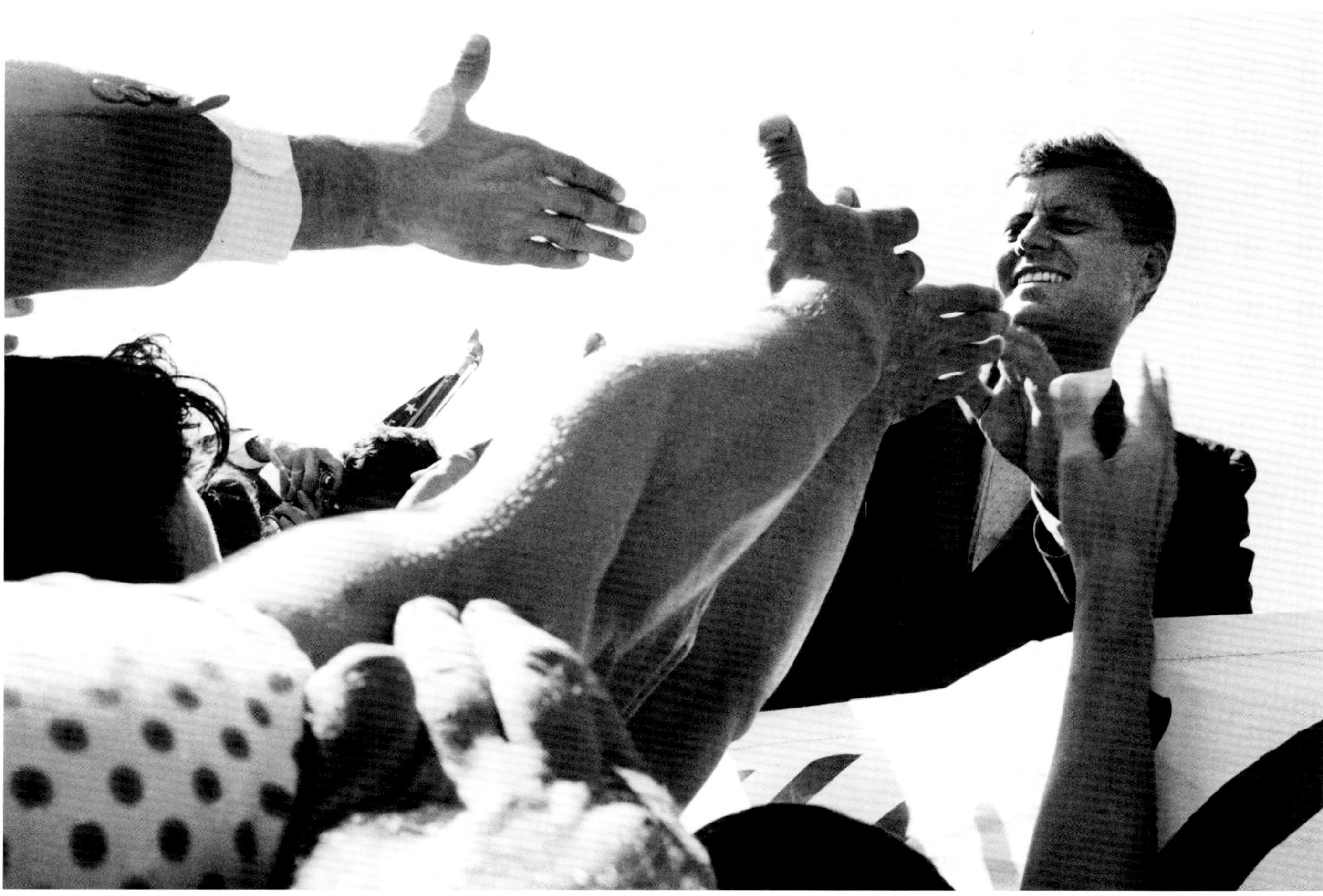

PREVIOUS SPREAD *September 25, 1960.* At the Cuyahoga County Democratic
Annual Steer Roast in Cleveland, Ohio, 20 days into the official campaign
against Nixon. Though now known as a great orator, JFK didn't excel at
public speaking in his early years as a congressman or when he first began
testing the waters for president. His skills grew on the campaign trail,
where he used his considerable talent and knowledge of history—as well as
that of his superb speechwriters—to connect with his listeners. From here
on out, the pace of his campaign would be frenetic. *Photo, Walter Sanders*

ABOVE *September 5, 1960.* Kennedy reaches out past the dais at a picnic in
Detroit, Michigan. The time-honored handshake could prove hazardous,
as many hundreds in the course of a day could leave JFK's hand swollen and
bleeding, along with torn sleeves and missing cuff links. *Photo, Cornell Capa*

OPPOSITE *September 5, 1960.* For Democratic presidential candidates a stop
at Detroit's Cadillac Square—where organized labor sponsors a big rally on
Labor Day—is compulsory. *Photo, Cornell Capa*

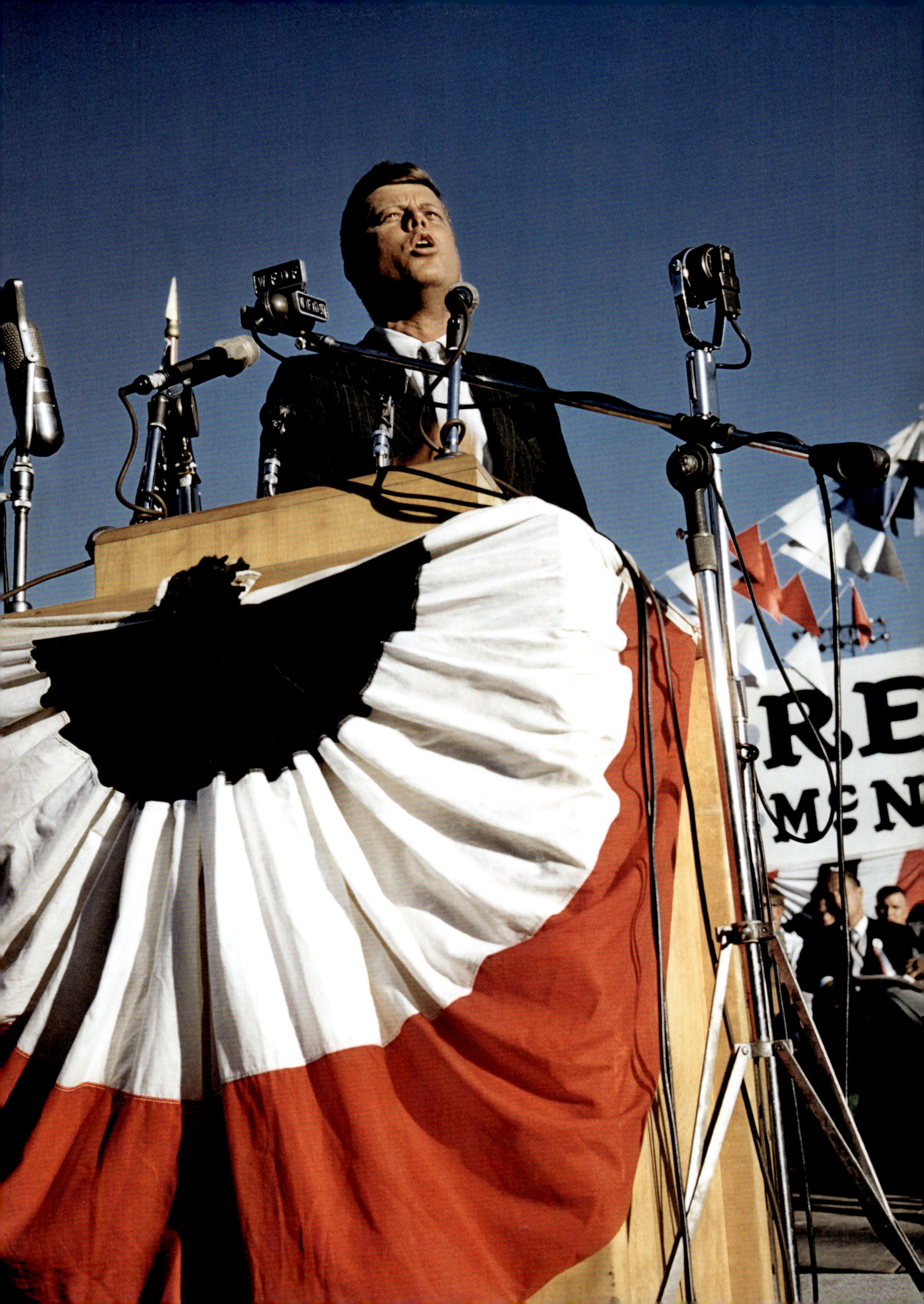

WFDF
RE
M N

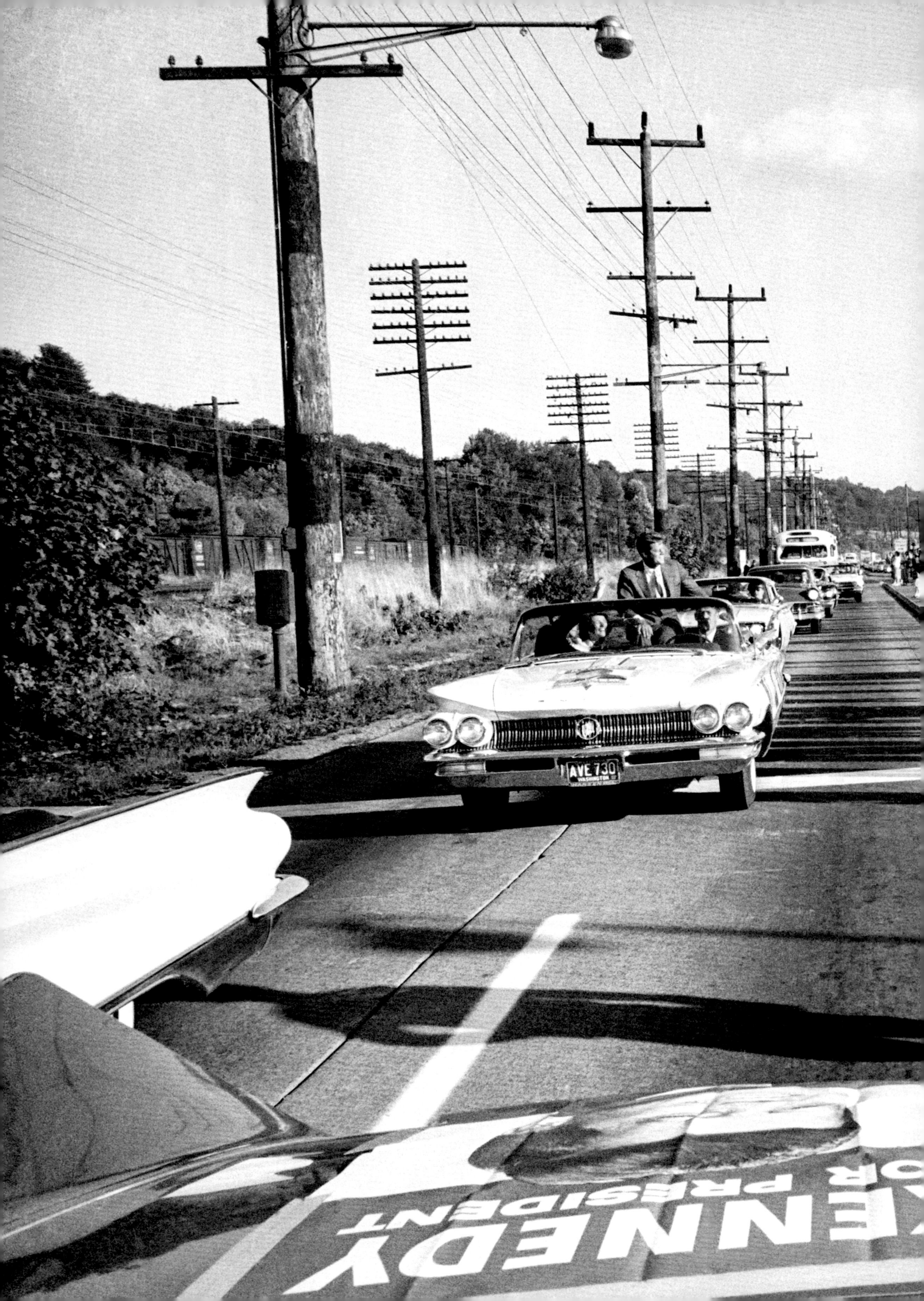
KENNEDY
FOR PRESIDENT

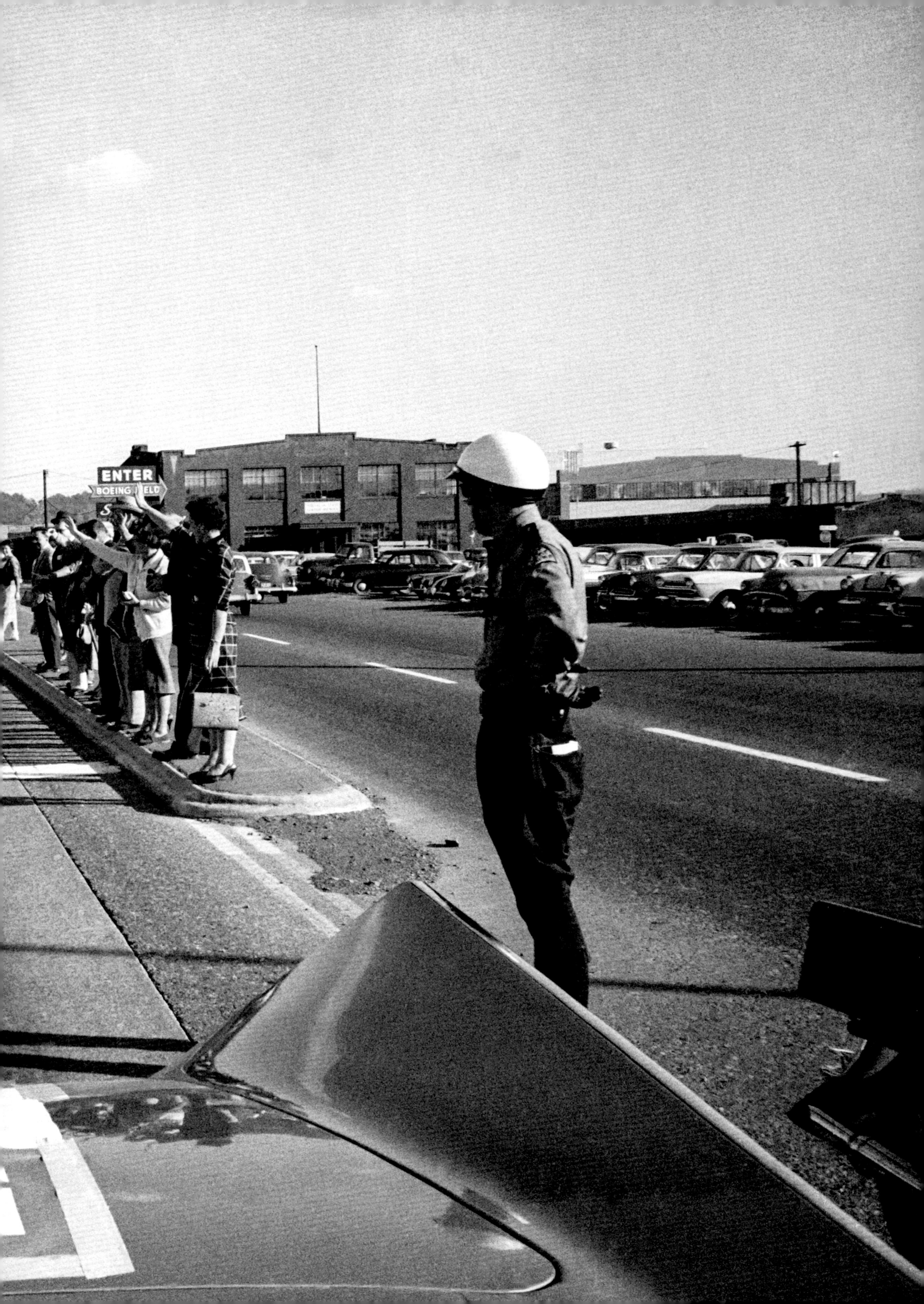

ENTER
BOEING FIELD

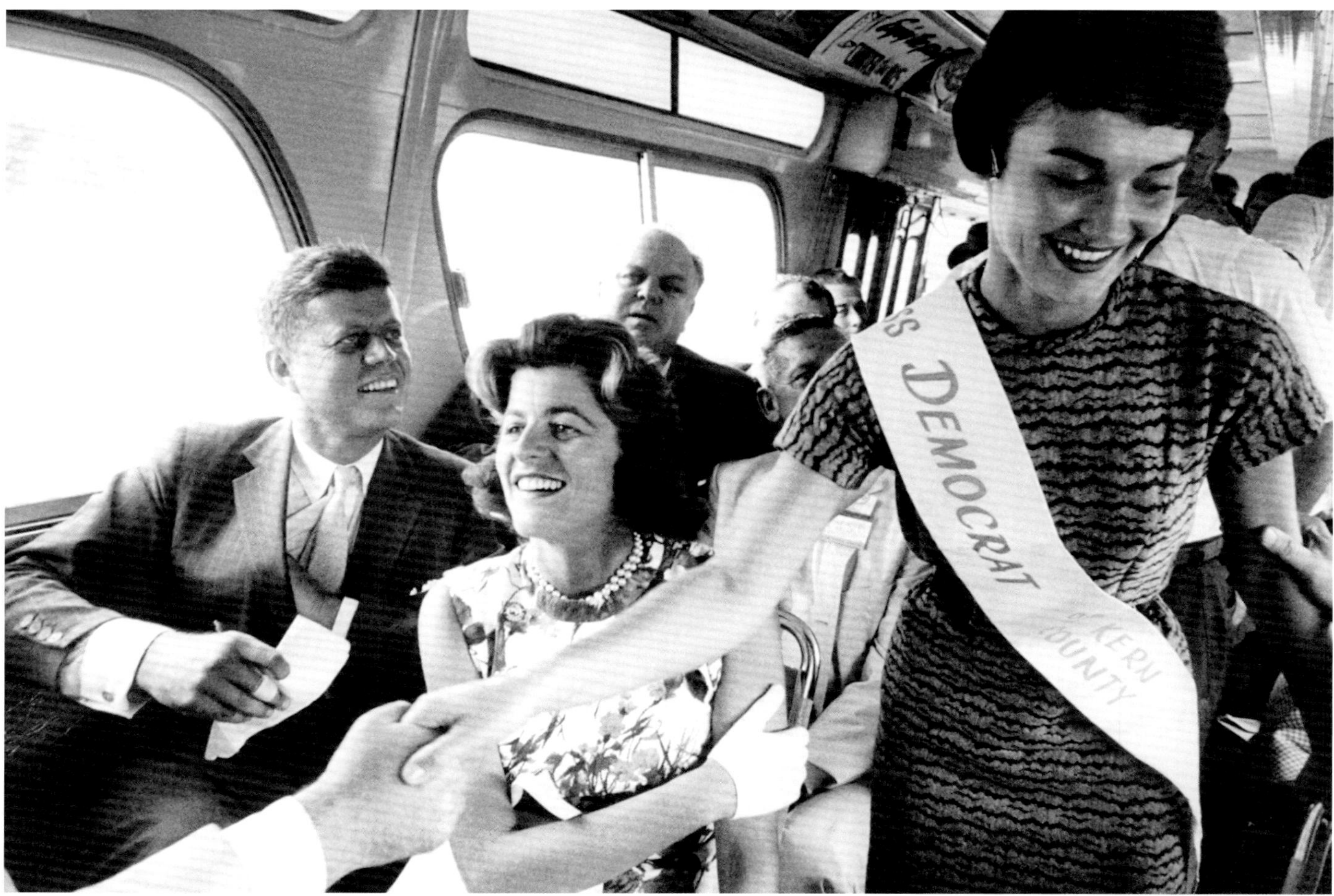

PREVIOUS SPREAD *September 7, 1960.* Kennedy's motorcade rolls though Seattle, Washington, on the way to the Olympic Hotel, where he gave a long speech touching on defense policy. In a 3,000-person rally at University Plaza in Victory Square the day before, he had reinforced the city's importance as a center for aeronautics and national defense. *Photo, Bob Peterson*

ABOVE *September 9, 1960.* With Jackie's travel limited, sister Pat was often a stand-in on the West Coast (she lived in Santa Monica), as on her brother's early September tour from Seattle to Los Angeles. *Photo, Paul Schutzer*

OPPOSITE *September 6, 1960.* After stops in Pocatello, Idaho, and Spokane, Washington, JFK lands in Seattle. Although Kennedy focused his campaign efforts on the large industrial states and the Northeast, he did campaign in the West, especially in California and the Pacific Northwest. (Brother Teddy coordinated efforts in the Western states.) Still, in the end, the West went largely to Nixon, with the exceptions of Nevada, New Mexico, and Lyndon Johnson's home state of Texas. *Photo, Bob Peterson*

"I am the first candidate for the Presidency to actively campaign in the State of Alaska. I left Washington, D.C., this morning at eight o'clock. I have come, I figure, about three thousand miles per electoral vote. And if I travel eight hundred thousand miles in the next two weeks, we might win this election."

—John F. Kennedy, Alaska State Fair, Palmer, Alaska, September 3, 1960

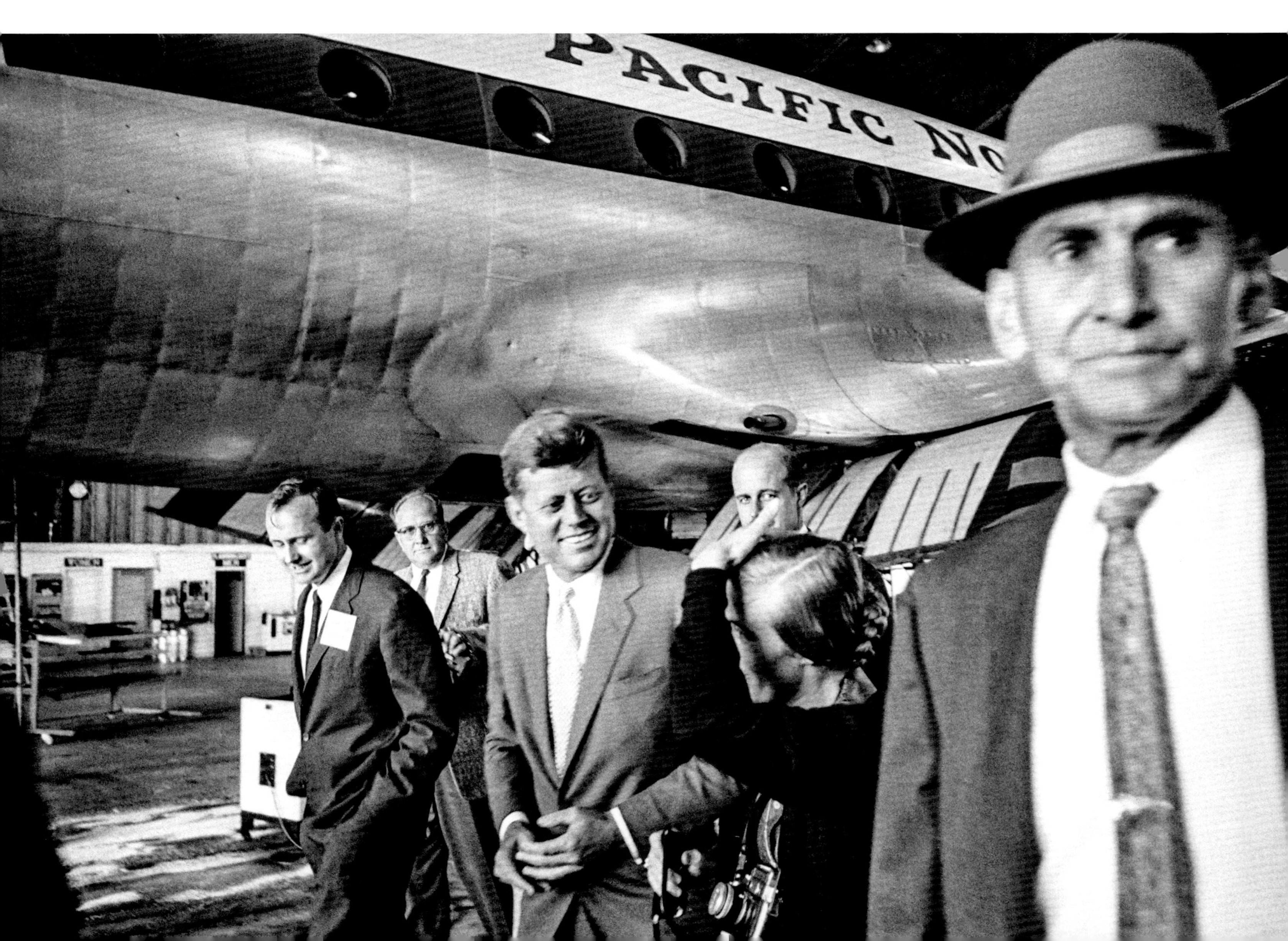

"I want to thank you all for coming to the station. This train
is going south, but it is also going toward Washington, and
I want your support in this campaign."

—John F. Kennedy, Redding, California, September 8, 1960

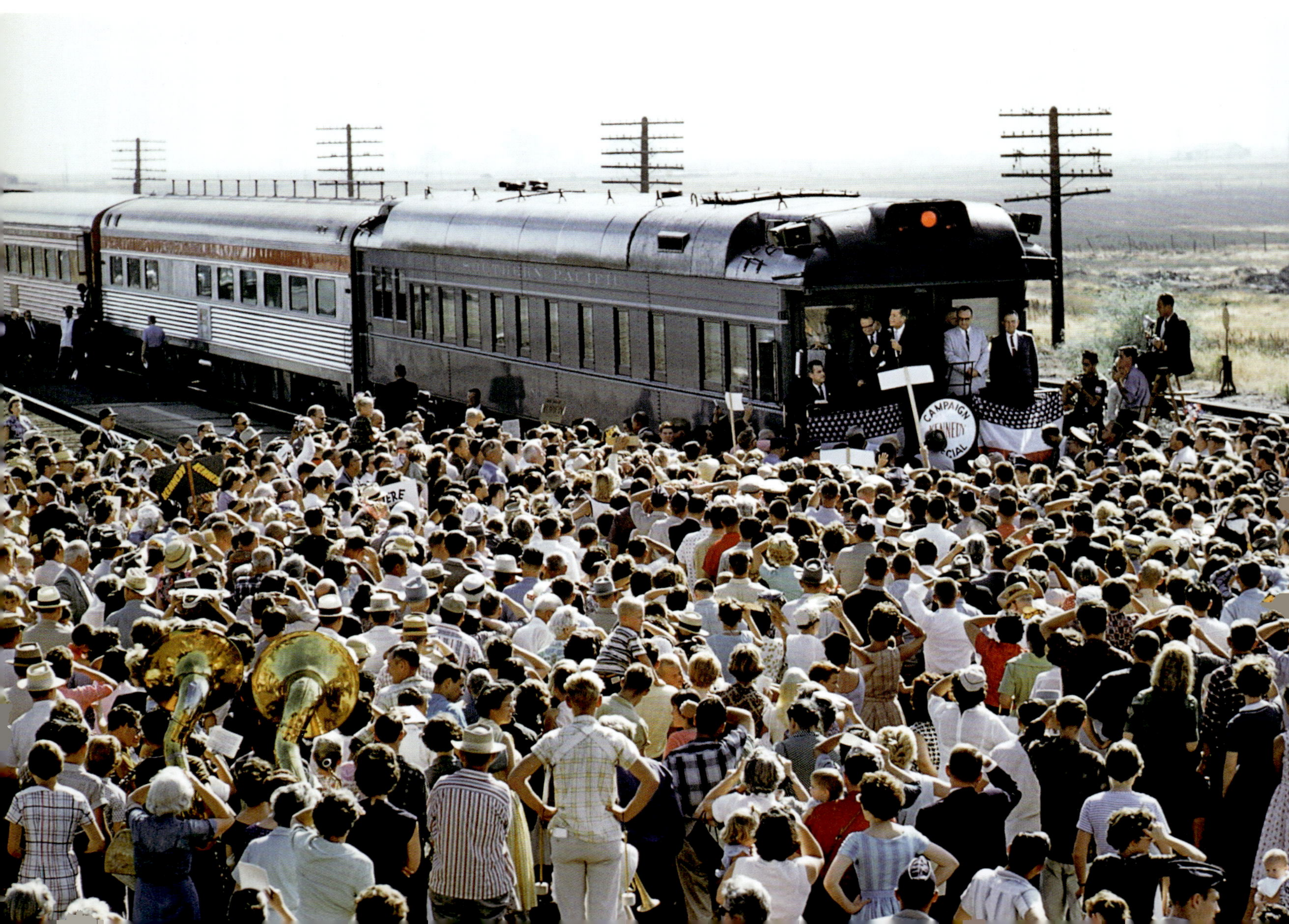

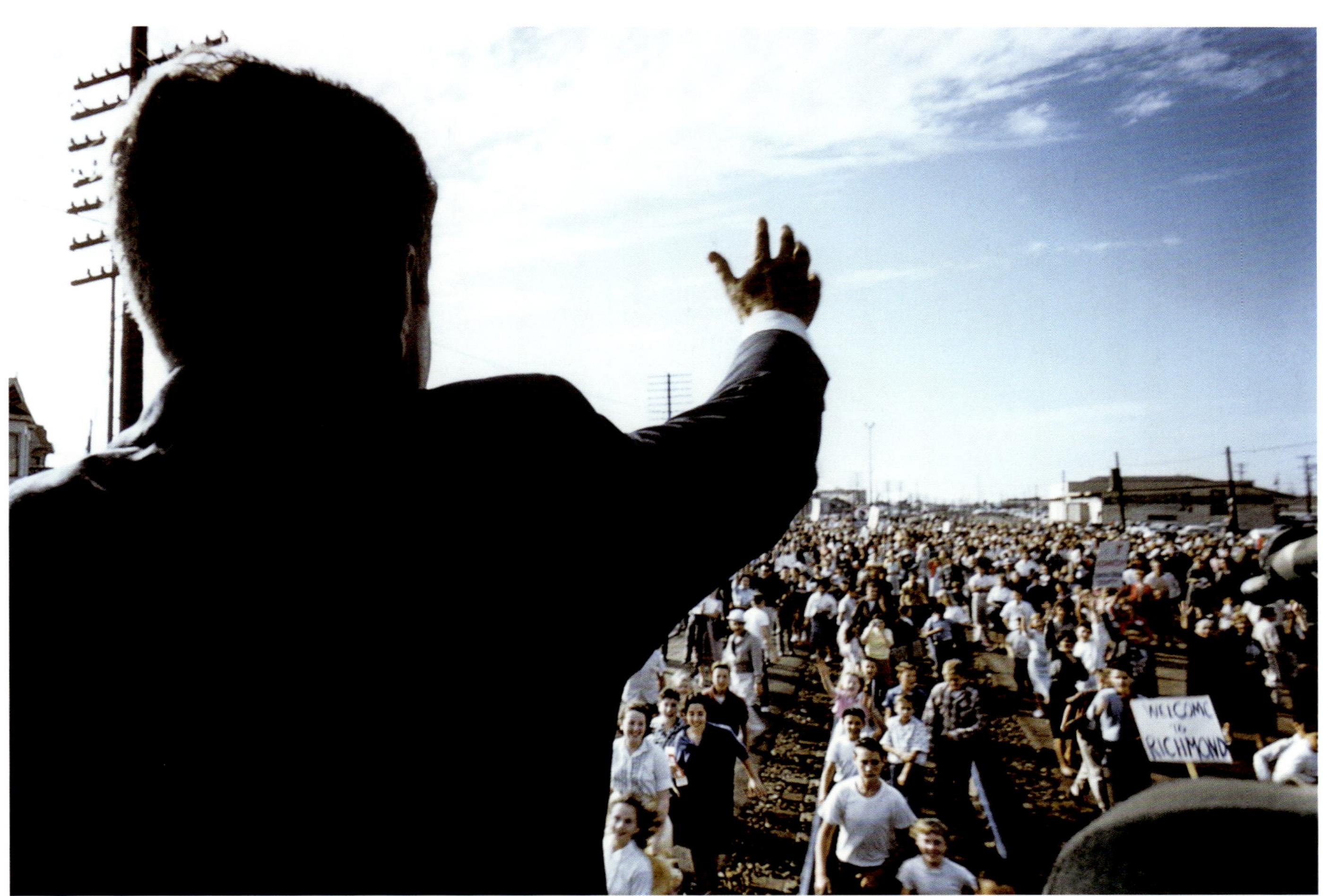

OPPOSITE AND ABOVE *September 8, 1960.* A two-day whistle-stop tour takes Kennedy from Portland, Oregon, south through the small towns of California's Central Valley. Often the residents of the agriculturally rich area brought Kennedy produce in return for journeying so far to see them, as journalist Teddy White reported, filling his train car with "peaches, grapes, olives, pears, prunes." *Photos, Cornell Capa*

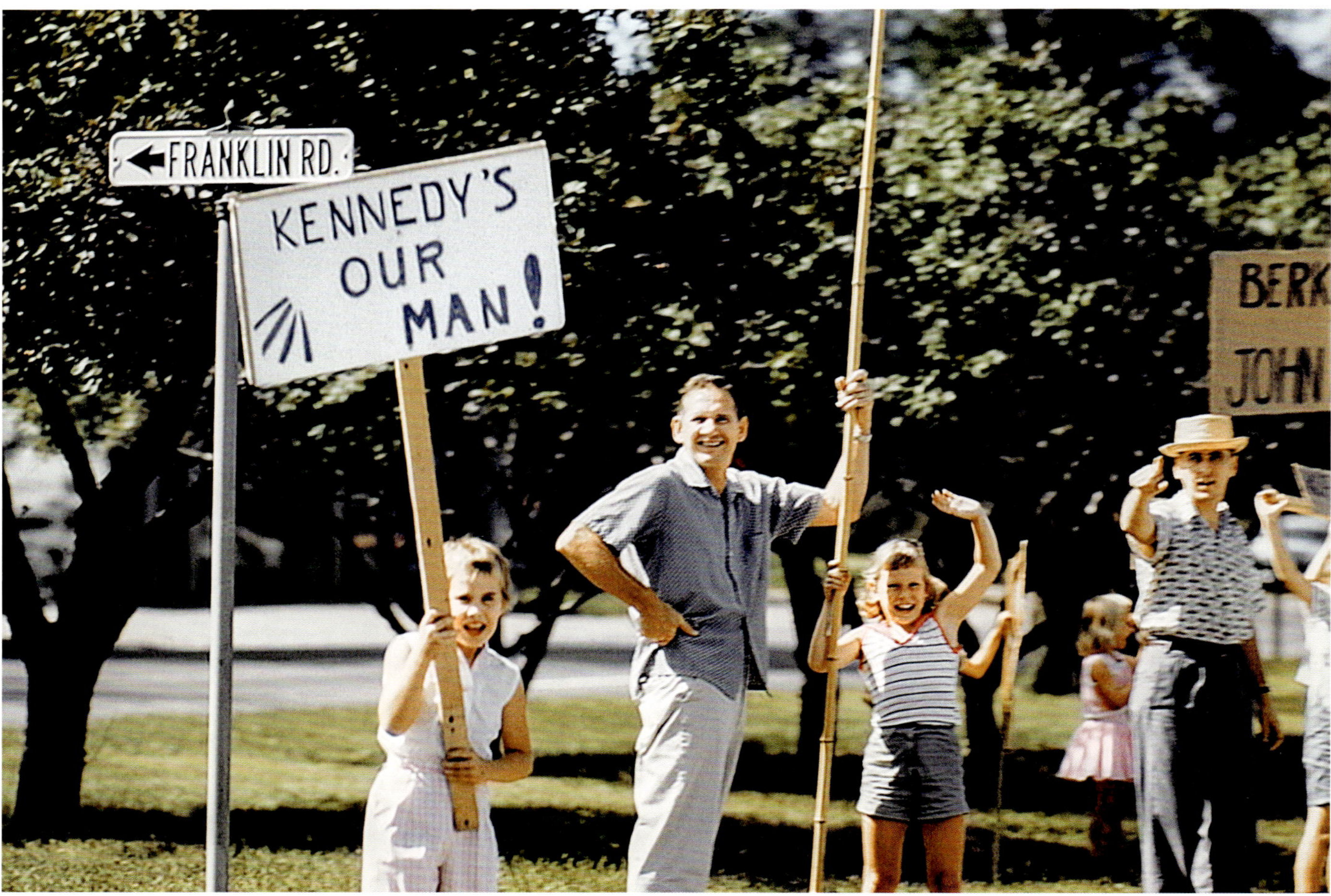

ABOVE *ca. September 8, 1960.* The imagery of campaigning by train conveyed nostalgia of an earlier America, an image that was effective with local voters. While he ended up losing California to native son Richard Nixon — but only by some 36,000 votes — Kennedy did win a number of the San Joaquin Valley counties he had visited, including Merced, Madera, Fresno, Kings, and Stanislaus. *Photo, Cornell Capa*

OPPOSITE *September 9, 1960.* The general fall campaign now underway, JFK's motorcade cruises along Laurel Canyon Boulevard in North Hollywood, California, with sister Patricia Kennedy Lawford. "Pat," as she was called, held considerable sway among the Hollywood elite, as both a producer and the wife of actor Peter Lawford. *Photo, Cornell Capa*

FOLLOWING SPREAD *September 9, 1960.* The Kennedy supporters at this event in North Hollywood, California, show the 43-year-old candidate's appeal among two important demographics: young people and women. *Photo, Cornell Capa*

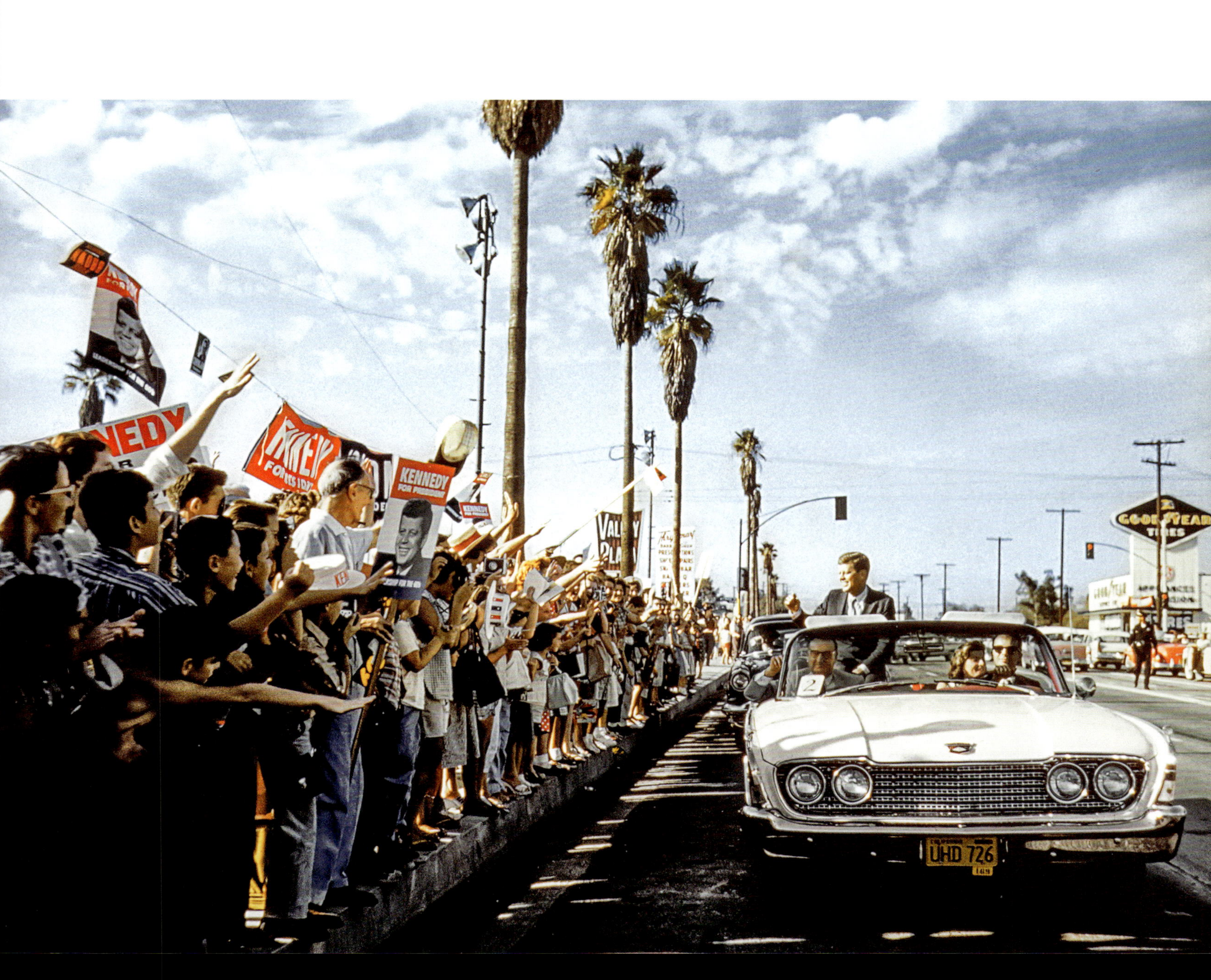

KENNEDY FOR PRESIDENT
KENNEDY
KENNEDY FOR PRESIDENT
VALLEY
GOODYEAR TIRES
UHD 726

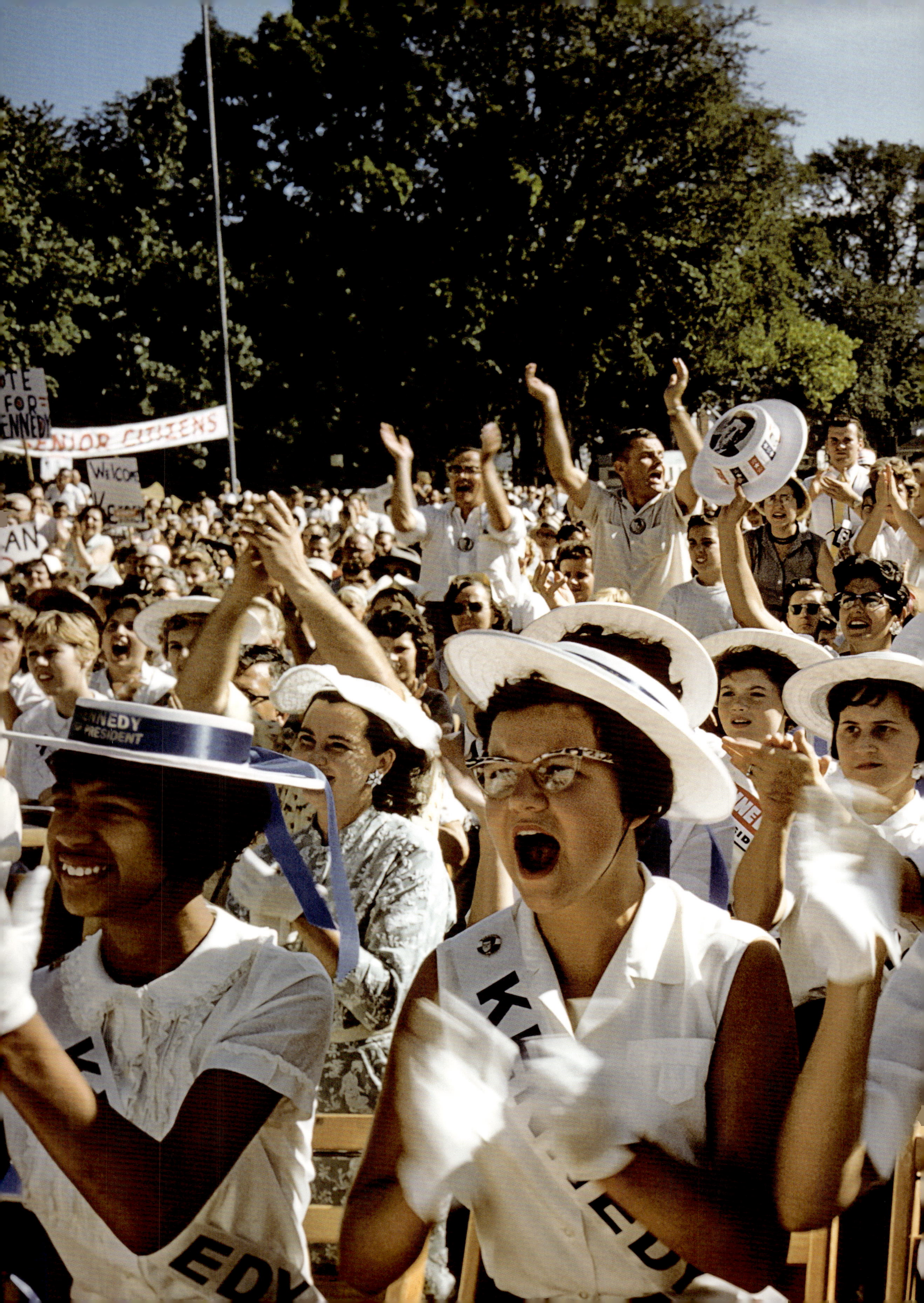
OTE
FOR
ENNEDY
SENIOR CITIZENS
WELCO
KENNEDY
FOR PRESIDENT
KENNEDY

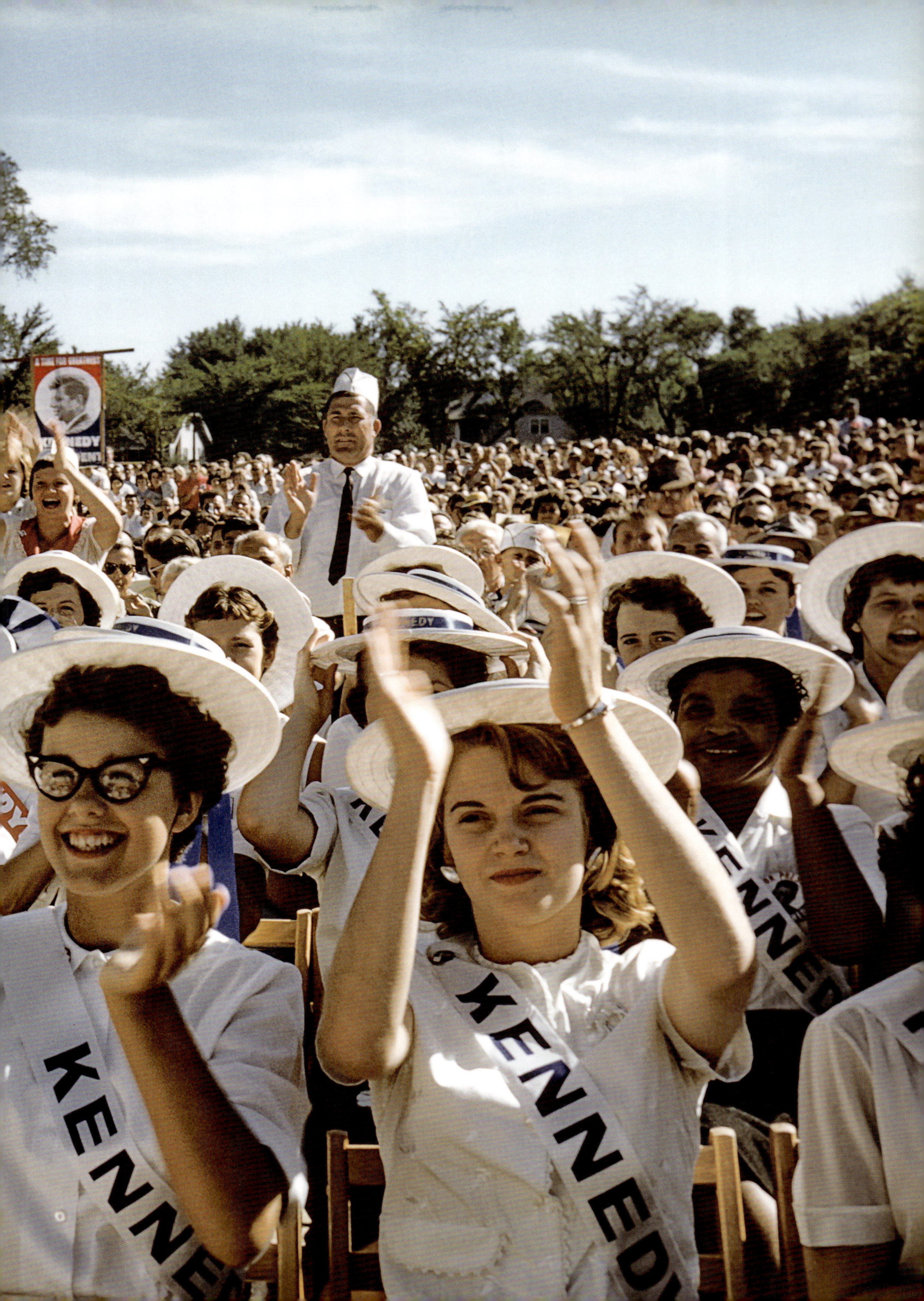
A TIME FOR GREATNESS
KENNEDY
KENNEDY

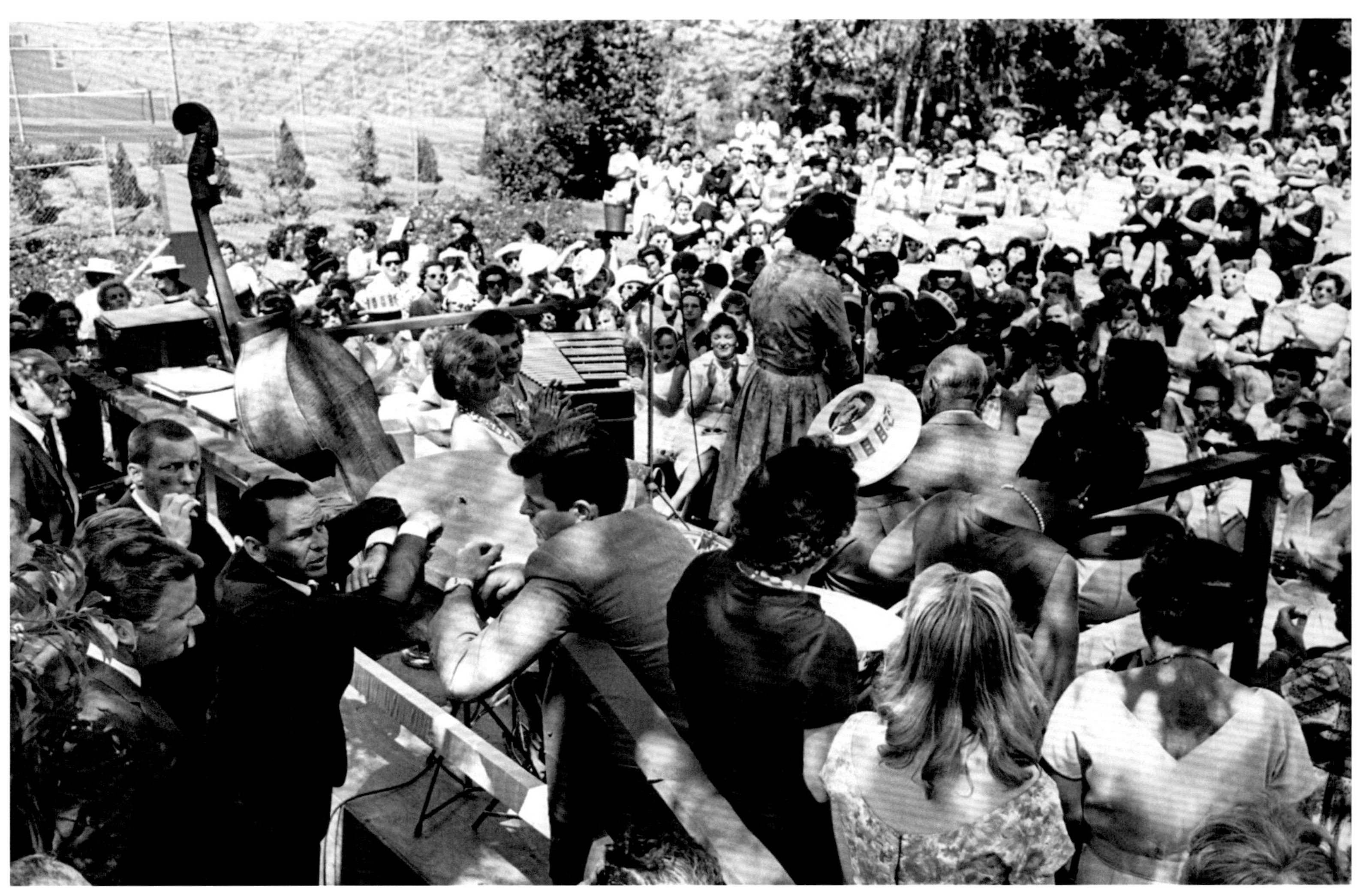

ABOVE *September 7, 1960.* While Jack barrels down the state on the back of a train, singer Frank Sinatra talks with Ted Kennedy at the Key Women for Kennedy fund-raiser held in the backyard of Hollywood actors Janet Leigh and Tony Curtis's home. Sinatra also performed at the Janet Leigh reception, and he would make other appearances on Kennedy's behalf, including a joint appearance with Eleanor Roosevelt in a radio appeal for Kennedy. *Photo, Ralph Crane*

OPPOSITE *September 7, 1960.* Movie star Janet Leigh speaks from the diving board of her pool during the rally held at her home. Women played an important role in campaigning for Kennedy, and in California the Key Women for Kennedy organization became a model for other such groups across the country. Leigh, Sinatra, and their friends weren't the only Hollywood glitterati helping Kennedy. Singer Harry Belafonte appeared in one campaign TV ad with Kennedy aimed at African American voters. In other radio and TV commercials, Lena Horne, Milton Berle, Gene Kelly, Myrna Loy, and Ella Fitzgerald also made pitches for Kennedy or performed on his behalf. *Photo, Ralph Crane*

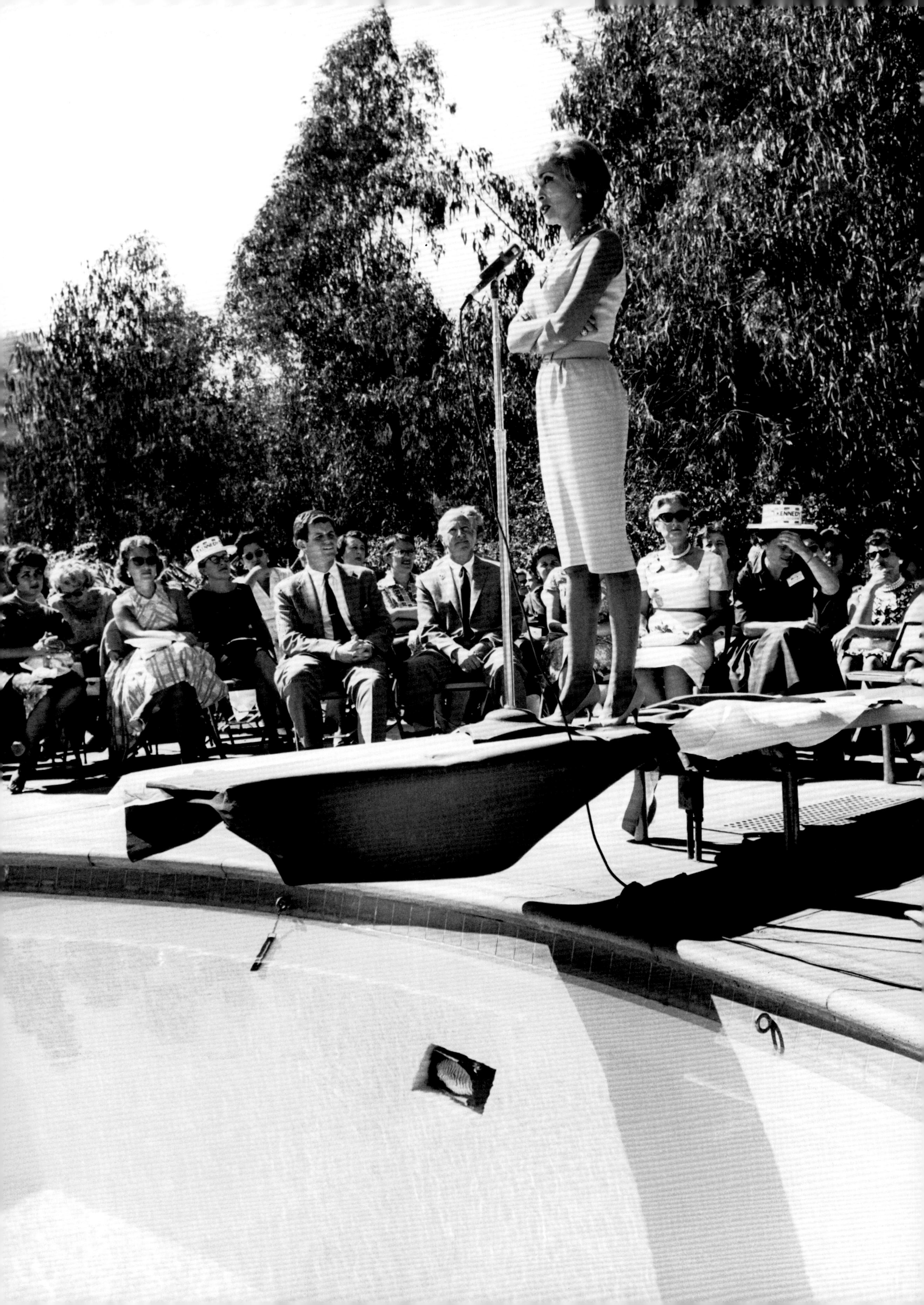

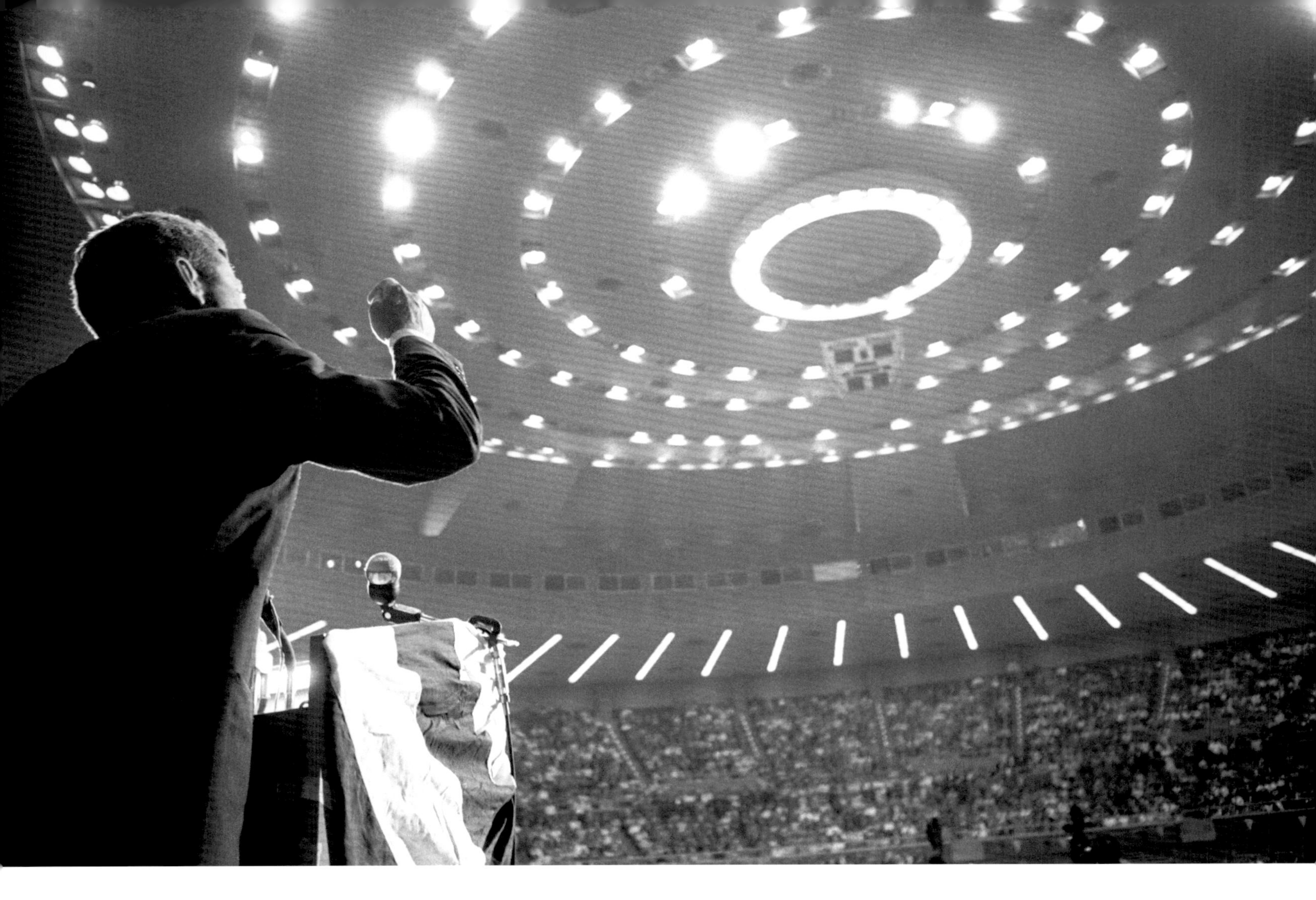

NORMAN MAILER · JFK

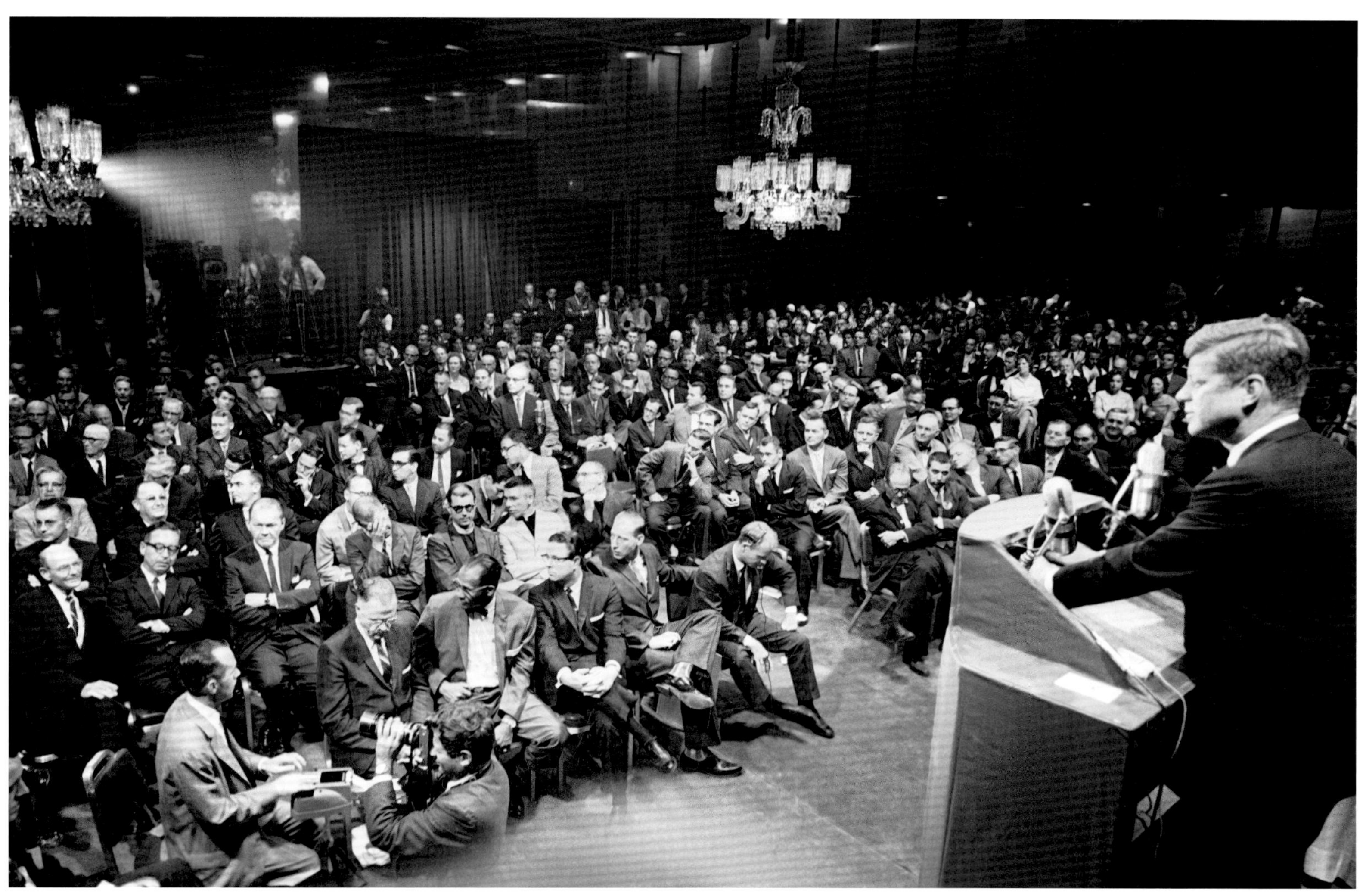

OPPOSITE *September 13, 1960.* Kennedy drew huge crowds at the Memorial Auditorium in Dallas. Kennedy had stated earlier that he had come to Texas, in part, "to melt the ice," as the Democratic Party was not held in high regard there. Eisenhower had carried the state in the 1952 and 1956 elections. Now, with Lyndon Johnson on the ticket, Kennedy and Democrats hoped to do better. *Photo, Paul Schutzer*

ABOVE *September 12, 1960.* In this speech before Houston ministers at the Rice Hotel, JFK faced an intimidating audience of 600 clergy and guests, most of whom were skeptical of electing a Catholic for president. Kennedy's performance was key to putting "the religion issue" to rest: He won over the audience, which included U.S. Representative and Speaker of the House Sam Rayburn, a longtime LBJ backer. "By God, look at him—and listen to him!" Rayburn is reported to have shouted while he watched Kennedy tear into the ministers on television. "He's eating them blood raw!" The next day, Rayburn delivered a fiery speech for Kennedy, hailing him as the greatest Northern Democrat since Franklin D. Roosevelt. *Photo, Anonymous*

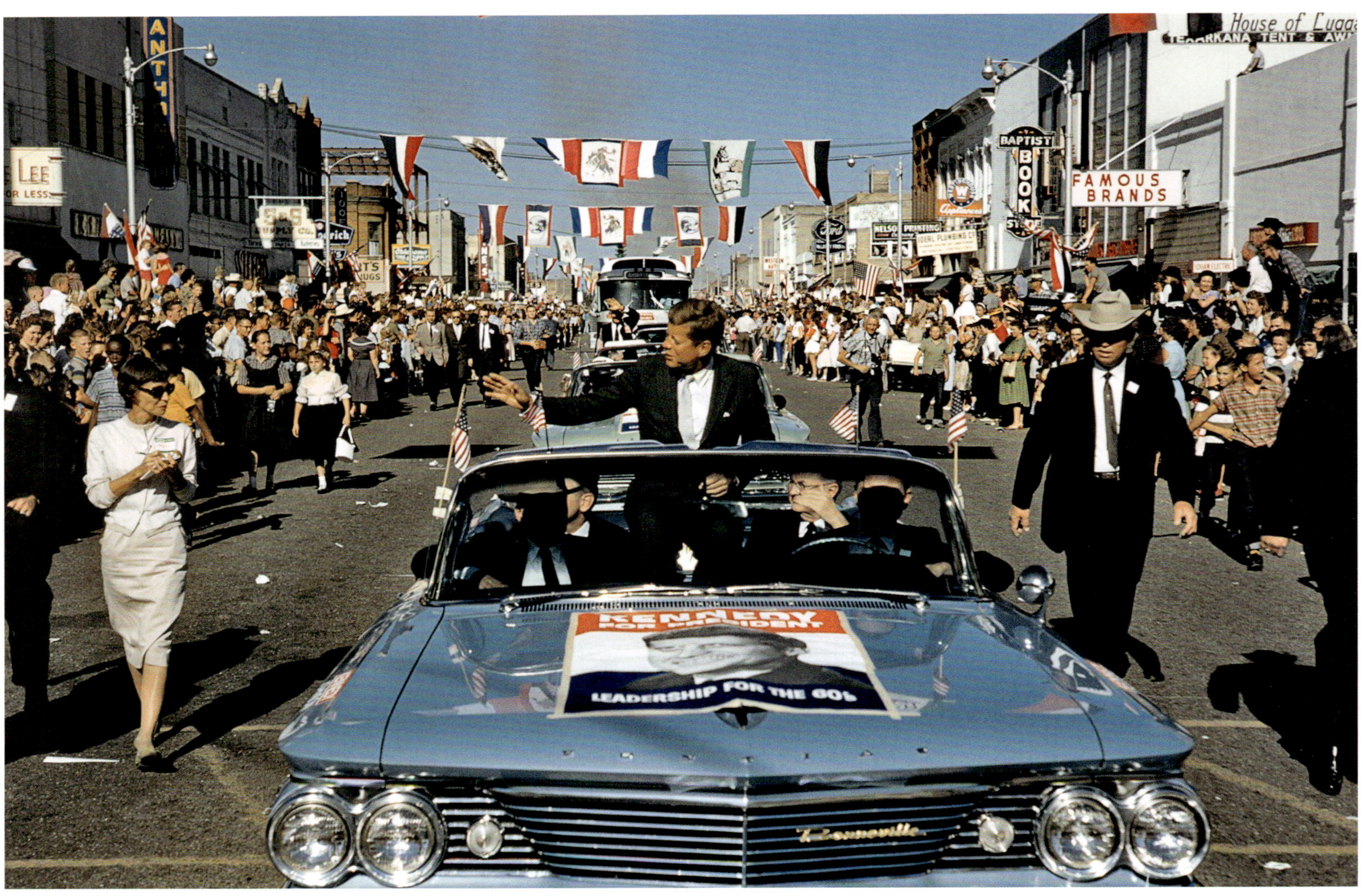

ABOVE *September 13, 1960.* JFK campaigns at the Texas–Arkansas border with Texas Congressman Wright Patman. According to Beverly Smith Jr., Washington editor of *The Saturday Evening Post*, "Crowds and confusion made motorcades the worst part of the tour" with "surging crowds block[ing] streets" and "sudden stops to spare lives and limbs among the frantic multitude." *Photo, Anonymous*

OPPOSITE *November 1, 1960.* Kennedy's opponent, Vice President Richard Nixon, was also drawing large audiences, especially in Republican bastions like Pennsylvania's Lancaster County, pictured here. An eight-year incumbent, Nixon was widely known and had extensive experience in politics, experience he liked to highlight his youthful rival as lacking. *Photo, Anonymous*

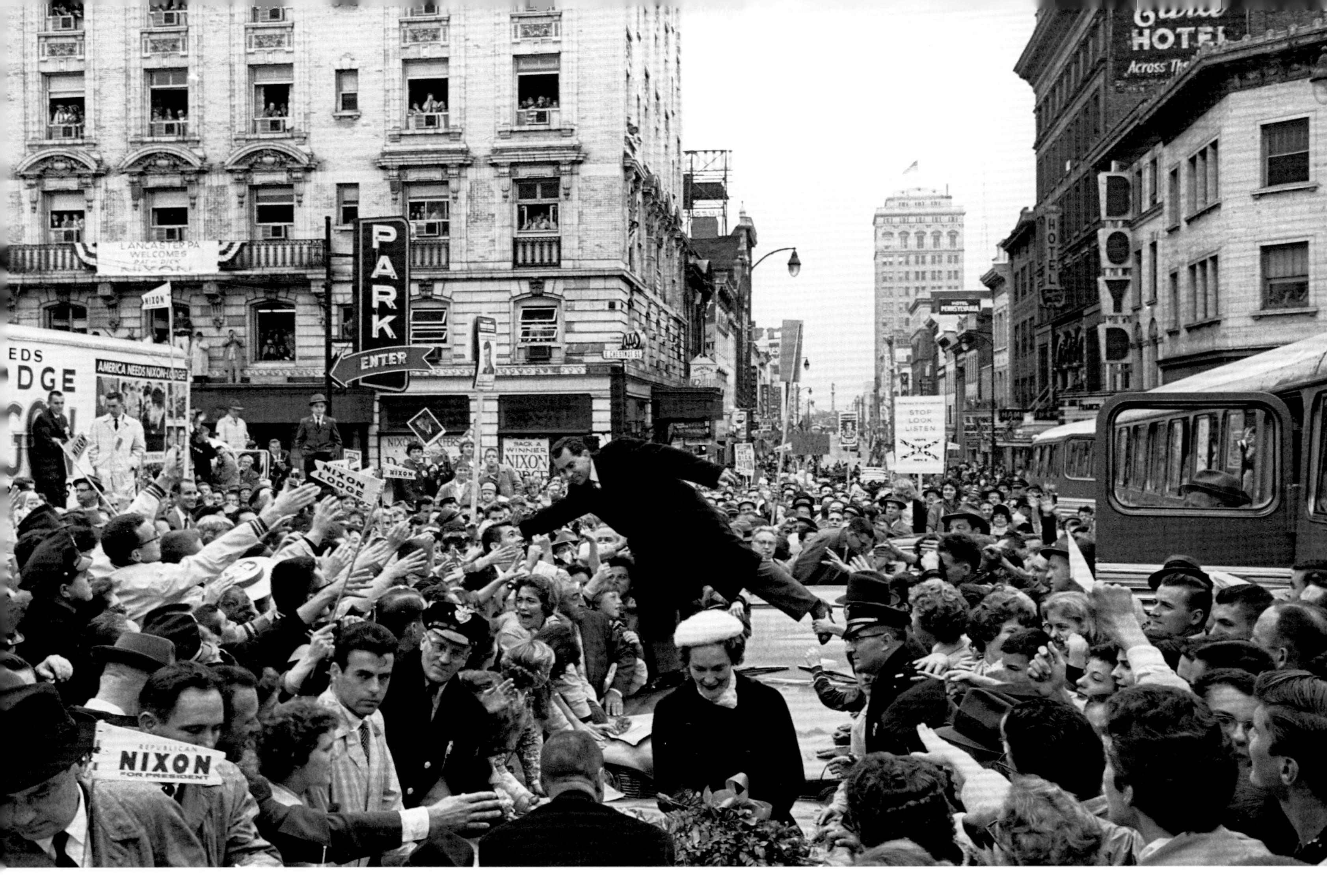

"I wonder when [Mr. Nixon] put his finger in Mr. Khrushchev's nose whether he was saying, … 'I know you are ahead of us in rockets, Mr. Khrushchev, but we are ahead of you in color television.' I would just as soon look at black-and-white television and be ahead of them in rockets."

—John F. Kennedy, Rally at Syria Mosque, Pittsburgh, Pennsylvania, October 10, 1960

OPPOSITE *September 14, 1960.* People gather outside the WMBD/CBS-TV studio in Peoria, Illinois, to watch a Nixon press conference, where foreign policy questions focused on the Russians. "We must not raise again the hopes of the world…and then have those hopes dashed by a completely irresponsible action on the part of Mr. Khrushchev," Nixon declared. Having made an impression on Americans who remembered him going toe-to-toe with Khrushchev in the famous Cold War "kitchen debate" of July 1959—so-called because it took place in front of a model suburban kitchen at the American National Exhibition in Moscow—Nixon was reinforcing his tough stance on the Soviets and Khrushchev. *Photo, Cornell Capa*

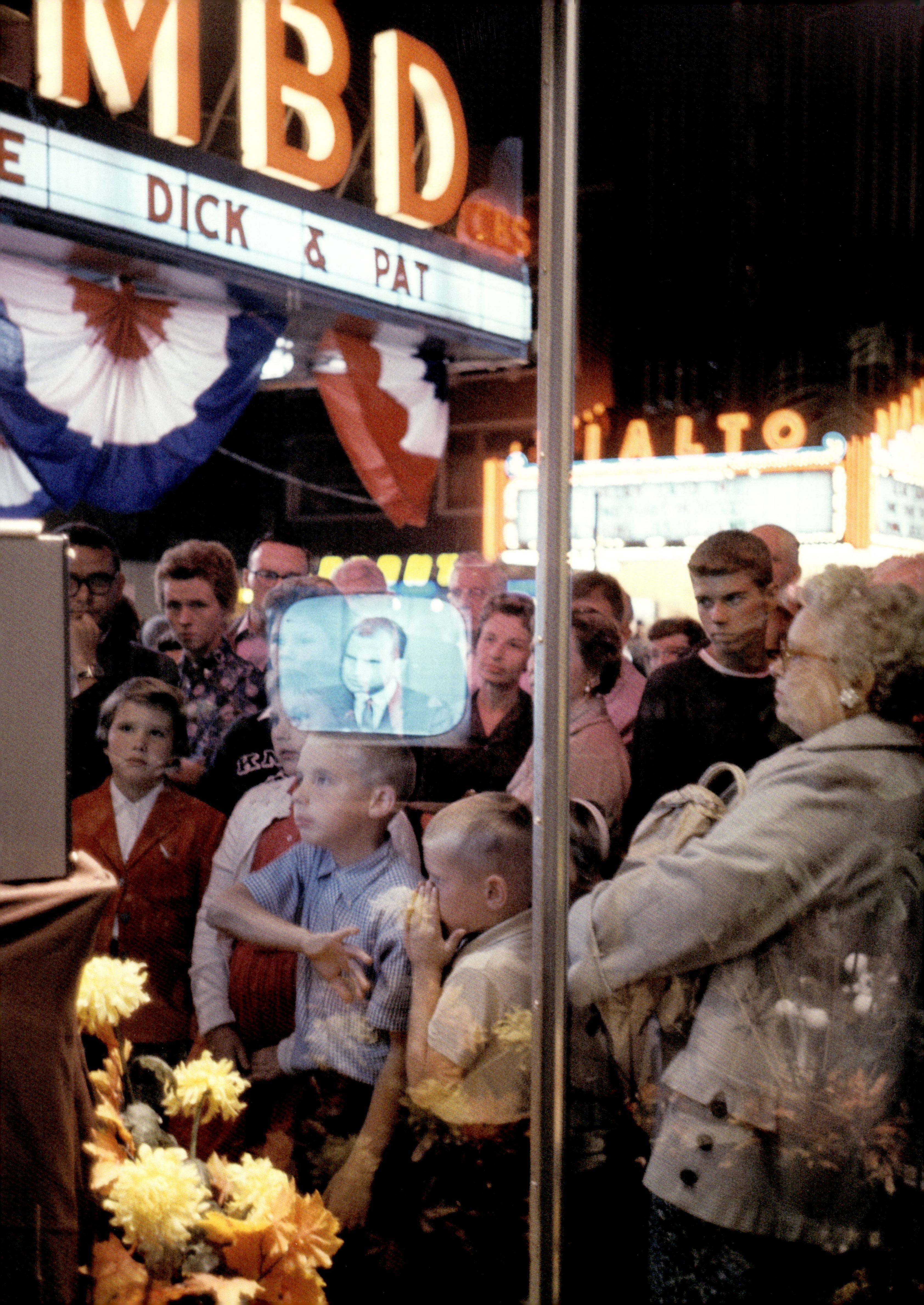
MBD
DICK & PAT
RIALTO

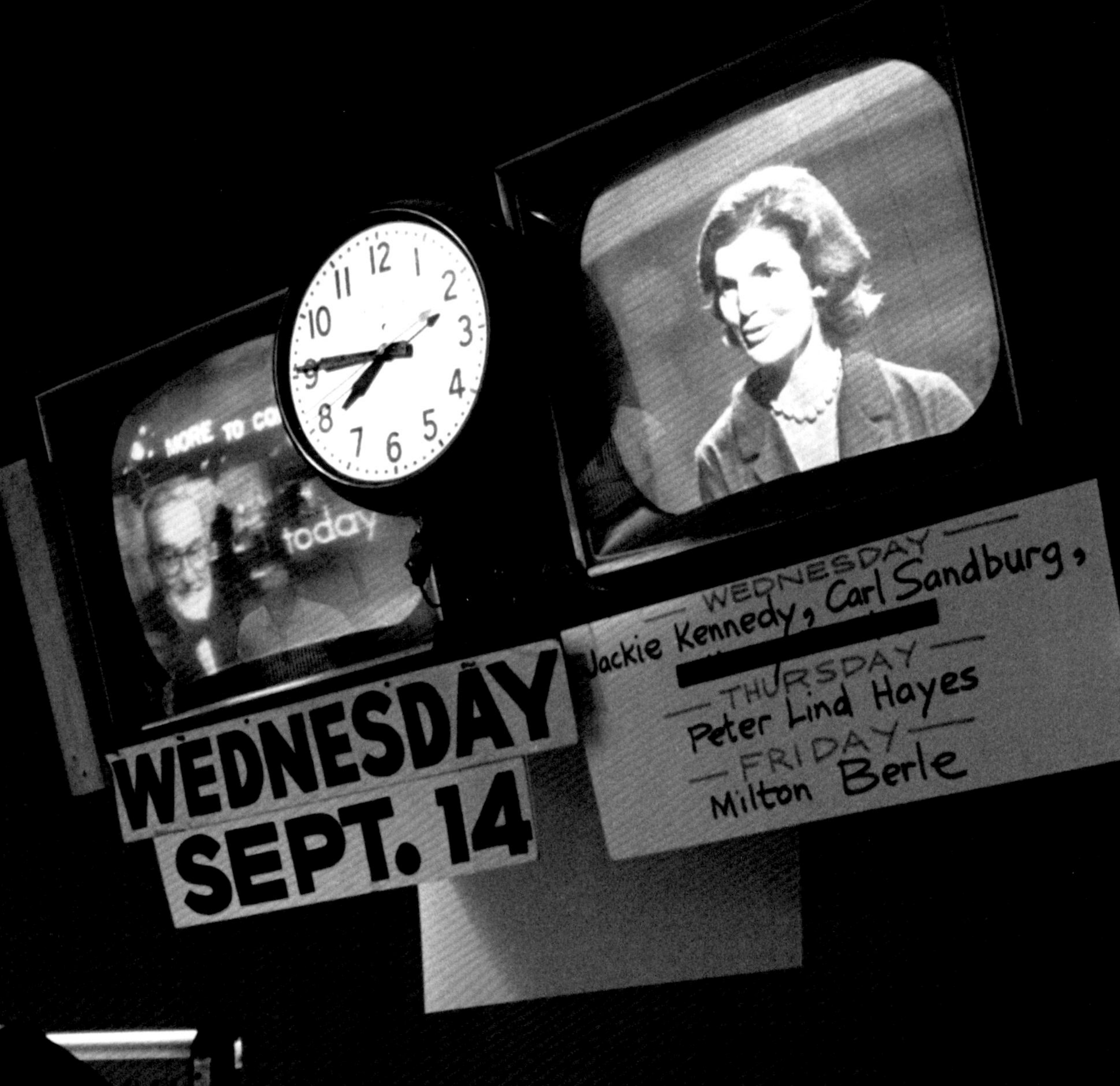
MORE TO C
today
WEDNESDAY
SEPT. 14
WEDNESDAY
Jackie Kennedy, Carl Sandburg,
THURSDAY
Peter Lind Hayes
FRIDAY
Milton Berle

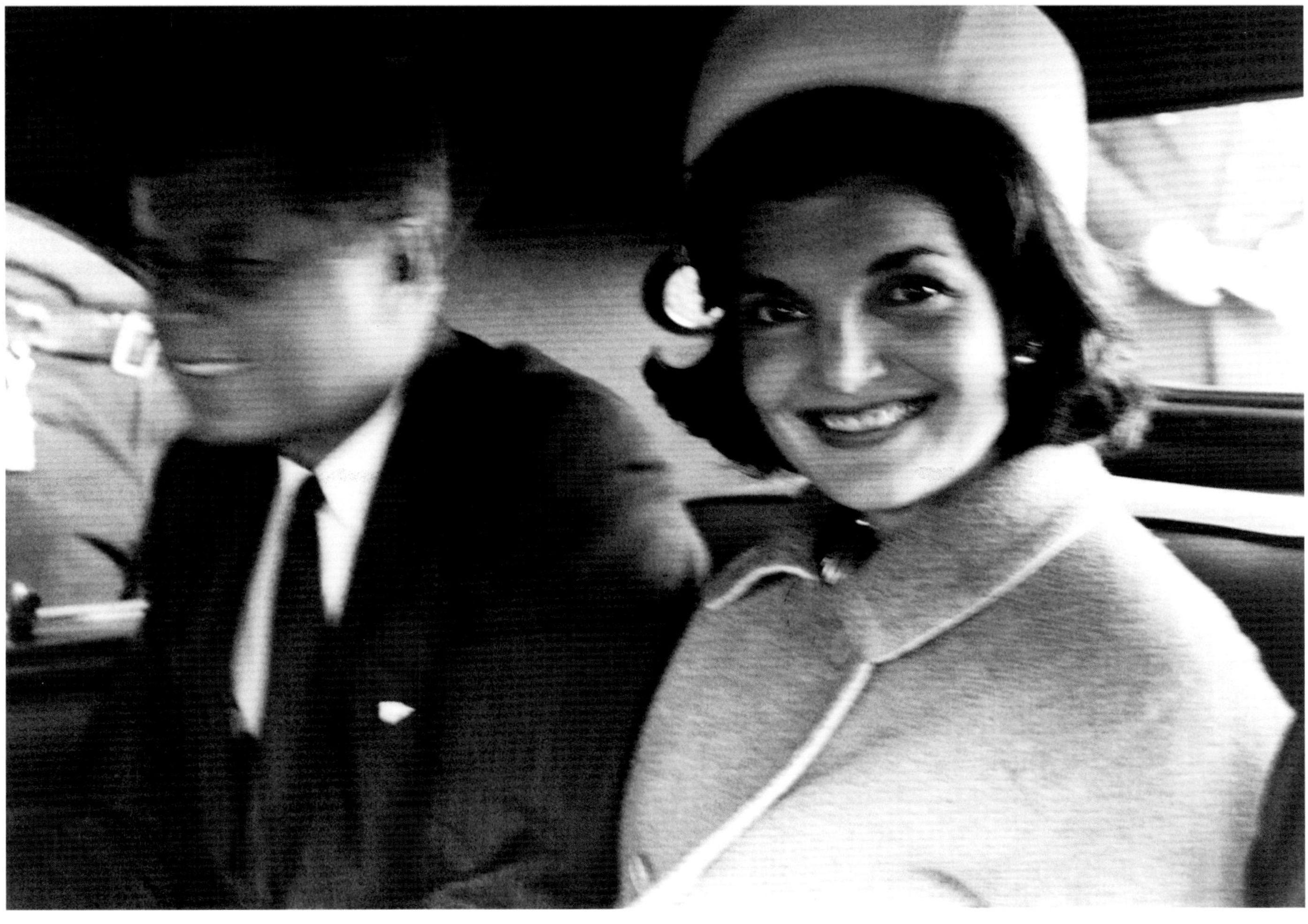

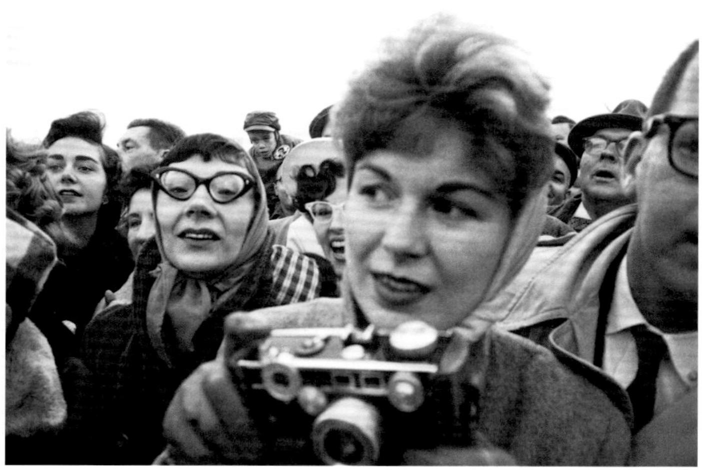

LEFT *November 6, 1960*. Fans at New York's Long Island Arena.
Photo, Burton Berinsky

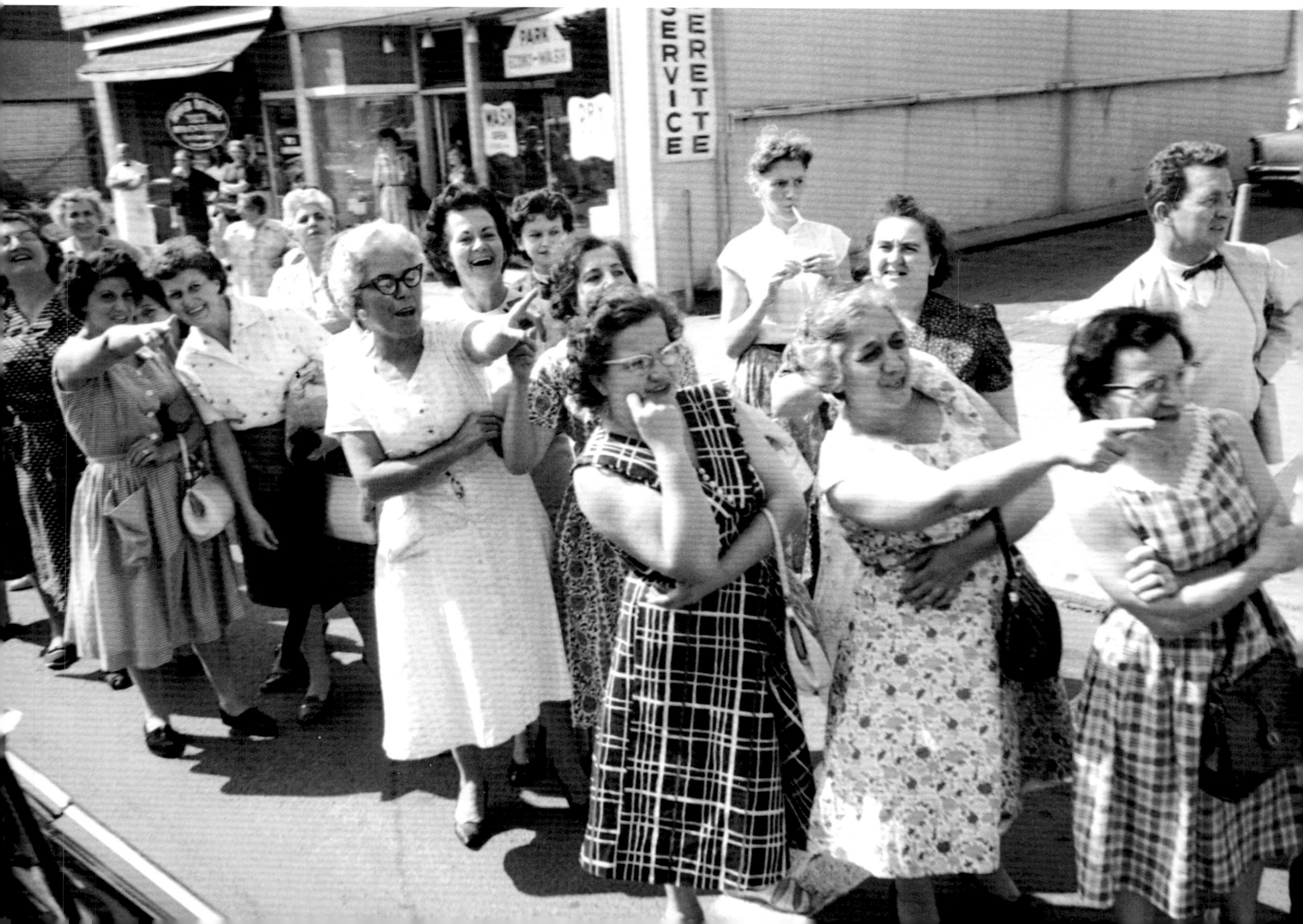

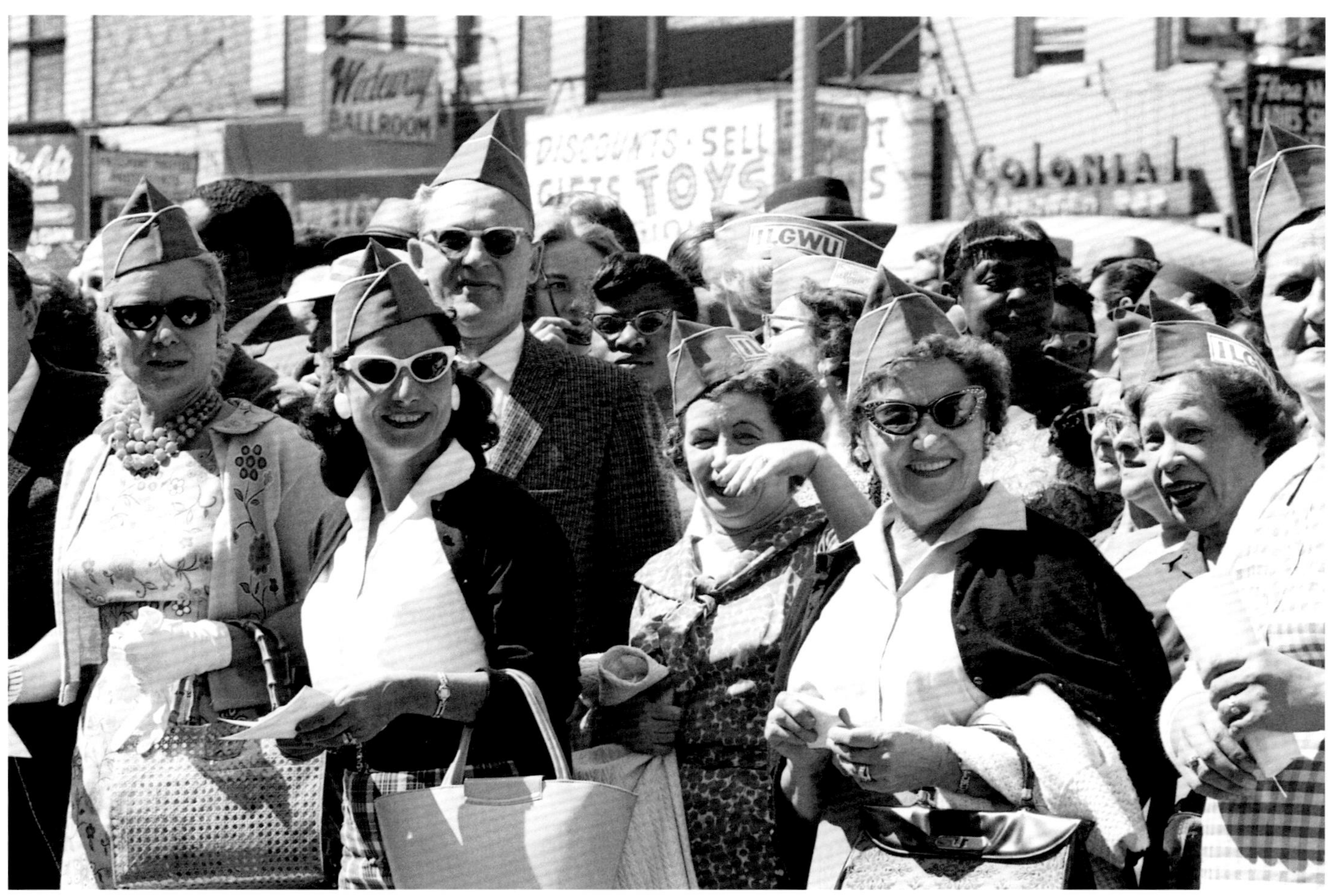

OPPOSITE (BOTTOM) AND ABOVE *September 15, 1960.* In Newark, New Jersey, members of the International Ladies' Garment Workers' Union rally for JFK. The ILGWU played an important role in the development of the Liberal Party of New York, which, the day before, had officially endorsed Kennedy. Proud to accept the nod of the progressive organization, JFK remarked: "A distinguished Republican said some time ago, 'I am a liberal abroad and a conservative at home.' Well, I am not.... Unless you are a liberal here, you can't be a liberal abroad." *Photos, Burton Berinsky*

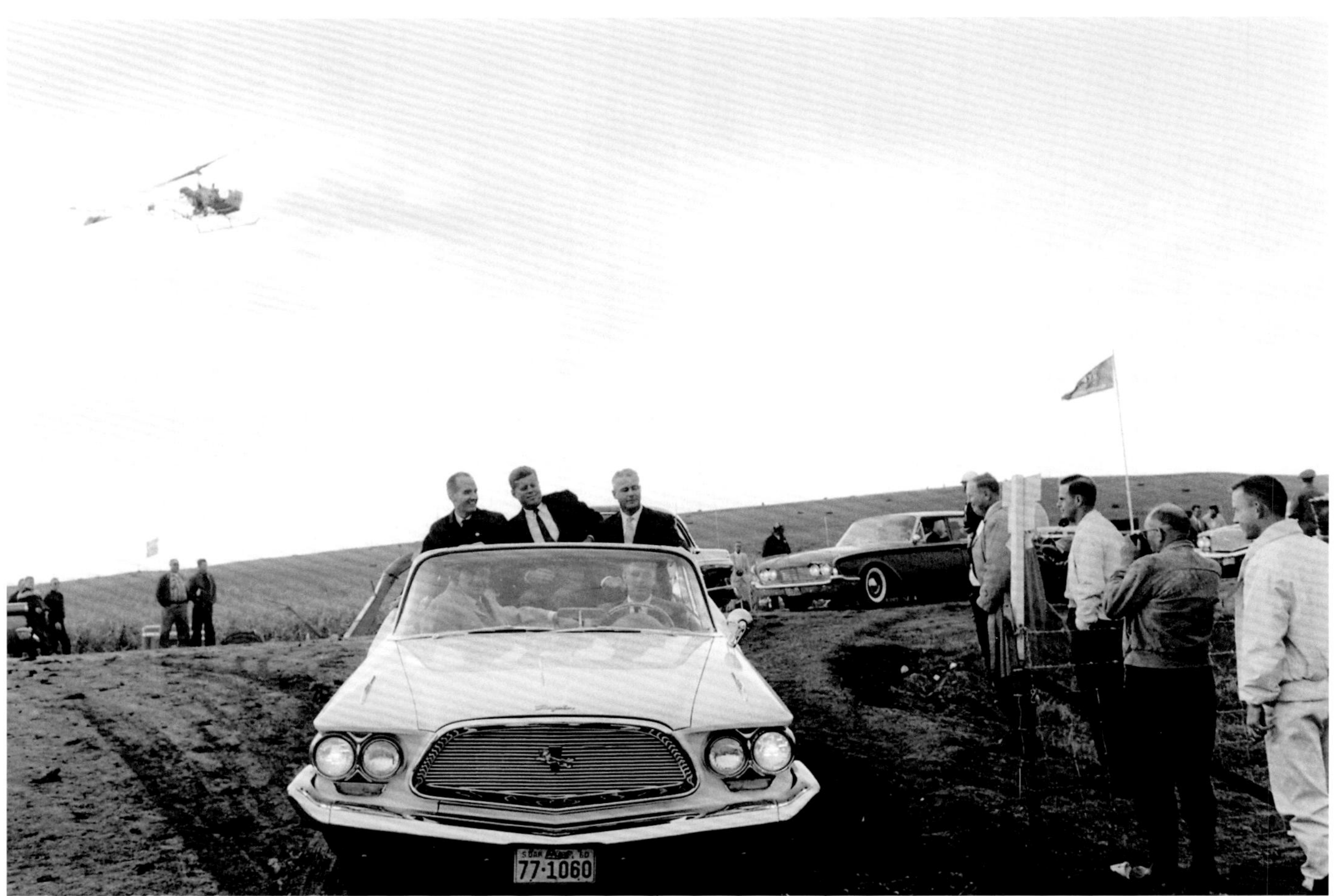

ABOVE *September 2, 1960.* JFK arrives at an agricultural event in Sioux Falls, South Dakota, with a delegation of state politicians, including Congressman George McGovern (above right). In his Sioux Falls speech (which made the front page of regional newspapers the next day, as well as *The New York Times*), Kennedy promised that he would work for "full parity of income" for farmers. According to aide and speechwriter Ted Sorensen, who was from Nebraska, "JFK was a Massachusetts boy and didn't have a lot of interest in farms." But under Sorensen's influence, Kennedy grew to believe that "the family farm should remain the backbone of American agriculture…," a sentiment he shared with voters when he campaigned in traditionally Republican agricultural areas. *Photo, Walter Sanders*

OPPOSITE *September 21, 1960.* Members of a marching band listen to Kennedy address an audience at the Tri-Cities Airport in Sullivan County, Tennessee. In his speeches he would often allude to a nation that could do better, positioning himself as the man to move the country ahead: "The people of the United States have a very clear choice to make between Mr. Nixon and myself," he said a few weeks later in Columbia, South Carolina. "He runs on a slogan of 'You have never had it so good.' I run on the slogan, 'This is a great country that must be greater.' I think we can do better." *Photo, Stanley Tretick*

"The farmer is the only man in our economy who has to
buy everything he buys at retail — sell everything he
sells at wholesale — and pay the freight both ways."

—John F. Kennedy, National Plowing Contest, Sioux Falls,
    South Dakota, September 22, 1960

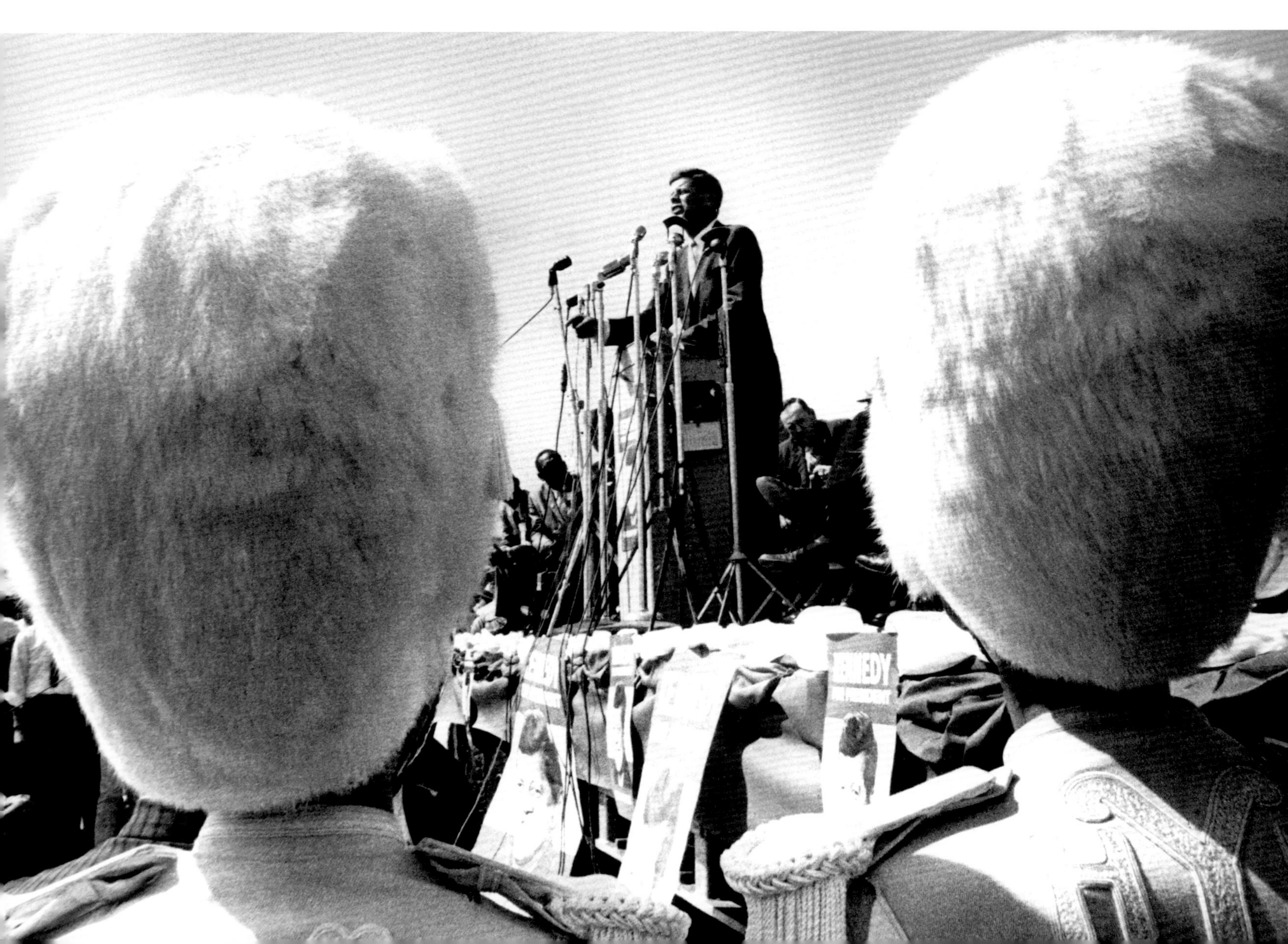

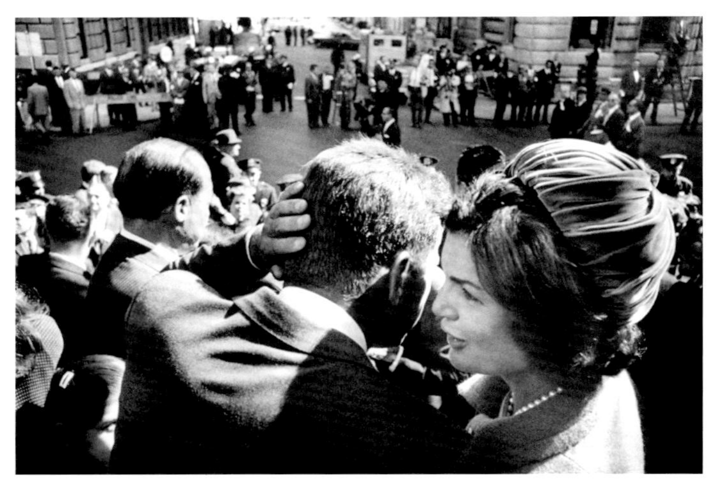

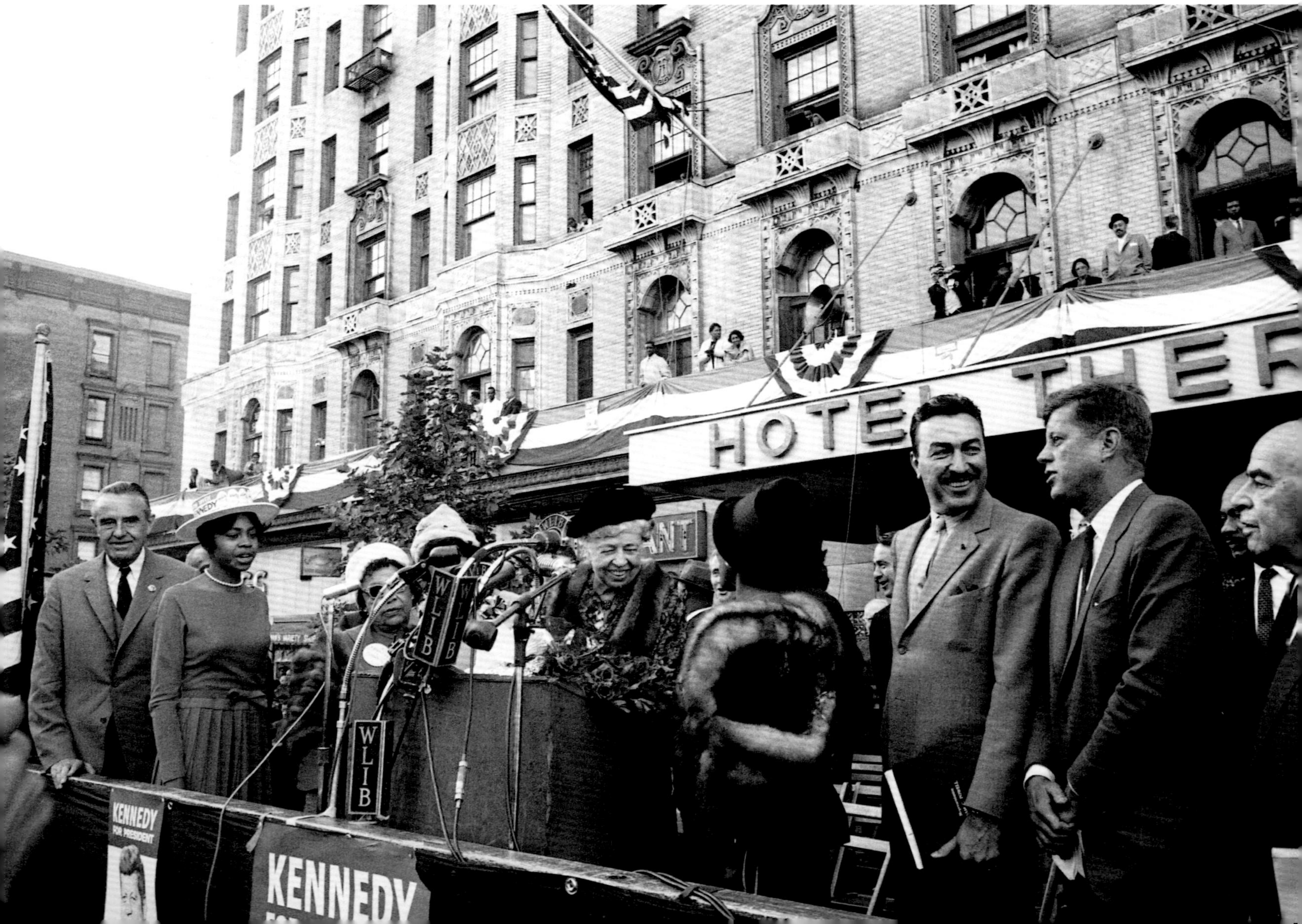

OPPOSITE (TOP) *October 12, 1960.* Jackie whispers to her husband during the Columbus Day Parade in New York City. *Photo, Paul Schutzer*

OPPOSITE (BOTTOM) AND BELOW *October 12, 1960.* On the eve of the third debate with Nixon, Kennedy held two important rallies in New York City, one in largely Puerto Rican East Harlem (below), and one outside the Hotel Theresa, the nexus of social life in Central Harlem (opposite). Only weeks earlier, when Fidel Castro was in town to address the U. N. General Assembly, he had stayed at the hotel and was famously visited by Soviet Premier Nikita Khrushchev. As he was joined onstage in Central Harlem by the liberal stalwart Eleanor Roosevelt, Congressman Adam Clayton Powell Jr., and former governor of New York W. Averell Harriman, it was no surprise that Kennedy began his address on a progressive note: "We should be glad they came to the United States. We should not fear the 20th century, for this worldwide revolution which we see all around us is part of the original American Revolution." *Photos, Burton Berinsky*

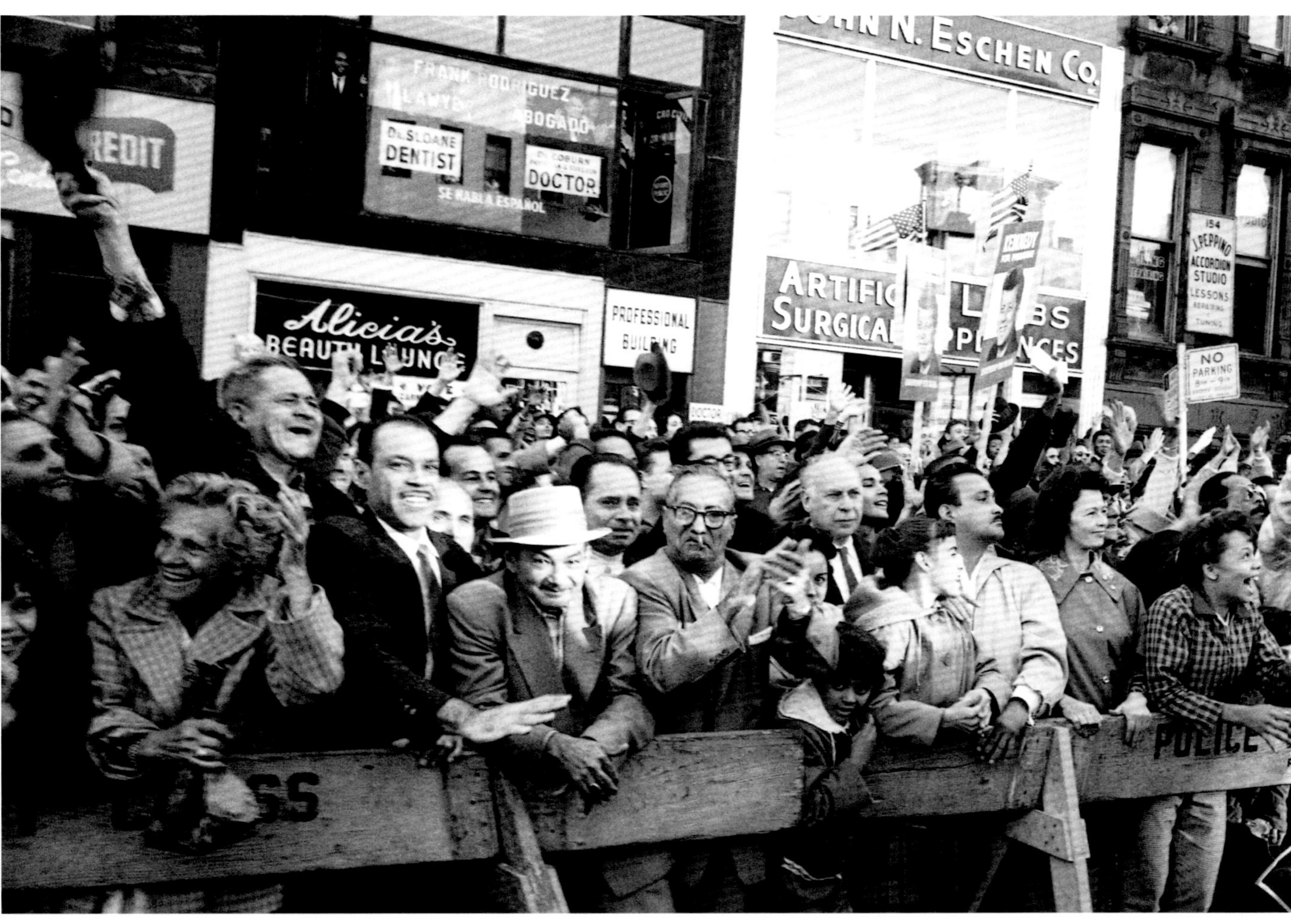

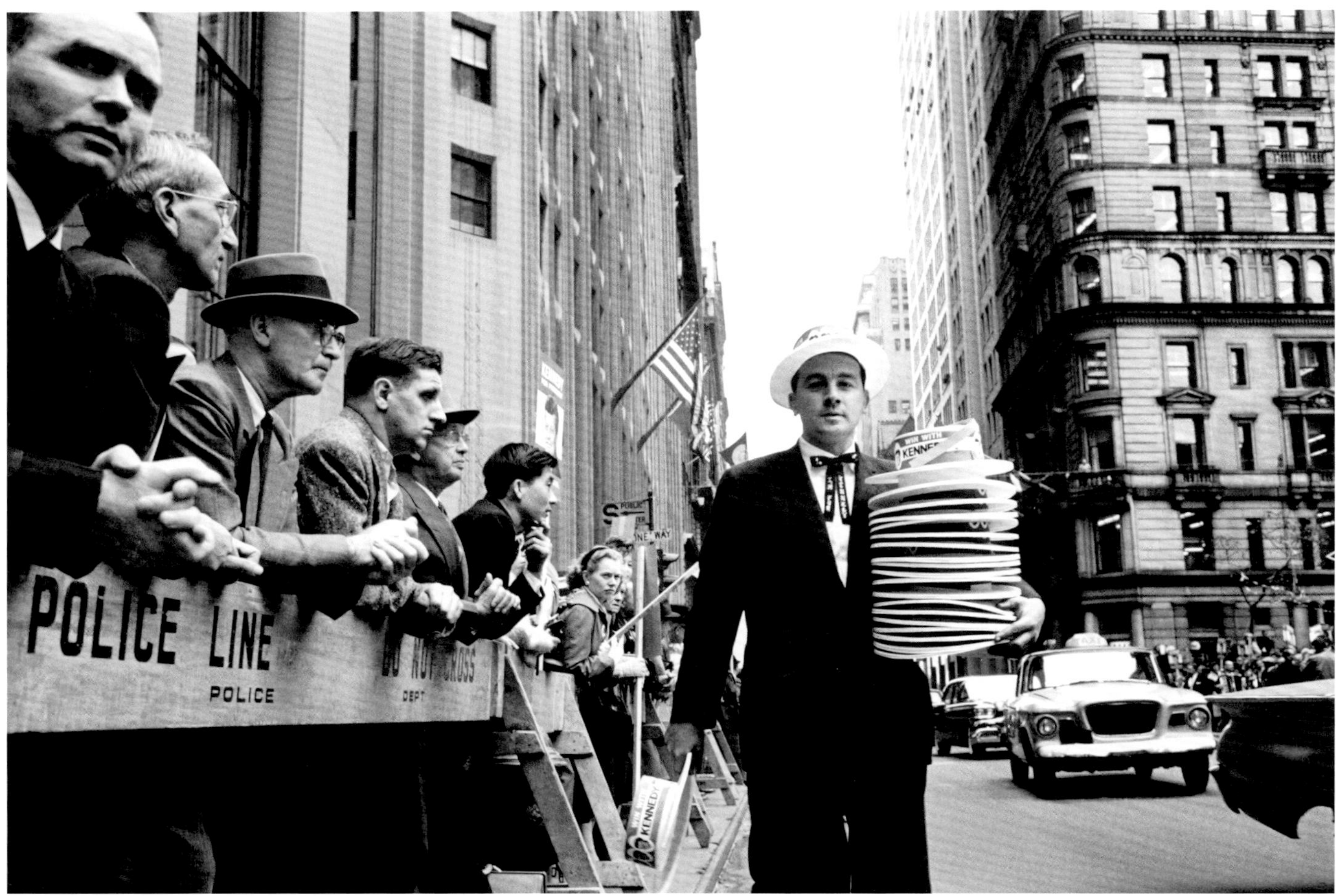

ABOVE *October 19, 1960.* As the campaign moved into its final weeks, New York City gave Kennedy a hero's welcome by hosting a ticker-tape parade through the Financial District from Whitehall and Broadway to City Hall, where Kennedy quoted Abraham Lincoln: "this Nation cannot exist half slave and half free." He continued, "I don't think in the long run the world can exist half slave and half free. Whether it moves in the direction of the Communists or whether it moves in the direction of freedom will depend in the final analysis upon us." *Photo, Cornell Capa*

OPPOSITE (TOP) *October 19, 1960.* Photographers at the ticker-tape parade, New York City. *Photo, Alfred Wertheimer*

OPPOSITE (BOTTOM) *October 19, 1960.* Workers in the office buildings that lined New York City's ticker-tape parade route not only got a bird's-eye view, they got to participate in the spectacle, hurling a snowstorm of shredded paper and confetti out of their windows and onto the passing motorcade. The next day the sanitation department reported that it had collected an estimated 100 tons of paper and debris along Broadway. *Photo, Burton Berinsky*

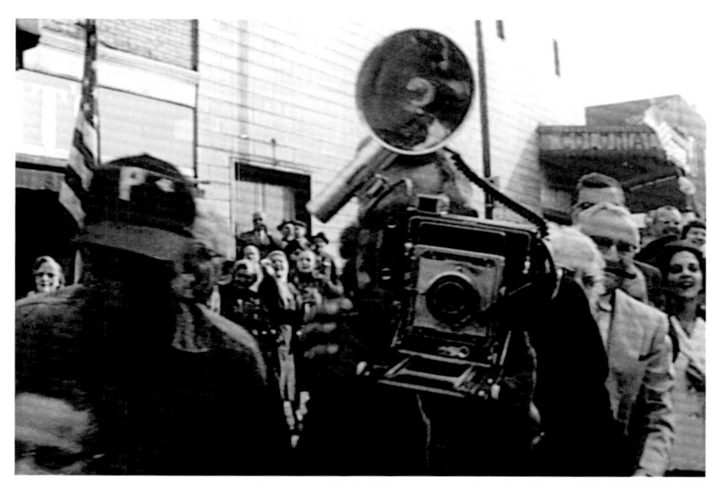

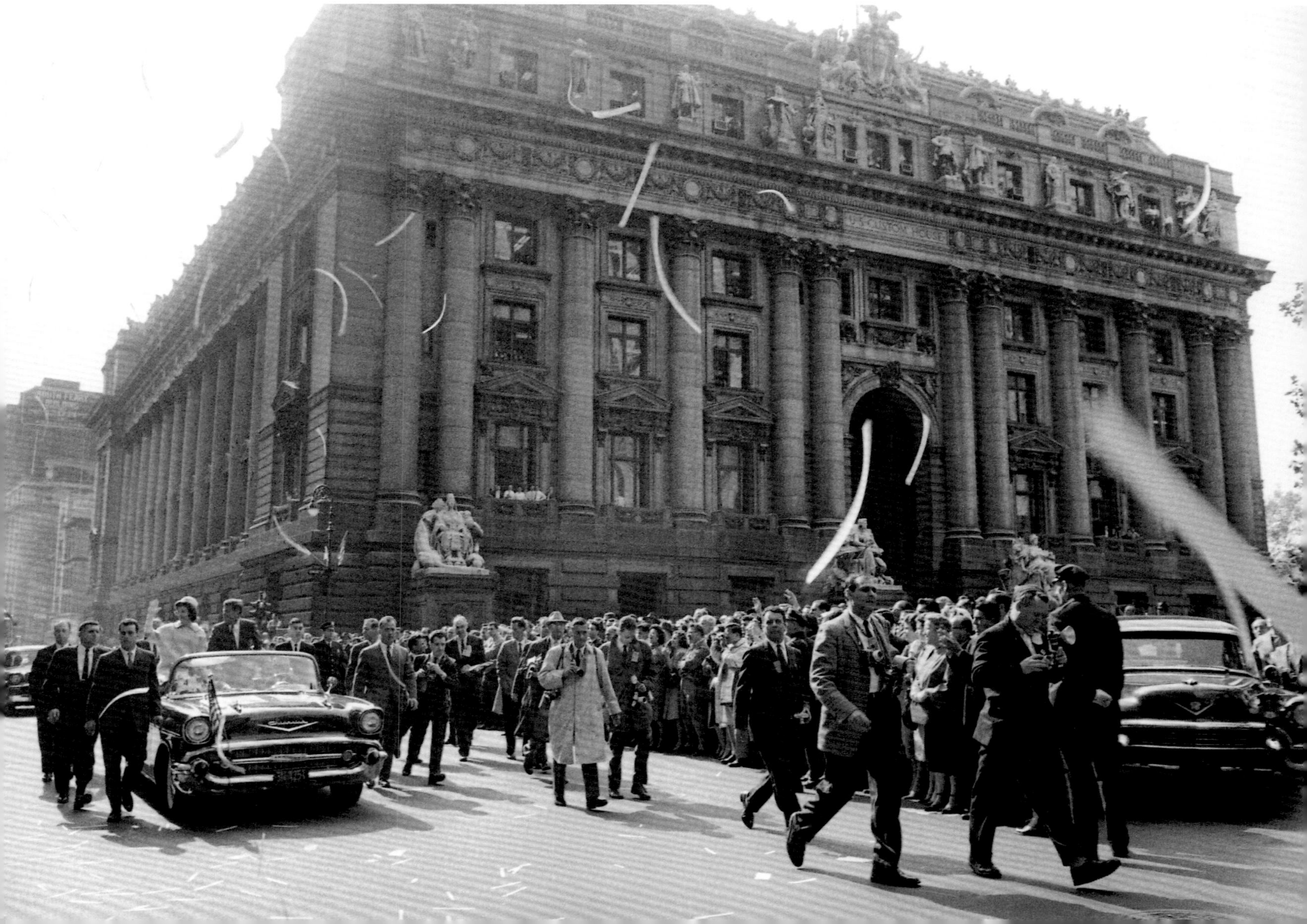

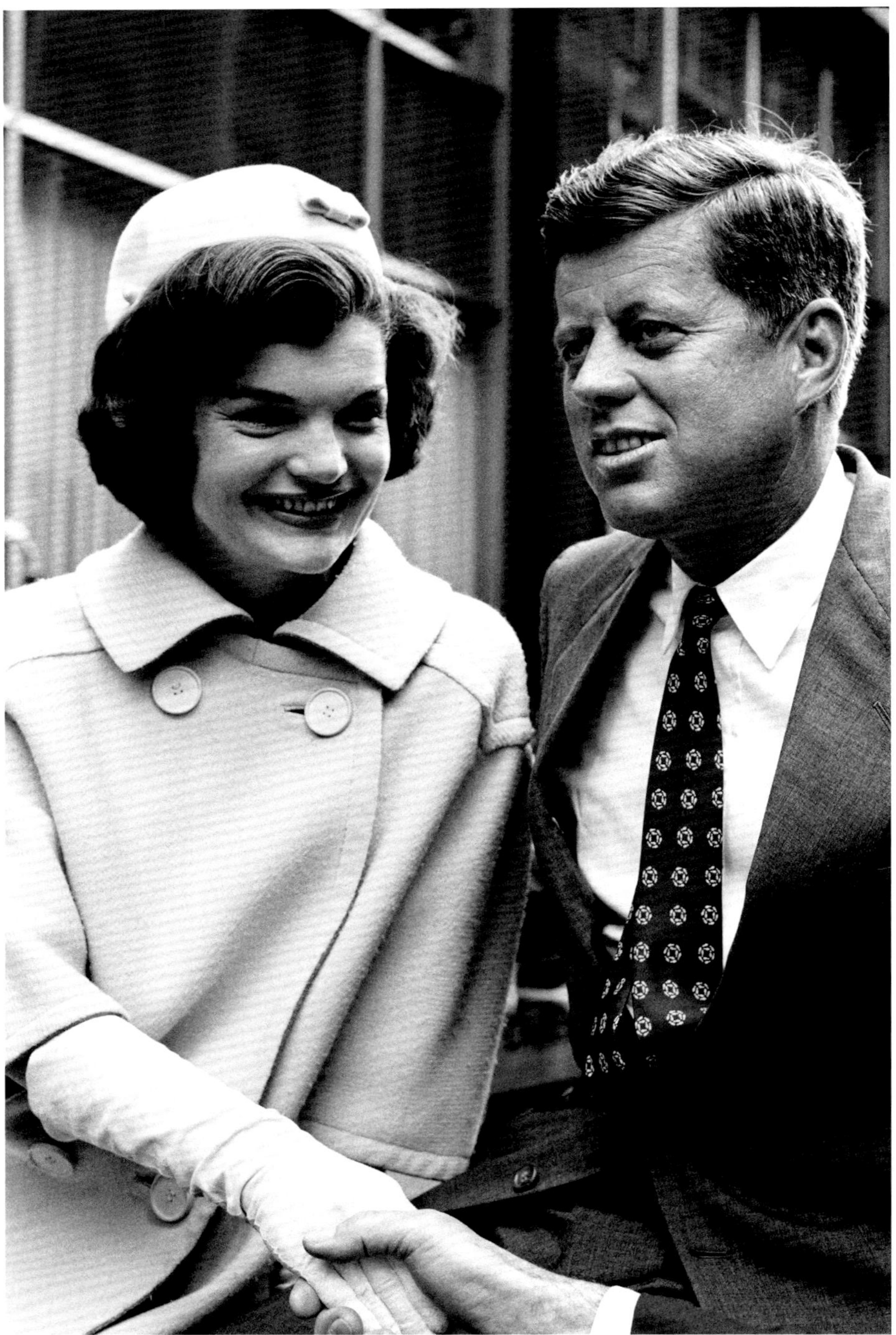

ABOVE *October 19, 1960.* When Jack and Jackie climbed into their convertible
for the parade, rain seemed imminent. But according to an enthusiastic
report in the next day's *New York Times*, "just as he was about to start up
Broadway from Whitehall Street, the sun shone as if a switch had been
turned on." By the time the motorcade reached Wall Street, the crush of the
crowd was so intense that Jackie told a reporter, "It felt like the sides of the
car were bending." *Photo, Henri Dauman*

OPPOSITE *October 19, 1960.* According to Mayor Robert Wagner Jr., the
turnout for Kennedy's ticker-tape parade was "the greatest reception anybody
has ever received in this section of the city in its history." Later that night,
JFK attended a dinner where he charmed the crowd by poking fun at
his family fortune: "I had announced earlier this year that if successful I
would not consider campaign contributions as a substitute for experience
in appointing ambassadors. Ever since I made that statement I have not
received one single cent from my father." *Photo, Anonymous*

"When President Roosevelt was running for a second term…
some garment workers unfolded a great sign that said, 'We love
him for the enemies he has made.' Well, I have been making some
good enemies lately. I find it a rather agreeable experience."

—John F. Kennedy, Citizens for Kennedy Rally, Waldorf Astoria Hotel,
  New York City, September 14, 1960

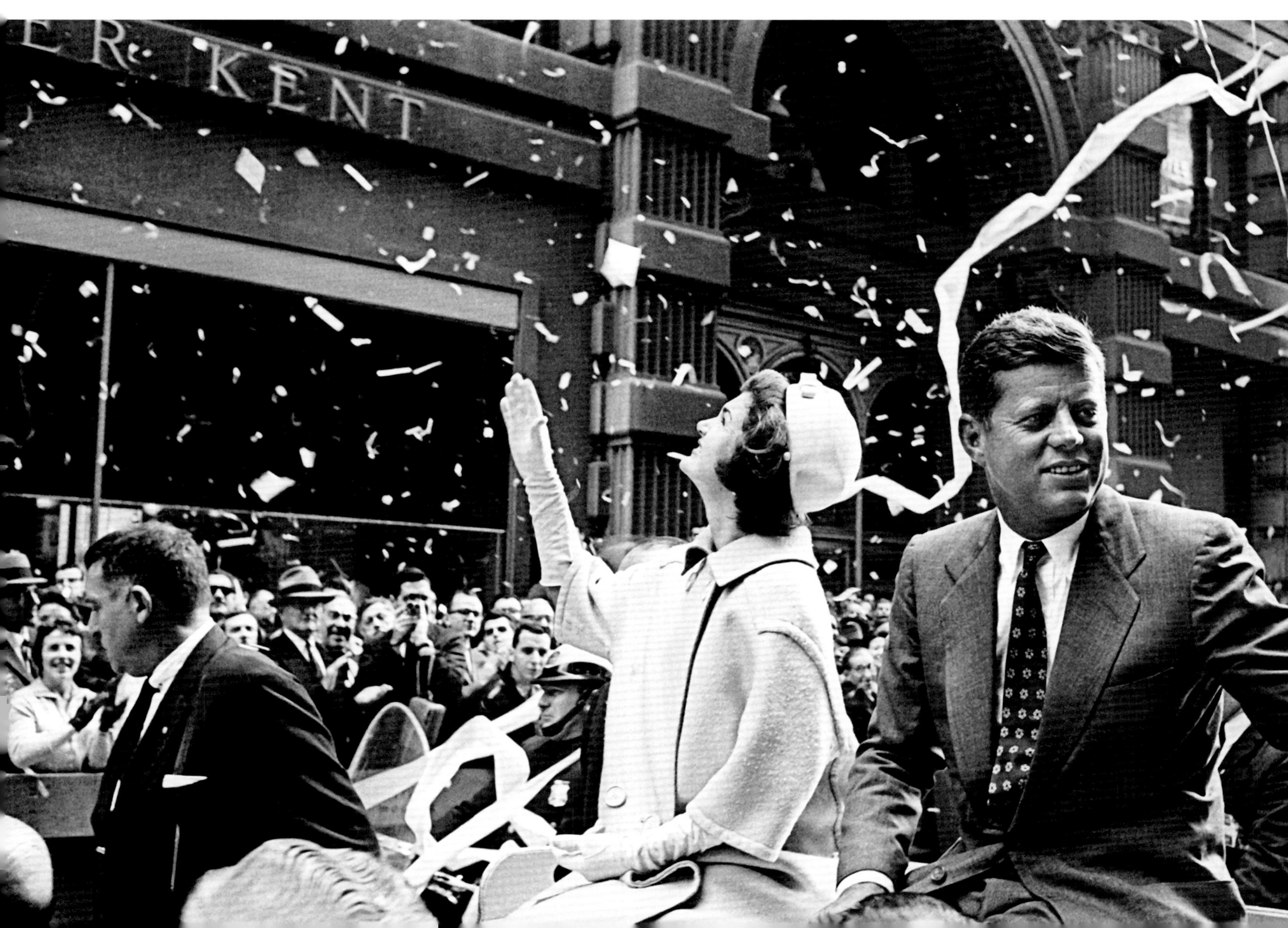

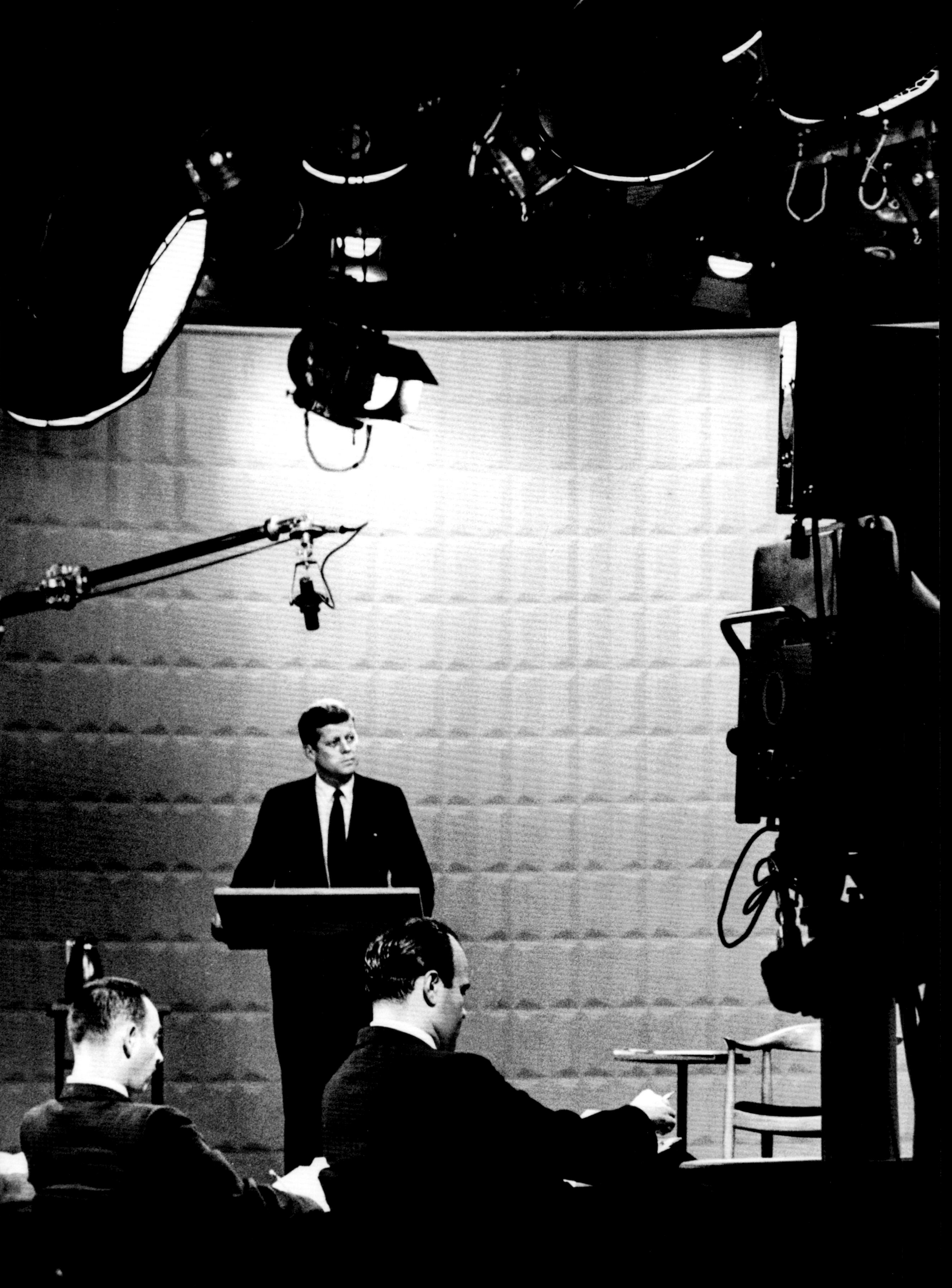

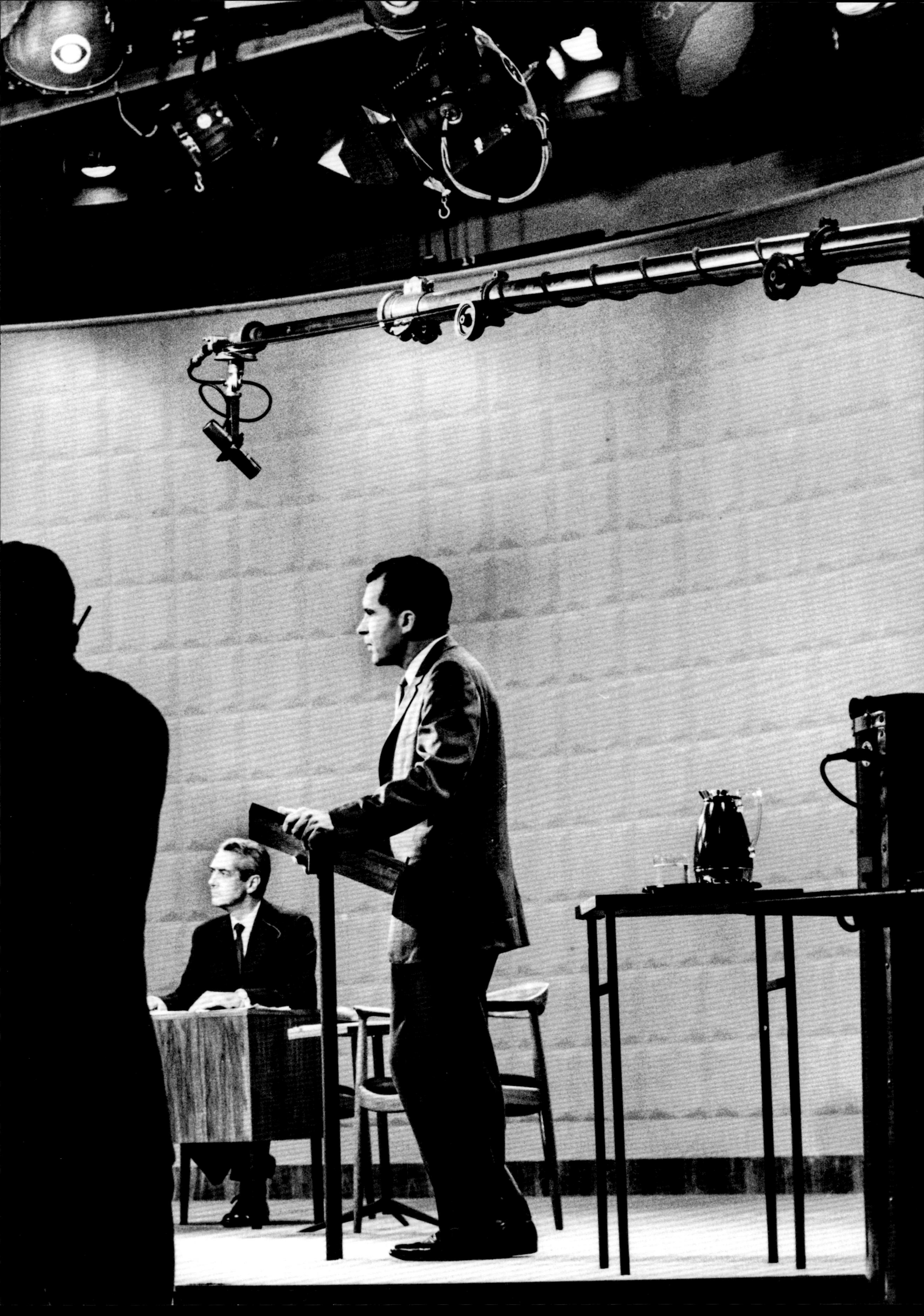

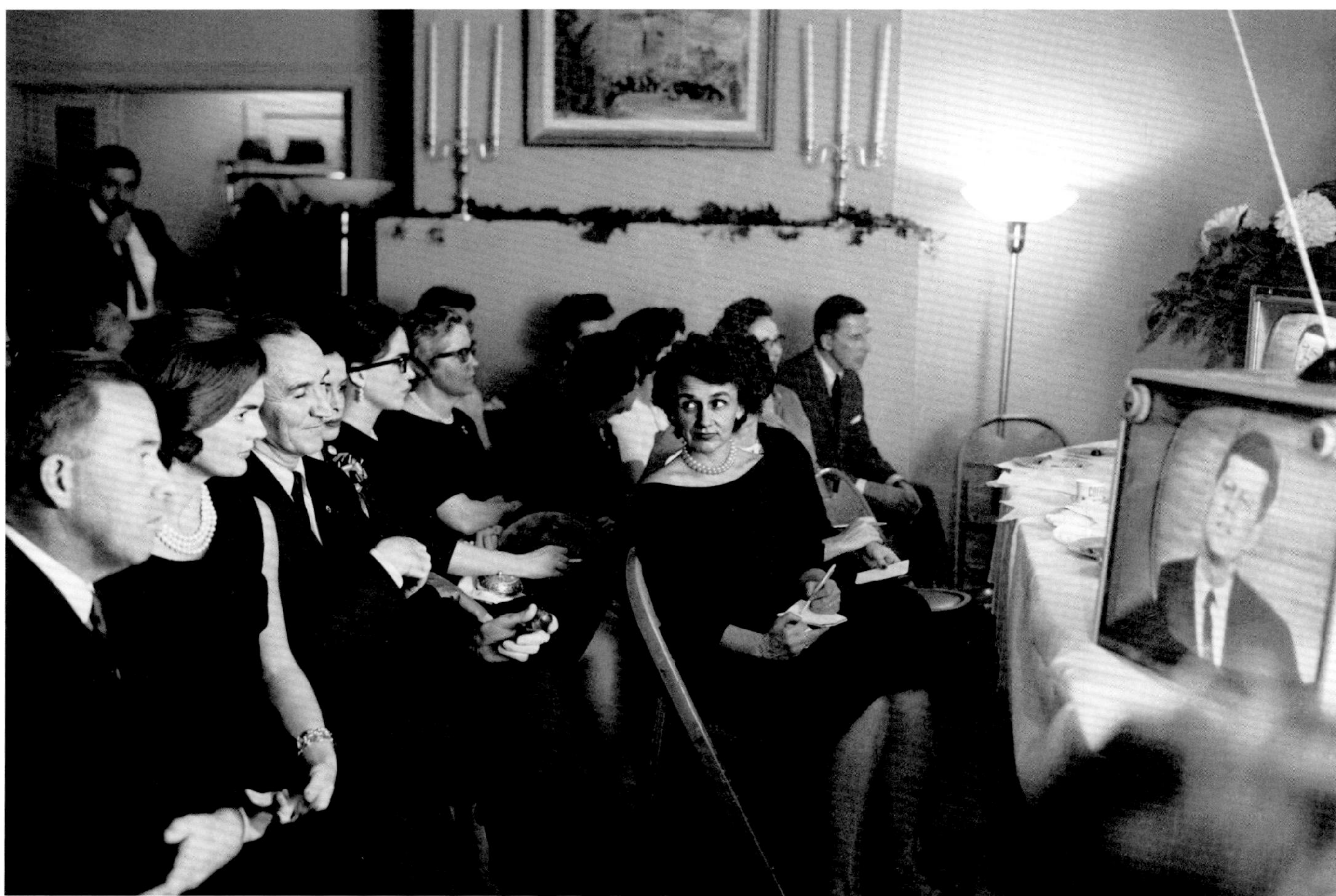

PREVIOUS SPREAD *September 26, 1960.* The first of the four televised debates between Nixon and Kennedy, held in Chicago and moderated by Howard K. Smith, changed the course of the election and altered political campaigns forever. Though people listening on the radio thought Nixon had prevailed, they were a small minority compared with the 74 million who watched on TV and saw Kennedy as the clear winner. Years later *Time* magazine would declare, "On the morning of September 26, 1960, John F. Kennedy was a relatively unknown senator from Massachusetts. He was young and Catholic… and facing off against an incumbent. But by the end of the evening, he was a star." *Photo, Paul Schutzer*

ABOVE *October 7, 1960.* Flanked by Senators Mike Mansfield of Montana and Henry "Scoop" Jackson of Washington at a debate-watching party in Washington, D.C., Jackie watches her husband take on Richard Nixon in their second televised duel. *Photo, Anonymous*

BELOW *October 7, 1960.* A couple in New York City watches the second Kennedy–Nixon TV debate from their Park Avenue terrace. Broadcast by NBC out of Washington, D.C., it was watched by an estimated 60 to 70 million viewers. Foreign policy was the central topic, engaging the candidates on subjects ranging from Cuba and Fidel Castro to U-2 spy planes. *Photo, Henri Dauman*

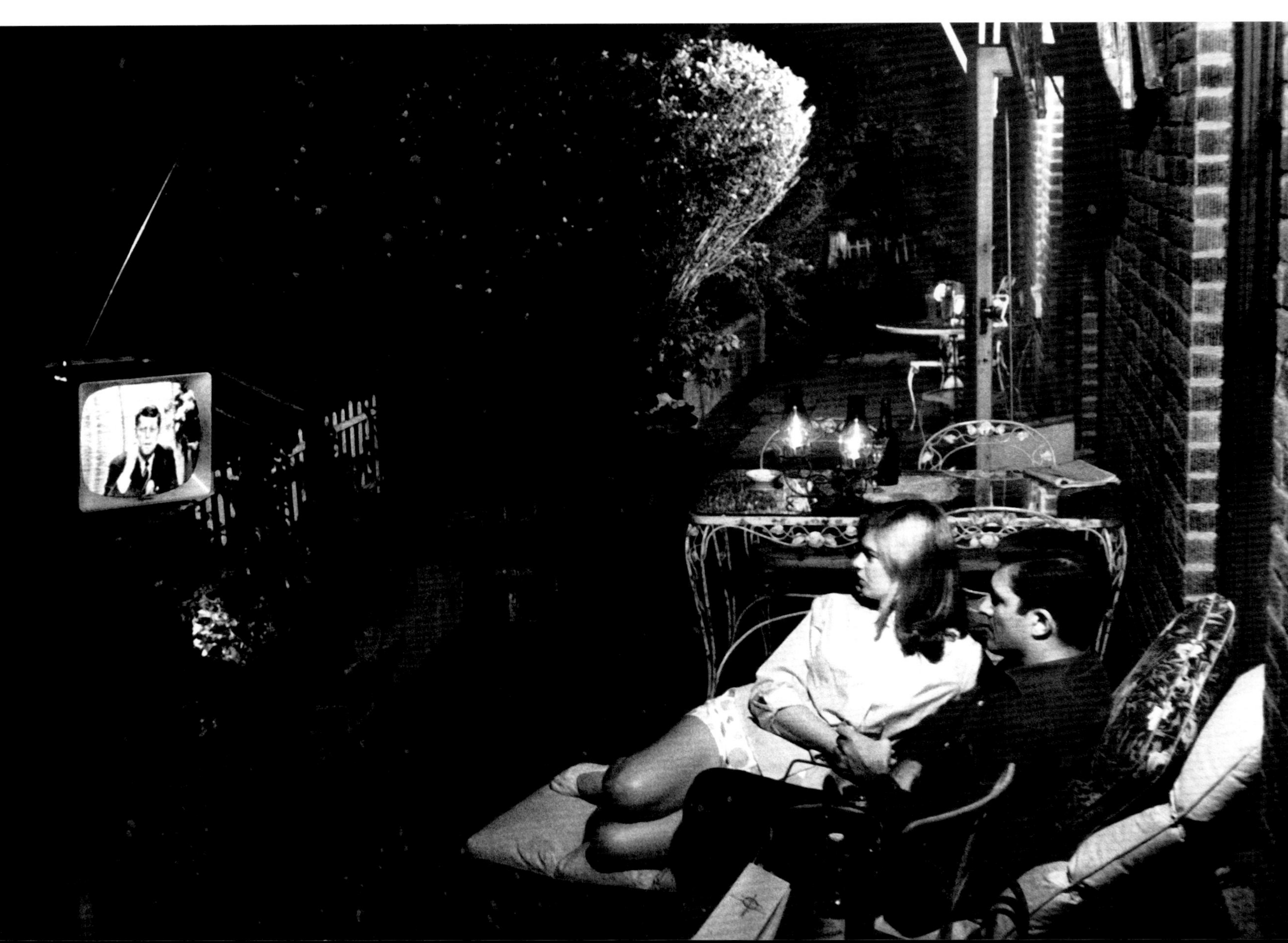

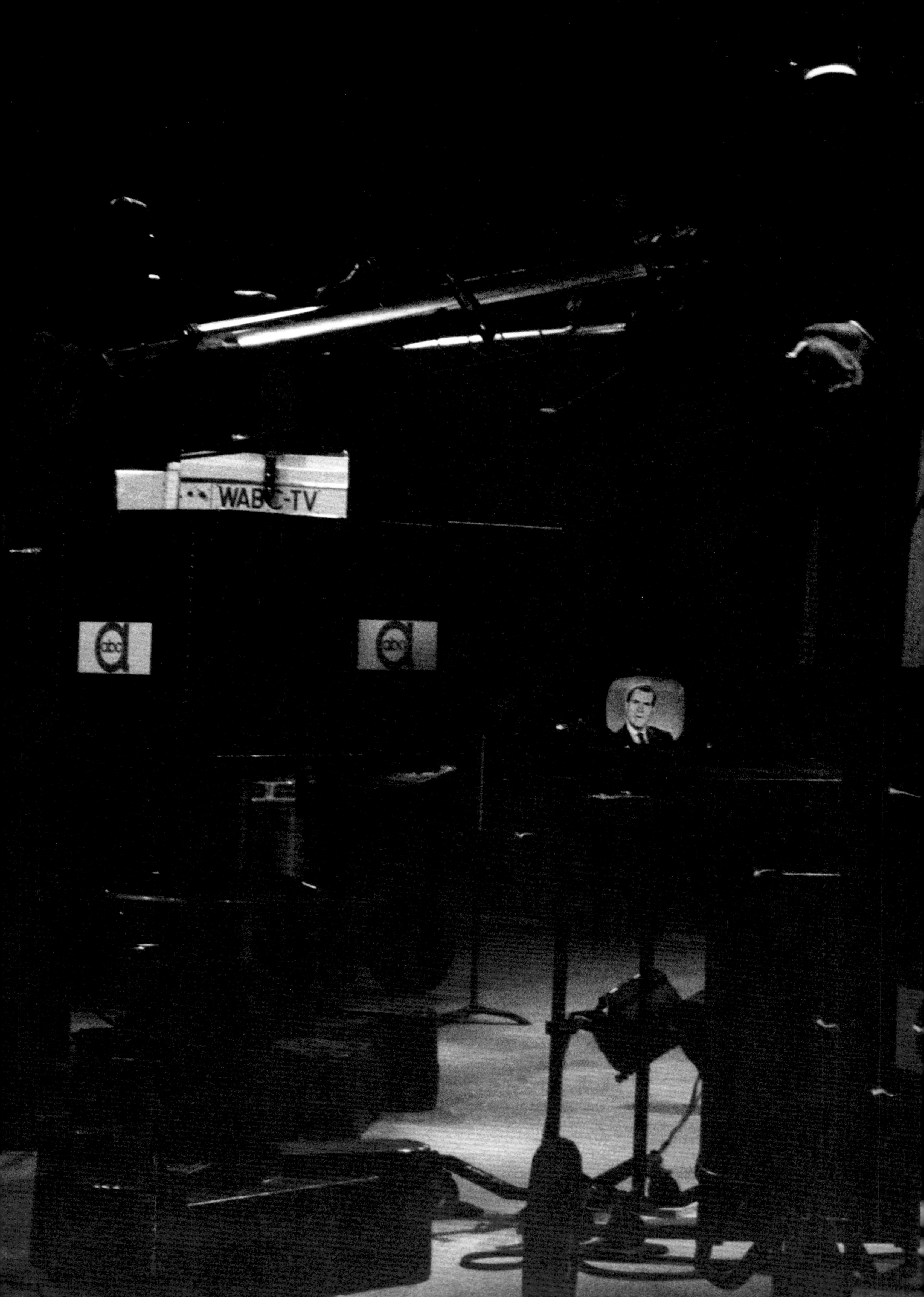

WABC-TV

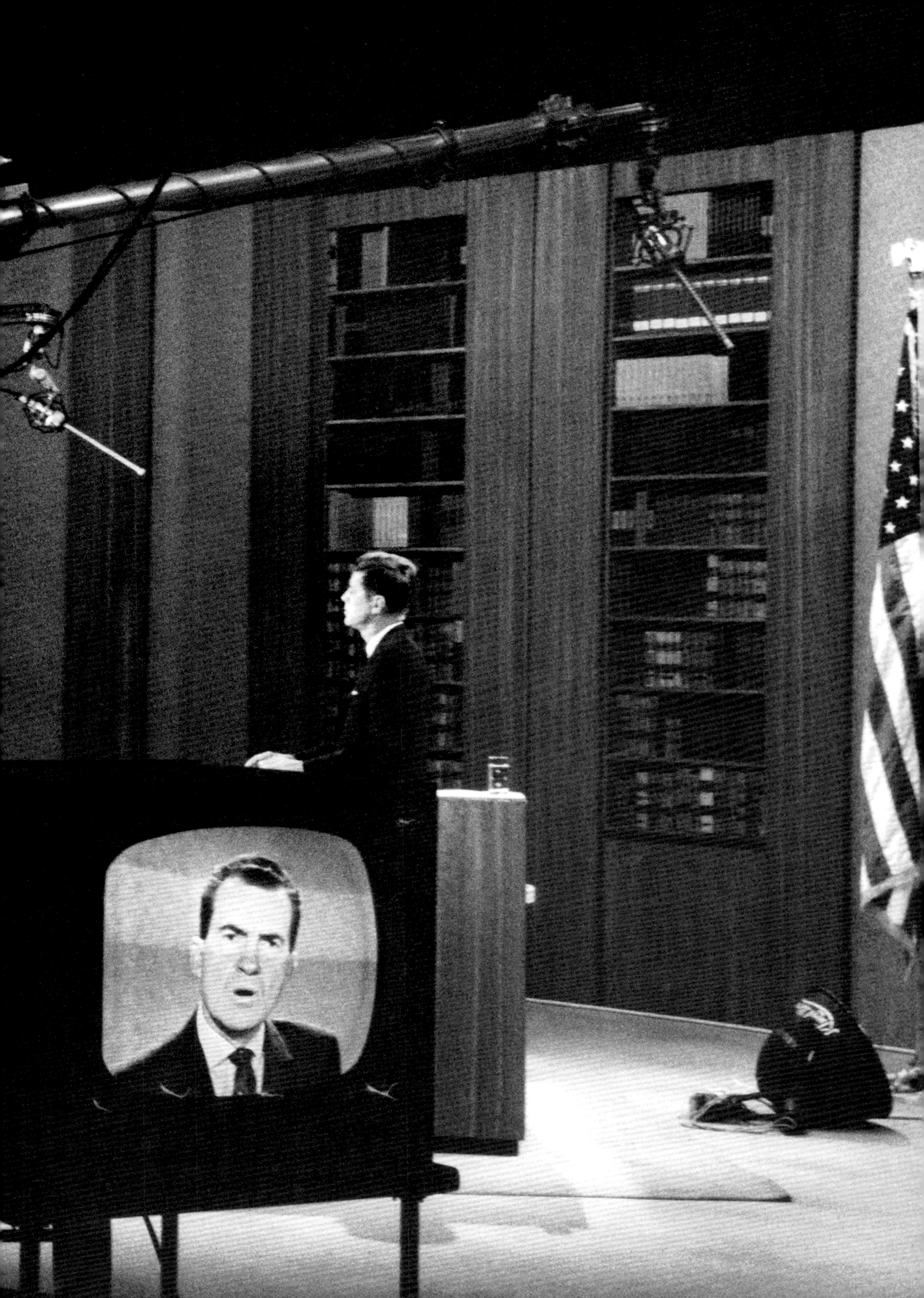

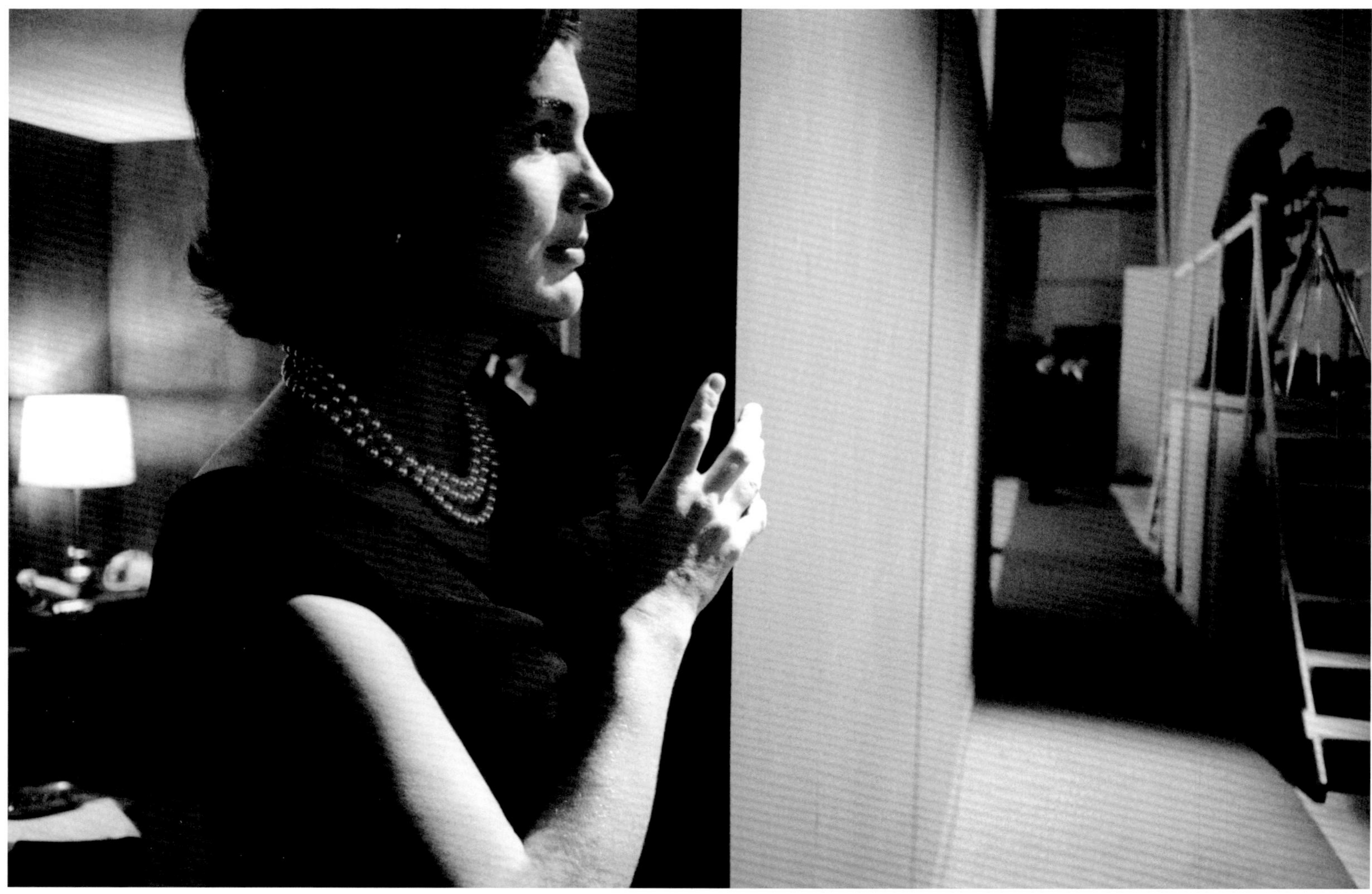

PREVIOUS SPREAD *October 13, 1960.* The third debate used split-screen technology, with Kennedy in New York and Nixon in Los Angeles. Though Nixon fared better in the second and third debates than he had in the first, the momentum from Kennedy's performance in September had made the indelible first impression on many voters. After it, his campaign was electrified, with crowds for rallies and motorcades much larger than they'd ever been. It was clear to his team that he had finally firmed up the full support of his party—and hopefully stolen some from the Republicans too. *Photo, Paul Schutzer*

ABOVE *October 21, 1960.* Jackie Kennedy watches a portion of the fourth Kennedy-Nixon debate from the wings of ABC-TV's studio in New York City. Photographer Jacques Lowe would later write: "When the debate ended, Kennedy came back and everybody shouted words of encouragement. But Jacqueline walked over to him and said softly, 'You looked wonderful, Jack.' He quickly responded to her compliment. 'You think so?…

You really think so?' And when he saw that she did, all the tension went from his face. He put his arm around her and they walked off—a couple alone for the moment in their private world." *Photo, Paul Schutzer*

OPPOSITE *September 20, 1960.* New York City's mayor, Robert Wagner Jr., gets Jackie's ear at a $100-a-plate fund-raising dinner in Washington, D.C. *Photo, Ed Clark*

FOLLOWING SPREAD *October 21, 1960.* Vice President Nixon appears to be trying to score one last point as Kennedy walks away from the podium at the end of the fourth debate. Both men performed well, and the debate was considered a draw. In mid-October, Kennedy had challenged Nixon to a fifth debate, and from the campaign trail he would continue to needle Nixon on that challenge. On October 31, Kennedy told students at Temple University in Philadelphia that he'd not only like to have a fifth debate with Nixon, but he wouldn't mind if President Eisenhower came along too. *Photo, Anonymous*

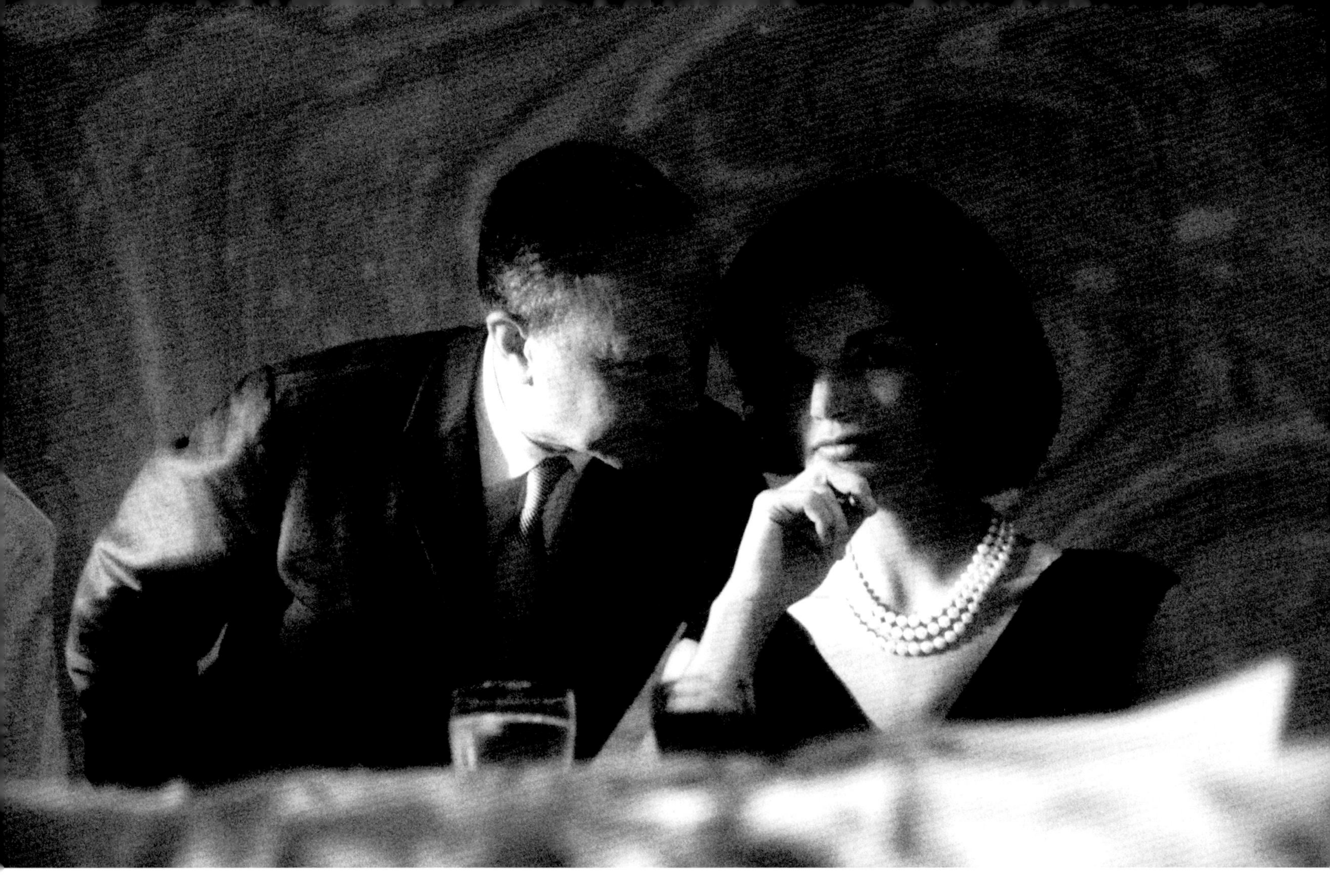

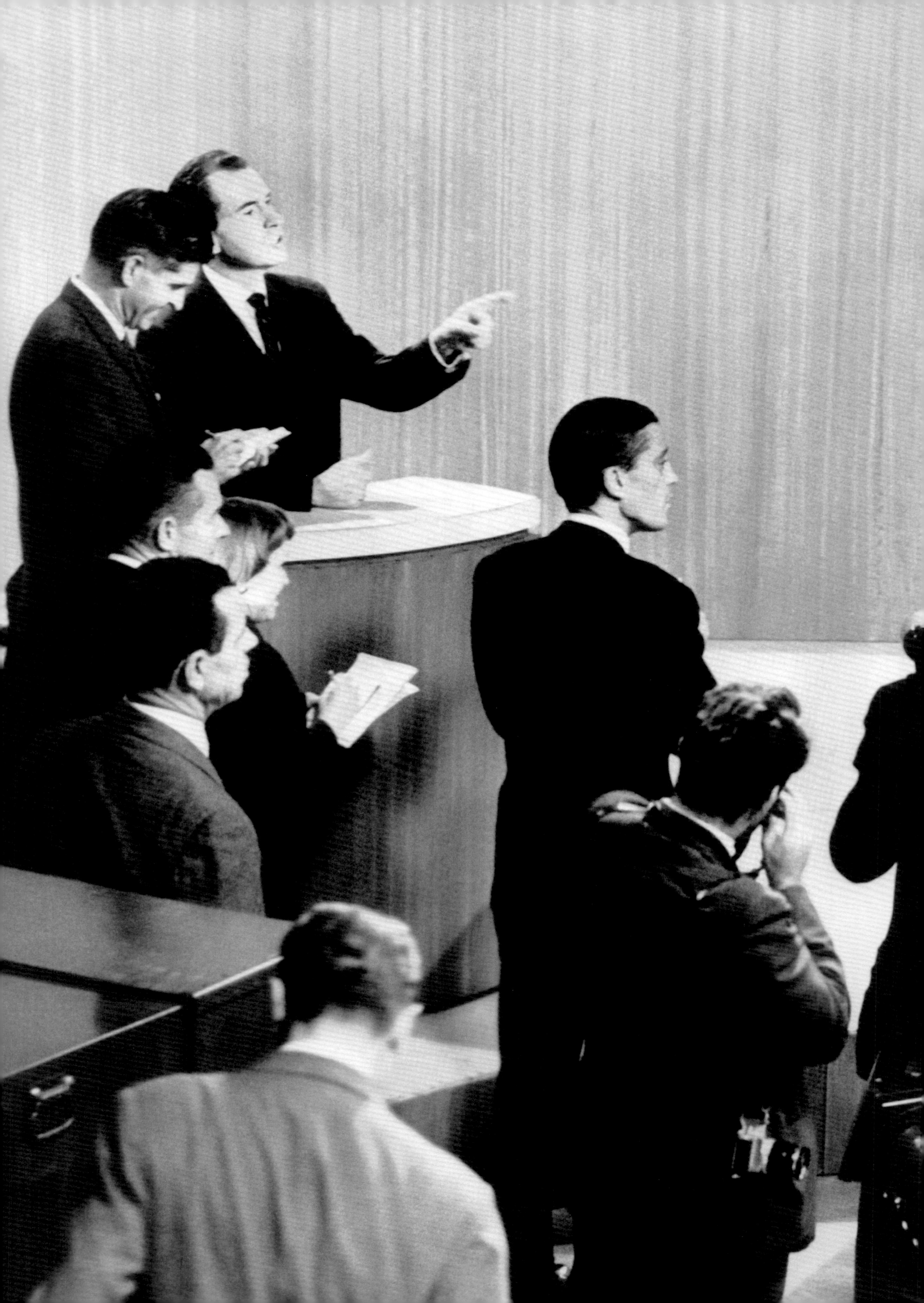

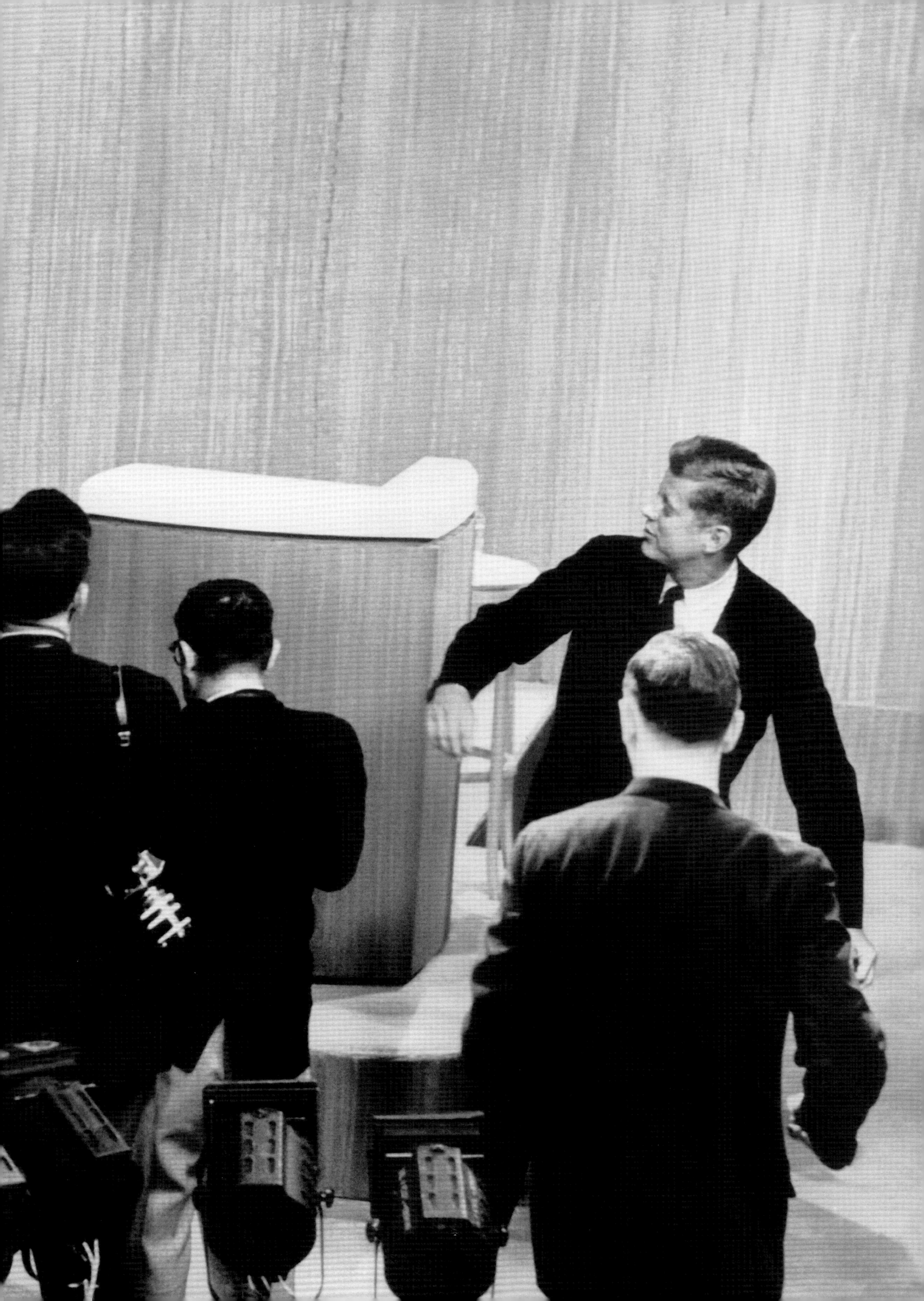

"I don't believe there's any burden, or any responsibility, that any American would not assume to protect his country, to advance the cause of freedom. And I believe it incumbent upon us now to do that."

—John F. Kennedy, the Fourth Debate, New York City, October 21, 1960

OPPOSITE *October 27, 1960.* Kennedy takes to the deck of the ferryboat *Cornelius G. Kolff* from Manhattan to Staten Island on one of half-a-dozen swings through New York City since the start of the general campaign. The 25-minute ride through New York's harbor passed the Statue of Liberty, an inspiring view even on a rainy day, offering Kennedy a rare moment of quiet before disembarking for his next stump speech of the day. *Photo, Paul Schutzer*

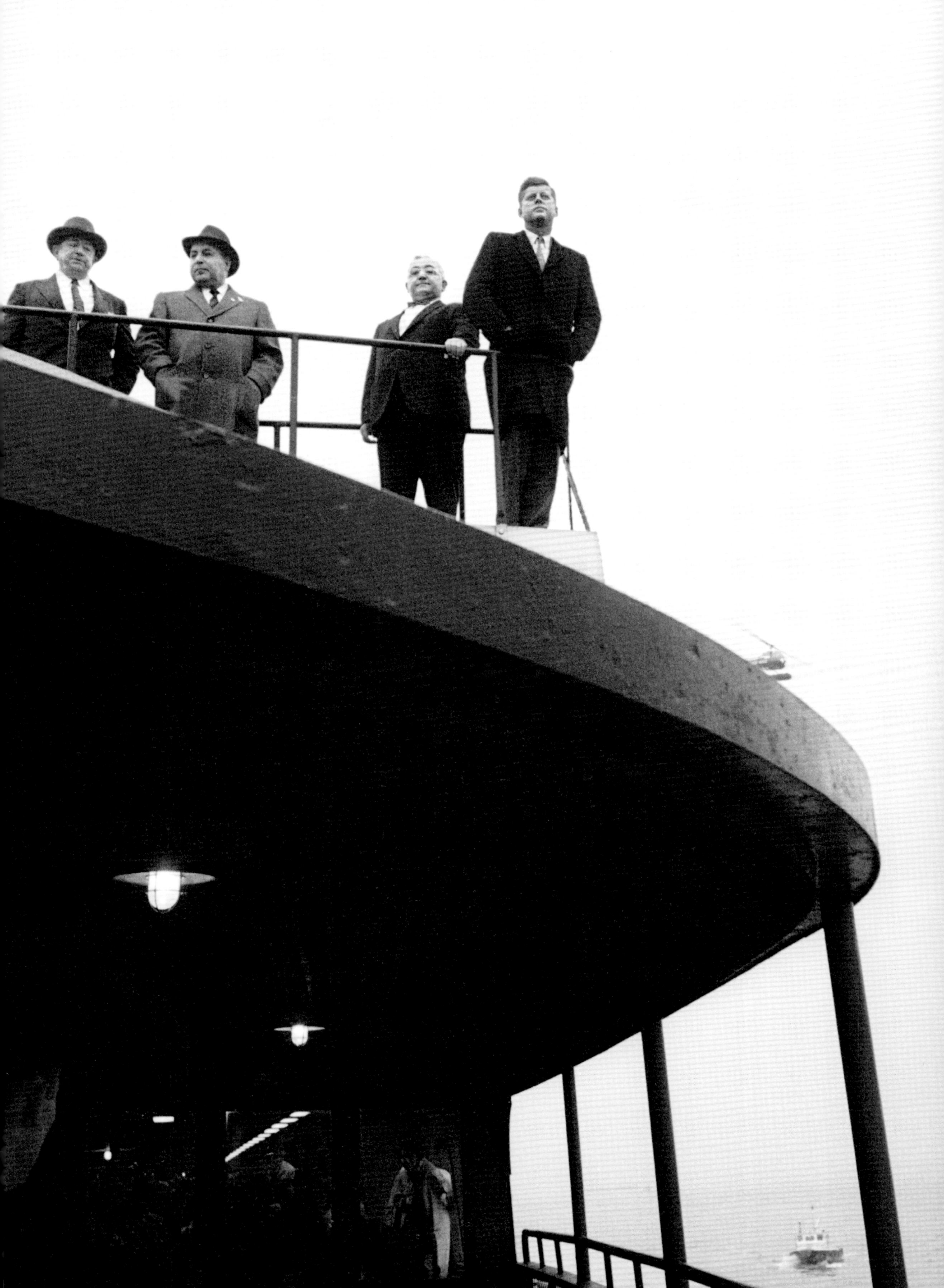

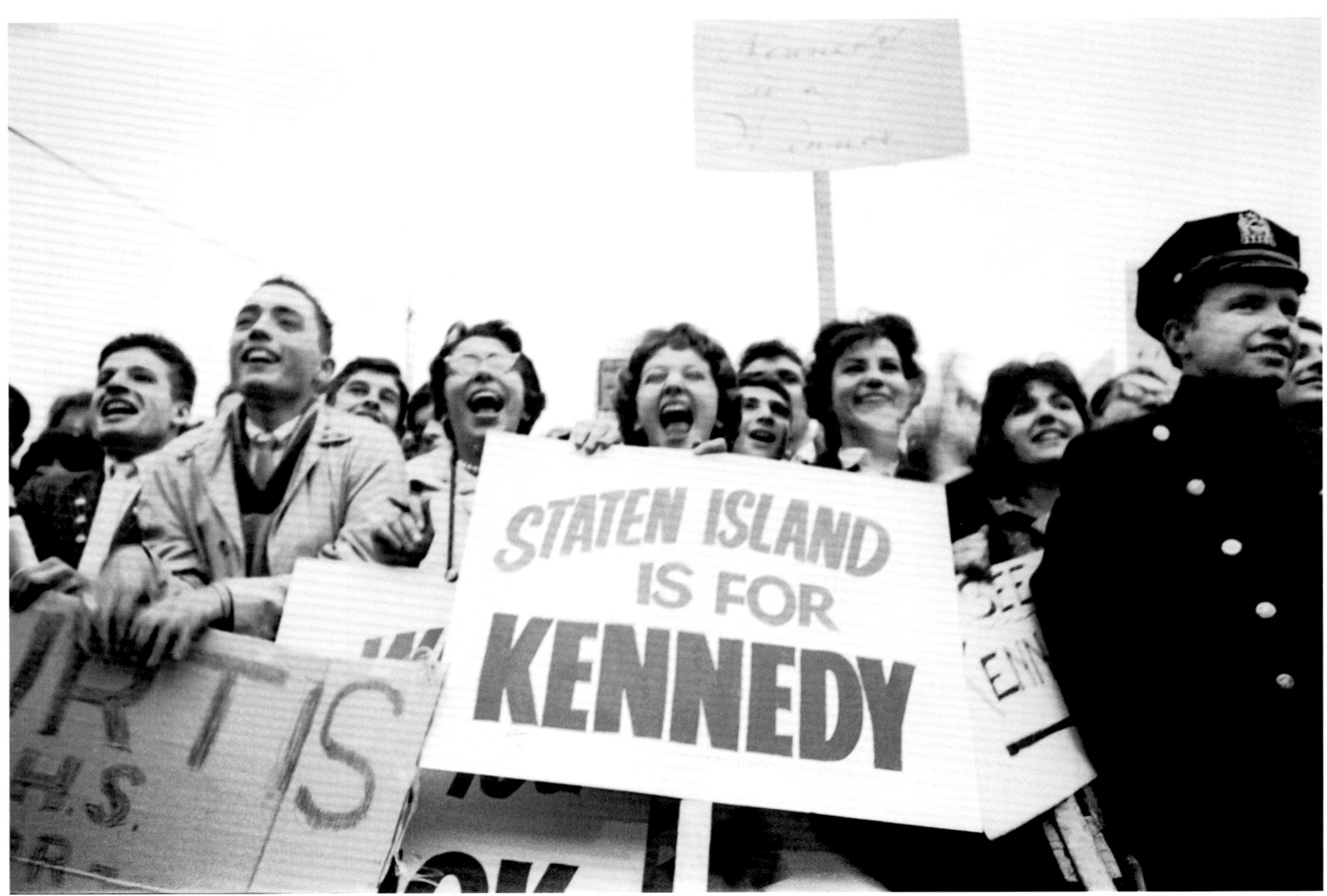

ABOVE *October 27, 1960.* A crowd of 15,000 fans spilled out of the St. George Ferry Terminal on Staten Island to hear Kennedy's half-hour address, where he charged that the Eisenhower-Nixon administration, in office since 1953, had been "manned by people who have been uninterested in the sweep of history and the revolutionary times in which they live. . . . " As a result, Kennedy said, "we are second-best in space [and] we are graduating one-half as many scientists and engineers as the Soviet Union." *Photo, Ted Russell*

OPPOSITE *October 27, 1960.* Seemingly all of New York City—including these youngsters at an afternoon rally in Union Square—turned out to see Kennedy just two weeks before Election Day. But it was in Brooklyn, where a scene "unparalleled in the campaign," according to the Associated Press, occurred when Kennedy stopped in a restaurant for a bite. Thousands surrounded the building, blocking the motorcade outside, and locking the candidate inside, where he was ordered by police to remain for an hour, safe from the "screaming, tumultuous mass." *Photo, Ted Russell*

RIGHT *October 27, 1960.* Kennedy's arrival on Staten Island snarled the commute of the rush hour crowd. "I want to express my regrets," he quipped over the microphone, in response to the chaos in the terminal, "if there are any Republican commuters who have been caught unwillingly in this crowd." *Photo, Alfred Wertheimer*

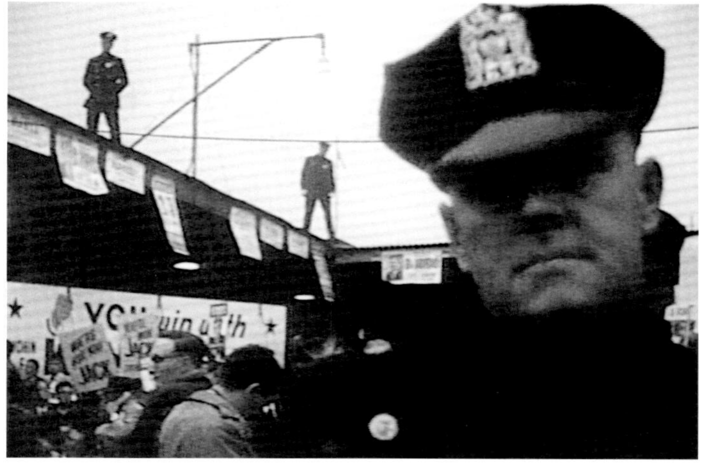

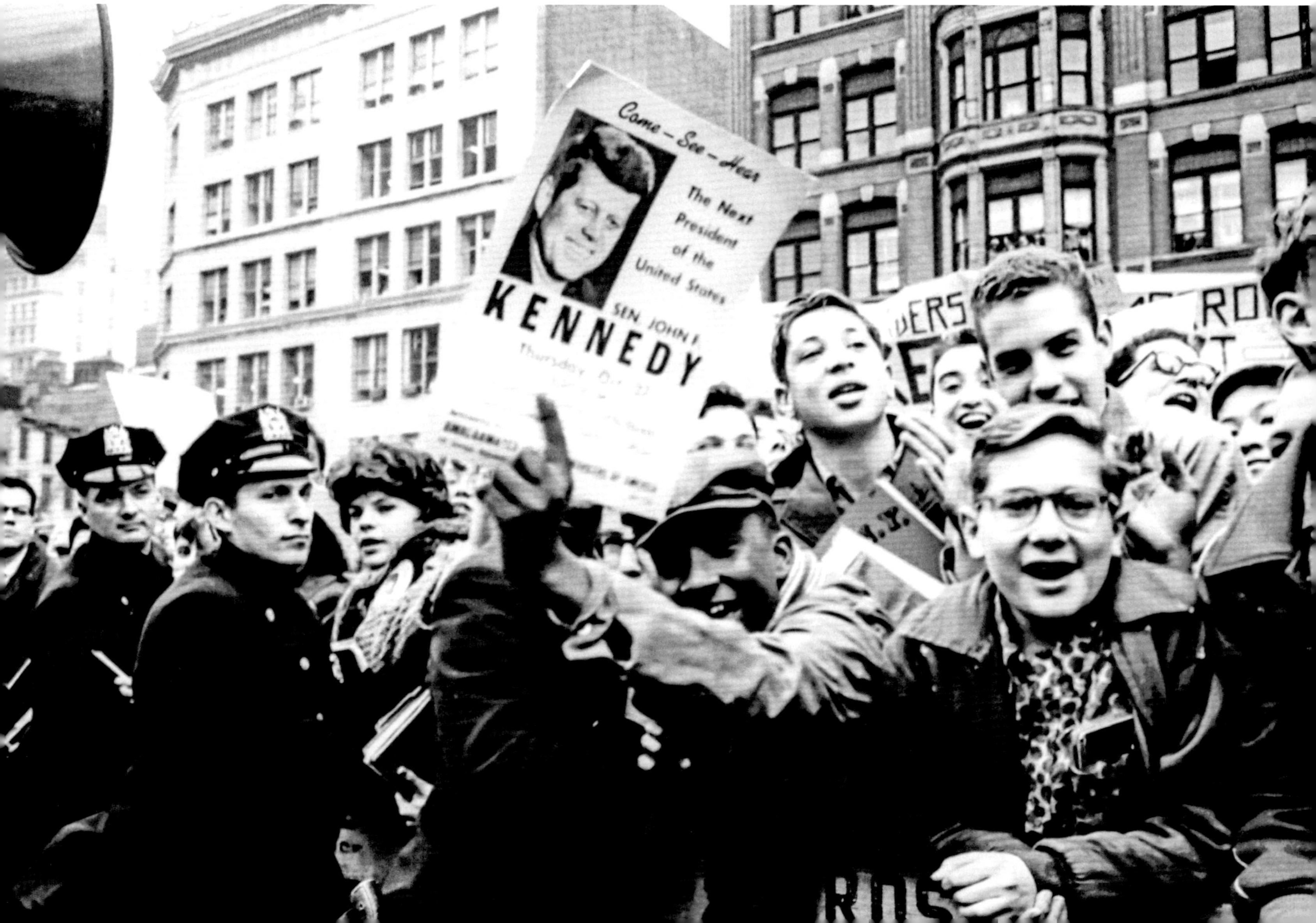

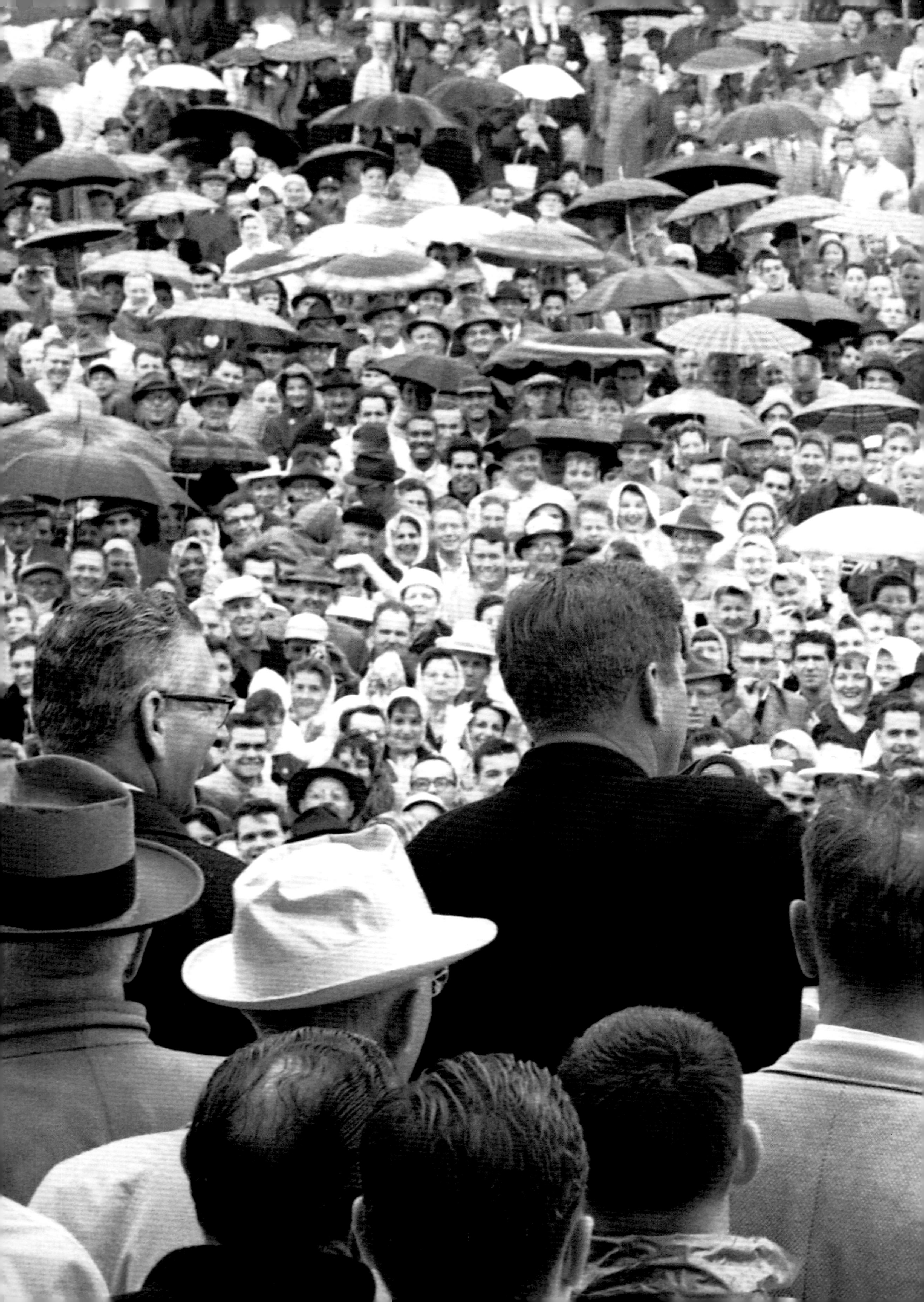

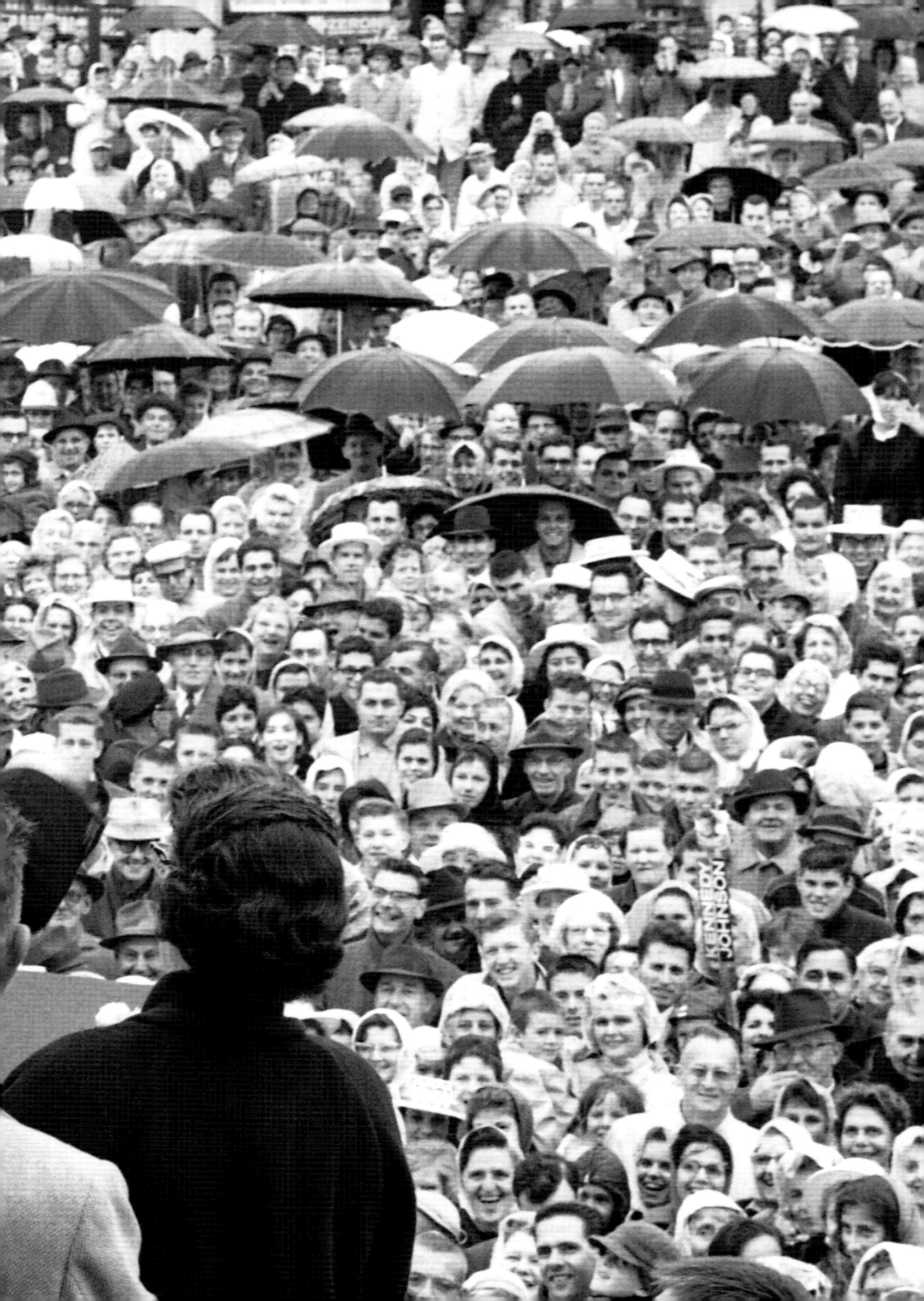

KENNEDY
JOHNSON

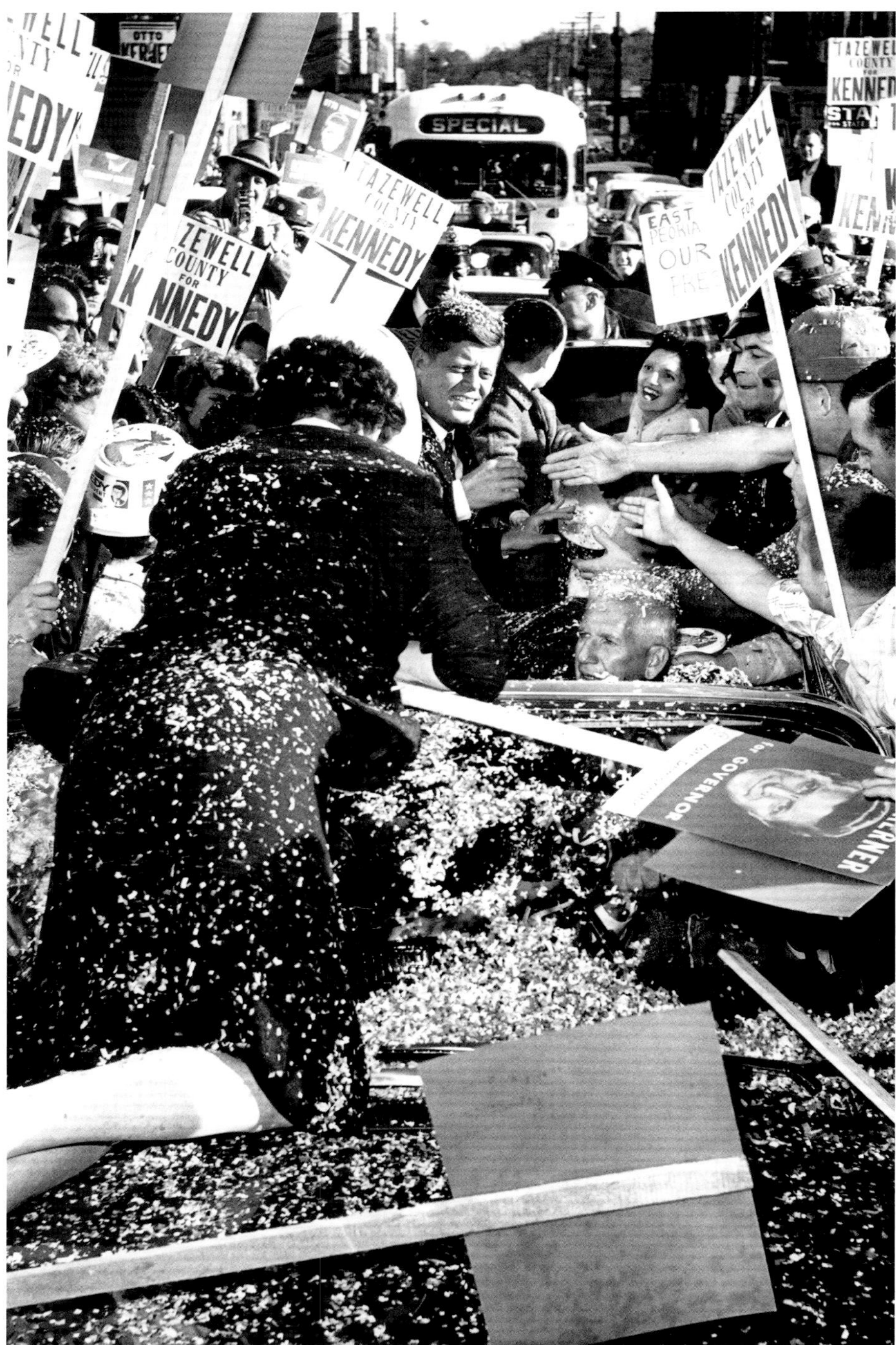

PREVIOUS SPREAD *October 29, 1960.* Thousands of people came to events in Philadelphia, even in the rain. A key battleground state, Pennsylvania held 32 electoral votes—as many as California and second only to New York. Between October 28 and October 31 Kennedy and his team made a blitz of appearances there, where Kennedy's message of economic opportunity resonated. *Photo, Burton Berinsky*

ABOVE *October 24, 1960.* "Frantic scenes like this one in Tazewell County, Illinois, became commonplace toward the close of the campaign," observed photographer Jacques Lowe, who also covered Kennedy's stop in the Peoria metro area. Illinois Senator Paul Douglas would later classify Kennedy's female acolytes as "jumpers, shriekers, huggers, lopers and touchers." And Russell Baker of *The New York Times*, writing in late October 1960, would observe, "…in the last month he has flowered into a magnificent campaigner with a Pied Piper magic over the street crowds, and especially the ladies, and with a considerable talent for what is ungraciously called rabble-rousing." *Photo, Stanley Tretick*

BELOW *November 6, 1960.* Demonstrators for JFK at a Newark, New Jersey, campaign rally. The last thing Kennedy could have wanted to see at this point was a sign like the one pictured, which said, "The election of Kennedy will be the greatest thing that happened in the world since Christ was born!" Having battled charges about his Catholic religion throughout the campaign—that he "would take orders from the Pope" and more—campaign placards like this one did him no favors. *Photo, Burton Berinsky*

FOLLOWING SPREAD *October 29, 1960.* Bleachers filled with Kennedy acolytes line the parade route in Upper Darby, Pennsylvania. *Photo, Burton Berinsky*

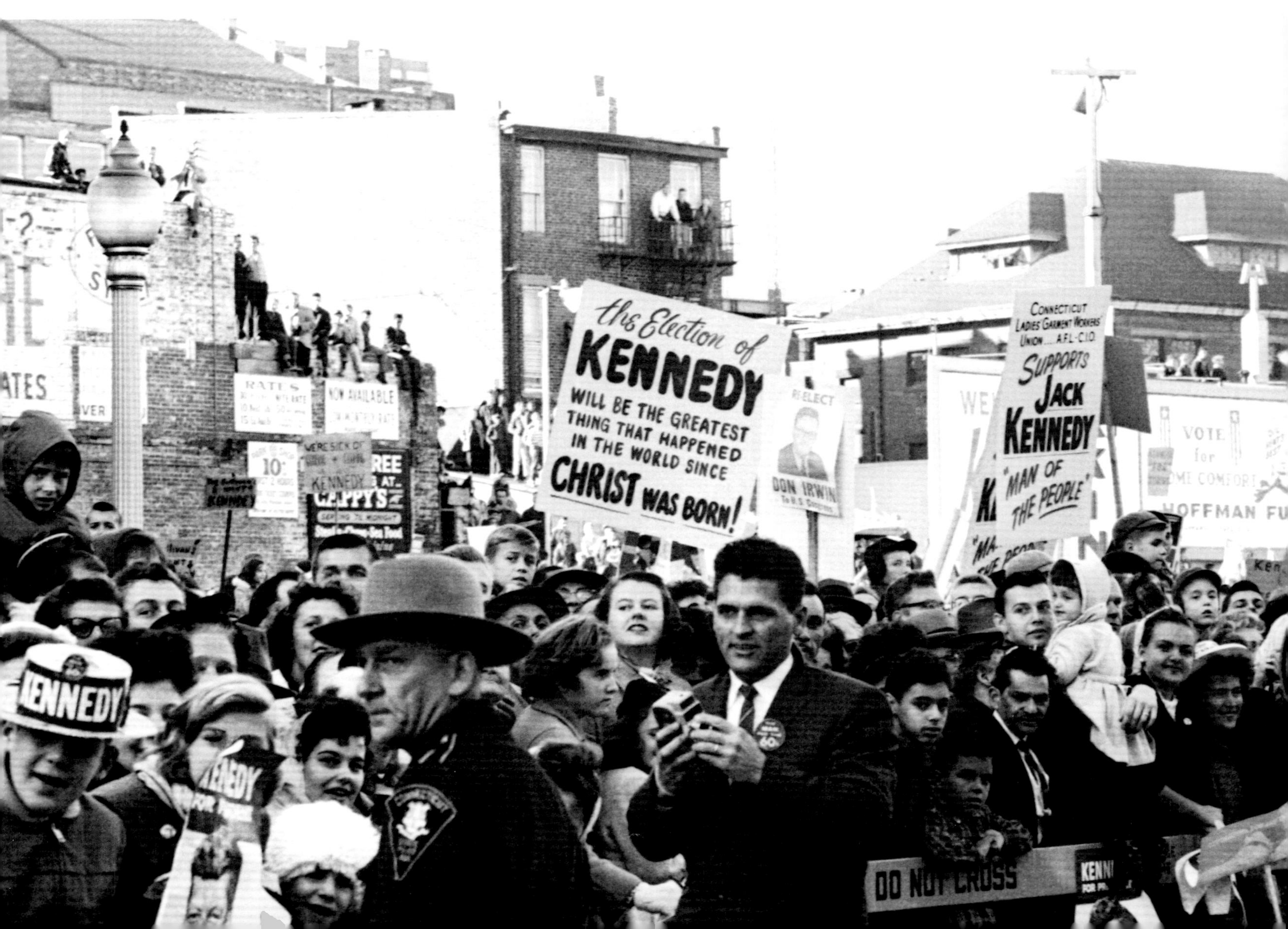
the Election of
KENNEDY
WILL BE THE GREATEST
THING THAT HAPPENED
IN THE WORLD SINCE
CHRIST WAS BORN!
CONNECTICUT
LADIES GARMENT WORKERS'
UNION ... A.F.L.-C.I.O.
SUPPORTS
JACK
KENNEDY
"MAN OF
THE PEOPLE"
RE-ELECT
DON IRWIN
VOTE
for
HOFFMAN FU
KENNEDY
DO NOT CROSS

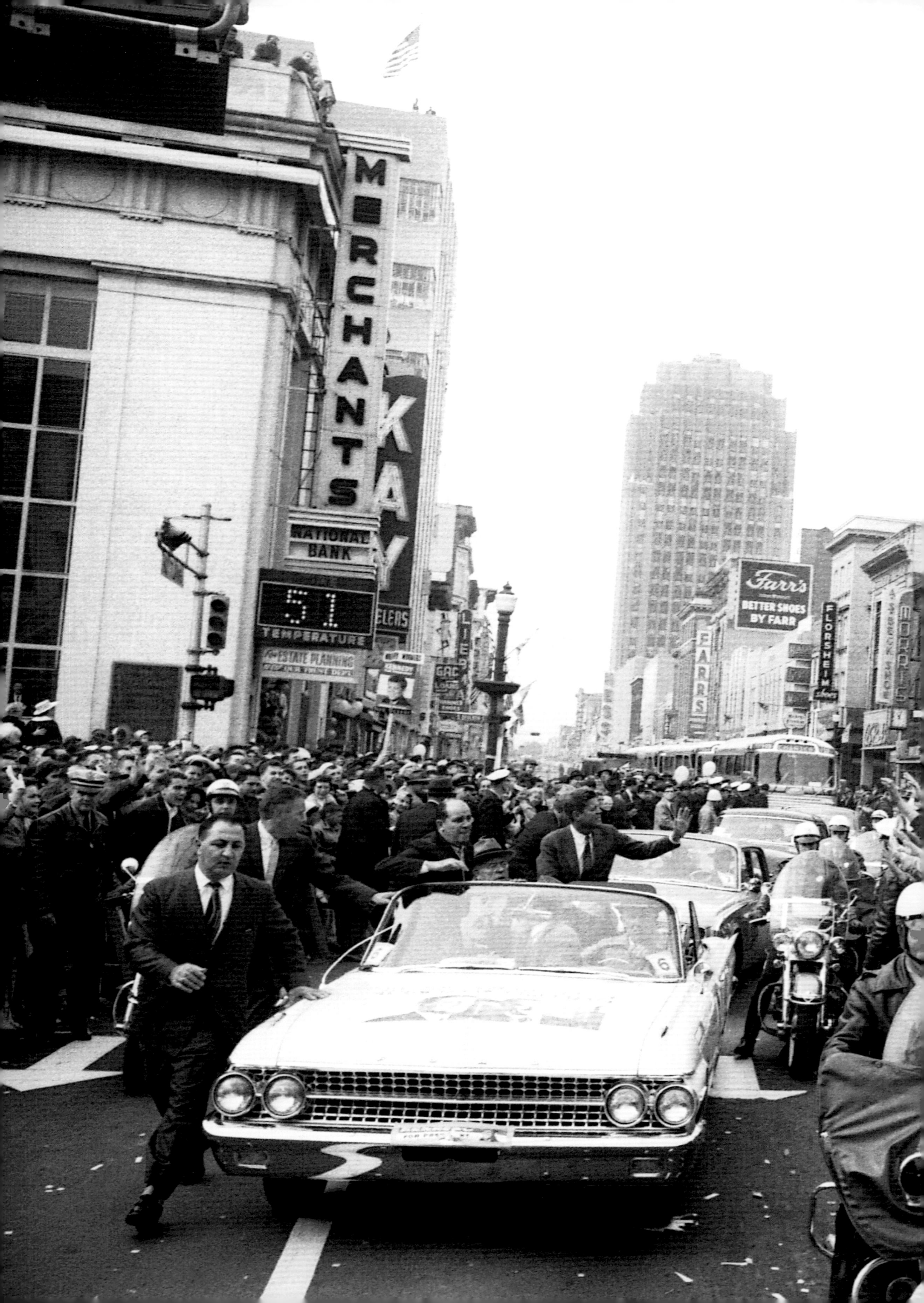

MERCHANTS
KAY
NATIONAL BANK
51
TEMPERATURE
ESTATE PLANNING
Farr's
BETTER SHOES
BY FARR
FARR'S
FLORSHEIM
FOR PRES.

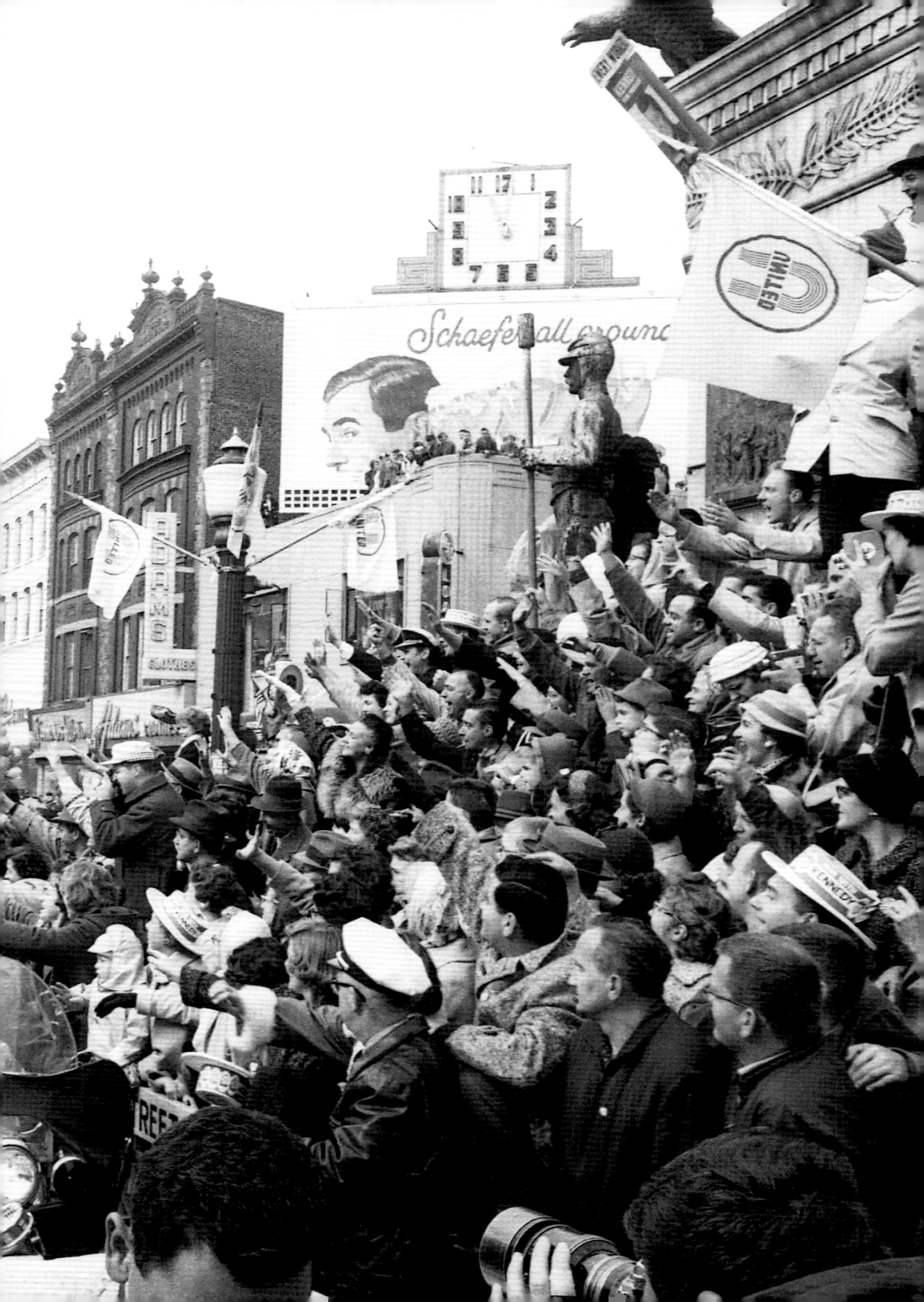

UNITED
Schaefer all around
UNITED
ADAMS
KENNEDY

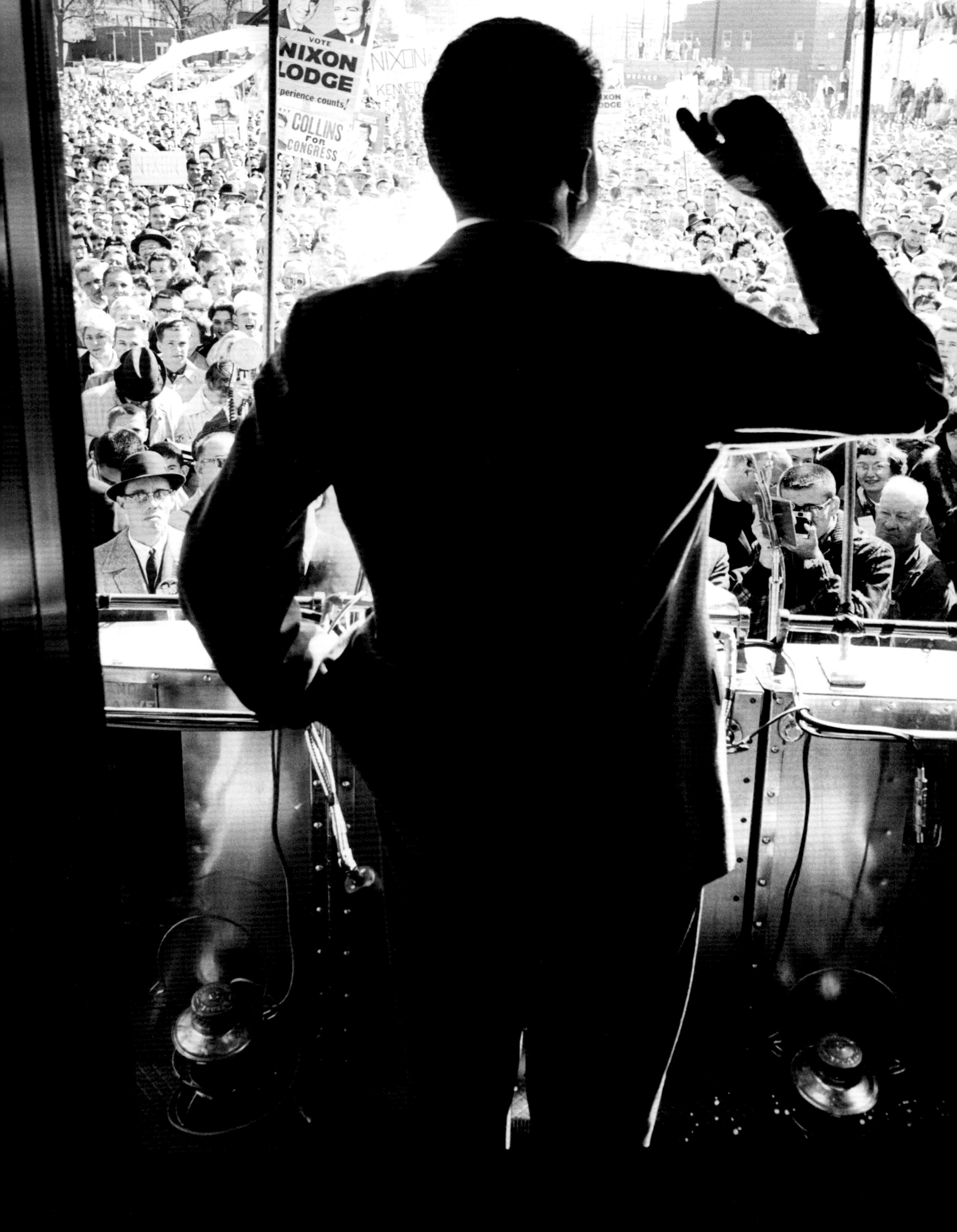

VOTE
NIXON
LODGE
Experience counts.
COLLINS
FOR
CONGRESS
NIXON
KENNEDY
NIXON
LODGE

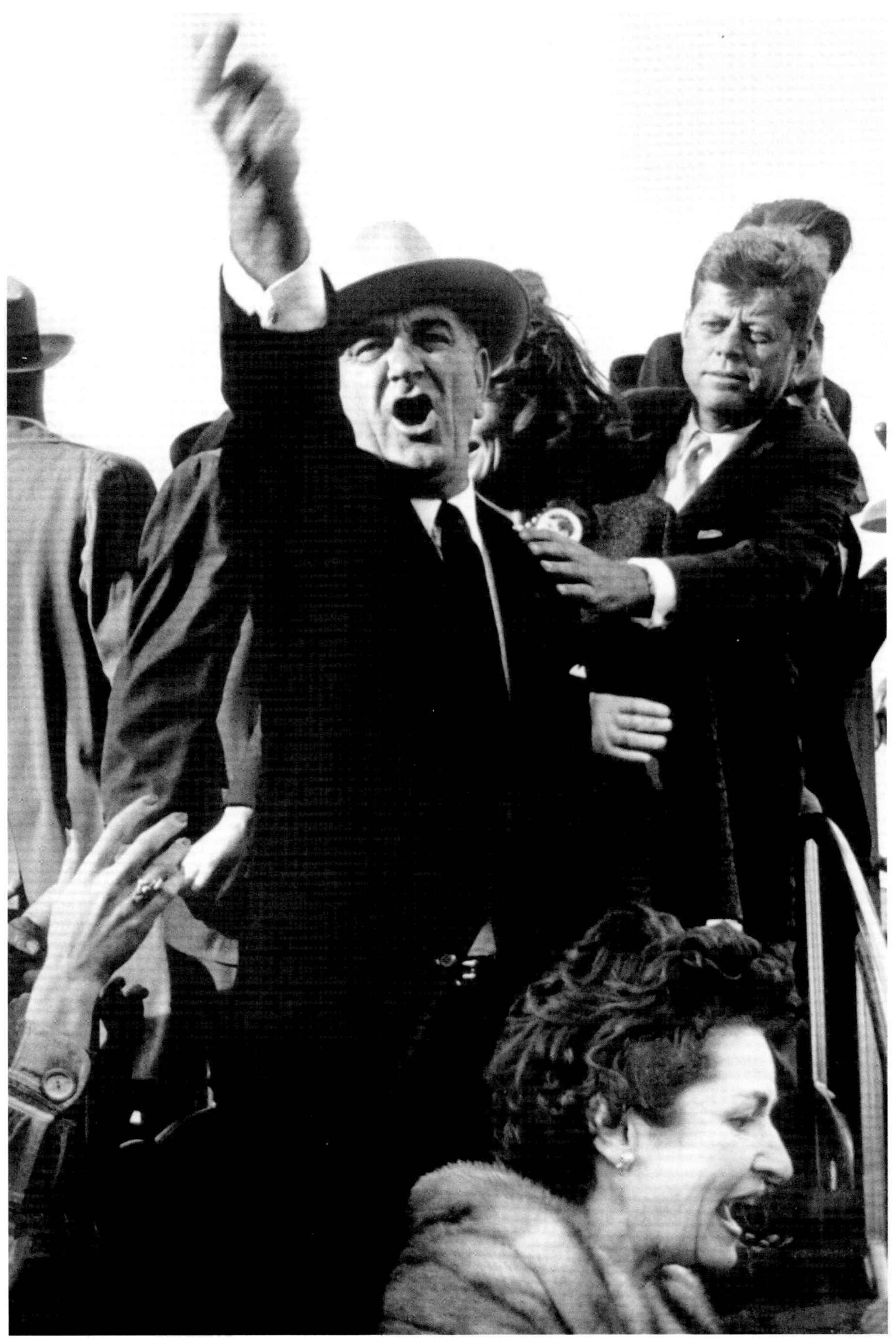

ABOVE *November 3, 1960.* Texas was tough terrain for Democrats. Even though air traffic was temporarily suspended for a short rally at the Amarillo airport, Republican pilots ran their engines to drown out the speakers, inciting Johnson's ire. A few days later, Johnson and his wife, Lady Bird, were jeered and jostled by a hostile crowd in Dallas—an event that prompted Senator Richard Russell of Georgia to take action on behalf of the campaign. News of Russell's endorsement was carried in newspapers throughout the South, helping to improve the ticket's chances in otherwise uncertain territory. *Photo, Richard Pipes*

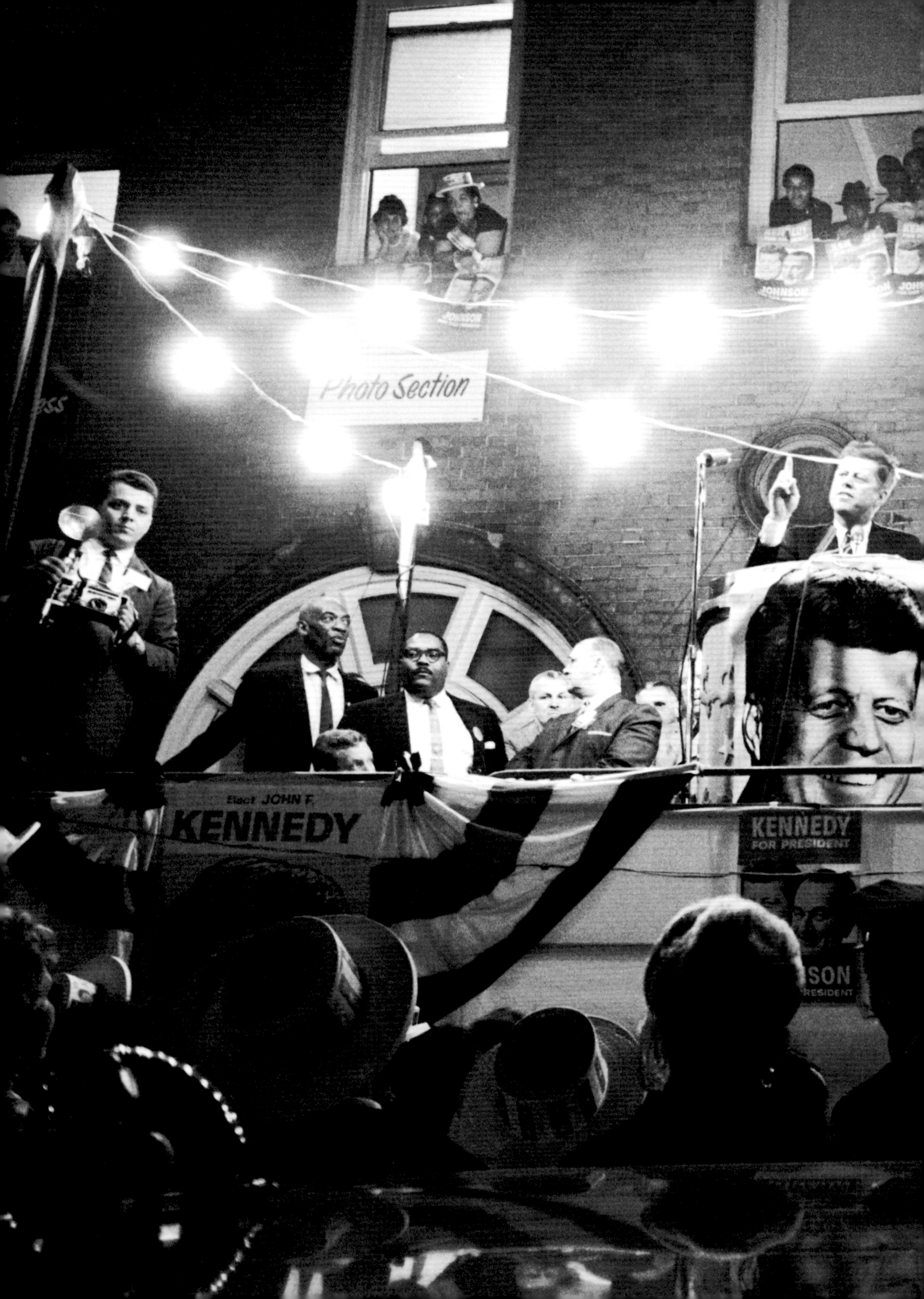

Photo Section
Elect JOHN F. KENNEDY
KENNEDY
KENNEDY FOR PRESIDENT
JOHNSON
SON
PRESIDENT

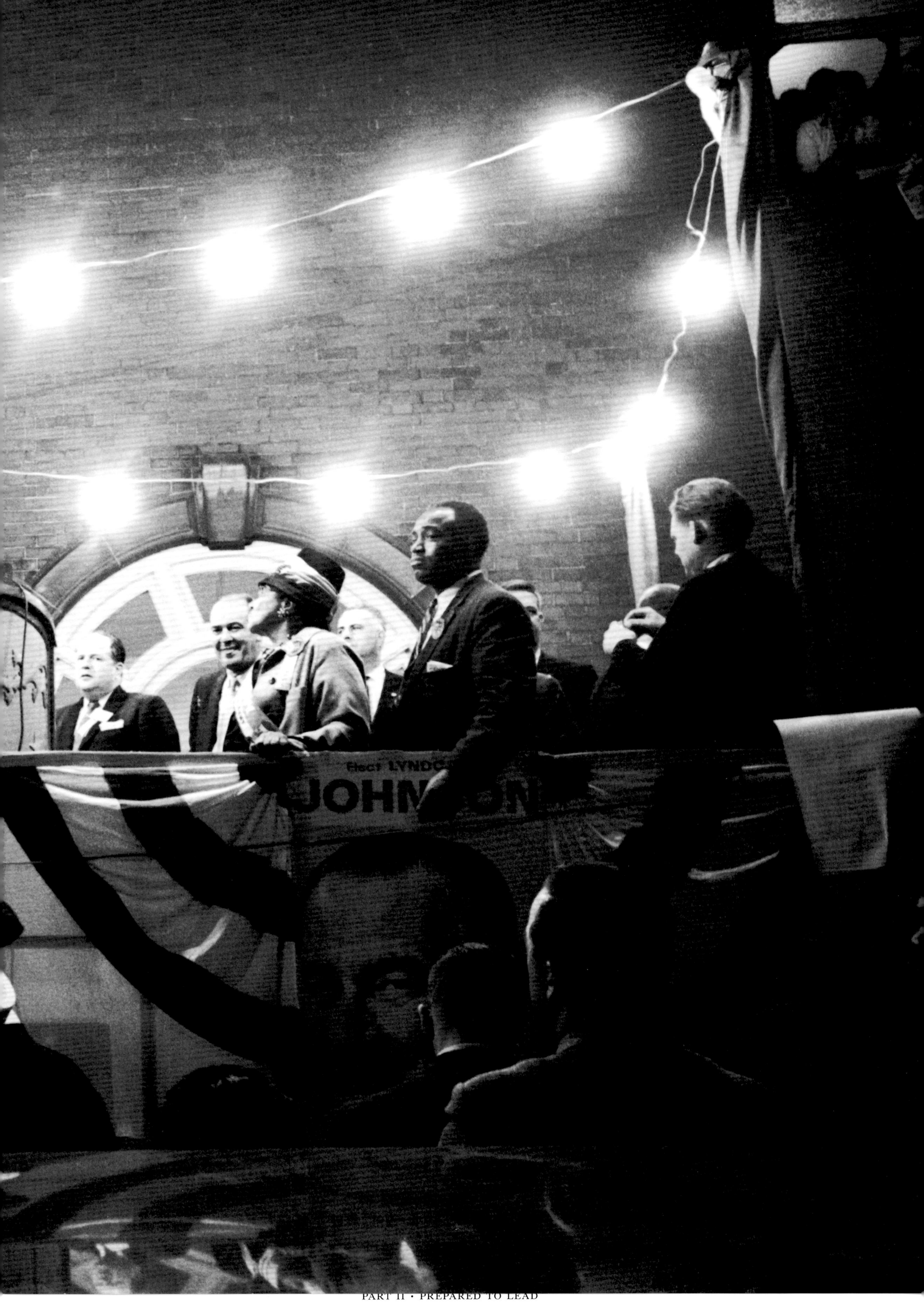

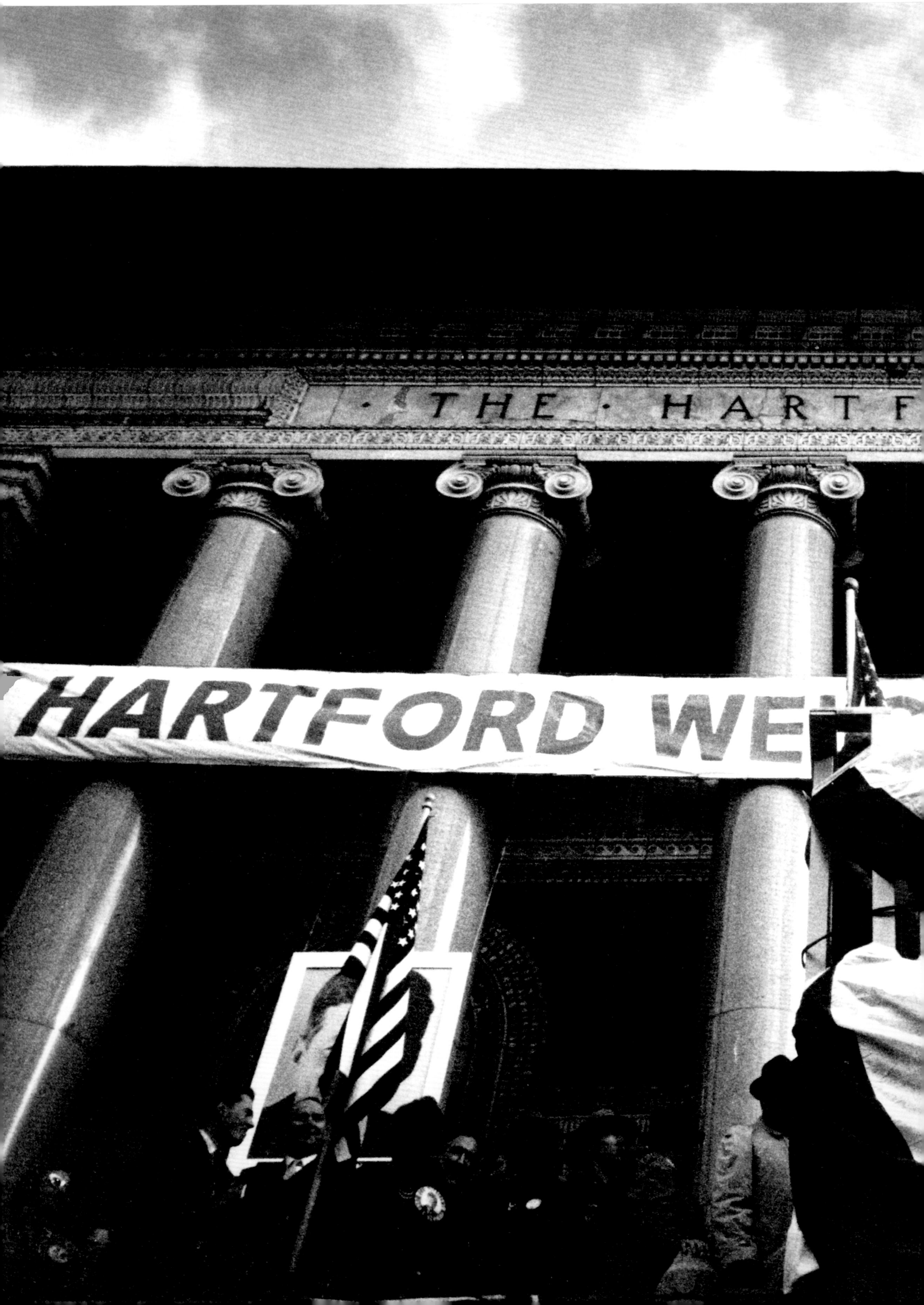

THE · HARTF
HARTFORD WE

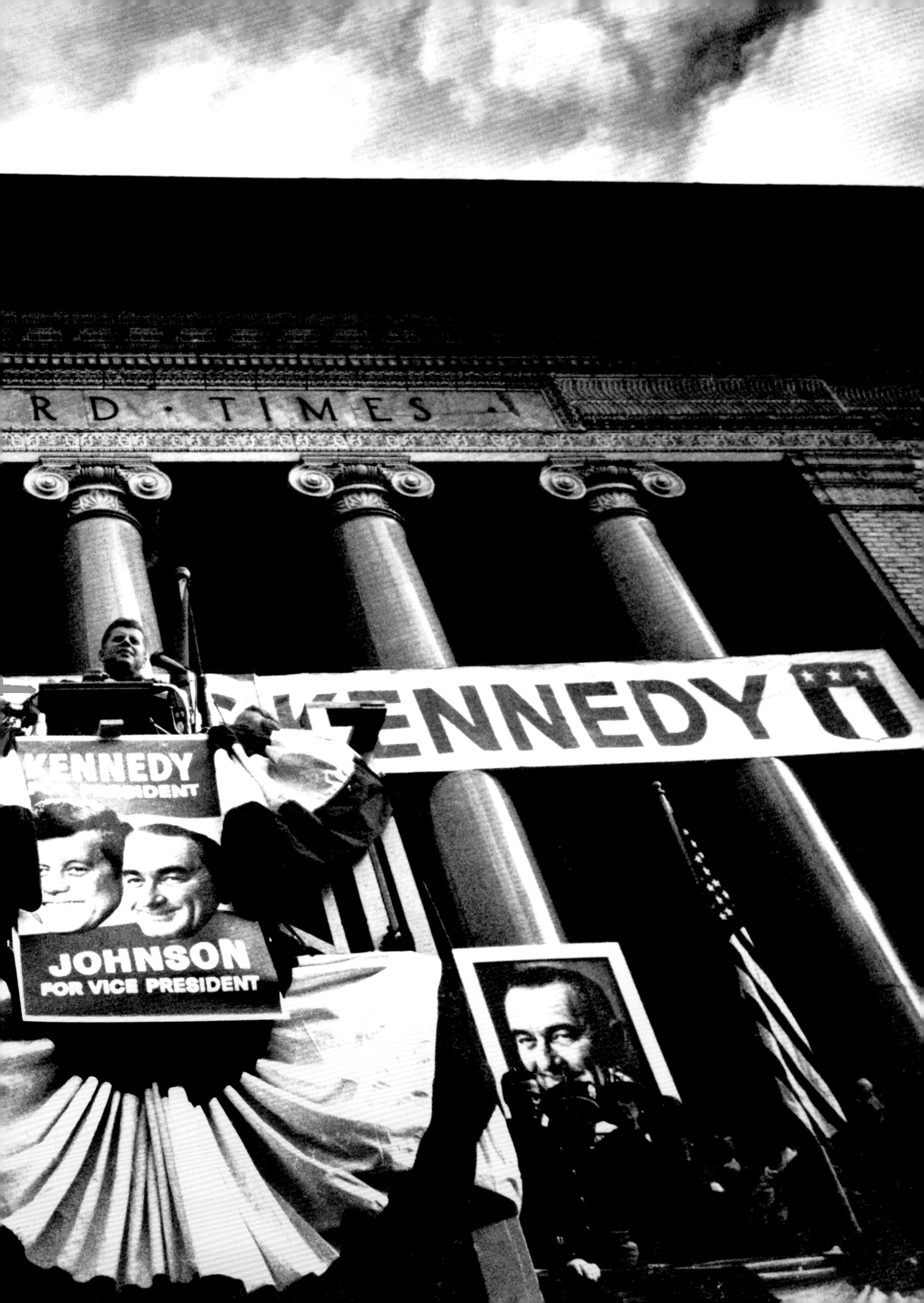

RD · TIMES
KENNEDY
KENNEDY
FOR PRESIDENT
JOHNSON
FOR VICE PRESIDENT

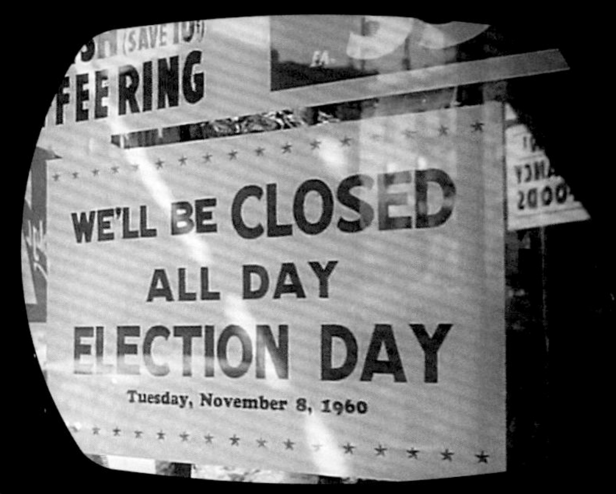
WE'LL BE CLOSED
ALL DAY
ELECTION DAY
Tuesday, November 8, 1960
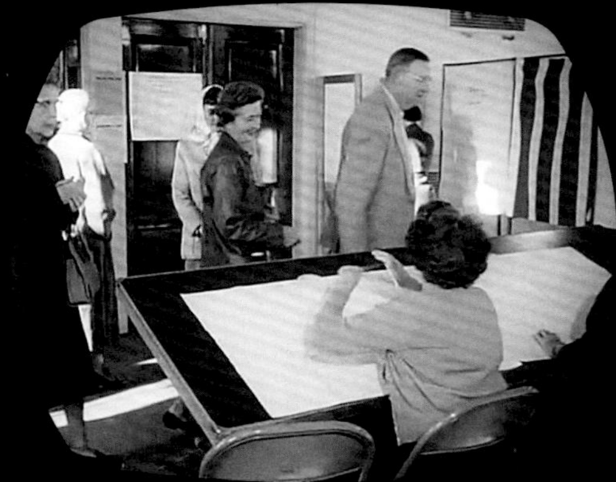
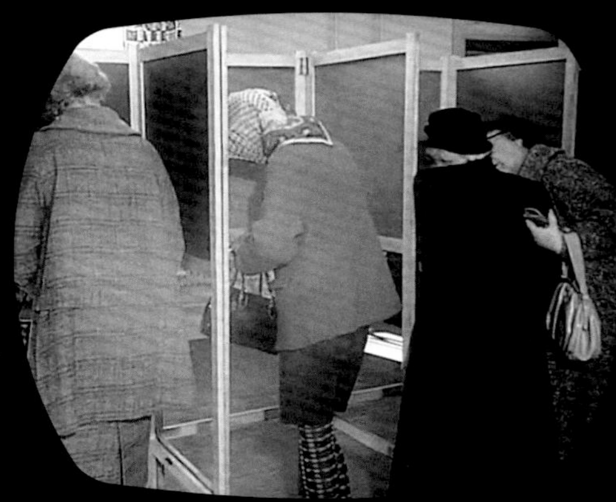
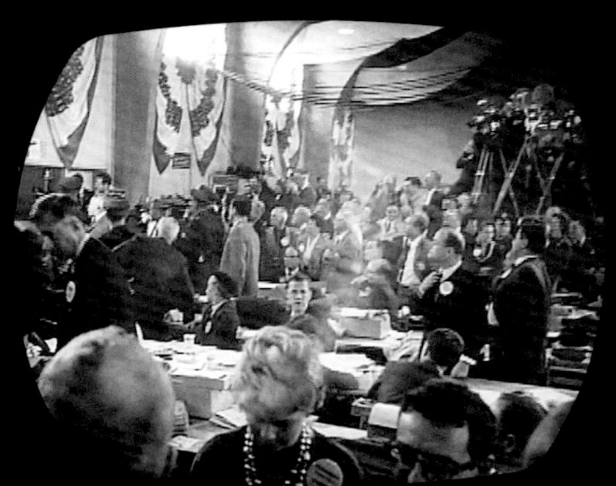
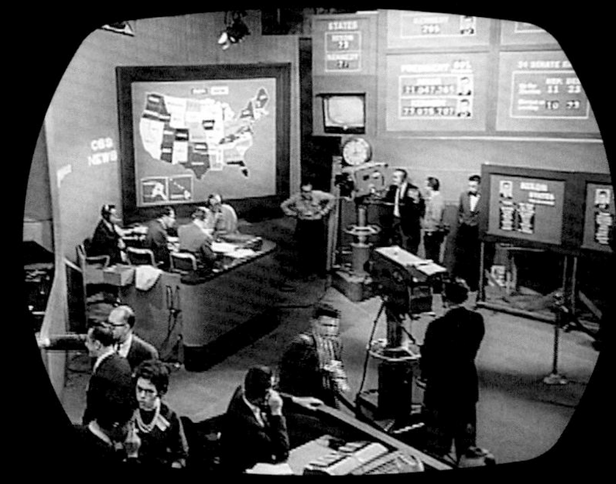
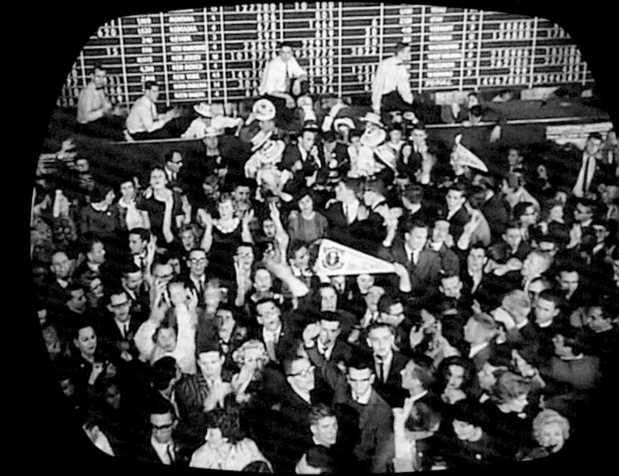
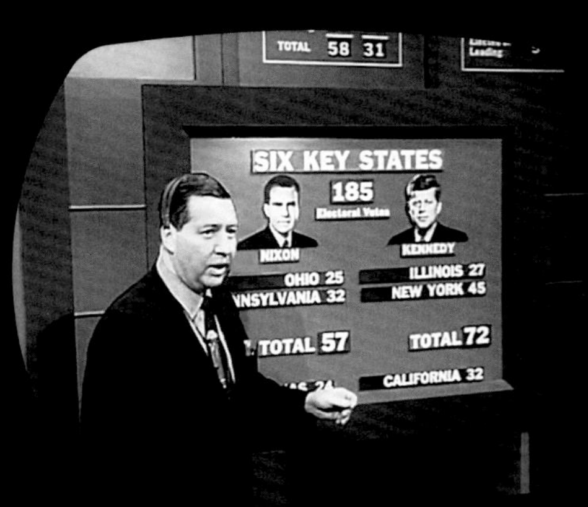
TOTAL 58 31
SIX KEY STATES
185
NIXON   KENNEDY
OHIO 25   ILLINOIS 27
NNSYLVANIA 32 NEW YORK 45
TOTAL 57   TOTAL 72
               CALIFORNIA 32
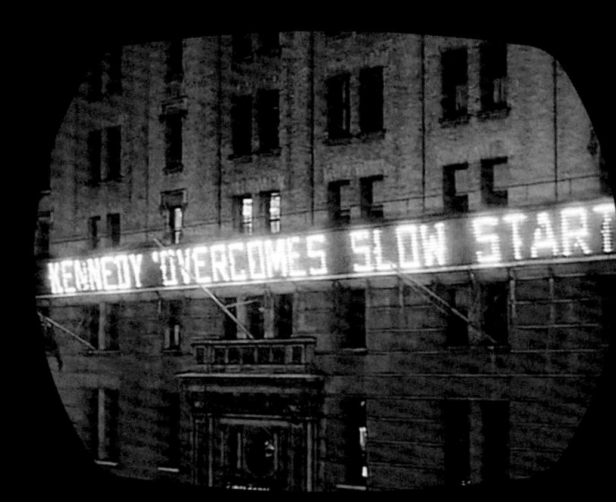
KENNEDY 'OVERCOMES SLOW START
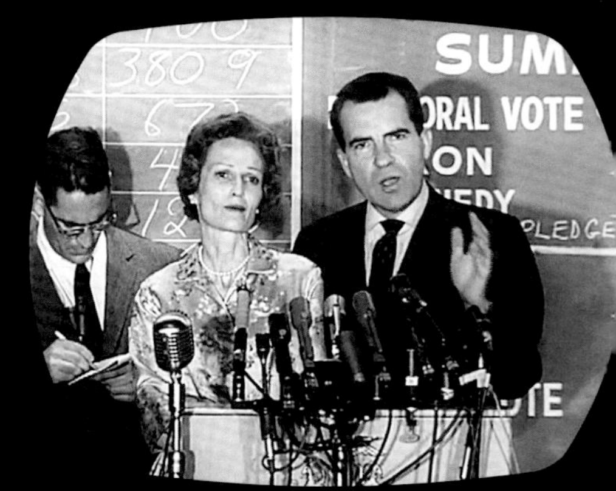
SUM
ORAL VOTE
ON
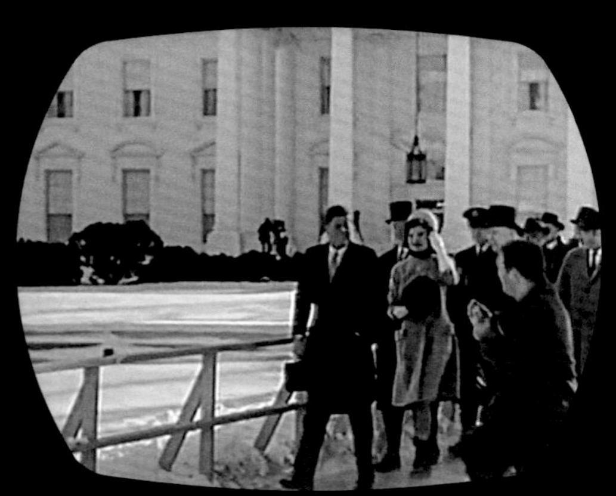
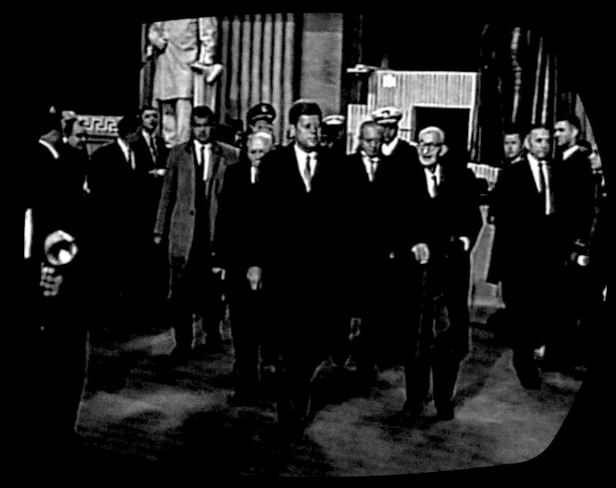
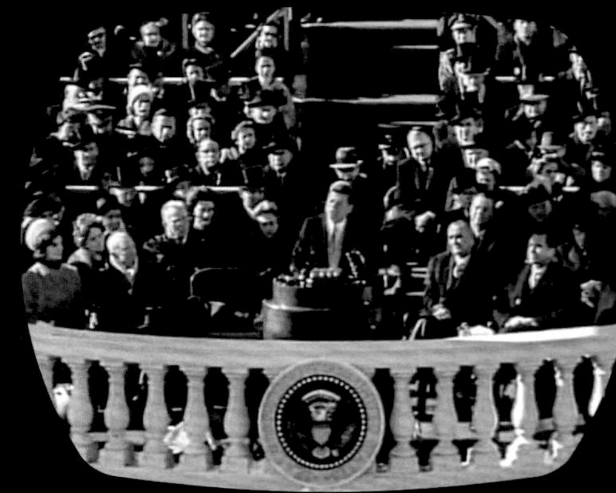
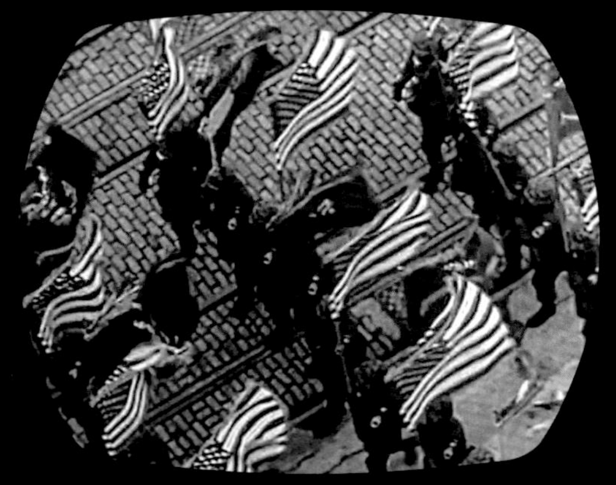
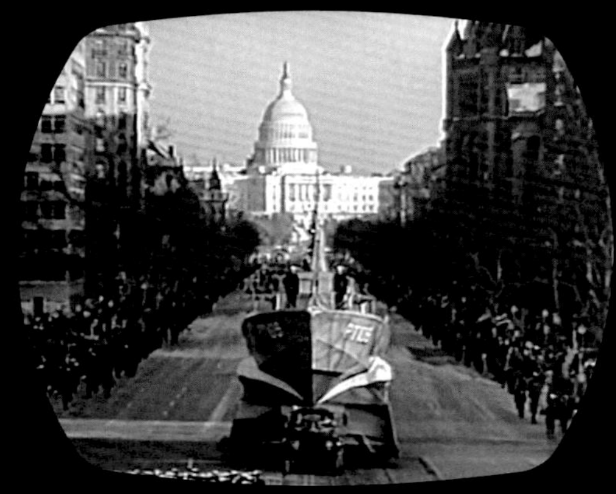
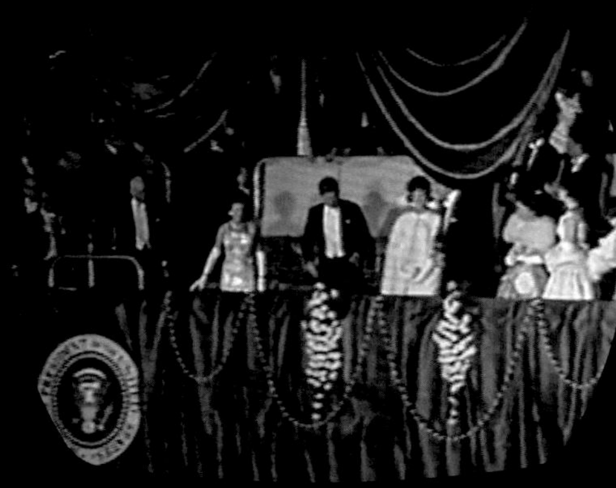

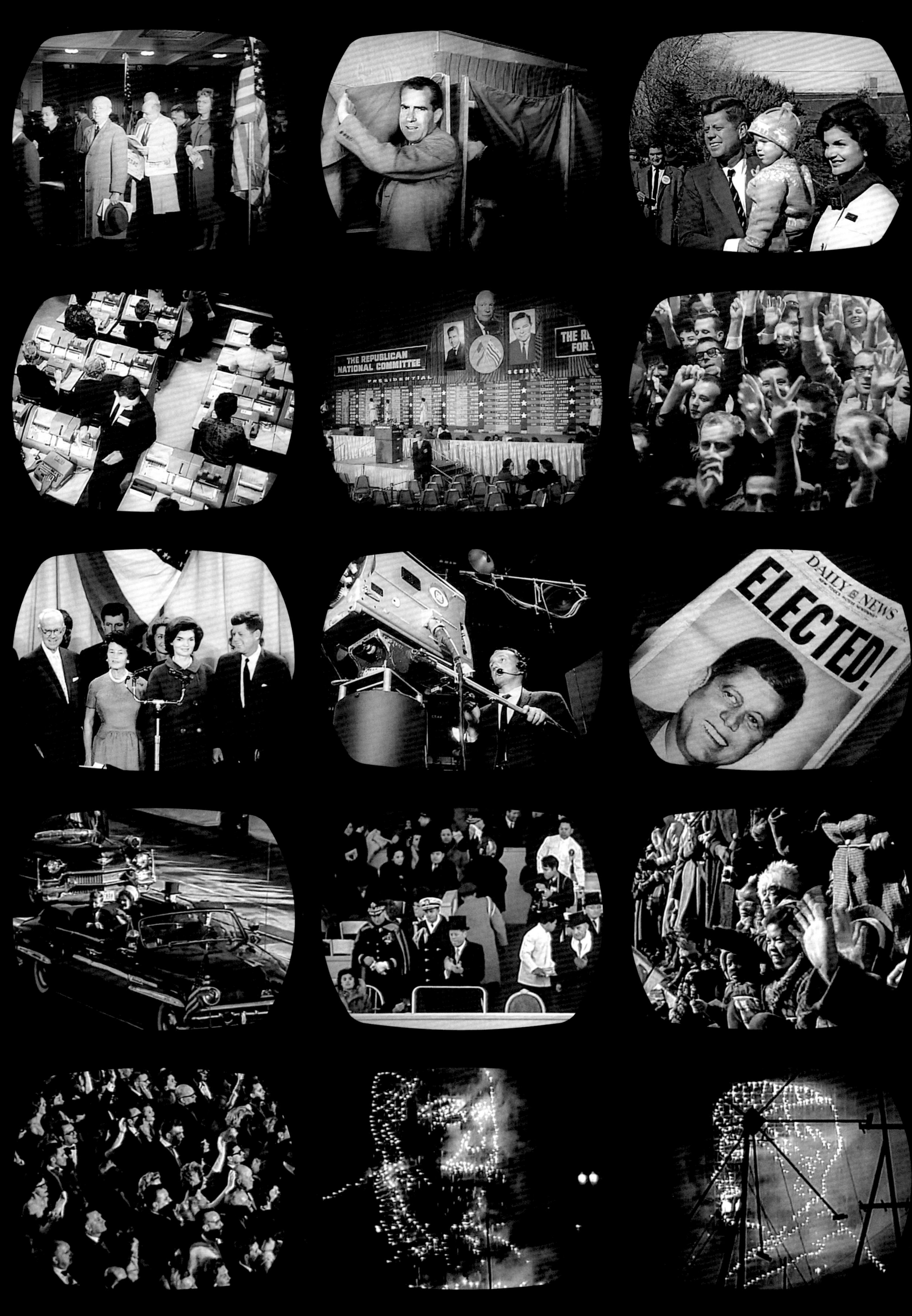

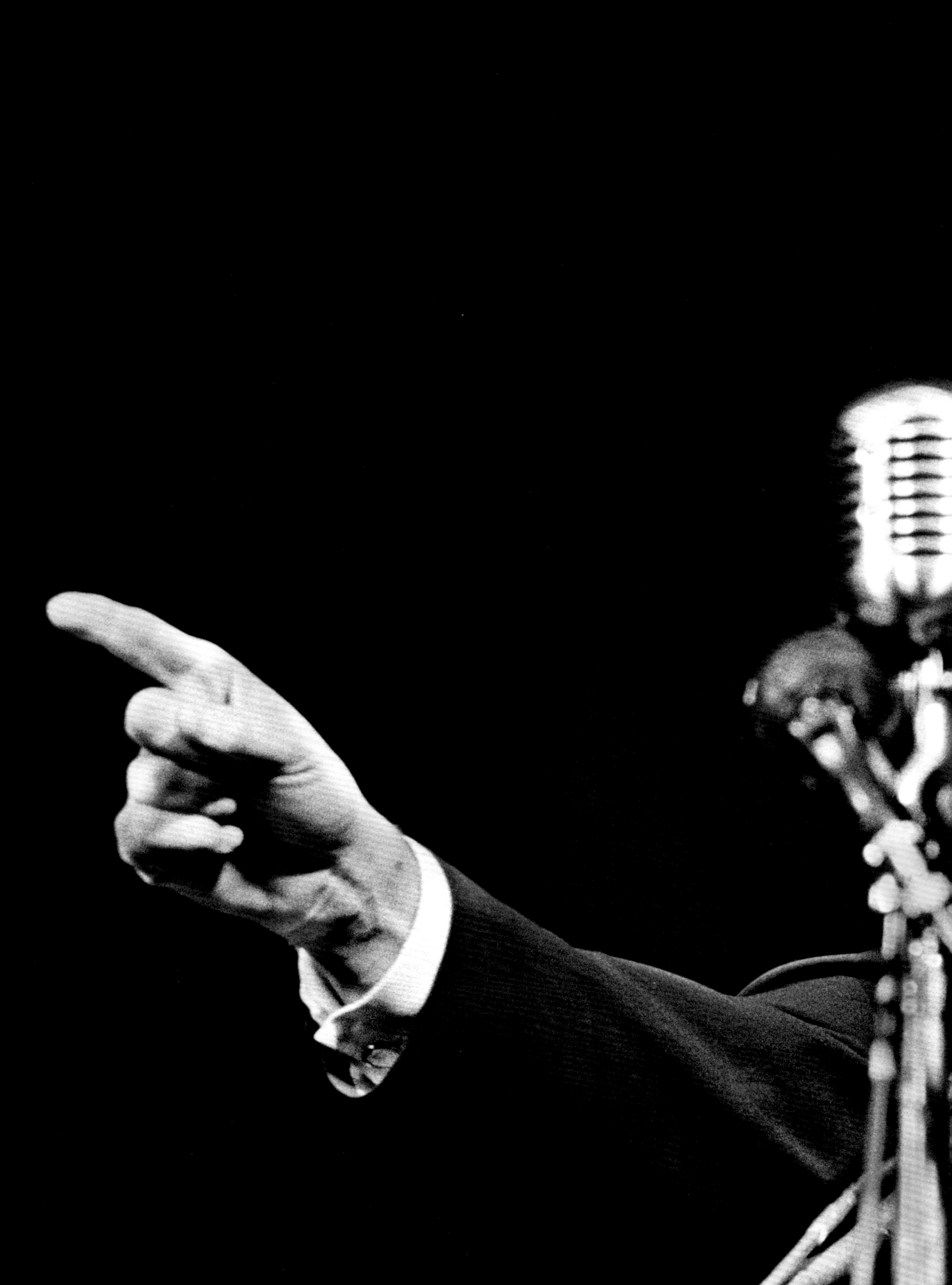

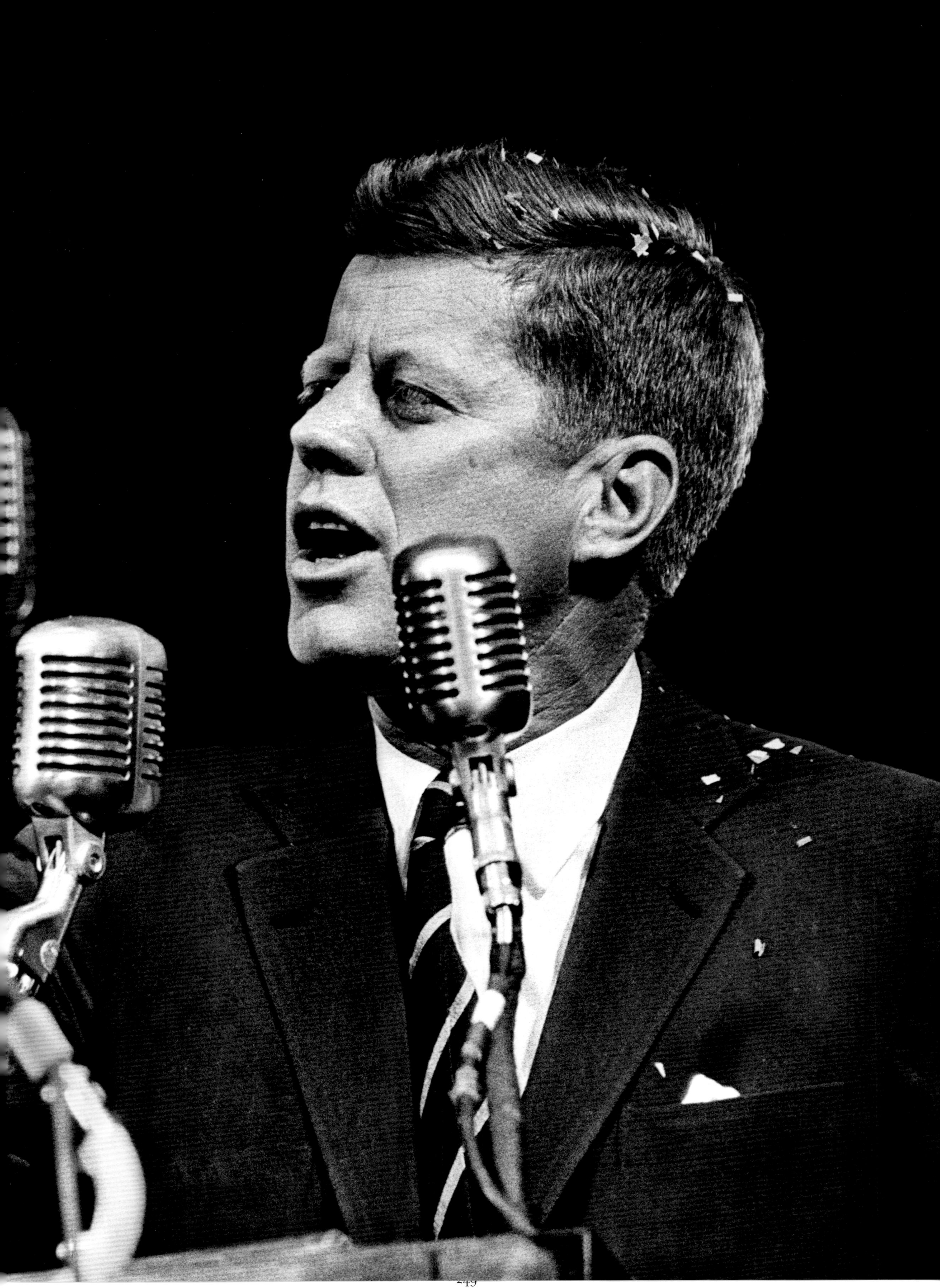

PART II · IN ALL THE TOMORROWS

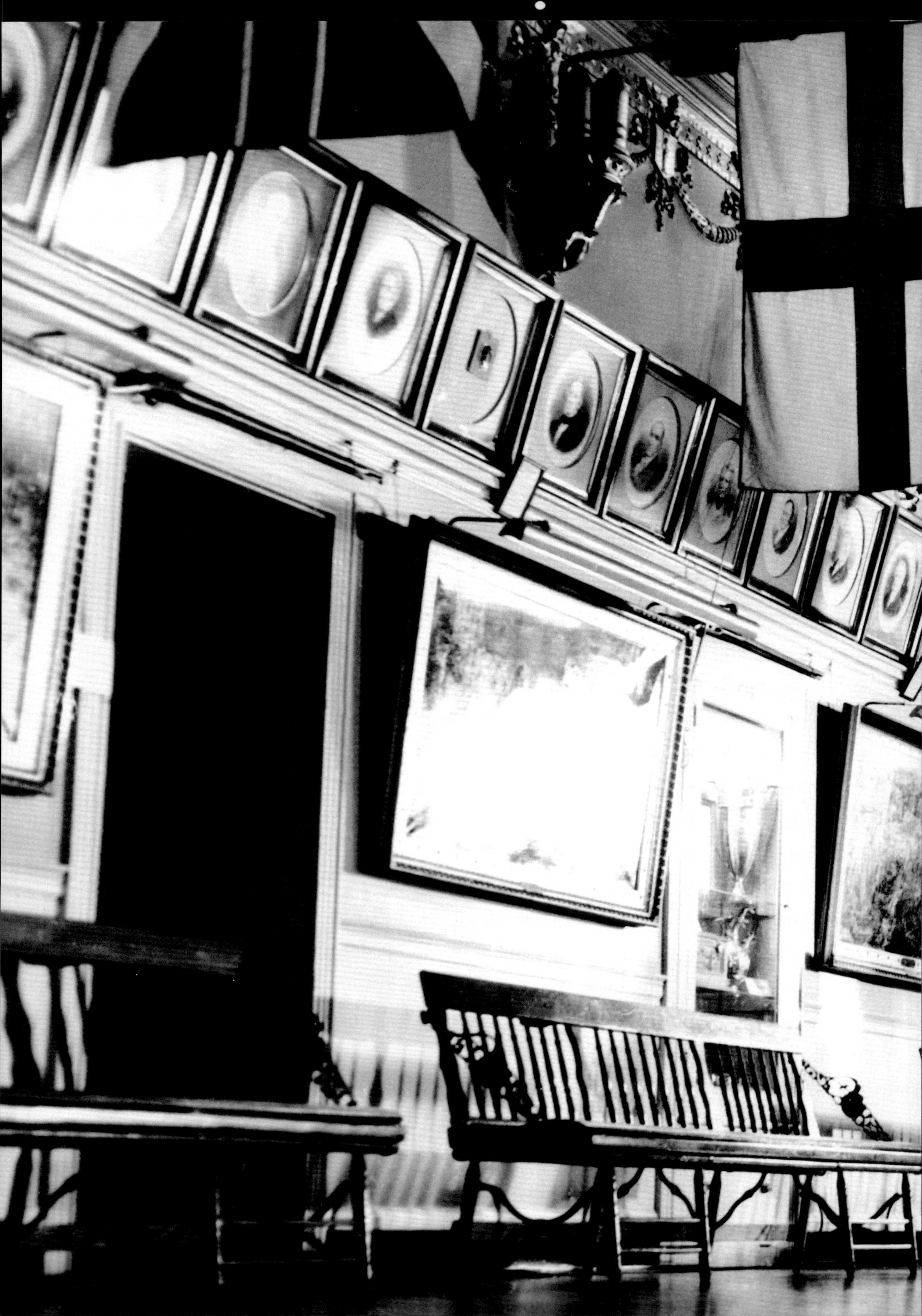

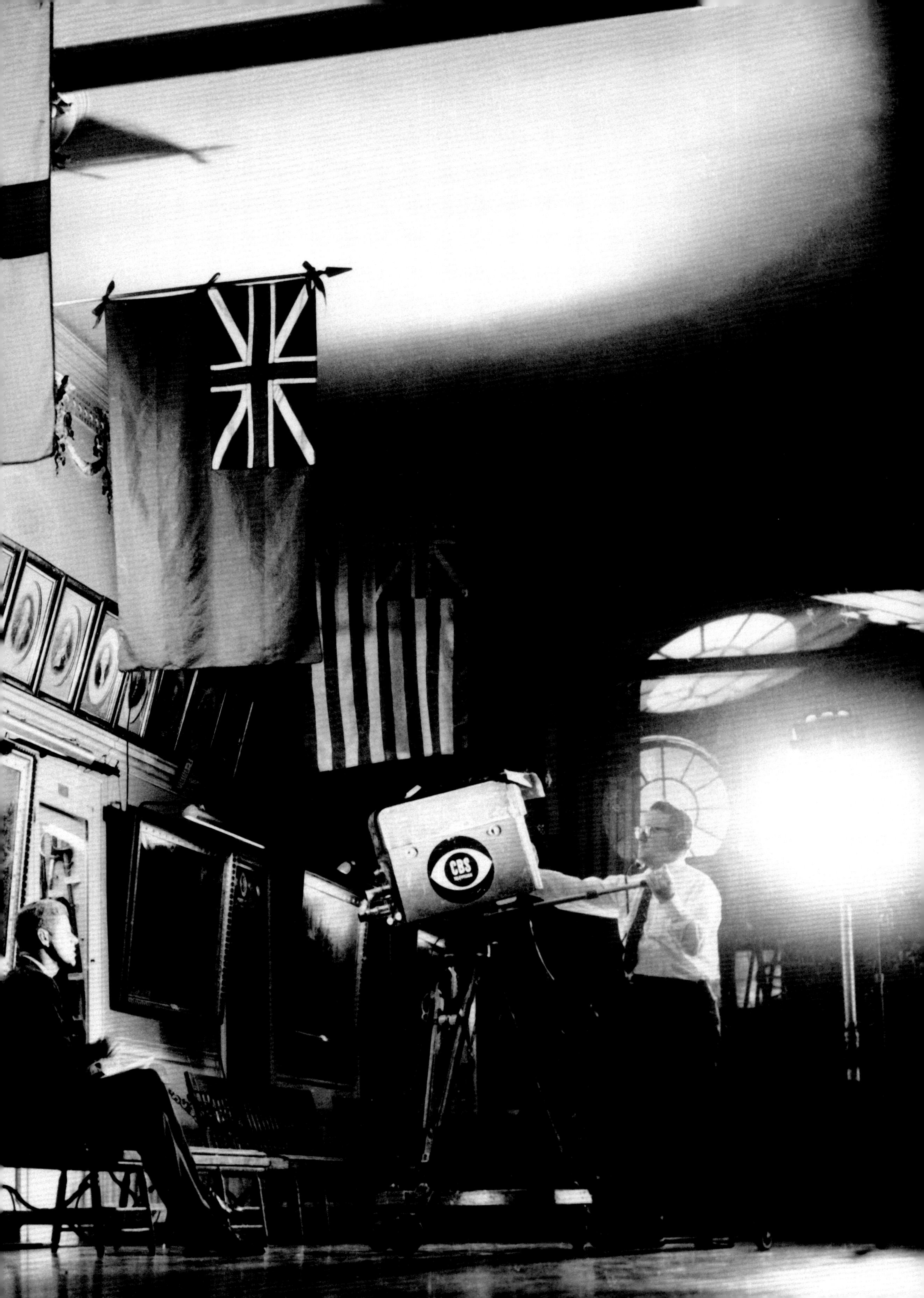

"This is the choice, then, in 1960. Shall we go forward? Shall we move with the times? Shall we progress again in the United States? Shall we stand as the great symbol of freedom around the world, or shall we sit still? Shall we lie at anchor?"

—John F. Kennedy, Citizens for Kennedy and Johnson Broadcast from Faneuil Hall,
Boston, Massachusetts, November 7, 1960

OPPOSITE *November 8, 1960.* Bobby and Ethel Kennedy vote in Hyannis Port. After years of crisscrossing the country and taking the measure of thousands of Americans, it all came down to pulling the lever in the voting booth. According to aides Kenny O'Donnell and Dave Powers, in the 70 days or so between late August 1960 and November 8th, JFK traveled to speaking appearances and rallies in 237 cities. Hundreds more visits occurred in the three previous years. So now—after speaking to tens of millions of Americans, logging countless miles of air travel, and partaking of too many parades, bad dinners, and airport rallies—the outcome would depend on what voting-booth decision tens of millions of Americans would make on Election Day. *Photo, Jacques Lowe*

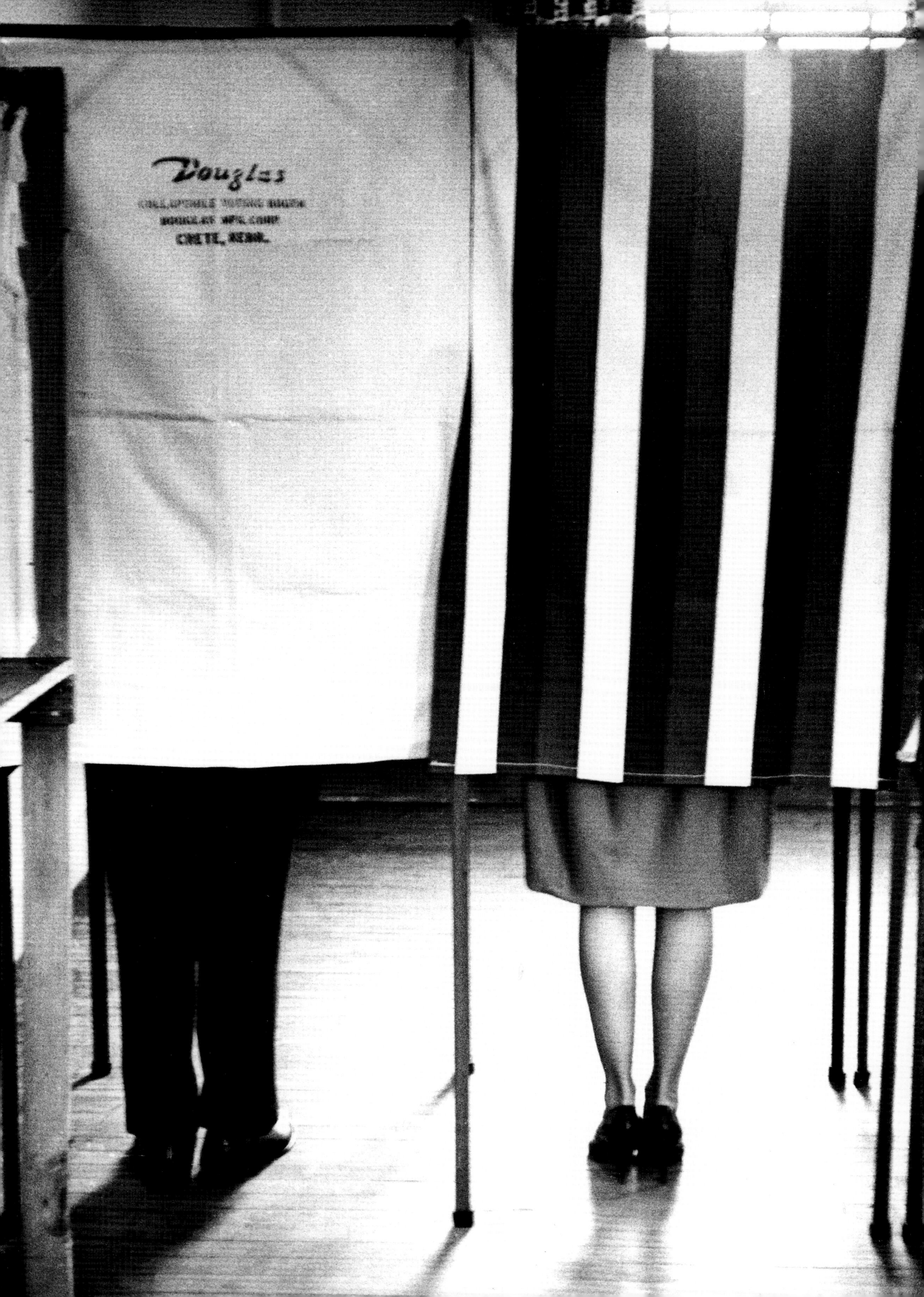
Douglas
CRETE, NEBR.

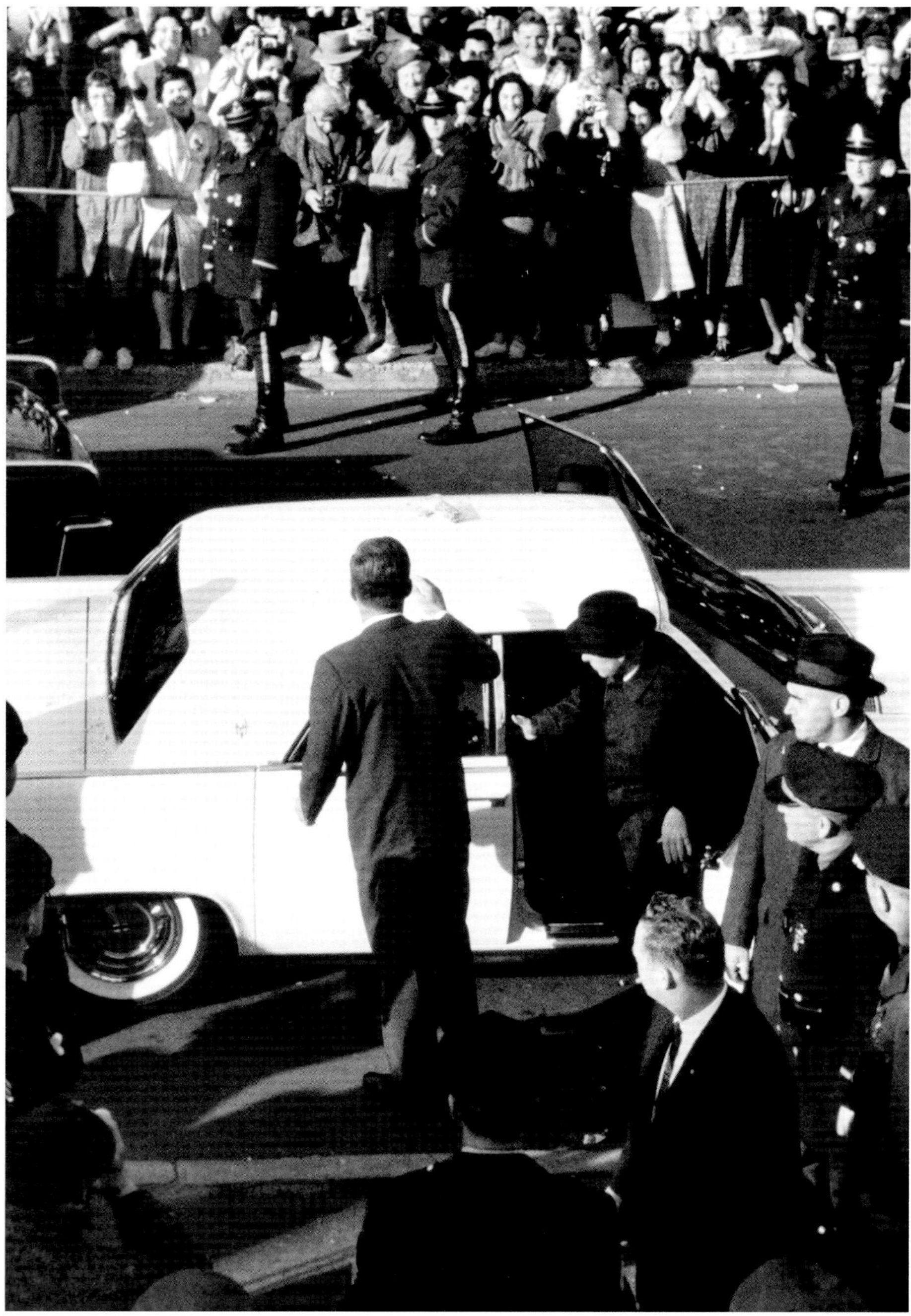

ABOVE *November 8, 1960.* Although increased security was out in Boston on
Election Day, when word went out that the Kennedys were at their polling place,
surging crowds surrounded their car upon their departure. *Photo, Yale Joel*

OPPOSITE *November 8, 1960.* The Kennedys cast their ballots in Boston at
around 8:45 A.M. at the West End Branch Library. A record 68.8 million
Americans (of nearly 110 million eligible) would go to the polls. Voter
turnout—at about 63 percent of voting age citizens—was then, and still is,
at the high point in modern U.S. presidential elections. Looking back,
photographer Jacques Lowe wrote that "Jacqueline Kennedy described the
period between the closing of the polls and the moment of victory as 'the
longest night in history.'" *Photo, Burton Berinsky*

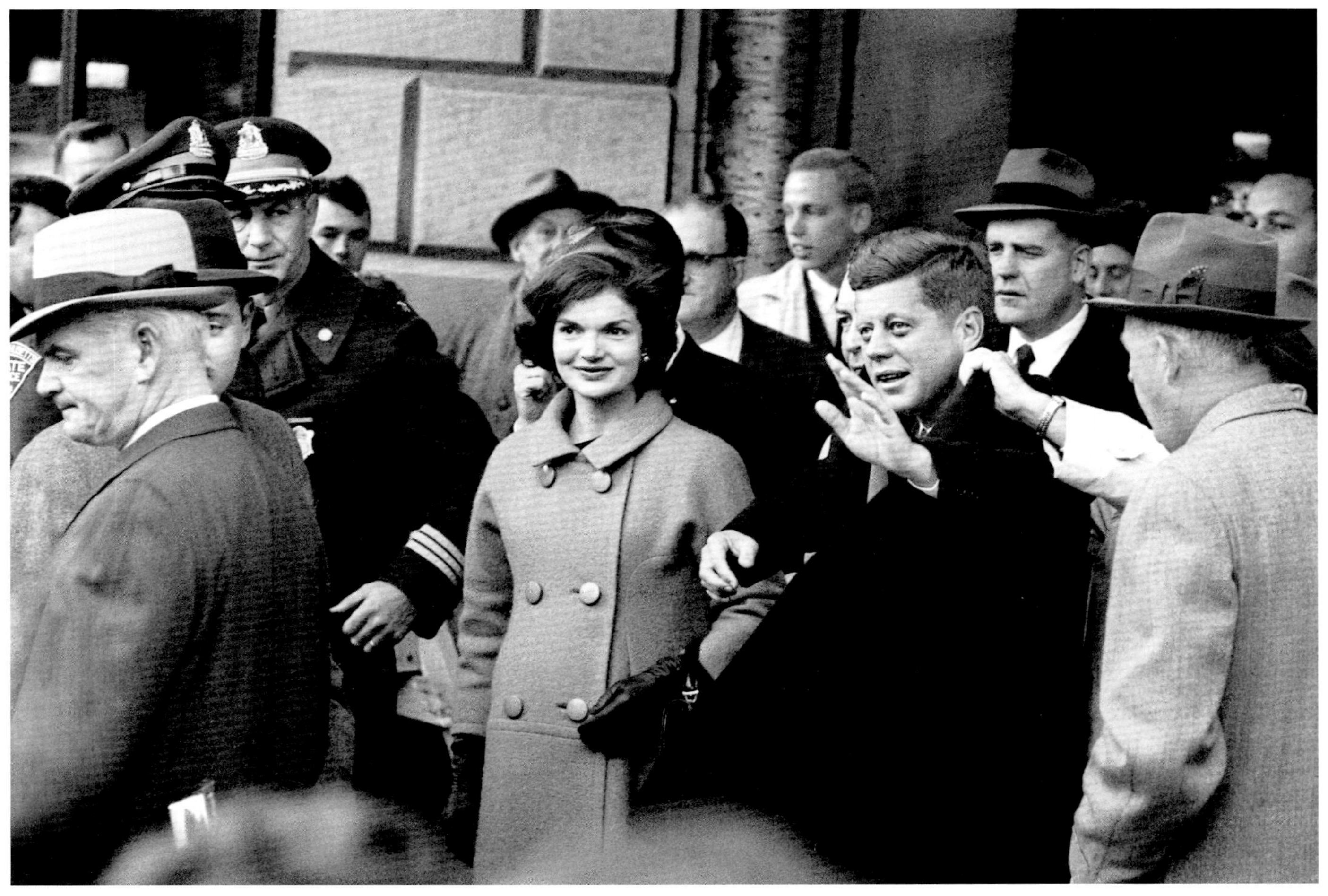

PART II · IN ALL THE TOMORROWS

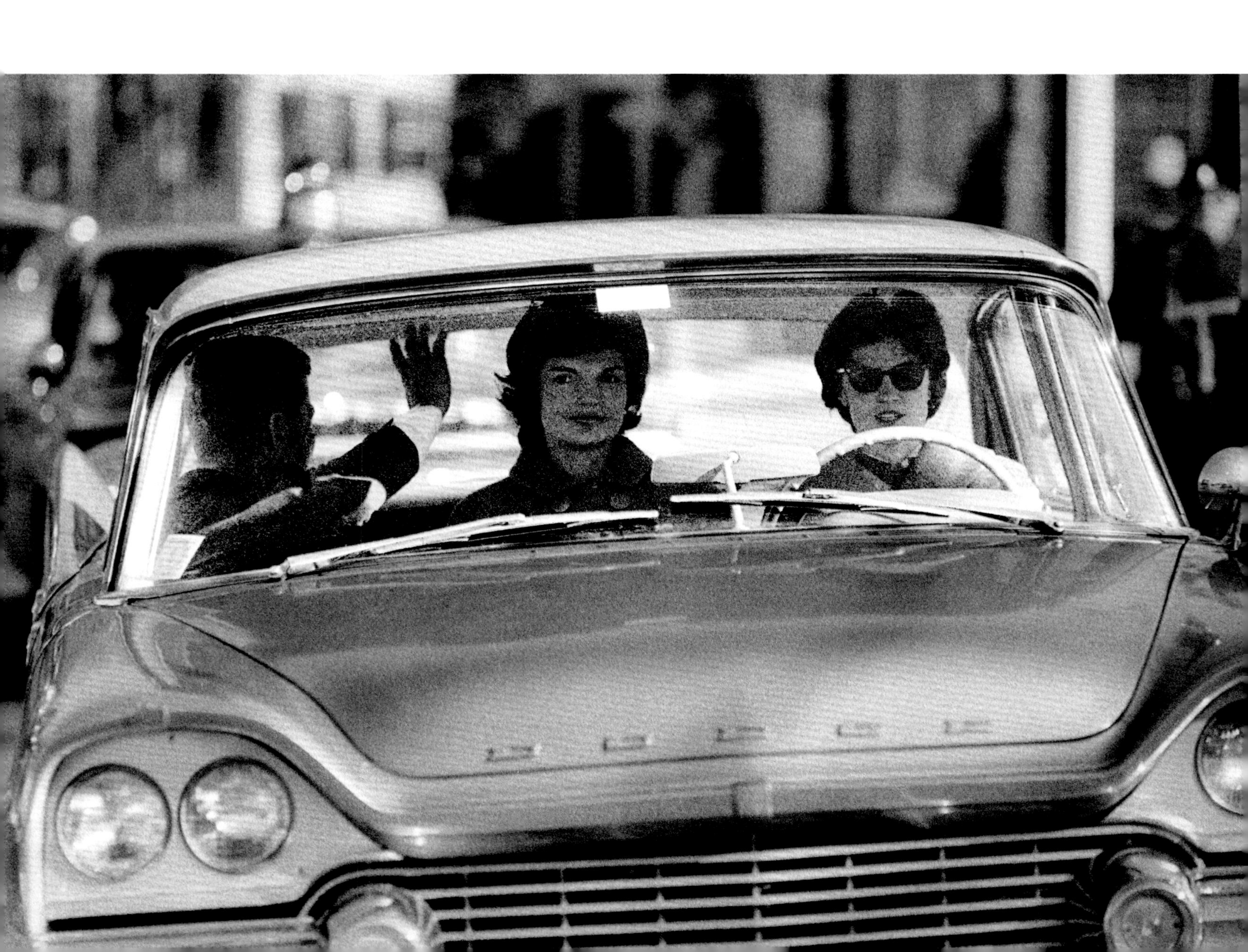

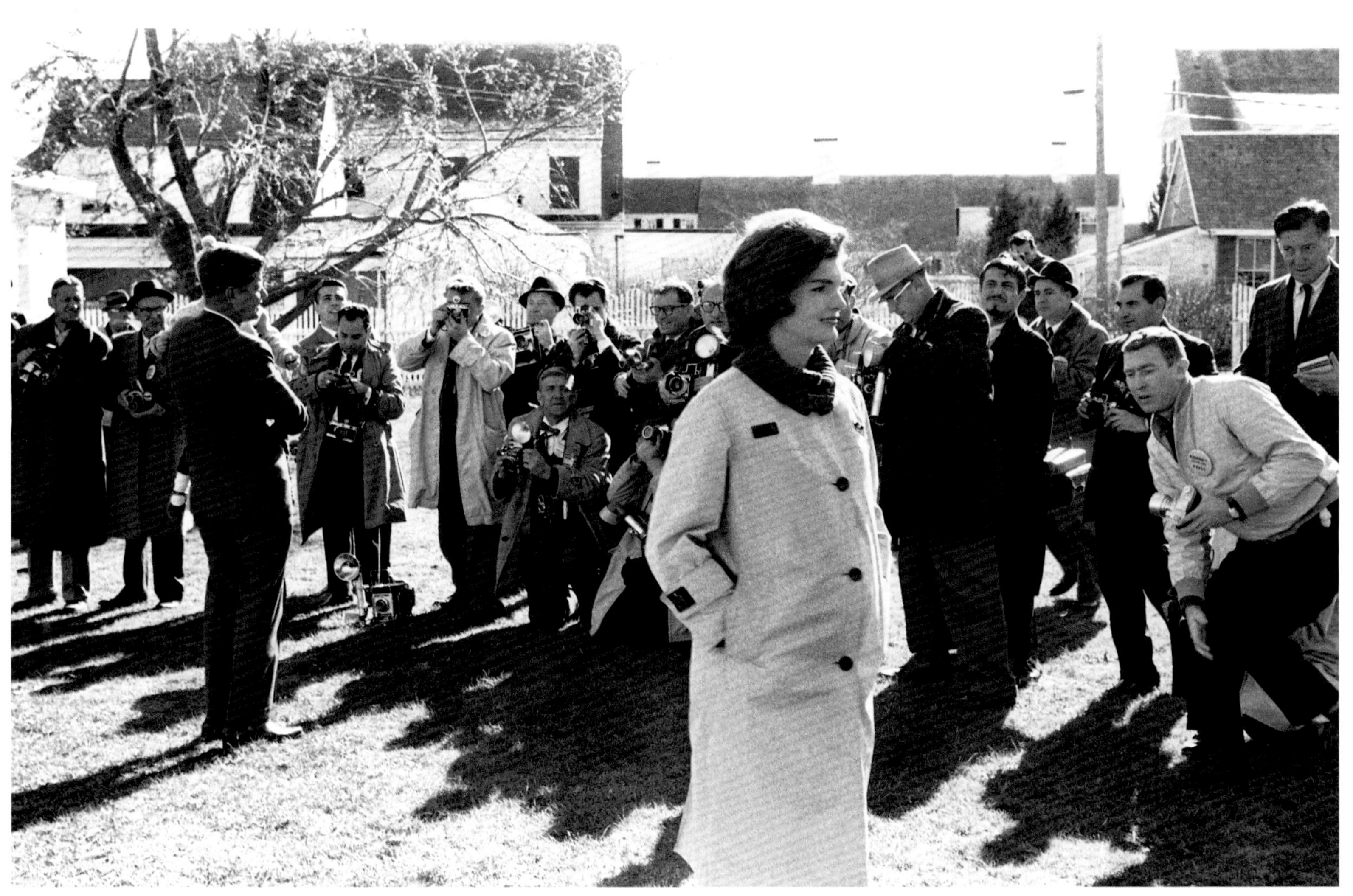

OPPOSITE *November 8, 1960.* A nondescript Dodge might have been a cover to avoid notice on the street, but Kennedy waves out the window nonetheless, perhaps hoping to sway one more vote. After voting the Kennedys took a short flight to Cape Cod on the *Caroline*, where they would wait out election results in Hyannis Port with family, a few friends, and key staff at the family's ocean-side compound. *Photo, Henri Dauman*

ABOVE *November 8, 1960.* The press descends on the house in Hyannis Port for a press conference before election returns come in. Jack and Jackie posed with Caroline, then almost three years old, before heading inside to await news. Though the couple understood how important the media's attention was and knew how to leverage it to their advantage, they differed in their dealings with the press, especially concerning their children. JFK knew the power of his image as a young father, posing with Caroline, and later John Jr., when he could; Jackie preferred to shield her children from the public eye. *Photo, Bob Sandberg*

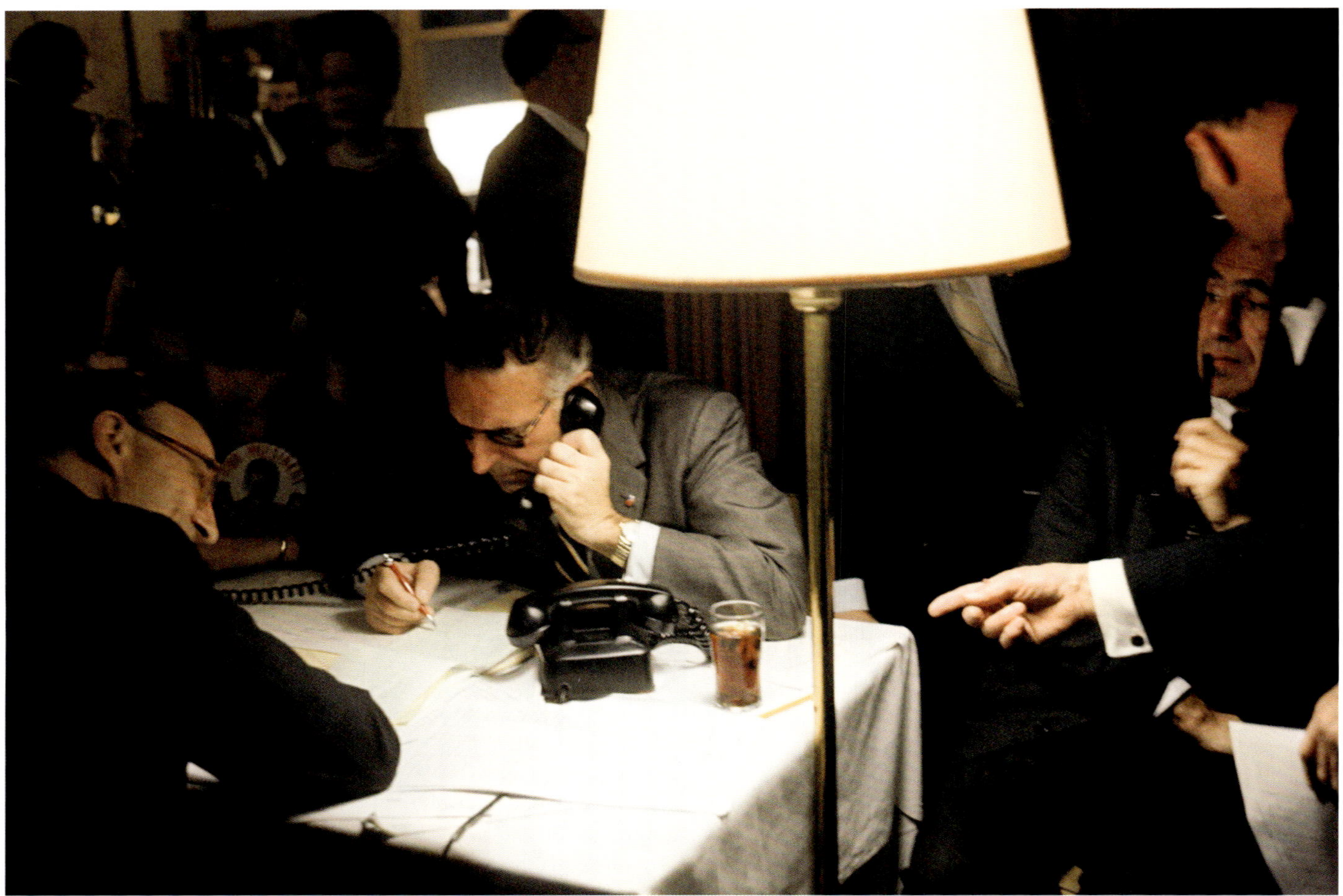

ABOVE *November 8, 1960.* Tammany Hall boss Carmine DeSapio stays on top of the results at the Democratic Party election-night headquarters, the Biltmore Hotel in New York City. *Photo, Cornell Capa*

OPPOSITE *November 8, 1960.* The vigil continued in front of the television at Bobby's house the morning after the election. From left, surrounding the candidate, artist Bill Walton; Pierre Salinger; Ethel and Bobby Kennedy; Bobby's secretary, Angie Novello; and campaign aide Bill Haddad. *Photo, Jacques Lowe*

FOLLOWING SPREAD *November 8, 1960.* The press assembles in the ballroom at the Ambassador Hotel in Los Angeles where the Republican National Committee had set up camp to await the results of the election. Covering Nixon that night was Lawrence Schiller on his first political assignment for *Paris Match* magazine; but Nixon was nowhere to be seen. "He was the vice president, so access to him was practically nonexistent," Schiller recalled. "Impatient, I decided to go up to his suite, but when I got off the elevator I was turned away by a Secret Service agent because my press pass was not valid for his floor." *Photo, Lawrence Schiller*

"We Democrats realize that the days when Presidential candidates can be nominated in smoke-filled rooms, by political leaders and party bosses, have forever passed from the scene."

—John F. Kennedy, Howard County Court House, Indiana, April 29, 1960

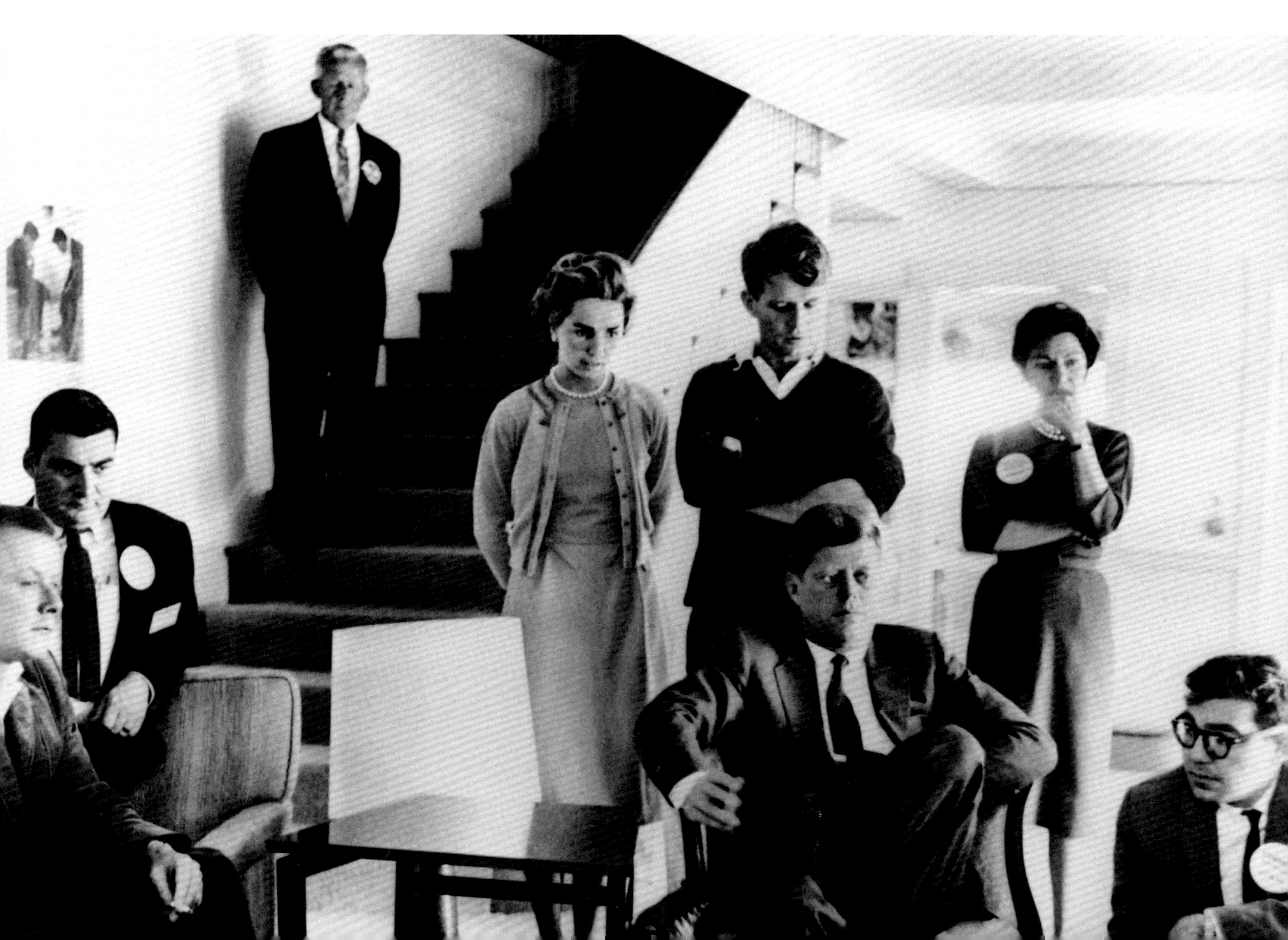

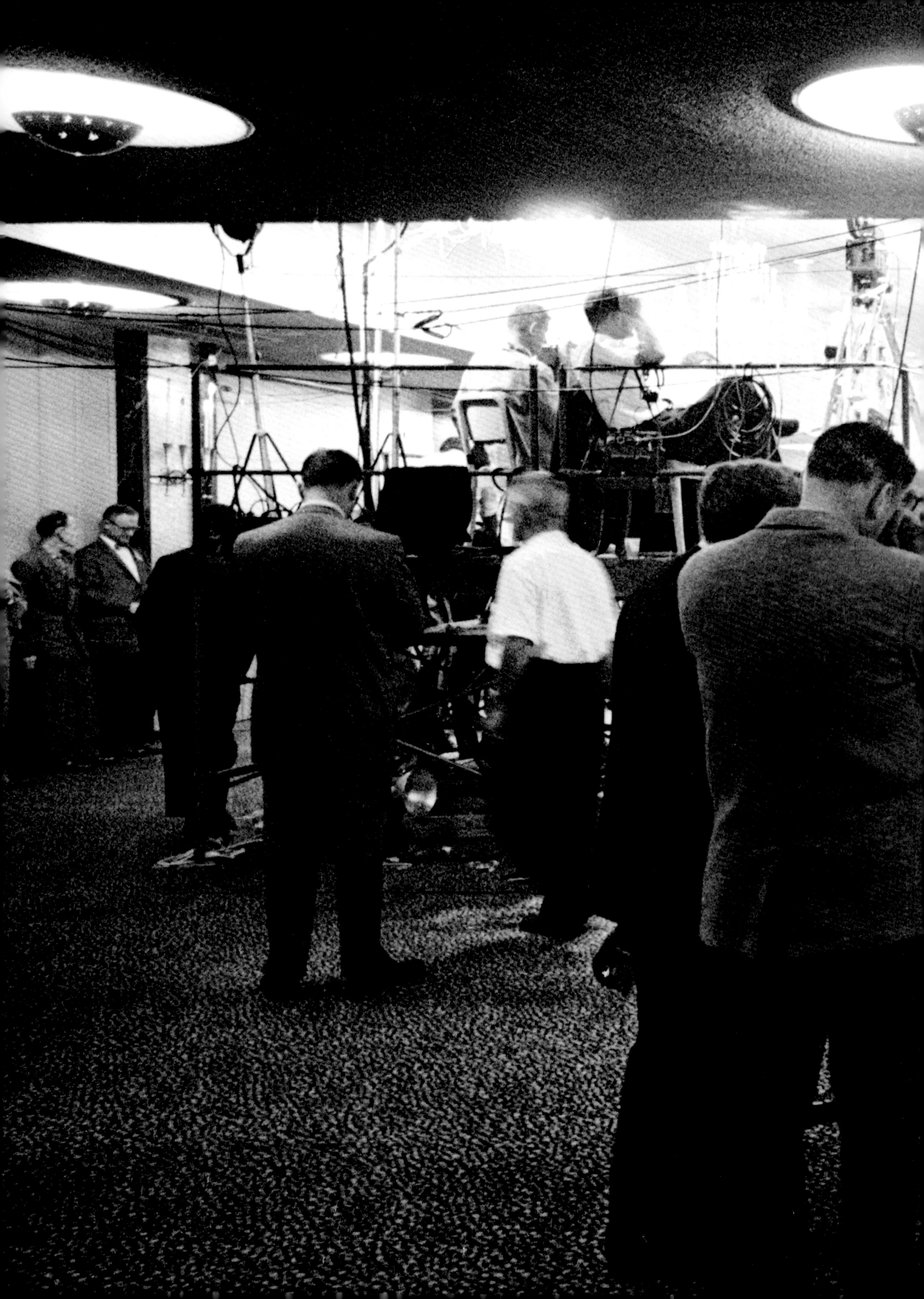

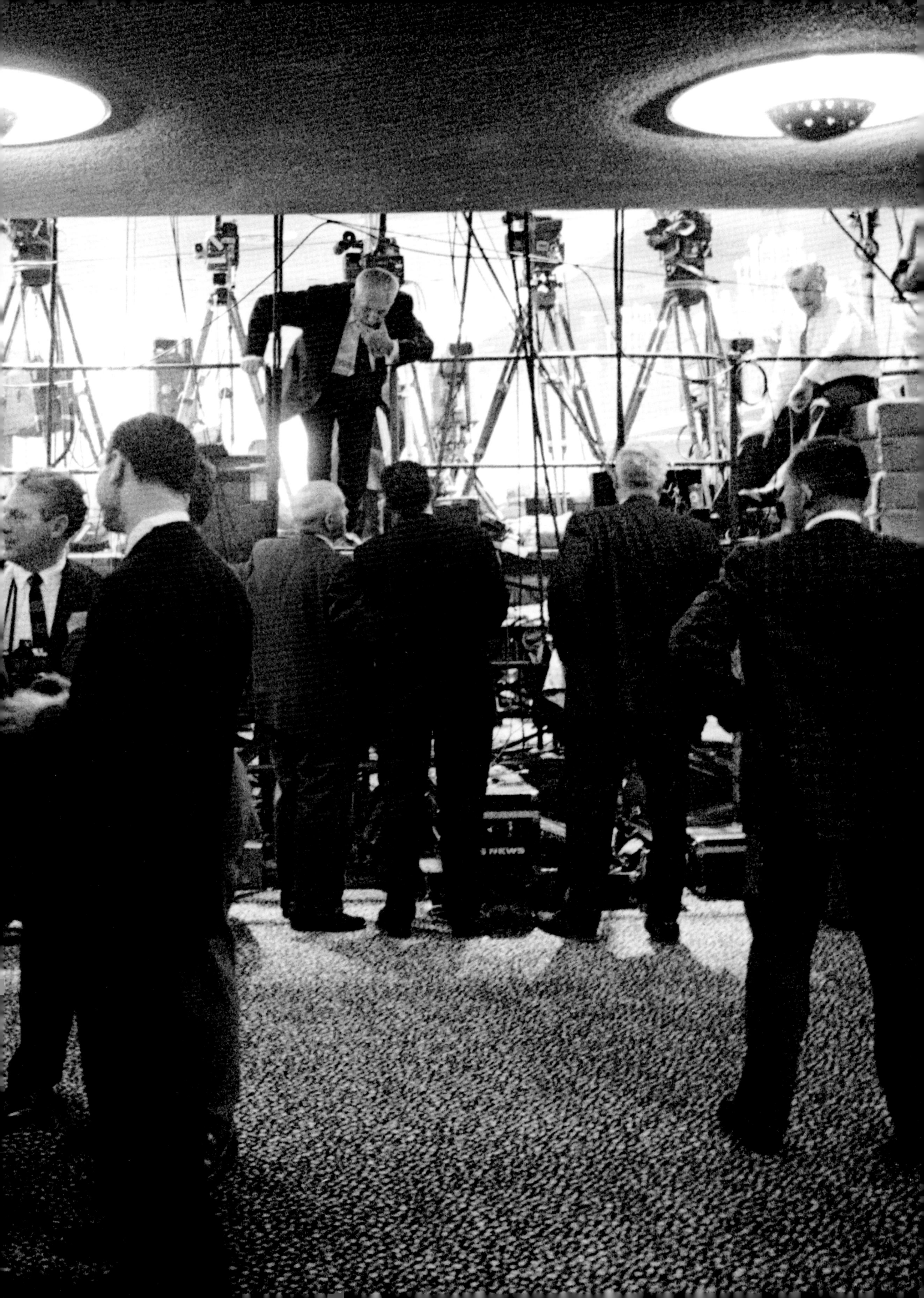

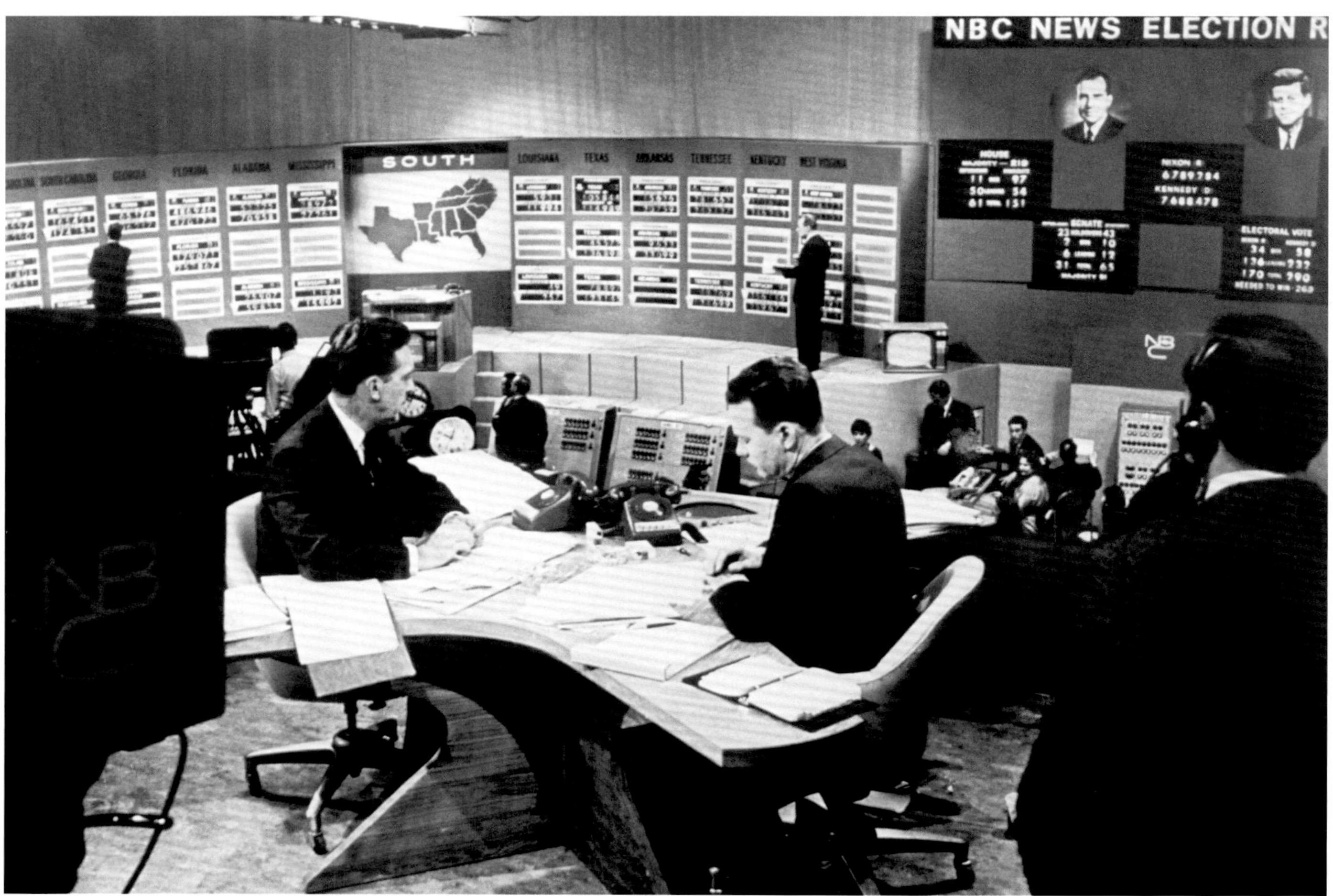

ABOVE *November 8, 1960.* The seasoned NBC-TV news duo of Chet Huntley (left) and David Brinkley (right) covered the election returns for more than 12 hours from their studio in New York's Rockefeller Center. One reason to watch NBC's coverage rather than other networks was its state-of-the-art RCA 501 computer, which computed projections of the final votes. Still, the TV news predictions and projections on election night were all over the map, seesawing between candidates with an uncertain outcome well into the early morning hours. CBS reversed itself at least once during the evening, and at one point, NBC had predicted a "Nixon sweep." *Photo, Anonymous*

OPPOSITE *November 8, 1960.* CBS's election-night newsroom studio and support areas are still calm around 6:30 P.M. EST, when the popular vote count is just beginning to be tabulated and electoral votes have been allocated only to known "sure win" states for each candidate. (At that hour, 15 states had gone for Nixon and eight for Kennedy.) The network's star newsmen, Eric Sevareid, Walter Cronkite, and Edward R. Murrow, would all participate in election-night coverage. By midnight, Kennedy would have a popular vote lead of about 2.3 million votes, a lead that shrank dramatically in the early A.M. hours as Midwestern and Western states reported. *Photo, Anonymous*

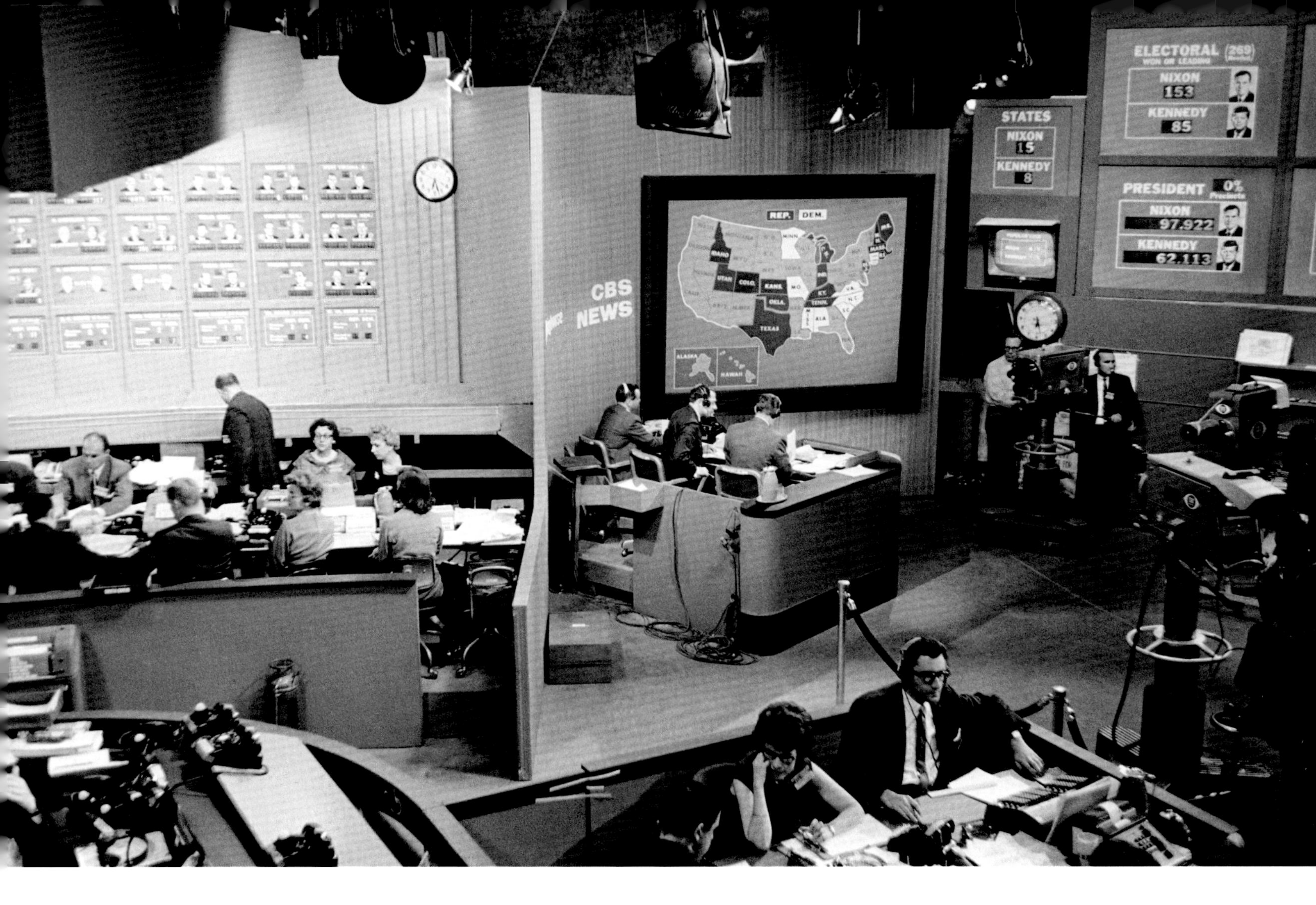

CBS NEWS
ELECTORAL (269)
NIXON 153
KENNEDY 85
STATES
NIXON 15
KENNEDY 8
PRESIDENT 0%
NIXON 97,922
KENNEDY 62,113
REP. DEM
TEXAS

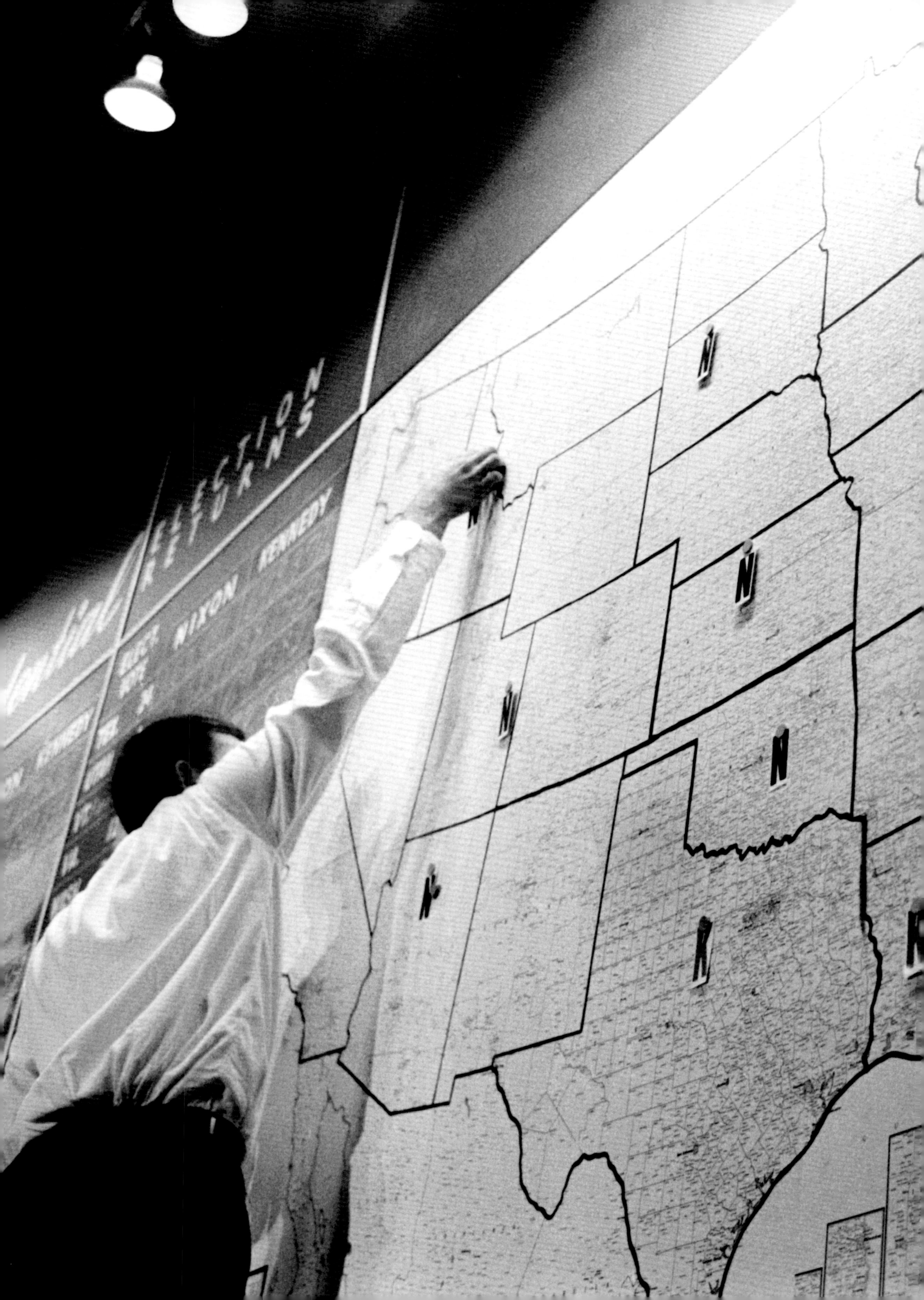
ELECTION
RETURNS
NIXON
KENNEDY

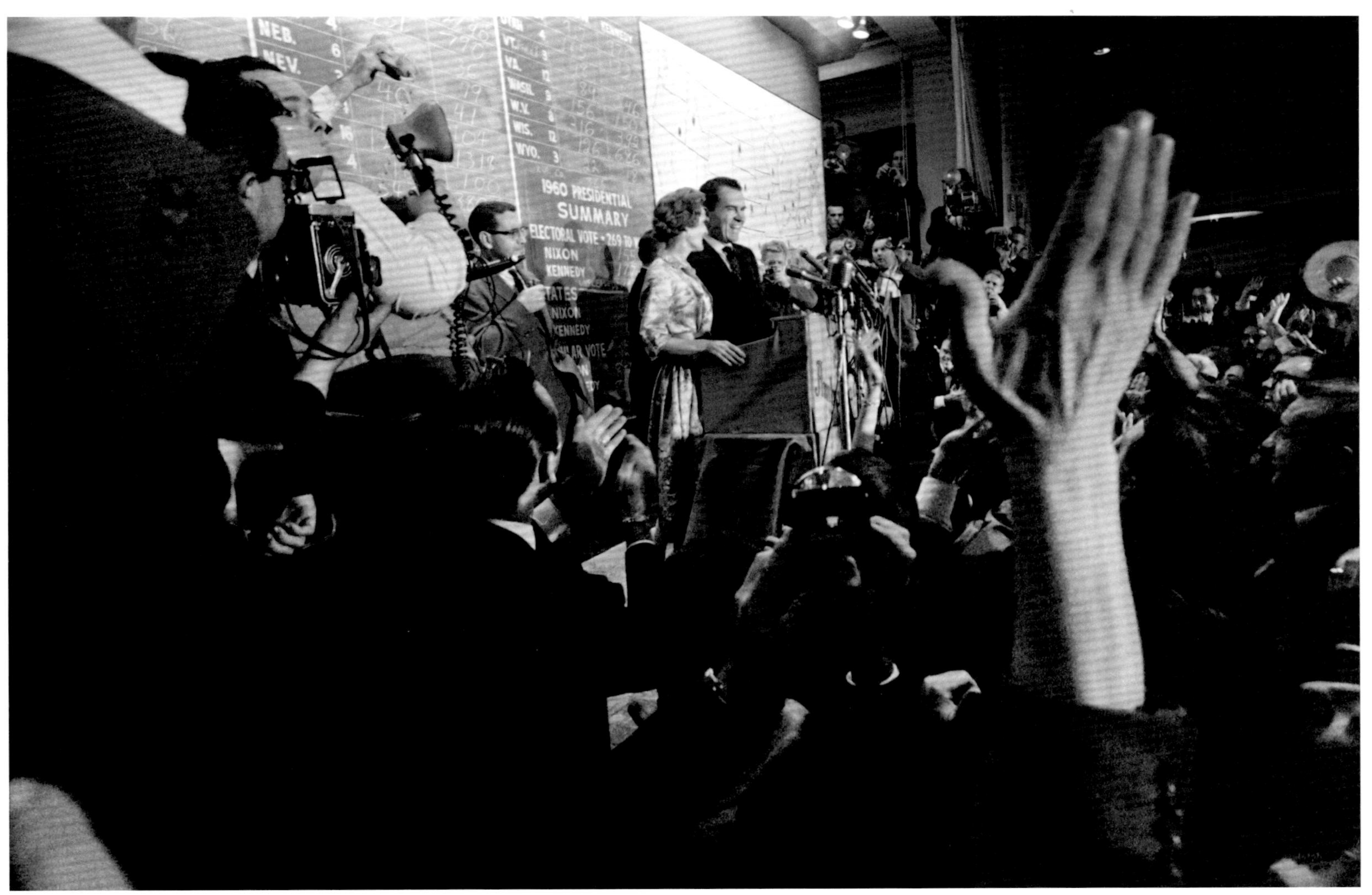

OPPOSITE *November 8, 1960.* A Nixon aide in Los Angeles pins another red "N" (this time on the state of Idaho) on the large map his team is using to tally the votes at the Ambassador Hotel. As election night continued, more Western states fell into Nixon's column. Still, the election was too close to call for the rest of the night. *Photo, Lawrence Schiller*

ABOVE *November 8, 1960.* When Nixon finally appeared at the podium with his wife, Pat, at the Ambassador Hotel in Los Angeles, it was after midnight on the West Coast and four key states were still undecided. If Kennedy lost all four of these states—California, Illinois, Michigan, and Minnesota—then Nixon would win. *Photo, Lawrence Schiller*

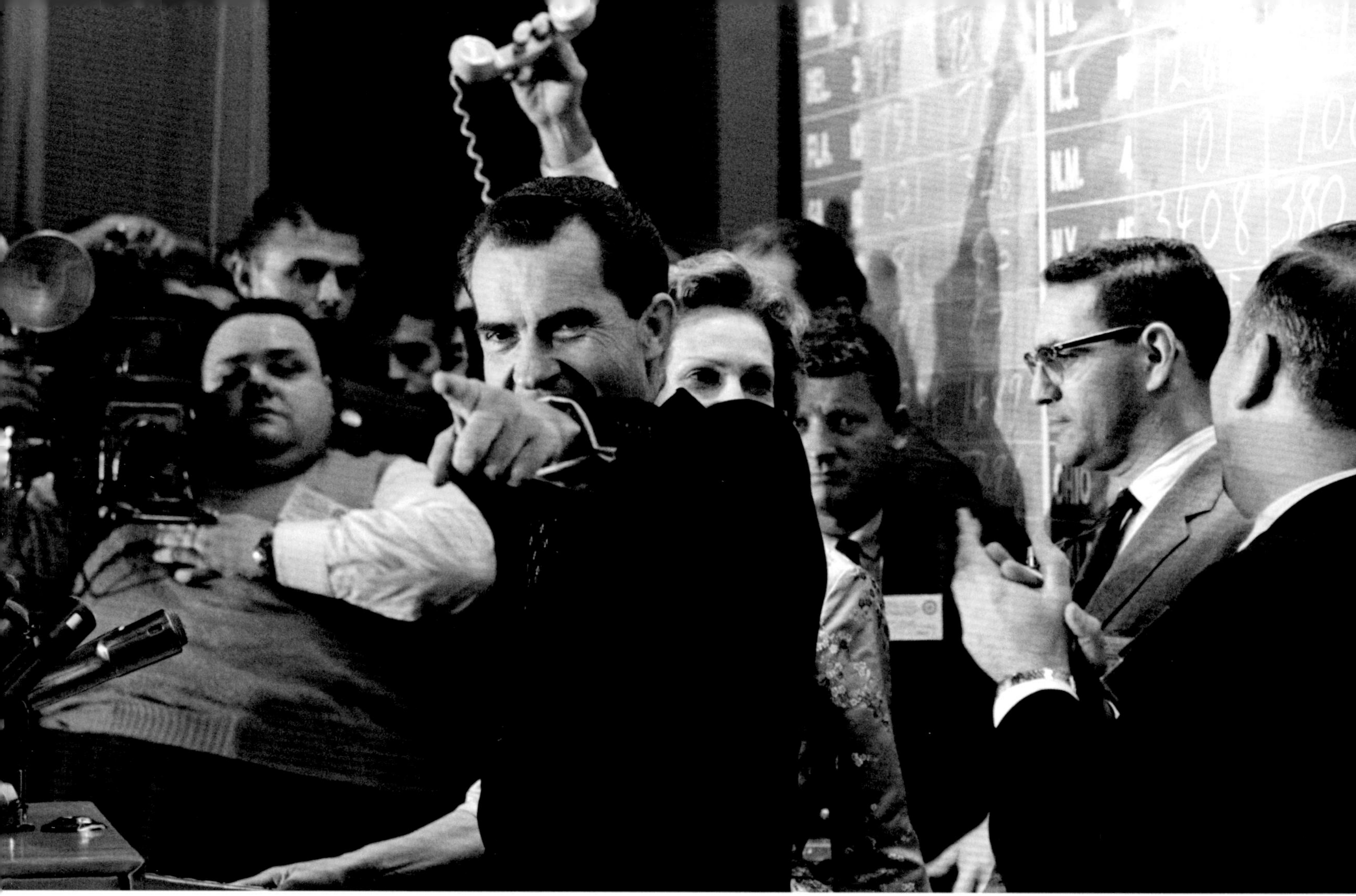

ABOVE *November 8, 1960.* By this point in the night, Kennedy's popular vote lead had nearly evaporated, and some commentators were saying he might win the presidency with the electoral vote, but lose the popular vote. As journalist Teddy White put it, "Though Nixon had almost certainly lost, Kennedy had yet not definitely won." *Photo, Lawrence Schiller*

OPPOSITE *November 8, 1960.* Though the outcome looked bleak for Nixon, he remained upbeat. No doubt, the upset of the 1948 presidential election (and the famous photo of winner Harry Truman holding a newspaper erroneously announcing his rival's victory) made people hesitant to call the race too soon. Also, Nixon, a savvy politician, knew not to go on stage defeated—the press always runs to the winner. *Photo, Cornell Capa*

FOLLOWING SPREAD *November 8, 1960.* In his televised address from the Ambassador Hotel, with a tearful Pat by his side, Nixon tells the crowd: "[A]s I look at the board here, while there are still some results to come in… if the present trend continues, Senator Kennedy will be the next president of the United States." This wasn't an official concession by Nixon, however, as one of his aides, Herb Klein, spelled out; rather it was a kind of conditional concession, leaving the door open in case of an upset. *Photo, Lawrence Schiller*

—John F. Kennedy, Boston Garden Rally, Boston, Massachusetts,
November 7, 1960

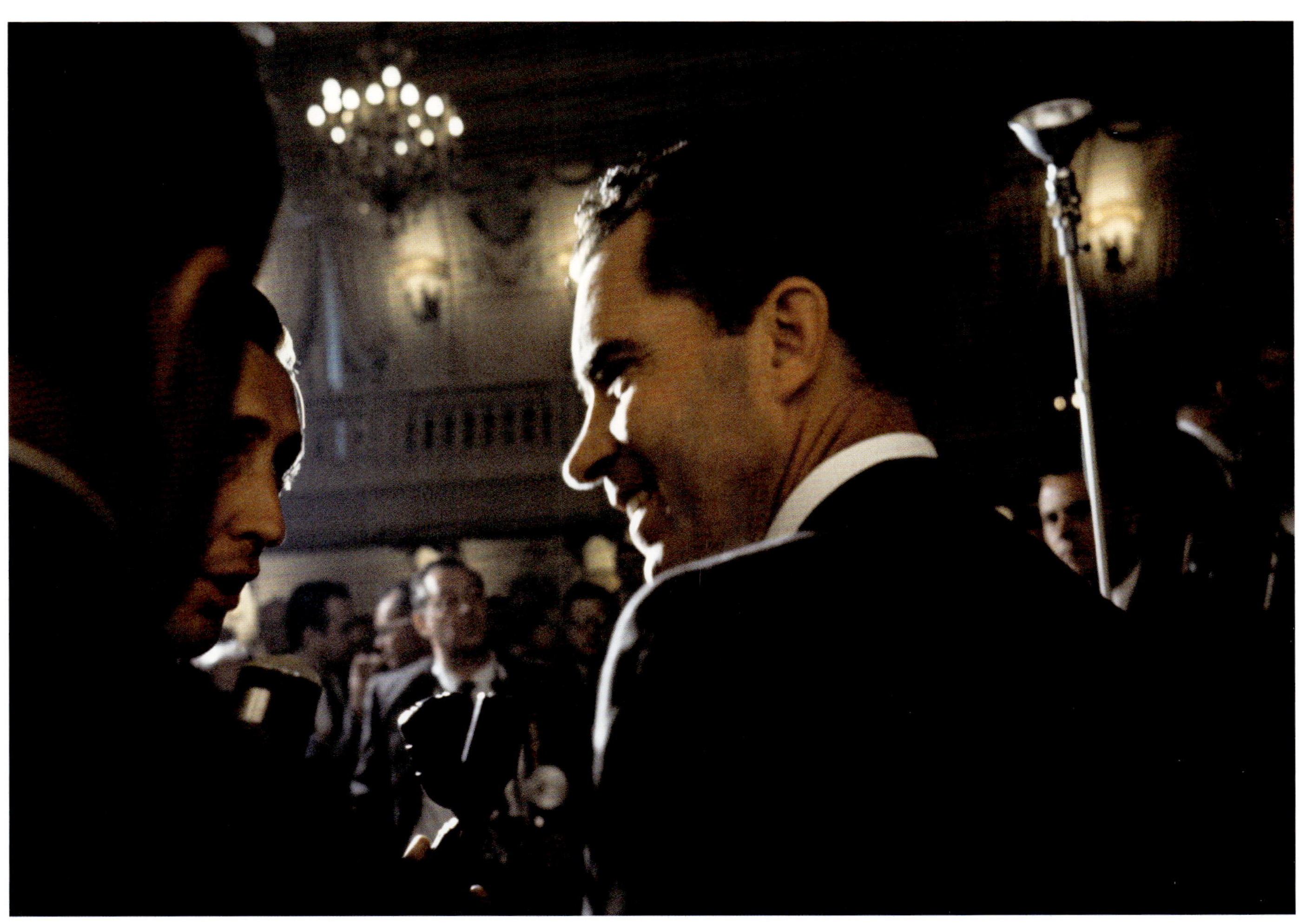

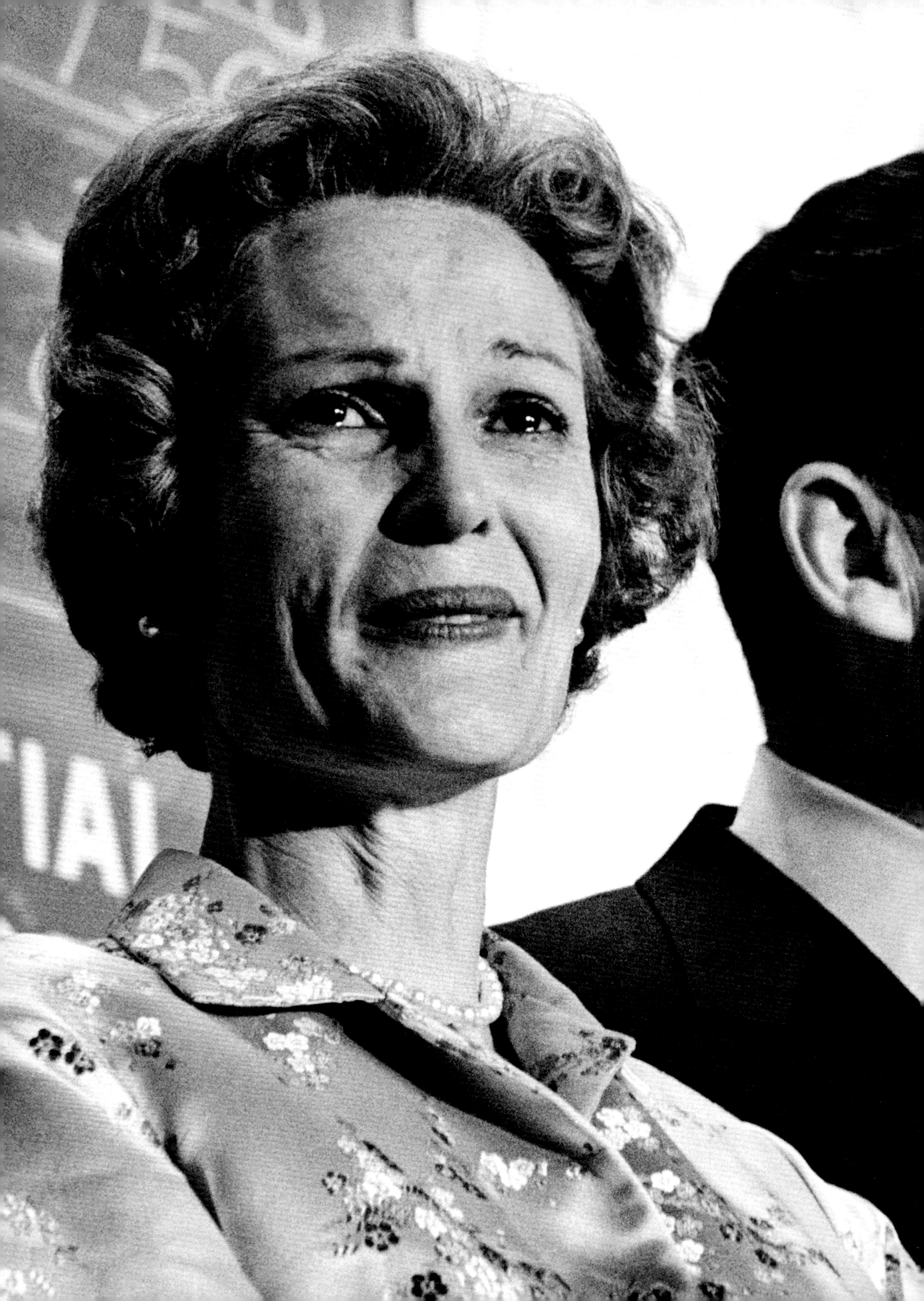

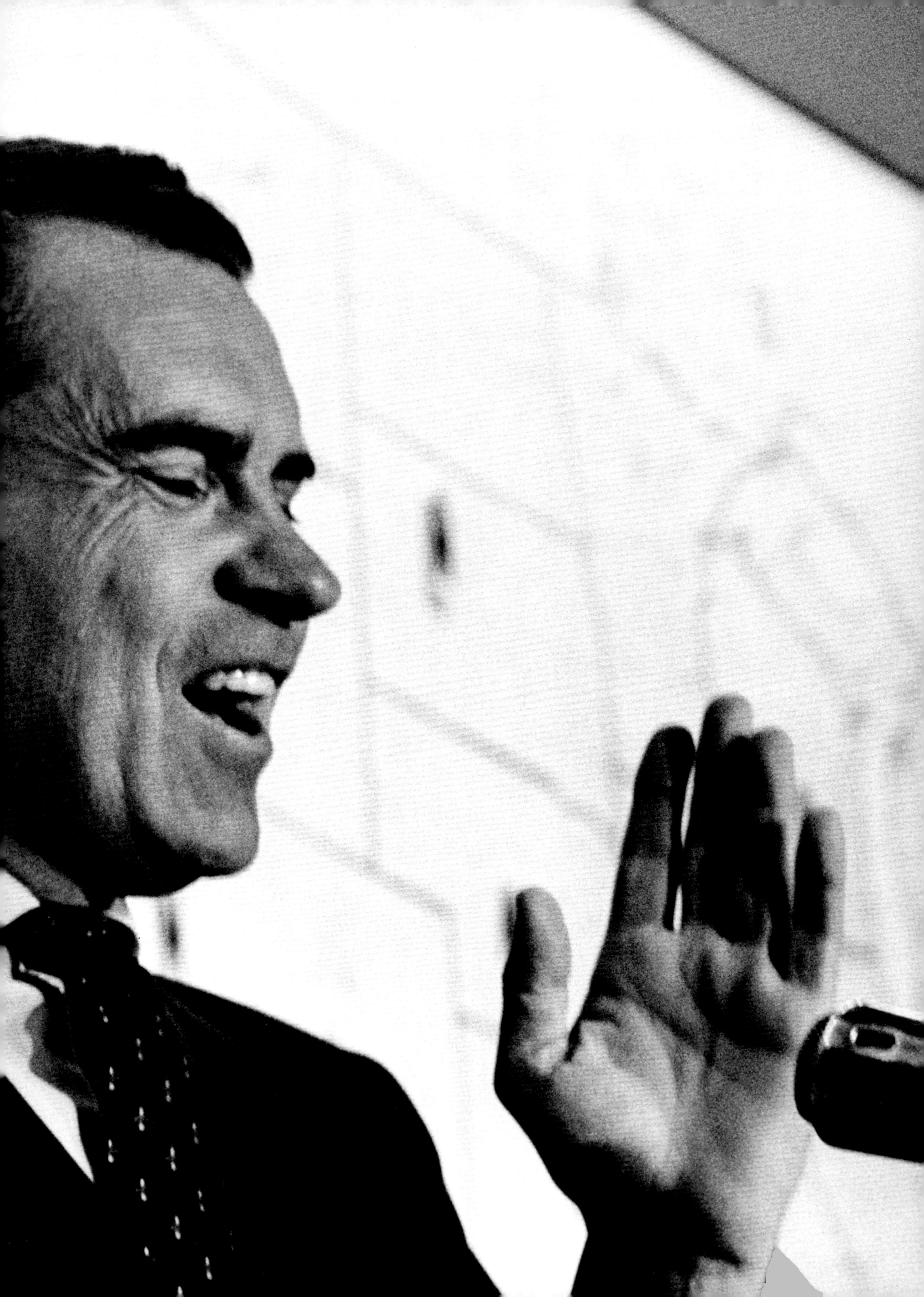

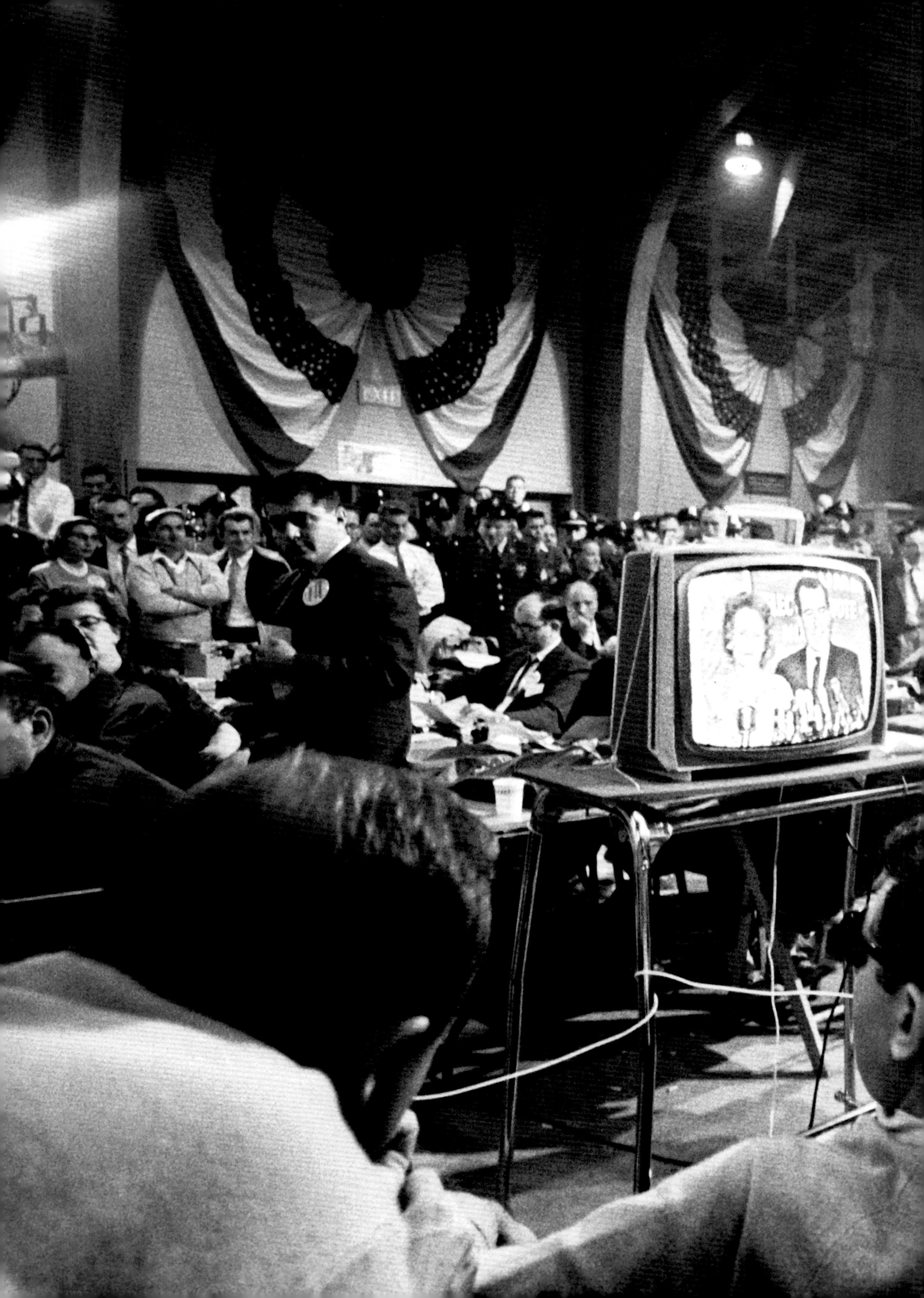

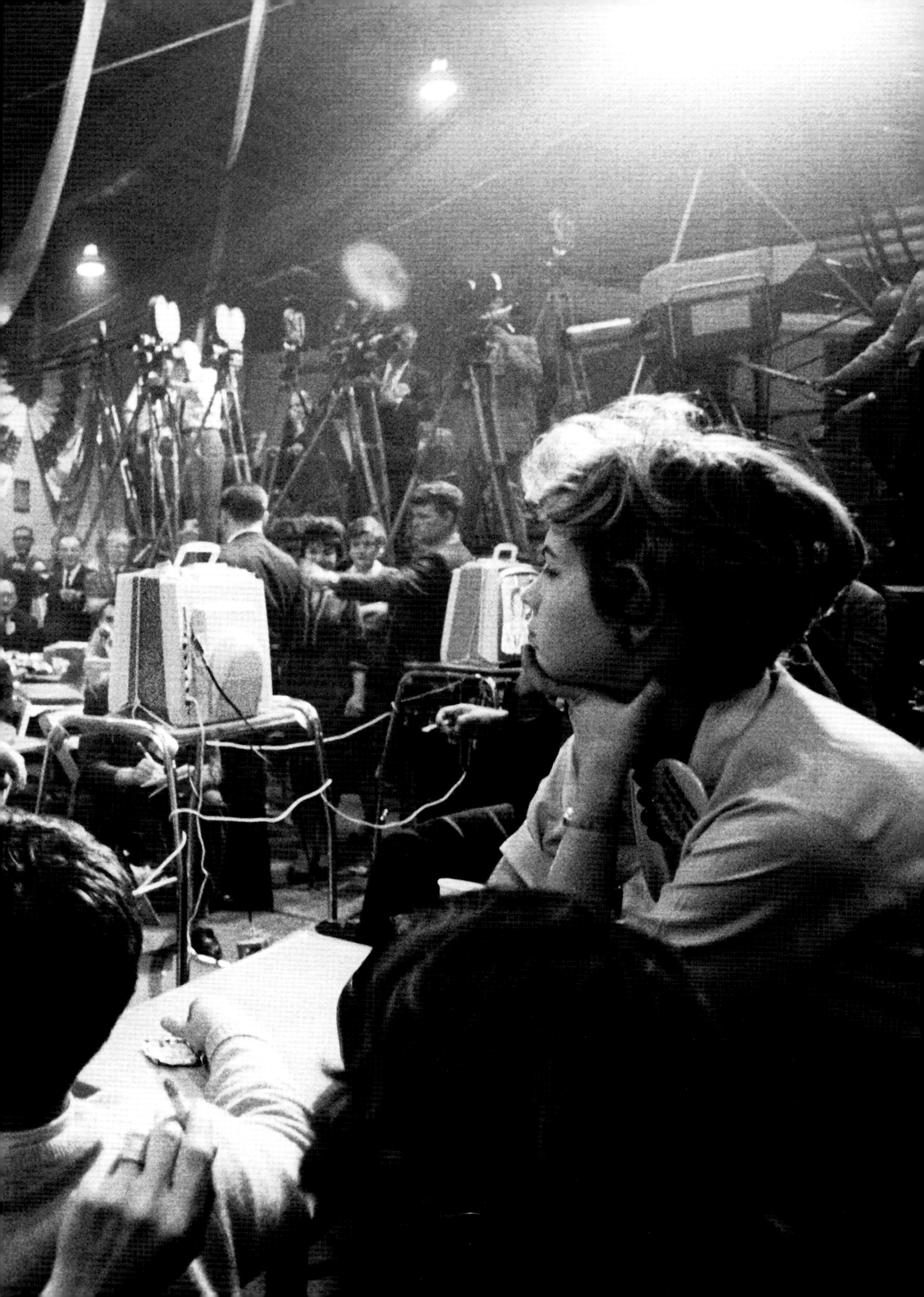

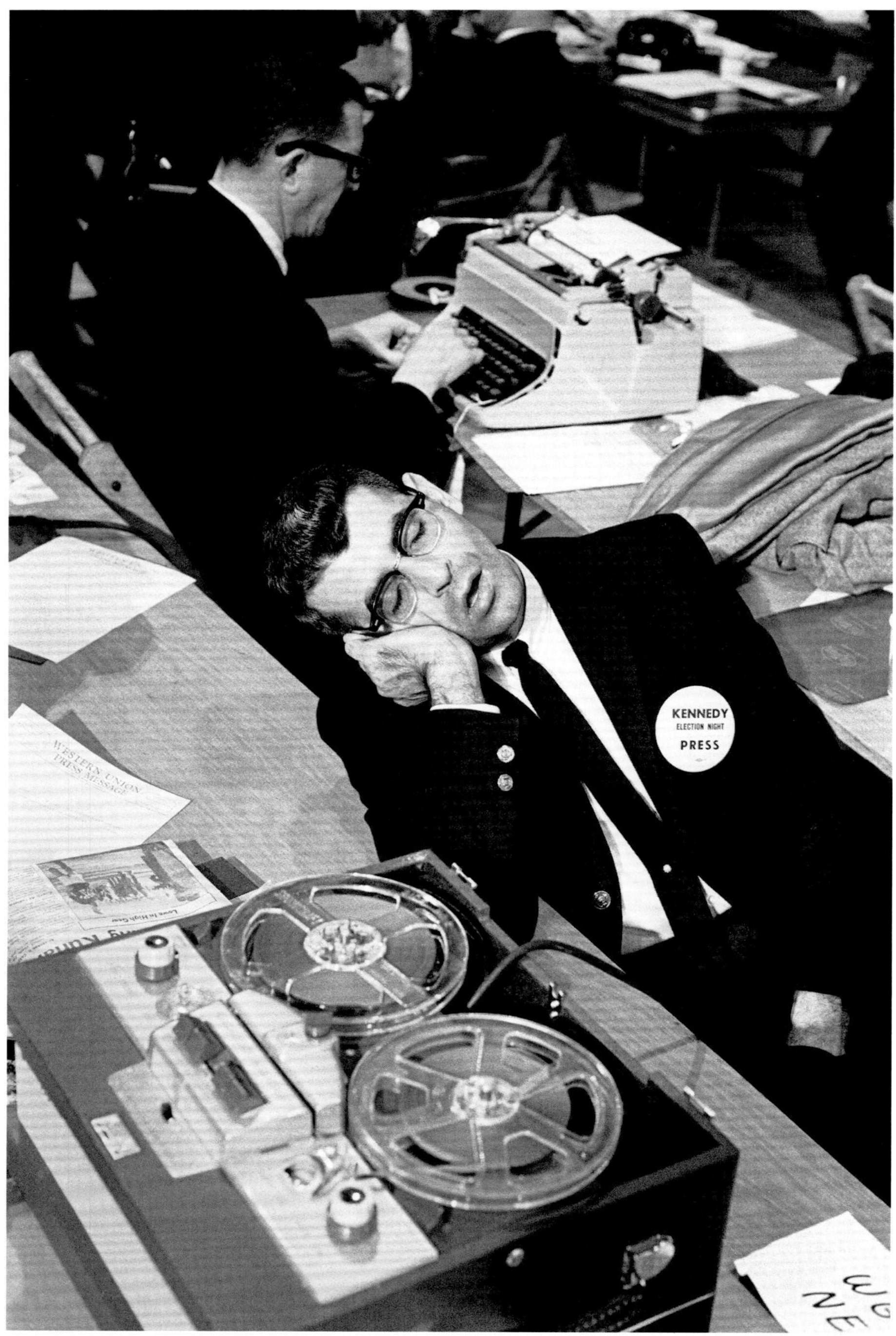

PREVIOUS SPREAD *November 9, 1960.* The crowd at Kennedy headquarters in the Hyannis Armory watches the live broadcast of Nixon's "conditional concession" at 3:30 A.M. EST. Kennedy's family and team, also watching the telecast, were furious. "Why should he concede?" Kennedy said. "I wouldn't." And with that, at nearly 4 in the morning, he went to bed, not knowing if he would be the next president of the United States. *Photo, Paul Slade*

ABOVE *November 8–9, 1960.* For Kennedy supporters, election night was fraught with the possibility of a nightmare scenario—that they would wake up in the morning to find he hadn't won. *Photo, Henri Dauman*

OPPOSITE *November 9, 1960.* Would-be revelers and exhausted members of the press at the Hyannis National Guard Armory in Barnstable, Massachusetts, await a possible appearance by Senator Kennedy after Nixon's "conditional concession." Given the uncertain election results in the early morning hours, Kennedy decided not to appear before the press until there was a formal statement from Nixon. *Photo, Anonymous*

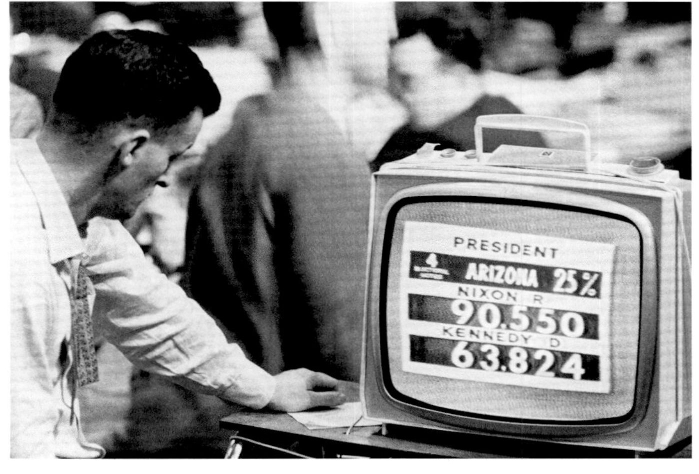

ABOVE *November 8–9, 1960.* Kennedy had visited Arizona a few times during the campaign, appearing in Tucson at an April luncheon, for example, with Congressman Stewart Udall, whom JFK would appoint as Secretary of the Interior. But on election night, the early voting shown here was indicative of the final outcome, as Nixon went on to win the state's 4 electoral votes beating JFK, 221,241 to 176,781. *Photo, Henri Dauman*

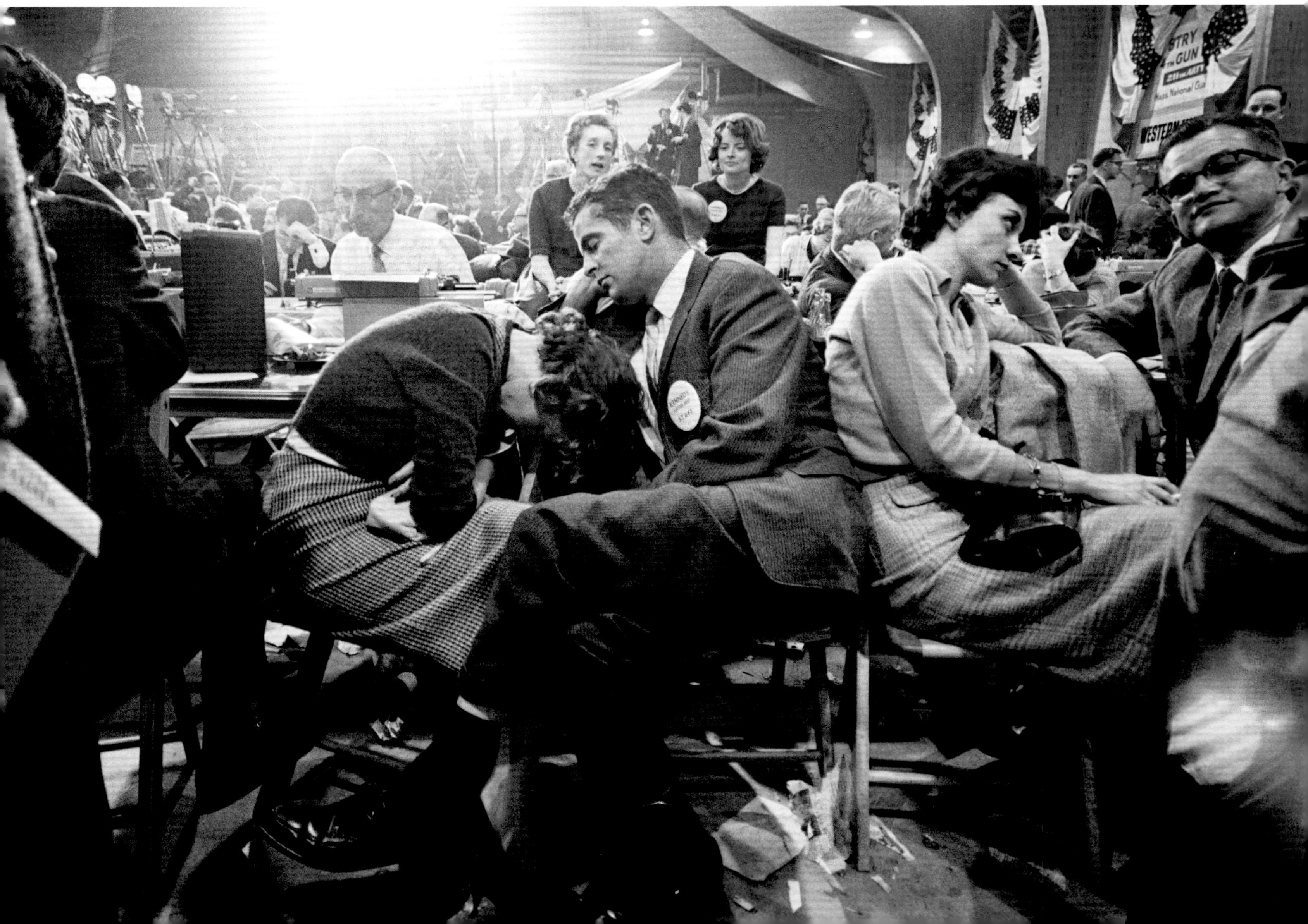

"I knew if he became President, it would be an existential event: he would touch depths in American life which were uncharted….America's tortured psychotic search for security would finally be torn loose from the feverish ghosts of its old generals…and we as a nation would finally be loose again in the historic seas of a national psyche which was…at last, again, adventurous. And that, I thought, that was the hope for America."

—Norman Mailer, *The Presidential Papers*, 1963

OPPOSITE *November 9, 1960.* By 11 A.M. EST on the day after the election, Nixon still hadn't conceded. Kennedy was still believed to be 11 electoral votes short of victory (though at least one TV network had called the election for him earlier that morning). An hour and a half later, Minnesota's votes took JFK over the top. A telegram soon arrived: "I want to repeat through this wire congratulations and best wishes I extended to you on television last night," it read. "I know that you have united support of all Americans as you lead this nation in the cause of peace and freedom during the next four years." Nixon aide Herb Klein read the same statement in a live television broadcast; finally, Nixon had admitted defeat. *Photo, Henri Dauman*

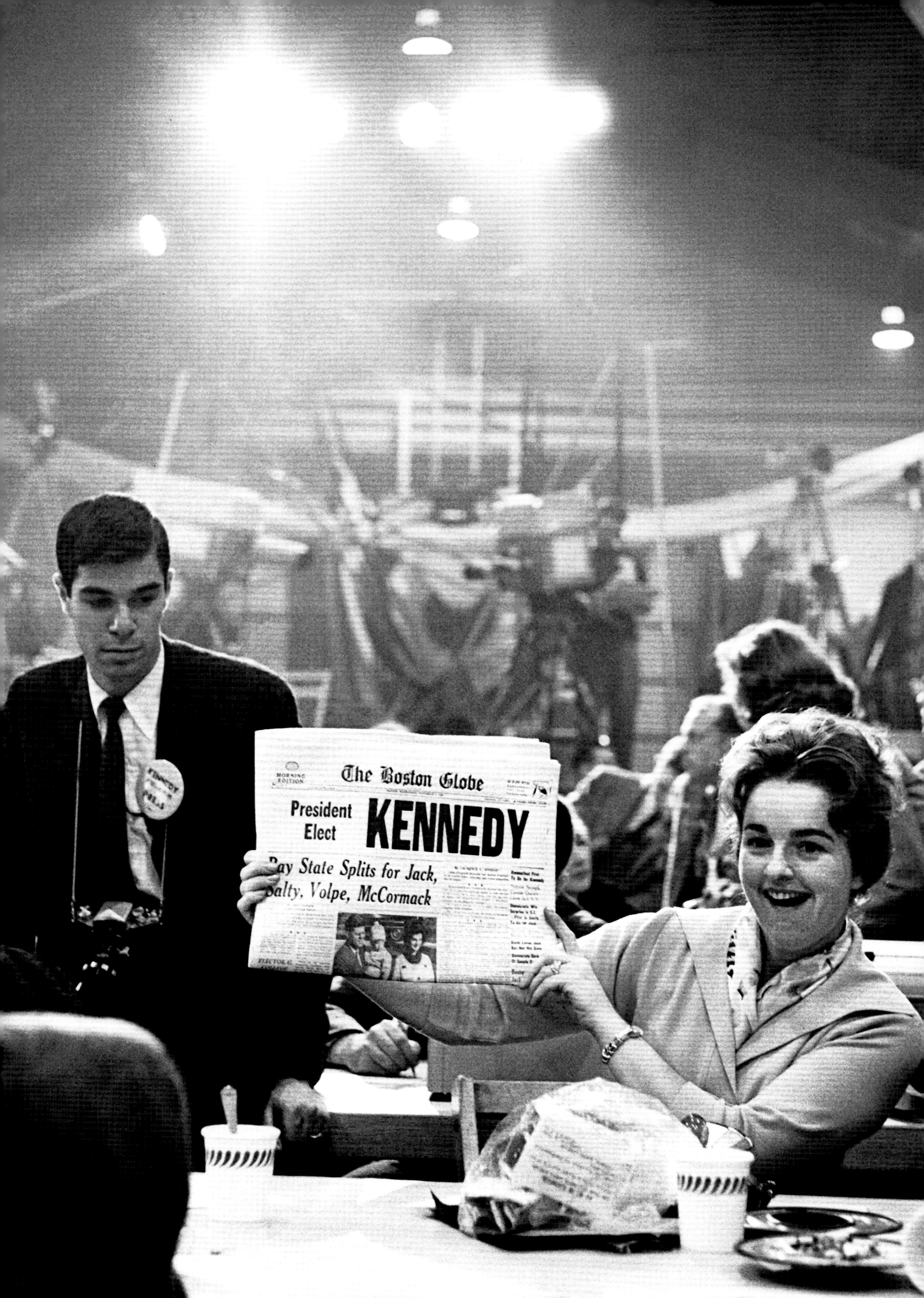

MORNING EDITION
The Boston Globe
President Elect KENNEDY
Bay State Splits for Jack, Salty, Volpe, McCormack

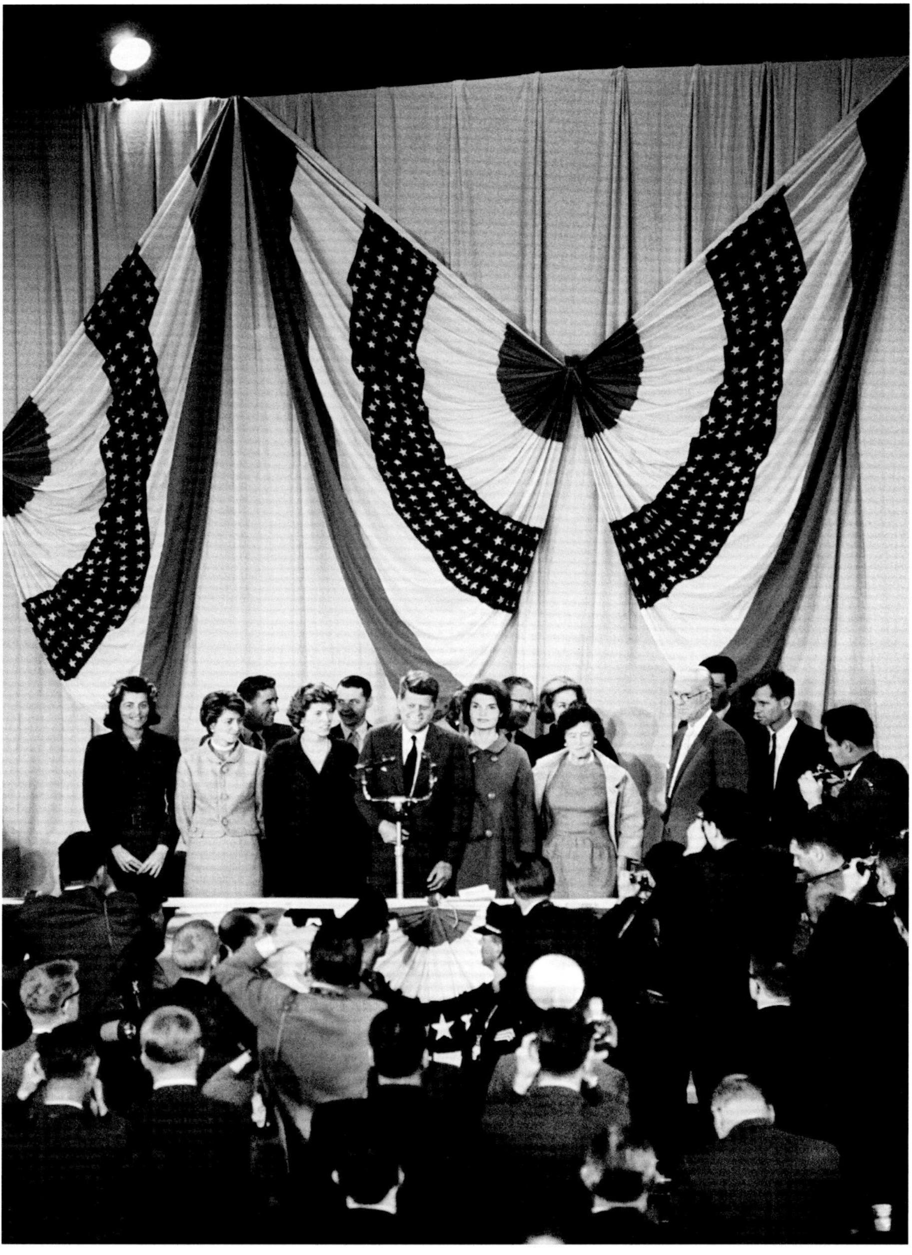

OPPOSITE *November 9, 1960.* An outtake from a portrait session of the
Kennedy family at their Hyannis Port home on the night after Kennedy's
win shows, sitting from the left, Eunice Shriver, Rose Kennedy, Joseph
Kennedy, Jackie Kennedy, and Ted Kennedy. On the back row, from the left
are Ethel Kennedy, Stephen Smith, Jean Smith, John F. Kennedy, Bobby
Kennedy, Patricia Lawford, Sargent Shriver, Joan Kennedy, and Peter
Lawford. *Photo, Paul Schutzer*

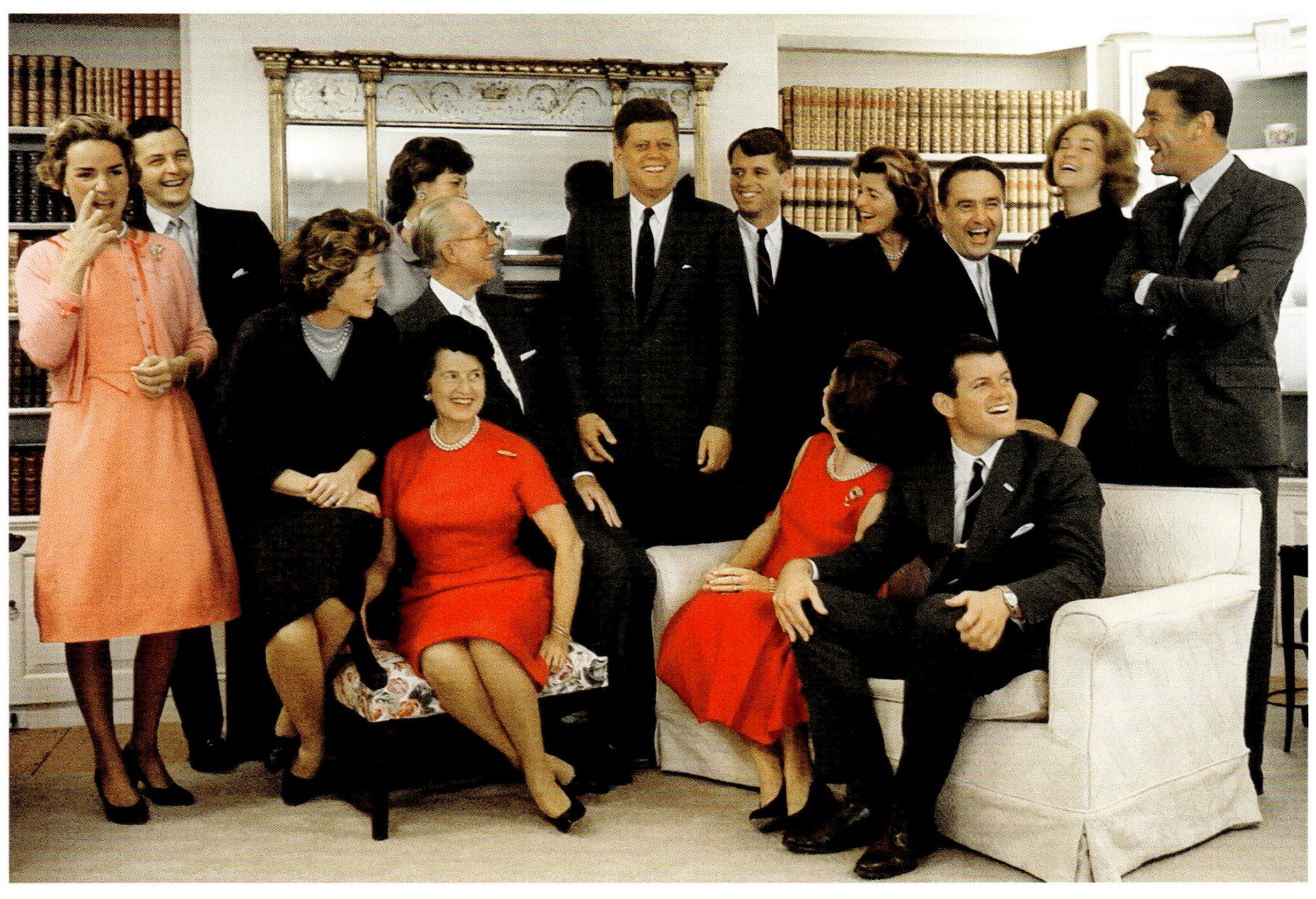

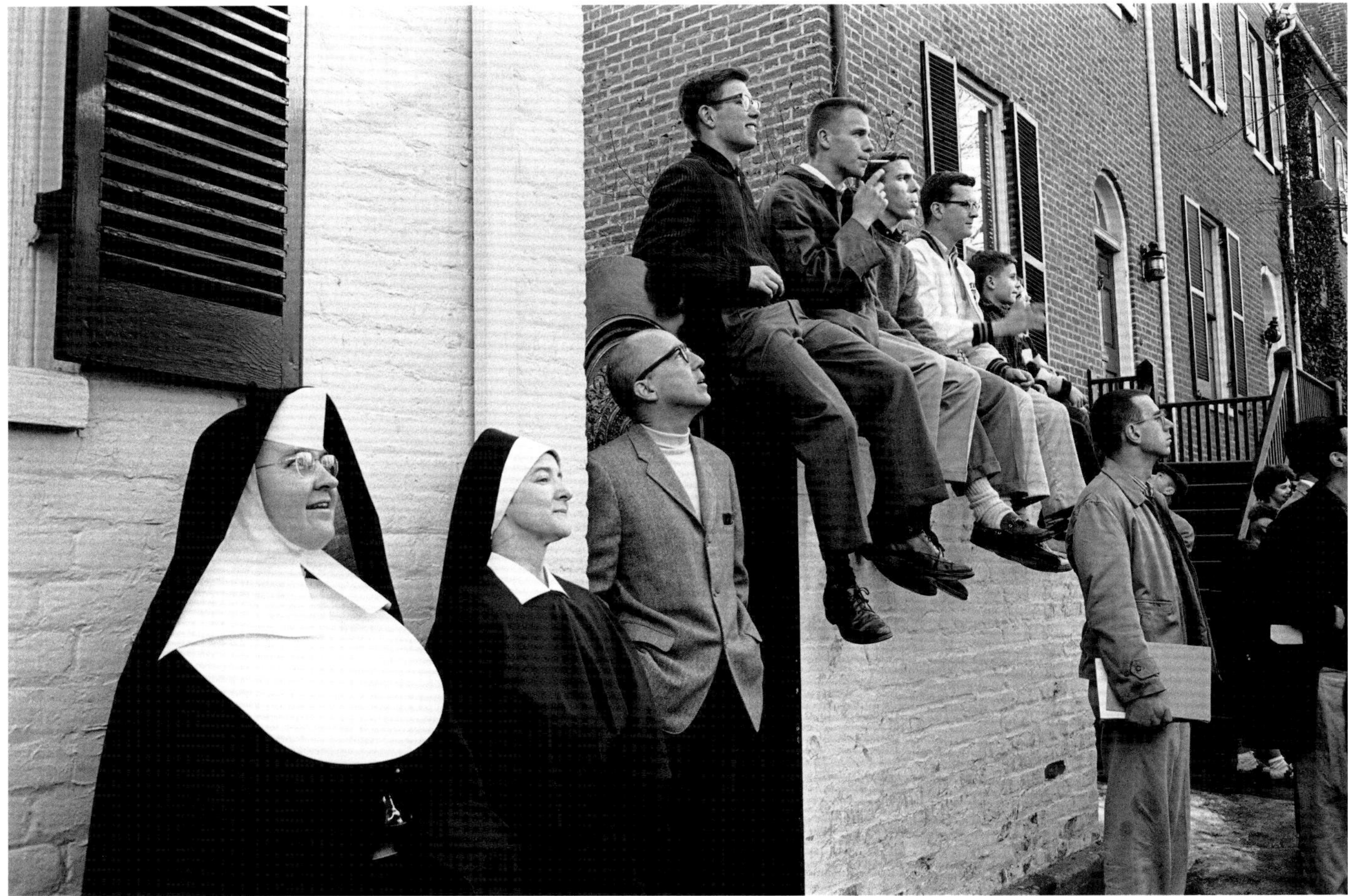

ABOVE *January 7, 1960.* On November 11, Kennedy returned from Cape Cod
to Washington, D.C., where crowds gathered outside his Georgetown home
until Election Day. But before he could finish assembling his cabinet and
planning for the transition from an Eisenhower White House to a Kennedy
White House, Jackie went into labor. *Photo, Henri Dauman*

OPPOSITE *December 9, 1960.* The Kennedys return home from Georgetown
University Hospital with their new son John F. Kennedy Jr., two weeks after
his birth on November 25. Luella Hennessey Donovan, the loyal Kennedy
family nurse who cared for three generations of Kennedy children (she
was present at the birth of 26 of them) carries the newborn baby. She would
soon be rocking him to sleep in the White House. *Photo, Ed Clark*

FOLLOWING SPREAD *January 2, 1961.* Incredibly—by today's security measures,
especially for a president-elect—JFK was just another fan as he sat in
the stands watching the Missouri vs. Navy Orange Bowl football game in
Miami, Florida. The Kennedys were spending some of their final days as
regular citizens with their family in nearby Palm Beach. *Photo, Neil Leifer*

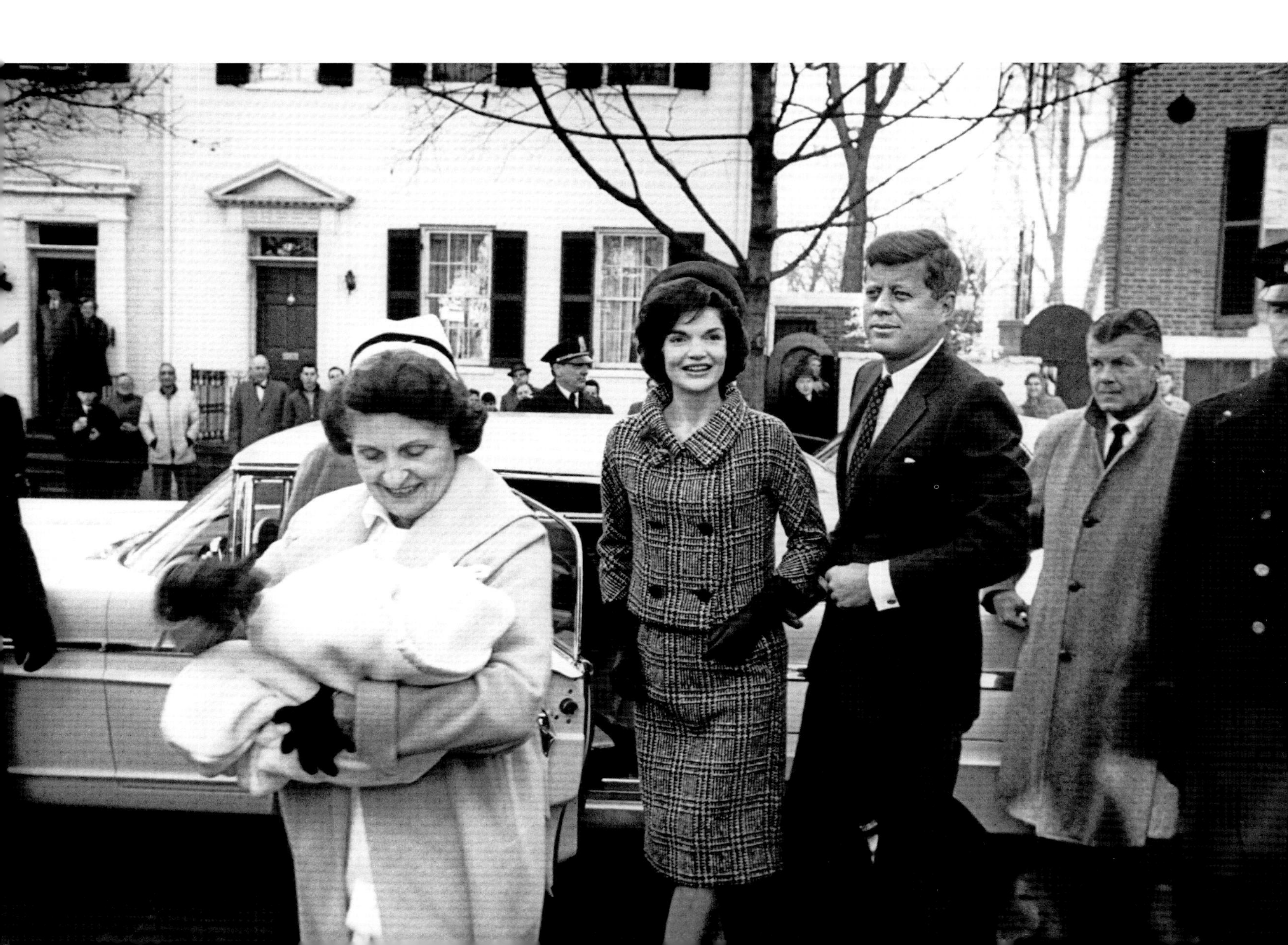

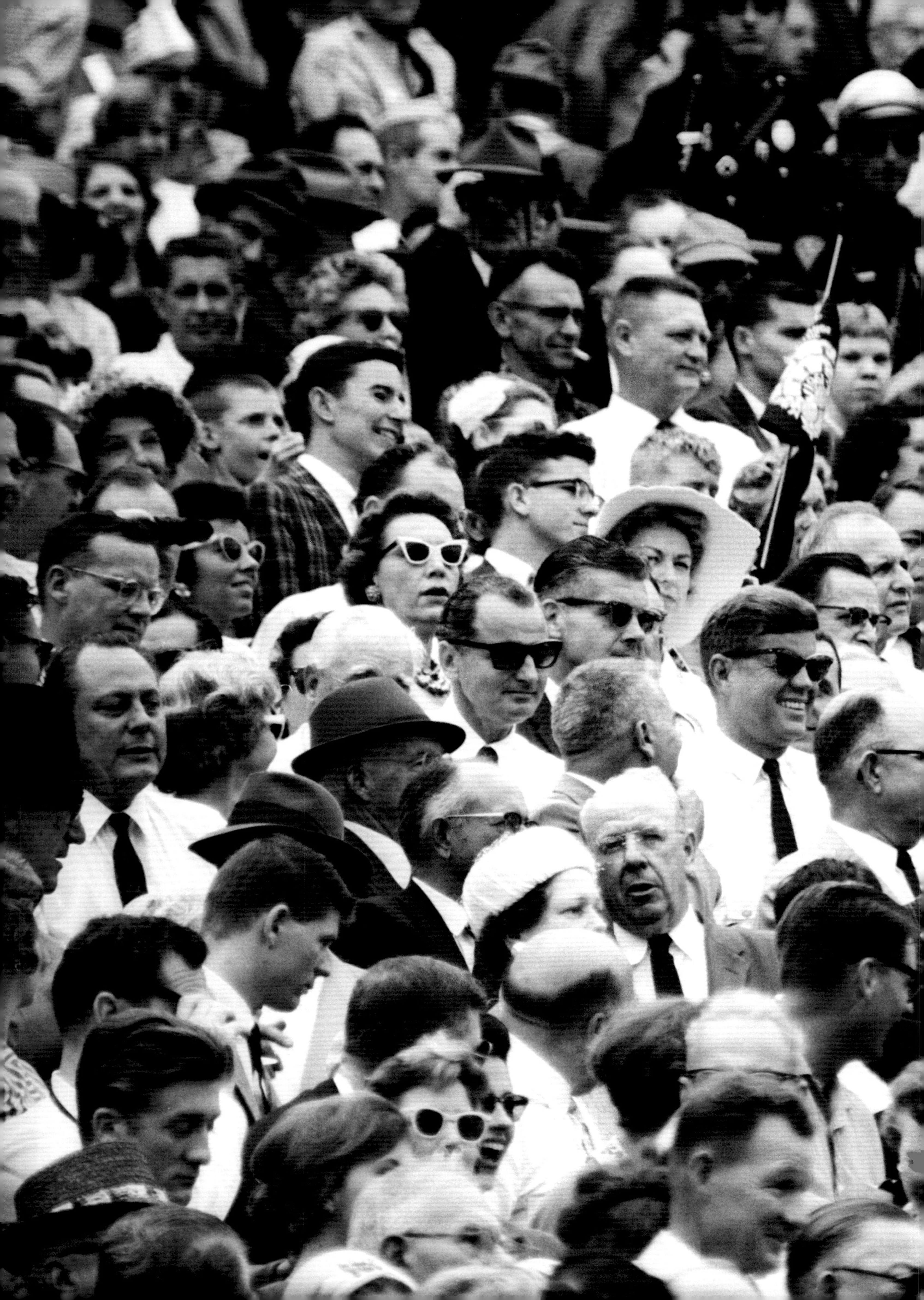

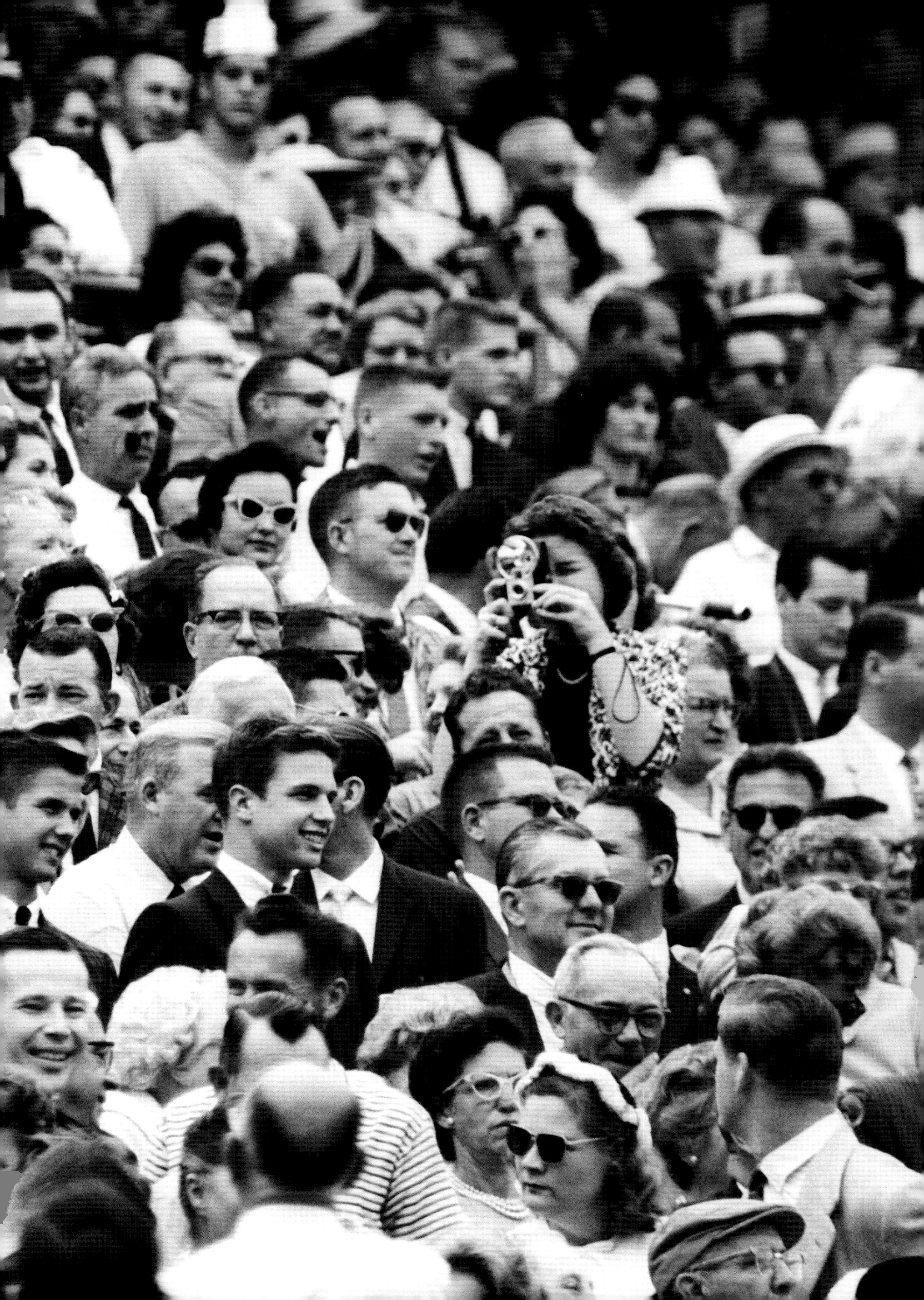

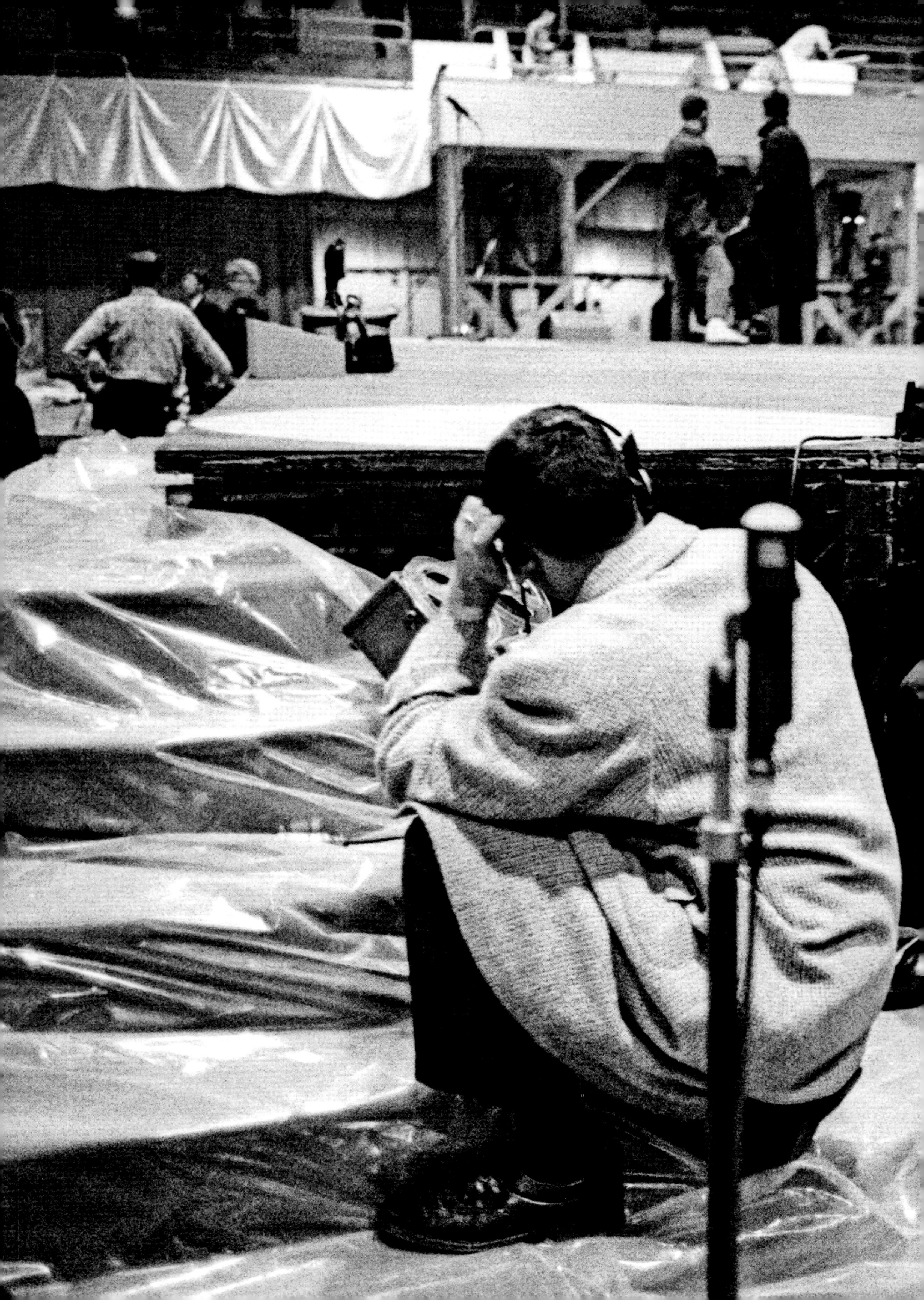

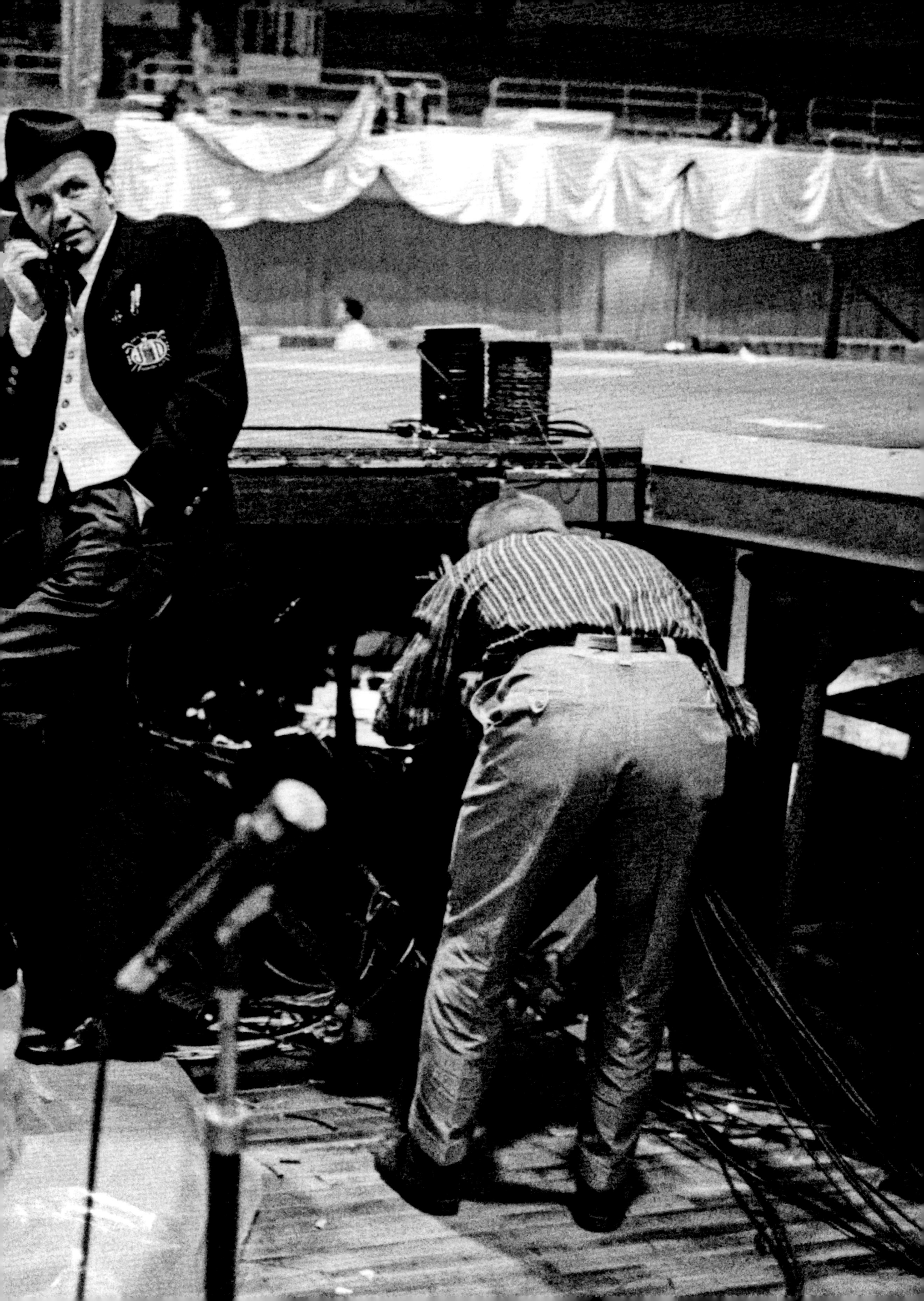

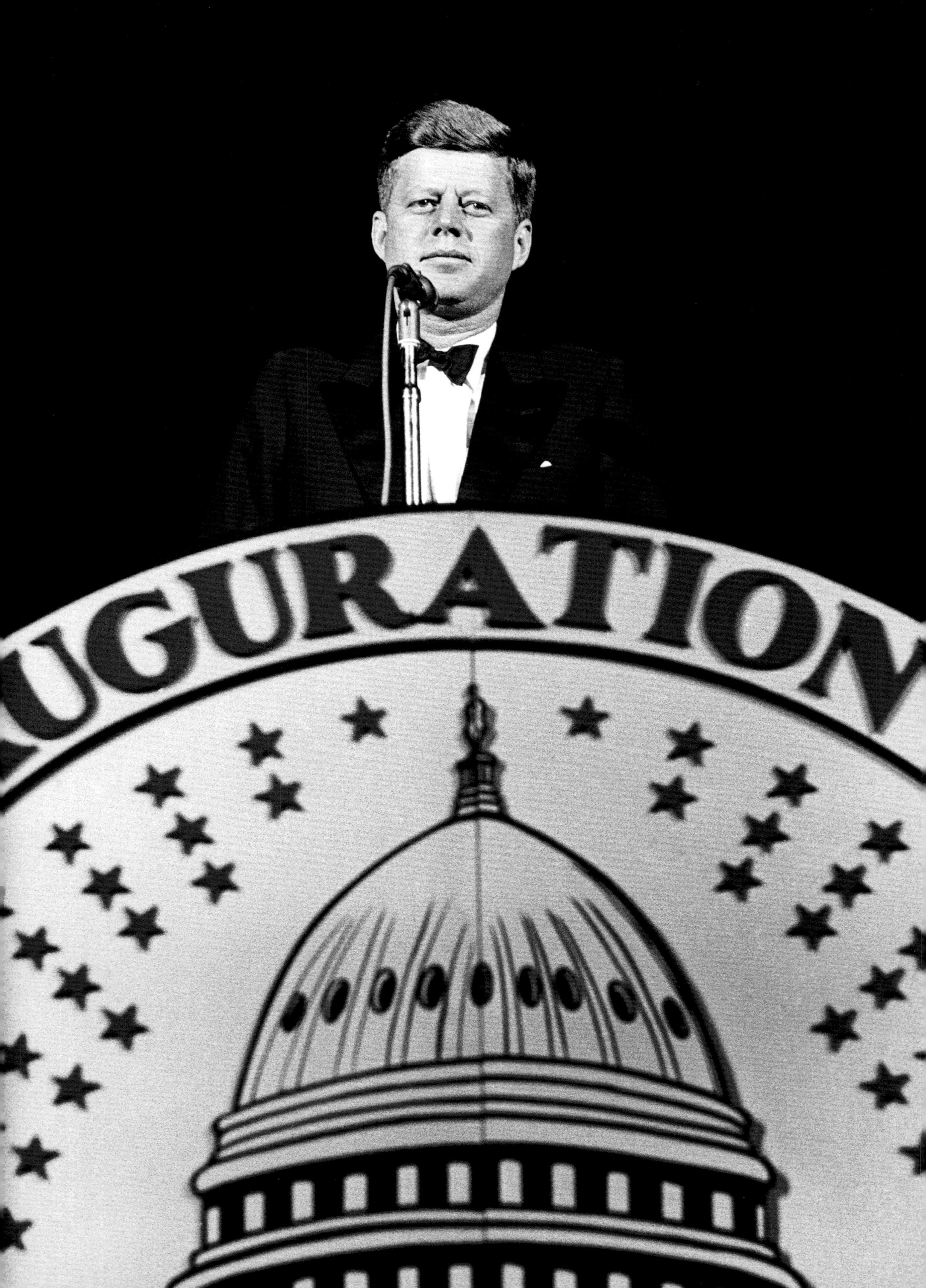
UGURATION

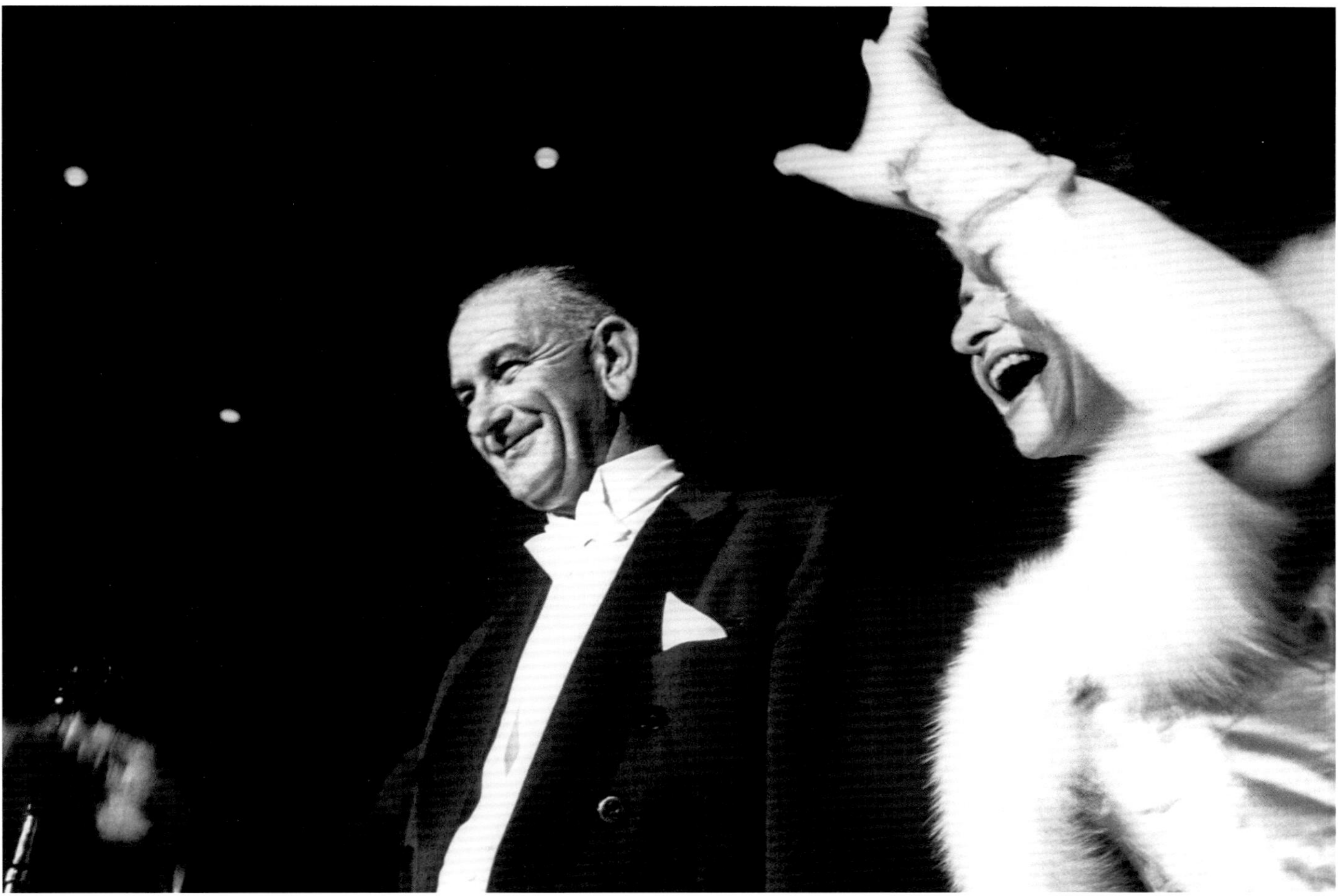

PREVIOUS SPREAD *Mid-January 1961.* In mid-December 1960, Frank Sinatra and Peter Lawford began planning a star-studded, celebrity-filled pre-inaugural gala and Democratic fund-raiser to be staged at the National Armory the night before JFK's official swearing in. The day of the party a storm dumped eight inches of snow on the city, but the show went on: Leonard Bernstein conducted; Gene Kelly danced; Bette Davis performed; and Nat King Cole sang—among many others. The inaugural gala would raise millions to help reduce the Democratic campaign debt and was one of the greatest Hollywood-on-the-Potomac fetes the city had ever witnessed. *Photo, Dennis Stock*

OPPOSITE *January 19-20, 1961.* It was 1:30 in the morning when President-elect John F. Kennedy addressed the crowd, thanking Sinatra and company. "And secondly," he continued, "I'm proud to be a member of a party which owes $4 million. Any party can balance its books. But to spend $4 million more than you've got in a close election is the kind of democratic tradition with which I choose to be associated. ..." *Photo, Henri Dauman*

ABOVE *January 19–20, 1961.* LBJ and Lady Bird join in the celebration. *Photo, Paul Schutzer*

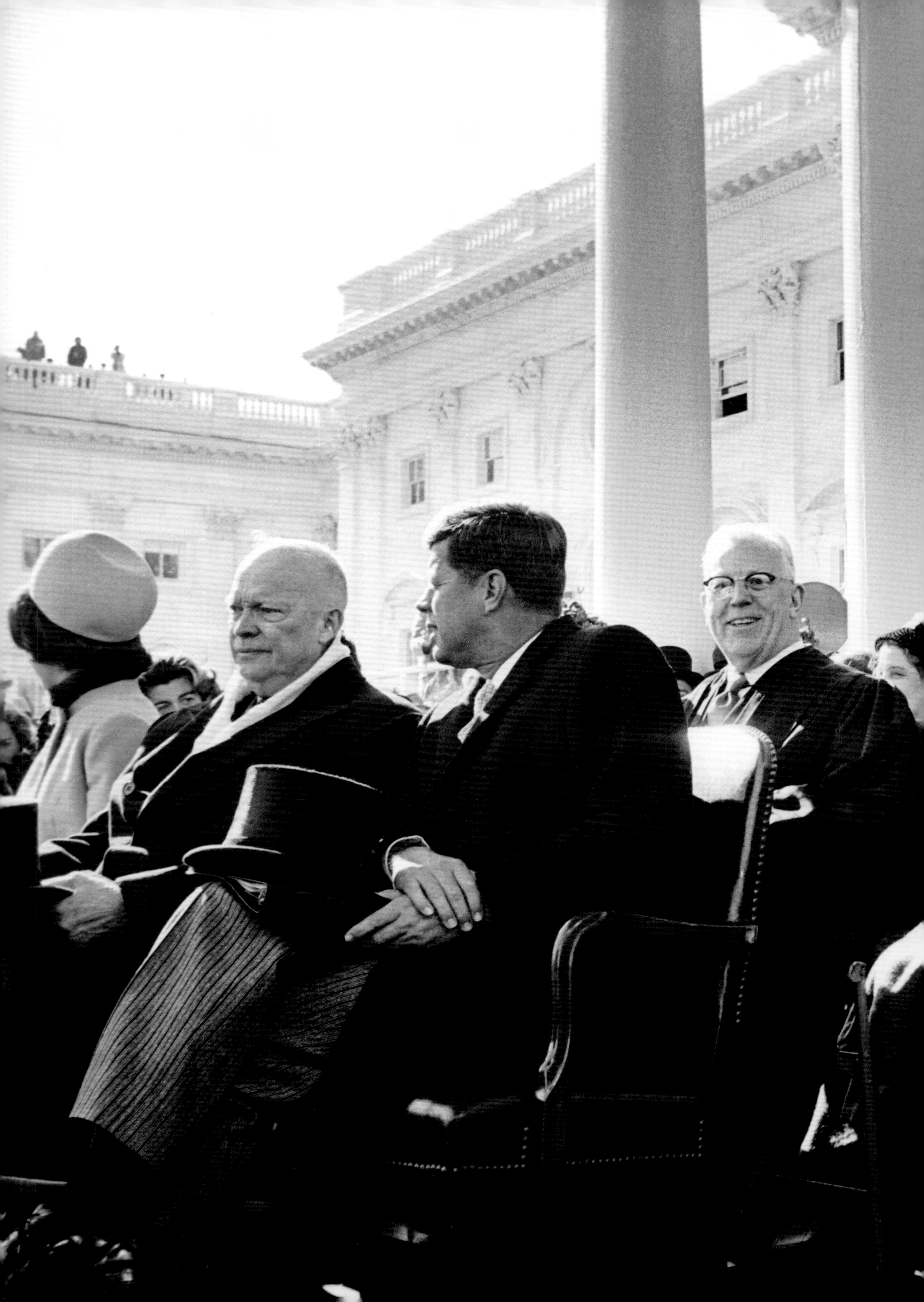

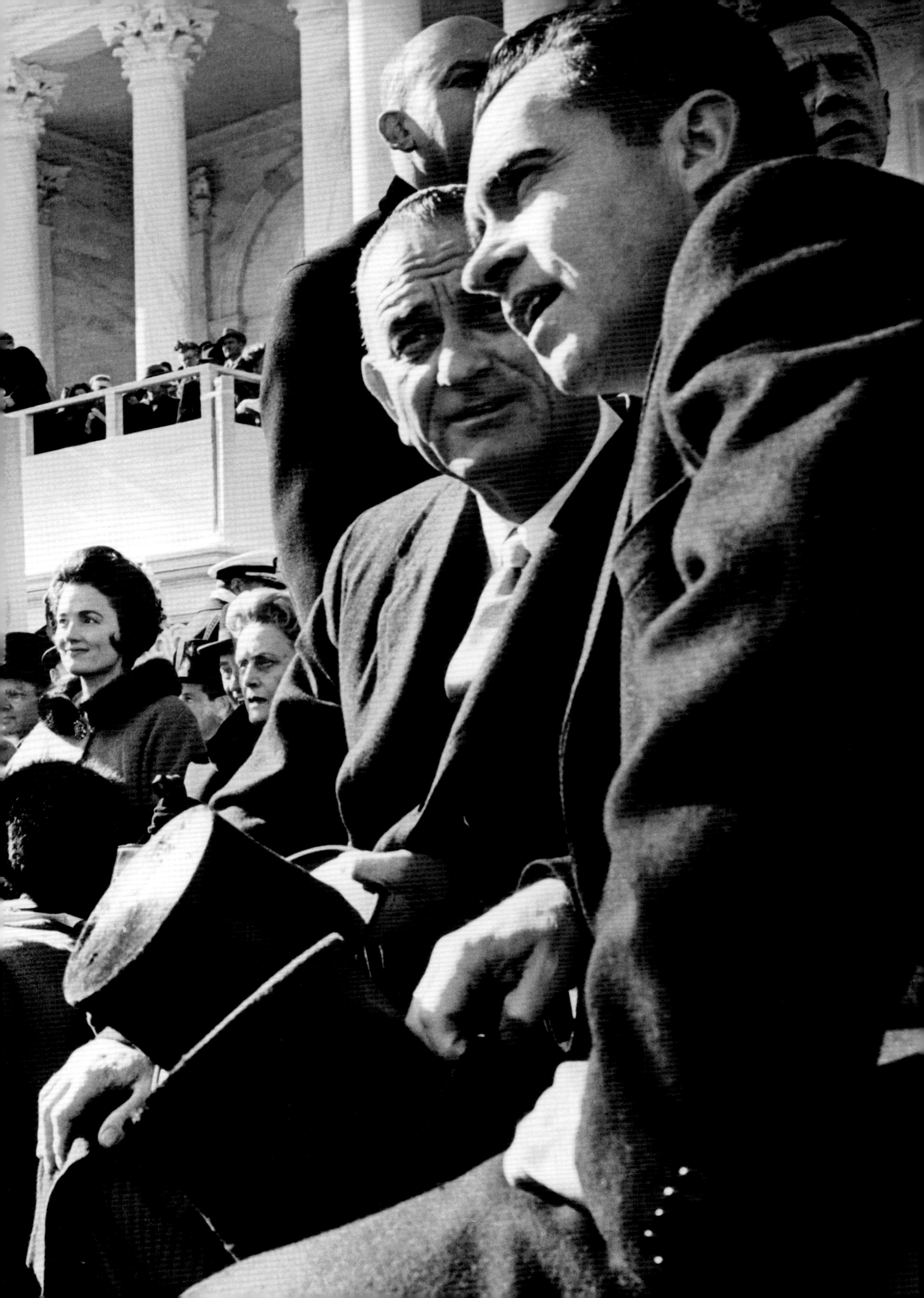

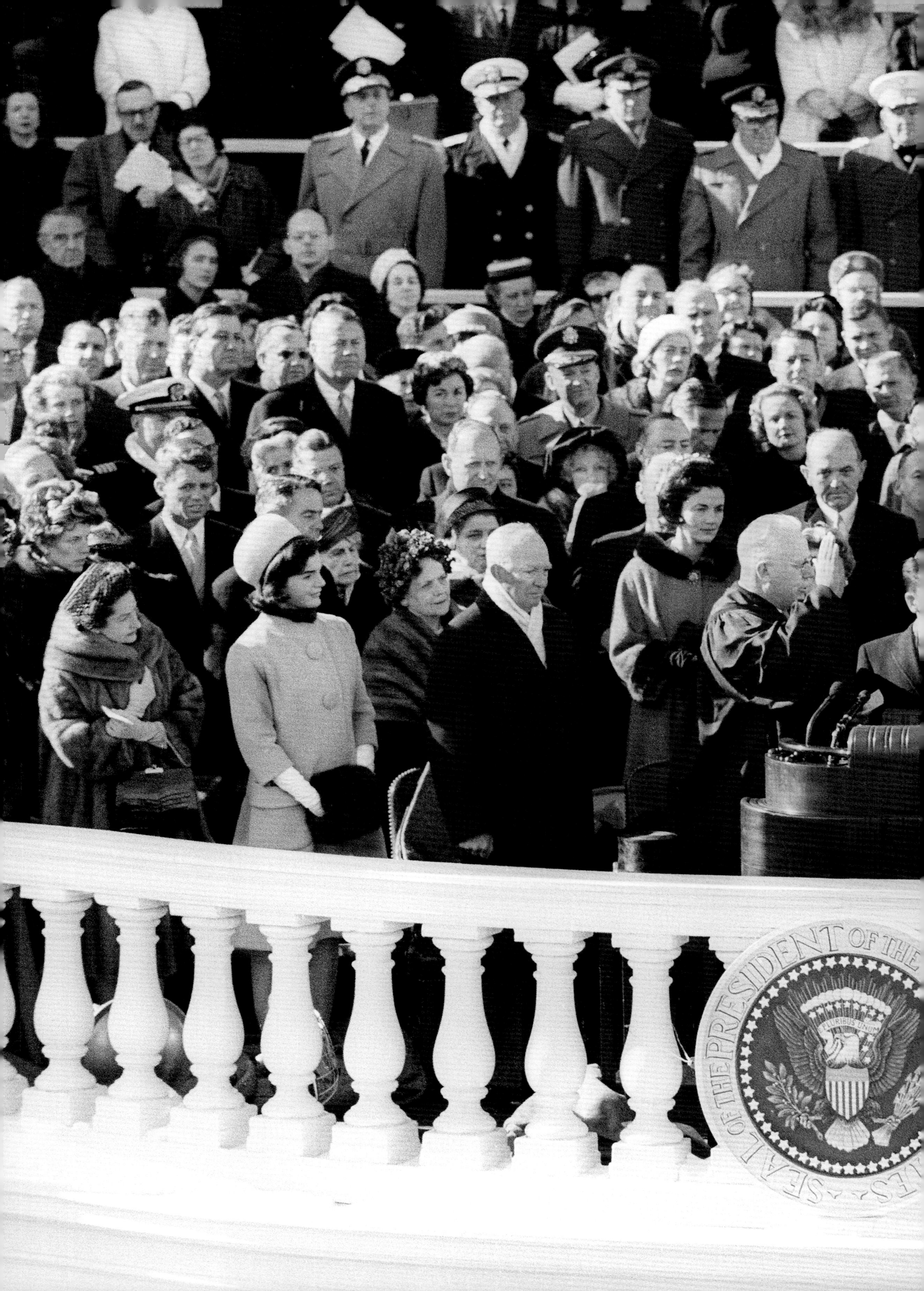
SEAL OF THE PRESIDENT OF THE
E PLURIBUS UNUM

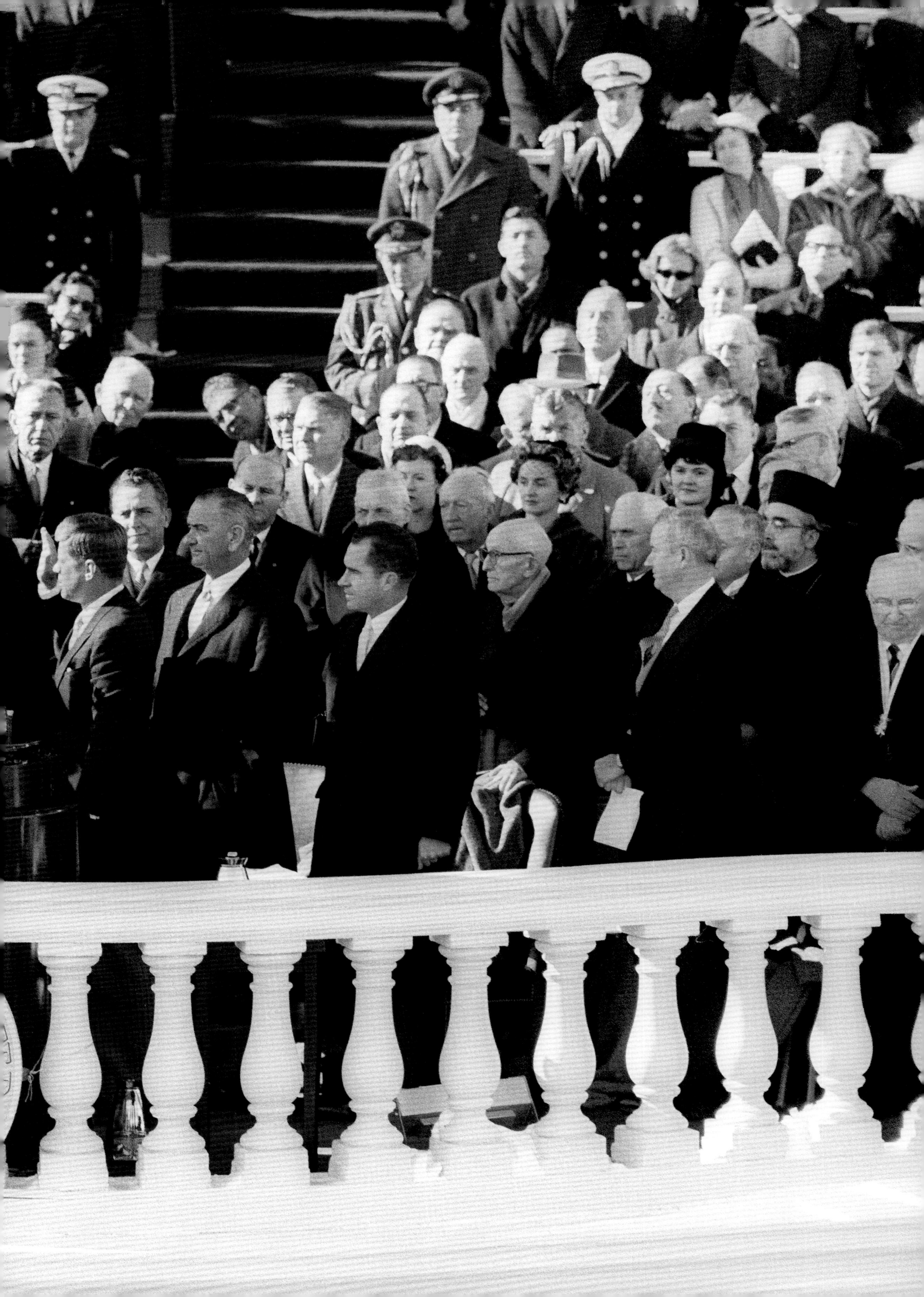

"Let every nation know, whether it wishes us well or ill, that we shall pay any price, bear any burden, meet any hardship, support any friend, oppose any foe, in order to assure the survival and the success of liberty. This much we pledge — and more."

—John F. Kennedy, Inaugural Address, Washington, D.C., January 20, 1961

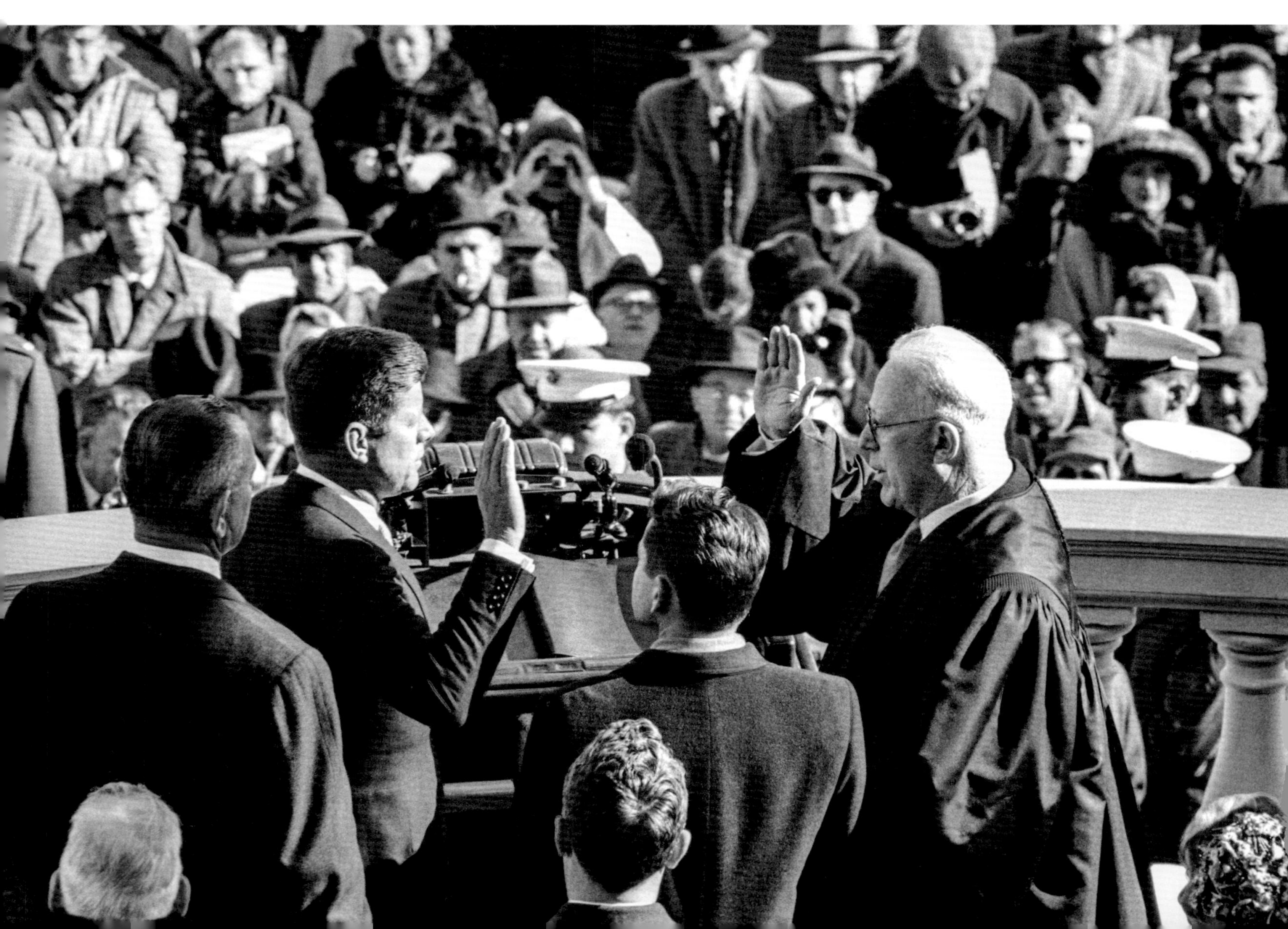

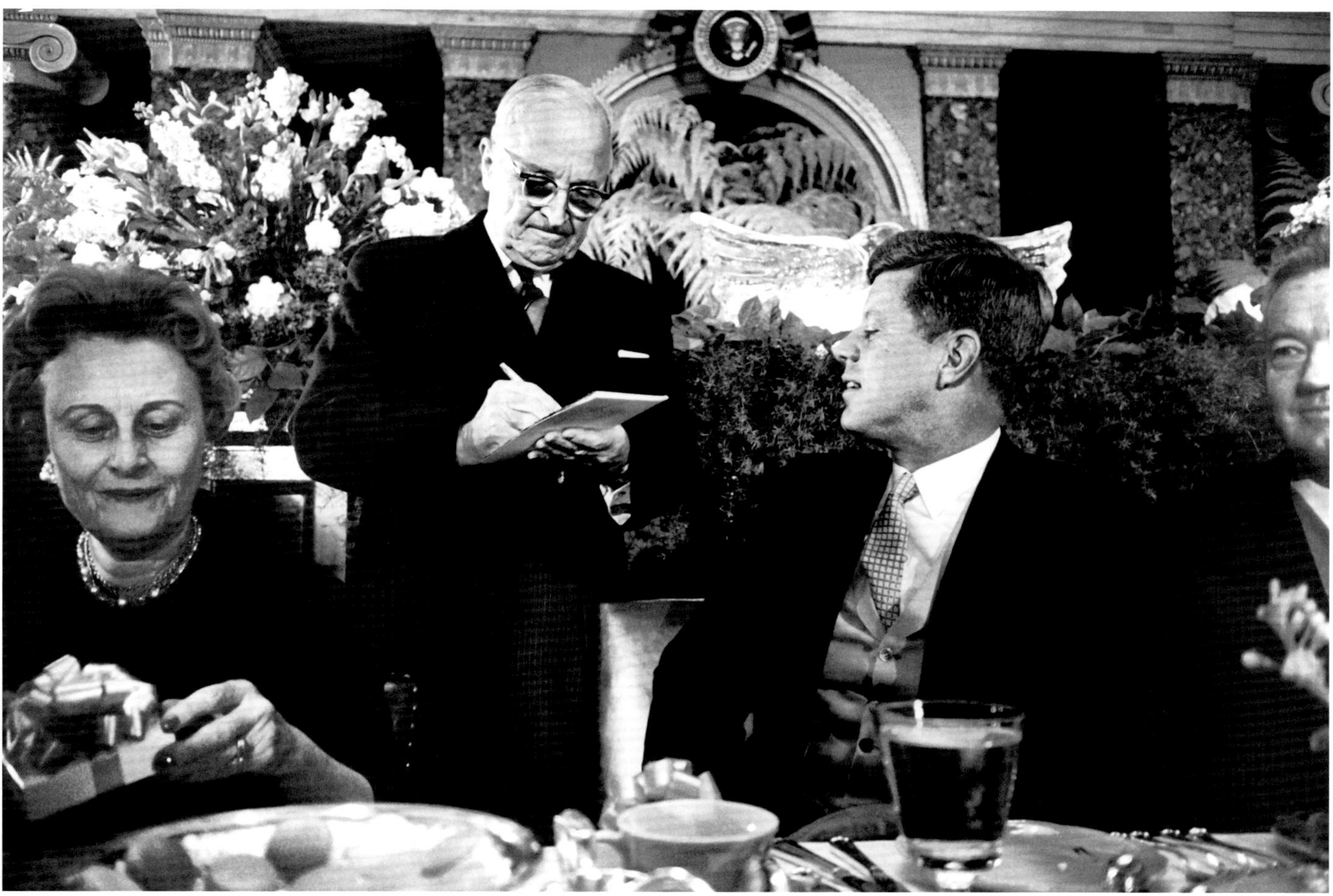

PAGES 288–289 *January 20, 1961.* At the Capitol it was a brisk, clear winter day following the previous evening's eight-inch snowfall. In the VIP seating section for the inauguration, waiting for the ceremony to begin, Lyndon Johnson and Richard Nixon chatted. Kennedy and President Eisenhower had a conversation about a book they both admired, *The Longest Day,* a history of the WWII allied landing on Normandy. *Photo, Paul Schutzer*

PREVIOUS SPREAD *January 20, 1961.* Chief justice of the U.S. Supreme Court Earl Warren swears in the new president. Kennedy was the first American president to be born in the twentieth century, the first Roman Catholic, and the youngest. At age 41 he took the mantle from Eisenhower, who at 70 was then the oldest president in office. *Photo, Henri Dauman*

OPPOSITE *January 20, 1961.* Kennedy's inaugural address included a great call to national service: "Ask not what your country can do for you," he famously said, "ask what you can do for your country." *Photo, Jacques Lowe*

ABOVE *January 20, 1961.* After the inauguration Kennedy joined former President Truman for a luncheon in the old Supreme Court Chamber of the U.S. Capitol. *Photo, Paul Schutzer*

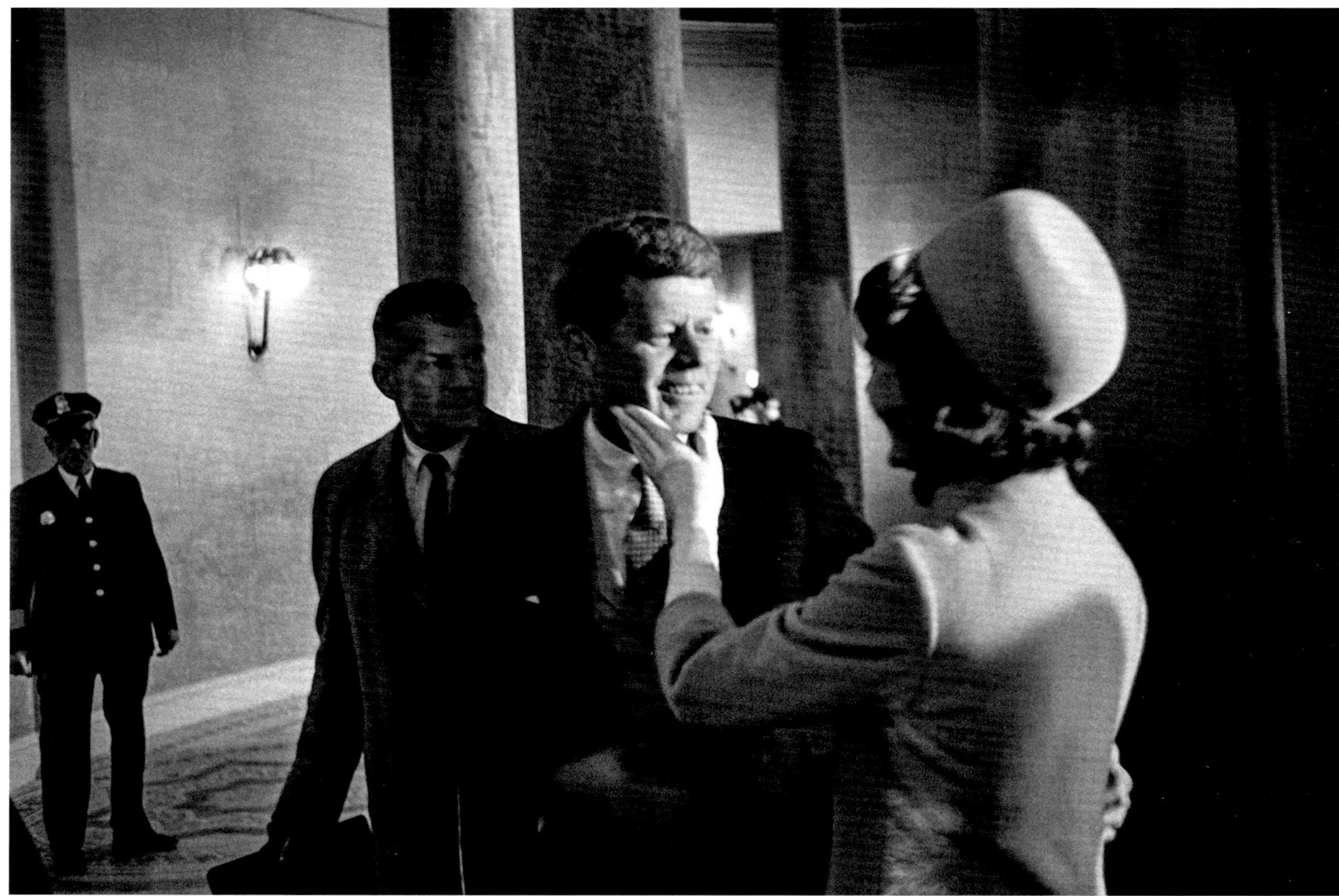

ABOVE *January 20, 1961.* The new president and First Lady have a tender moment in the Capitol building on the morning of the inauguration. With her sophisticated knowledge of the arts and love of fashion, she brought style and glamour into the general election campaign and, later, into the White House. Tom Wolfe would later call Kennedy's inviting Robert Frost to read a poem from the Capitol steps that morning one of the greatest coups of Frost's career, noting that Kennedy "did recognize, quite correctly, that art and culture have become the religion of the educated classes."
Photo, Henry Burroughs

OPPOSITE *January 20, 1961.* On Inauguration Day, the newly sworn-in President and First Lady attend a reception in the U.S. Capitol. It had been a long day already. The night before, Kennedy had attended Frank Sinatra's lavish inaugural gala along with several other parties and went to bed at 4 A.M. Still, he rose early for Mass, walking in the snow to nearby Holy Trinity Catholic Church. After Mass, he and Jackie then went to the White House to meet President Eisenhower and his wife, Mamie, who joined them in travelling to Capitol Hill for the inauguration. *Photo, Ed Clark*

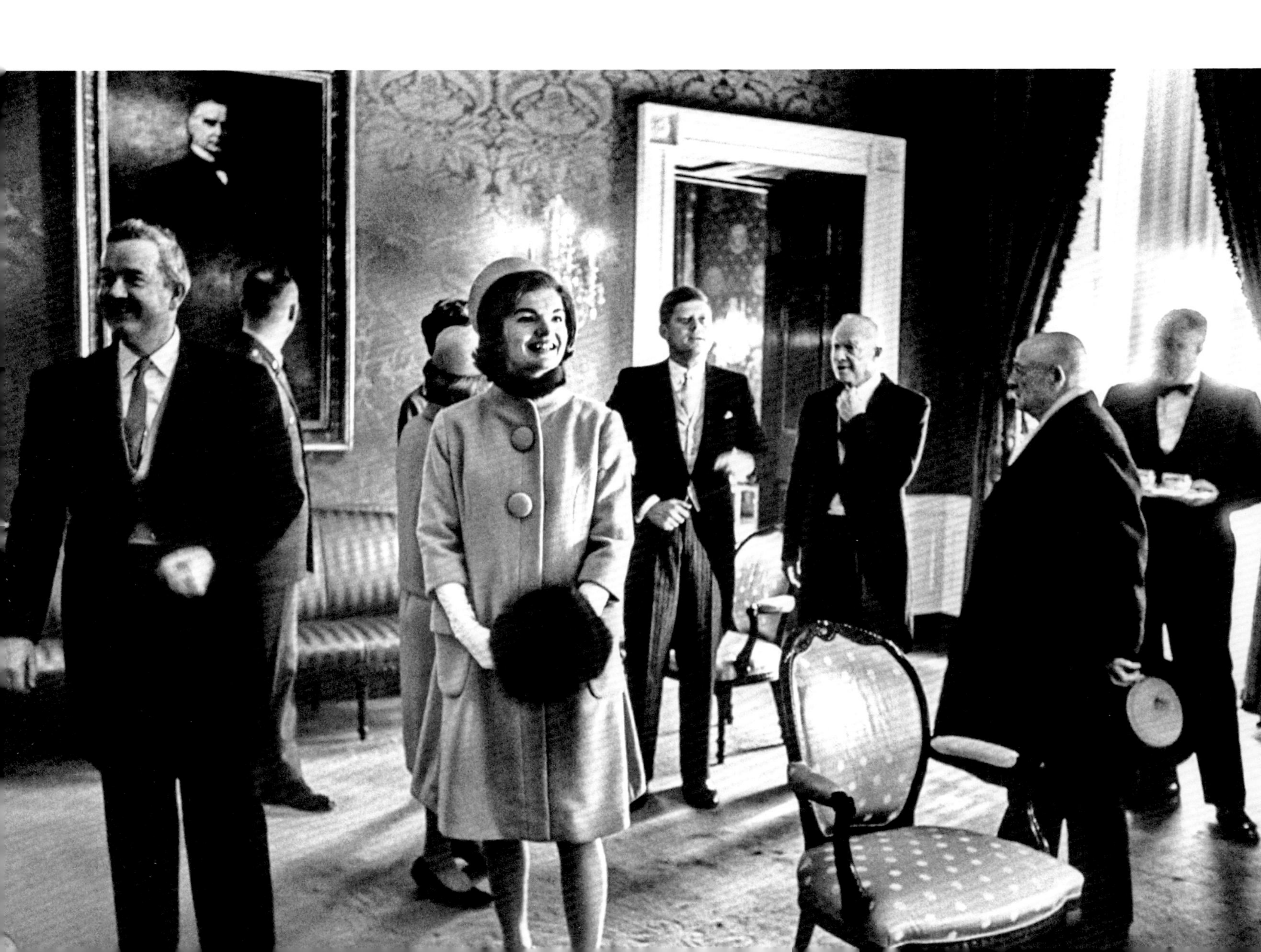

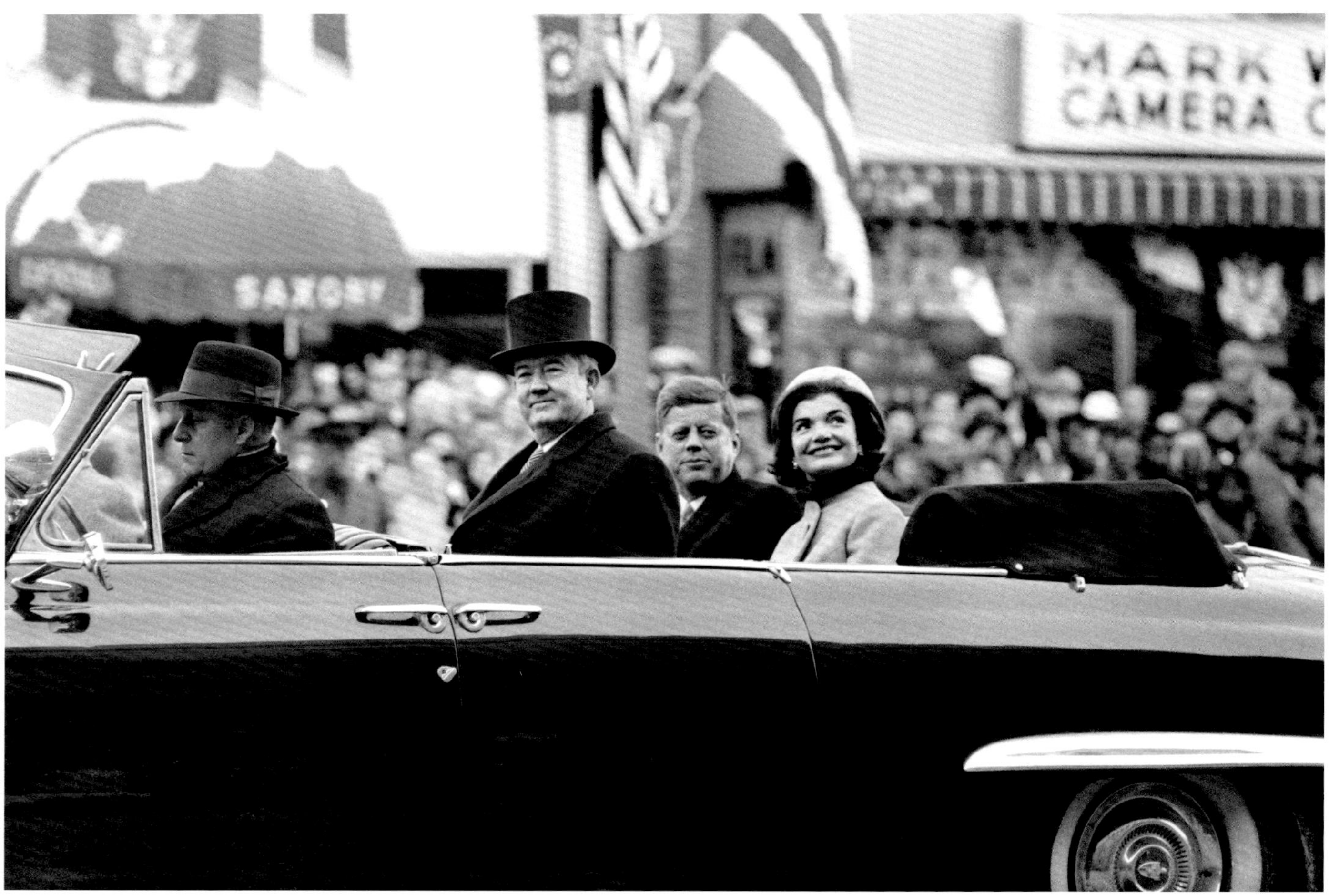

ABOVE *January 20, 1961.* Following the inauguration and a luncheon, President Kennedy and the First Lady ride in an open convertible down Pennsylvania Avenue to the White House. *Photo, Henri Dauman*

OPPOSITE BELOW *January 20, 1960. The Washington Post* reported that "hundreds of thousands of enthusiastic well-wishers braved numbing cold and biting winds . . . to cheer President John F. Kennedy along his Inaugural parade route to the White House." *Photo, Henri Dauman*

RIGHT *January 20, 1960.* Presidential inaugurations brim with photo ops—packed as they are with political VIPs of every description, world leaders, corporate executives, and celebrity figures from every walk of life. No news organization wants to be left out, so media coverage is intense. And in 1960, perhaps more than ever before given the emergence of television, thousands of reporters, photographers, and correspondents, domestic and foreign, were present for the event, as well as additional amateurs, all compiling a visual and literary record that will continue to inform for generations to come. *Photo, Alfred Wertheimer*

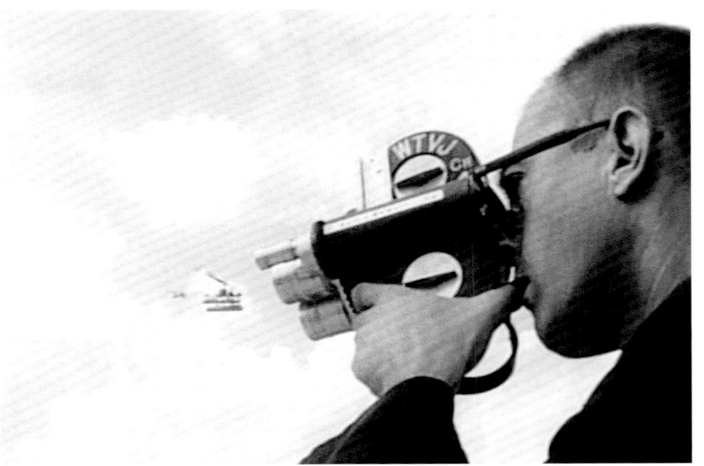

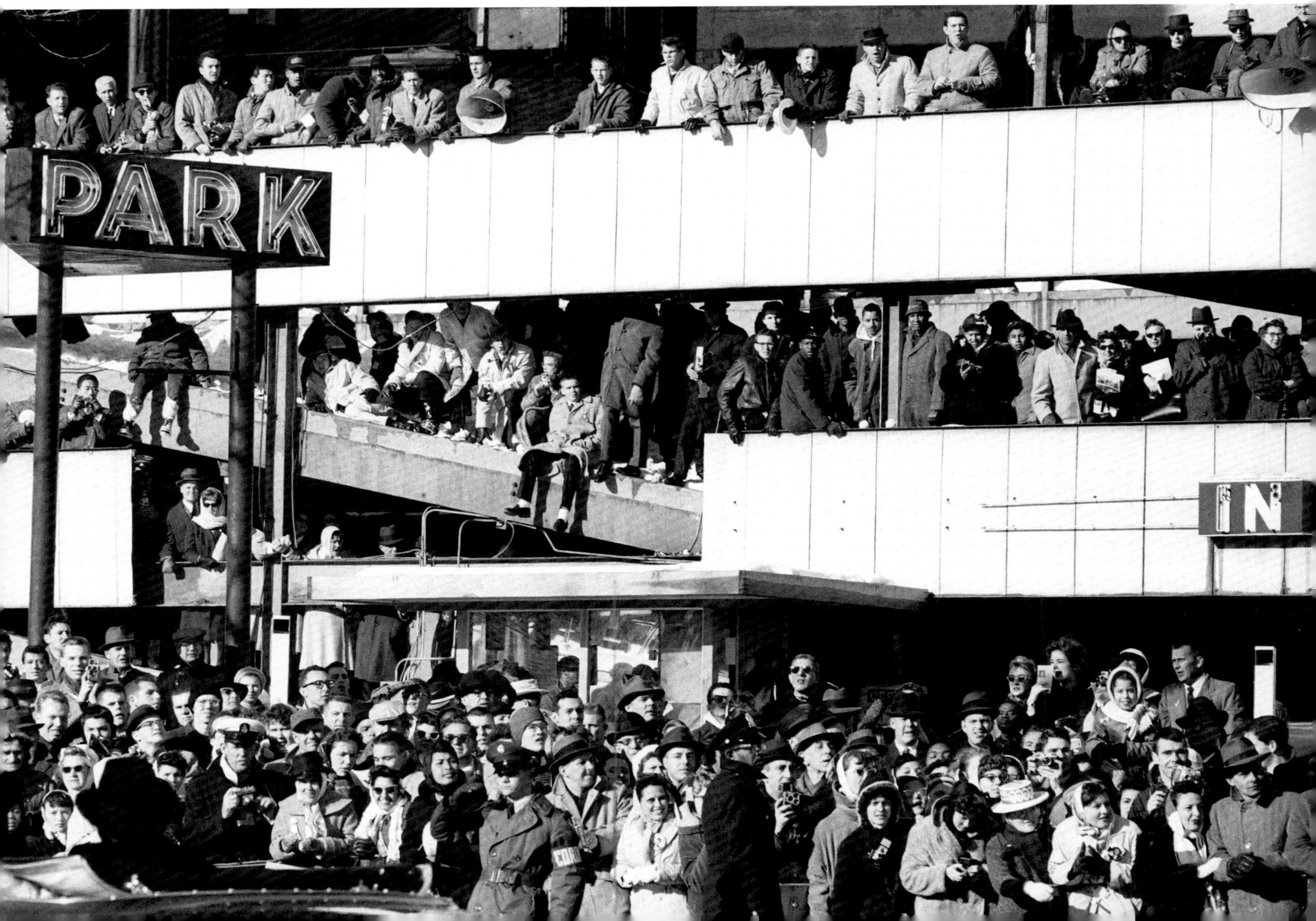

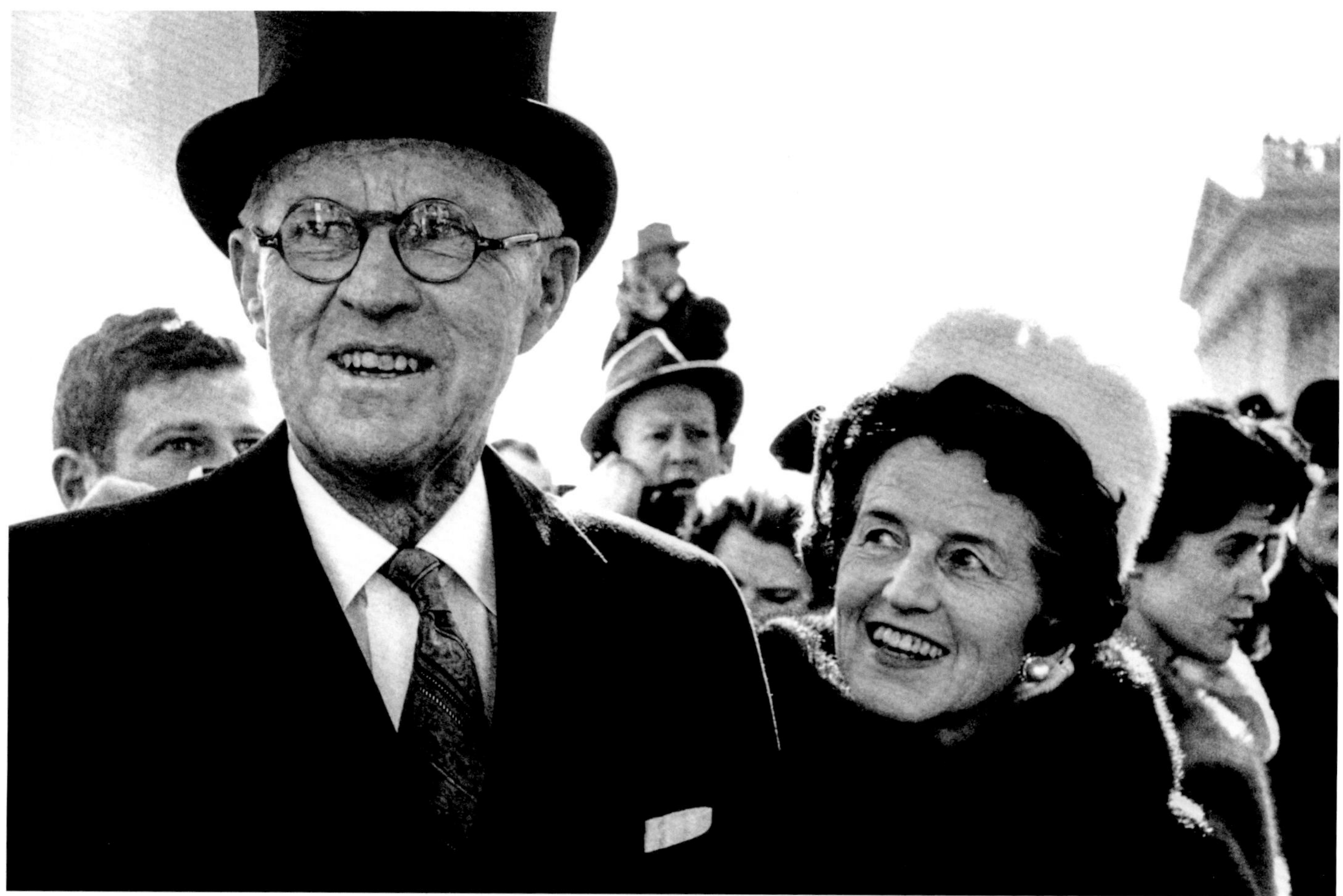

ABOVE *January 20, 1961.* JFK's proud parents, Joseph P. and Rose Kennedy, on the day of their son's inauguration as the thirty-fifth president of the United States. A former ambassador and one-time presidential possibility, Joe Kennedy played a very powerful, but behind-the-scenes, role in his son's election, using his money and his wide network of political and financial connections to help elect his son. *Photo, Jacques Lowe*

OPPOSITE *January 20, 1961.* From a viewing stand outside the White House, President Kennedy and Vice President Johnson endured subfreezing temperatures while watching the inaugural parade for most of the afternoon. The parade featured more than 30,000 marchers, including West Point cadets and Annapolis midshipmen, dozens of bands, assorted military hardware, and numerous floats, one of which was a PT-109 float with members of JFK's wartime crew. A man dressed like Buffalo Bill even rode a bronking bison past the viewing stand. While the First Lady and Rose Kennedy adjourned to the White House early on, JFK and LBJ stayed until about 6:15 P.M., after the last floats had passed. *Photo, Jacques Lowe*

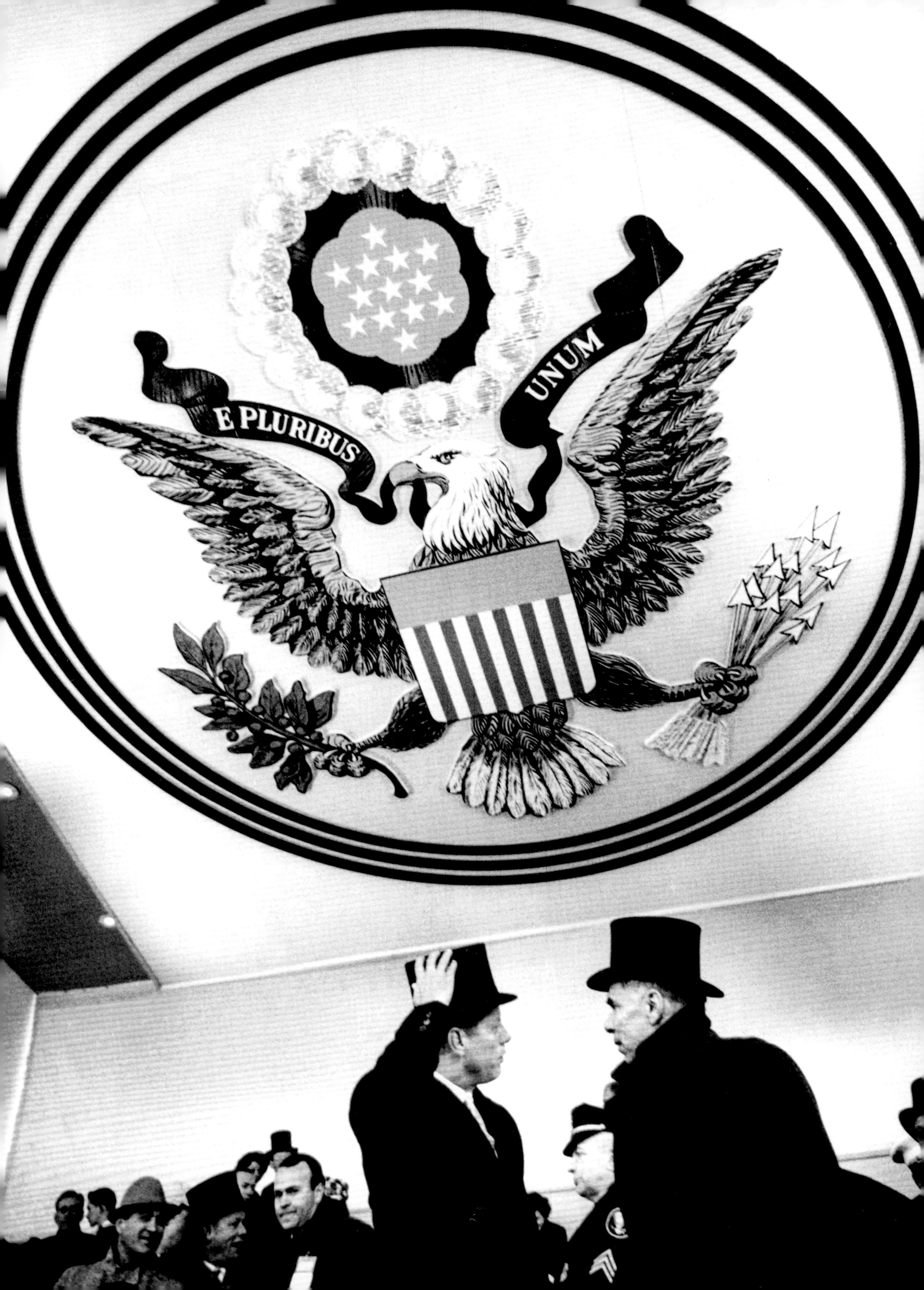
E PLURIBUS UNUM

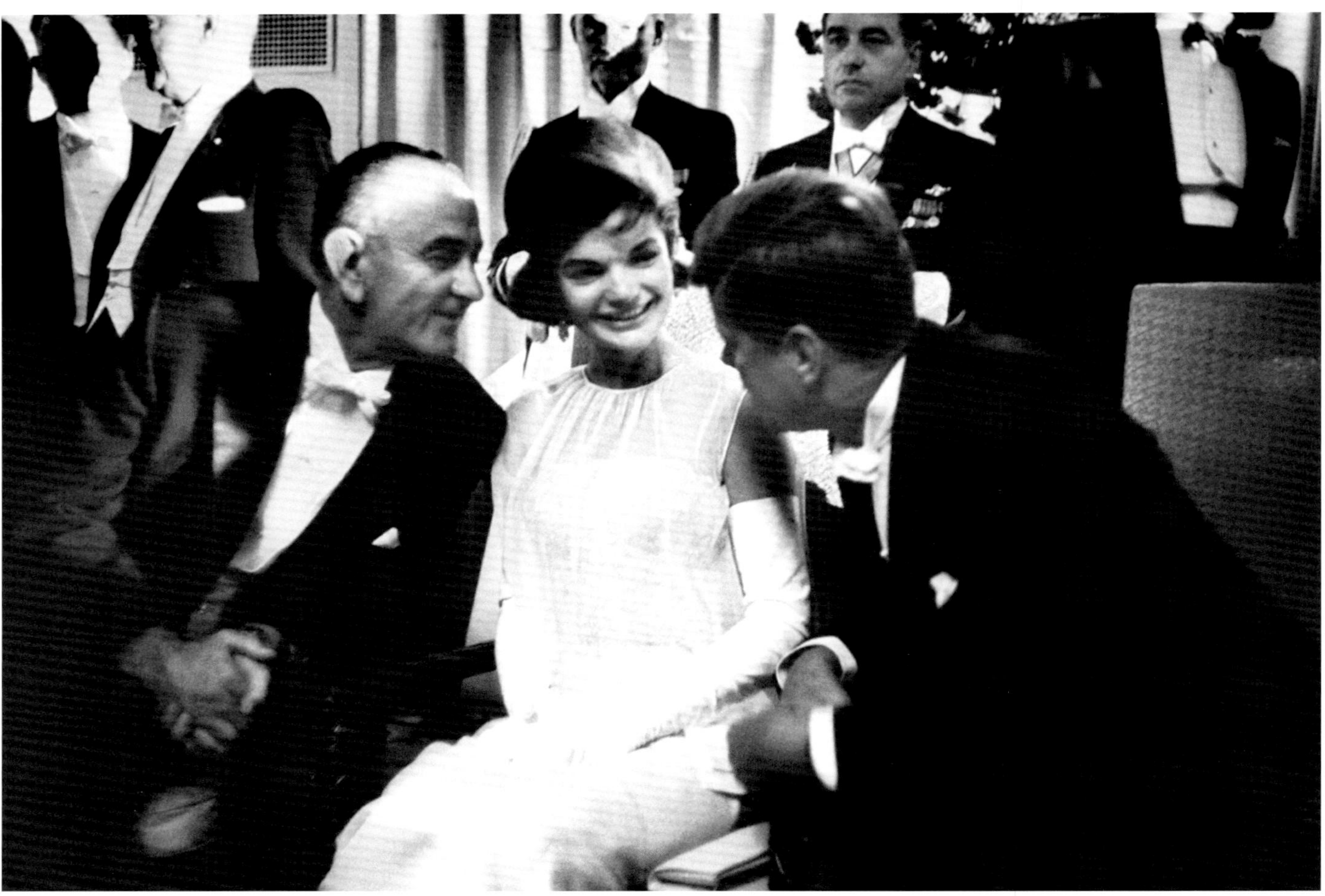

ABOVE *January 20, 1961.* Seated between the newly sworn-in vice president
and president, the First Lady and her Oleg Cassini gown were the subject of
much attention at an inaugural ball. While she loved fashion, Jackie tried to
downplay it, especially on the campaign trail. While campaigning in 1960
she denied a gossip item claiming that she and her mother-in-law spent a
combined $30,000 a year on clothes from Paris with the line, "I couldn't
spend that much unless I wore sable underwear." *Photo, Alfred Eisenstaedt*

OPPOSITE *January 20, 1961.* Of the five inaugural balls that evening, the
biggest was held at the National Armory in Washington, D.C., where,
as one account put it, "two-and-a-half acres of Kennedy fans waited elbow-
to-elbow." *Photo, Jacques Lowe*

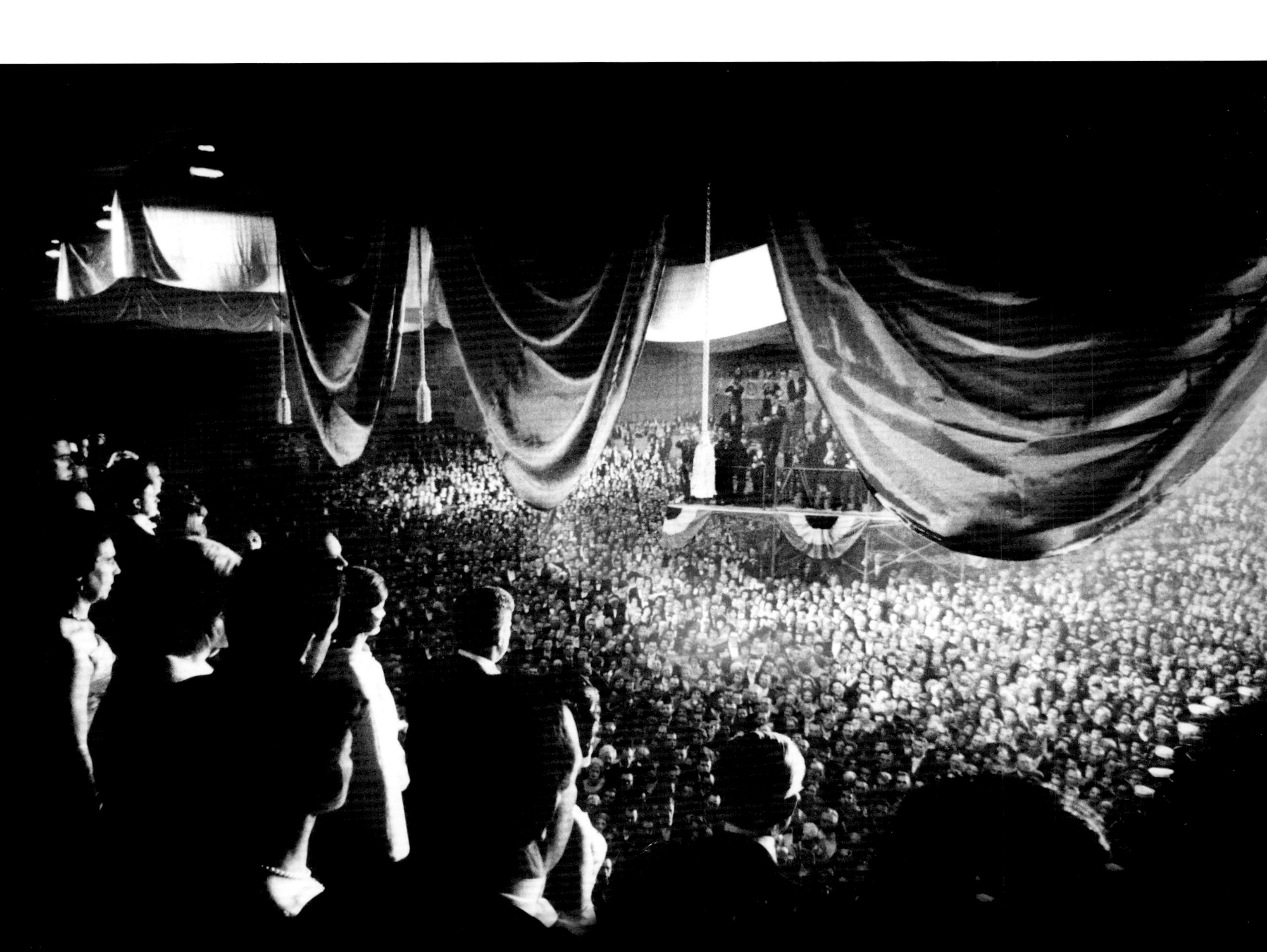

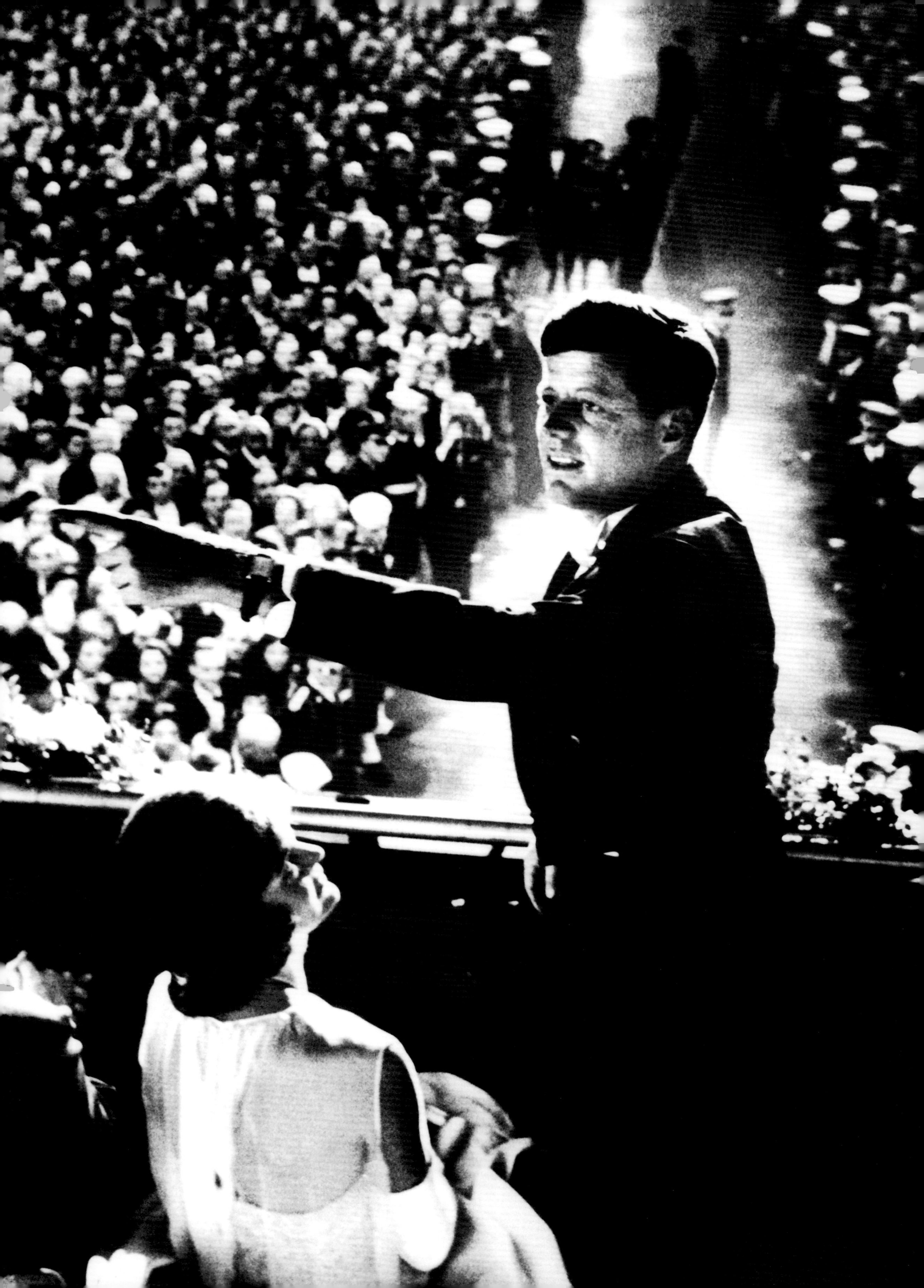

"The torch has been passed to a new generation of Americans, born in this century, tempered by war, disciplined by a hard and bitter peace, proud of our ancient heritage — and unwilling to witness or permit the slow undoing of those human rights to which this nation has always been committed, and to which we are committed today at home and around the world."

—John F. Kennedy, Inaugural Address, Washington, D.C., January 20, 1961

OPPOSITE *January 20, 1961.* Though Jackie retired early after attending three of the inaugural balls, at 1 A.M., Jack continued on for all five, with a few more stops during and after the balls. The president managed to slip away to Sinatra's cast party at the Statler-Hilton and mingle with the guests there. And later that night, at about 2 A.M., the new president visited the Georgetown home of Joseph Alsop, a newspaper columnist and old friend, where another party was underway. It was 3:30 by the time JFK made it to the White House where he would sleep for the first time, briefly, before beginning his administration the next day, a Saturday, with a staff meeting at 9 A.M. *Photo, Paul Schutzer*

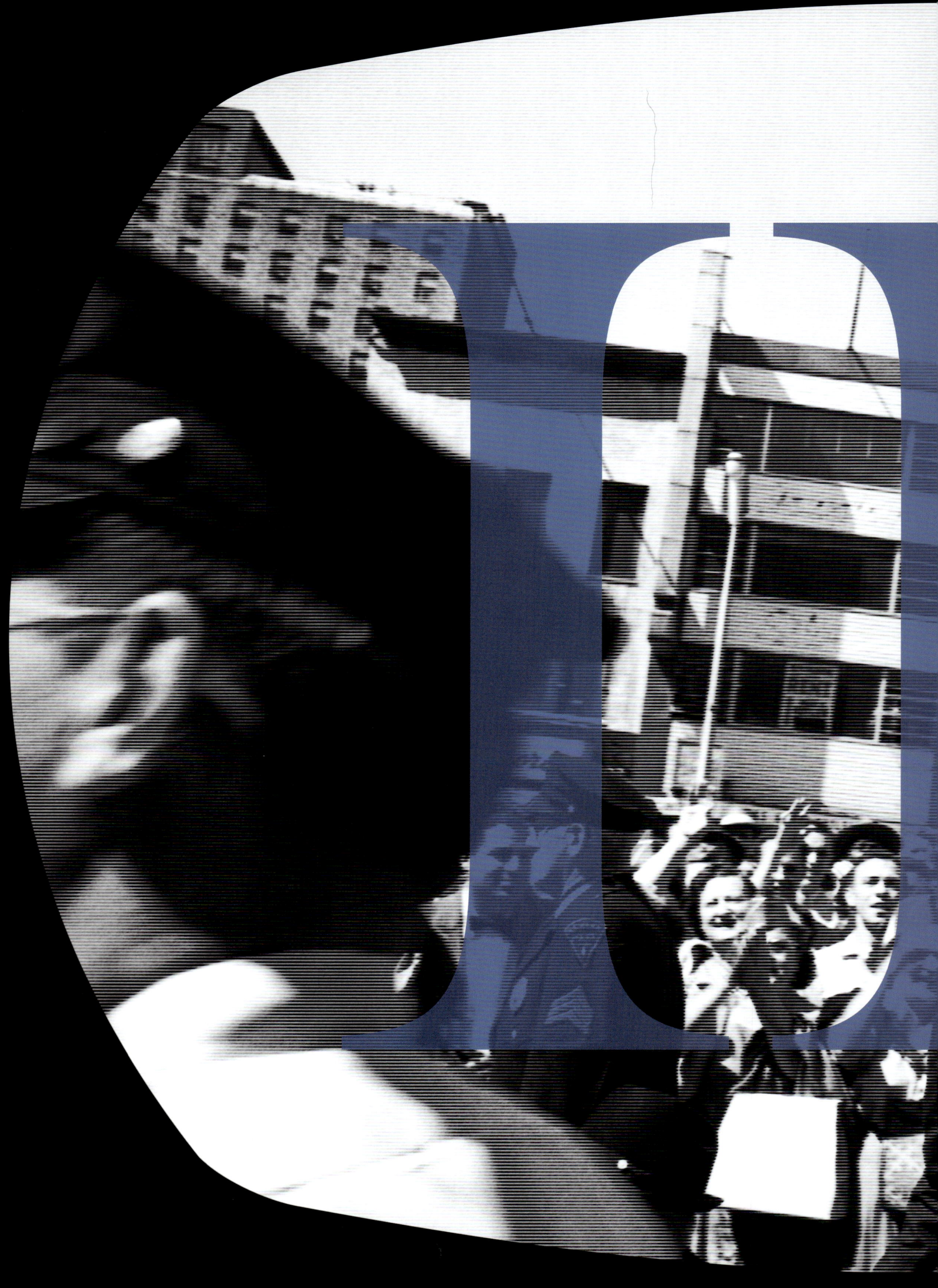

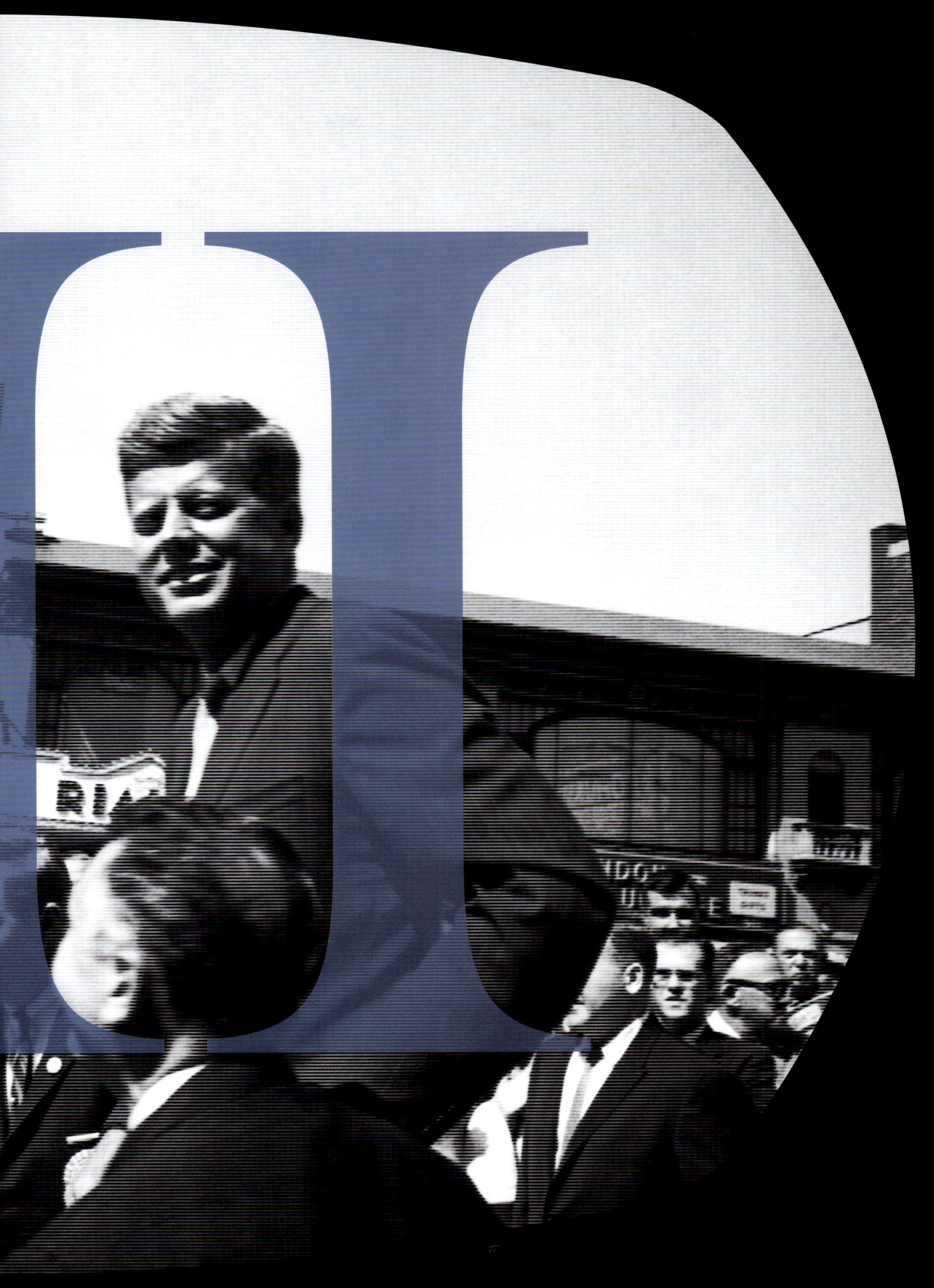

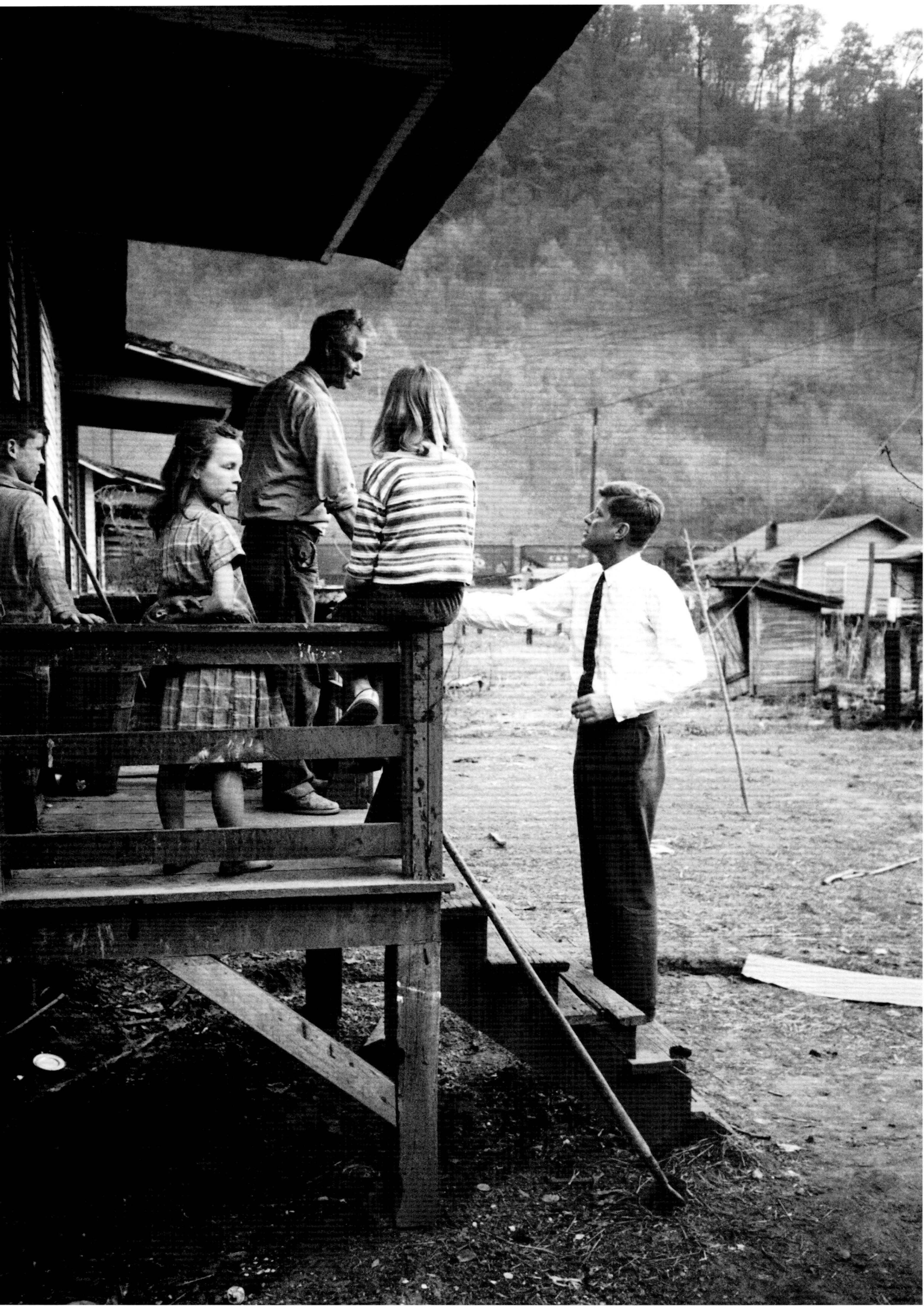

January 2, 1960: John F. Kennedy announces candidacy for Democratic presidential nomination from the U.S. Senate Caucus Room.

January 3: First TV interview as presidential candidate on NBC's *Meet the Press.*

January 14: Addresses National Press Club in Washington, D.C., with speech, "The Presidency in 1960," criticizing Eisenhower administration while calling for activist presidency ahead.

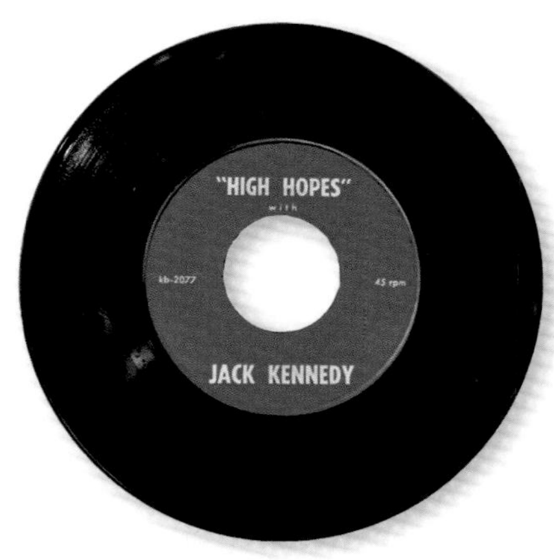

PREVIOUS SPREAD **The crowds thicken in the final days of the campaign, Long Island, New York, November 6.** *Photo, Burton Berinsky*

OPPOSITE **Kennedy greets a family in rural West Virginia during the primaries.** *Photo, Hank Walker*

ABOVE **In February 1960 Frank Sinatra recorded "High Hopes" with lyrics that "back Jack," making the popular tune the unofficial song of the campaign.**

January 21: Announces bid for Wisconsin's April 5 primary in Milwaukee, battling Minnesota Senator Hubert Humphrey. Going up against popular liberal from neighboring state regarded as highly risky move.

January 25: Despite frigid weather, crowds turn out to meet Jack and Jackie in Nashua, New Hampshire. Visit makes front-page news.

January 30: Meets with David O. McKay, president of LDS (Mormon) Church, in Salt Lake City, Utah.

January 31: Reno, Nevada.

February: Frank Sinatra records "anonymous" version of his 1959 hit song "High Hopes" for campaign. Released as 45-rpm record for promotional use and jukebox distribution with "Vote for Kennedy" lyrics, and B-side recording of "All the Way."

February 1: First sit-in by four black students at "whites only" lunch counter in Greensboro, North Carolina.

February 7–8: Stop in Las Vegas with younger brother, Teddy, Western states coordinator, and campaign staff. While there, they take in some "Rat Pack" shows at Sands Hotel. Sinatra introduces and applauds JFK from stage, and invites him and entourage for private dinner. Guests include Judith Campbell, who will become Kennedy's mistress.

February 9–12: Oregon and California.

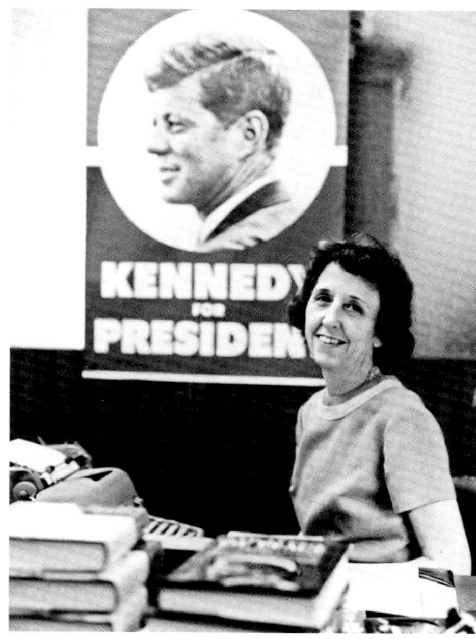

ABOVE **Evelyn Lincoln, JFK's longtime personal secretary, in her office, 1960.** *Photo, Genevieve Naylor*

March 4: Gallup poll ranks Kennedy and Nixon evenly matched (up from JFK's 47 percent in previous January poll).

March 5–7: Three-day swing through New Hampshire, whose right-wing Republican Governor Wesley Powell accuses JFK of being "soft on Communism."

March 8: Kennedy and Nixon win respective parties' primaries in New Hampshire, home of country's first primary election. JFK garners more votes than previous Democratic candidates.

March 16: Opens campaign headquarters in Charleston, West Virginia.

March 21: Enters Indiana primary set for May 3. Baptist demonstrators in Indianapolis challenge him to debate on the Catholic president question.

March 24: Missouri Senator Stuart Symington announces candidacy for Democratic presidential nomination. Says he will not run in any primaries because he believes results do not reflect voter preferences as accurately as convention will.

April: Jackie Kennedy takes hiatus from campaigning on the road. She is pregnant with son John, and given earlier history with difficult pregnancies, doctors insist she keeps campaign appearances local. Jack's sisters will take active role in appearing by his side as he crisscrosses the country.

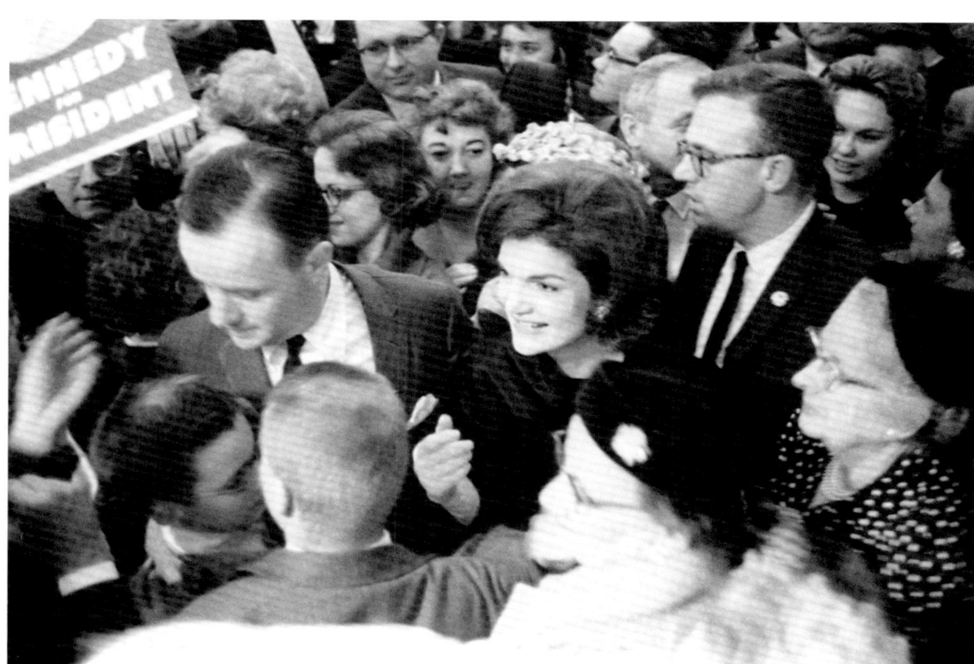

LEFT **Jackie was a major presence on the road throughout the spring primaries.** *Photo, Bob Sandberg*

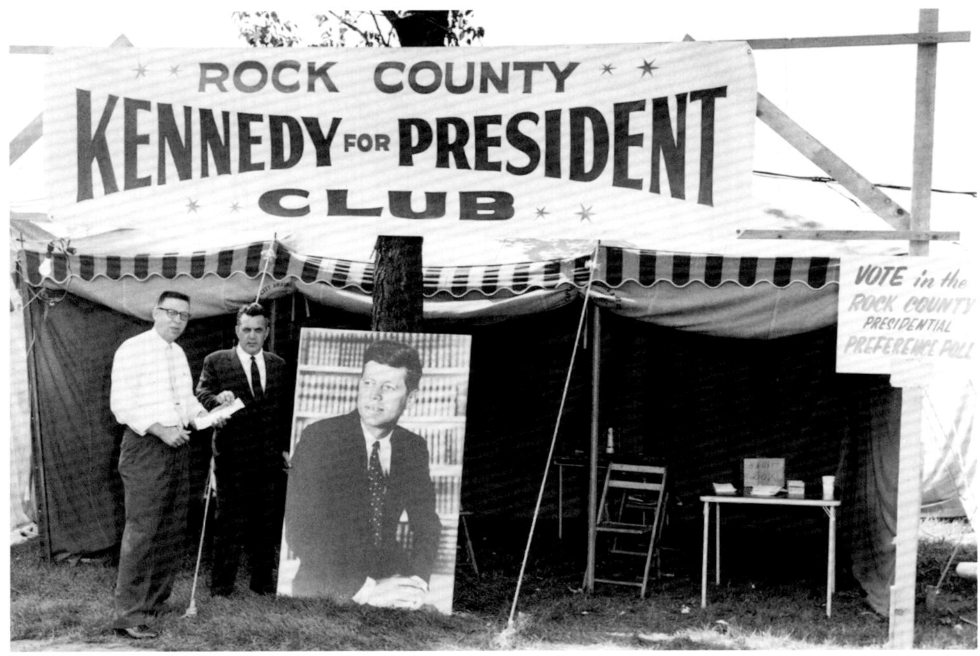

ABOVE A Kennedy Club in Janesville, Wisconsin, 1959. *Photo, Anonymous*

April 5: Kennedy defeats Hubert Humphrey in Wisconsin—478,118 to 372,034. Huge margin of victory, won in part from heavily Catholic districts, does not impress Democratic party bosses who remain doubtful of JFK's broader appeal.

April 5 – 6: Campaign manager Bobby Kennedy and team arrive in West Virginia, where JFK has suffered a serious reversal in the polls. Coverage of the "Catholic issue" in the heavily Protestant state has reversed JFK's earlier 70 – 30 advantage over Humphrey to 60 – 40 for Humphrey.

April – May: West Virginia now key battleground state. Candidates, campaign staff, friends, family, and various West Virginia surrogates — celebrities and politicians alike — blanket state, covering large cities and small towns, coal fields and factory floors, using outdoor rallies, radio broadcasts, TV ads, and more. It is a political fight to the death, as winner gains significant momentum for nomination.

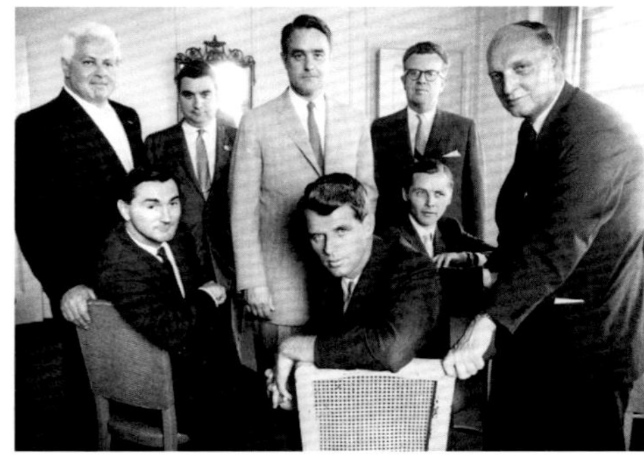

ABOVE Bobby Kennedy and campaign staffers, counter-clockwise from center: scheduler Kenneth O'Donnell, communications aide Hy Raskin, press secretary Pierre Salinger, organizer Sargent Shriver, director Lawrence O'Brien, finance chairman Steve Smith, and political strategist John Bailey. *Photo, Hank Walker*

April 11: "Stop Kennedy" drive within Democratic Party backed by West Virginia's Senator Robert Byrd, who tells voters at one point, "If you are for Adlai Stevenson, Senator Stuart Symington, Senator [Lyndon] Johnson or John Doe, this primary may be your last chance to stop Kennedy."

April 12: JFK defeats four rivals in Illinois primary.

April 15: (SNCC) Student Nonviolent Coordinating Committee formed in Raleigh, North Carolina.

April 26: Wins Pennsylvania primary with 71 percent of vote and Massachusetts with 92 percent of vote.

May 1: American U2 spy plane shot down in Soviet Union.

May 3: Wins in Indiana with 81 percent.

May 4: In what is considered to be first televised "debate" between U.S. presidential candidates, Kennedy and Humphrey go head-to-head on West Virginia television. Most consider JFK to be winner.

May 8: Two days before West Virginia primary, Franklin Delano Roosevelt Jr., whose father was a much-loved figure throughout state, hosts TV spot with Kennedy to discuss his religion and hopes for presidency. According to Theodore H. White, author of *The Making of the President, 1960*, JFK's reply at the moment ("made from the gut") was "the finest TV broadcast I have ever heard any political candidate make."

May 10: Wins West Virginia and Nebraska primaries. In West Virginia, JFK soundly defeats Humphrey with 61 percent of vote, carrying 48 of 55 counties. Next day Humphrey withdraws from race. Aides Dave Powers and Kenny O'Donnell will later write: "[Y]ou could say that Hubert Humphrey nominated Jack by

running against him in that primary and giving him that opportunity to lick the religious issue in a showdown test that certainly must be a monument in American political history." Still, JFK's religion will dog him through election day.

May 13: Students and teachers in San Francisco organize major demonstration against House Committee on Un-American Activities (HUAC).

May 17: JFK sweeps Maryland primary with 71 percent of vote.

May 20: Takes 51 percent of vote in Oregon, defeating favorite son Senator Wayne Morse, as well as Missouri's Senator Stuart Symington and Senate Majority Leader Lyndon Baines Johnson from Texas.

May 29: Meets with Adlai Stevenson at his home in Libertyville, Illinois. Stevenson tells JFK he is remaining "neutral," but JFK privately believes Stevenson is "neutral for Lyndon Johnson."

May 31: All 19 Scripps-Howard newspapers, including *New York World-Telegram & Sun*, endorse Johnson.

June 4: JFK woos several delegates away from LBJ in New Mexico primary.

June 10: Former first lady Eleanor Roosevelt endorses Stevenson, who is not officially seeking Democratic nomination.

June 16: Guest appearance on *The Jack Paar Show*.

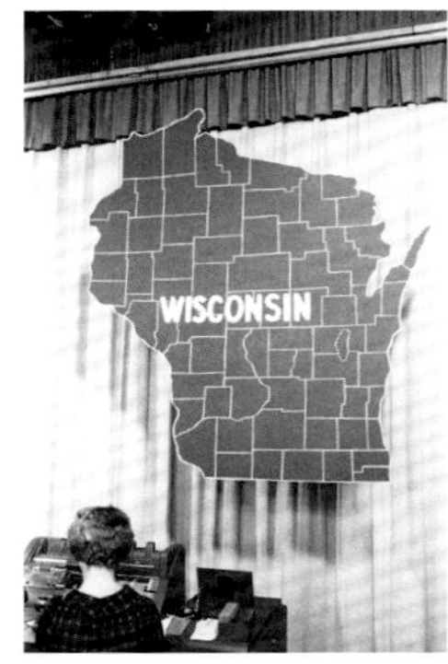

LEFT CBS affiliate WITI reports that the state of Wisconsin goes for Kennedy on April 5 after hotly contested primary battle. *Photo, Bob Sandberg*

July 2: In week before Democratic National Convention, former President Harry S. Truman holds televised news conference from hometown of Independence, Missouri, where he asserts that JFK is too young to be president and should decline nomination. Also claims to prefer Stuart Symington, Lyndon Johnson, and other candidates, and charges that Kennedy's people will rig convention.

July 4: In reply to Truman's remarks, JFK holds press conference in New York. Replies that his 14 years in the House and Senate give him more experience in national elective office than any successful president candidate in the 20th century, including Woodrow Wilson, FDR, and Truman.

July 5: Lyndon B. Johnson officially announces candidacy. Has eschewed primaries in favor of "cloakroom" campaign in Washington, wooing key congressman and senators to help win nomination at convention. Johnson asserts that Kennedy has less than 600 of required 761 delegates needed for nomination. Johnson claimed he had at least 500.

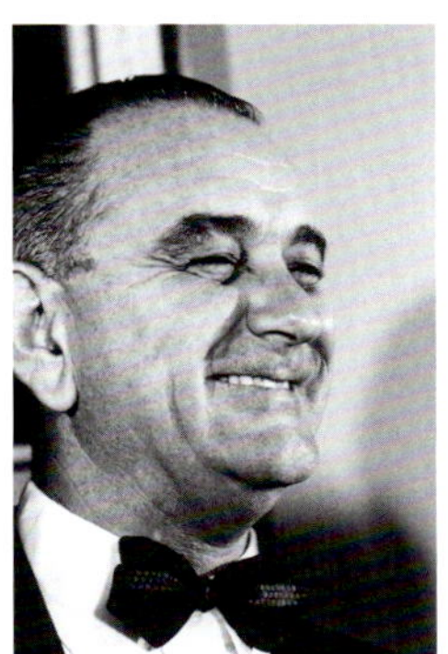

LEFT **Of LBJ Mailer observed, "When he smiled the corners of his mouth squeezed gloom; when he was pious, his eyes twinkled irony…."** *Photo, Bob Gomel*

July 5 or 6: Norman Mailer arrives in Los Angeles to cover the Democratic National Convention with press pass from *Esquire* magazine. It is his first political reporting assignment. His celebrity gives him access to key events at convention, though he is not granted an interview with JFK until later in month.

July 8–9: Adlai Stevenson emerges as stealth candidate, telling followers and media just prior to the Democratic National Convention that if drafted he would do his utmost to win. The Democratic presidential nominee in 1952 and 1956, he had lost on both occasions to Republican opponent Dwight D. Eisenhower.

July 9: Kennedy arrives in Los Angeles for convention.

July 10 (morning): Addresses meeting of National Association for the Advancement of Colored People (NAACP) at Shrine Auditorium. Crowd is initially cold to him, with some booing, but JFK eventually wins audience over when he vows to end segregation.

July 10 (day): Amidst pre-convention politicking, California's Governor Pat Brown also endorses JFK and Illinois delegation, led by Mayor Richard Daley, delivers 59.5 votes for Kennedy.

July 10 (evening): Sinatra and friends help fill "big donors" fund-raising dinner at the Beverly Hilton Hotel. Sinatra and Judy Garland perform for more than 2,800 guests.

July 11: Opening ceremony for Democratic National Convention in Los Angeles Sports Arena. Many Hollywood guests appear, including Sinatra, Janet Leigh, Tony Curtis, Peter Lawford, Nat "King" Cole, Shirley MacLaine, Lee Marvin, Edward G. Robinson, Lloyd Bridges, and Vincent Price. When Sammy Davis Jr. is introduced, he is booed by Mississippi and Alabama

delegations in protest of his imminent marriage to Swedish actress May Britt. Devastated by the racist slurs of the crowd, Davis manages to sing through the national anthem, but leaves immediately after.

July 12 (day): After LBJ challenges JFK to debate, they meet before joint gathering of Texas and Massachusetts delegations at Biltmore Hotel, a debate which most believe Kennedy wins. Author David Pietrusza describes it thus: "Johnson used an axe, Kennedy wielded a rapier, leaving LBJ in shreds." Afterward, Johnson is not able to expand his delegate support beyond the South.

July 12 (evening): Nominations begin with Orville Freeman for Kennedy, Sam Rayburn for Johnson, and Eugene McCarthy, in the most crowd-stirring speech of the night, for Stevenson.

July 13: John F. Kennedy wins nomination on first ballot. With 761 votes needed, JFK receives 806. LBJ comes in second with 409.

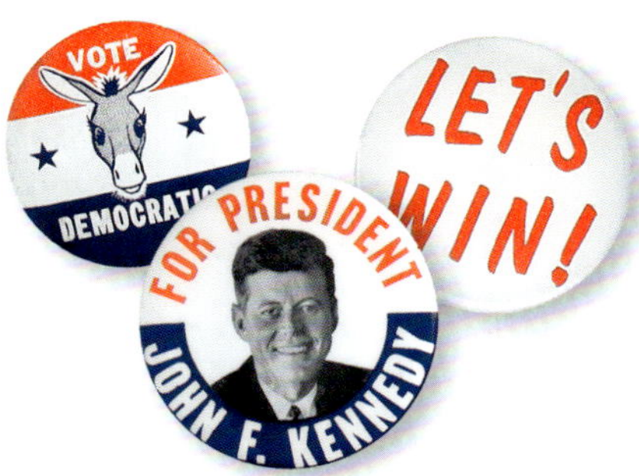

July 14: Against the wishes of many of his closest advisors, JFK invites LBJ to share the presidential ticket. Much to his surprise, Johnson accepts.

July 15: Kennedy appears before crowd of some 80,000 in the Los Angeles Memorial Coliseum to deliver his formal acceptance speech, "The New Frontier."

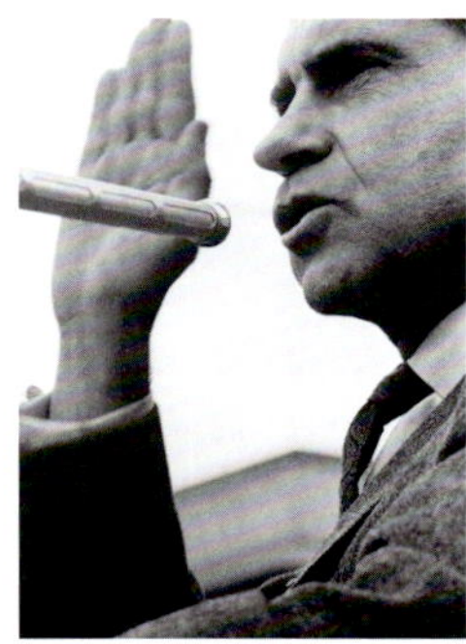

LEFT **Republican rival and sitting Vice President Richard Nixon at a campaign fund-raiser in the last week of the general campaign.** *Photo, Ron Galella*

July 16: Following the convention, JFK returns to Boston and Hyannis Port, for period of post-convention rest, meetings with party leaders, and planning for fall campaign.

July 25–28: Republican National Convention held at International Amphitheater in Chicago, Illinois.

July 29: JFK holds separate meetings with Stevenson, Johnson, and others at home in Hyannis Port.

Early August: Mailer visits Hyannis Port on two occasions, where he interviews the candidate and is especially charmed by Jackie.

August 14: JFK meets with Eleanor Roosevelt in Hyde Park, New York.

August 20: Flies to Harry Truman's hometown of Independence to seek support from former president.

September 3–7: General campaign kicks off Labor Day weekend with stops in Maine, Alaska, Michigan, Idaho, Washington, and Oregon.

BELOW **Kennedy accepts his party's nomination on July 15, the last day of the Democratic National Convention. He delivered his "New Frontier" speech to an estimated 80,000 people at the Los Angeles Memorial Coliseum.** *Photo, Ed Clark*

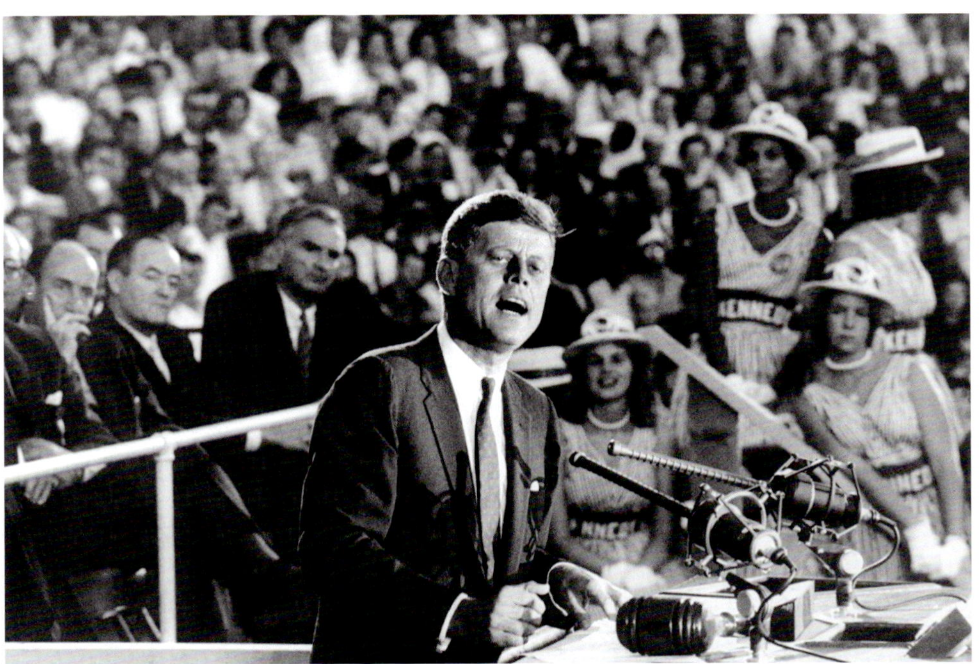

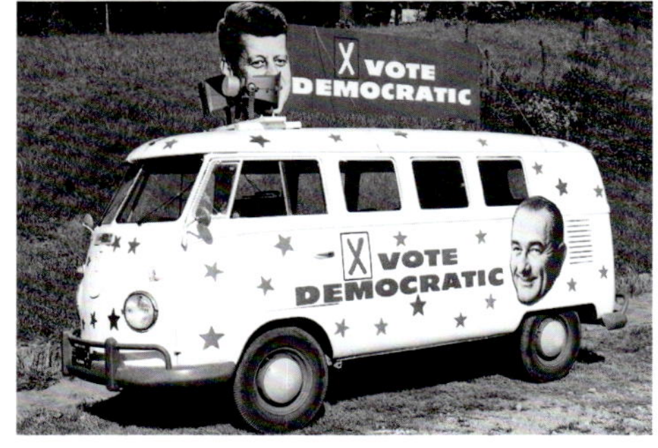

ABOVE **A campaign wagon for the Democratic State Campaign Committee of Alabama.** *Photo, Anonymous*

September 7: Hollywood film stars Janet Leigh and Tony Curtis open home to Ted Kennedy and 2,000 guests for "Key Women for Kennedy" fund-raiser. Sinatra performs.

September 8–10: Whistle-stop tour through Central California.

September 11: Arrives in Texas, where he will draw large crowds in El Paso, Forth Worth, and San Antonio.

September 12: In speech before Greater Houston Ministerial Association, declares, "I am not the Catholic candidate for president. I am the Democratic Party candidate for president who also happens to be a Catholic. I do not speak for my church on public matter—and the church does not speak for me."

September 14–19: Campaigns at more than 20 locations throughout New York, New Jersey, Pennsylvania, Maryland, and North Carolina. While in New York, makes first visit to "Dr. Feelgood," Max Jacobson, who prescribes painkillers.

September 19: CBS airs Walter Cronkite interview, "Mr. Kennedy: A Profile."

September 23: Salt Lake City, Utah; Cheyenne, Wyoming; Denver, Colorado.

September 25: Arrives in Chicago, ahead of first TV debate with Nixon.

September 26: First nationally televised presidential debate, produced by CBS from Chicago. An estimated 70 million viewers tune in to watch. Another 15 million listen on radio. Producer Don Hewitt will later say, "When that [first] debate was over, I realized that we didn't have to wait for an election day. We just elected a president. It all happened on television."

September 30: Interviewed by NBC's Chet Huntley and David Brinkley at home in Hyannis Port.

October 1–6: Illinois, Minnesota, Indiana, and Ohio.

October 4: Republican "truth squad" charges that JFK was absent on more than one quarter of

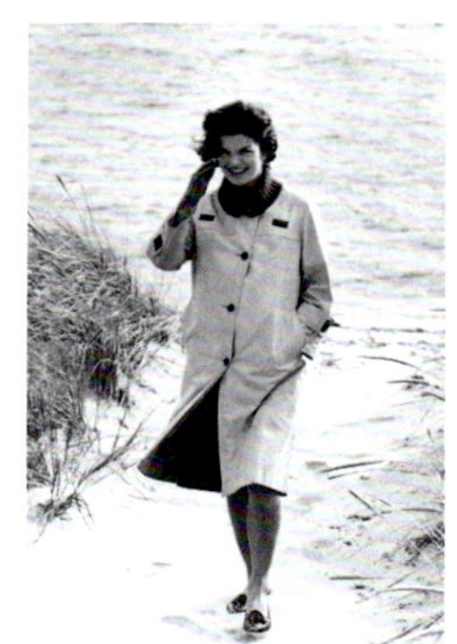

LEFT Although Jackie Kennedy joined her husband campaigning in the early and late months of the 1960 presidential race, due to her pregnancy, she spent a good deal of time resting at Hyannis Port. *Photo, Anonymous*

record votes taken in Senate between 1953–1960, asserting that presidency "is no job for a playboy."

October 7: Second "Great Debate," broadcast from Washington, D.C., by NBC. Nixon is given a slight edge.

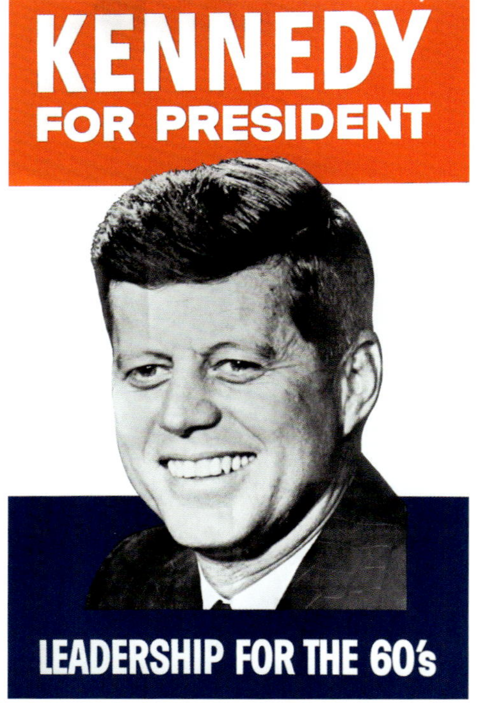

October 18: November issue of *Esquire* magazine hits newsstands with Mailer's essay, "Superman Comes to the Supermarket," inside. Essay will come to be regarded as important breakthrough for "New Journalism" of the 1960s, and launchpad for author's interest in politics.

October 8–10: Kentucky, Ohio, Georgia, South Carolina, Pennsylvania.

October 12: Breakfast with Mrs. Roosevelt in New York City. Followed by appearances at Columbus Day Parade, Long Island Fair, and East Harlem Puerto Rican rally; and speech before National Council of Women in New York. Although limited in her travel due to her pregnancy, Jackie rejoins the campaign for appearances in New York area.

October 13: Third Nixon–Kennedy debate shows candidates on split screen for first time in TV history—Kennedy from New York and Nixon from Los Angeles. Night flight to Ann Arbor, Michigan, where JFK first proposes the idea of the Peace Corps to late-night audience at University of Michigan.

October 14–17: Michigan, Pennsylvania, New Jersey, Delaware, Maryland, Ohio.

October 18: Miami, Tampa; Jacksonville, Florida.

October 19: Ticker-tape parade through New York City and rally at Rockefeller Plaza, with Jackie

ABOVE **Campaign poster, Summer 1960.** *Designers, Donald Wilson and Bernard Quint*

LEFT "You can only vote once on election day," Kennedy said, "but if you will go out and register one person between now and the time of the election in November, then you can vote twice." *Photo, Burton Berinsky*

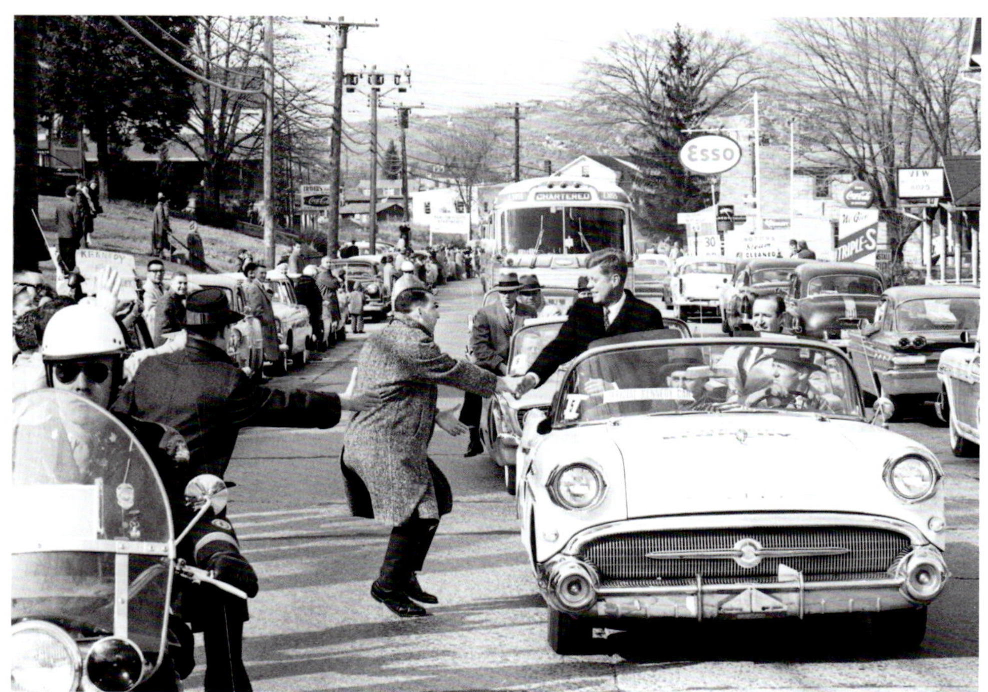

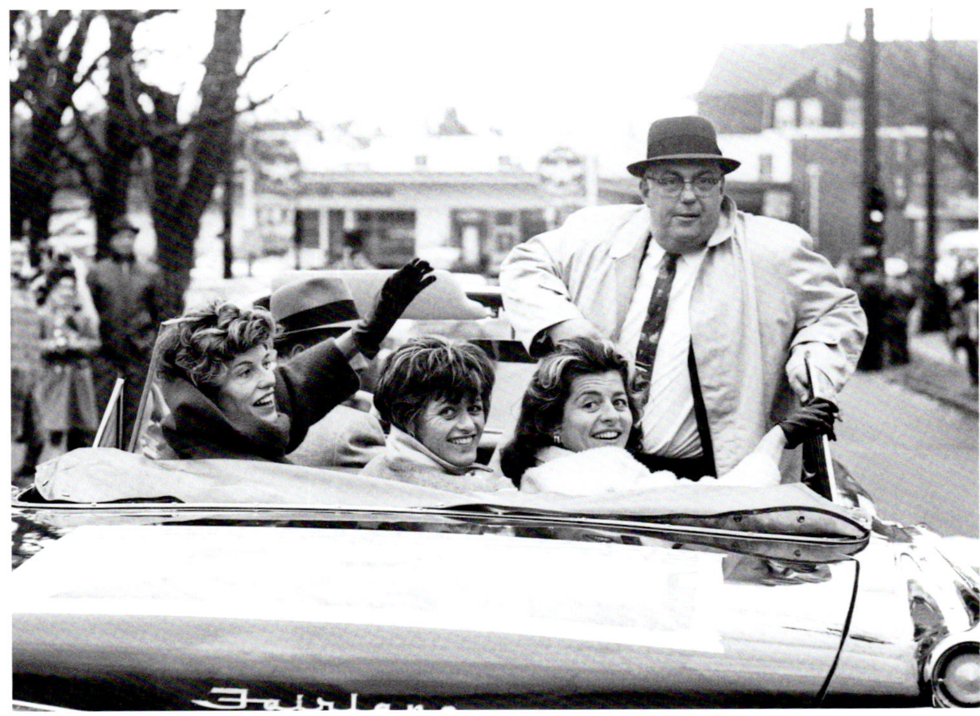

ABOVE Sisters Eunice, Jean, and Pat give a last push in Hartford on election eve. *Photo, Burton Berinsky*

BELOW Hosted by ABC, the third of four "great debates" was a television milestone, utilizing split-screen technology to broadcast the first bicoastal presidential debate. *Photo, Anonymous*

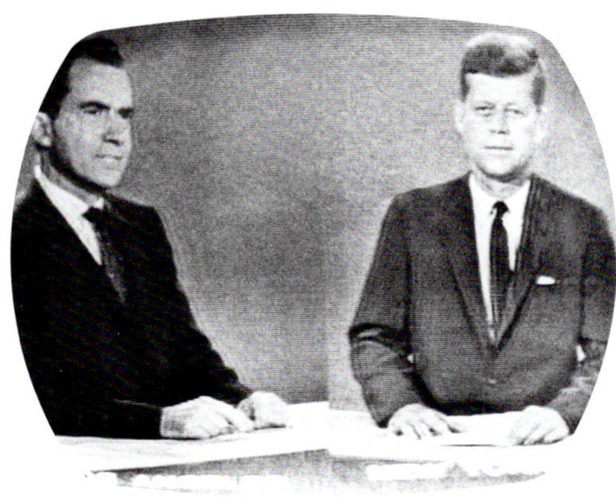

by his side. Later that evening, JFK attends Alfred E. Smith dinner, as do Nixon and New York Governor Nelson Rockefeller.

October 21: Fourth and final "Great Debate" from ABC's studios in New York City. Survey of viewers in 23 major cities calls it a draw.

October 22–23: Missouri, Kansas, Wisconsin.

October 24: *Life* magazine endorses Nixon for president.

October 24–27: Illinois, Michigan, New Jersey, New York.

October 26: JFK phones MLK's wife, Coretta Scott King, to express support of husband after arrest during a lunch counter sit-in. RFK appeals to

Georgia's Governor Ernest Vandiver and judge Oscar Mitchell to release MLK on bail. He walks free the following day.

October 28–31: Pennsylvania.

October 30: Kennedy appears on *Face the Nation*. *Chicago Tribune* endorses Nixon.

November 1–3: California, Arizona, New Mexico, Texas, Oklahoma.

November 1: MLK publicly thanks JFK for support in release from prison in Reidsville, Georgia. While not an official endorsement of the candidate, statement thought to help turn out black vote.

November 2: Actor Henry Fonda does one-hour television program with Jackie for campaign.

November 4: Torchlight parade through Chicago. Estimated 1.5 million turn out along parade route and to hear JFK speech at Chicago Stadium.

November 5: New York City; Waterbury, Connecticut.

November 6: Nixon runs 32-page advertising supplements in Sunday newspapers, and on TV preempts CBS's *General Electric Theater* with 30-minute appeal to voters. Gallup poll results: JFK 49 percent, 48 percent Nixon, 3 percent undecided.

November 7 (afternoon): Nixon campaign runs first televised telethon in presidential campaign history on all three networks — ABC, CBS, and NBC. The four-hour special (2 P. M. – 6 P. M. EST) features Nixon and Hollywood celebrities such as Ginger Rogers, Lloyd Nolan, and Robert Young.

November 7 (evening): JFK follows Nixon on ABC with his sisters from Manchester, New Hampshire. Republican Thomas E. Dewey, former New York governor and presidential candidate, follows JFK in rebuttal.

November 8 (Election Day): Jack and Jackie vote near their Boston home then travel to Hyannis Port, joining family, friends, and core campaign staff to monitor election returns. Early results from large cities in the East and Midwest give JFK large initial lead in both popular and electoral vote. It appears he has certain victory. However, after some premature TV declarations of JFK winning in selected states — and some retractions — an hours-long "too close to call" contest sets in, stretching into the next day.

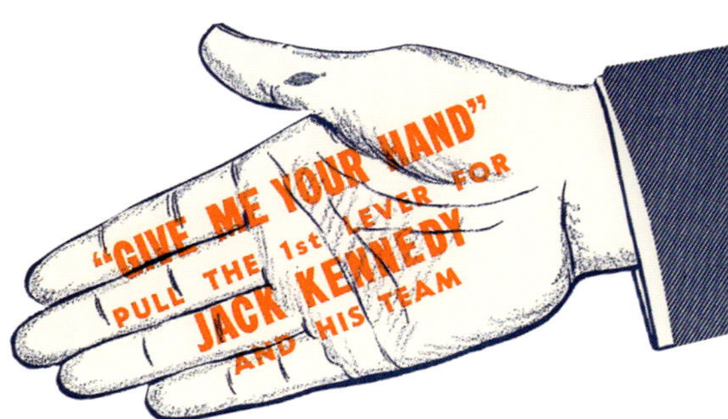

November 9 (early morning): As last election returns come in during early morning hours from rural and suburban Midwest and Western states, Nixon begins to catch up. Some newspapers, including *The New York Times*, prepare "Kennedy Elected" headline copy, but still not confirmed.

BELOW Kennedy addresses a crowd outside Central Harlem's Hotel Theresa on October 12. Only weeks earlier, Fidel Castro and Nikita Khrushchev had met in this very location during the U.N. General Assembly. *Photo, Burton Berinsky*

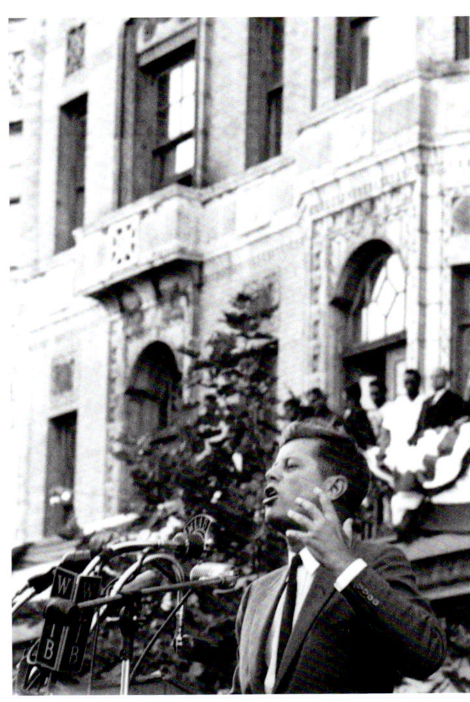

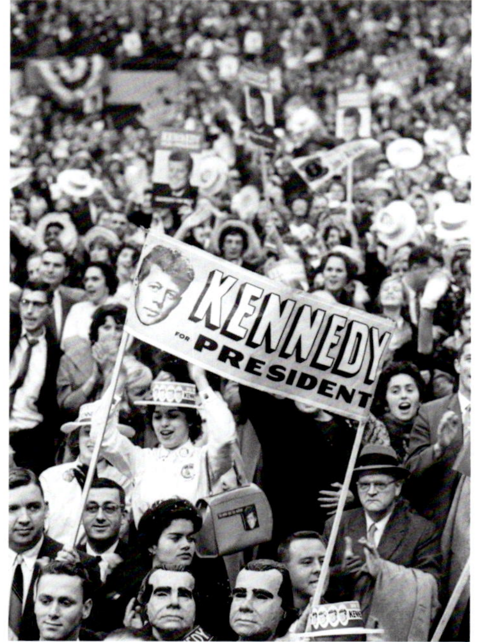

ABOVE In his last live appearance of the campaign, Kennedy gets a hero's welcome at Boston Garden on election eve. *Photo, Burton Berinsky*

BELOW With wife Pat by his side, Richard Nixon delivers his "conditional concession" speech, admitting the tide had turned in Kennedy's favor. *Photo, Burton Berinsky*

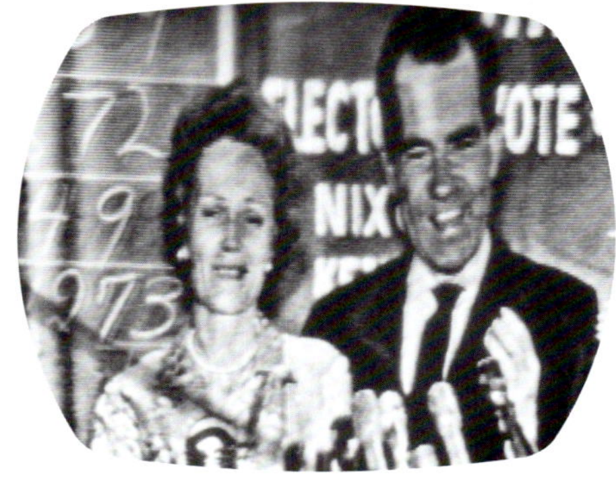

November 9 (early morning): Nixon makes television appearance from the Ambassador Hotel in Los Angeles after midnight, but does not formally concede. Watching on television from Hyannis Port, Kennedy decides to go to bed around 4 A.M.

November 9 (afternoon): After Minnesota's 11 electoral votes put JFK over the top, Nixon sends Kennedy congratulatory telegram. At Hyannis Armory President-elect John F. Kennedy makes brief acceptance speech to press and supporters, many of whom have waited up all night. Kennedy has defeated Nixon in closest presidential election of 20th century.

November 10: JFK heads to Palm Beach, Florida, for short rest at family home there.

November 14: Kennedy and Nixon meet privately in Key Biscayne, Florida, and later with press

RIGHT Kennedy delivers his inaugural speech from the East Portico of the U.S. Capitol in Washington, D.C., January 20, 1961. *Photo, Anonymous*

to unify the nation after such a close national election. On this date, absentee ballots are still being counted in California, where JFK's narrow lead of 24,091 votes is later overtaken by Nixon, who is awarded California's 32 electoral votes. But JFK takes Pennsylvania and New York in final electoral count.

November 25: John Fitzgerald Kennedy Jr. is born at Georgetown University Hospital.

November–December: JFK begins thinking about and assembling his cabinet. Releases names of selections one or two at a time, ending on December 17 with California insurance executive J. Edward Day to serve as postmaster general. One controversial appointment is that of brother Bobby to serve as attorney general.

December 6: President-elect John F. Kennedy meets with President Eisenhower to discuss handover.

December: Frank Sinatra and Peter Lawford start to plan star-studded, preinaugural gala and Democratic Party fund-raiser to be staged at National Armory in Washington, D.C.

December 25: Kennedys spend Christmas holidays with family in Palm Beach, where they will stay through early January.

January 3, 1961: Photographer Richard Avedon makes series of portraits of Jack and Jackie with Caroline and John-John, some of which appear in February issues of *Harper's Bazaar* and *LOOK* magazines.

January 19: On eve of inauguration, inaugural gala opens amid a snowstorm in Washington. Among the performers are Frank Sinatra, Harry Belafonte, Milton Berle, Nat King Cole, Ella Fitzgerald, Gene Kelly, Jimmy Durante, Mahalia Jackson, Bette Davis, Sidney Poitier,

and others. JFK and JBK attend, with JFK staying until 1:30 A.M., then attending another party thrown by his father until 3:30 A.M.

January 20 (morning): Attends Mass. Reviews inaugural address. Meets with outgoing president, Dwight D. Eisenhower.

January 20 (noon): John F. Kennedy becomes 35th president of the United States of America. At inaugural ceremony, Marian Anderson sings "The Star-Spangled Banner" and poet Robert Frost recites "The Gift Outright." JFK is administered the oath of office by Chief Justice Earl Warren. In his address, JFK declares: "the torch has been passed to a new generation of Americans." He appeals to Americans to "ask not what your country can do for you, ask what you can do for your country." The day's activities also include a luncheon, inaugural parade, and five inaugural balls that evening.

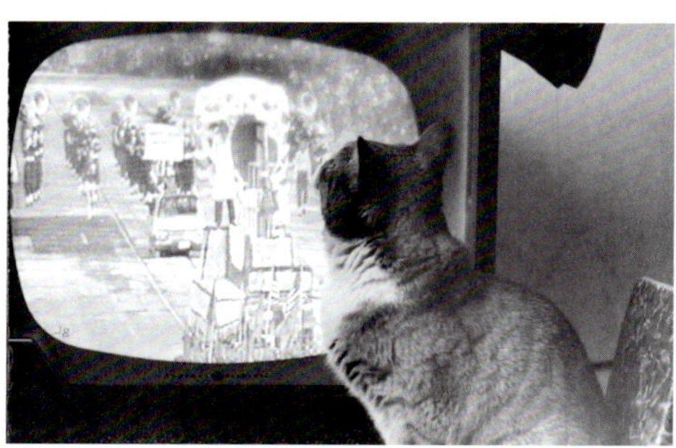

ABOVE An estimated 80 million Americans tuned in to watch the inauguration. Millions more around the world heard it on the radio. *Photo, Isidore Leff*

OPPOSITE If Yousuf Karsh made Jackie look like royalty, he made Jack look like he was president already. When their portrait sitting began in JFK's Senate office in fall 1960, Kennedy asked if he could trade ties with the photographer. Karsh accepted, and kept the swapped tie in the bargain. *Photo, Yousuf Karsh*

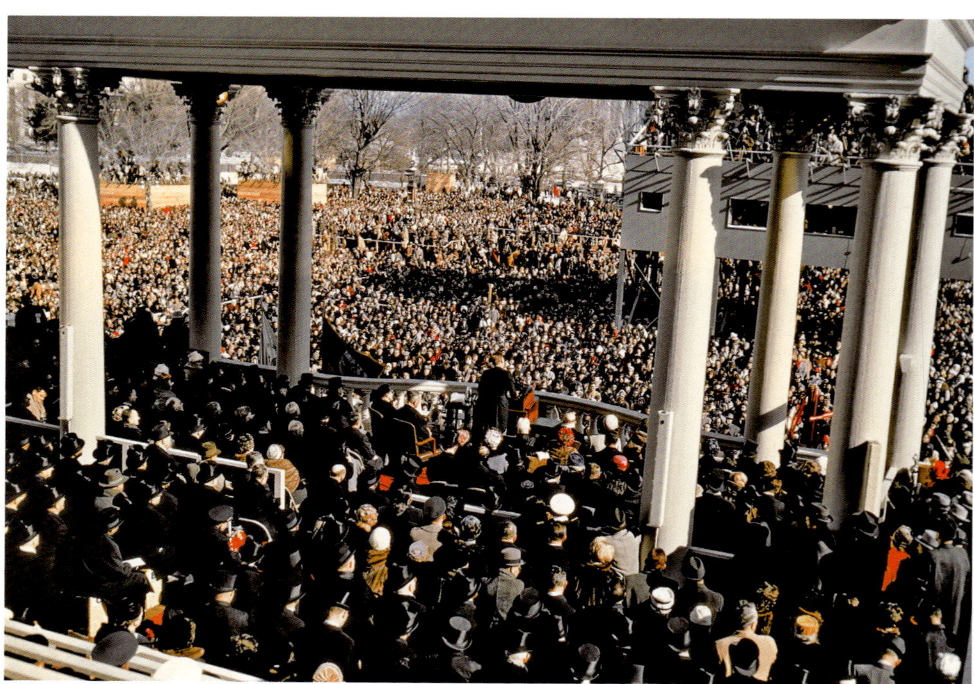

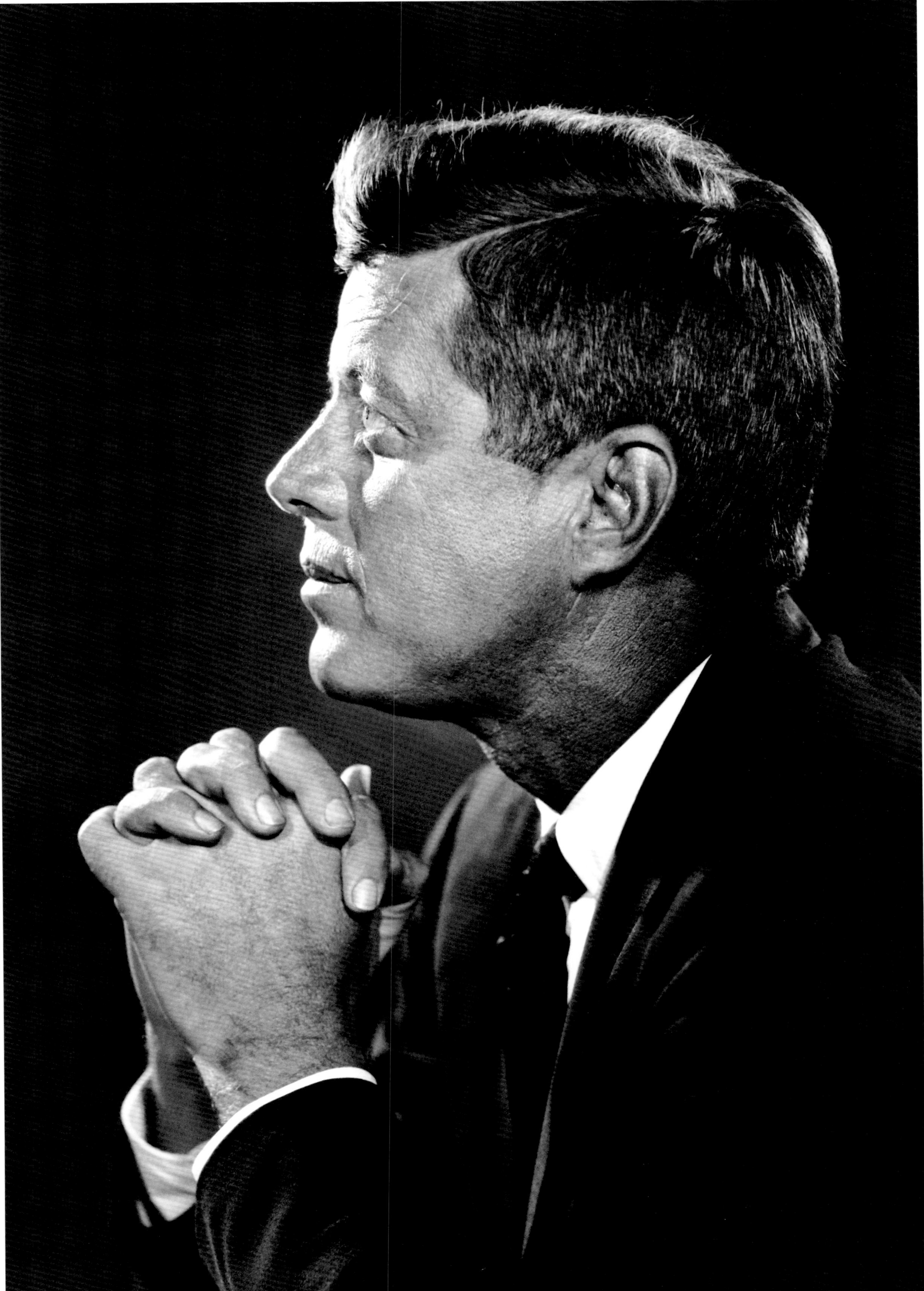

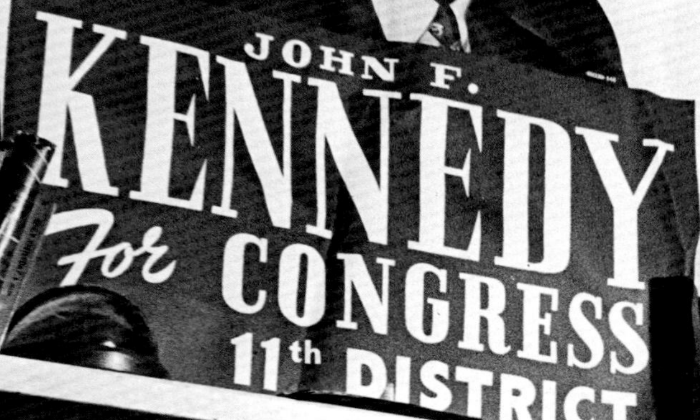

The New Generation
Offers a Leader
JOHN F.
KENNEDY
For CONGRESS
11th DISTRICT

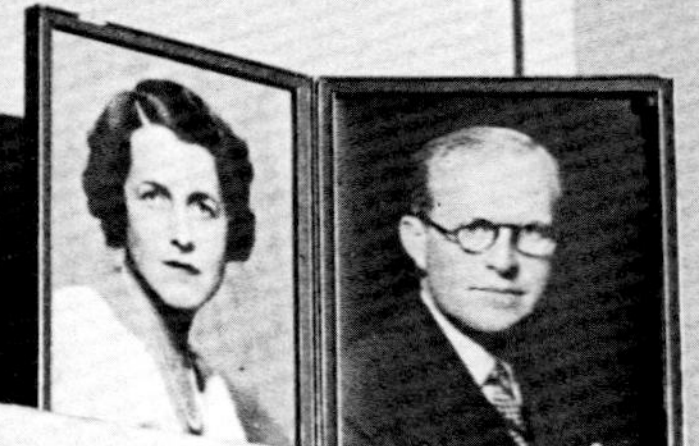

May 29, 1917: Born John Fitzgerald Kennedy (JFK) in Brookline, Massachusetts, son of Joseph and Rose Fitzgerald Kennedy and great grandson of Irish immigrants. He is second of nine Kennedy children: Joe Jr. (b. 1915), Rosemary (b. 1918), Kathleen "Kick" (b. 1920), Eunice (b. 1921), Patricia (b. 1924), Robert "Bobby" (b. 1925), Jean (b. 1928), and Edward "Teddy" (b. 1932).

1919: Contracts scarlet fever around third birthday and is hospitalized for two months.

1921: Joins kindergarten class of Edward Devotion Elementary School, a Brookline public school.

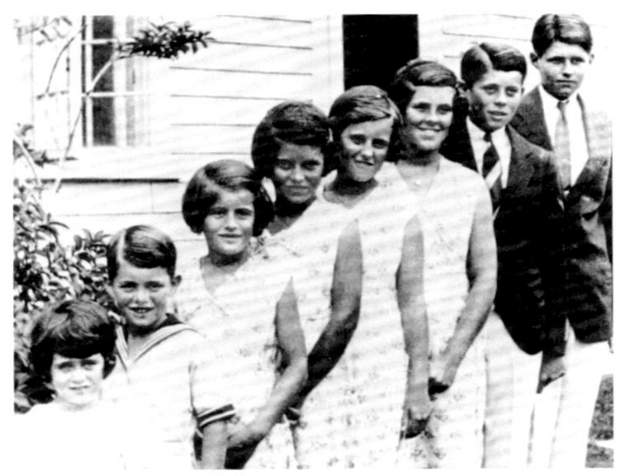

OPPOSITE **Kennedy campaigns for Congress, Boston, Massachusetts, September 1946.** *Photo, Yale Joel*

ABOVE **A young Jack, age 12 (second from right) in 1930, with his siblings. Left to right: Jean, Bobby, Pat, Eunice, Kathleen, Rosemary, and Joe. Teddy would be born two years later.** *Photo, Anonymous*

1926: With brother Joe, transfers to private Noble and Greenough School and later the Dexter School with the children of the Protestant elite.

Summer 1926: Joe Sr. rents summer cottage at 28 Marchant Avenue in Hyannis Port, Massachusetts, on Cape Cod along Nantucket Sound. Two years later, he will purchase it, and family will spend summers there.

September 1927: The Kennedys move to Riverdale in the Bronx, New York.

July 28, 1929: Jacqueline Lee Bouvier is born in Southampton, New York, the oldest child of John and Janet Bouvier.

1930–1931: JFK attends Canterbury School, New Milford, Connecticut.

1931–1935: Attends elite boarding school, Choate Hall, in Wallingford, Connecticut. Despite high intelligence and academic potential, earns mediocre grades.

Summer 1935: Attends London School of Economics.

Fall 1935: Enrolls in Princeton, but drops out later that year due to illness.

January 1936: President Roosevelt names Joseph Kennedy as U.S. ambassador to Great Britain.

Fall: Enters Harvard University, Cambridge, Massachusetts.

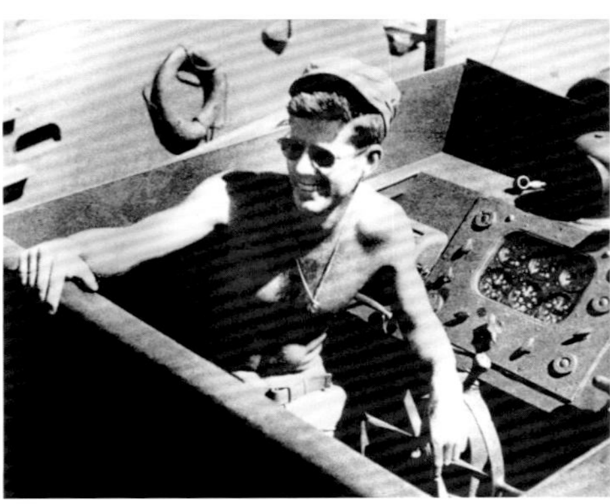

ABOVE **Lieutenant Kennedy aboard the PT-109 in the South Pacific, May 1943.** *Photo, Anonymous*

Summer 1937: Tours Europe with friend Lem Billings for 10 weeks, traveling through France, Italy, Austria, Germany, the Netherlands, and England.

June 1938: Sails overseas with older brother Joe Jr. to work with father.

1939: Spends second semester of junior year working at the American Embassy in Paris and travels through Poland, Moscow, and Berlin. After WWII begins in September, British passenger ship *The Athenia* torpedoed and sunk off coast of Scotland. Ambassador Kennedy sends JFK to aid American survivors.

June: Graduates cum laude from Harvard with a bachelor of science in international affairs.

August 1: With help of his father, publishes his Harvard thesis as book with introduction by magazine magnate Henry Luce. Originally called "Appeasement at Munich," book titled *Why England Slept*, a play on Winston Churchill's book *While England Slept* (1938).

1941: Helps father write memoir. Travels throughout South America.

September: At age 24, enlists in U.S. Navy. Brother Joe Jr. is already training to be a navy pilot.

December 7: Japanese bomb Pearl Harbor, compelling U.S. to enter World War II.

March 1943: After eight-week training course in Rhode Island, assigned to command PT-109 command boat in the South Pacific as lieutenant, junior grade. Sails west from San Francisco, and arrives a month and a half later at destination in Solomon Islands.

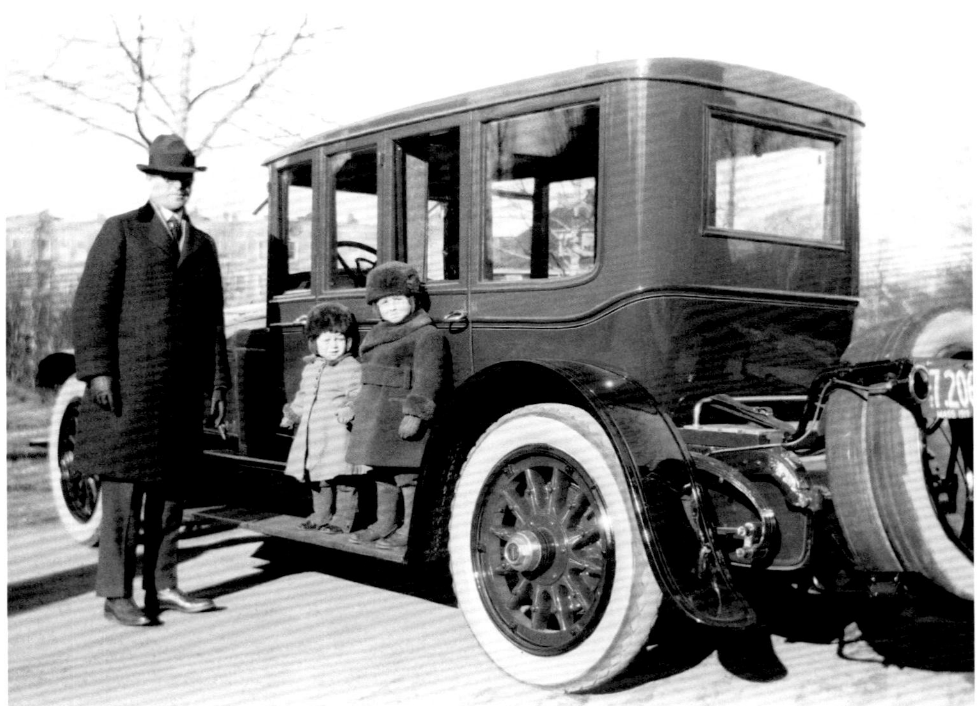

LEFT **Joseph P. Kennedy with sons Jack (left) and Joe Jr., Brookline, Massachusetts, 1919.** *Photo, Anonymous*

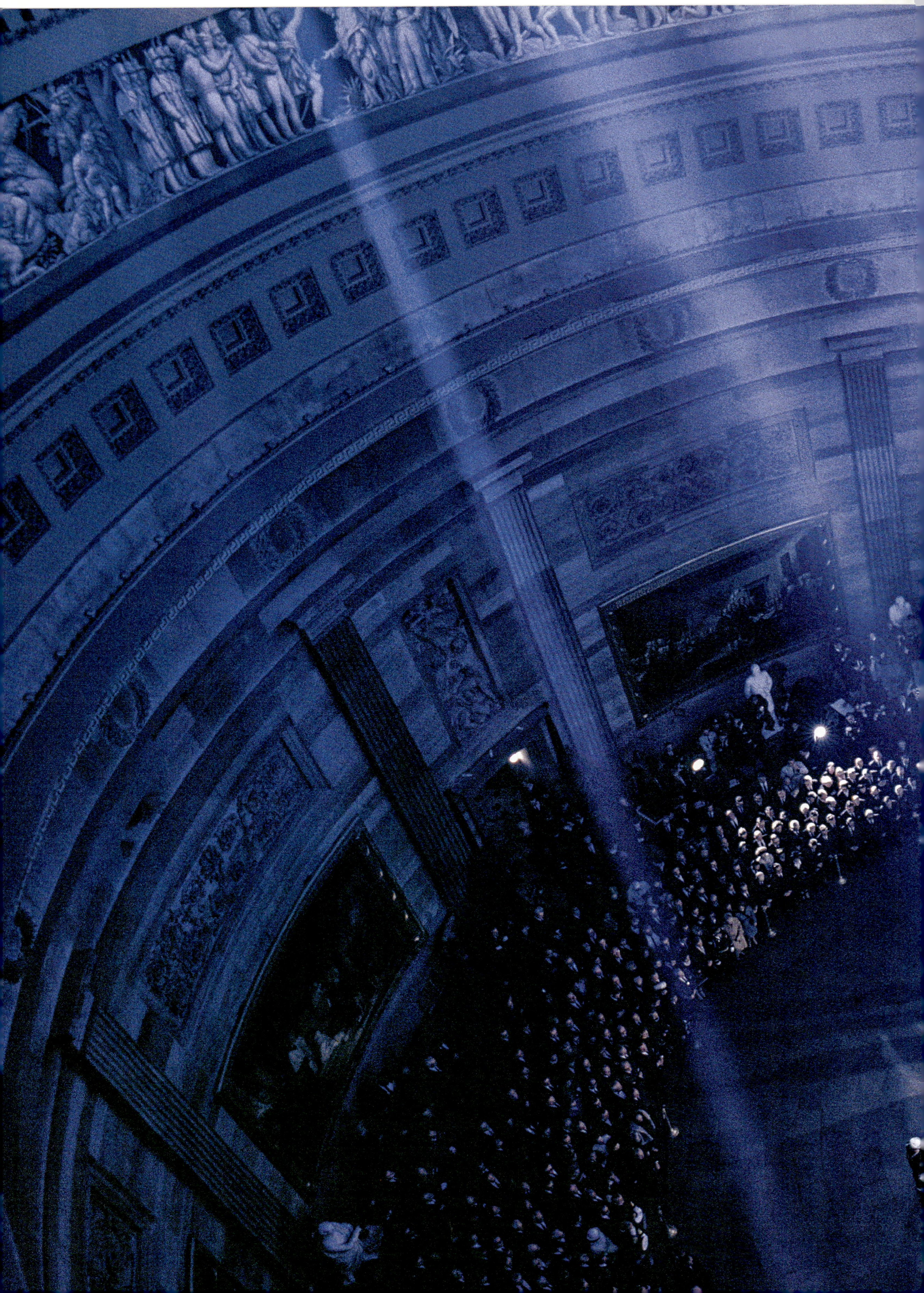

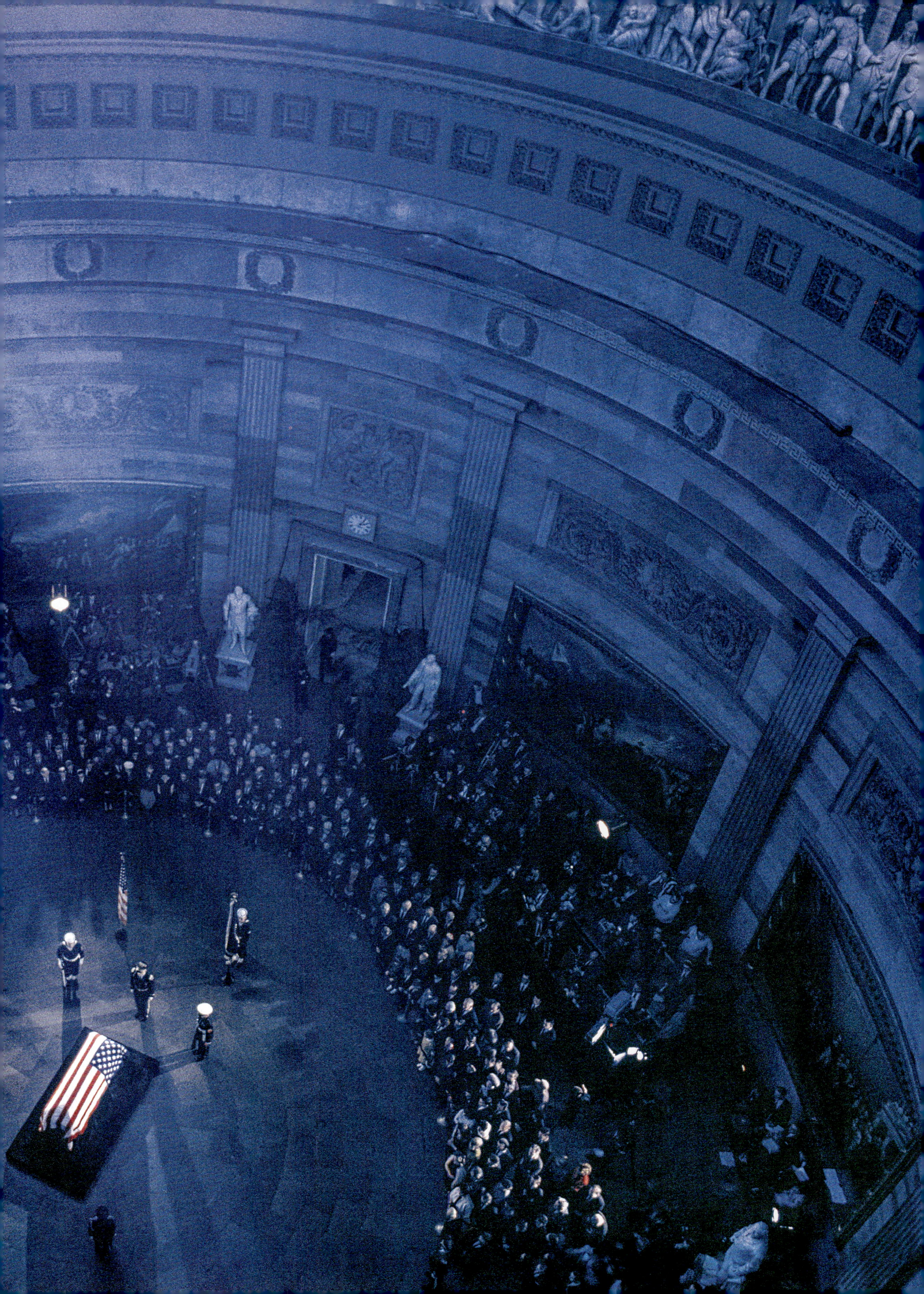

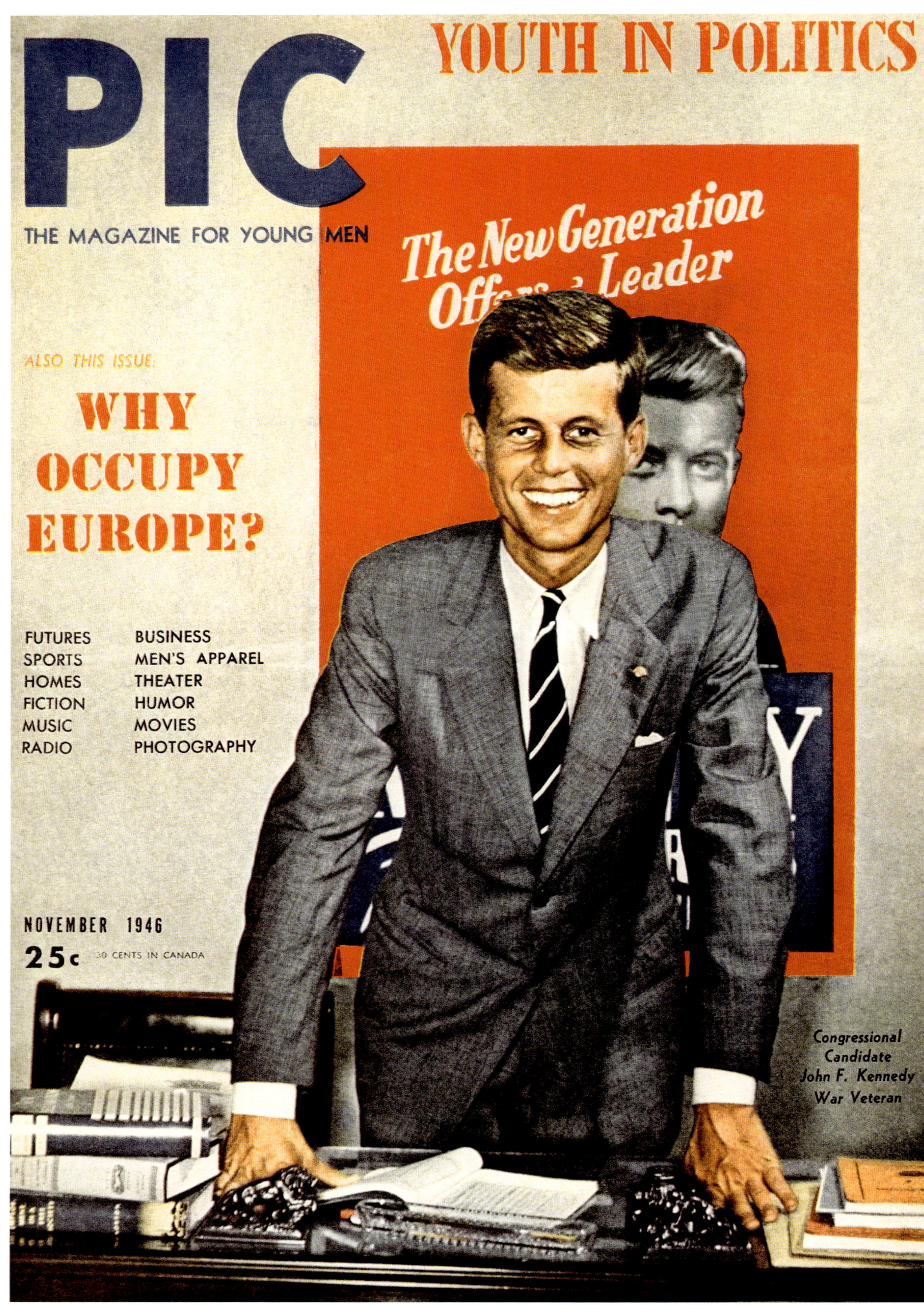

PIC
YOUTH IN POLITICS
THE MAGAZINE FOR YOUNG MEN
The New Generation Offers a Leader
ALSO THIS ISSUE:
WHY OCCUPY EUROPE?
FUTURES
SPORTS
HOMES
FICTION
MUSIC
RADIO
BUSINESS
MEN'S APPAREL
THEATER
HUMOR
MOVIES
PHOTOGRAPHY
NOVEMBER 1946
25c
30 CENTS IN CANADA
Congressional Candidate John F. Kennedy War Veteran

THE CANDIDATE IN PRINT

JUNE 1944–FEBRUARY 1961

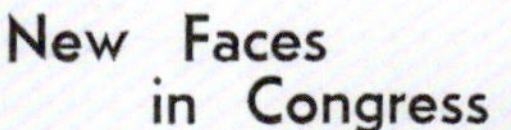
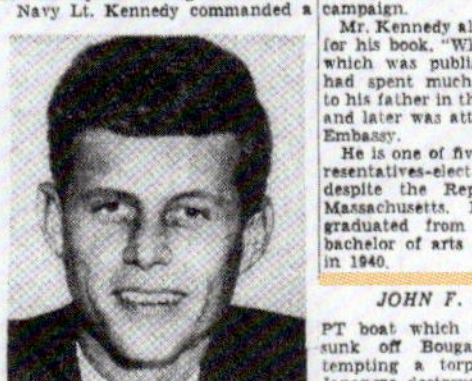

The Evening Star, November 26, 1946

"New Faces in Congress"

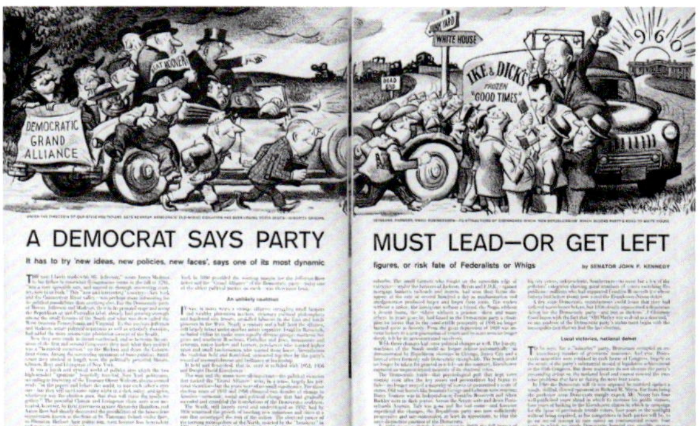

Life, March 11, 1957

"A Democrat Says Party Must Lead—
or Get Left" by John F. Kennedy

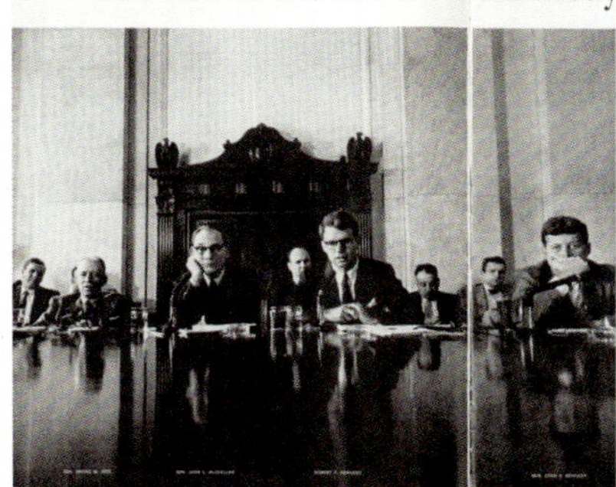

Look, August 6, 1957

"The Rise of the Brothers Kennedy"

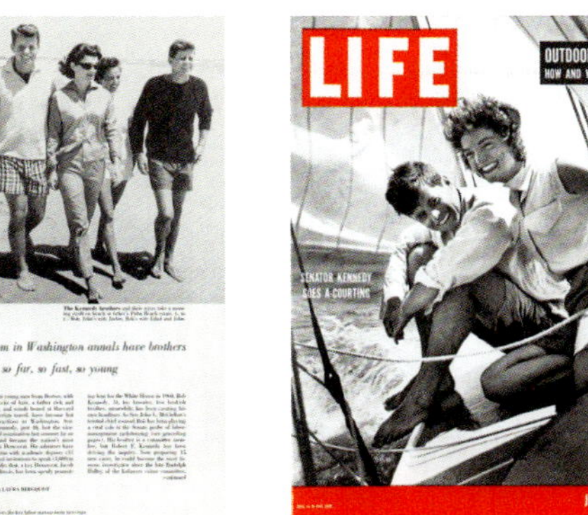

Life, July 20, 1953

"Senator Kennedy Goes
A-Courting"

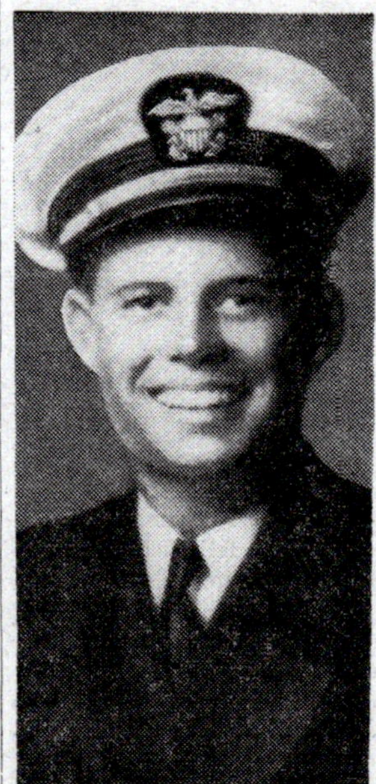

The New York Times, June 12, 1944

"Lieut. Kennedy Cited as Hero by the Navy"

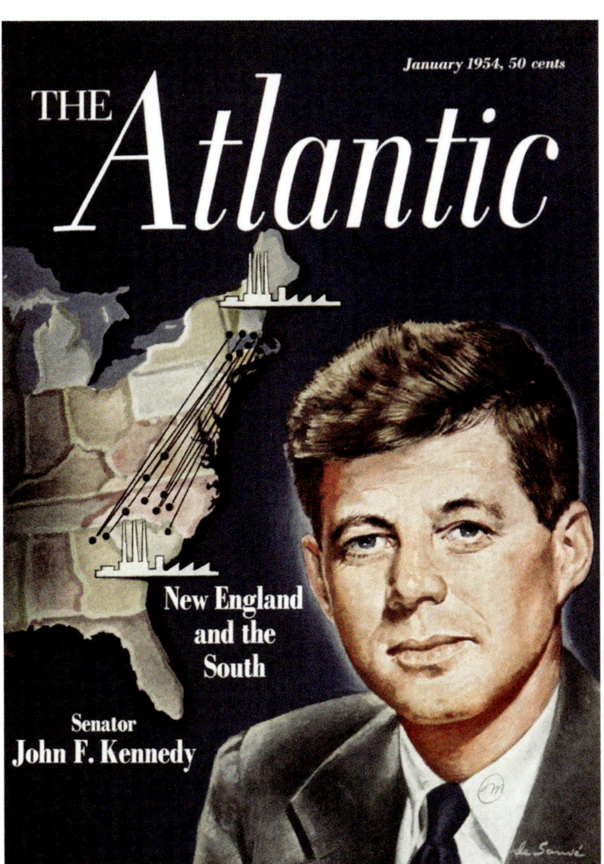

(OPPOSITE) *PIC*, November 1946

"Congressional Candidate
John F. Kennedy: War Veteran"

The Atlantic, January 1954

"Senator John F. Kennedy"

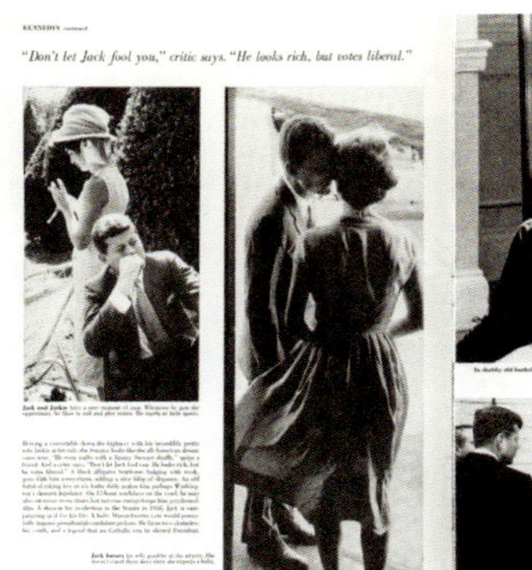

Look, August 6, 1957

"The Rise of the Brothers Kennedy: Don't Let Jack
Fool You. He Looks Rich but Votes Liberal"

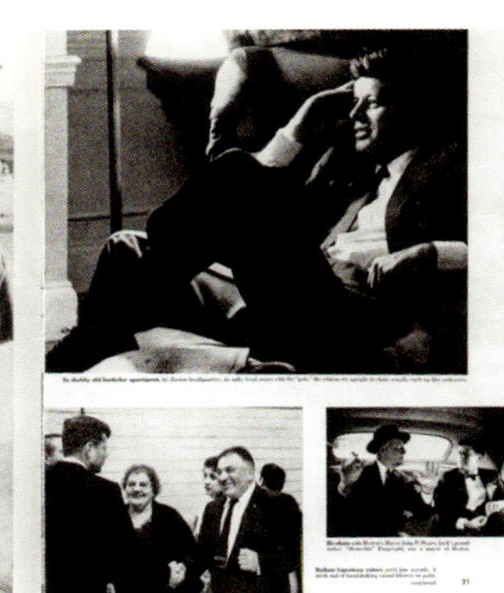

The Sign, August 1958

"With God It's Never Too Late"

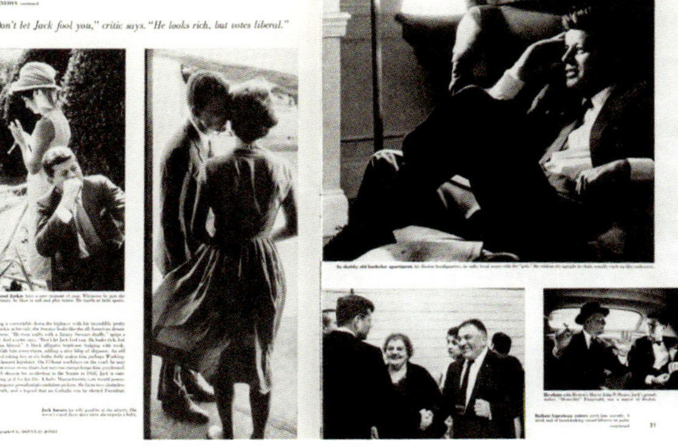

Time, November 24, 1958

"Democratic Hopefuls"

The New York Times Magazine, October 25, 1959

"Two Candidates on the Road"

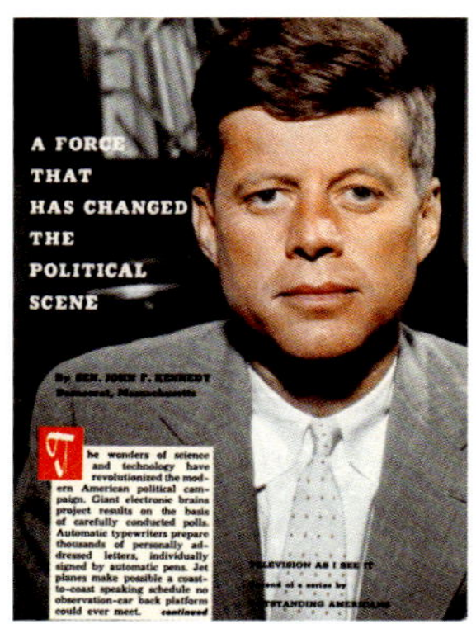

TV Guide, November 14, 1959

"Television as I See It" by Sen. John F. Kennedy

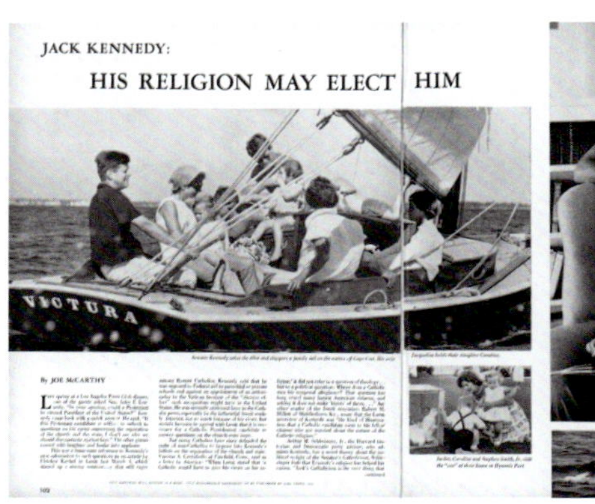

Life, November 10, 1959

"Jack Kennedy: His Religion May Elect Him"

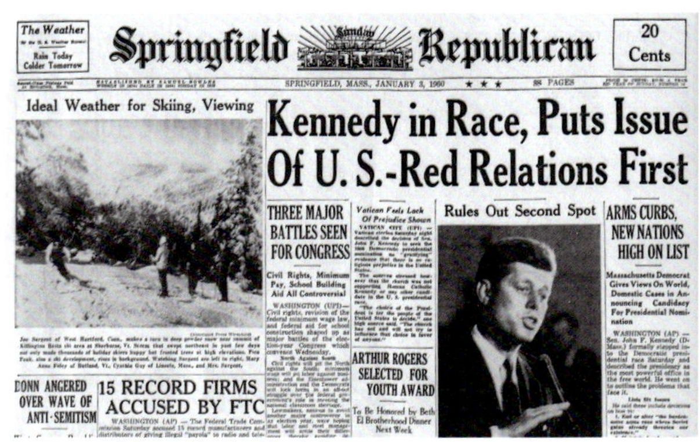

Springfield Republican, January 3, 1960

"Kennedy in Race, Puts Issue of U.S.– Red Relations First"

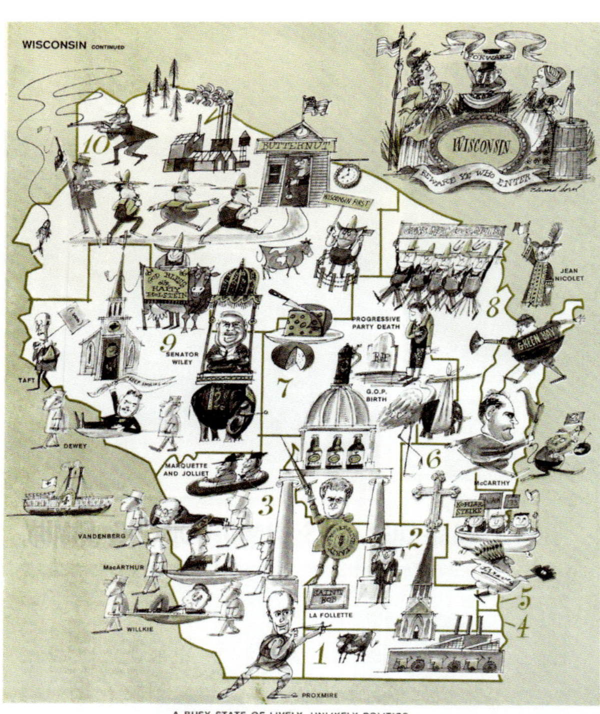

Life, March 28, 1960

"Strategic Warpath in Wisconsin: A Busy State of Lively, Unlikely Politics"

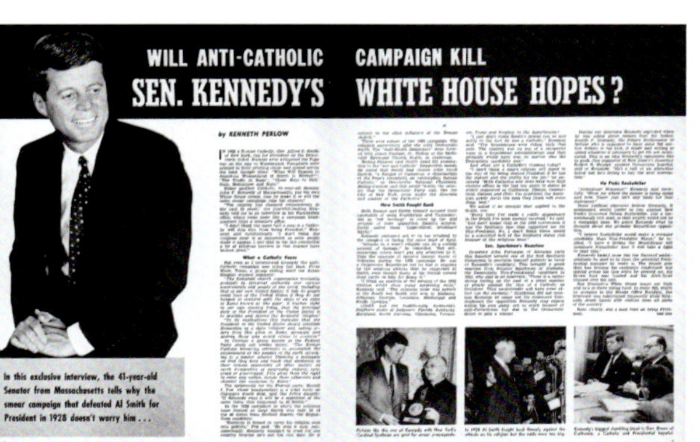

The National Police Gazette, September 1, 1959

"Will Anti-Catholic Campaign Kill Sen. Kennedy's White House Hopes?"

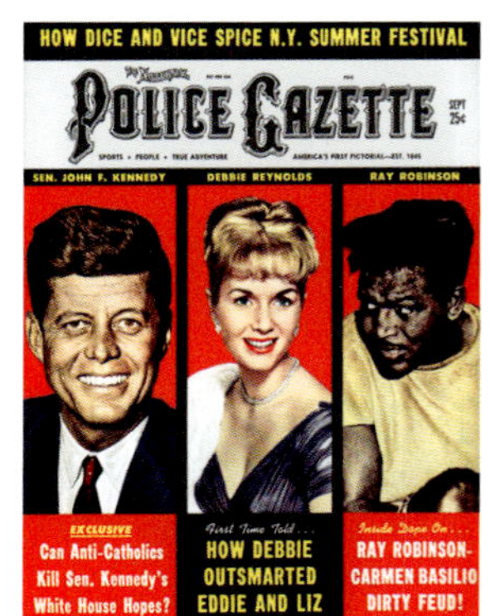

The National Police Gazette, September 1, 1959

"Can Anti-Catholics Kill Sen. Kennedy's White House Hopes?"

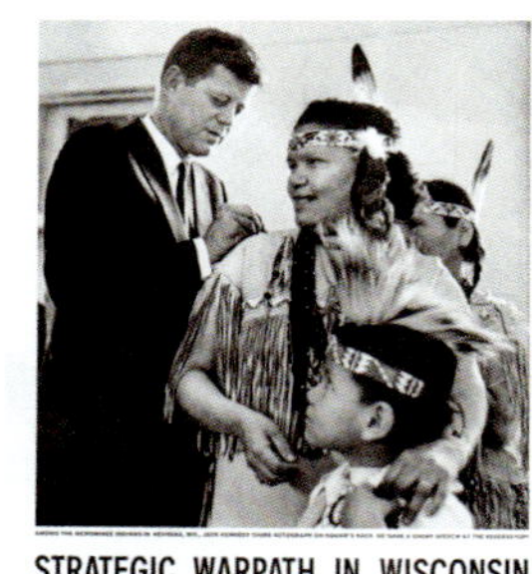

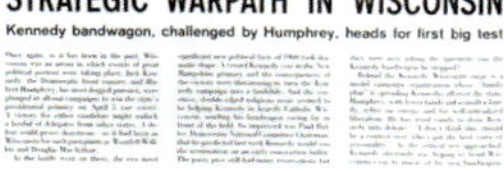

Life, March 28, 1960

"Strategic Warpath in Wisconsin"

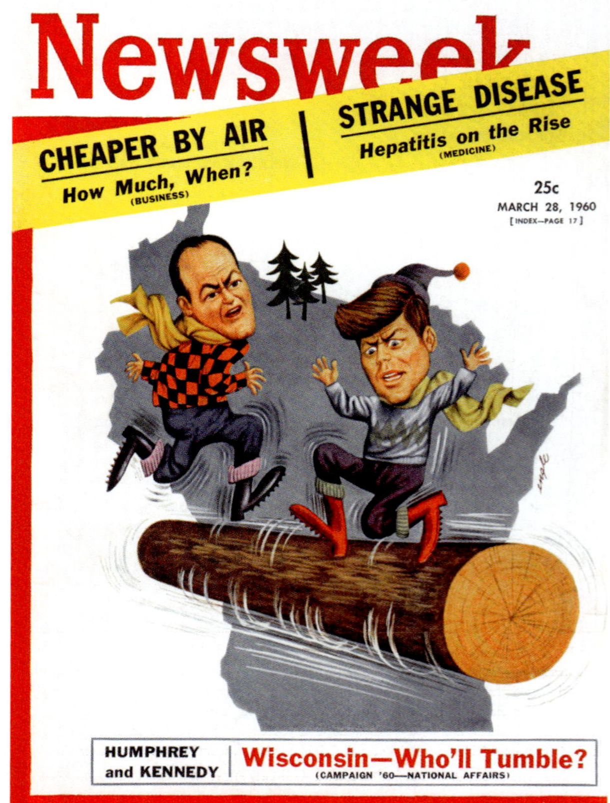

Newsweek, March 28, 1960

"Humphrey and Kennedy: Wisconsin—Who'll Tumble?"

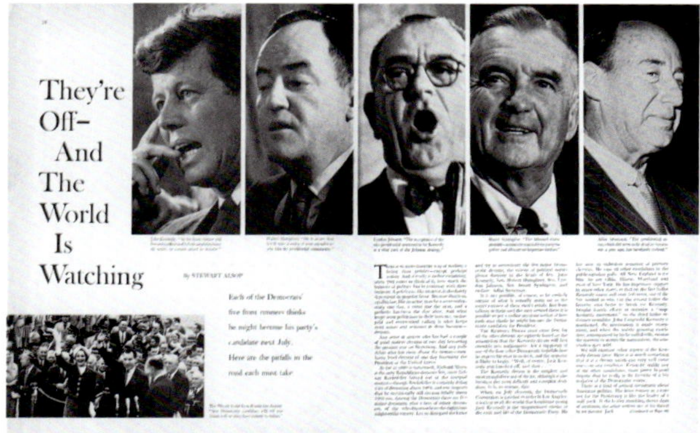

The Saturday Evening Post, March 19, 1960

"They're Off — and the World Is Watching"

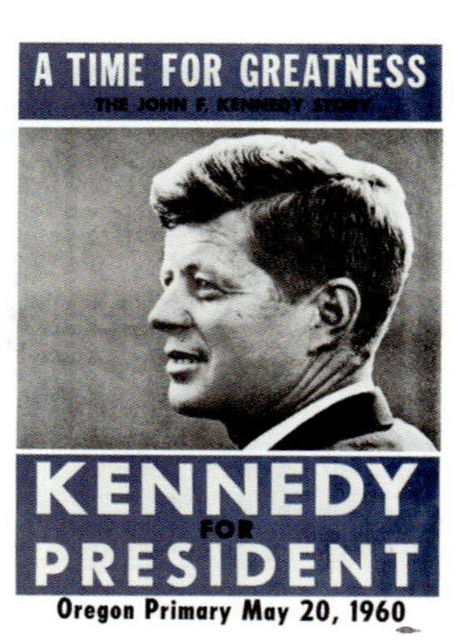

Oregon for Kennedy, May 20, 1960

Campaign brochure for Oregon

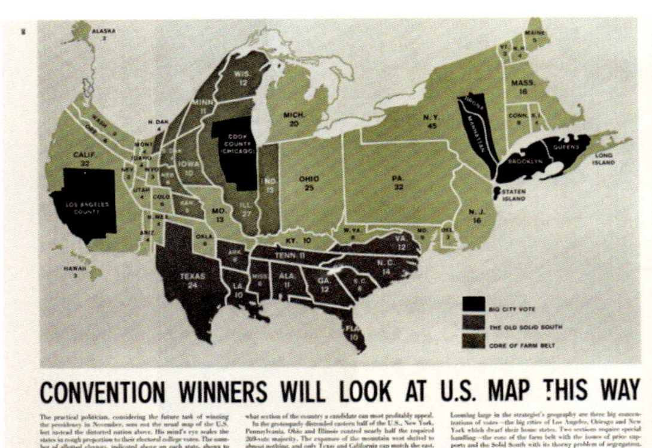

Life, July 4, 1960
"Convention Winners Will Look at U.S. Map This Way"

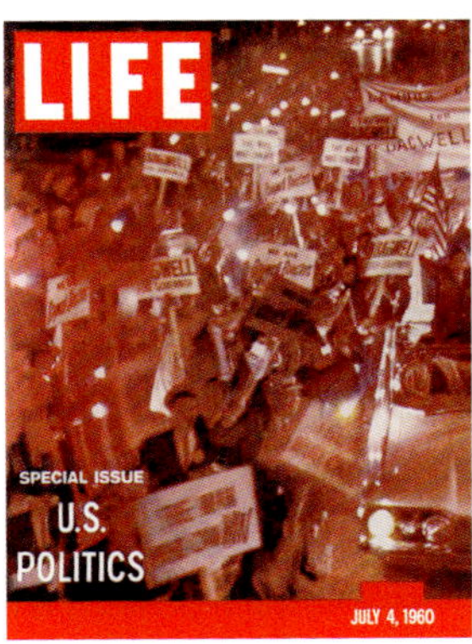

Life, July 4, 1960
"Special Issue: U.S. Politics"

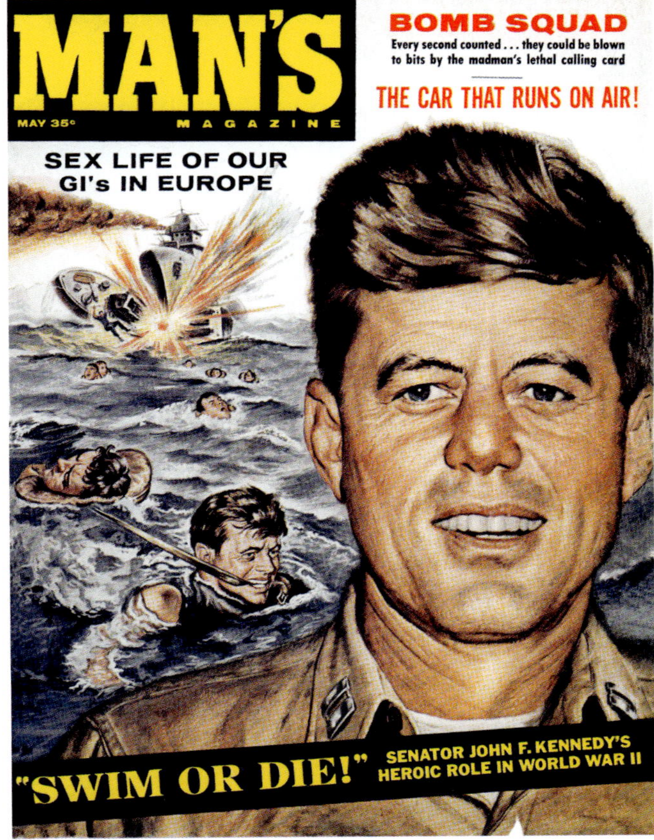

Man's Magazine, May 1960
"'Swim or Die!' Senator John F. Kennedy's Heroic Role in World War II"

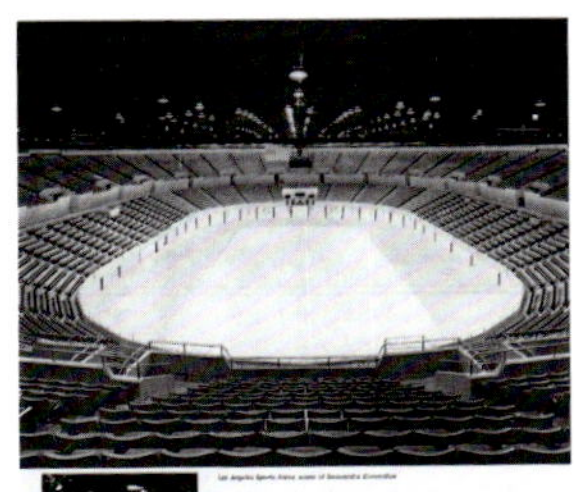

Westinghouse advertisement, 1960
"Los Angeles Sports Arena, Scene of Democratic Convention"

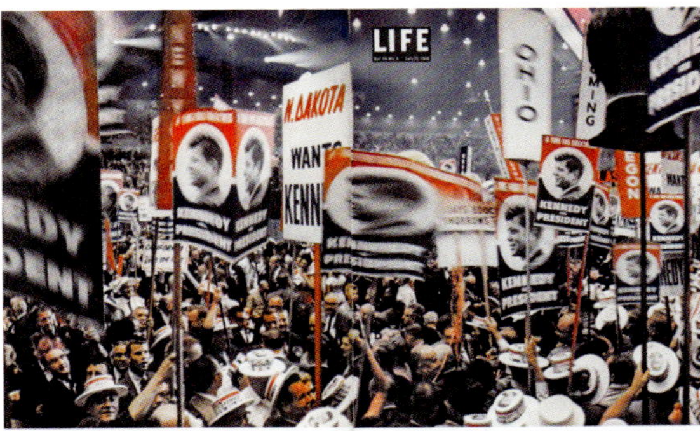

Life, July 25, 1960
"Kennedy's Organized Forces Nail Down Margin of Victory"

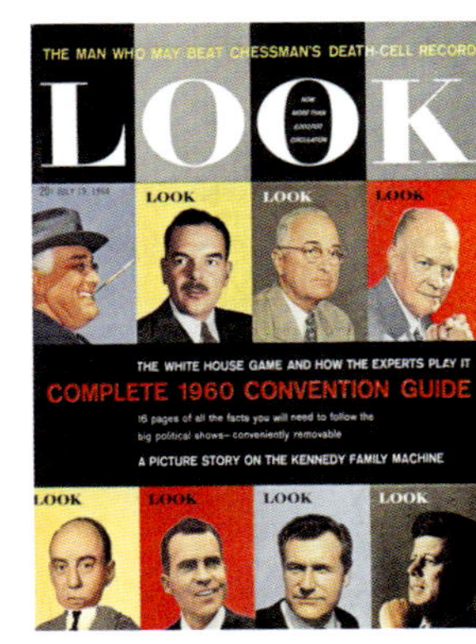

Look, July 19, 1960
"Complete 1960 Convention Guide"

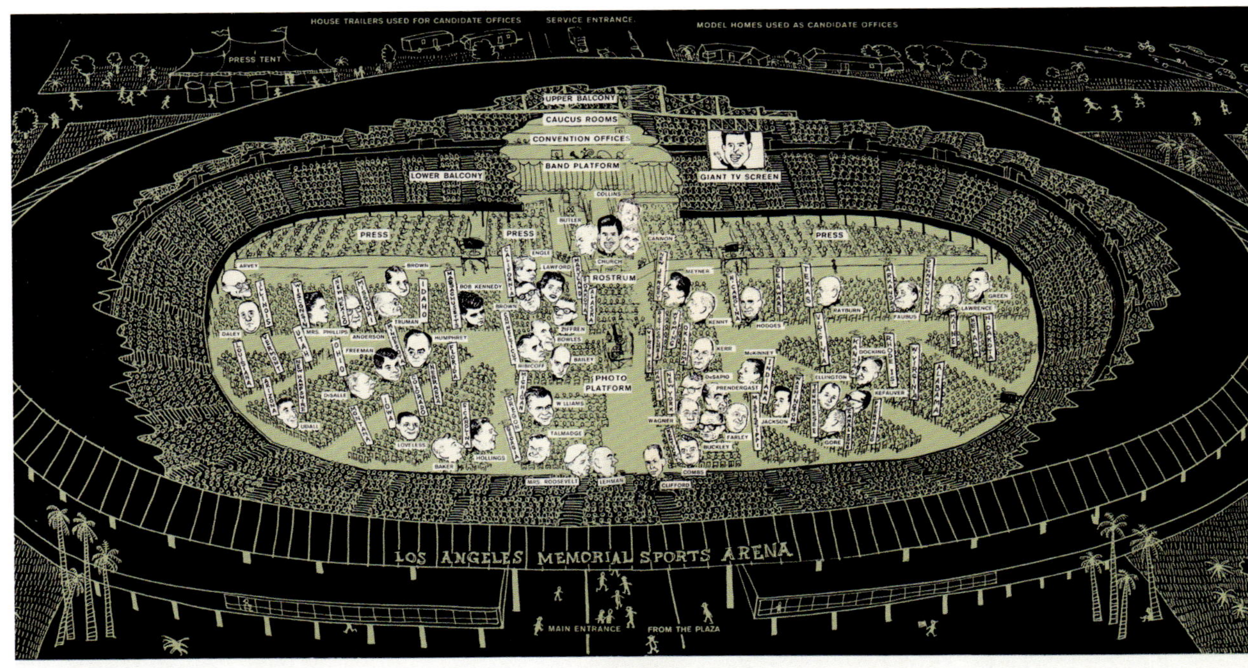

DEMOCRATIC BATTLE RING

Here are faces to watch in Los Angeles—and why

Life, July 4, 1960
"Democratic Battle Ring"

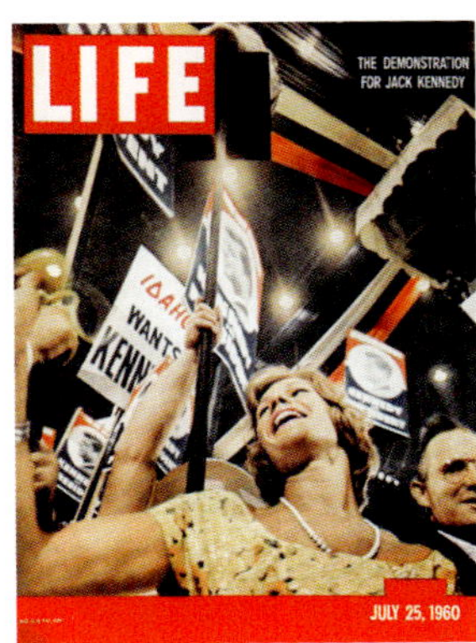

Life, July 25, 1960
"The Demonstration for Jack Kennedy"

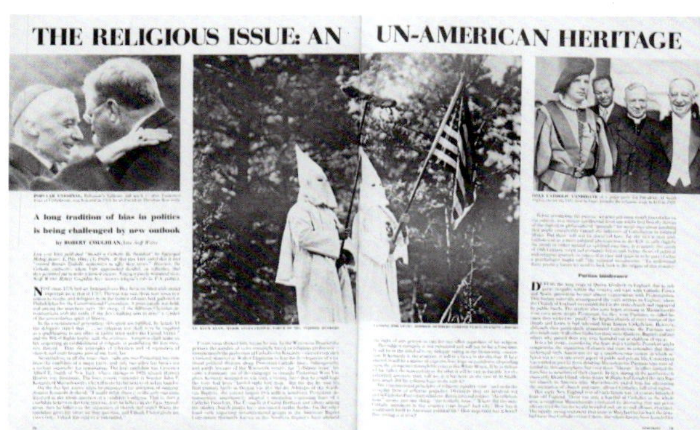

Life, July 4, 1960

"The Religious Issue: An Un-American Heritage"

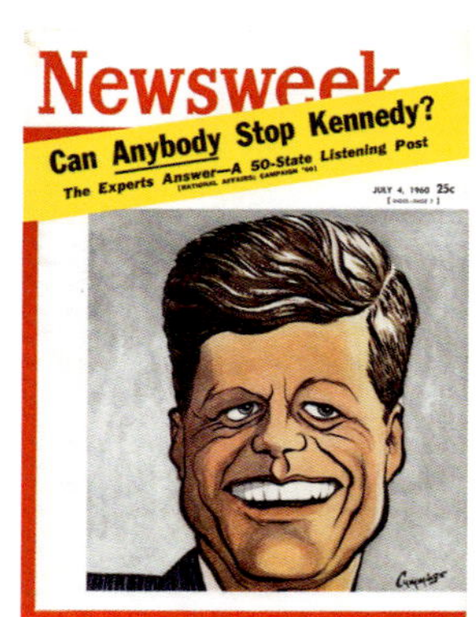

Newsweek, July 4, 1960

"Can Anybody Stop Kennedy?"

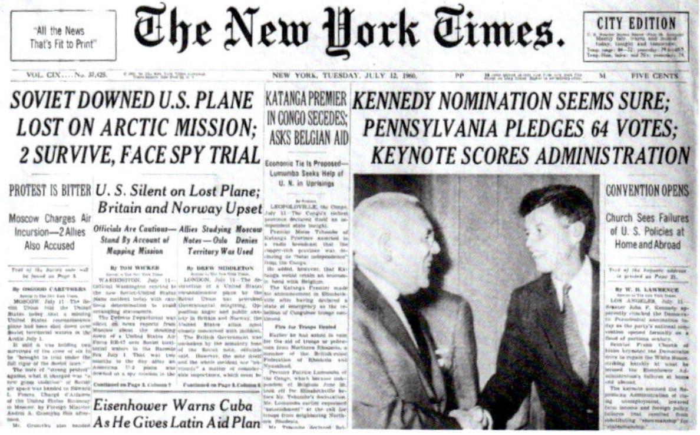

The New York Times, July 12, 1960

"Kennedy Nomination Seems Sure; Pennsylvania Pledges 64 Votes; Keynote Scores Administration"

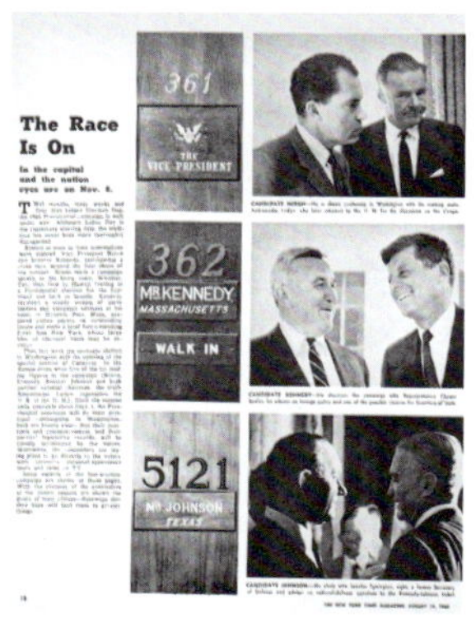

The New York Times Magazine, **August 14, 1960**

"The Race Is On"

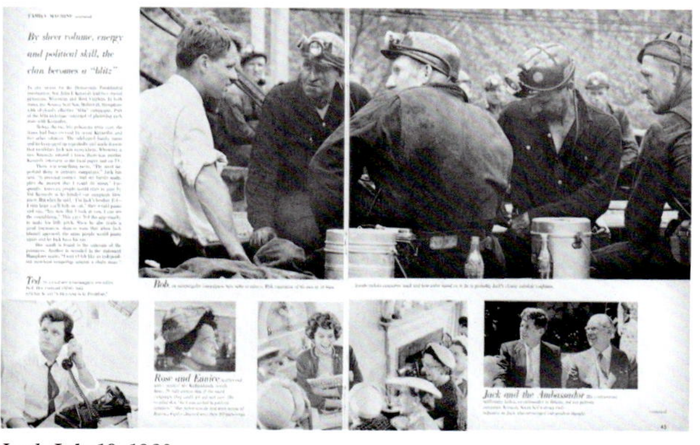

Look, July 19, 1960

"The Kennedys: A Family Political Machine"

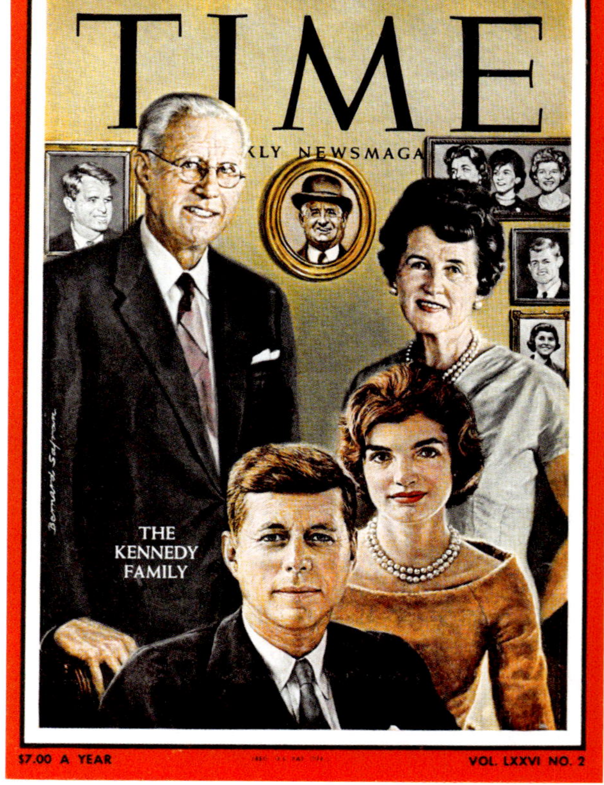

Time, July 11, 1960

"The Kennedy Family"

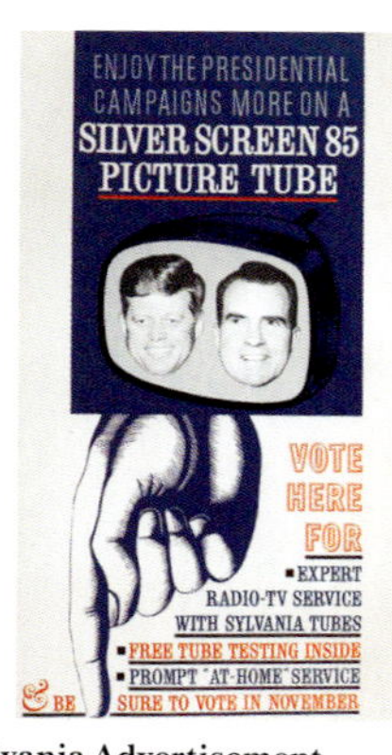

Sylvania Advertisement, Fall 1960

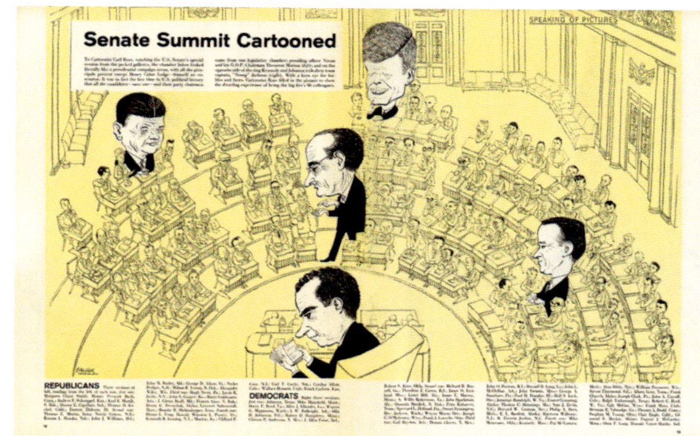

Look, July 19, 1960

"The Kennedys: A Family Political Machine"

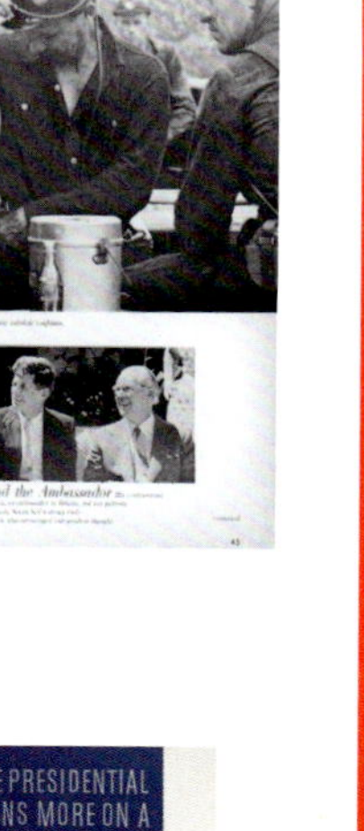

Life, August 29, 1960

"Senate Summit Cartooned"

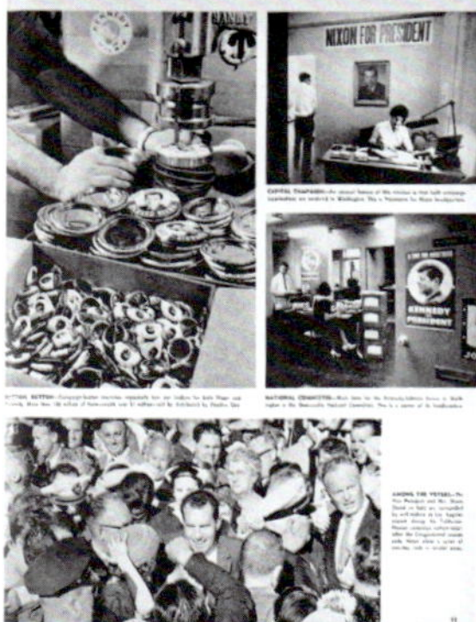

The New York Times Magazine, **August 14, 1960**

"The Race Is On: Button, Button"

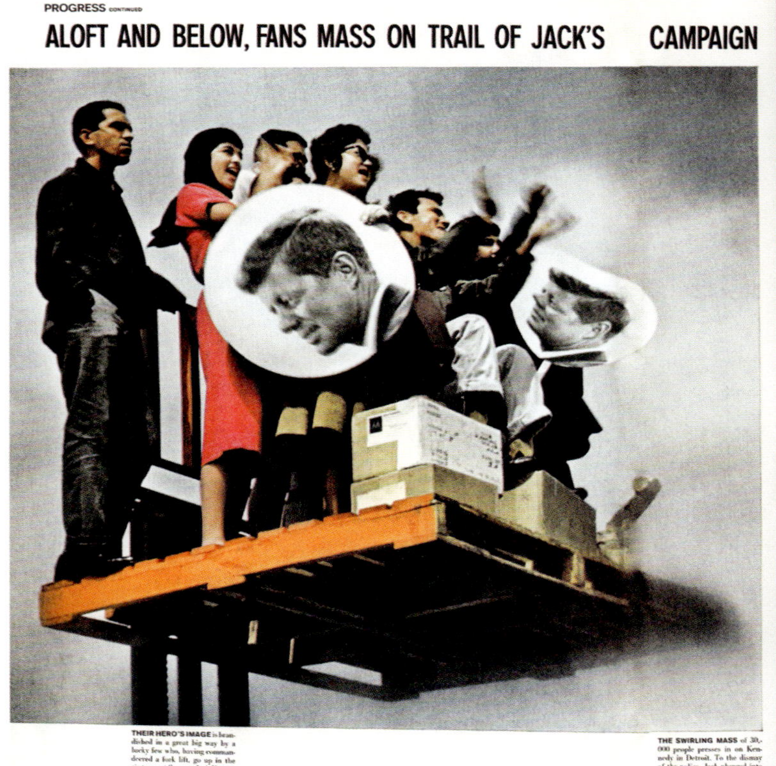

Life, October 10, 1960

"Aloft and Below, Fans Mass on Trail of Jack's Campaign"

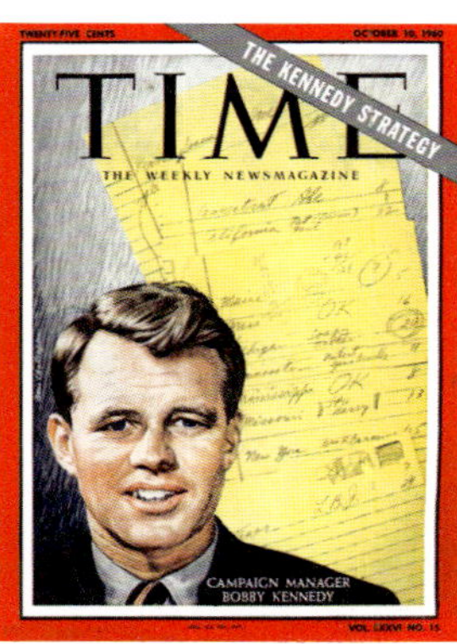

Time, October 10, 1960

"Campaign Manager Bobby Kennedy"

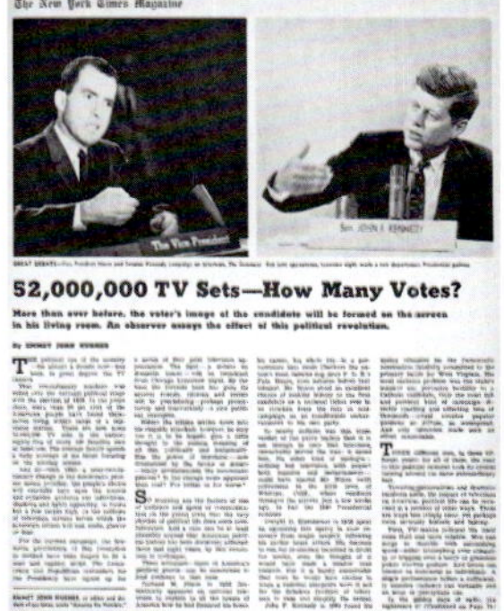

The New York Times Magazine,
September 25, 1960

"52,000,000 TV Sets—How Many Votes?"

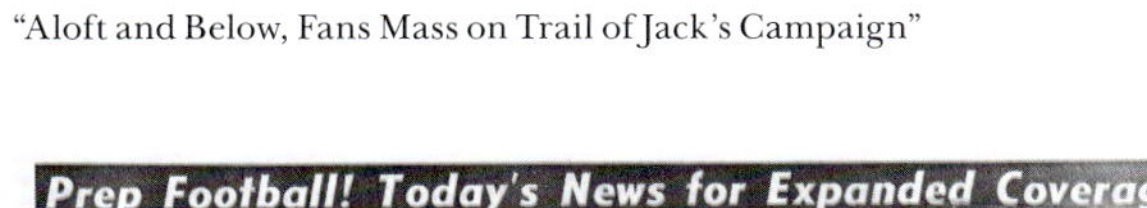

The Detroit News, October 26, 1960

"Hoover, Dewey Urge V.P. to OK 5th Debate"

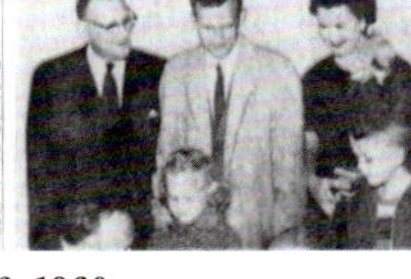
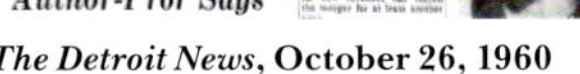

Life, October 10, 1960

"What Really Happened
Before the TV Debate"

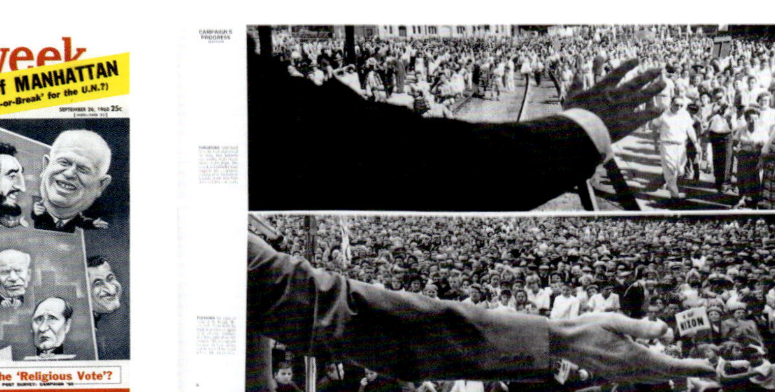

Newsweek, September 26, 1960

"How Important the
'Religious Vote'?"

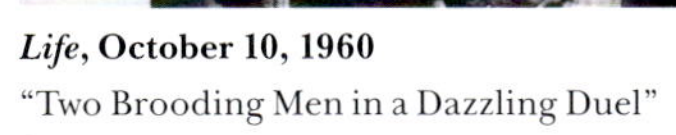

Life, October 10, 1960

"Two Brooding Men in a Dazzling Duel"

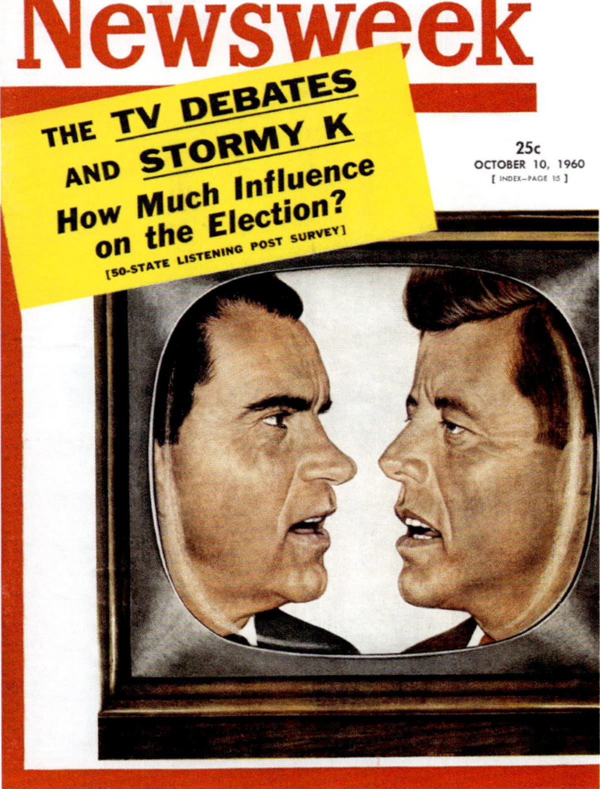

Newsweek, October 10, 1960

"The TV Debates and Stormy K:
How Much Influence on the Election?"

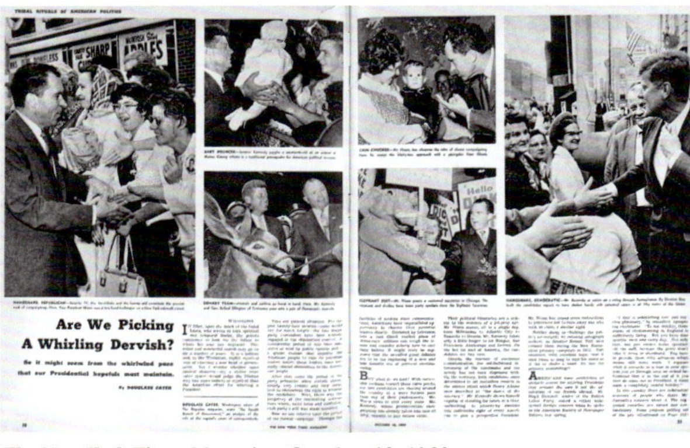

The New York Times Magazine, October 16, 1960

"Are We Picking a Whirling Dervish?"

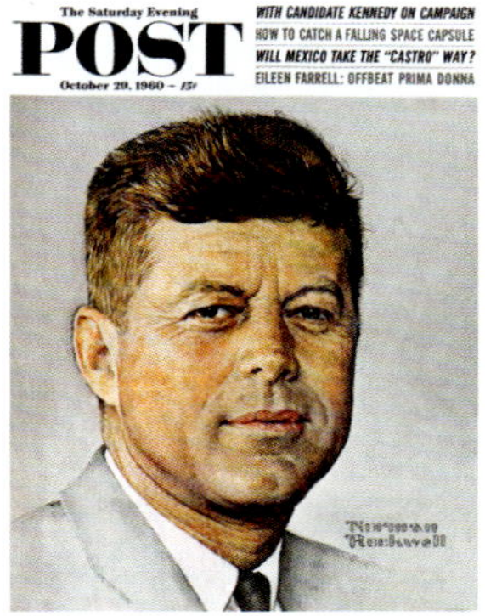

The Saturday Evening Post,
October 19, 1960

"With Candidate Kennedy
on Campaign"

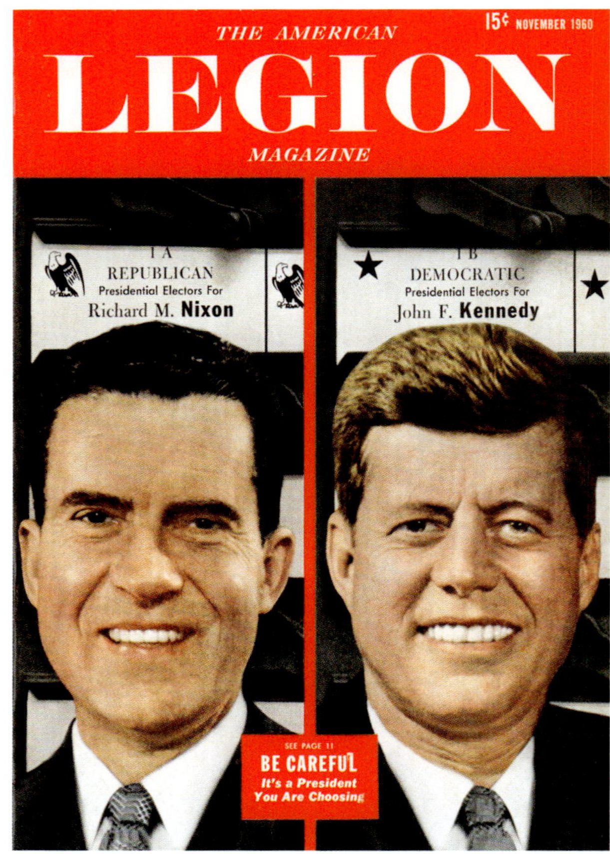

The American Legion Magazine, November 1960

"Be Careful: It's a President You Are Choosing"

Look, October 11, 1960

"The Kennedy Women"

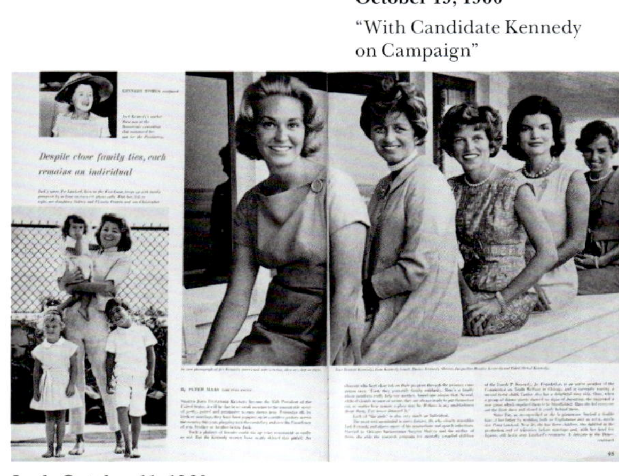

Look, October 11, 1960

"The Kennedy Women: Despite Close
Family Ties, Each Remains an Individual"

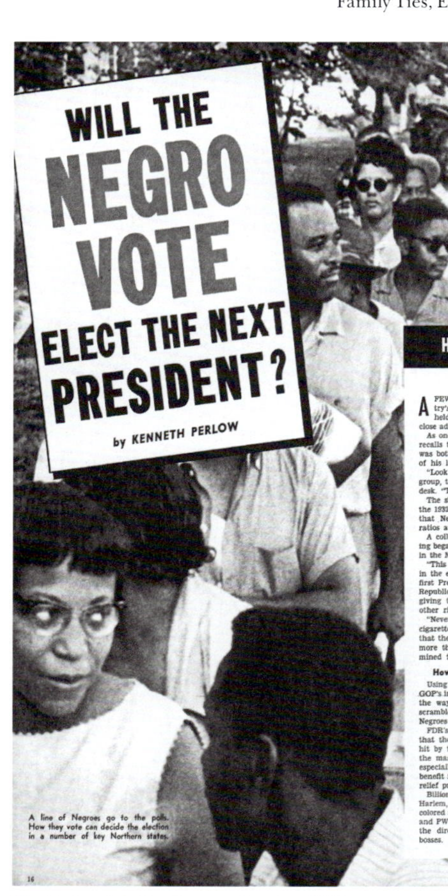

The National Police Gazette, October 1960

"Will the Negro Vote Elect the Next President?"

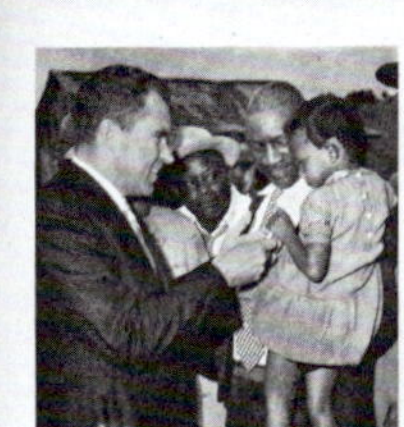

Richard Nixon, the Republican candidate, offers a gift to a Negro girl. Nixon was active in bringing about passage of "right-to-vote" laws in 85th Congress, which won him praise of Negro leaders.

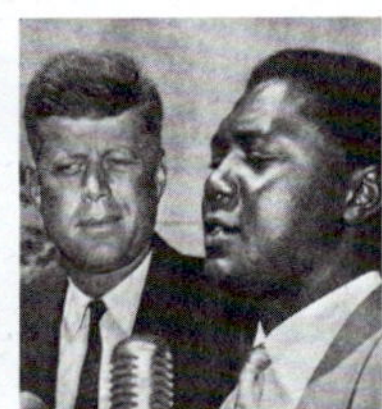

John F. Kennedy, Democratic nominee, discussed African problems with Tom Mboya, head of Kenya labor federation. Kennedy has assured Negro leaders he'll support civil rights legislation if elected.

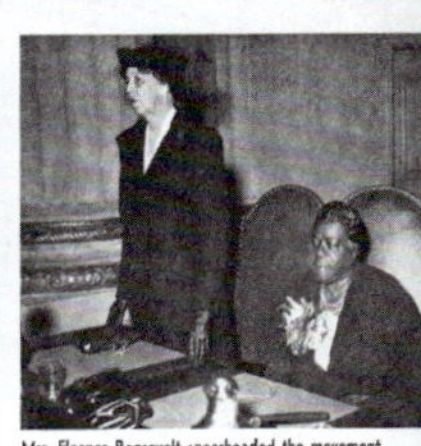

Mrs. Eleanor Roosevelt spearheaded the movement to convince Negroes that only through the Democratic Party could they expect progress in civil rights. Here she's addressing a Negro conference.

Here's the inside story of the frantic behind-the-scene political battle for the Negro vote — and what it really means . . .

A FEW months after his election as the country's 32nd President, Franklin D. Roosevelt held a highly secret conference with six close advisers in his paneled study at Hyde Park. As one member of FDR's original "braintrust" recalls that meeting in 1933, the new President was both puzzled and worried about one aspect of his landslide victory over Herbert Hoover.

"Look at these statistics," Roosevelt told the group, tossing a sheaf of ruled paper across his desk. "This is something we've got to change."

The sheets listed details of the Negro vote in the 1932 Roosevelt-Hoover election. They showed that Negro districts had gone for Hoover by ratios averaging nearly four to one.

A college professor at the Hyde Park gathering began an explanation of the historical factors in the Negro vote.

"This loyalty to the Republican Party began in the election of 1868," he said. "That was the first Presidential vote after the Civil War. The Republicans were enacting Reconstruction laws giving the Negro the right to vote and many other rights he had never had before. . . ."

"Never mind all that," said FDR, raising his cigarette holder impatiently. "I'm well aware that there's been no change in the situation for more than 60 years. But I'm absolutely determined that there will be a change now."

How Roosevelt Captured Negro Vote

Using brand new methods, Roosevelt broke the GOP's iron grip on the Negro vote. He thus paved the way for today's frantic behind-the-scenes scramble by both parties to win the support of Negroes in certain key northern states.

FDR's big weapon was the relief dollar. Noting that the Negro had been among those hardest hit by the devastating depression of the 1930s, the master politician made sure that Negroes, especially those in the big northern cities, would benefit from federally endowed and administered relief projects.

Billions of dollars were poured into New York's Harlem, Chicago's South Side and other major colored areas. The alphabet agencies—WPA, CCC and PWA, among others—doled out funds under the direction of handpicked local Democratic bosses.

But Roosevelt did more than approach Negroes through their pocketbooks. While Democratic politicos handed out federal cash, Mrs. Eleanor Roosevelt spearheaded a movement to convince colored people that only through the Democratic Party could they expect real progress in civil rights.

Harold Ickes, Roosevelt's first secretary of the interior, once told a Negro audience in Chicago:

"Abraham Lincoln freed the slaves, but what have the Republicans done for you *lately?*"

The Negro vote swung solidly to the Democrats in 1936, when FDR won his second term. In general, it has stayed Democratic ever since.

Vote Can Be Crucial

Top strategists in the camps of both Richard M. Nixon and John F. Kennedy told *Police Gazette* reporters this summer that they believe the Negro vote can be crucial if this year's election is close.

What's more, Republicans are hopeful that for the first time since 1932 a majority of the Negro votes will go to the GOP column.

How best to woo Negro votes has been a matter of personal concern to both Nixon and Kennedy.

Although they were never publicized, many secret conferences between Kennedy and leaders of national Negro organizations were held during the summer at the Senator's vacation retreat in Hyannis Port, Massachusetts. Some of these same Negro bigwigs also met secretly with Nixon in Washington during the summer.

One of the leaders has told the *Police Gazette* that the attitude of the two candidates was virtually identical.

"They both asked us what the Negro people really wanted," he recalls. "We told them we want more civil rights and more job opportunities.

"They both promised us everything in sight, if only we'd come through on Election Day."

Unknown to the general public, both parties are employing big, well-heeled special staffs whose only task is to try to bring in the Negro vote.

Mrs. Roosevelt, whose popularity among Negroes remains as high as ever, made a remark at the Democratic convention which still upsets Kennedy.

Although she eventually gave Kennedy her support, Mrs. Roosevelt told a small group of reporters at the Los Angeles conclave last July that Kennedy "cannot win the election, nor can he win the Negro vote."

Why would he be unpopular among Negroes?

"It's because of a few things he has said," she explained, "and perhaps they've been taken in the wrong context."

Mrs. Roosevelt refused to amplify on this remark, but Harlem's Negro Congressman, Adam Clayton Powell Jr., made this statement to a group of New York delegates at a convention caucus held behind closed doors:

"Until just a few weeks ago, Kennedy's campaign managers disregarded Negro areas, the Negro vote and the Negro leadership."

Powell predicted flatly that Kennedy could not carry New York State this fall. "If the election were held today," he said, "the bulk of the state's Negro votes would go to Nixon."

Ike Won Without Negro Vote

One great irony in the emphasis on the Negro vote today is the fact that President Eisenhower won landslide triumphs in 1952 and 1956 even though Negro districts in the larger northern cities went overwhelmingly for Adlai Stevenson. In Detroit, for example, typical big Negro districts gave Stevenson 90.5 percent of their ballots in 1952 and 85.7 percent in 1956. Michigan as a whole went to Eisenhower in both elections by big margins.

In Kennedy's sweeping victories of 1936, 1940 and 1944, the Negro vote was equally superfluous. FDR would easily have won without it.

But both sides fear this year's election will be much closer than those won by either FDR or Ike.

In a close election, the Negro vote could be decisive in 14 states with a total electoral vote of 281—only eight short of the 269 needed to elect the next President. These northern, border and West Coast states have Negro populations ranging from 5 to 15 percent.

One of Kennedy's closest associates sat with a *Police Gazette* reporter in New York last July and watched the climactic moments of the Republican convention on television. After Nixon was nominated, this Democratic professional remarked:

"I have an idea that this election will be 1954 all over again. You remember what happened that year here in New York State? Averell Harriman was elected Governor by only 11,000 votes out of five million cast.

"If Harriman had failed to keep the Negro vote, he would have lost. That's why our greatest single concern this year will be to reassure the northern Negroes on civil rights."

Political Hot Potatoes

The smoldering struggle over civil rights flared into the open in August when the Senate convened in special session.

The maneuvers of both parties were prime examples of political cynicism. After treating civil rights like a political hot potato for years, both parties rushed forward with efforts to win the Negro vote.

It can now be revealed that the Republican strategy was drawn up at a breakfast conference in the White House on August 9. Present were Eisenhower, Nixon and several key GOP Senators.

"We've got to put the squeeze on the Democrats," one eastern Senator said at the parley.

Senator Everett McKinley Dirksen, the Republican minority leader, then outlined a plan by which the GOP would introduce a flurry of civil rights bills. The idea was to embarrass northern Democrats by forcing them to take clearcut action against the interests of either their southern colleagues or the Negro.

The plan was approved by a majority of those at the meeting. Later that same day, Dirksen introduced one of the bills.

The proposed law consisted of two hotly controversial sections that had been deleted from the civil rights bill passed by Congress last April. These two sections—cut out because they had aroused all-out southern opposition—would have provided for federal grants to school districts seeking to desegregate and would also have made the Federal *(Continued on page 26)*

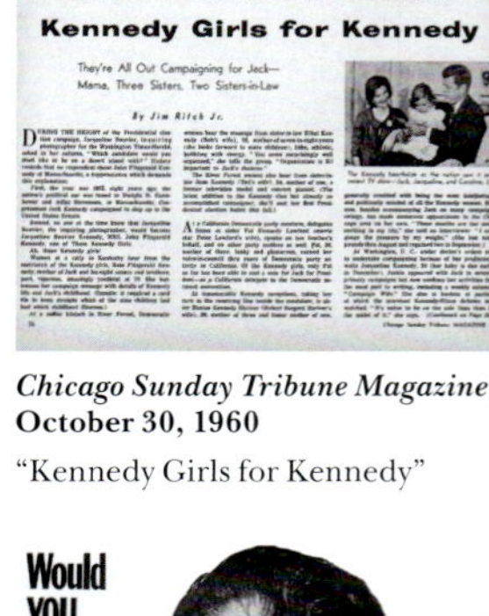

Chicago Sunday Tribune Magazine,
October 30, 1960

"Kennedy Girls for Kennedy"

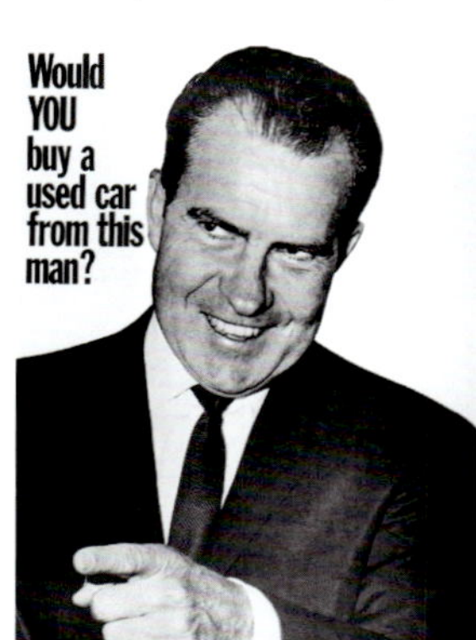

Pro-Kennedy Advertisement, 1960

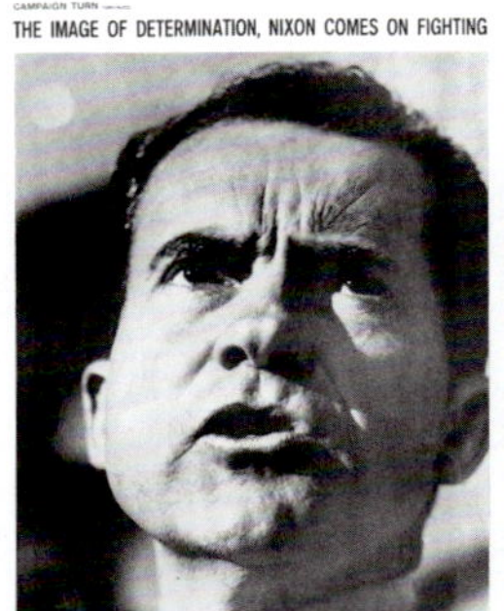

Life, October 31, 1960

"The Image of Determination, Nixon Comes on Fighting"

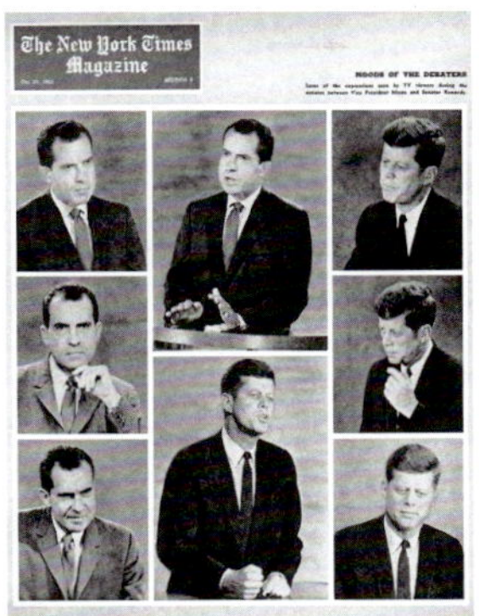

The New York Times Magazine, October 23, 1960

"Moods of the Debaters"

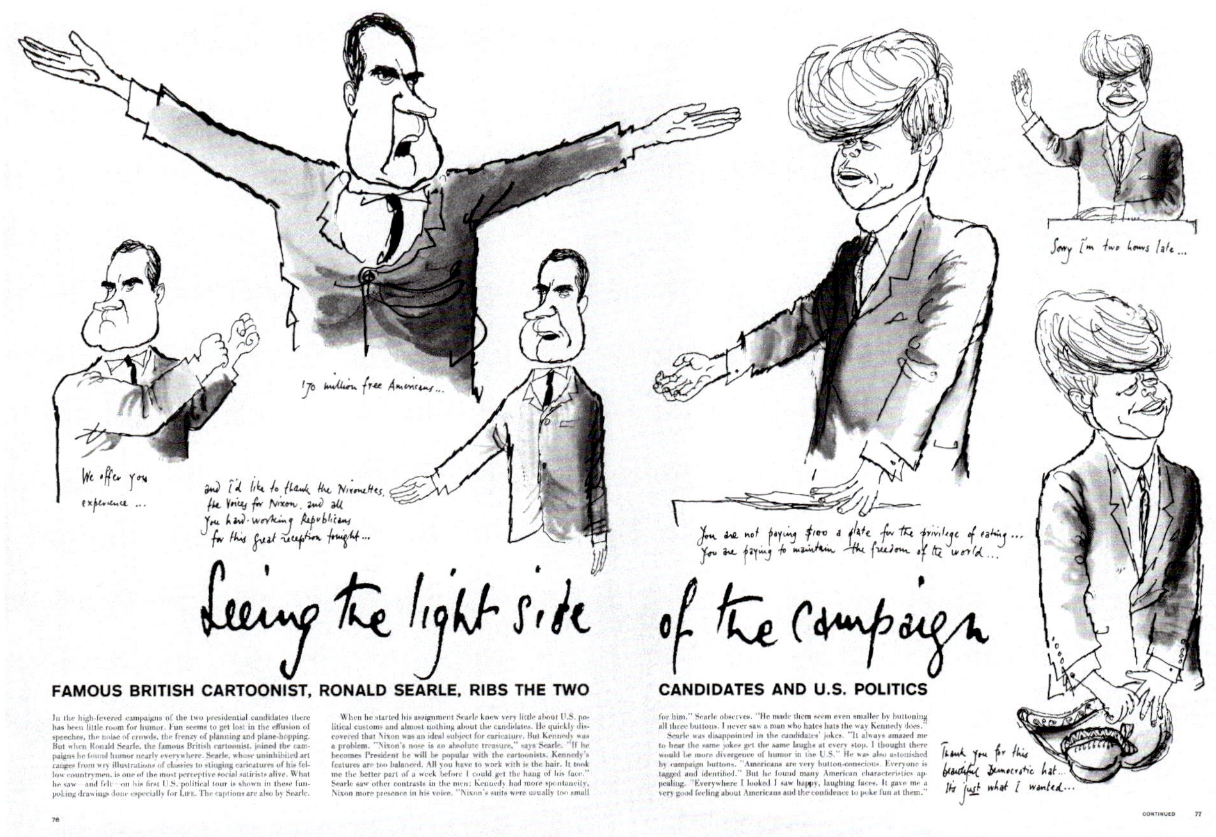

Life, October 31, 1960

"Seeing the Light Side of the Campaign: Famous British Cartoonist, Ronald Searle, Ribs the Two Candidates and U.S. Politics"

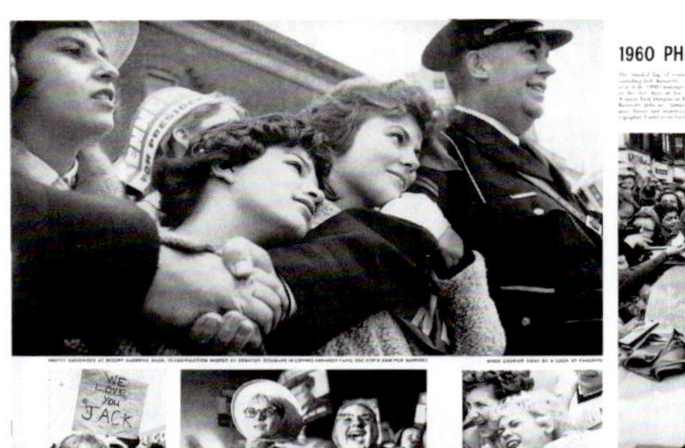

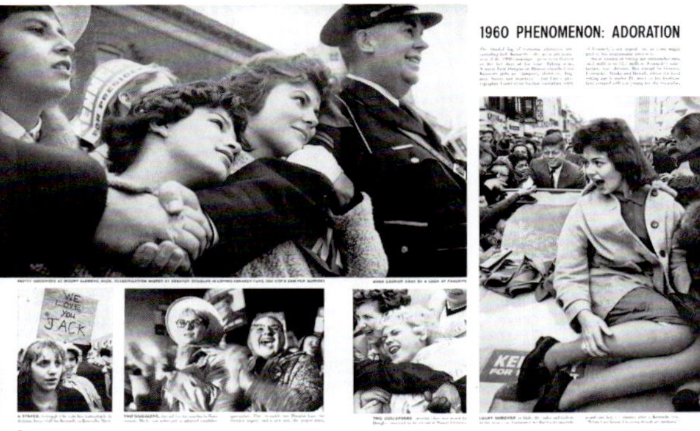

Life, November 7, 1960

"1960 Phenomenon: Adoration"

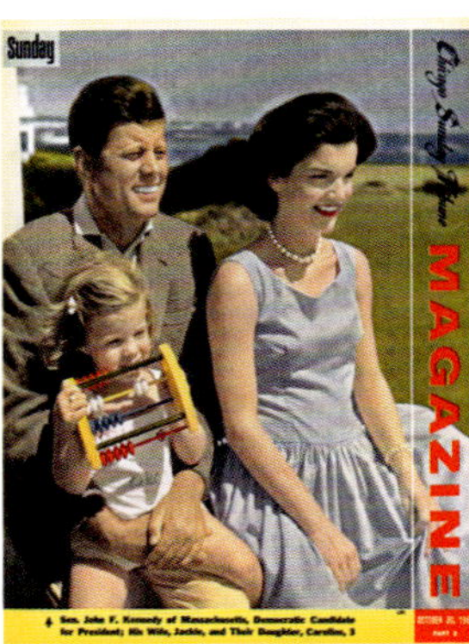

Chicago Sunday Tribune Magazine, October 30, 1960

"Sen. John F. Kennedy of Massachusetts . . ."

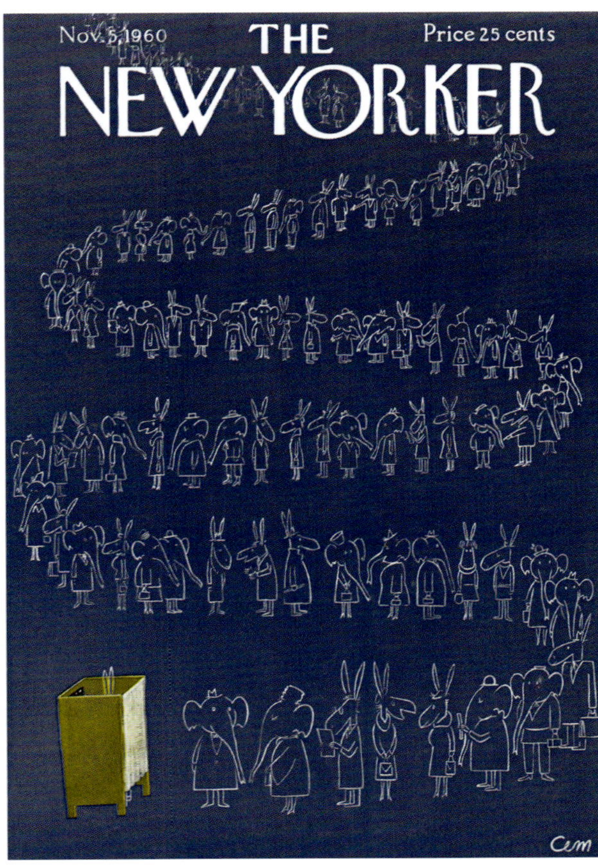

The New Yorker, November 5, 1960

Election edition

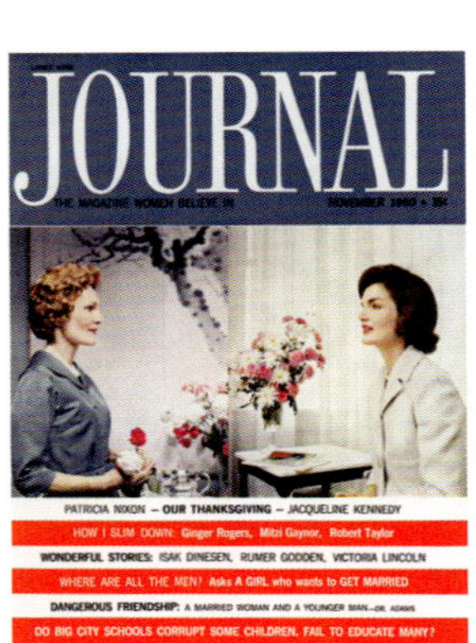

Ladies Home Journal, November 1960

"Our Thanksgiving: Patricia Nixon and Jacqueline Kennedy"

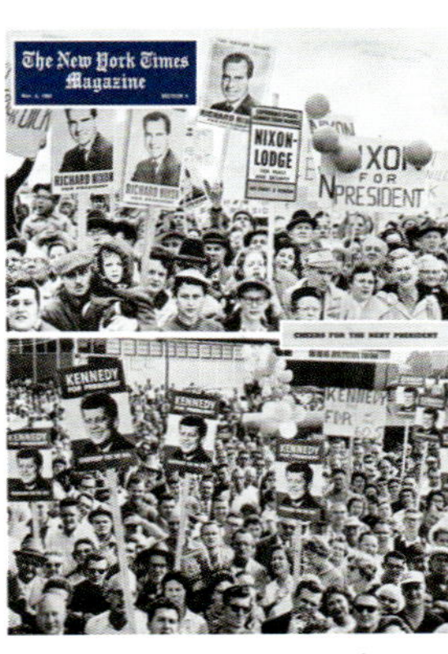

The New York Times Magazine, November 6, 1960

"Cheers for the Next President"

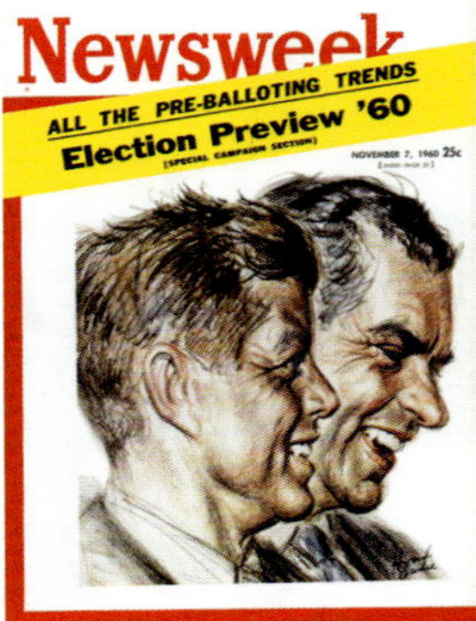

Newsweek, November 7, 1960

"All the Pre-Balloting Trends: Election Preview '60"

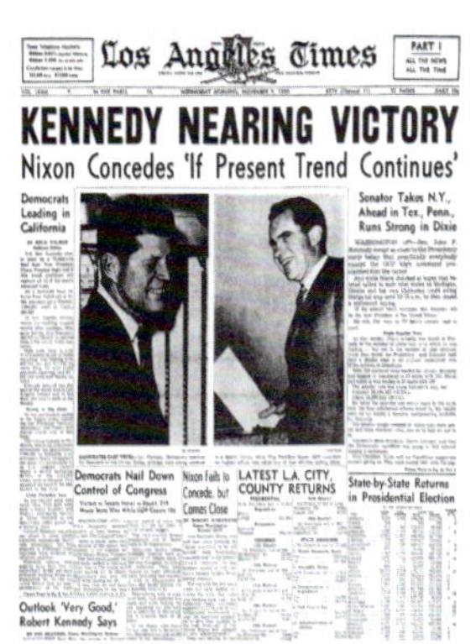

Los Angeles Times, November 9, 1960
"Kennedy Nearing Victory"

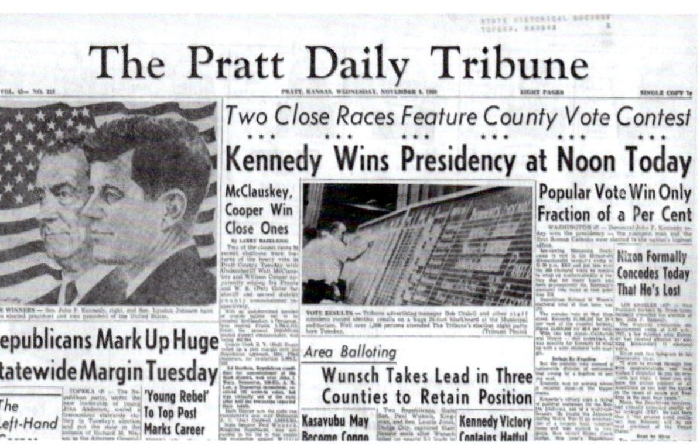

The Pratt Daily Tribune, November 9, 1960
"Kennedy Wins Presidency at Noon Today"

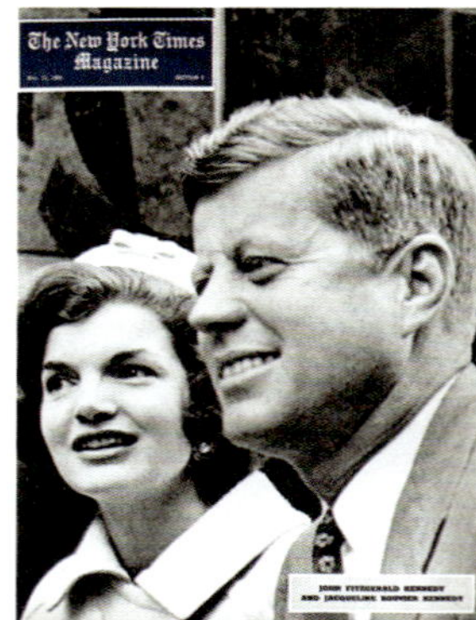

Boston American, November 9, 1960
"Kennedy for Sure!"

The New York Times Magazine, November 13, 1960
"John Fitzgerald Kennedy and Jacqueline Bouvier Kennedy"

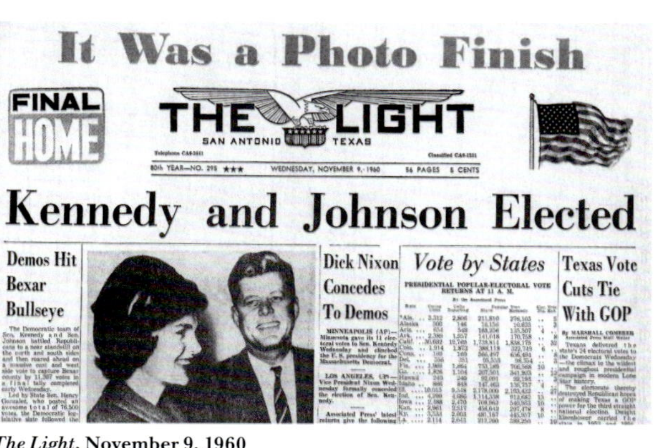

The Light, November 9, 1960
"Kennedy and Johnson Elected"

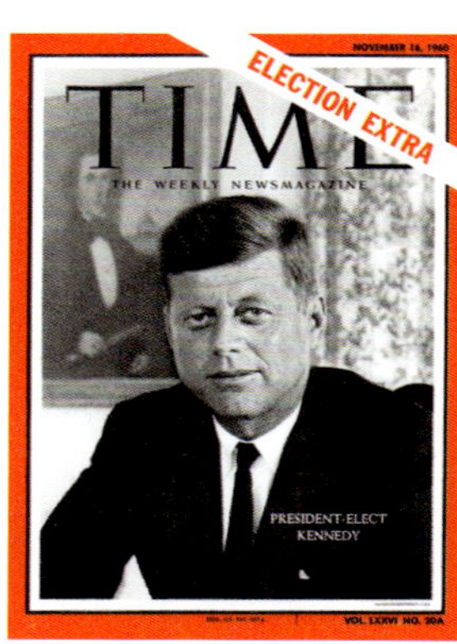

Time, November 16, 1960
"President-Elect Kennedy"

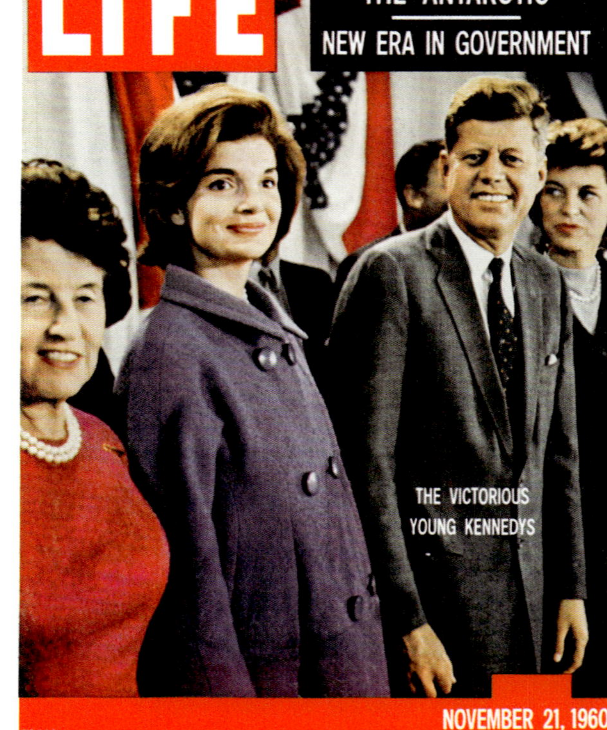

Life, November 21, 1960
"The Victorious Young Kennedys"

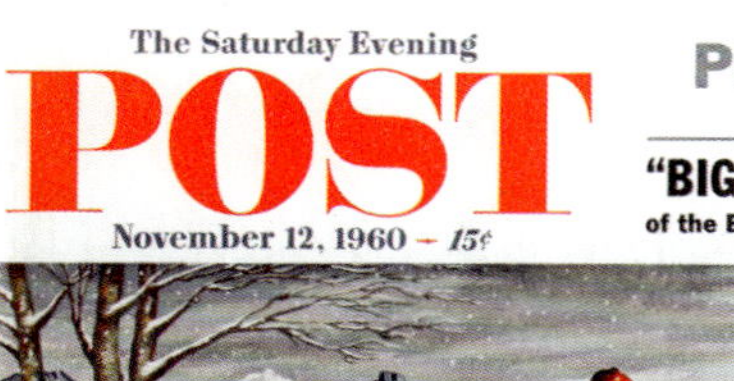

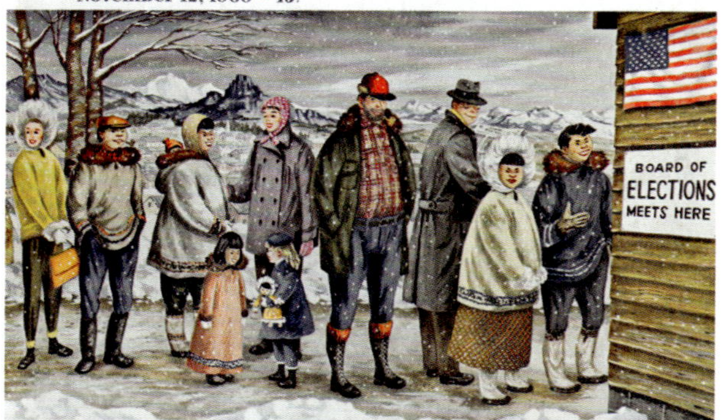

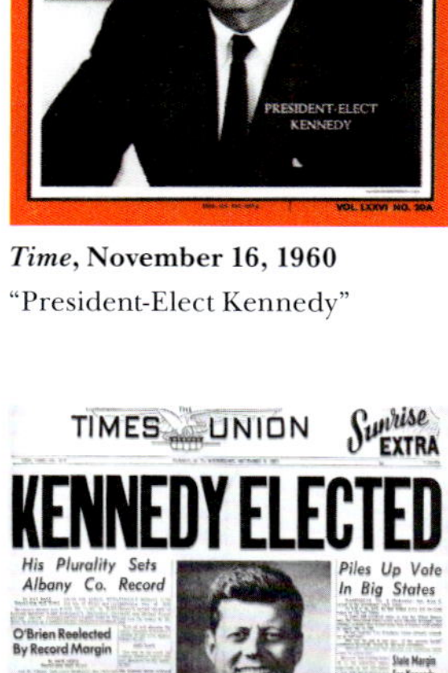

The Times Union, November 9, 1960
"Kennedy Elected: His Plurality Sets Albany Co. Record"

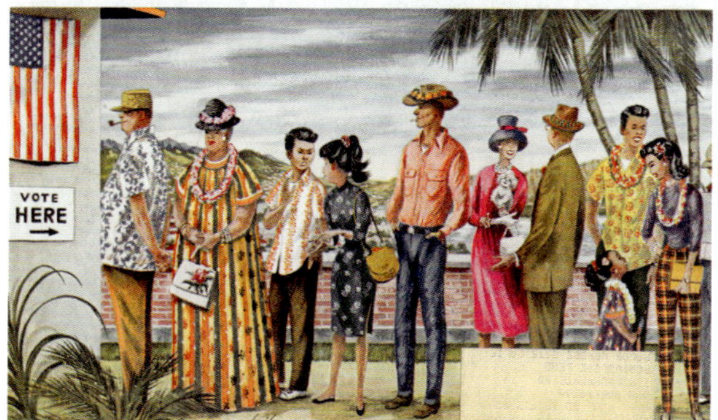

The Saturday Evening Post, November 12, 1960
"First Vote in the New States"

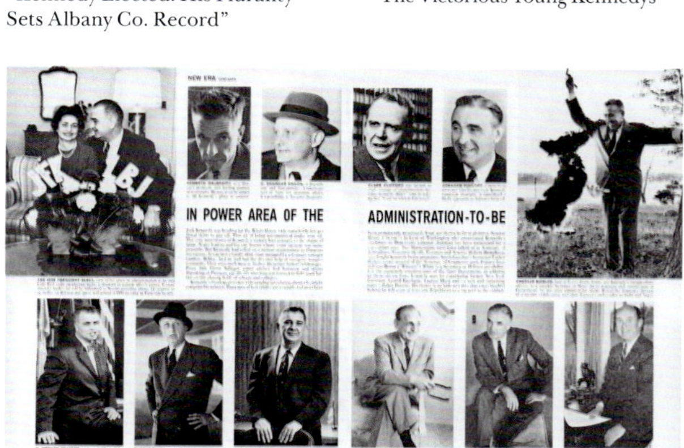

Life, November 21, 1960
"In Power Area of the Administration-To-Be"

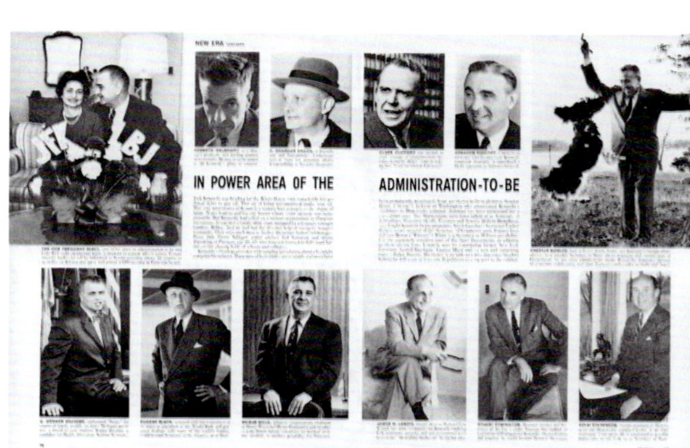

San Francisco Examiner, November 9, 1960
"Kennedy Wins!"

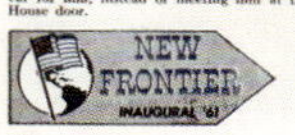

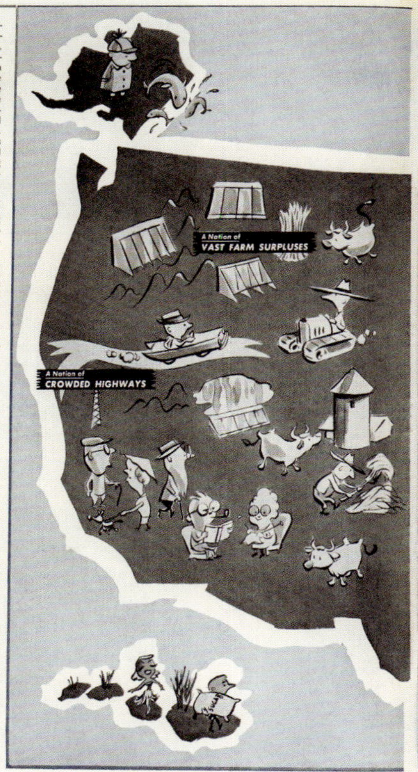

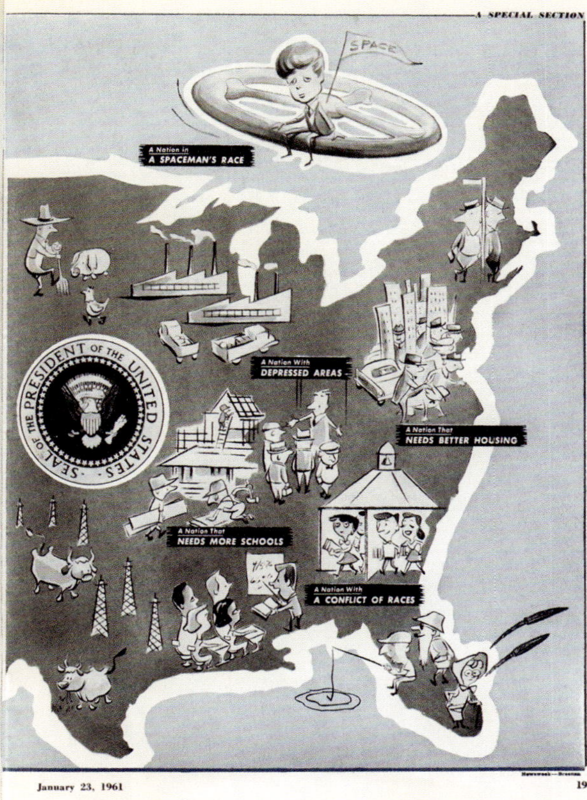

Newsweek, **January 23, 1961**

"'New Frontier'—Special Section"

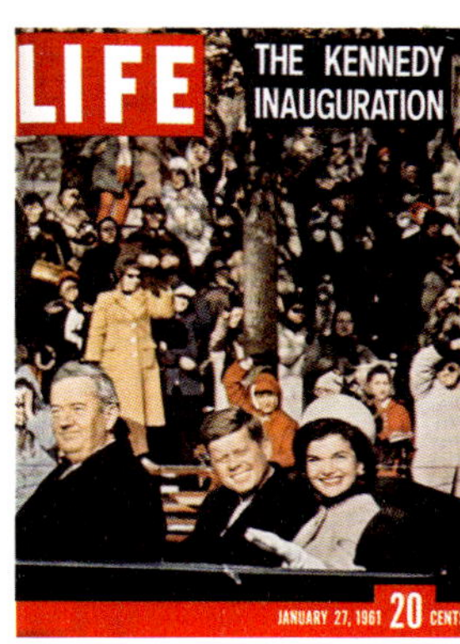

Life, **January 27, 1961**

"The Kennedy Inauguration"

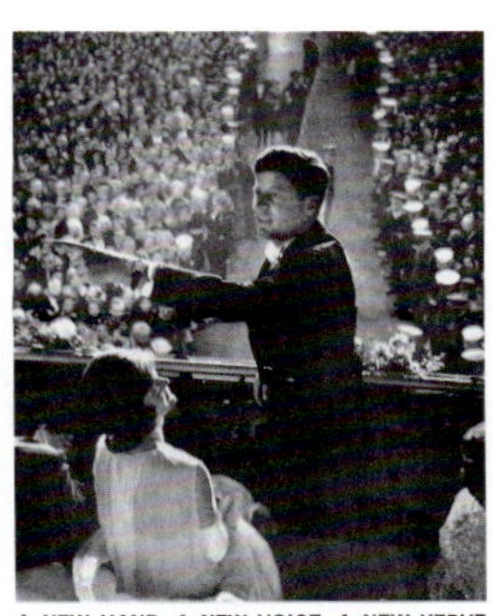

Life, **January 27, 1961**

"A New Hand, A New Voice,
A New Verve"

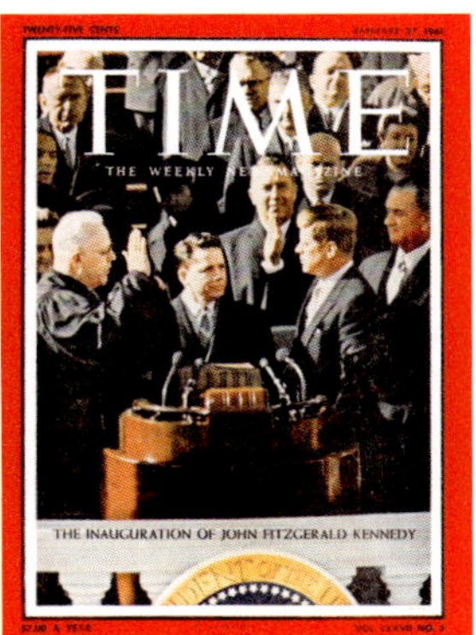

Time, **January 27, 1961**

"The Inauguration of John
Fitzgerald Kennedy"

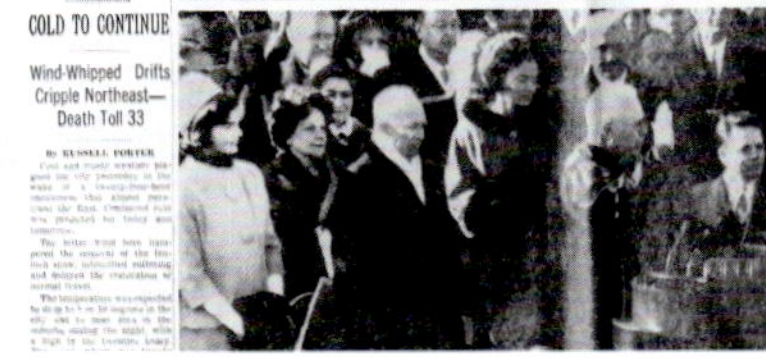

The New York Times, **January 21, 1961**

"Kennedy Sworn In, Asks 'Global Alliance'
Against Tyranny, Want, Disease, and War"

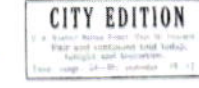

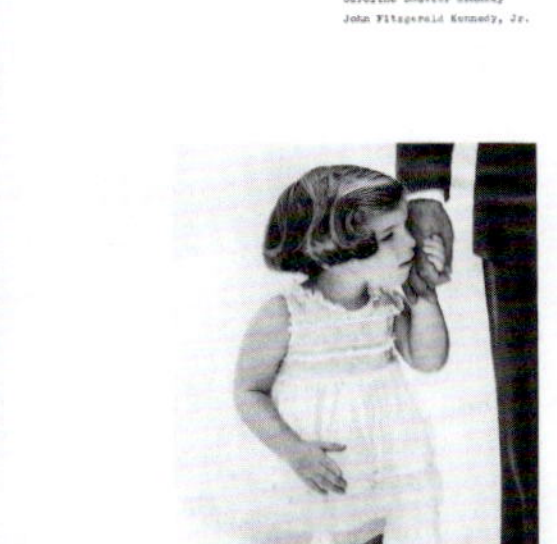

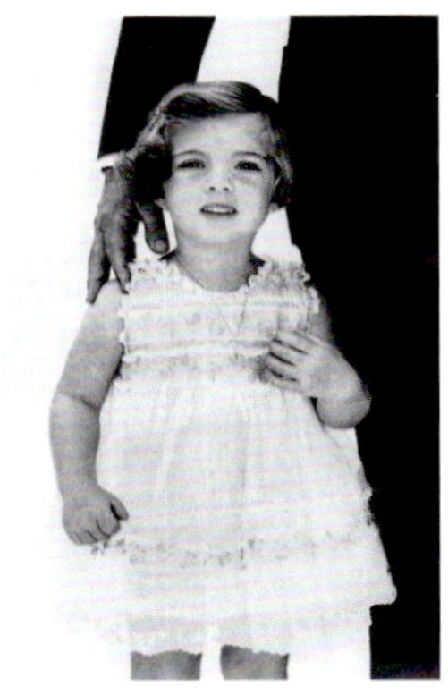

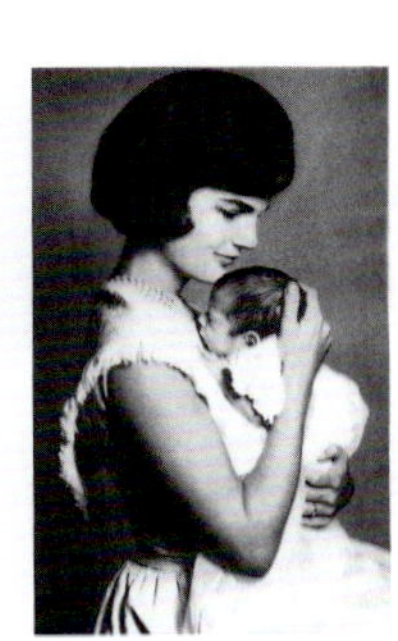

(ABOVE AND RIGHT) *Harper's Bazaar*, **February 1961**

"Avedon: Observations on the 34th First Family"

Newsweek, **January 23, 1961**

"'New Frontier'—Special Section"

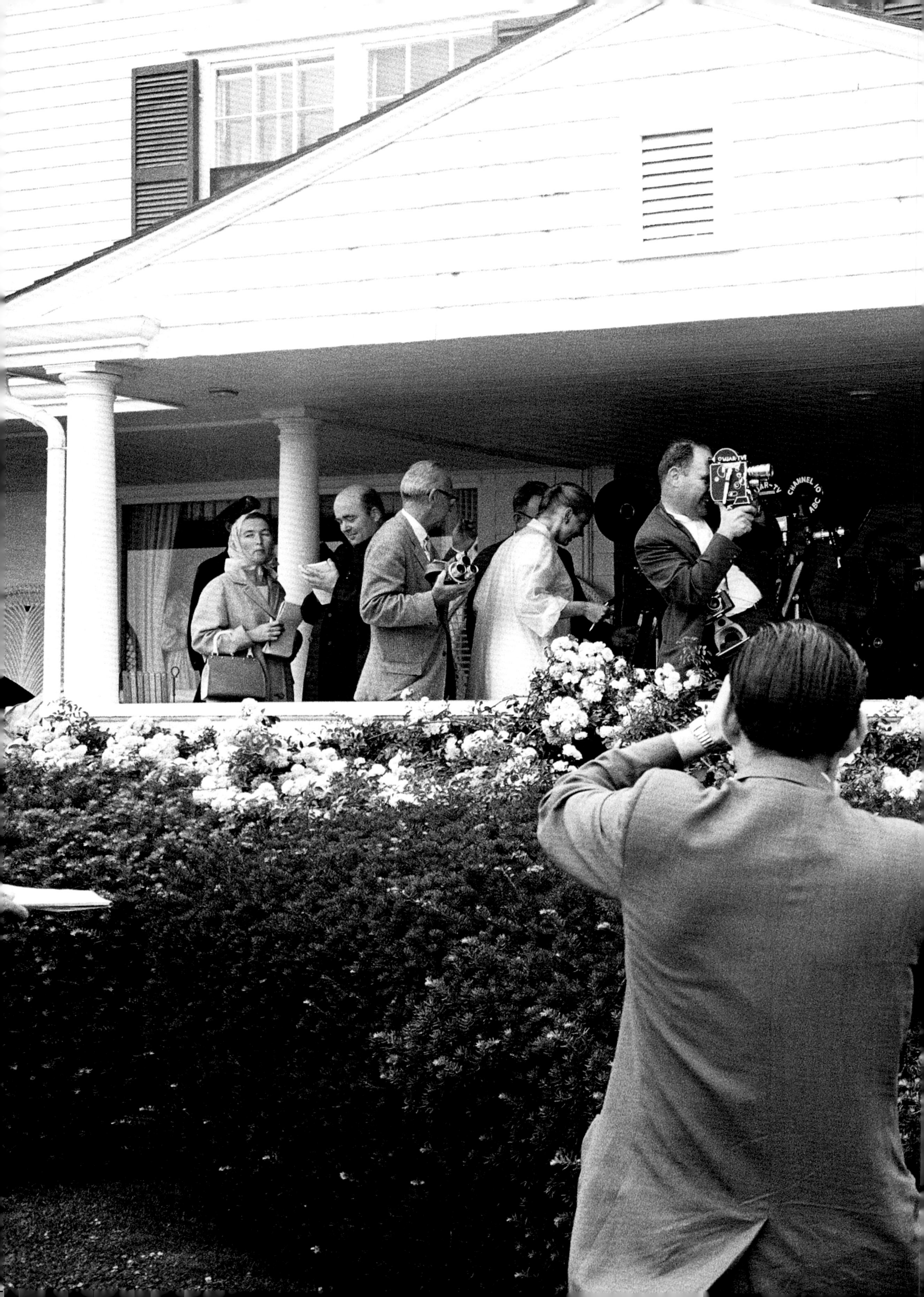

WSAR-TV
CHANNEL 10
ABC

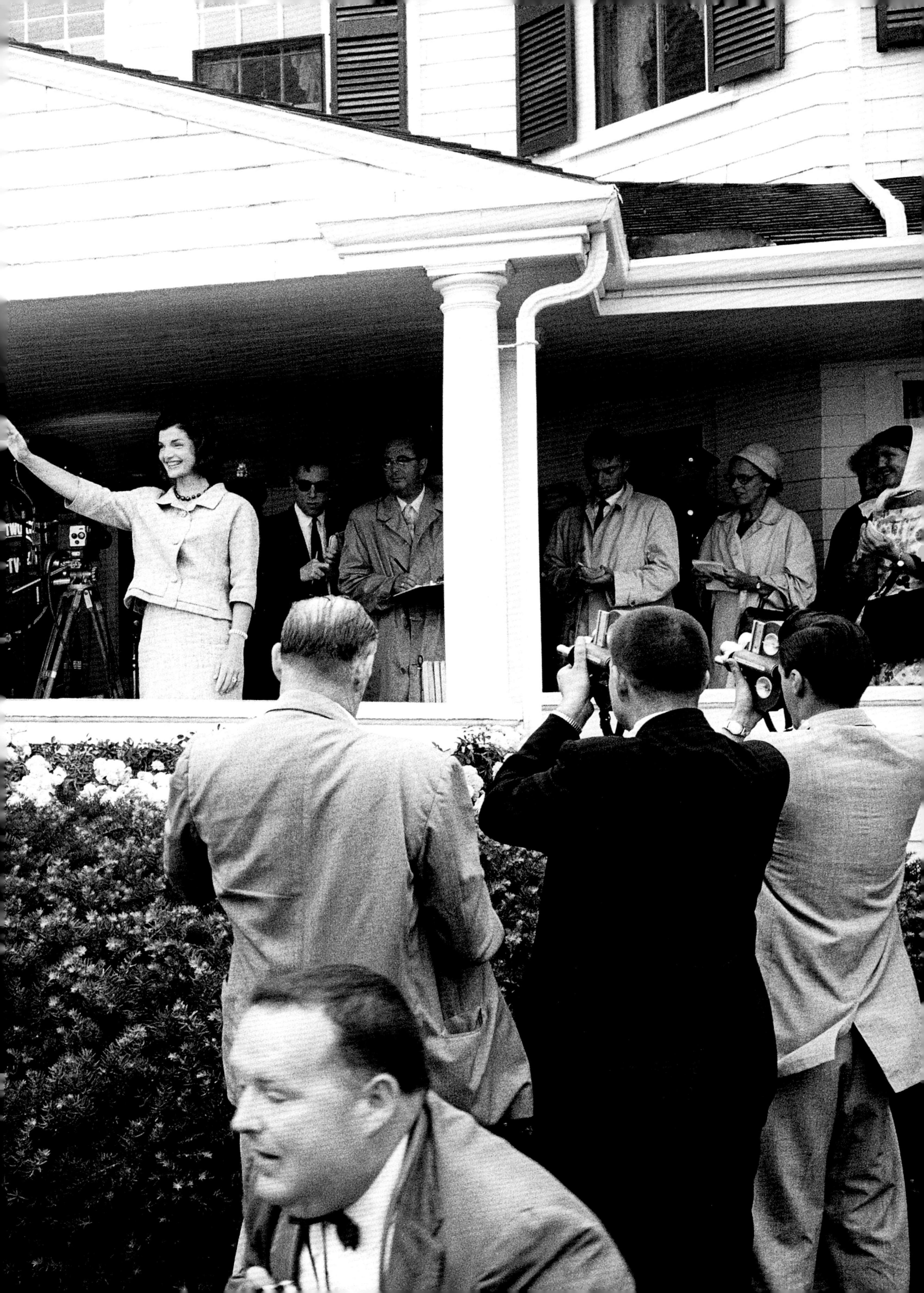

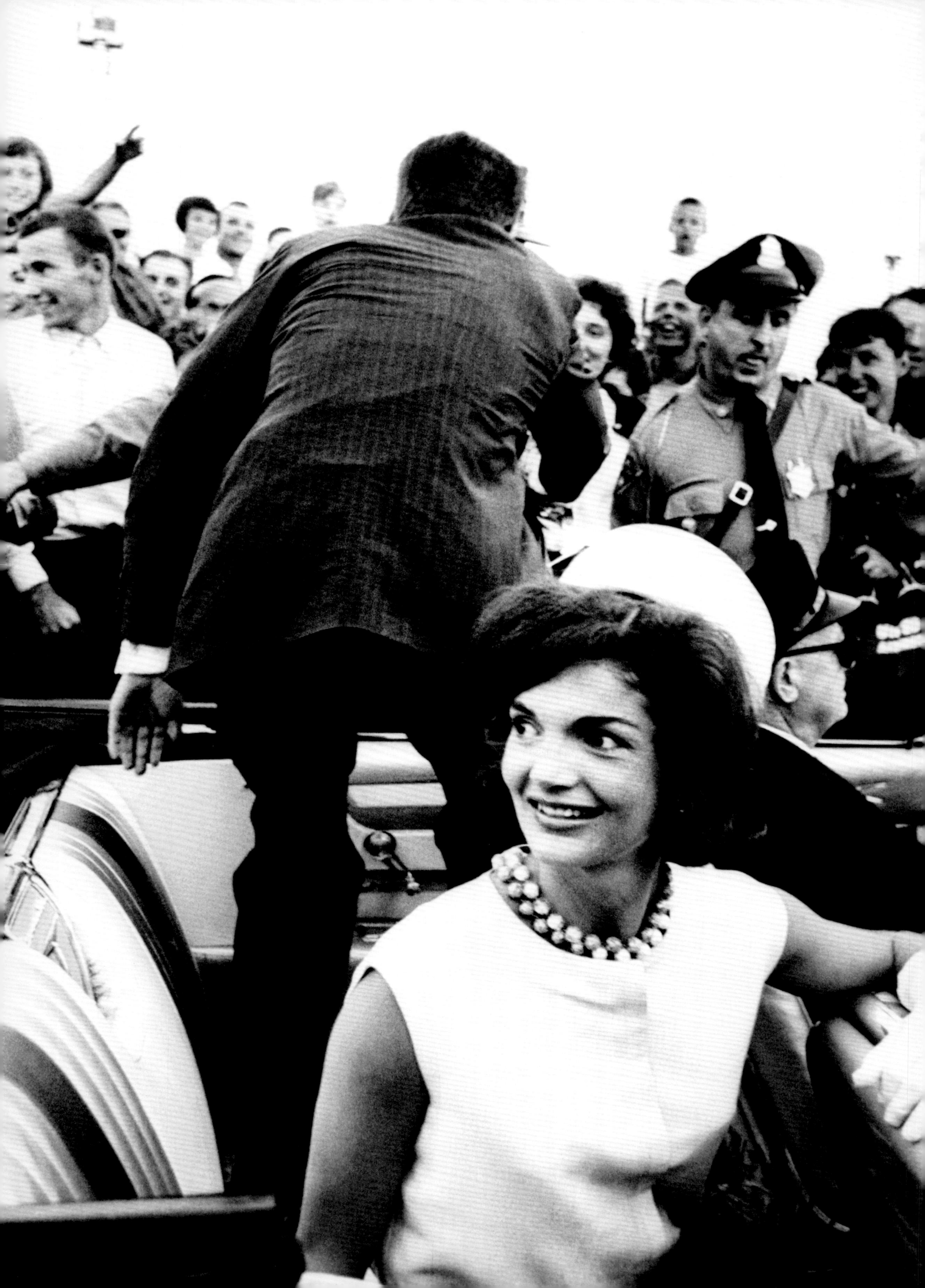

AN EVENING WITH
JACKIE KENNEDY...

...or, the Wild Wild West of the East *by Norman Mailer*

[…] It was the Summer of 1960, after the Democratic Convention, before the presidential campaign had formally begun, at Hyannis Port, site of the Summer White House — those of you who know Hyannis ("High-anus," as the natives say) will know how funny is the title — all those motels and a Summer White House too: the Kennedy compound, an enclosure of three summer homes belonging to Joe Kennedy, Sr., RFK, and JFK, with a modest amount of lawn and beach to share among them. In those historic days the lawn was overrun with journalists, cameramen, magazine writers, politicians, delegations, friends and neighboring gentry, government intellectuals, family, a prince, some Massachusetts state troopers, and red-necked hard-nosed tourists patrolling outside the fence for a glimpse of the boy. He was much in evidence, a bit of every-where that morning, including the lawn, and particularly handsome at times as one has described elsewhere (*Esquire*, November, 1960), looking like a good version of Charles Lindbergh at noon on a hot August day. Well, Jackie Kennedy was inside in her living room sitting around talking with a few of us, Arthur Schlesinger Jr. and his wife Marian, Prince Radziwill, Peter Maas the writer, Jacques Lowe the photographer, and Pierre Salinger. We were a curious assortment indeed, as oddly assembled in our way as some of the do-gooders and real baddies on the lawn outside. It would have taken a hostess of broad and perhaps dubious gifts, Perle Mesta, no doubt, or Ethel Merman, or Elsa Maxwell, to have woven some mood into this occasion, because pop! were going the flashbulbs out of the crazy August sun on the sun-drenched terrace just beyond the bay window at our back […]

And I had the impression that Jackie Kennedy was almost suffering in the flesh from their invasion of her house, her terrace, her share of the lands, that if the popping of the flashbulbs went on until midnight on the terrace outside she would have a tic forever in the corner of her eye. Because that was the second impression of her, of a lady with delicate and exacerbated nerves. She was no broad hostess, not at all; broad hostesses are monumental animals turned mellow: hippopotami, rhinoceri, plump lion, sweet gorilla, warm bear. Jackie Kennedy was a cat, narrow and wild, and her fur was being rubbed every which way. This was the second impression. The first had been simpler. It had been merely of a college girl who was nice. Nice and clean and very merry. I had entered her house perspiring — talk of the politician, I was wearing a black suit myself, a washable, the only one in my closet not completely unpressed that morning, I had been forced to pick a white shirt with button-down collar: all the white summer shirts were in the laundry. What a set-to I had had with Adele Mailer at breakfast. Food half-digested in anger, sweating like a goat, tense at the pit of my stomach for what I would be interviewing Kennedy in a half hour, I was feeling not a little jangled when we were introduced, and we stumbled mutually over a few polite remarks, which was my fault I'm sure more than hers for I must have had a look in my eyes—I remember I felt like a drunk marine who knows in all clarity that if he doesn't have a fight soon it'll be good for his character but terrible for his constitution.

She offered me a cool drink—iced verbena tea with sprig of mint no doubt—but the expression in my face must have been rich because she added, still standing by the screen in the doorway, "We do have something harder of course," and something droll and hard came into her eyes as if she were a very naughty eight-year-old indeed. More than one photograph of Jackie Kennedy had put forward just this saucy regard—it was obviously the life of her charm. But I had not been prepared for another quality, of shyness conceivably. There was something quite remote in her. Not willed, not chilly,

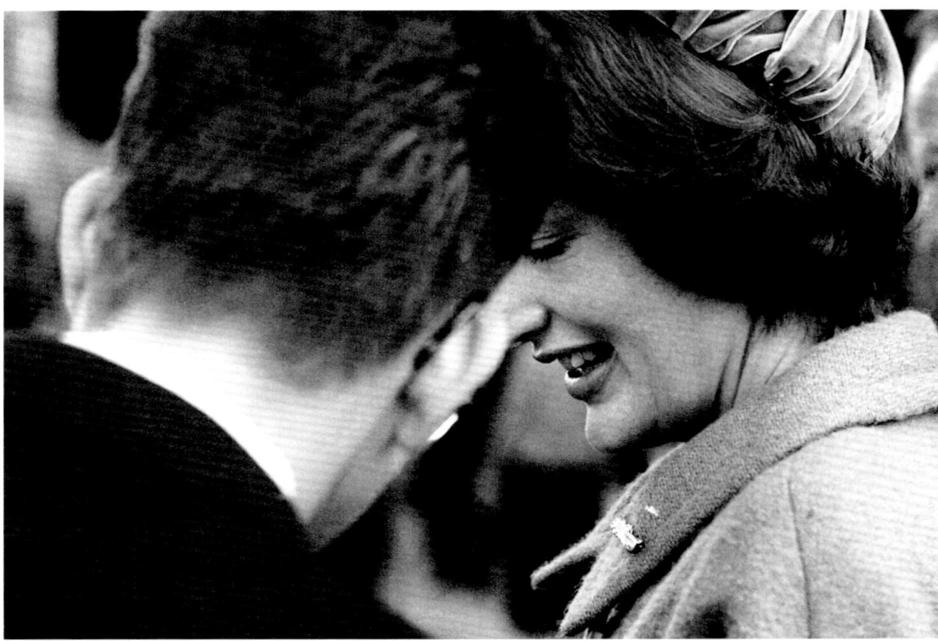

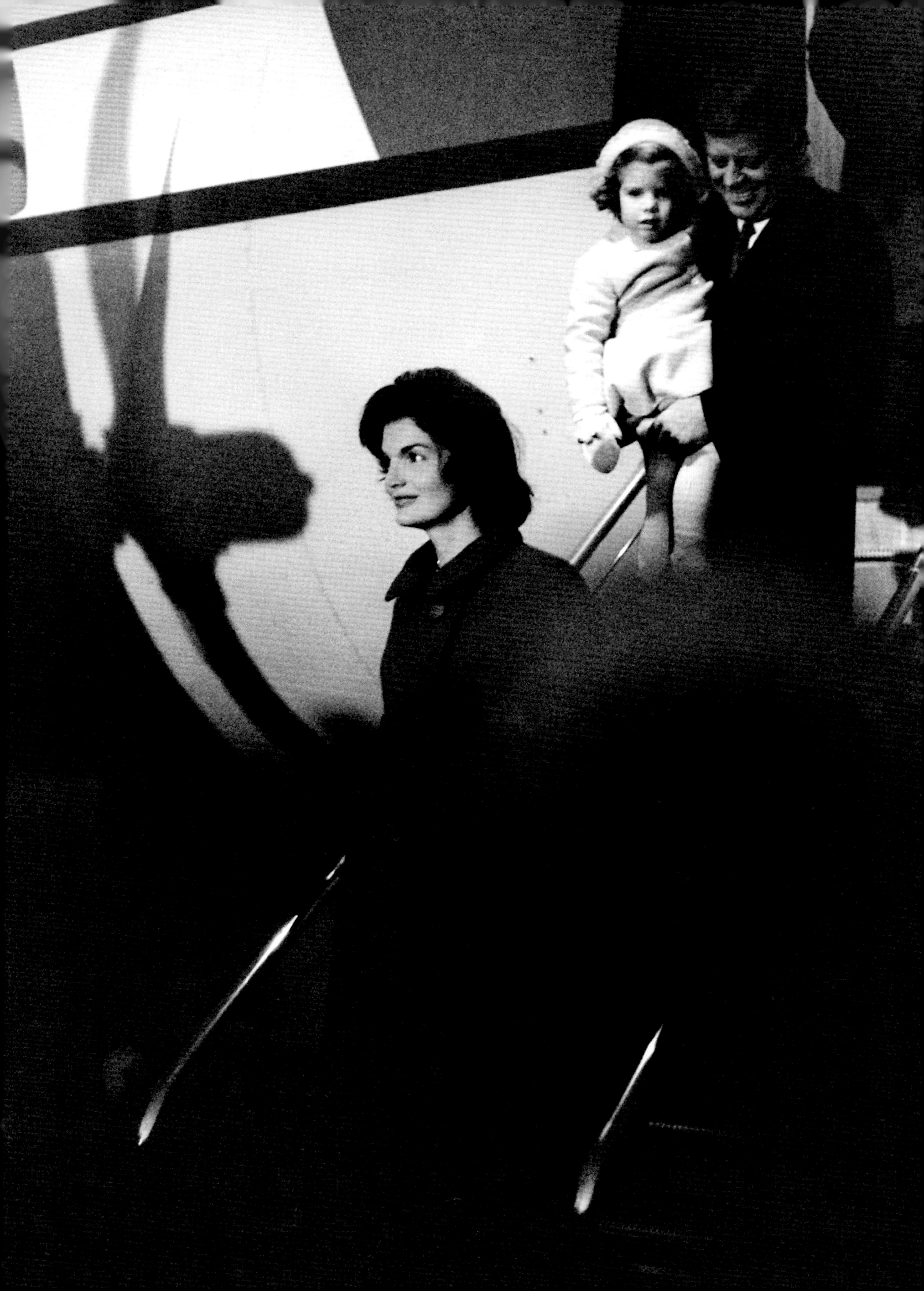

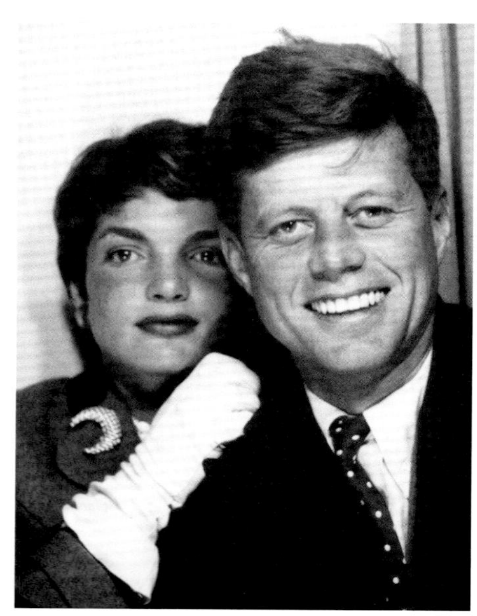

not directed at anyone in particular, but distant, detached as the psychologists say, moody and abstracted the novelists used to say. As we sat around the coffee table on summer couches, summer chairs, a pleasant living room in light colors, lemon, white and gold seeming to predominate, the sort of living room one might expect to find in Cleveland, may it be, at the home of a fairly important young executive whose wife had taste, sitting there, watching people go by, the group I mentioned earlier kept a kind of conversation going. Its center, if it had one, was obviously Jackie Kennedy. There was a natural tendency to look at her and see if she were amused. She did not sit there like a movie star with a ripe olive in each eye for the brain, but in fact gave conversation back, made some of it, laughed often. We had one short conversation about Provincetown, which was pleasant. She remarked that she had been staying no more than fifty miles away for all these summers but had never seen it. She must, I assured her. It was one of the few fishing villages in America which still had beauty. Besides it was the Wild West of the East. The local police were the Indians and the beatniks were the poor hard-working settlers. Her eyes turned merry. "Oh, I'd love to see it," she said. But how did one go? In three black limousines and fifty police for escort, or in a sports car at four A. M. with dark glasses? "I suppose now I'll never get to see it," she said wistfully.

She had a keen sense of laughter, but it revolved around the absurdities of the world. She was probably not altogether unlike a soldier who has been up at the front for two weeks. There was a hint of gone laughter. Soldiers who have had it bad enough can laugh at the fact some trooper got killed crossing an open area because he wanted to change his socks from khaki to green. The front lawn of this house must have been, I suppose, a kind of no-man's-land for a lady. The story I remember her telling was about Stash, Prince Radziwill, her brother-in-law, who had gone into the second-story bathroom that morning to take a shave and discovered, to his lack of complete pleasure, that a crush of tourists was watching him from across the road. Yes, the house had been besieged, and one knew she thought of the sightseers as a mob, a motley of gargoyles, like the horde who riot through the last pages in *The Day of the Locust*.

Since there was an air of self-indulgence about her, subtle but precise, one was certain she liked time to compose herself. While we sat there she must have gotten up a half-dozen times, to go away for two minutes, come back for three. She had the exasperated impatience of a college girl. One expected her to swear mildly. "Oh

""I liked Jackie Kennedy, that she was not at all stuffy, that she had perhaps a touch of that artful madness which suggests future drama."

—Norman Mailer

Christ!" or "Sugar!" or "Fudge!" And each time she got up, there was a glimpse of her calves, surprisingly thin, not unfeverish. I was reminded of the legs on those adolescent Southern girls who used to go out together and walk up and down the streets of Fayetteville, North Carolina, in the Summer of 1944 at Fort Bragg. In the petulant Southern air of their boredom many of us had found something luminous that summer, a mixture of languor, heat, innocence and stupidity which was our cocktail vis-à-vis the knowledge we were going soon to Europe or the other war. One mentions this to underline the determinedly romantic aura in which one had chosen to behold Jackie Kennedy. There was a charm this other short Summer of 1960 in the thought a young man with a young attractive wife might soon become President. It offered possibilities and vista; it brought a touch of life to the monotonies of politics, those monotonies so profoundly entrenched into the hinges and mortar of the Eisenhower administration. It was thus more interesting to look at Jackie Kennedy as a woman than as a probable First Lady. Perhaps it was out of some such motive, such a desire

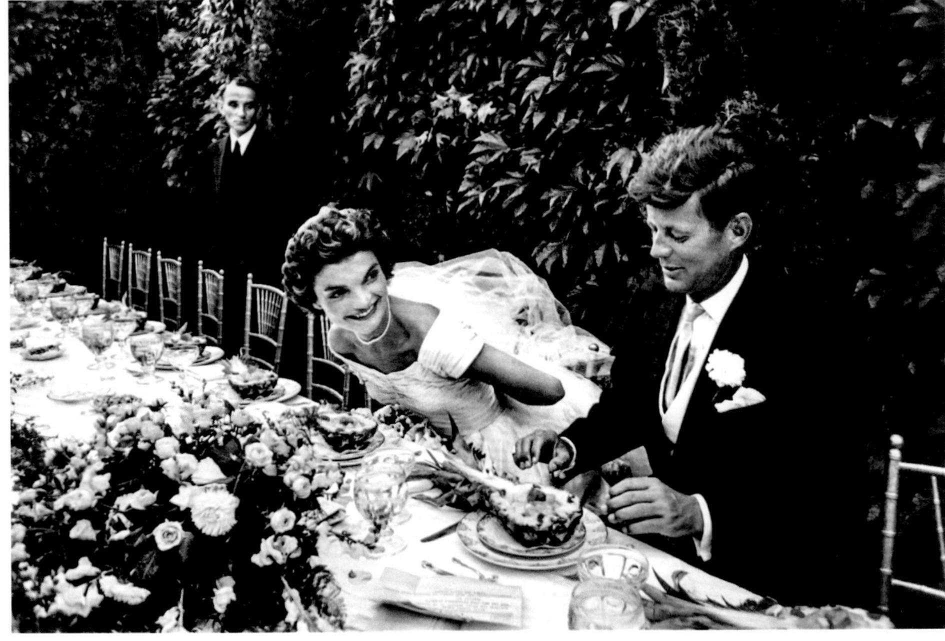

LEFT *September 12, 1953.* The couple's highly publicized wedding reception took place at the home of Jackie's mother, Mrs. Hugh Auchincloss. It took them two hours to shake the hands of all 1,200 guests in attendance, practically making the event a coronation. *Photo, Lisa Larsen*

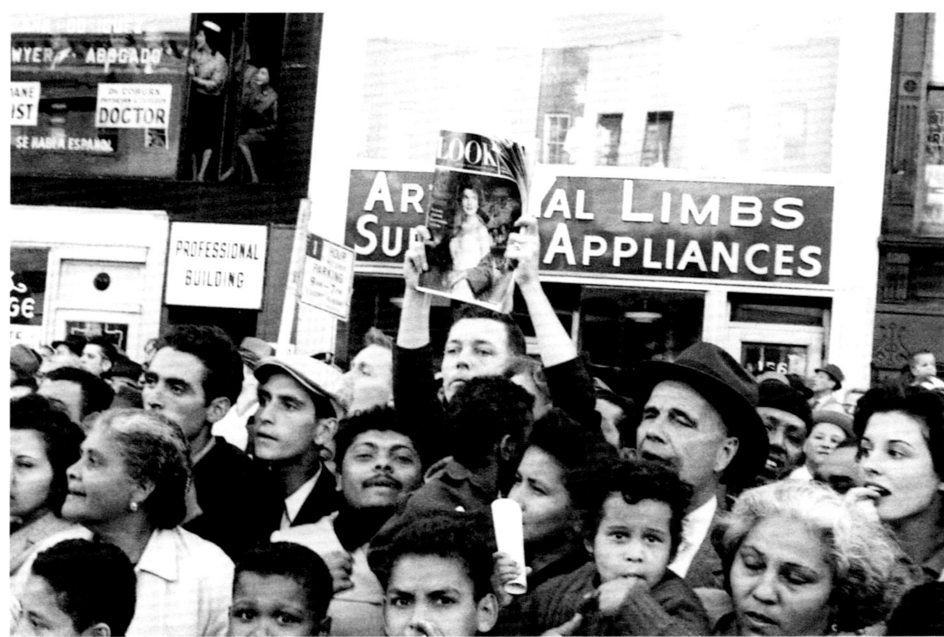

for the clean air and tang of unexpected montage, that I spoke about her in just the way I did later that afternoon.

"Do you think she's happy?" asked a lady, and old friend on the beach at Wellfleet.

"I guess she would rather spend her life on the Riviera."

"What would she do there?"

"End up as the mystery woman, maybe, in a good murder case."

"Wow," said the lady, giving me my reward.

It had been my way of saying I liked Jackie Kennedy, that she was not at all stuffy, that she had perhaps a touch of artful madness which suggests future drama.

My interview the first day had been a little short, and I was invited back for another one the following day. Rather nicely, Senator Kennedy invited me to bring anyone I wanted. About a week later I realized this was part of his acumen. You can tell a lot about a man by whom he invites in such a circumstance. Will it be a political expert or the wife? I invited my wife. The presence of this second lady is not unimportant, because this time she had the conversation with Jackie Kennedy. While I was busy somewhere or other, they were introduced. Down by the Kennedy family wharf. The Senator was about to take Jackie for a sail. The two women had a certain small general resemblance. They were something like the same height, they both had dark hair, and they had each been wearing it in a similar style for many years. Perhaps this was enough to create a quick political intimacy. "I wish," said Jackie Kennedy, "that I didn't have to go on this corny sail, because I would like very much to talk to you, Mrs. Mailer." A stroke. Mrs. M. did not like many people quickly, but Jackie now had a champion. It must have been a pleasant sight. Two attractive witches by the water's edge.

[…] After I saw the Kennedys I added a few paragraphs to my piece about the convention, secretly relieved to have liked them, for my piece was most favorable to the Senator, and how would I have rewritten it if I had not liked him? With several mishaps it was printed three weeks before the election. Several days later, I received a letter from Jackie Kennedy. It was a nice letter, generous in its praise, accurate in its details. She remembered, for example, the color of the sweater my wife had been wearing, and mentioned she had one like it in the same purple. I answered with a letter which was out of measure. I was in a Napoleonic mood, I had decided to run

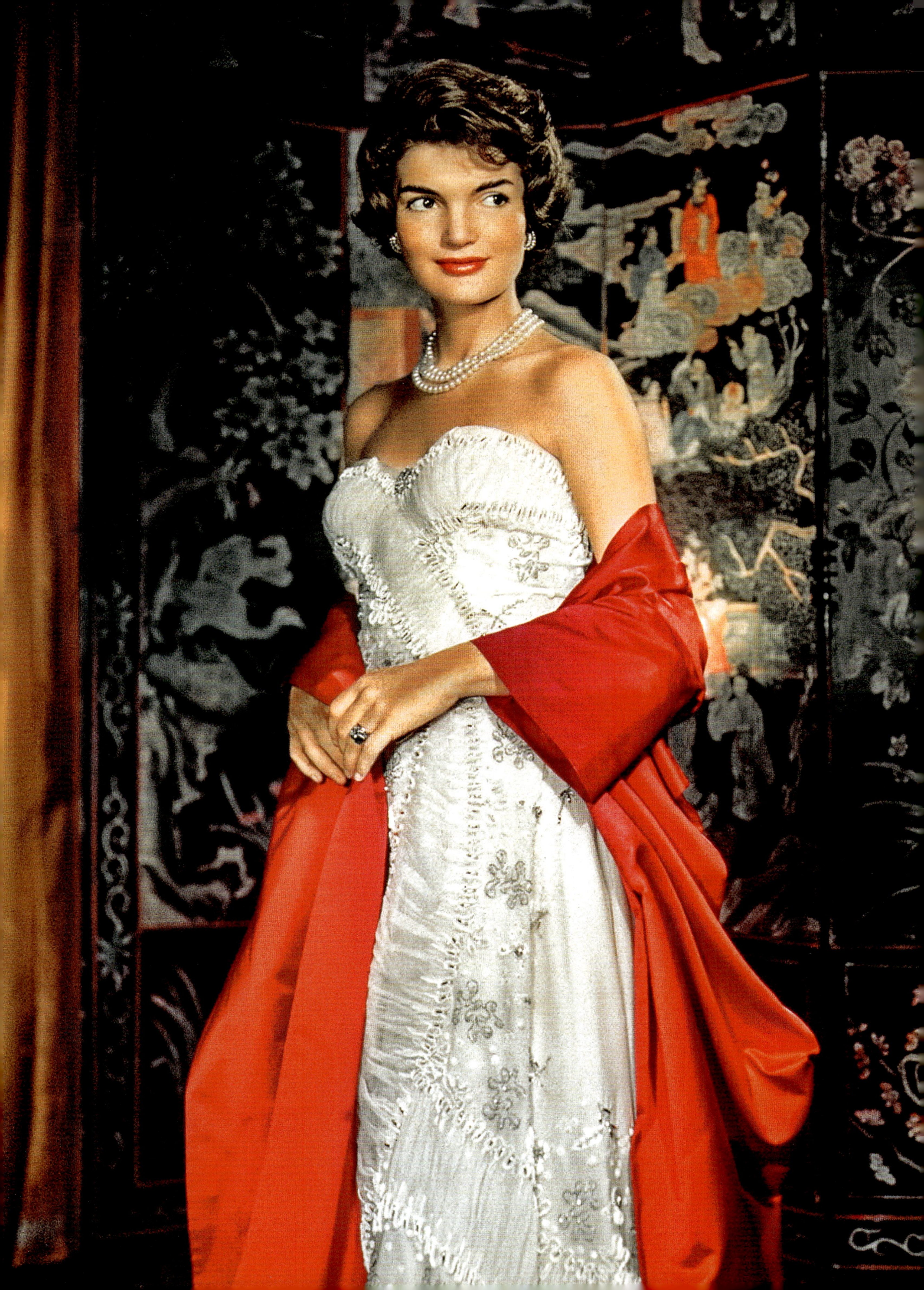

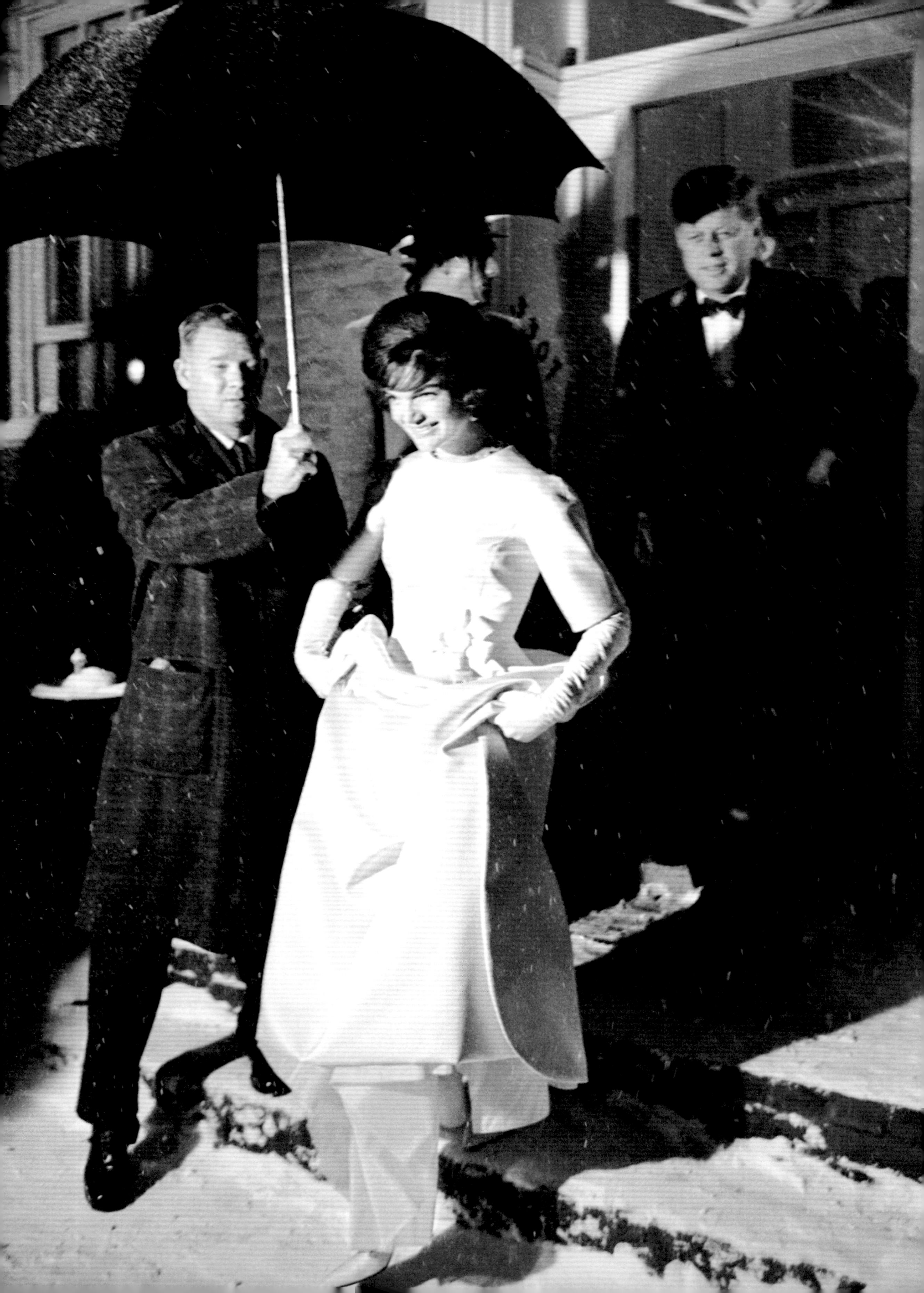

—Norman Mailer

for Mayor of New York; in a few weeks, I was to zoom and crash—my sense of reality was extravagant. So in response to a modestly voiced notion by Mrs. Kennedy that she wondered if the "impressionistic" way in which I had treated the convention could be applied to the history of the past, I replied in the cadence of a Goethe that while I was now engaged in certain difficulties of writing about the present, I hoped one day when work was done to do a biography of the Marquis de Sade and the "odd strange honor of this man."

I supposed this is as close to the edge as I have ever come. At the time, it seemed reasonable that Mrs. Kennedy, with her publicized interest in France and the eighteenth century, might be fascinated by de Sade. The style of his thought was, after all, a fair climax to the Age of Reason.

Now sociology has few virtues, but one of them is sanity. In writing such a letter to Mrs. Kennedy I was losing my sociology. The Catholic wife of a Catholic candidate for President was not likely to find de Sade as familiar as a tea cozy. I received no reply.

OPPOSITE *January 19, 1961.* On the snowy evening before Kennedy's inauguration, he and Jackie emerge from their home in Georgetown to attend a gala fund-raiser organized by friend Frank Sinatra. *Photo, Paul Schutzer*

BELOW *January 12, 1961.* At the Hotel Pierre in New York City, fashion editors gather around designer Oleg Cassini, who would be Jackie's exclusive couturier in her years in the White House, as he shows them sketches of three gowns he has designed for her inaugural activities. The first lady's love of clean lines and understated elegance, known as the "Jackie Look," ushered in a new era of American fashion. *Photo, Anonymous*

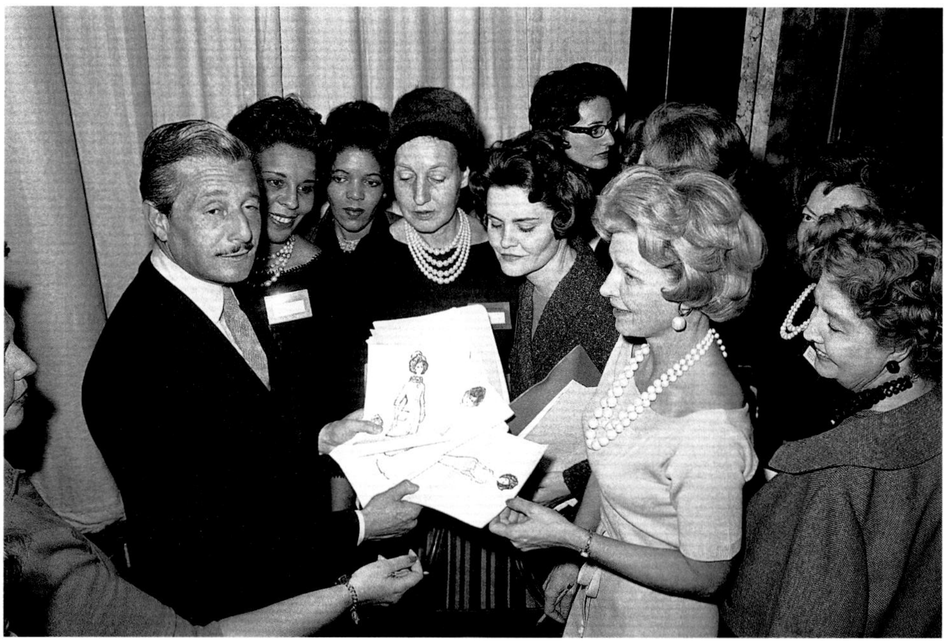

PART III · AN EVENING WITH JACKIE KENNEDY...

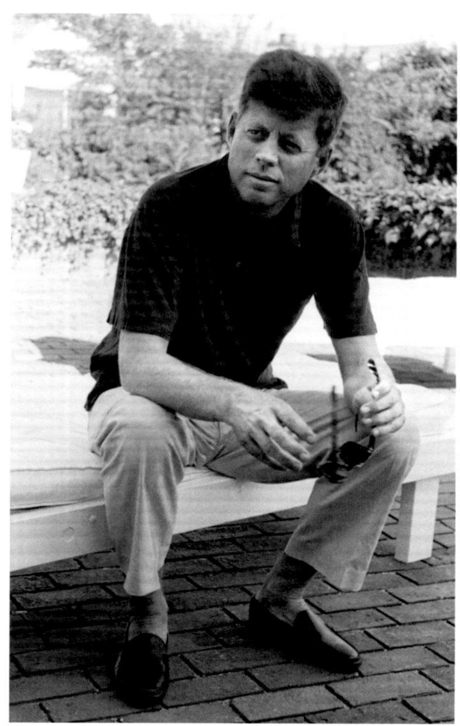

I had smashed the limits of such letter-writing. In politics a break in sociology is as clean as a break in etiquette. [...]

Now if I have bothered to show my absence of proportion, it is because I want to put forward a notion which will seem criminal to some of you, but was believed in by me, is still believed in by me, and so affects what I write about the Kennedys.

Jack Kennedy won the election by one hundred thousand votes. A lot of people could claim therefore to be the mind behind his victory. Jack Arvey could say the photo-finish would have gone the other way if not for the track near his Chicago machine. J. Edgar Hoover might say he saved the victory because he did not investigate the track. Lyndon Johnson could point to LBJ Ranch, and the vote of Texas. *Time* Magazine could tell you that the abstract intrepidity of their support for Nixon gave the duke to Kennedy. Sinatra would not be surprised if the late ones who glommed onto Kennedy were not more numerous than the early-risers he scattered. And one does not even need to speak of the Corporations, the Mob, the money they delivered by messenger, the credit they would use later. So if I came to the cool conclusion I had won the election for Kennedy with my piece in *Esquire*, the thought might be high presumption, but it was not unique. I had done something curious but indispensable for the campaign—succeeded in making it dramatic. I had not shifted one hundred thousand votes directly, I had not. But a million people might have read my piece and some of them talked to other people. The cadres of Stevenson Democrats whose morale was low might now revive with an argument that Kennedy was different in substance from Nixon. Dramatically different. The piece titled *Superman Comes to the Supermarket* affected volunteer work for Kennedy, enough to make a clean critical difference through the country. But such counting is a quibble. At bottom I had the feeling that if there were a power which made presidents, a power which might be termed Wall Street or Capitalism or The Establishment, a Mind or Collective Mind of some Spirit, some Master, or indeed *the* Master, no less, that then perhaps my article had turned that intelligence a fair hair in its circuits. This was what I thought. Right or wrong, I thought it, still do. [...]

[From "An Evening With Jackie Kennedy, or, the Wild West of the East," originally published in *Esquire*, July 1962]

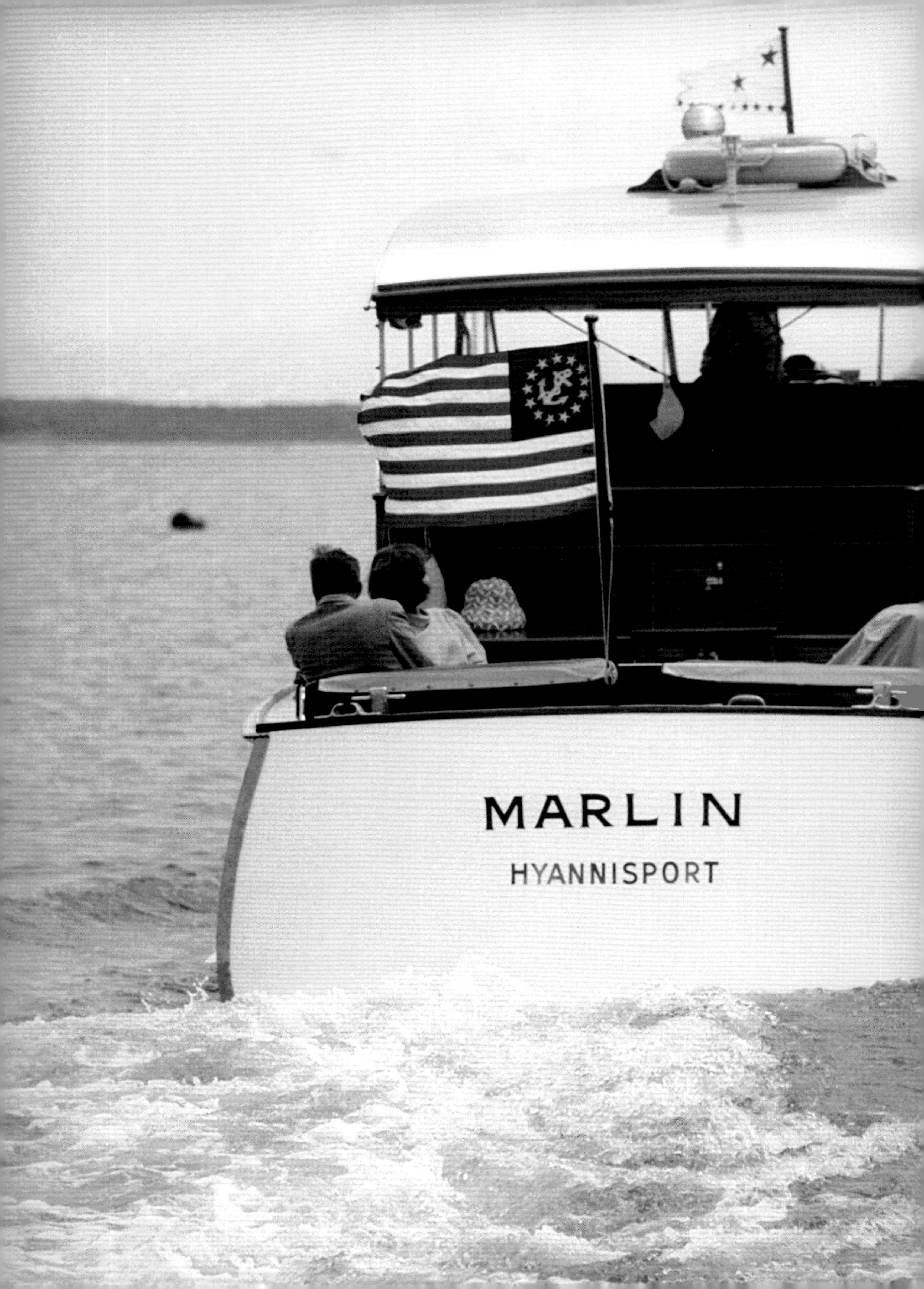

MARLIN
HYANNISPORT

[ ] ~~This lurching,~~ unhappy, pompous and most corrupt nation—
could it have the courage finally to take on a new image for
itself, ~~could it accept the hero whose lineaments had already
been formed by myth~~ was it brave enough to put into office not
only one of its ablest men, its most efficient, its most conquistadorial (for Kennedy's capture of the Democratic Party deserves
the word) but also one of its more ~~enigmatic~~ [mysterious] men, (the national
psyche must shiver in its sleep at the image of Mickey Mantle-cum-
Lindbergh in office, and a First Lady with an Eighteenth-century
face.) Yes, America was at last ~~moving toward the destiny of~~ [engaging the fate of]
its myth, its consciousness about to be accelerated or cruelly
depressed in its choice between two young men in their forties
who, no matter how close, dull, or indifferent their stated
politics might be, were radical poles apart, for one was ~~sober, x~~
the apotheosis of ~~plugging~~ opportunistic lead, all radium spent,
the other ~~royal,~~ handsome as a ~~king~~ [prince] in the unstated aristocracy
of ~~all~~ [the] American ~~myths of the flesh.~~ [dreams] So, finally, ~~through these
mass-techniques, mutations, bastards, idiots and simple~~ [ponderous] monsters
~~of historic birth which are the mass-media in America, through
the papers, magazines, televisions, press agents and advertisements
of a presidential campaign~~ would come a choice which history had
never presented to a nation before— one could vote for glamour
or for ugliness, a staggering and most stunning choice— would
the nation be brave enough to ~~vote for~~ [enlist] the romantic dream of
itself, ~~to~~ [would it] vote for the ~~new~~ image in the ~~unconscious mirror it~~ [mirror of its unconscious,]
~~had wrought,~~ [were] the people indeed brave enough to ~~vote~~ [hope] for ~~that~~
an acceleration of Time, ~~that augment of drama in its destiny which~~ [for that new life of drama which]

NORMAN MAILER
A BRIEF HISTORY

Biography by J. Michael Lennon

Norman Mailer was one of the most prolific, outspoken, and accomplished writers of the second half of the 20th century. A relentless innovator and connoisseur of narrative forms and techniques, he published over 40 books in virtually every literary genre, and was acclaimed as one of the pioneers of the New Journalism, a mode of writing in which fictional techniques are used in nonfiction works. He was also a leading public intellectual who spoke out on a broad range of issues, from the dangers of plastic and television's deadening effects to the Women's Liberation Movement and the Iraq War. His dramatic interpretations of American cultural phenomena and his idiosyncratic views on sex, violence, power, technology, architecture, identity, and the art of writing appeared in a 60-year run of novels and nonfiction narratives, plays, poems, sports reporting, political essays, biographies, and countless media interviews.

Born in Long Branch, New Jersey, in 1923 to Jewish immigrant parents, he grew up in Brooklyn, New York, and graduated from Harvard University in 1943, where he studied engineering. Mailer was drafted into the U.S. Army in 1944 and served as a

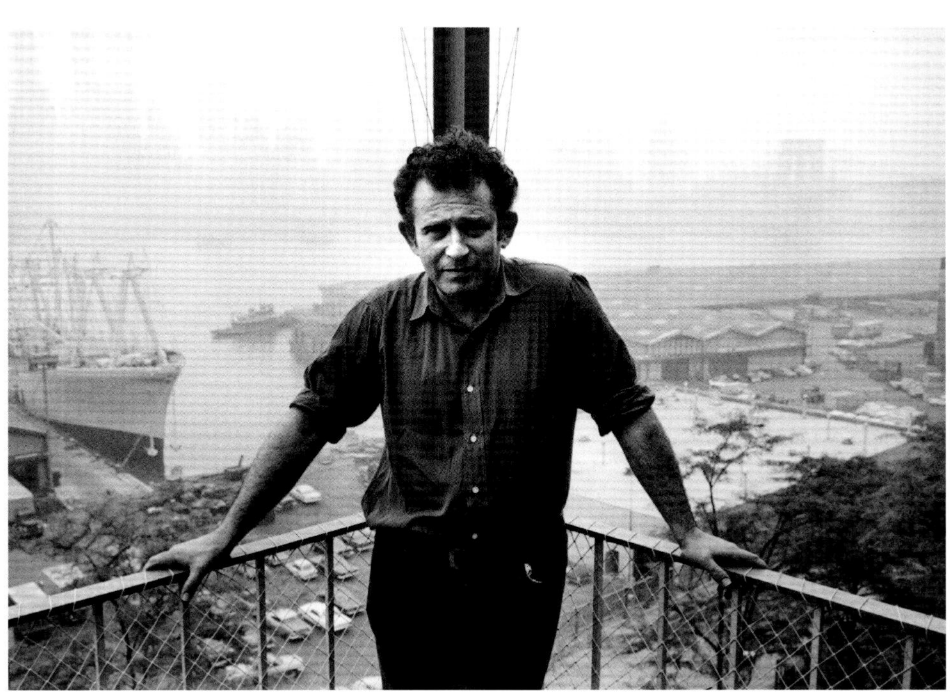

OPPOSITE *Summer 1960.* Mailer wrote rapidly, beginning in late July, and finishing in mid-August after interviewing Kennedy in Hyannis. He wrote a longhand draft, and then worked over the typescript before submitting it for publication in *Esquire*'s November issue, on the newsstands on October 18, exactly three weeks before Election Day.

LEFT *1965.* Mailer on the balcony of his Brooklyn Heights apartment overlooking the Buttermilk Channel of the East River directly across from the southern tip of Manhattan. He lived there from 1962 to 2007. *Photo, Inge Morath*

BELOW *Spring 1969.* From late April to early June 1969, Mailer campaigned in the Democratic mayoral primary, speaking in all five New York City boroughs, and getting strong media coverage. Come Election Day—June 17—former mayor Robert Wagner Jr. took the day, leaving Mailer to come in fourth in a field of five. *Photo, Anonymous*

OPPOSITE *November 1960.* Infuriated when *Esquire* publisher Arnold Gingrich changed the last word of the essay's title without his permission, Mailer broke ties with the magazine until mid-1962. In later years, he often corrected the title of the essay when he autographed copies of the November 1960 issue.

rifleman and cook in the Pacific theater from 1944–46. While attending the Sorbonne on the G.I. Bill after the war, he published his first novel, *The Naked and the Dead* (1948). The book traces the campaign to take a Japanese-held island, and is widely considered to be one of the finest novels of WWII. It has never gone out of print and has been translated into a score of languages. Other major novels include *The Deer Park* (1955), *An American Dream* (1965), *Why Are We in Vietnam?* (1967), *Ancient Evenings* (1983), and *Harlot's Ghost* (1991). His eleventh and final novel, *The Castle in the Forest*, an exploration of Adolf Hitler's boyhood, was published in 2007, months before his death. Mailer is the only major American author to have best sellers in seven consecutive decades.

A cofounder of *The Village Voice* in 1955, Mailer also wrote for *Life*, *Esquire*, *The New Yorker*, *Playboy*, *Harper's*, *Partisan Review*, *The Paris Review*, *Parade*, and *Vanity Fair*, as well as many counterculture and underground publications. His magazine work appears in several collections, including *Advertisements for Myself* (1959), the book where he established his characteristic voice—bold, acerbic, and self-referenced.

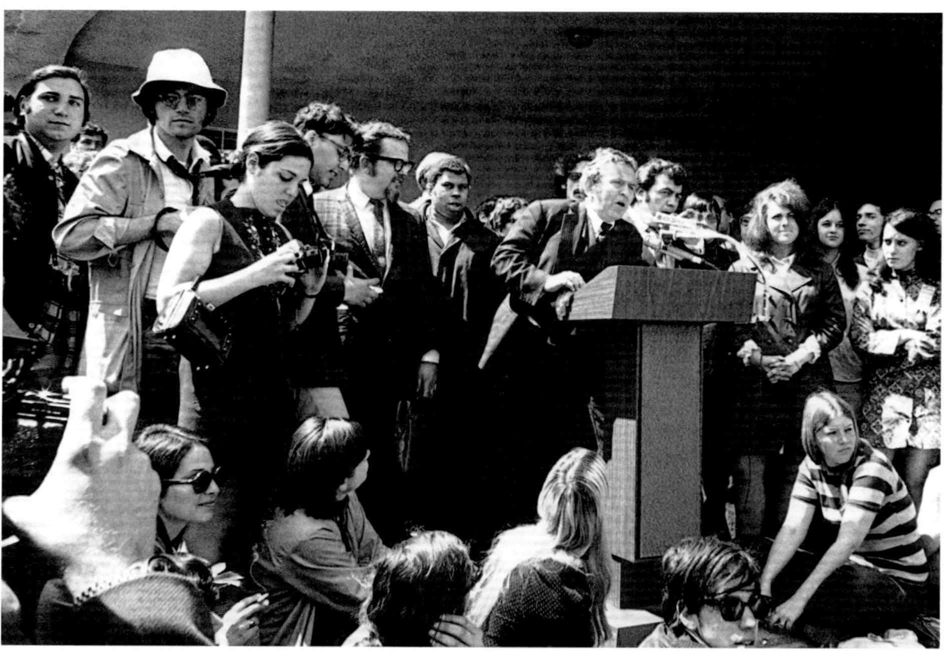

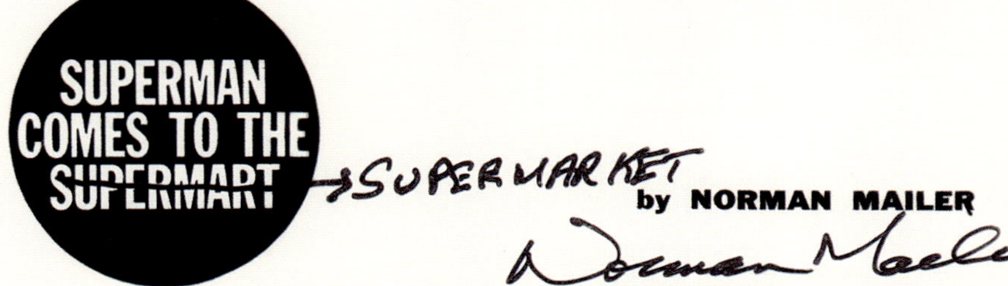

FOR once let us try to think about a political convention without losing ourselves in housing projects of fact and issue. Politics has its virtues, all too many of them—it would not rank with baseball as a topic of conversation if it did not satisfy a great many things—but one can suspect that its secret appeal is close to nicotine. Smoking cigarettes insulates one from one's life, one does not feel as much, often happily so, and politics quarantines one from history; most of the people who nourish themselves in the political life are in the game not to make history but to be diverted from the history which is being made.

If that Democratic Convention which has now receded behind the brow of the Summer of 1960 is only half-remembered in the excitements of moving toward the election, it may be exactly the time to consider it again, because the mountain of facts which concealed its features last July has been blown away in the winds of High Television, and the man-in-the-street (that peculiar political term which refers to the quixotic voter who will pull the lever for some reason so salient as: "I had a brown-nose lieutenant once with Nixon's looks," or "that Kennedy must have false teeth"), the not so easily estimated man-in-the-street has forgotten most of what happened and could no more tell you who Kennedy was fighting against than you or I could place a bet on who was leading the American League in batting during the month of June.

So to try to talk about what happened is easier now than in the days of the convention, one does not have to put everything in—an act of writing which calls for a bulldozer rather than a pen—one can try to make one's little point and dress it with a ribbon or two of metaphor. All to the good. Because mysteries are irritated by facts, and the 1960 Democratic Convention began as one mystery and ended as another.

Since mystery is an emotion which is repugnant to a political animal (why else lead a life of bad banquet dinners, cigar smoke, camp chairs, foul breath, and excruciatingly dull jargon if not to avoid the echoes of what is not known), the psychic separation between what was happening on the floor, in the caucus rooms, in the headquarters, and what was happening in parallel to the history of the nation was mystery enough to drown the proceedings in gloom. It was on the one hand a dull convention, one of the less interesting by general agreement, relieved by local bits of color, given two half hours of excitement by two demonstrations for Stevenson, buoyed up by the class of the Kennedy machine, turned by the surprise of Johnson's nomination as vice-president, but, all the same, dull, depressed in its over-all tone, the big fiestas subdued, the gossip flat, no real air of excitement, just moments—or as they say in bullfighting—details. Yet it was also, one could argue—and one may argue this yet—it was also one of the most important conventions in America's history, it could prove conceivably to be the most important. The man it nominated was unlike any politician who had ever run for President

in the history of the land, and if elected he would come to power in a year when America was in danger of drifting into a profound decline.

II.

A Descriptive of the Delegates: Sons and Daughters of the Republic in a Legitimate Panic; Small-time Practitioners of Small-town Political Judo in the Big Town and the Big Time

Depression obviously has its several roots: it is the doubtful protection which comes from not recognizing failure, it is the psychic burden of exhaustion, and it is also, and very often, that discipline of the will or the ego which enables one to continue working when one's unadmitted emotion is panic. And panic it was I think which sat as the largest single sentiment in the breast of the collective delegates as they came to convene in Los Angeles. Delegates are not the noblest sons and daughters of the Republic; a man of taste, arrived from Mars, would take one look at a convention floor and leave forever, convinced he had seen one of the drearier squats of Hell. If one still smells the faint living echo of a carnival wine, the pepper of a bullfight, the rag, drag, and panoply of a jousting tourney, it is all swallowed and regurgitated by the senses into the fouler cud of a death gas one must rid oneself of—a cigar-smoking, stale-aired, slack-jawed, butt-littered, foul, bleak, hard-working, bureaucratic death gas of language and faces ("Yes, those *faces*," says the man from Mars: lawyers, judges, ward heelers, *mafiosos*, Southern goons and grandees, grand old ladies, trade unionists and finks), of pompous words and long pauses which lay like a leaden pain over fever, the fever that one is in, over, or is it that one is just behind history? A legitimate panic for a delegate. America is a nation of experts without roots; we are always creating tacticians who are blind to strategy and strategists who cannot take a step, and when the culture has finished its work the institutions handcuff the infirmity. A delegate is a man who picks a candidate for the largest office in the land, a President who must live with problems whose borders are in ethics, metaphysics, and now ontology; the delegate is prepared for this office of selection by emptying wastebaskets, toting garbage and saying yes at the right time for twenty years in the small political machine of some small or large town; his reward, one of them anyway, is that he arrives at an invitation to the convention. An expert on local catch-as-catch-can, a small-time, often mediocre practitioner of small-town political judo, he comes to the big city with nine-tenths of his mind made up, he will follow the orders of the boss who brought him. Yet of course it is not altogether so mean as that: his opinion is listened

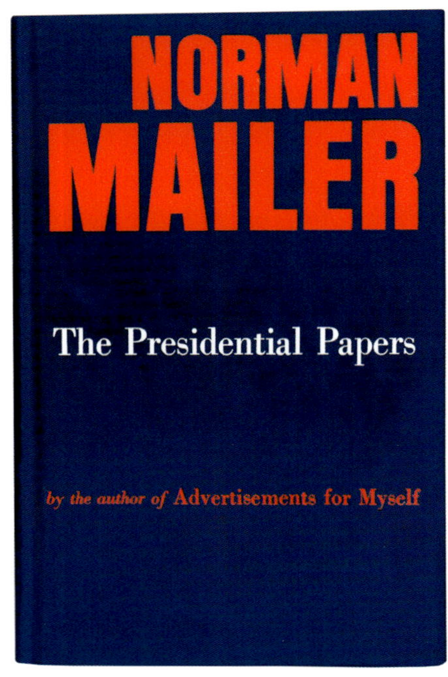

ABOVE *1963.* Two weeks before Kennedy's November 22, 1963, assassination, *The Presidential Papers*, Mailer's collection of politcal essays, including "Superman Comes to the Supermarket," was published by Putnam's. Mailer's intention had been to capture the president's attention with his ideas.

OPPOSITE *Spring 1969.* "Vote the Rascals In" was one of several slogans used by the Mailer-Breslin campaign. Another was: "No More Bullshit." *Photo, Bob Peterson*

In the late 1960s he made three experimental films, including *Maidstone*, his most famous movie, in which the action and dialogue were improvised. All three were influential, as was his 1987 film *Tough Guys Don't Dance* (based on his 1984 mystery novel of the same name), his only foray into commercial filmmaking. He also ran for mayor of New York City in the 1969 Democratic primary, campaigning on a platform that called for New York City to become the 51st state. That same year, his nonfiction narrative about the anti-Vietnam War movement, *The Armies of the Night*, won the Pulitzer Prize and the National Book Award. Mailer discovered in the 1960s that he needed a new way to see the fantastic and unpredictable events of the decade: the optics of conventional journalism were simply too clumsy. He decided to interweave reportorial perseverance, fictional technique, and the urgent promptings of his own intuition into a new narrative mode that would capture the momentous happenings of the era. "Superman Comes to the Supermarket," his long, trail-blazing essay profiling John F. Kennedy's ascent into the American imagination, is an instance of this narrative mode, and one of the icons of the New Journalism.

Mailer is the only person to win Pulitzers in both fiction and nonfiction. Five of his books have been finalists for National Book Awards, including *Of a Fire on the Moon* (1971), his nonfiction narrative of the Apollo 11 moon shot, which was serialized in *Life*. Aquarius, as he referred to himself in *Fire*, solidified his position as the most acute observer of contemporary American reality with his sensuous and analytic examination of the space program. He won a second Pulitzer for *The Executioner's Song* (1979), an account of the life and death of Utah murderer Gary Gilmore. He explores other lives at great length, but nowhere else does he display his acumen for psychological spelunking with such verve. Other biographical works include portraits of Muhammad Ali, Marilyn Monroe, Henry Miller, Pablo Picasso, Lee Harvey Oswald, Madonna, Jesus Christ, and Hitler. In 2006 he was recognized for his many contributions to literature and culture with the National Book Award Foundation's Lifetime Achievement Award. Married six times, he was the father of nine children and had ten grandchildren. For the last 33 years of his life, he and his sixth wife, the painter and novelist Norris Church Mailer, lived in Brooklyn Heights, New York, and Provincetown, Massachusetts.

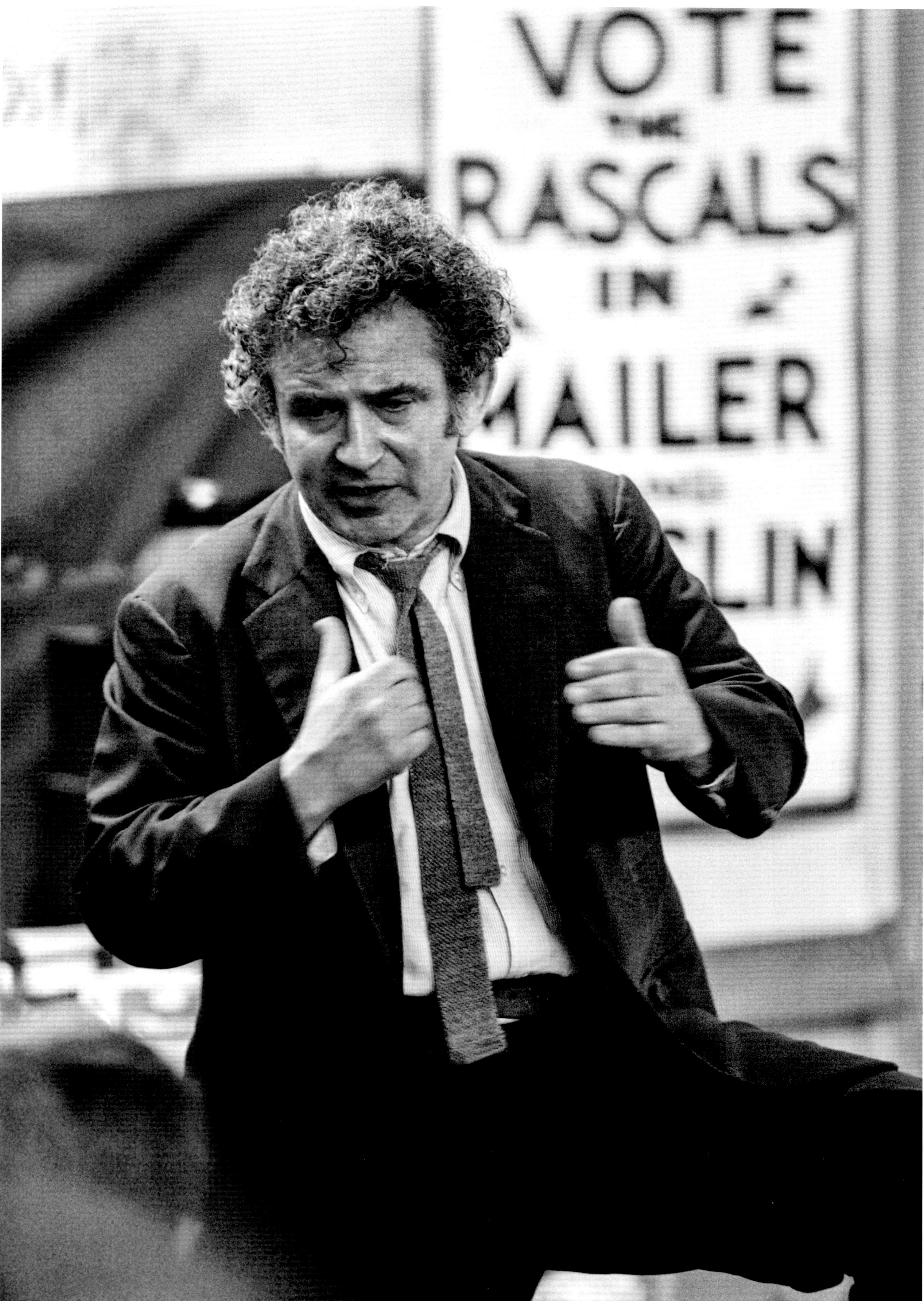

VOTE
THE
RASCALS
IN
MAILER
AND
BRESLIN

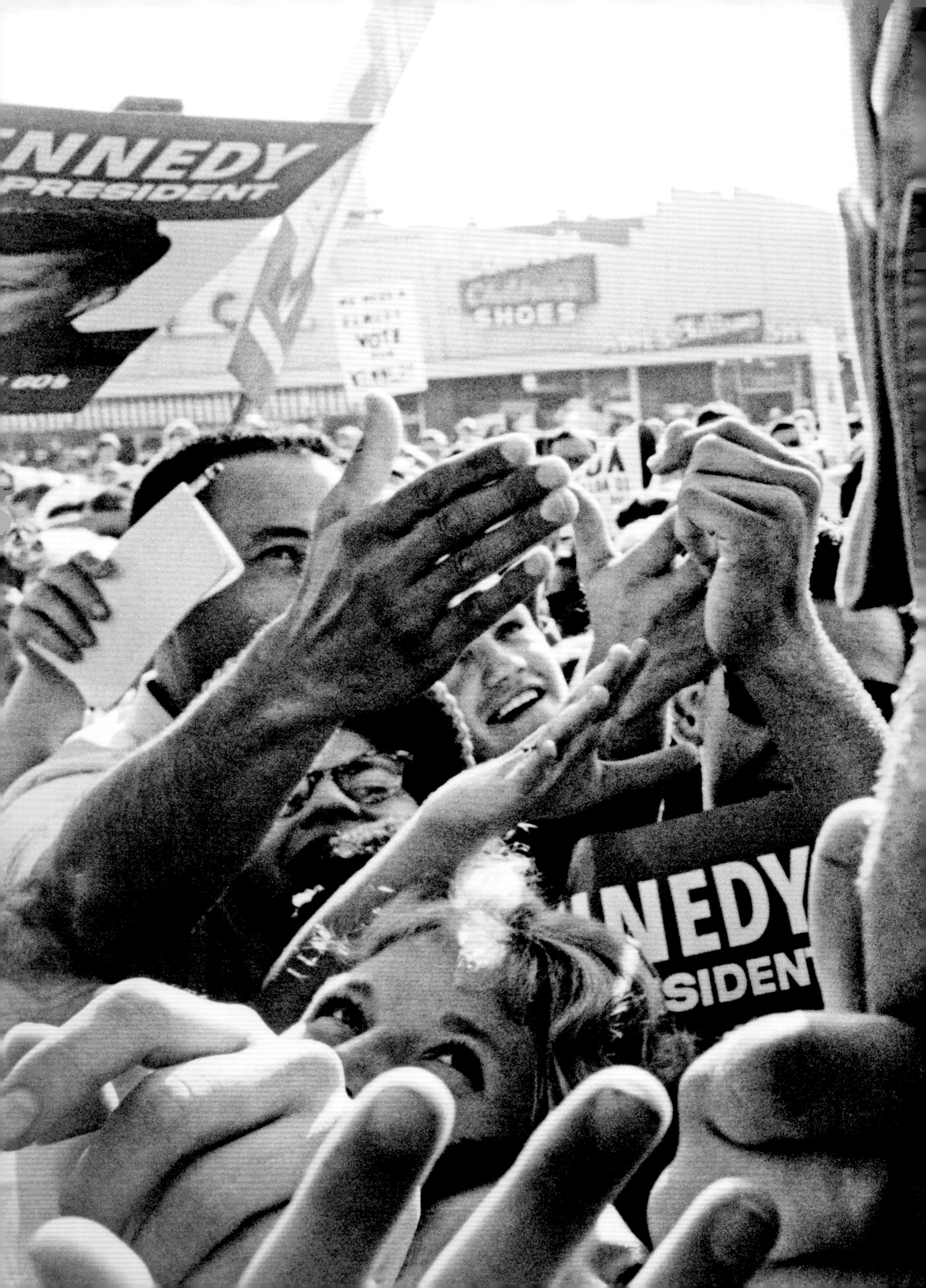

NNEDY
PRESIDENT
SHOES
VOTE
NNEDY
SIDENT

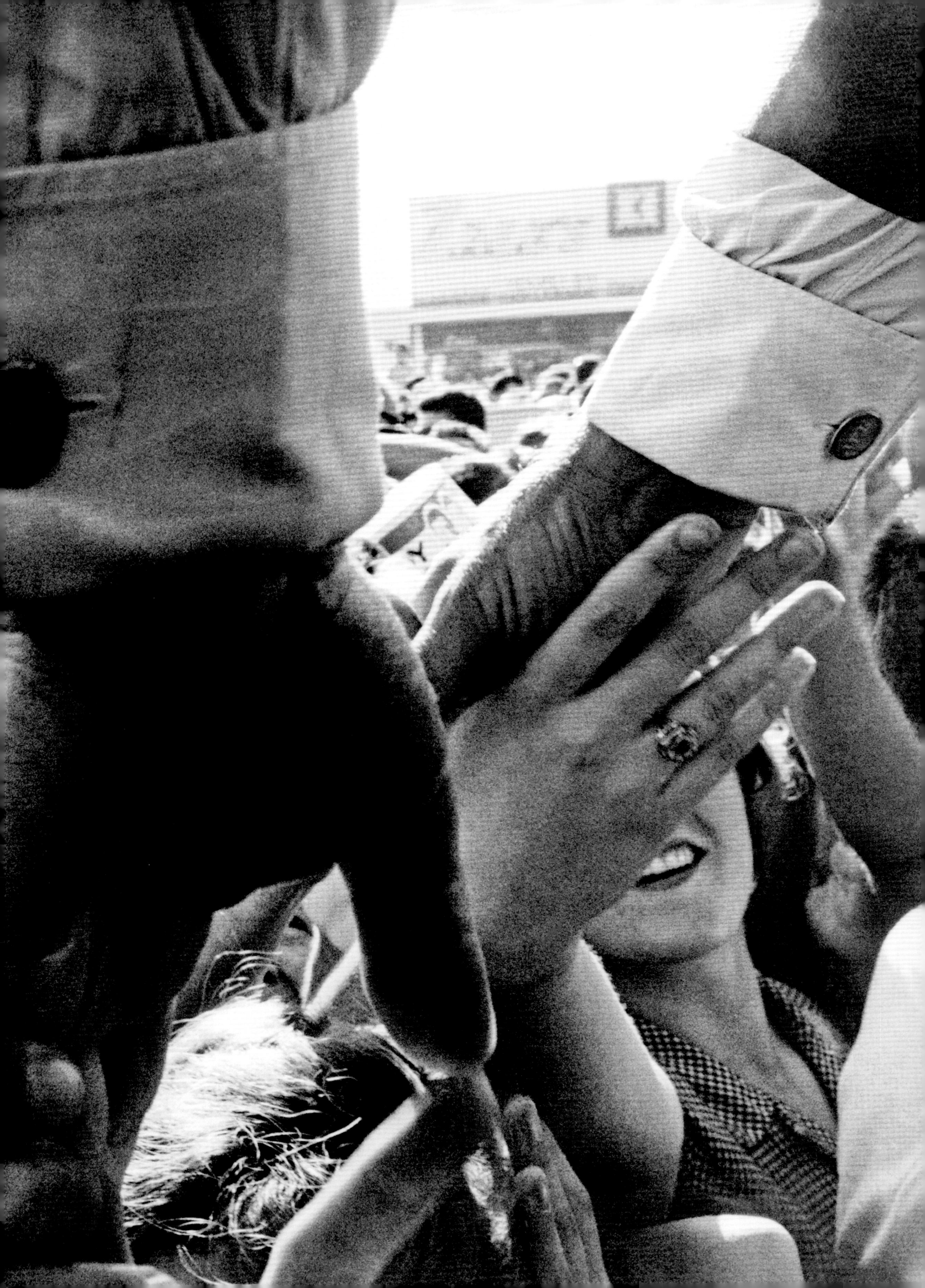

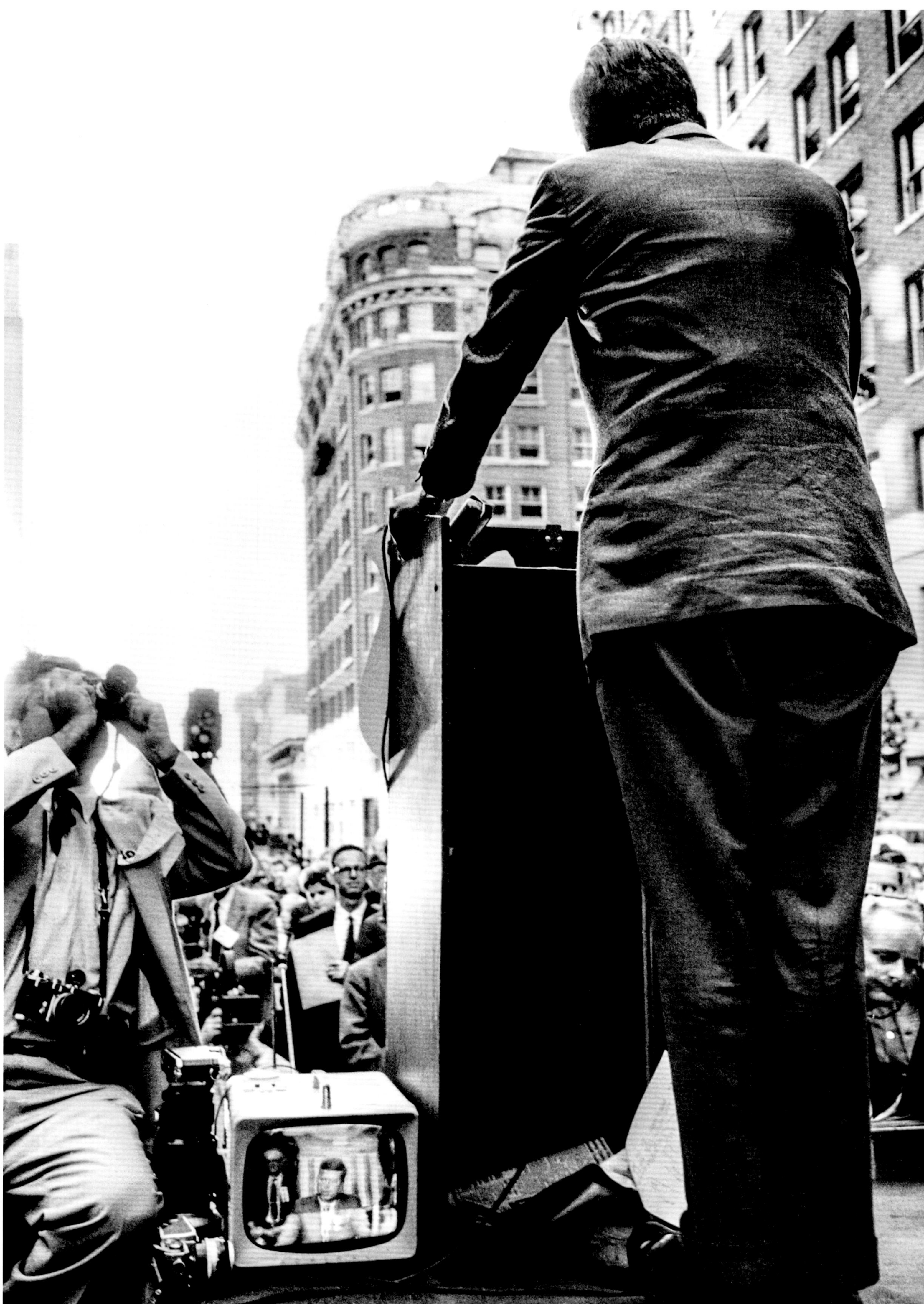

THE PHOTOGRAPHERS

Berinsky, Burton (1931–1991) An American writer, photographer, union organizer, and hat designer, Burton Berinsky began his career in 1954 working as a representative for the International Ladies' Garment Workers' Union in New Jersey, taking part in the Matawan Undergarment Work Stoppage of 1956 and the Dress Joint Board General Strike in 1958. Berinsky then served as the ILGWU's photographer before embarking on a career as a freelance photographer, journalist, and hat designer. In 1960 he met then–Senator John F. Kennedy and became an unofficial photographer of the Kennedy entourage. In 1980 he took over his father-in-law's hat business, Jay Lord Hatters, and won a Coty American Fashion Critics' Award.

Bryson, John (1923–2005) John Bryson, a Texas native, was a correspondent, bureau chief, and picture editor for *Life* then became a freelance photographer for the magazine, as well as for *Look* and *Holiday* in 1955. Famous for photographing the rich and famous (at home and at work), his subjects included Salvador Dalí, Clint Eastwood, Ernest Hemingway, John F. Kennedy, Robert F. Kennedy, Marilyn Monroe, Frank Sinatra, Elizabeth Taylor, Armand Hammer, and Katharine Hepburn. Bryson was also an actor, appearing in three films by director Sam Peckinpah; and playing himself in John Frankenheimer's *Grand Prix* (1966).

Capa, Cornell (1918–2008) Younger brother of war photographer Robert Capa, the Hungarian-born Cornell Capa established New York's International Center of Photography in 1974 with help from Jacqueline Kennedy. He moved to New York City from Paris in 1937 to work in *Life* magazine's darkroom. In 1946, after serving in the U.S. Air Force, he joined the magazine as a junior photographer. After the death of his brother in 1954 he left *Life* for Magnum Photos, which had been cofounded by Robert in 1947. As color television began to permeate the culture, Capa mirrored the use of color in still photography, bringing his unique view of the everyday rituals in American life — from Elks clubs gatherings to small-town politics. In 1961 he and nine fellow Magnum photographers published the seminal book on Kennedy's first 100 days in office, *Let Us Begin*.

Cartier-Bresson, Henri (1908–2004) The French photographer considered the father of modern photojournalism, Henri Cartier-Bresson was a pioneering street photographer for over three decades and a proponent of "the decisive moment," knowing exactly the right instant to take a photograph. Though he studied painting in his early 20s, he laid down his paintbrush for a Leica in 1930, embracing its flexibility and quick reaction time. Cartier-Bresson got his start as a photojournalist covering King George VI's coronation in 1937; within ten years he had became one of the cofounders of the legendary Magnum Photo agency. In 2003 he and his family established the Henri Cartier-Bresson Foundation in Paris with the aim of preserving his legacy and continuing to encourage generations of photographers in their work.

Clark, Ed (1911–2000) Nashville-native Ed Clark began his photojournalism career on the staff of *The Nashville Tennessean*. He began contributing to *Life* as a stringer in 1936 and joined the staff as a photographer in 1944. His most famous photograph depicted navy accordion player Graham W. Jackson Sr. weeping as he played "Goin' Home" during President Franklin Delano Roosevelt's funeral procession. After the war, Clark photographed the Nuremberg Trials; spent time in Los Angeles covering movie stars such as Marilyn Monroe, Humphrey Bogart, and Lauren Bacall; and photographed presidents Roosevelt, Truman, Eisenhower, and Kennedy. An Ed Clark photograph of then-Senator Kennedy playing peekaboo with baby daughter Caroline hung in the Oval Office during JFK's term.

Crane, Ralph (1913–1988) Ralph "Rudy" Crane was a German-born photographer. He moved to England in 1934 and began freelancing for *Life* in 1936. In 1941 he emigrated to the United States, where he photographed the stars of the era from Kim Novak and Brigitte Bardot to Twiggy and Joan Baez from his Los Angeles base. He also covered school desegregation in the South and the "astrochimps" of the U.S. space program. One of Crane's most famous images is a 1962 photograph of people in a Los Angeles department store watching JFK's television announcement of the blockade of Cuba during the Cuban missile crisis.

Dauman, Henri (1933–) Henri Dauman's work brings an extraordinary, invaluable visual record that reflects American and European styles, urban landscapes, icons, cultural values, and political concerns of the twentieth century. Born in France, Dauman established a name for himself in New York in the 1960s as a feature photographer for Life; and was published over four decades in publications such as *The New York Times, New York Magazine, Newsweek, Forbes, Smithsonian,* and *Town & Country.* He photographed personalities of the day such as Marilyn Monroe, Elvis Presley and Andy Warhol, and documented John F. Kennedy's presidential campaign and his funeral. Dauman's photograph of a veiled Jackie was brought into further notoriety by Andy Warhol's unauthorized use in dozens of multiple silk screens. For television, he has produced, directed, and photographed for PBS, BBC, and Granada Television.

Eisenstaedt, Alfred (1898–1995) Alfred Eisenstaedt served in the German army in World War I and, in the 1920s, took photographs on the side while working as a belt and button salesman. In 1929 he became a freelance photographer in Berlin, working for publications such as the *Berliner Tageblatt.* In 1935 he moved to the United States and joined *Life* magazine in 1936 as one of four staff photographers when it was still known as "Project X." He was with the magazine for more than 50 years, shot 80 covers, and worked on 2,500 assignments. In 1945 he took one of the most famous photographs of all time — a sailor passionately embracing a young woman in Times Square during the V-J Day celebrations. He published numerous books, including *Witness to Our Time* (1966).

Erwitt, Elliot (1928–) The documentary photographer Elliot Erwitt is known for the ironic wit and unusual juxtaposition of his photographs. Many of his photographs depict odd, even absurd moments of everyday life, often featuring dogs; but Erwitt has also photographed many public figures, from Marilyn Monroe and Che Guevara to Richard Nixon and John F. Kennedy. He photographed JFK during his presidential campaign and presidency and also his funeral. Born in Paris of Russian immigrant parents, Erwitt studied photography at Los Angeles City College and the New School for Social Research before serving as a photographer's assistant with the U.S. Army in Germany and France in the 1950s. He joined the Magnum Photos agency in 1953.

Gomel, Bob (1933–) Born and raised in New York City, Gomel began working for *Life* in 1959, where he photographed celebrities and sports figures like Muhammad Ali, Marilyn Monroe, and the Beatles; and world events from

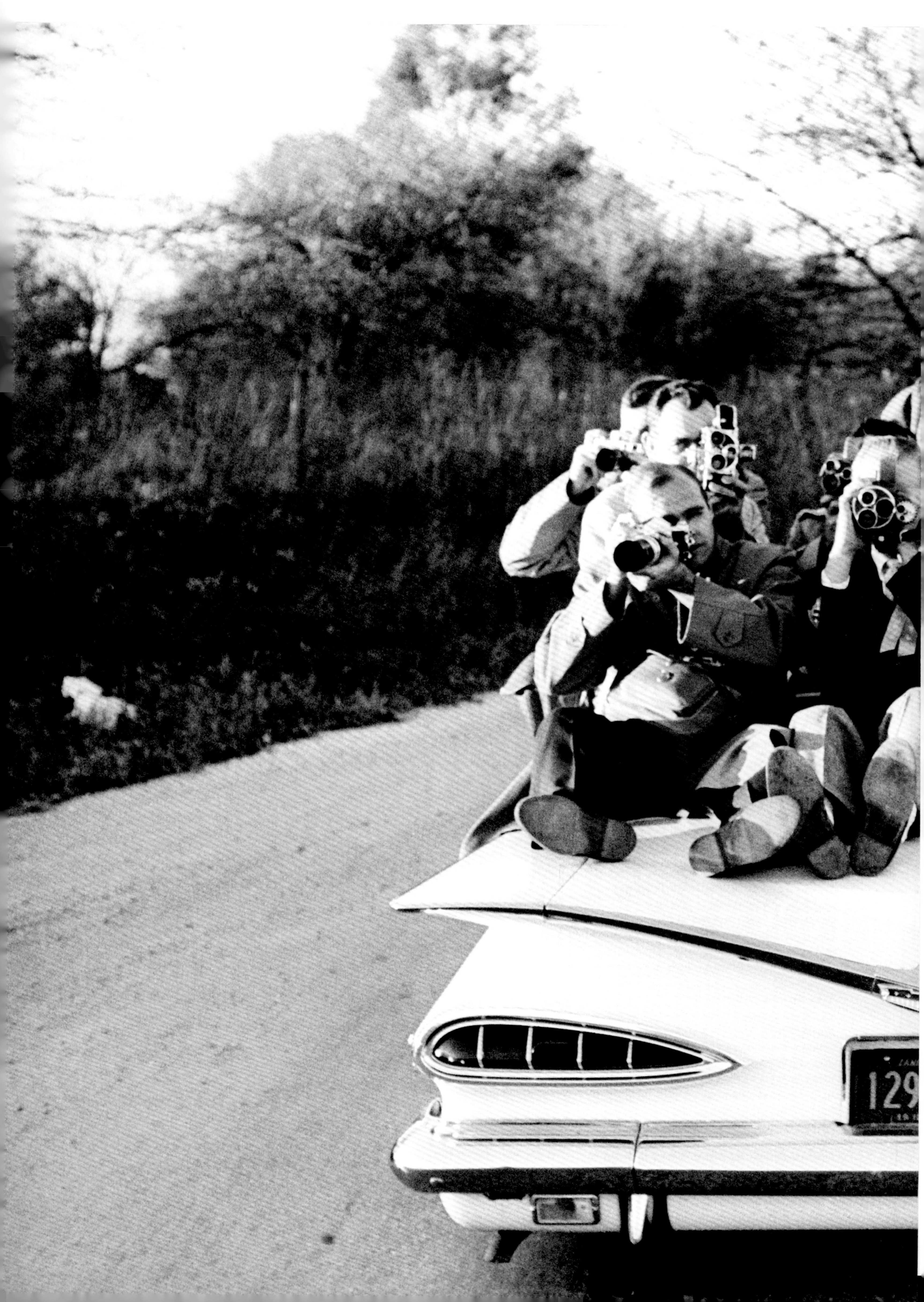

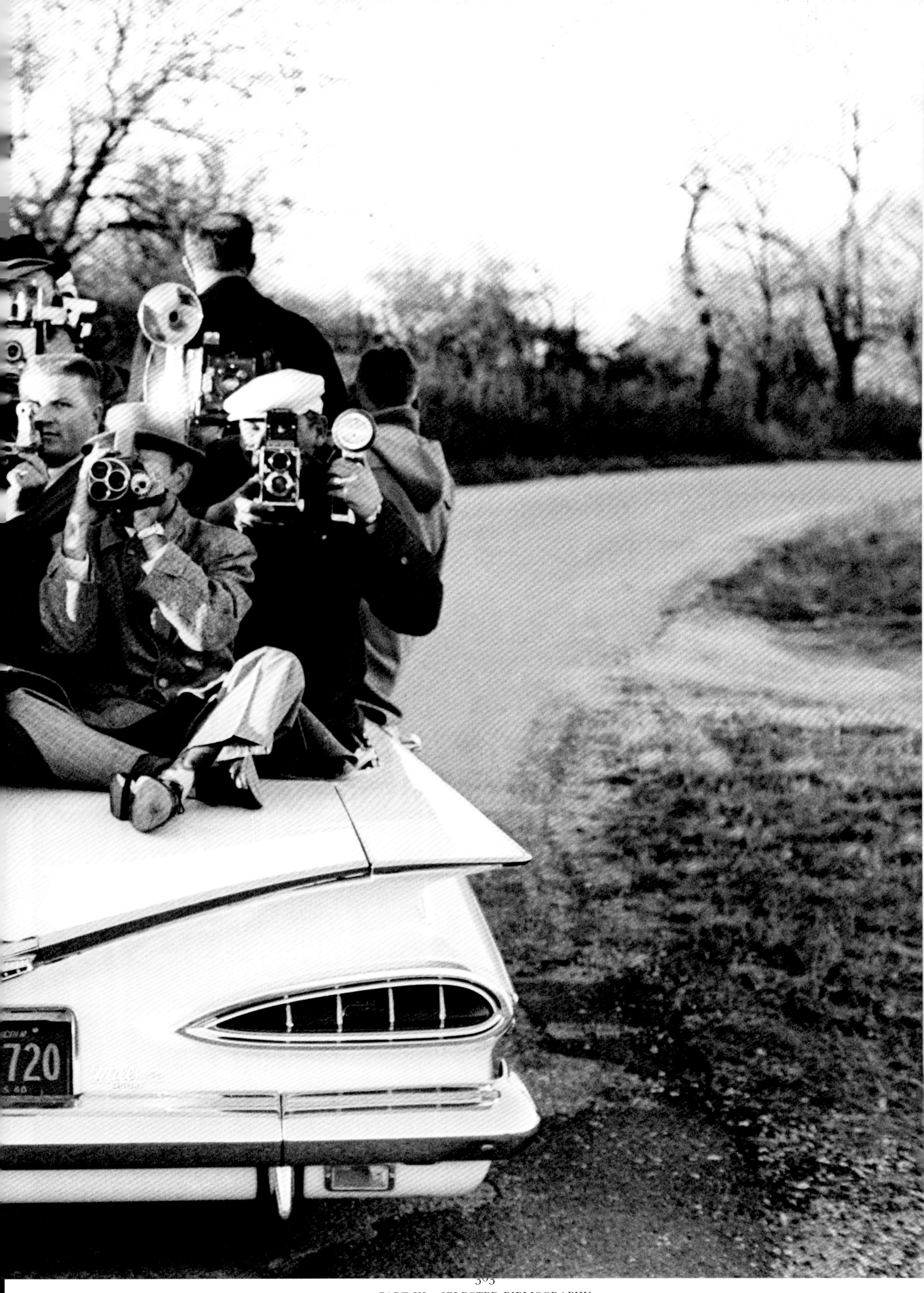720

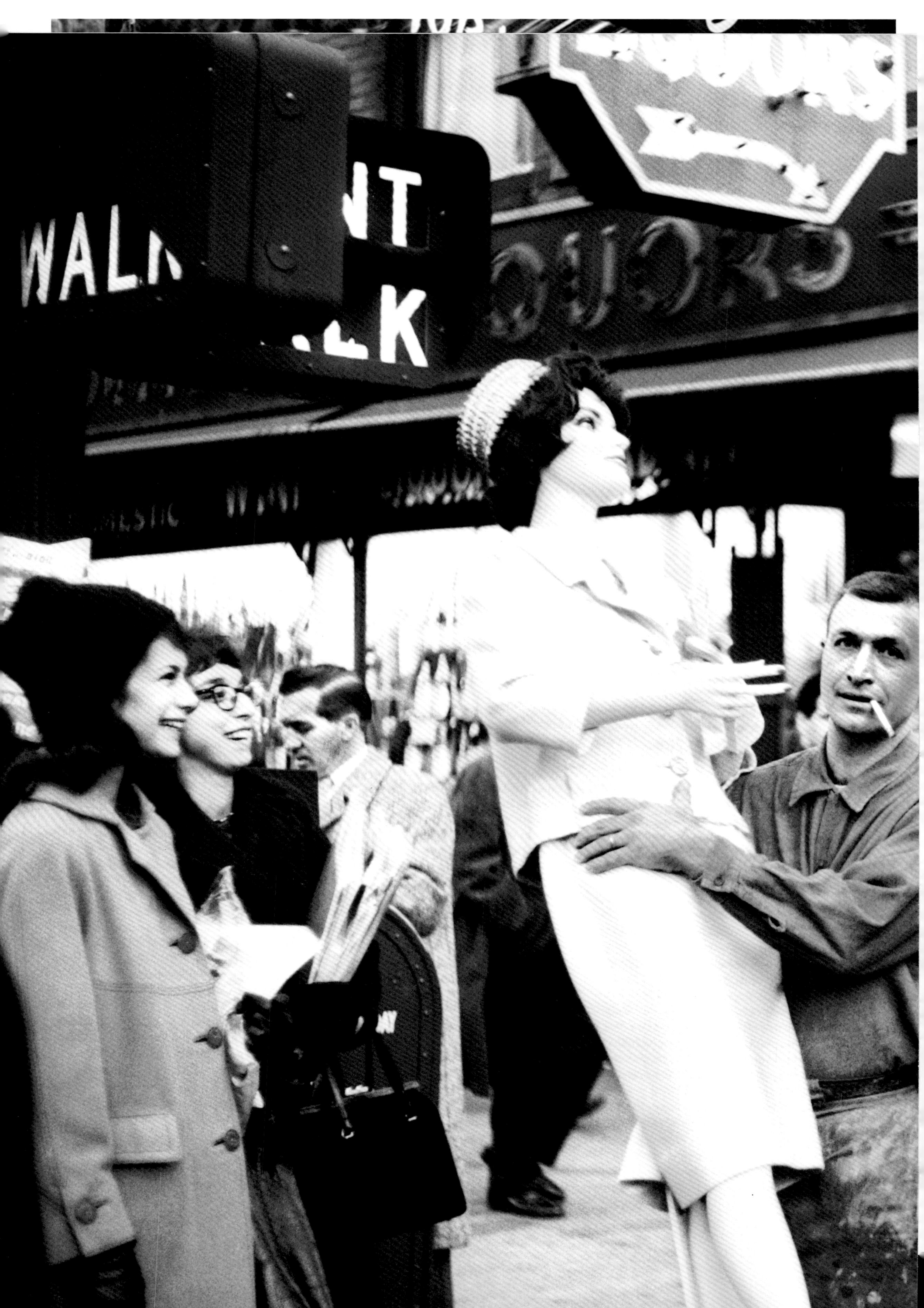

WALK
DON'T
WALK

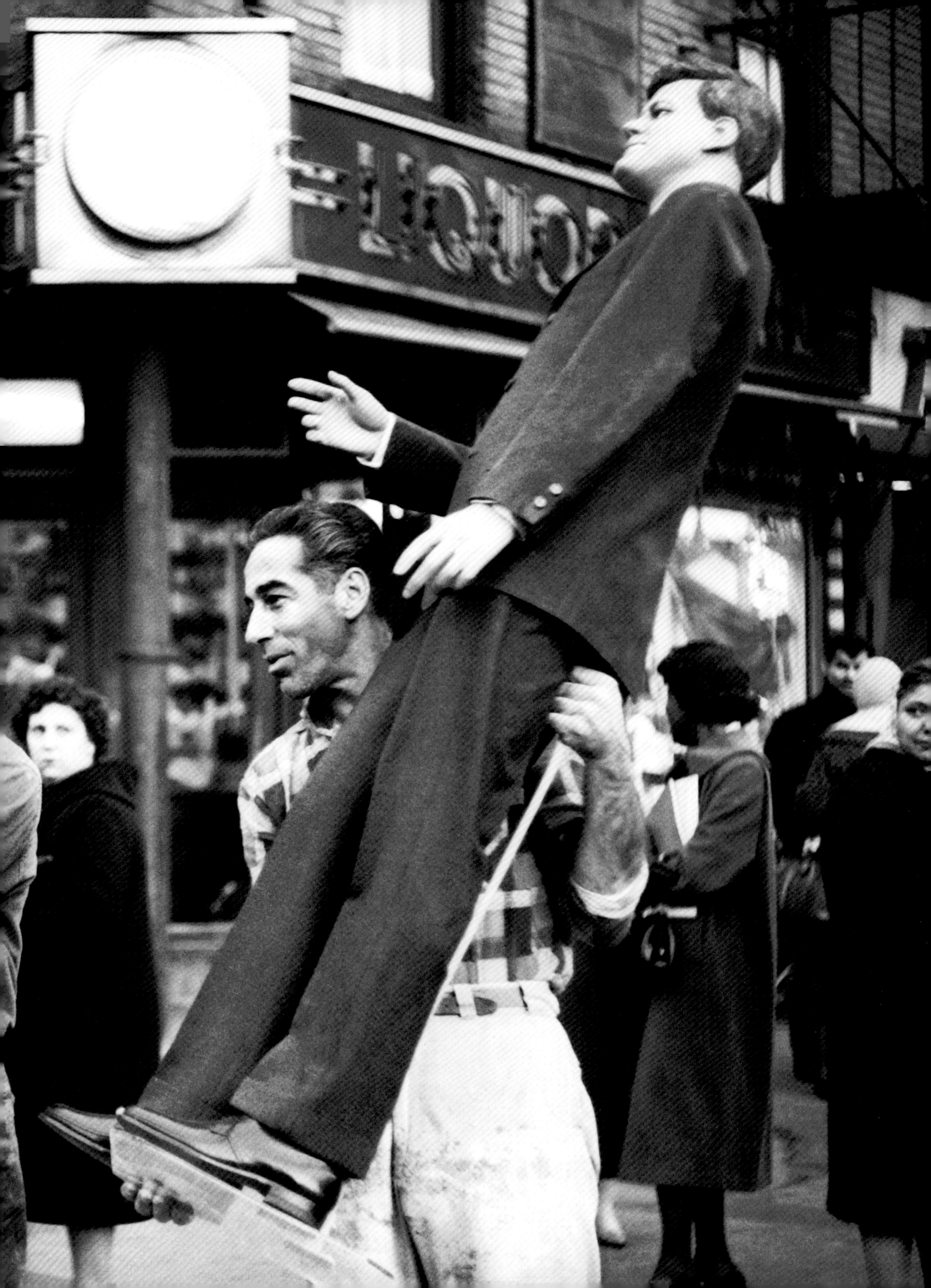

ACKNOWLEDGMENTS

ENDPAPERS *1960.* Campaign buttons for Kennedy.

PAGE 2 *July 15, 1960.* On the last night of the Democratic National Convention, John F. Kennedy accepted his party's nomination for president. "The New Frontier" is what Kennedy called the coming decade in his twilight acceptance speech at the Los Angeles Memorial Coliseum, and it was his message of giving America a fresh start that would carry him to a win in November. *Photo, Garry Winogrand*

PAGE 4 *October 21, 1960.* The fourth—and final—televised presidential debate between Kennedy and Richard Nixon plays in a New York bar. The election was less than a month away. *Photo, Cornell Capa*

PAGES 88–89, 126–127, 176–177, 242–243, AND OPPOSITE *1960-61.* "It was TV more than anything else that turned the tide," Kennedy is reported to have said after the election. But it wasn't just the Kennedy–Nixon debates that garnered attention from the voting public. It was also the commercials produced for television by his campaign and newsreels played primarily in theaters that also helped to pave the way, dozens of which have been preserved by the John F. Kennedy Presidential Library in Boston. *Moving picture stills, various sources*

PREVIOUS SPREAD *January 1961.* In honor of JFK's upcoming inauguration, some clothing stores in New York City decided to capitalize on the future president and his wife's style, employing sidewalk mannequins in their likenesses. The Jackie mannequin shown here was used to point customers to the John Frederics shop, where pillbox hats were then selling for $35 to $70. *Photo, Yale Joel*

There are over 500 books on the life and times of John F. Kennedy. This is now one of them, published with the intent to document the critical year in which he ran for president of the United States. In that year of 1960 no single voice in American letters could have covered Kennedy with more depth and humanity than Norman Mailer, whose essay "Superman Comes to the Supermarket" changed journalism as we know it. This is the third book by Mr. Mailer that TASCHEN has been fortunate enough to publish, thanks to the blessing of Norris Church Mailer and the Estate of Norman Mailer; the enthusiasm of Lawrence Schiller and Benedikt Taschen, who have supported the Mailer–TASCHEN collaboration since 2008; and the guidance of Mr. Mailer's biographer, J. Michael Lennon, who also contributed two essays to this volume.

Much credit is due to Jack Doyle—creator of the fascinating website pophistorydig.com—for many months spent researching and writing picture captions and the two chronologies of Kennedy's campaign and life; to Edgar Beem for his biographies of the featured photographers; and to Edwin Fotheringham for his delightful illustrations.

It wouldn't be TASCHEN without the incredible team of collaborators, in-house and out-, but especially Jessica Trujillo, Jonathan Newhall, Josh Baker, Anne Sauvadet, Thomas Grell, Anna Skinner, Nicole Depolo, and Andrea Richards. Thanks also to Frank Goerhardt, Florian Kobler, Jennifer Patrick, Maurene Goo, Jim Heimann, J. C. Gabel, Keith Krick, Martha Davidson, Nemuel DePaula, Robert Noble, and James Harrison.

Our gratitude goes out to the individual photographers and private collectors who generously opened their archives for publication in this volume: Henri Dauman, Lawrence Schiller, Bob Peterson, Neil Leifer, Alfred Wertheimer, Ted Russell, Robert Lerner, Ted Hake, Christen Carter, and Bill Everheart.

The bulk of the photographs could never have been included without the participation of many photo archives. In particular we want to thank the following people who went above and beyond the call of duty. Getty Images: Joelle Sedlmeyer, Michelle Butnick-Press, and Jonathan Hyams; Focus: Olga Neufeld; the International Center for Photography: Claartje van Dijk; Landov Media: Uri Davidov and Cornelia Schnall; Content Partners: Hugo Fleischmann; Jacques Lowe Archive: Michelle Wild; the Winogrand Estate: Eileen Adele Hale; Fraenkel Gallery: Rebecca Herman, Carin Johnson, and Emily Lambert; the Center for Creative Photography: Tammy Carter and Leslie Squyres; Historic Image Licensing: Victoria Ann Rehberg; the Yousuf Karsh Estate: Julie Grahame; Camera Press:

Elizabeth Kerr; *Sports Illustrated*: Karen Carpenter; the Harry Ransom Center: Rick Watson; the Newseum: Shelby Coffey, Carrie Christoffersen, Cathy Trost, and Indira Williams Babic; and John Frost Newspapers: Andrew Frost.

Special thanks to the researchers, archivists, and reproduction specialists at the John F. Kennedy Library and Museum in Boston, Massachusetts: Maryrose Grossman, Stephen Plotkin, Stacey Chandler, John Buzunga, and Heather Joines; as well as Lee Statham of the JFK Library Foundation. They were instrumental not only in providing access to much of the critical research and many of the photographs included in this volume, but they serve as the faithful guardians of this historic library's deep and varied collections.

We were honored to have Richard Reeves review the book prior to publication. And salutations to my great aunt, Rosalind Wyman, who thrilled me with her first-hand stories of organizing the Democratic National Convention in Los Angeles in 1960.

—Nina Wiener, 2014

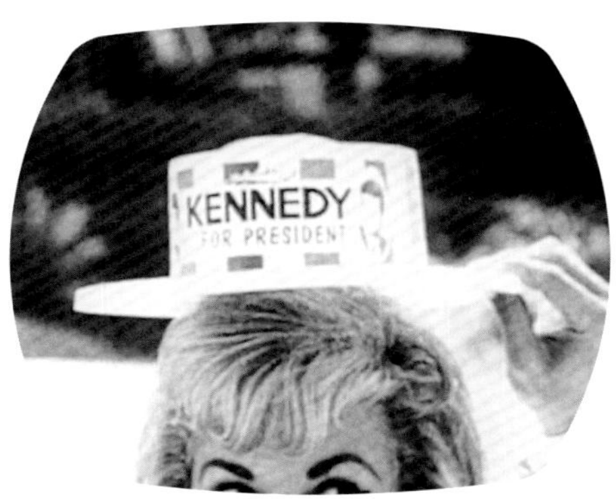

To stay informed about TASCHEN and our upcoming titles, please subscribe to our free magazine at www.taschen.com/magazine, follow us on Twitter, Instagram, and Facebook, or e-mail your questions to contact@taschen.com.

ORIGINAL EDITION © 2014 TASCHEN GmbH
DESIGN Jessica Trujillo, Los Angeles
EDITORIAL COORDINATION Jascha Kempe, Cologne;
    Anne Sauvadet, Cologne;
    Jonathan Newhall, New York
PRODUCTION Thomas Grell, Cologne
CAPTIONS Jack Doyle, New Market, Maryland,
    with Nina Wiener, New York,
    and Andrea Richards, Los Angeles
PHOTOGRAPHERS' BIOGRAPHIES Edgar Beem,
    Yarmouth, Maine

PRINTED IN ITALY
ISBN 978-3-8365-6253-9

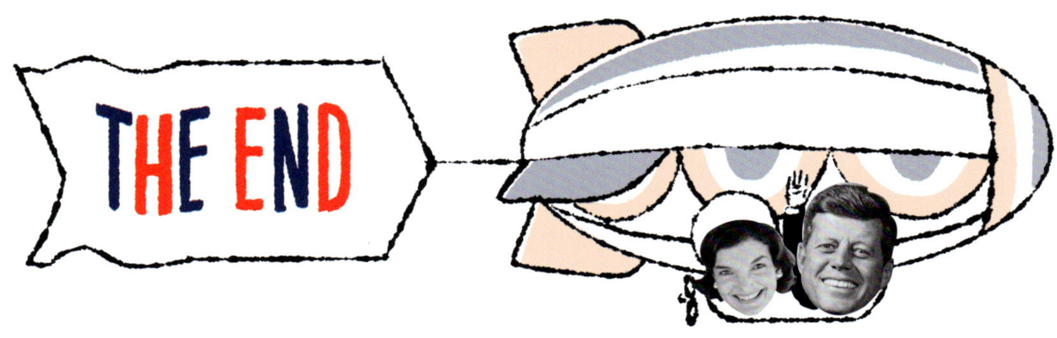
THE END

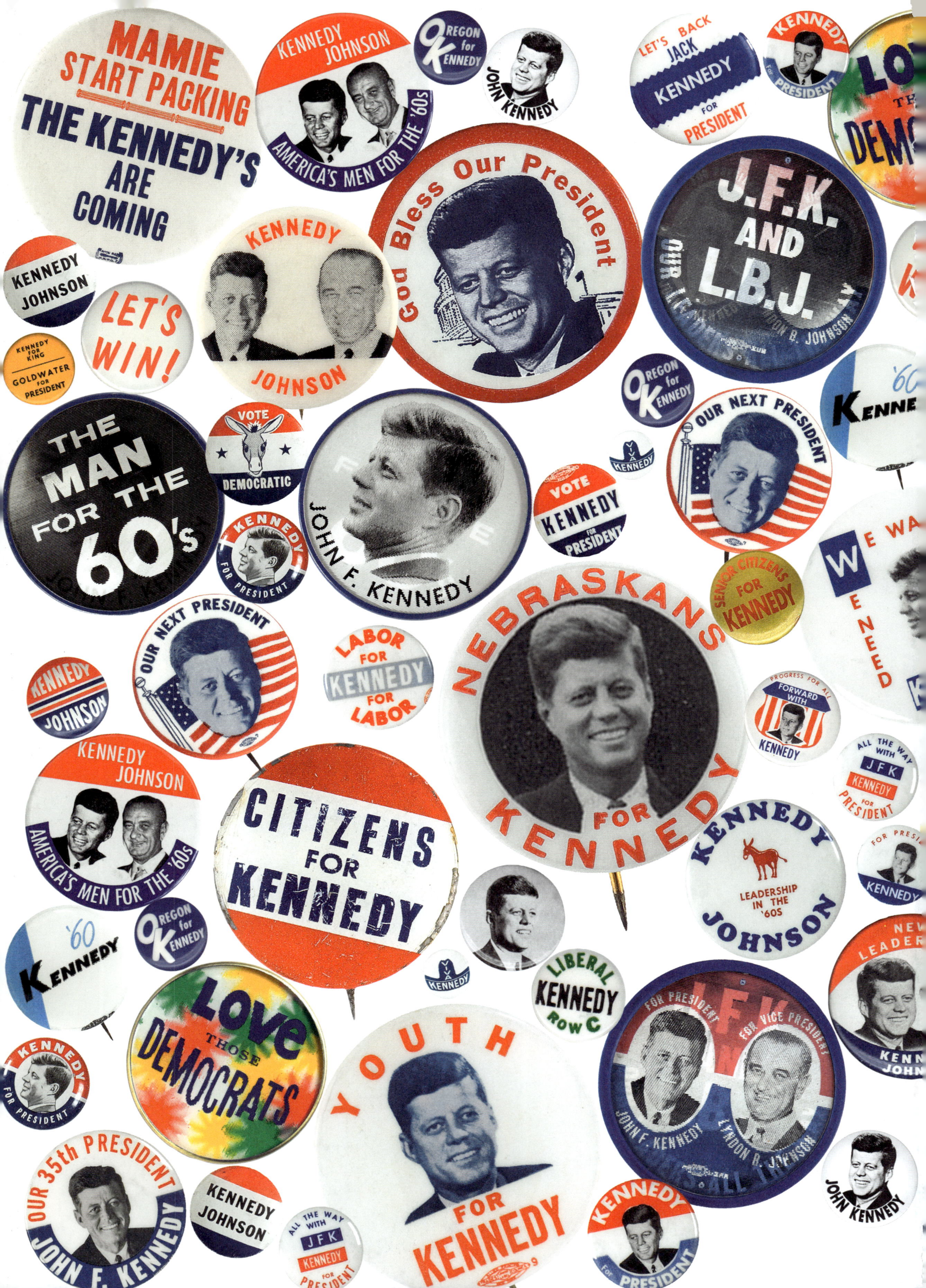

MAMIE START PACKING THE KENNEDY'S ARE COMING
KENNEDY JOHNSON
AMERICA'S MEN FOR THE '60s
OREGON for KENNEDY
JOHN KENNEDY
LET'S BACK JACK KENNEDY FOR PRESIDENT
KENNEDY FOR PRESIDENT
LOVE THE DEMO
KENNEDY JOHNSON
KENNEDY JOHNSON
God Bless Our President
J.F.K. AND L.B.J.
K
LET'S WIN!
KENNEDY FOR KING GOLDWATER FOR PRESIDENT
'60 KENNE
THE MAN FOR THE 60's
JOHN F. KENNEDY
VOTE DEMOCRATIC
JOHN F. KENNEDY
OREGON for KENNEDY
VIVA KENNEDY
OUR NEXT PRESIDENT
WE WA
VOTE KENNEDY FOR PRESIDENT
KENNEDY FOR PRESIDENT
SENIOR CITIZENS FOR KENNEDY
WE NEED
K
OUR NEXT PRESIDENT
LABOR FOR KENNEDY FOR LABOR
NEBRASKANS FOR KENNEDY
PROGRESS FOR ALL FORWARD WITH KENNEDY
ALL THE WAY WITH J F K KENNEDY FOR PRESIDENT
KENNEDY JOHNSON
KENNEDY JOHNSON
AMERICA'S MEN FOR THE '60s
CITIZENS FOR KENNEDY
KENNEDY JOHNSON LEADERSHIP IN THE '60s
FOR PRESIDENT KENNEDY
NEW LEADER
'60 KENNEDY
OREGON for KENNEDY
VIVA KENNEDY
LIBERAL KENNEDY Row C
FOR PRESIDENT J.F.K. FOR VICE PRESIDENT JOHN F. KENNEDY LYNDON B. JOHNSON
KENN JOHN
KENNEDY FOR PRESIDENT
Love THOSE DEMOCRATS
YOUTH FOR KENNEDY
KENNEDY FOR PRESIDENT
JOHN KENNEDY
OUR 35th PRESIDENT JOHN F. KENNEDY
KENNEDY JOHNSON
ALL THE WAY WITH J F K KENNEDY FOR PRESIDENT